The Literature
of Terrorism

The Literature of Terrorism

A SELECTIVELY ANNOTATED BIBLIOGRAPHY

Compiled by Edward F. Mickolus

GREENWOOD PRESS · WESTPORT, CT • LONDON, ENGLAND

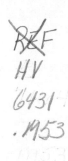

Library of Congress Cataloging in Publication Data

Mickolus, Edward F
   The literature of terrorism.

   Includes indexes.
   1. Terrorism—Bibliography. I. Title.
Z7164.T3M53   [HV6431]   016.3036'2   80-541
ISBN 0-313-22265-7

Library of Congress Catalog Card Number: 80-541
ISBN 0-313-22265-7

First published in 1980

Greenwood Press
A division of Congressional Information Service, Inc.
88 Post Road West, Westport, Connecticut 06881

Printed in the United States of America

10 9 8 7 6 5 4 3 2 1

For Delores Tucker

CONTENTS

PREFACE

If we are to believe statistics, more ink than blood has been spilled as a result of terrorist attacks in the past decade. To date this vast outpouring of commentary and research on terrorism has escaped formal categorization and comparison. This study is designed to impose some order on this chaos and provide researchers with a comprehensive survey of literature dealing with various aspects of terrorism. Day-to-day press reports have not been noted, although several noteworthy news analyses receive mention. Although the majority of the entries are in English and written by Americans, numerous citations from other languages are included to illustrate contributions available around the world.

Care has been taken to minimize duplicate listings. Because some entries relate to more than one category, each item is placed under the heading deemed most appropriate to the central theme of the book or article cited and cross-referenced by citation number at the end of additionally relevant headings. In some cases, annotations given by authors or sponsoring organizations have been quoted. Where appropriate, such instances are noted at the beginning of a commentary. FAR notations refer to documents that have been reprinted for general public distribution by the Foreign Affairs Research service of the U.S. Department of State.

The organization of this annotated bibliography is as follows. The *General Treatments* section includes books and articles discussing definitions, theories, the history of terrorism, notes on terrorist tactics, and trends in various forms of terrorism. The *Tactics of Terrorists* section has five sub-categories: *Assassinations* includes works on the killing of highly placed political leaders, as well as murders of lesser-known individuals for political reasons. *Bombings* notes articles on bombing campaigns, types of bombs, firebombs and arson attempts, letter bombs, and effects of bombing on civilian morale. *Hijackings* includes general treatments on skyjacking and aircraft sabotage, discussions of preventive security and international legal solutions. *Hostage Incidents* includes works on kidnapping, barricade and hostage situations, extortionate threats made against individuals or installations, strategies of negotiation by terrorists and victims, and related issues. *Potential Nuclear Threats* includes discussions of safeguards measures against governmental and private diversion and nuclear materials safeguards against attack and theft, and types of demands which could be made. (The reader should also refer to the

Disaster Response category for discussions of societal responses.) The *Terrorist and Guerrilla Philosophies* listing includes books and articles by well-known terrorists and commentaries on their thoughts. The *Links of Terrorist Groups* section includes articles on the funding, training, and exchanges of personnel between known organizations. The *Terrorism by Geographic Area* section is divided into six subcategories, with discussions of terrorism, revolutionary movements, and civil uprisings, with separate sections on major countries. The *State Terrorism* section notes the use of terrorism by governmental authorities and the effects of such state-sanctioned violence upon society.

Having noted terrorist motivations and trends in their behavior, we move to a discussion of *Responses*, which is divided into four major sections. *General* treatments note governmental and societal reactions, and mutually reinforcing cycles of terrorism and counterterrorism. The effects on democracy of antiterrorist responses are also included. *Physical Security* notes guidelines on preventing attacks, how police and military forces should respond, and antiterrorist hardware. The section on *International Legal Approaches* has several subcategories. The *General* treatments relate to international legal responses, discussions in international fora, and suggestions for future work. The *Law of War* includes discussions of how the legal conventions and customs on the conduct of war might apply or be modified to handle terrorism. *Extradition Law* lists discussions of the political offenses exemption to most extradition agreements, which is frequently cited by jailed terrorists. *Domestic Legislation against Terrorism* catalogs some of the literature on municipal antiterrorist laws. *State Responsibility for Terrorist Acts* draws on the literature calling for action to halt governments fomenting subversion overseas, and notes present-day attempts to halt patron state support to terrorists. *Measures of Self-Help in Combating Terrorism* concentrates on the development of unilateral measures to deal with terrorism, including kidnapping of fugitives and Entebbe-style paramilitary rescue teams. The *General Legal Observations* category of the *Hijacking* section includes overall reviews of the international legal conventions on aerial hijacking, the problem of piracy, and suggestions for future measures. Separate treatment is given the *Tokyo, Hague,* and *Montreal Conventions. Other International Legal Conventions* includes the *League of Nations Antiterrorist Actions, Organization of American States Convention, United Nations Antiterrorist Actions,* and *Inter-European Legal Conventions.* The *Disaster Response* section includes books and articles from the social sciences on responses to catastrophes, and may be helpful in considering society-wide plans for coping with nuclear terrorism, chemical or biological attacks.

Several miscellaneous sections complete the bibliography. The *Media and Terrorism* section includes arguments on the proper role of the media in the tactical and strategic responses to terrorism. *Psychological and Medical Ap-*

proaches to Terrorism includes studies of terrorist motivations, psychiatric notions about the causes of murderous behavior, selection of political targets, and the effects of society upon unstable individuals. *Guerrilla Warfare* catalogs works on guerrilla war and revolutionary behavior in general, especially those campaigns that frequently resort to terrorist activity. *Related Studies* refers to behavioral science approaches to causes of political violence in general and criminal activity, defining relationships between forces, governments, and society. *Events Data Research* notes the development of computerized data sets on terrorism, including the author's ITERATE, which are built upon relevant findings in this area. This section is generally limited to published reports or easily obtainable monographs. *Fiction* concentrates on contemporary novels on transnational terrorism, although a few earlier works are represented. *Bibliographies* concentrates on compilations of works on terrorism in general. Listings on specialized topics are included in the appropriate regional or functional section of this bibliography. Author and title indexes are found at annex.

The list of people who have aided me by providing copies of their drafts and published works, as well as others who have provided leads in tracking down fugitive or obscure citations, is too extensive to list here. Rather let me offer a plenary thanks and invite the readers of this guide to send copies or citations of their recent works for inclusion in future editions of this bibliography.

This book has been reviewed by the Central Intelligence Agency's Publications Review Board to assist me in avoiding the unauthorized disclosure of classified information; however, neither that review nor my own affiliation with CIA either constitutes or implies CIA authentication of factual material or endorsement of my views.

The Literature
of Terrorism _____

GENERAL TREATMENTS

1. Adam, Frances Cruchley. "Terrorist Images." *Chitty's Law Journal* 24 (September 1976): 246-248.

2. Alexander, Yonah. "Contemporary Terrorism: Perspectives." Paper presented to the Conference on Psychopathology and Political Violence, November 16-17, 1979, at the University of Chicago.

3. ———, ed. *International Terrorism: National, Regional and Global Perspectives.* New York: Praeger, 1976. 414 pp. Also in paperback from New York: AMS, 1976. 412 pp.

Reviewed by Daniel C. Turack *Annals of the American Academy of Political and Social Science* 427 (September 1976): 135-136. A collection of studies on terrorism in specific regions, and United Nations responses.

4. ———. "Introduction." In his *International Terrorism: National, Regional, and Global Perspectives,* pp. xi-xx. (New York: AMS, 1976).

Discusses problems of defining terrorism, some of its current-day manifestations in various areas of the world, and its philosophical underpinnings.

5. ———. *The Role of Terrorism in World Power Assessment.* Washington, D.C.: Georgetown Center for Strategic and International Studies, forthcoming.

Alexander will use the conceptual framework enunciated by Ray Cline in looking at Soviet, Chinese, and Third World attitudes towards terrorism. He will look at the power characteristics of groups, and give an assessment of the future.

6. ———. "Some Perspectives on International Terrorism." *International Problems* 14, (Fall 1975): 24-29.

Gives a brief survey of the worldwide manifestations of terrorism, along with the feeble attempts to counteract it. Alexander argues that all terrorists "regard themselves to be beyond the limits of any society and system of government." He believes that a time may come in which all targets will be vulnerable, leading to a collapse of civilization. Action is therefore urgently needed.

7. ———. "Super-Terrorism." In Yonah Alexander and John M. Gleason, eds. *Terrorism: Behavioral Perspectives*. New York: Pergamon, 1980.

8. ———, ed. *Terrorism: Moral Aspects*. Boulder: Westview, 1980.

9. Alexander, Yonah; Carlton, David; and Wilkinson, Paul, eds. *Terrorism: Theory and Practice*. Boulder: Westview, 1979. 280 pp.
    Surveys academic theories of terrorism, responses to the problem, and probable future courses.

10. Alexander, Yonah, and Kilmarx, Robert A., eds. *Political Terrorism and Business: The Threat and Response*. New York: Praeger, 1979. 540 pp.
    Surveys the nature of corporate vulnerability, suggests security precautions, details infringements on personal freedoms, and notes hostage conduct.

11. Allan, Ray. "The Terror Business." *New Leader*, December 19, 1977.

12. Allemann, Fritz R. "How Effective Is Terrorism?" In *International Summaries: A Collection of Selected Translations in Law Enforcement and Criminal Justice*, 3:73-80. Washington, D.C.: U.S. Department of Justice, National Criminal Justice Reference Service, April 1979.
    Looks at terrorist successes and failures and makes predictions on the ETA, IRA, and PLO.

13. Amon, Moshe. "The Devil's Righteousness: A Romantic Model of Secular Gnosticism." Paper presented to the Conference on the Moral Implications of Terrorism, March 14-16, 1979, at UCLA.

14. ———. "Terrorism: Problems of Good and Evil." Paper presented to the Conference on Psychopathology and Political Violence, November 16-17, 1979, at the University of Chicago.

15. Anable, David, "Terrorism: Violence as Theater." *Inter-Dependent* 3 (January 1976): 1, 6.
    Summarizes the incidents of December 1975. Mentions the oft-heard conventional wisdom on terrorism.

16. Analyses of Group Size. Vienna, Va.: BDM Corporation, submitted to the Nuclear Regulatory Commission under Contract AT (49-24)-0131, BDM/ W-75-247-TR, December 2, 1975.
    Using the BDM data base of 1,204 terrorist incidents, the study concludes that "a majority of incidents are committed by individuals and seldom by

groups larger than 6; occurrences of internal collusion or assistance are remote; the primary motivation among incidents with known group size are bargaining and financial gain; few incidents were perpetrated that had a potential for impacting on general public safety; and unprotected or minimally protected targets are attacked the majority of the times.''

17. Andreski, S. ''Terror.'' In Julius Gould and William L. Kolb, eds., *A Dictionary of the Social Sciences*, p. 719. New York: Free Press, 1964.

Defines terror as a special kind of tyranny, which does not allow the victims any method of safety from the possibility of being attacked, and which is indiscriminate, aiming at creating fear.

18. Arblaster, Anthony. ''Terrorism: Myths, Meaning and Morals.'' *Political Studies* 25 (September 1977): 413-424.

A review of books by Wilkinson, Hyams, Bell, Clutterbuck, Burton, Carlton and Schaerf, Dobson, Styles, Alexander, Halperin, and Ellis. Arblaster argues that one must define terrorism and also consider state terrorism.

19. Arendt, Hannah. ''Ideologie und Terror.'' In *Offener Horizont: Festschrift fur Karl Jaspers*. Munich: R. Piper, 1953.

20. Atala, Charles, and Groffier, Ethel. *Terrorisme et Guérilla: La révolte armée devant les nations*. Ottawa: Dossiers Interlex, Les Editions Lemeac, 1973. 181 pp.

Atala's essay, ''La violence sans rivages,'' strings together a series of quotations from social scientists (who are judged to be failures in providing guidance) and terrorist theoreticians. Groffier, in ''Aspects juridiques,'' presents documents from international and Canadian law on the question of terrorism.

21. ''Atlas Report: Curbing Terrorism.'' *Atlas World Press Review* (January 1978): 31-37.

22. Atwater, James. ''Time to Get Tough with Terrorists: An Interview with Brian Crozier.'' *Reader's Digest* (April 1973): 89-93.

Crozier answers the following questions: How serious is the threat of terrorism today? How did Japanese terrorists become involved in the Arab-Israeli quarrel? How actively have the Red Chinese supported terrorism? What do terrorists hope to gain by attacking democracies? How are the terrorist groups around the world linked together? How successful do you think terrorism has been? Can we do anything to combat terrorism?

23. Avery, William P. "Terrorism, Violence and the International Transfer of Conventional Armaments." Paper presented at the Annual Meeting of the Midwest Political Science Association, April 1978, Chicago. Available as FAR 29178-N and published in Yonah Alexander and John M. Gleason, eds., *Terrorism: Behavioral Perspectives*. New York: Pergamon, 1980.

24. Barber, C. "Application of Terrorism Typology to Regional Security Arrangements." Paper presented to the annual meeting of the Midwest Political Science Association, April 20-22, 1978, Chicago.

25. Baron, Dominic Paul. *The Increasing Vulnerability of Computers to Terrorist Attack*. London: Foreign Affairs Research Institute, 1978. 10 pp.

Shows that terrorists could gain access to classified data by chance acquisition of passwords or by kidnapping computer specialists authorized to hold such material. Notes the dependence of industrialized societies upon sophisticated computers and points out that Western export of computers to the Soviets could also pose a problem.

26. Barsy, Janet. "International Terrorism: No End in Sight." *Student and Foreign Affairs* 1 (December 1972): 3-4.

Reviews a conference on terrorism held at Georgetown University's School of Foreign Service.

27. Bartos, Milan. "International Terrorism." *Review of International Affairs* (Belgrade) 23 (April 1972): 25-26.

28. Bassiouni, M. Cherif. "Prolegomenon to Terror Violence." *Creighton Law Review* 12 (Spring 1979): 745-779.

Author seeks to distinguish terrorist attacks from structurally similar criminal violence by examining the motives of the attacker, the selection of targets, and the audience for the crime. Includes an excellent summary of the potential role of the media in promoting terrorism as well as combating it. Concludes with a discussion of proposed methods of controlling antistate and state terrorism.

29. The BDM Corporation's Terrorism Data Base. Vienna, Va.: BDM Corporation, n.d.[1976]. 7 pp.

Explains the types of variables used to describe the 4,700 incidents of terrorism and other forms of violent behavior that occurred from 1965-1975 listed in nine sources used by BDM. The data set is 75 percent American based and is not solely related to terrorist incidents (a definition of terrorism not being provided), but including cases selected according to twelve criteria. Seventy percent of the data set's incidents are bombings.

30. Beckett, Brian. "Chemical Warfare Is Available to Terrorists." *New Scientist*, October 12, 1978.

Shows that a search through the British Patent Office, bolstered by digging through business libraries, can uncover the formulas for V and G series nerve agents.

31. Bell, J. Bowyer. "Academic Analysis: The Common Wisdom." Paper presented to the Transnational Terrorism panel of the 19th Annual Convention of the International Studies Association, February 22-25, 1978, Washington, D.C.

32. ———. "Contemporary Revolutionary Organizations." In Robert O. Keohane and Joseph S. Nye, Jr., eds. *Transnational Relations and World Politics*, pp. 153-168. Cambridge: Harvard University Press, 1973.

Observes that the vast majority of revolutionary groups, while professing solidarity with the international movement, are fundamentally national in character, tactics, and immediate aspirations. The fortunes of groups in third world regions are outlined, and the evolution of successful movements into state governments (with subsequent radical changes in their behavior) is discussed.

33. ———. "Future Trends in Terrorism." Paper presented to the conference on Terror: The Man, the Mind, and the Matter, October 15-16, 1976, at the John Jay School of Criminal Justice, New York City.

34. ———. *On Revolt: Strategies of National Liberation*. Cambridge: Harvard University Press, 1976. 272 pp.

Based upon hundreds of interviews with terrorists and security forces, Bell discusses terrorism in Palestine, Malaya, Kenya, Cyprus, South Arabia, and Ireland. A useful review of the literature on the revolts in these areas is appended.

35. ———. "Revolutionary Organizations: Special Cases and Imperfect Models." In David Carlton and Carlo Schaerf, eds., *International Terrorism and World Security*, pp. 78-92. London: Croom Helm, 1975.

Argues that current theorizing on terrorism is too general to be useful and uses case studies of the IRA Provisionals, EOKA-B, and the ELF to show that they differ in many important ways that cannot be handled by a general theory of terrorist behavior.

36. ———. "Terror: An Overview." In Marius Livingston, ed., *International Terrorism in the Contemporary World*, pp. 36-43. Westport, Conn.: Greenwood Press, 1978.

37. ———. "Terrorism and Academic Analysis: A Common Wisdom." Paper presented to the Joint National Meeting of the Operations Research Society of America and the Institute of Management Sciences, May 1-3, 1978, New York City.

The author's abstract states: "This discussion will examine the rise in the perception of terrorism by the public, the media, the policy people, and the academics; the academic response, rituals, and institutions; the conclusions of the common wisdom; the future: methodological problems and real terrorists."

38. ———. *Transnational Terror* (Stanford, Calif., and Washington, D.C.: Hoover Institution and American Enterprise Institute, 1975. 91 pp.

A good overview of the major contemporary terrorist campaigns, save for a curious silence about Asia. Gives many case studies, good descriptions of main incidents, and a serviceable typology of terrorists and terrorist actions. The discussion of responses taken is good.

39. ———. "Transnational Terror and World Order." *South Atlantic Quarterly* 74 (Autumn 1975): 404-417.

Argues that revolutionaries use terrorism for functional, provocative, and symbolic purposes, illustrating each type. Bell finds that world order can be disrupted but not destroyed by such actions. Conversely, he suggests that terrorism is more easily tolerated than prevented.

40. ———. "Trends on Terror: The Analysis of Political Violence." *World Politics* 24 (April 1977): 476-488.

Laments the poor response of academe in analyzing terrorism, arguing that most work is unsystematic, uncoordinated, and very much divorced from reality. Books reviewed include those of Clutterbuck, Hyams, Wilkinson, Kohl and Litt, and Willrich and Taylor.

41. Beloff, Max. "Terrorism and the People." In *Ten Years of Terrorism: Collected Views*, pp. 109-127. New York: Crane-Russak, 1979.

42. Beres, Louis René. "Guerrillas, Terrorists, and Polarity: New Structural Models of World Politics." *Western Political Quarterly* (December 1974): 624-636.

One of the rare attempts to incorporate the activities of terrorists into macromodels of world politics. Unfortunately the discussion is at a very low level of sophistication and quickly becomes an exercise in multiplication of 2-by-2 and 3-by-3 tables. The models are presented in such limited detail as to make the exercise of little value.

43. Bergier, Jacques. *La troisiéme guerre mondial est commencée.* Paris: Albin Michel, 1976. 183 pp.

Discusses the increase of world terrorism, focusing on Western Europe. Also mentions funding sources of groups, as well as possible nuclear terrorism. Notes the possibility of a worldwide north-south guerrilla conflict developing.

44. Bite, Vita. *International Terrorism.* Issue Brief Number 1B74042. Washington, D.C.: Library of Congress, CRS, October 31, 1975. 15 pp.

An update of an earlier CRS report, it gives an issue definition; policy analysis; lists of legislation, congressional hearings, reports, and documents; and chronology of terrorist events.

45. Bobrow, Davis B. "Preparing for Unwanted Events: Instances of International Political Terrorism." Paper delivered at the International Seminar on Research Strategies for the Study of International Political Terrorism. May 30-June 1, 1977, Evian, France. Published in *Terrorism* 1 (1978): 397-422.

Evaluates four police models of hostage situations and suggests that models of extrication, cooptation through payoffs, and deterrence may be appropriate for mass destruction cases. The possibilities of diagnostic gaming are explored.

46. Bocca, Geoffrey. *The Secret Army.* Englewood Cliffs, N.J.: Prentice-Hall, 1968.

47. Bonanate, L. *Political Violence in the Contemporary World.* Milan: Franco Angeli, 1979.

48. Bouthoul, Gaston. "Definitions of Terror." In David Carlton and Carlo Schaerf, eds., *International Terrorism and World Security*, pp. 50-59. London: Croom Helm, 1975.

Covers most of the points made by the earlier paper in the conference by Jenkins. Bouthoul, president of the Institut française de polemologie, mentions characteristics of terrorism, forms of terrorism, new techniques, problems of getting adequate statistics on incidents, and effects of terrorism.

49. ———. "On International Terrorism: Historical and Contemporary Aspects 1968-1975." Paper distributed at the State Department Conference on International Terrorism in Retrospect and Prospect, March 25-26, 1975. 36 pp. FAR document 24837-S.

Presents statistics on terrorist activities.

50. ———. ''Le terrorisme.'' *Etudes polemoligiques* 8 (April 1973): 37.

51. Bracher, Karl Dietrich. *Terrorismus in der demokratischen Gesell-schaft.* Hamburg, 1978.

52. Bradshaw, Jon. ''The Dream of Terror.'' *Esquire*, July 18, 1978, pp. 24-50.

53. Brewer, Gary D. *Existing in a World of Institutionalized Danger.* New Haven, Conn.: School of Organization and Management, Yale University, Technical Report No. 102. March 1976. Published in *Yale Studies in World Public Order* 3 (Spring 1977): 339-387.

While concerned with larger strategic questions, Brewer mentions some problems in the current study of terrorism. In Brewer's view, little attention has been paid to deterrence and prevention of terrorism. We should consider the common structural features of the terrorist act (audience, terrorist, victim, media, spectator, authorities, allies, and sanctuaries), as well as its phases, including preparation, execution, climax, and denouement.

54. Brown, Larry C. ''Transnational Terrorism and Foreign Policy: A Summary of Workshop Deliberations.'' In *Proceedings of the 13th International Affairs Symposium of the Foreign Area Officer Course*, pp. 46-54. Fort Bragg, N.C.: U.S. Army Institute for Military Assistance, December 5-7, 1977.

Presentations were made by Eugene Methvin of *Reader's Digest*, Robert Taubert of FBI, and Ed Mickolus of CIA. The group discussed the media, intelligence, psychology, U.S. policy and response, and nuclear terrorism.

55. Browne, Marjorie Ann, and Nanes, Allan S. *International Terrorism: Issue Brief Number IB74042.* Washington, D.C: Library of Congress Congressional Research Service, March 10, 1978.

A review of major domestic and international legislation against terrorism. Appended is an extensive chronology of recent actions related to terrorism.

56. Buckley, Jr., William F. *UN Journal: A Delegate's Odyssey.* New York: G. P. Putnam's Sons, 1974.

57. Burnham, James. ''Notes on Terrorism.'' *National Review*, October 13, 1972.

58. ———. ''Roots of Terrorism.'' *National Review*, March 16, 1974.

59. ———. ''The Protracted Conflict.'' *National Review*, January 5, 1973.

60. Burton, Anthony. *Revolutionary Violence: The Theories*. New York: Crane, Russak, 1978.

Reviews several revolutionary theories, including those of Carlos Marighella, Camilo Torres, Kim Il Sung, Giap, Mao, and Lawrence of Arabia and notes the long history of fascist theories. In considering the future, Burton believes that transnational terrorism will continue to grow if states are unable to cooperate against it.

61. Campbell, Donald G. ''The Growth of Transnational Terrorism.'' Research Report No. 299 Air War College, Air University, April 1978. Available as FAR 29085-N AD B029 119L.

62. Carlton, David. ''The Future of Political Substate Violence.'' In Yonah Alexander, David Carlton, and Paul Wilkinson, eds., *Terrorism: Theory and Practice*, pp. 201-230. Boulder: Westview, 1979.

A speculative essay on the future, suggesting that terrorism will grow in an uneven fashion, some countries will continue to be vulnerable (particularly technologically sophisticated ones), most groups will prefer not to use mass destruction weapons and will instead copy others' actions, partronage of terrorism will be self-limiting, and some international cooperation on specific issues will be possible.

63. Carlton, David, and Schaerf, Carlo, eds. *International Terrorism and World Security*. London: Croom Helm, and New York: Halstead Press of John Wiley, 1975. 332 pp.

European and Middle East security, the arms race, peace teaching, and international terrorism were four topics discussed in the fifth course of the International School on Disarmament and Research on Conflicts held at Urbino, Italy, in August 1974. This volume is a record of their proceedings. Articles on terrorism are by Brian Jenkins, Gaston Bouthoul, Steven J. Rosen, Robert Frank, George Sliwowski, J. Bowyer Bell, and Daniel Heradstveit.

64. Carmichael, D. J. C. ''Terrorism: Some Ethical Issues.'' *Chitty's Law Journal* 24 (September 1976): 233-239.

65. Carson, John, ed. *Terrorism in Theory and Practice: Proceedings of a Colloquium*. Toronto: Atlantic Council of Canada, 1978.

66. Chisholm, Henry J. *''The Function of Terror and Violence in Revolution.''* Master's Thesis, Georgetown University, 1948.

67. Clandestine Tactics and Technology Data Service. Gaithersburg, Md.: International Association of Chiefs of Police.

The service, offered to only selected applicants, covers documents on terrorist groups, activities, tactics, and countermeasures.

68. Clarity, James F. "Terrorists' Techniques Improve, and So Do Efforts to Block Them." *New York Times*, July 23, 1976.
A rundown of the modus operandi of the major terrorist groups around the world, their links, sources of arms and other support, and methods of recruitment. Most of the article is derived from interviews with intelligence sources.

69. Clutterbuck, Richard. "The Police and Urban Terrorism." *Outpost: The Magazine of B.S.A. Police* 53 (July 1975): 204-214.
Gives an overview of left-wing terrorism.

70. ———. *Protest and the Urban Guerrilla.* London: Abelard-Schuman, 1973.
Compares the lack of violence in England, Scotland, and Wales to the situation in Northern Ireland. Discusses the spread of such forms of dissent and their effects upon society, industry, and individual rights.

71. Cobb, Richard. *Terreur et subsistances, 1793-1795.* Paris: Librairie Clavreuil, 1964.

72. Cohen, Bernard L. "Potentialities of Terrorism." *Bulletin of the Atomic Scientists* 32 (June 1976): 34-35.

73. Connelly, Ralph William. "Third Party Involvement in International Terrorist Extortion." Master's thesis, Naval Postgraduate School, 1976.
Using a refined version of Mickolus's ITERATE data set, Connelly looked at 166 cases of hostage taking to determine whether success in obtaining demands leads to further incidents. The variables indicating success were so interrelated that no single determinant of success could be isolated. Connelly's contribution is a method of coding the amount of publicity an incident receives and relating that to future terrorist behavior.

74. Constance, George. "International Terrorism and the United States." Ph.D. dissertation, New School for Social Research, in preparation.

75. Cooper, H. H. Anthony. "The International Experience with Terrorism." In *Report of the Task Force on Disorders and Terrorism*, pp. 419-442. Washington, D.C.: National Advisory Committee on Criminal Justice Standards and Goals, December 1976.
Presents an overview of contemporary terrorism, pointing out its limited efficacy in the long run. The arguments in the debate over negotiations are

discussed in greater detail than normally found, with attention being given to the relevant legal context. Airline security is given special mention, although the author is silent about the U.S.-Cuba agreement. Comparative legal responses to terrorism, bolstered by detailed explication of specific laws, conclude the work.

76. ———. "The Menace of Terrorism." Paper presented at the Conference on Terrorism in the Contemporary World: An International Symposium, April 1976, at Glassboro State College. Available as FAR 25658-N.

77. ———. "Terrorism and the Intelligence Function." *Chitty's Law Journal* 24 (March 1976): 73.

78. ———. "Terrorism and the Intelligence Function." In Marius Livingston, ed., *International Terrorism in the Contemporary World*, pp. 287-296. Westport, Conn.: Greenwood Press, 1978.

79. ———. "Terrorism: The Problem of the Problem of Definition." *Chitty's Law Journal* 26 (March 1978): 105ff.

80. ———. "Terrorism: The Problem of a Problem of Definition." Paper presented to the panel on Violence and Terror of the Conference on Complexity: A Challenge to the Adaptive Capacity of American Society, sponsored by the Society for General Systems Research, March 24-26, 1977. Columbia, Maryland.

Cooper, director of a major national commission study on terrorism and violence, notes the uses of definitions in research and centers on the problem of subjectivity in such endeavors. Agreement on parts of the general definition, rather than the definition itelf, may prove more fruitful.

81. ———. "The Terrorist and His Victim." *Victimology* I (June 1976).

82. ———. "Whither Now? Terrorism on the Brink." *Chitty's Law Journal* 25 (1977): 181-190.

Surveys trends in terrorism during the previous year, noting the rise of state terrorism, as well as domestic and international patterns. The role of states in acting as restraints on terrorists they support is noted, as are the possibilities of alterations in terrorists tactics as security measures improve.

83. Copley, Gregory. "A Sociological Profile of Terrorism." *Defense and Foreign Affairs Digest* 4 (1978): 38-39.

A summary of Russell and Miller's comparisons of terrorists.

84. Crelinsten, Ronald D. "International Political Terrorism: A Challenge for Comparative Research." *International Journal of Comparative and Applied Criminal Justice*. In press.

85. Crozier, Brian. "Anatomy of Terrorism." *Nation* 188 (1959): 250-252.

86. ———, ed. *Annual of Power and Conflict 1972-73: A Survey of Political Violence and International Influence*. London: Institute for the Study of Conflict, 1973.
    Surveys the actions of the world's extremist groups and looks at changes in the political balance of power.

87. ———, ed. *Annual of Power and Conflict 1973-74*. London: Institute for the Study of Conflict, 1974.
    Country-by-country record of events involving extremist movements. Crozier contributes an introductory chapter on aid for terrorism and analyzes the causes, trends, and consequences of revolutionary violence. Appendixes on communist parties and extremist movements are also presented.

88. ———, ed. *Annual of Power and Conflict 1974-75*. London: Institute for the Study of Conflict, 1975.
    In addition to its annual area studies, has a lead article on subversion and the Soviet Union.

89. ———, ed. *Annual of Power and Conflict 1975-76*. London: Institute for the Study of Conflict, 1976.
    Includes introductory articles on Russia's revolutionary base and the shifting balance of power.

90. ———, ed. *Annual of Power and Conflict 1976-77*. London: Institute for the Study of Conflict, 1977.
    The *Annual's* format changed with this issue and now includes a chronology of security-related events after each country discussion. While still a useful survey, the authors' acceptance of unsubstantiated press stories at times detracts from the volume's credibility.

91. ———, ed. *New Dimensions of Security in Europe*. London: Institute for the Study of Conflict, 1975.
    Among other threats discussed is that of terrorists. The presentation is akin to an APC country-by-country profile, along with suggestions for combating such insurgent attacks.

92. ———. *The Rebels: A Study of Post-War Insurrections*. Boston: Beacon Press, 1960.

Discusses cases of guerrilla warfare and anti-government uprisings in the 1950s. Terrorism receives mention in one of five major sections. Among the conclusions: ''Terrorism is the weapon of the weak.'' To succeed, terrorists need the support of the population and arms.

93. ———. ''Terrorism: The Problem in Perspective.'' Paper presented to the Department of State Conference on International Terrorism in Retrospect and Prospect, March 25-26, 1976, Washington, D.C.

Begins with a history of major terrorist campaigns from 1944 to the present. The growth of transnational terrorists armed with high technology and backed by state sponsors is discussed, as are options for combating them.

94. ———. ''Transnational Terrorism.'' Testimony before the subcommittee on Internal Security of the Committee on the Judiciary, U.S. Senate, May 14, 1975. 9 pp.

Gives definitions and discusses phases of revolutionary groups versus terrorism for its own sake, objects of terrorism (disruptive versus coercive), types of terrorist groups, subversive centers, and responses to terrorism.

95. d'Astorg, Bertrand. *Introduction du monde de la terreur*. Paris: Editions du Sevil, 1945.

96. Davidson, William H. ''Terrorism Now and in the Future.'' *Pilot* 34 (Fall 1977): 6-7.

A pithy description of what terrorists have done and are capable of doing, as well as a checklist of how to react if faced with a terrorist situation.

97. Davies, Donald M. ''Terrorism: Motives and Means.'' *Foreign Service Journal* (September 1962): 19-21.

98. Davies, Thomas Russell. ''Feedback Processes and International Terrorism.'' Ph.D. dissertation, Florida State University, 1977.

99. Demaitre, Edmund. ''Terrorism and the Intellectuals.'' *Washington Star*, April 15, 1973.

100. D'Hondt, J. ''Terrorism and Politics.'' *Etudes internationales de psycho-sociologie criminelle* 24 (1973): 72-77.

Claims that the roots of terrorism can be found in the world situation and the righteous reaction to repression.

101. Dobson, Christopher, and Payne, Ronald. *The Terrorists: Their Weapons, Leaders, and Tactics.* New York: Facts on File, 1979. Simultaneously published as *Weapons of Terror*. London: Macmillan, 1979.

Two investigative journalists give an update on the major international terrorist groups (although they ignore Central American organizations), their weapons, and a chronology of their operations through January 1979. Also provides a discussion of how democracies fight back.

102. Dror, Yehezkel. ''TFB: Terror, Fanaticism, Blackmail as a Strategic Problem.'' Paper presented to the Conference on Terrorism, Pre-emption and Surprise, sponsored by the Leonard Davis Institute of International Relations June 1975, at Hebrew University, Jerusalem, Israel.

103. Drummond, William. ''Scholars Examine Political Terrorism: Academic Meeting in Israel Probes Problems, Solutions.'' *Los Angeles Times*, May 4, 1975.

Coins term *TFB* (terrorism, fanaticism, and blackmail). Mentions three-day March conference in Jerusalem under the aegis of the Leonard Davis Institute for International Relations, where Tanter argued that Israeli reprisals are effective for only about thirty days and have no long-range effect in quelling attacks. Dror suggested that mass media should reduce publicity. Quester argued that value on life has increased, making TFB's job easier. Technology has increased vulnerability of society.

104. Dugard, John. ''International Terrorism and the Just War.'' *Stanford Journal of International Studies* 12 (Spring 1977): 21-38.

105. Eggers, William. *Terrorism: The Slaughter of Innocents.* Chatsworth, Calif.: Major, 1975.

106. Elliott, John D. ''Contemporary Terrorism: Catalyst or Agent of Revolution?'' Unpublished manuscript, Washington, D.C.

107. ———. ''International Terrorism: Threat to US Security?'' *Armed Forces Journal International* 114 (September 1976): 38-39.

108. ———. ''Primers on Terrorism.'' *Military Review* (October 1976).

109. ———. ''Terrorism Examined.'' *Marylander* (Spring 1977).

110. ———. ''Transitions of Contemporary Terrorism.'' *Military Review* (May 1977): 3-15.

111. ———. "Transitions of Contemporary Terrorism Related to Changes in Technology." Paper presented to the NASA Summer Faculty Institute, July 23, 1976, Houston, Texas.

112. Elliott, John D., and Gibson, Leslie K., eds. *Contemporary Terrorism: Selected Readings.* Gaithersburg, Md.: International Association of Chiefs of Police, 1978.

Articles are taken from previously published works by noted academics, journalists, private researchers, and government officials. General chapter headings are "Perspectives on Contemporary Terrorism," "Response of Threatened Societies," and "Emerging Patterns of Terrorism."

113. Elser, Anthony. *Bombs, Beards and Barricades: 150 Years of Youth Revolt.* New York: Stein and Day, 1971.

114. Ermlich, Fred. "Ethical Implications of Terrorism." Paper presented to the Eighteenth Annual Convention of the International Studies Association, March 16-20, 1977, St. Louis, Missouri.

115. Esson, D. M. R. "The Secret Weapon: Terrorism." *Army Quarterly* 78 (1959): 167-180.

116. Evans, Ernest. "Terrorism and International Politics." Paper presented at the annual convention of the Northeast Political Science Association, November 11-13, 1976 at South Egremont, Massachusetts.

The third chapter of Evans's MIT dissertation, it analyzes the effects that terrorism has had and could have on the international order, illustrating its points with case studies of major incidents. Evans argues that terrorism has five major implications: it aggravates relations between nations, it can cause already serious international situations to escalate to war, it raises important international legal questions, it introduces surrogate warfare, and it endangers international order.

117. Evron, Yair, ed. *International Violence: Terrorism, Surprise, and Control.* Jerusalem: Hebrew University, Leonard Davis Institute for International Relations, 1979.

A compilation of papers presented at a 1975 conference by scholars from the United States, Western Europe, and Israel.

118. Executive Risk Assessment. Alexandria, Va.: Risks International.

Each monthly issue looks at a specific aspect of terrorism. Six regional assessments are published every two months. For an annual fee, subscribers may use the Risks data base for twelve updates of materials.

119. Fabricius-Brand, Margarete. "Women in Isolation." In *International Summaries: A Collection of Selected Translations in Law Enforcement and Criminal Justice*, 3: 55-62. Washington, D.C.: U.S. Department of Justice, National Criminal Justice Reference Service, April 1979.

Discusses three theses on the behavior of terrorists: withdrawal from productive society, rejection of personal interests, and terrorism as the inadequate solution of female terrorists to the process of social status reduction experienced by female intellectuals.

120. Falk, Richard A. "Terror, Liberation Movements, and the Processes of Social Change." *American Journal of International Law* 63 (1969): 423-427.

121. Fattah, Ezzat A. "Terrorist Activities and Terrorist Targets: A Tentative Typology." In Yonah Alexander and John Gleason, eds., *Terrorism: Behavioral Perspectives*. New York: Pergamon, 1980.

122. Fearey, Robert A. "Introduction to International Terrorism." In Marius Livingston, ed., *International Terrorism in the Contemporary World*, pp. 25-35. Westport, Conn.: Greenwood, 1978.

123. ———. "Remarks before the Los Angeles World Affairs Council and the World Affairs Council of Orange County on International Terrorism." Available from the U.S. Department of State, Office of the Special Assistant to the Secretary of State and Coordinator for Combating Terrorism, February 19, 1976.

Gives the official State Department view of the scope of the problem, types of effective responses and methods of combating terrorism, prospects for terrorism in the future, and possible responses. U.S. policy in combating terrorism includes intelligence, physical security measures, and apprehension and punishment of terrorists.

124. Fields, Rona. "Victims of Terror." Paper presented at the Conference on Moral Implications of Terrorism, March 14-16, 1979, UCLA.

125. Finger, Seymour Maxwell, and Alexander, Yonah, eds. *Terrorism: Interdisciplinary Perspectives*. New York: John Jay Press, 1977.

A collection of the papers presented to the conference on international terrorism sponsored by the Ralph Bunche Institute, held in New York City, June 9-11, 1976.

126. Fogel, Lawrence. *Predictive Antiterrorism*. Decision Sciences, April 1977.

Greisman, H. C. "Social Meanings of Terrorism: Reification, Violence, and Social Control." *Contemporary Crises* 1 (July 1977): 303-318.
Argues that social meanings assign perceived morality to specific behaviors. Morality changes as a function of this social attribution.

Griffith, G. W. "Biological Warfare and the Urban Battleground." *Enforcement Journal* 14 (1975): 405.
Argues that biological agents would not be difficult for a terrorist to obtain or disperse.

Groom, A. J. R. "Coming to Terms with Terrorism." *British Journal of International Studies* 4 (April 1978): pp. 62-77.
A review of several early works on terrorism by Wilkinson, Walter, Bell, Hutkins, Clutterbuck, Burton, Sobel, Deane-Drummond, and the United Nations. Most of the common arguments are raised.

Gros, Bernard. "Terrorism and Literature." In Marius Livingston, ed., *International Terrorism in the Contemporary World*, pp. 447-453. Westport, Conn.: Greenwood Press, 1978.

Gross, Feliks. "The Social Setting for Emergent Terrorism." Paper presented to the Conference on Terror: The Man, the Mind, and the Matter, October 15-16, 1976, at the John Jay School for Criminal Justice, New York City.

Gurr, Ted Robert. "Proposals for Research on Political Terrorism." April 1973. 23 pp. Available as FAR 17081-N.
Aims at policy-relevant research by focusing on origins, processes, and outcomes of terrorism at the macrolevel and microlevel. Gurr hoped to look at growth and decline of activities and how long- and short-term policies would alter these outcomes.

———. "Some Characteristics of Political Terrorism in the 1960s." Paper presented to the Department of State Conference on International Terrorism in Retrospect and Prospect, March 25-26, 1976. Published in Michael Stohl, ed., *The Politics of Terrorism*, pp. 23-49. New York: Dekker, 1979.
Surveys episodes and campaigns of domestic terrorism in eighty-seven countries between 1961 and 1970, looking at destructive violence by stealth rather than open combat against political targets conducted by groups operating clandestinely and sporadically. Despite most of the conventional wisdom on terrorism, Gurr found that campaigns were conducted by small groups and were short-lived. Their public motives did not differ from those of groups

Uses an epidemiological analogy to analyze the spread of terrorist campaigns, tactics, and ideologies.

127. Fooner, M. "Vulnerable Society: Crisis in Technology, Terror and Victimization." *Police Chief* 41 (February 1974).

129. Frank, Robert S. "The Prediction of Political Violence from Objective and Subjective Social Indicators." Paper presented to the International Psychoanalytical Congress, 1976, Edinburgh.

130. Freedman, Lawrence Z. "Messianic and Prophetic Terrorism." Paper delivered to the Conference on the Moral Implications of Terrorism: Justifications and Consequences, March 14-16, 1979, UCLA.

131. ———. "Problems of the Polistaraxic: Terrorism, Policy, Pathology, Politics." *University of Chicago Magazine* 66 (Summer 1974): 7-10.

132. Friedlander, Robert A. "Historical Perspectives on Terrorism" Paper presented to the Conference on International Terrorism, sponsored by the Ralph Bunche Institute on the United Nations of the Graduate School and University Center of the City University of New York and the State University College at Oneonta of the State University of New York, June 9-11, 1976. Published as "The Origins of International Terrorism," in Seymour Maxwell Finger and Yonah Alexander, eds., *Terrorism: Interdisciplinary Perspectives*, pp. 30-45. New York: John Jay Press, 1977.
Suggests that the prevailing confusion regarding the origin and composition of terror violence has led to an understandable disagreement over solutions to the problem. Shows how the strategy of terrorism has developed over the centuries, with philosophical justifications closely paralleling this evolution.

133. ———. "The Origins of International Terrorism: A Micro Legal-Historical Perspective." *Israel Yearbook on Human Rights* 6 (1978).

134. ———. "Terrorism and Political Violence: Some Preliminary Observations." *International Studies Notes* 2 (Summer 1976).
Friedlander strenuously denounces the growing rise of terrorism, along with an apparent willingness by society to accept such high levels of violence, and calls upon national leaders to express their moral outrage at these attacks by implementing tough legislation.

135. ———. "Terrorism and Violence: Some Preliminary Observations." *International Studies Notes* 3 (Summer 1976): 1-3.

Friedlander makes a distinction between terrorism by states and by non-governmental actors, accepting Moss's threefold typology of repressive, defensive, and offensive uses (see entry 319). Discusses the history of international legal remedies, finding the world community wanting.

136. Fromkin, David. "The Strategy of Terrorism." *Foreign Affairs* 53 (July 1975): 683-698.

Through the use of historical case studies of the Irgun, Robespierre, Irish terrorists in the early 1900s, and FLN in Algeria, Fromkin argues that the strategy of terrorism is in determining the countermove of those who are attacked. Terrorism cannot be prevented, but it can be defeated by not giving in to terrorist demands or engaging in the repressive behavior that loses the government's societal support.

137. Funke, Manfred, ed. *Terrorism: Investigations of the Strategy and Structure of the Revolutionary Political Power.* Dusseldorf: Droste Verlag, 1977.

138. Garrigan, Timothy B. and Lopez, George A. *Terrorism: A Problem of Political Violence.* Richmond, Indiana: Earlham College, a Learning Package Prepared for the Consortium for International Studies Education of the International Studies Association, February 1978.

The authors aim at introducing students to groups that practice political terrorism; to the causes and patterns of this form of political violence; and to the problems of responding to terrorist activity. Uses case studies, simulations, statistical analysis, and questionnaires.

139. Gaucher, Roland. *The Terrorists: From Tsarist Russia to the OAS.* Translated by Paula Spurlin. London: Secker and Warburg, 1968.

Gives a historical overview of domestic terrorism, beginning with nineteenth-century Russian anarchism, 1920s German and Macedonian groups, Rumania's Iron Guard, the original IRA, and Stern Gang and Irgun, and the Algerian problem, which receives a much more extensive treatment than the other cases. Originally published as *Les terroristes.* Paris: Albin Michel, 1965.

140. Geraghty, Tony. "Ten Years of Terrorism." In Jennifer Shaw, E. F. Gueritz and A. E. Younger, eds., *Ten Years of Terrorism: Collected Views*, pp. 170-187. New York: Crane, Russak, 1979.

141. Gertz, Dwight L. "Terrorist Weapons and the Terrorist Threat." U.S. Naval Institute *Proceedings* 101 (October 1975): 113-114.

142. Gladwin, Thomas N. *Terrorism and the Mu* Forthcoming.

143. Glaser, H. "Die Diskussion ueber den Terroris *Zeitgeschichte*, June 24, 1978.

144. Gleason, John M. "Third World Terrorism: Per tive Research." In Yonah Alexander and John M. Gle *Behavioral Perspectives.* New York: Pergamon Press,

145. Glines, C. V. "Is Terrorism Still a Threat?" *A* 1977): 21-23.
Yes, according to a CIA study, and an interview wi Sloan of the University of Oklahoma.

146. Golob-Nick, Mirjana. "New Aspects of Interna *Review of International Affairs* (March 1975).

147. Gonzales-Mata, Luis M. *Terrorismo Internacio Derecha la Extrema Izquierda, y los Crimenes del Estado.* Editorial Argos, S.A., 1978.

148. Goode, Stephen. *Guerrilla Warfare and Terrorism.* N Watts, 1977.

149. Gotovitch, M. Hose. "Quelques réflexions historique isme." In *Réflections sur la définition et la répression du terro* Brussels: Editions de l'Université de Bruxelles, 1974.

150. Grabosky, P. N. "The Urban Context of Political Michael Stohl, ed., *The Politics of Terrorism*, pp. 51-76. Nev 1979.
Studies the urban environment, exploring those characte port terrorist operations. Discusses recruitment, organization, port, strategic considerations, and urban-oriented tactics, targe measures.

151. Graham, N. F. "International Terrorism." *Army Jour* 1975): 43-63.

153. Green, Leslie C. "International Terrorism." Address de Edmonton branch of the Canadian Institute of International Affai 1973.

using other means. They were motivated by hostility to specific policies rather than by revolutionary goals. Their actions did not seriously threaten society.

161. Hacker, Frederick J. *Crusaders, Criminals, Crazies: Terror and Terrorism in Our Time.* New York: Norton, 1976.

Sees terror as being practiced by governments, while terrorism is engaged in by those wanting to obtain government power. Crusaders have an ideology, criminals seek personal gain, and crazies have mental disorders. Gives many case examples of how his typology can classify. Of interest are Hacker's accounts of the Hearst and Vienna cases, in which he was a consultant during negotiations. He argues that we should consider a type of preincident bargaining and that bargains made by negotiators should be judicially binding. In postscript, he dissents from the popular view of the Entebbe raid. Reviewed by Diane Johnson "The Blood Dimmed Tide," *Washington Post Book, World,* January 30, 1977, pp. E5-E6, and Robert A. Friedlander "Tanya Lives!" *Student Lawyer* 5 (April 1977): 61-62.

162. ———. *Terror: Mythos, Realitat, Analyse.* Vienna: Verlag Fritz Molden, 1973.

A presentation of various spectacular terrorist incidents such as the Munich massacre, with discussion of popular views and theories of terrorist behavior.

163. Hamilton, Lawrence C. "A Causal Theory of Terrorism." Paper presented to the Joint National Meeting of the Operations Research Society of America and the Institute of Management Sciences, May 1-3, 1978, New York City.

The paper's abstract reads: "The literature on terrorism contains a number of competing hypotheses about its structural causes and effects. These hypotheses may be stated as propositions which could be integrated into formal causal theories in which the existence, signs, and magnitude of the possible relationships are problematic. One such theory, a non-recursive path model, is proposed and evaluated through the use of numerical data on 86 nations from 1960-1970."

164. ———. "Ecology of Terrorism." Ph.D. dissertation, University of Colorado, 1978.

165. Hamilton, Michael P. "Terrorism: Its Ethical Implications for the Future." *Futurist* 11 (December 1977): 351-354.

166. Hamilton, Peter. *Espionage, Terrorism, and Subversion.* Surrey: Peter A. Heims, 1979.

167. Hannay, William A. "International Terrorism: The Need for a Fresh Perspective." *International Lawyer* 8 (1974): 268-284.

168. Hardman, J. B. S. "Terrorism." *International Encyclopedia of the Social Sciences* 14 (1968): 575-580.
An update of his 1933 treatment of the subject, Hardman distinguishes terrorism from intimidation, government use of extreme force, mass insurrection, and coups. He discusses the role of terrorism in revolutionary theory, concentrating on the activities of the early Russian anarchists.

169. Heren, Louis. "Curing Terrorism: The New Romantics—Myth and Reality." *Atlas World Press Review* 25 (January 1978): 31-33.
A review of two papers by the CIA on international terrorism.

170. Heyman, Edward S. "The Diffusion of Transnational Terrorism." Paper presented to the annual meeting of the International Studies Association, March 1979, at Toronto.
After introducing innovative methods of studying diffusion by computer and mapping, Heyman surveys the mechanisms of the spread of terrorism.

171. ———. "Monitoring the Diffusion of Transnational Terrorism: A Conceptual Framework and Methodology." Master's thesis, University of North Carolina, 1979. Revised and published by Technical Notes, Clandestine Tactics and Technology, Gaithersburg, Md.: International Association of Chiefs of Police, 1979.

172. ———. "The Moral Implications of the Diffusion of Terror among States." Paper delivered to the Conference on Moral Implications of Terrorism, March 14-16, 1979. UCLA.

173. ———. "Risk Assessment." In Stephen Sloan and Richard Shultz, eds., *Responding to the Terrorist Threat: Prevention and Control*. New York: Pergamon, 1980.
Applies random outlaw models to study terrorist behavior.

174. Heyman, Edward and Mickolus, Edward. "Imitation by Terrorists: Quantitative Approaches to the Study of Diffusion in Transnational Terrorism." Paper presented to the joint national meeting of the Operations Research Society of America and the Institute for Management Sciences, May 1-3, 1978, New York City. Published in Yonah Alexander and John Gleason, eds., *Terrorism: Behavioral Perspectives*. New York: Pergamon, 1980.

A computer data set is used to generate a series of maps that illustrate the spread of certain forms of transnational attacks during the past decade. Markov chain models are used to assess the stability of this process.

175. Higgins, R. "Can Terrorism Be Justified?" *Listener* 99 (May 1978): 558-559.

176. Historical Evaluation and Research Organization. "An Approach to the Use of Historical Case Material to Develop a Behavioral Theory of Terrorism." McLean, Va., n.d. [July 1975].

Suggests using case historians in studying terrorist groups. Four or five behavioral scientists would use the historians as data bases, developing propositions on behavior which could then be tested by other means. Revision of opinion in the light of new data is allowed for, and generation of new propositions by these new data is called for. Creates propositions by sequential analysis of cases, rather than looking at cases in combinations. Their weakest point is central to their method: "Although it appears reasonable to this time to suggest examination of a dozen cases, the actual number should be based on 2 empirical factors; 1. when the number of new propositions generated reaches a point of diminishing returns and 2. when the level of support (certainty) for 'critical' propositions reaches an acceptable point."

177. Hobsbawm, Eric J. "Appraisal of Terrorism." *Canadian Dimension* 9 (1972): 11-14.

178. Hodgson, Godfrey. "Terrorism." *Ditchley Journal* 6 (Spring 1979): 35-44.

Reviews the proceedings of a conference of North American and Western European dignitaries on the causes of and responses to terrorism.

179. Hofmann, Paul. " 'Terrorism' or 'Liberation Struggle'? Violence Begets Many New Nations." *New York Times*, October 31, 1974.

180. Holton, Gerald. "Reflections on Modern Terrorism." *Bulletin of the Atomic Scientists* (November 1976): 8-9.

Suggests that the distinctions between terrorism by non-state groups (which is generally unsuccesful and uses a low level of technology) and that by governments (always successful, which is arguable, and using sophisticated technology) will in the future become blurred, with states hiring bands of mercenaries. This will lead some states to give these groups technological boosts, forcing other states to adopt unconventional means of defense. We may also see technical failures in the initial stages of the new type of terrorist campaign, but the future looks bleak for targeted societies.

181. Honderich, Ted. *Political Violence: A Philosophical Analysis of Terrorism.* Ithaca: Cornell, University Press, 1976.

Review by Mulford Q. Sibley, *American Political Science Review* 72 (September 1978): 1028-1029, complains that the book is lacking in illustrative examples to back Honderich's conclusion that some violence is justified.

182. Horowitz, Irving Louis. "Political Terrorism and State Power." *Political and Military Sociology* 1 (Spring 1973): 147-157.

Originally a discussion draft of remarks prepared for the special Ad Hoc Conference on International Terror, directed by Ambassador Armin H. Meyer, U.S. Department of State, October 24, 1972, the paper's abstract explains that this work "attempts to locate the problem of political terrorism within the larger context of the current blending and fusion of radical political practice and social deviance generally. Beyond that, it attempts to develop a profile of the terrorist that distinguishes the terrorist from the guerrilla or the national revolutionary. It also seeks to show how the problem of terrorism manifests particular concern within the Marxist tradition, where this issue of the use of terror remains a viable theoretical and pragmatic consideration—unlike the older western democratic political traditions. Finally, the paper offers some brief remarks on the control of terror and the limits of such control within a democratic society."

183. ——. "Toward a Qualitative Micro-politics of Terror: Remarks Delivered at the Conference on International Terrorism." Washington, D.C.: U.S. Department of State, S/CCT, March 25, 1976. Reprinted as FAR 24506-N.

Horowitz comments on Ted Gurr's conference presentation, arguing that there are many ways to measure the success of a terrorist campaign. Mere counting of deaths does not do justice to the extent of societal disarray caused by such attacks. One must also consider the extent of state-sponsored activities against its citizens.

184. ——. "Unicorns and Terrorists." Mimeographed. Statement prepared for the Conference on International Terrorism, Washington, D.C.: U.S. Department of State, S/CCT, March 25-26, 1976. Reprinted as FAR 24507-N.

Argues that there is no such thing as international terrorism, which can be viewed as an organized transnational conspiracy to overthrow the world's constituted governments. Rather we have many forms of national terrorism, and further research should be conducted with this in mind.

185. Howe, Irving. "The Return of Terror." *Dissent* 22 (Summer 1975): 227-237.

Sees terrorism as taking four main types: eradication of individuals crucially representative of autocratic power, dynastic assassination, focused random killing aimed at appropriate targets, and random killings.

186. Hutchinson, Martha Crenshaw. "Comments on a Paper Presented by Dr. Thomas P. Thornton." Mimeographed. Washington, D.C.: U.S. State Department Conference on International Terrorism, March 25, 1976. Reprinted as FAR 24510-S

Attempts to provide the most useful directions for the conduct of research on terrorism. Suggests consideration of a group's legitimacy potential, principal audiences, direct and permissive causes of terrorism, and consequences of terrorism and government response.

187. ———. "The Concept of Revolutionary Terrorism." *Journal of Conflict Resolution* 16 (September 1972): 383-396.

This is a highly theoretical discussion that brings in Gurr and relative deprivation; however, there is very little empirical backing to her statements, other than a few examples from Algeria's FLN. Her concept of terrorism is limited solely to insurgent strategy: "neither one isolated act nor a series of random acts is terrorism." The author views terrorism as an efficient choice and organizes the essay, after definitional preliminaries, around risks of terrorist strategies, including "(1) the danger of creating hostility rather than fear in the civilian masses; (2) the possibility that the governmental response may destroy the revolutionary organization; and (3) the risk that the use of terrorism may emotionally harm the terrorists themselves."

188. ———. "Implications of the Pattern of Transnational Terrorism." Paper presented to the International Studies Association convention, February 20, 1975, Washington, D.C.

The ISA abstracts reads "The expansionary potential of terrorism—its tendency to spread beyond the borders of the nations or regions directly involved in conflict—reveals the facility with which the political grievances of sub-national organizations can be made international issues. Policy responses to terrorism, while seeming to necessitate cooperation among the affected actors, are hampered by different levels of vulnerability to the threat of terrorist violence, as well as the linking of the issue to other areas of foreign policy controversy."

189. ———. "Transnational Terrorism and World Politics." *Jerusalem Journal of International Relations* 1 (Winter 1975): 109-129.

An earlier version of this paper was presented at the 1974 APSA convention. Hutchinson views transnational terrorism as "an externalization of internal warfare," deliberately defying national borders, and believes a trend toward escalation of violence is evident. Hutchinson touches on most of the points made elsewhere in the literature but is weak in presenting evidence backing her statements. Her three typological tables are interesting and could be used as a basis for quantitative work, although some of her categories are too dependent upon the Arab-Israeli conflict. Also of note is the assertion: "While holding prisoners clearly increases the probability of terrorism, submission to terrorist demands does not."

190. ———. "Transnational Terrorism as a Policy Issue." Paper presented to American Political Science Association's annual convention, August 29-September 2, 1974, Chicago.

191. ———. "Transnational Terrorism as a Policy Issue." Summary of 1974 APSA paper. In William D. Coplin, ed., *The Analysis of Transnational Policy Issues: A Summary of the International Relations Panels of the 1974 American Political Science Convention*, pp. 15-16. St. Louis: University of Missouri, Consortium for International Studies Education.

Notes the common factors shared by Latin and Palestinian revolutionary groups employing transnational terrorism, including their exclusively political aims, the vulnerability of the nation-state to them, and their transnational character. There had been little uniformity of response to terrorism because of differences in perception. Efforts have been made at the ICAO and the UN, but the most successful protective measures have been unilateral, reinforcing national autonomy.

192. Hyams, Edward. *Terrorists and Terrorism.* London: J. M. Dent, and New York: St. Martin's Press, 1975.

The book is badly written, with poor use of evidence in confronting propositions about terrorist behavior. However, information can still be gleaned from author's discussion of the theorists of terrorism: Max Stirner, Sergei Nechayev, Michael Bakunin, and Johann Most. Historical discussions are given of early terrorists and their societies: the Populists, anarchists, the original IRA, the Irgun, Azev's work as a double agent, and a present-day analysis of the IRA and PLO. Concludes with a sympathetic apologia for terrorism, colored with Marxist rhetoric. Reviewed by Mary Ann Frantz, "Terrorism: Historical Vignettes," *Stanford Journal of International Studies* 12 (Spring 1977): 175-178.

193. Ikor, Roger. *Lettre ouverte à de gentils terroristes. [Open letter to terrorists]* Paris: A. Michel, 1976.

194. International Summaries: A Collection of Selected Translations in Law Enforcement and Criminal Justice. Washington, D.C.: U.S. Department of Justice, National Criminal Justice Reference Service, April 1979. Vol. 3. 172 pp.

An anthology of nineteen articles from pamphlets, journals, and conferences from Belgium, Italy, West Germany, and Yugoslavia, on terrorism.

195. "International Terrorism." *FAR Horizons* (Spring 1976): 1-4.

A description of the Department of State's March 1976 conference on international terrorism.

196. "International Terrorism." *Senior Scholastic* 109 (October 7, 1976): 22-25.

197. "International Terrorism: 'Do Something!—But What?" In *Great Decisions '79*, pp. 74-85. New York: Foreign Policy Association, 1979.

Explores the legitimacy of political violence, protection of innocents, reponding to terrorists, and the future of terrorism.

198. "International Terrorism in 1976." Washington, D.C.: Central Intelligence Agency, RP 77-10034U, July 1977.

An update of earlier CIA research, giving statistics on terrorist incidents worldwide and discussing recent trends in political violence.

199. "International Terrorism in 1977." Washington, D.C.: CIA National Foreign Assessments Center, RP 78-10255U, August 1978.

An update of previous statistics, the report notes an overall decline of attacks in general, as well as in those directed against Americans. Terrorists in 1977 preferred simple operations, finding governmental paramilitary rescue squads effective responses to complex hostage episodes. Reviewed in "The Growing Psychological Aspects of International Terrorism," *Defense and Foreign Affairs Digest* 6 (October 1978): 36-37.

200. "International Terrorism in 1978." Washington, D.C.: CIA National Foreign Assessment Center, RP 79-10149, March 1979.

An update of CIA statistics, which notes various terrorist reverses and governmental cooperation in combating terrorism.

201. International Terrorism. Proceedings of an Intensive Panel at the 15th Annual ISA Convention, St. Louis, Missouri, March 23, 1974. Global Focus Series No. 16.

Available from the International Studies Association, University of Wisconsin, Institute of World Affairs, Milwaukee, Wisconsin 53201.

202. International Terrorism. Proceedings of the Third Annual Conference of the Canadian Council on International Law held at the University of Ottawa, October 18-19, 1974.

203. Irish, Joss. *Terrorismo Internacional.* Barcelona: Producciones Editoriales, 1975.

204. Irnberger, Harold. *Die Terrormultis* (Munchen: Jugend und Volk, 1976.

In addition to a general overview of international terrorism, Irnberger discusses the Baader-Meinhof Group, the Ustasha, IRA, ETA, neofascist Italian groups, Palestinians, the JRA, and Chilean leftists.

205. Janke, Peter. "Institute for the Study of Conflict." *Police Journal* 47 (January-March 1974): 48-52.

A discussion of the activities of the British research group.

206. Jay, Martin. "Politics of Terror." *Partisan Review* 38 (1971): 95-103.

Discussion of aestheticization of politics, terror as an art form; it is dissatisfaction expressed in a style that no longer asks serious questions or suggests alternatives. Its primary function appears to be the self-definition of the participant through actions. Terrorists have perverted Marx's concept of praxis from "making" to "doing." More disturbing the new terrorism signals a return to the antitheoretical bias of American political life.

207. Jenkins, Brian Michael. "High Technology Terrorism and Surrogate War: The Impact of New Technology on Low-Level Violence," in Geoffrey Kemp, Robert L. Pfaltzgraff, Jr., and Uri Ra'anan, eds., *The Other Arms Race: New Technologies and Non-Nuclear Conflict.* Lexington, Mass.: Lexington Books, 1975.

208. ———. "High Technology Terrorism and Surrogate War: The Impact of New Technology on Low-Level Violence." Santa Monica, Calif: RAND Corporation, P-5339, January 1975.

RAND abstract states: In the future the world will be "an unstable collection of nations, ministates, autonomous ethnic substates, governments in exile, national liberation fronts, guerrillas, and ephemeral but destructive terrorist organizations, some linked in vague alliances, some protégés of foreign states."

209. ———. "International Terrorism." In *Major U.S. Foreign and Defense Policy Issues*, a Compilation of Papers prepared for the Commission on the

Operation of the Senate by the Congressional Research Service of the Library of Congress (1977), pp. 18-26.

Provides an overview of the problem of terrorism and notes what the U.S. policy response has been and can be.

210. ———. "International Terrorism: A Balance Sheet." *Survival* (July-August 1975): 158-164.

A shortened version of his paper, in David Carlton and Carlo Schaerf, eds., *International Terrorism and World Security*. London: Croom Helm; New York: Halstead Press of John Wiley, 1975.

Discusses the purposes of terrorism, which attempts to inspire and manipulate fear: wringing specific concessions, gaining publicity, causing widespread social disorder, deliberately provoking repression, enforcing obedience, punishing a guilty symbol. Mentions the effects of terrorism: in the 1968-1974 period, 520 killed, 830 wounded; much written on the subject. International cooperation against terrorism has been feeble. Possible trends include growing links between groups, more extravagant and destructive acts, surrogate warfare.

211. ———. "International Terrorism: A New Kind of Warfare." Santa Monica, Calif.: RAND Corporation, P-5261, June 1974.

Discusses how international terrorism operates, how and why it seeks international attention, its new targets and new capabilities.

212. ———. "International Terrorism: A New Mode of Conflict." Santa Monica: California Arms Control and Foreign Policy Seminar Research Paper 48; Los Angeles: Crescent, January 1975.

The chronology of incidents—January 1970 to July 1974—goes three months further than his RAND chronology (see entry 223). Portions of the paper were contained in an earlier written statement submitted to the Subcommittee on the Near East and South Asia, Committee on Foreign Affairs, House of Representatives, 24 June 1974. Contents: defining terrorism; promiscuous use of the term; theory of terrorism; purposes; indiscriminate or selective violence; defining international terrorism; actual effects of terrorism; the effect on the international order; a feeble response; new targets and new capabilities; "simultaneous revolution" or surrogate warfare; beyond terrorism.

213. ———. "International Terrorism: A New Mode of Conflict." In David Carlton and Carlo Schaerf, eds., *International Terrorism and World Security*, pp. 13-49 London: Croom Helm, 1975.

A revision of entry 212. Defines terrorism, discusses motivations and possible future trends, and offers an appended chronology.

214. ———. "International Terrorism as a New Mode of Conflict." Paper presented to the International Studies Association Convention, February 20, 1975, Washington, D.C.

Overview of terrorism and possible trends.

215. ———. "International Terrorism: Trends and Potentialities." Paper presented at the Conference on International Terrorism, U.S. Department of State, March 25-26, 1976. Reprinted as FAR 24509-S.

A summary of Jenkins's presentation of the future of terrorism.

216. ———. "International Terrorism: Trends and Potentialities: A Summary." Santa Monica: RAND Corporation, October 1977. Published in *Journal of International Affairs* 32 (Spring-Summer 1978): 115-124.

Updates Jenkins's study presented to the 1976 conference held at the Department of State. The fortunes of the major terrorist groups are outlined, as are possibilities for the development of a terrorist subculture whose ideology is terrorism, and growing restrictions on civil liberties.

217. ———. "Position Paper for International Scientific Conference on Terrorism." Paper presented to the conference held by the Institute for International Scientific Exchange, November 14-18, 1978, West Berlin.

218. ———. "Rand's Research on Terrorism." Santa Monica: RAND Corporation, P-5969, August 1977. Reprinted in *Terrorism: An International Journal* 1 (1977): 85-95.

Brings together the types of research RAND has engaged in since 1973 and suggests its relevance to policy makers.

219. ———. "The Study of Terrorism: Definitional Problems." in Yonah Alexander and John Gleason, eds., *Terrorism: Behavioral Perspectives*. New York: Pergamon Press, 1980.

220. ———. "Terrorism: Definitional Problems and the Rand Research." Paper presented to the Joint National Meeting of the Operations Research Society of America and the Institute of Management Sciences, May 1-3, 1978, New York City.

The author's abstract states: "In the course of its continuing research on terrorism, the Rand Corporation has compiled a chronology of international terrorism incidents that have occurred since 1968. This chronology now contains close to 1000 incidents. . . .The chronology allowed researchers to assess the magnitude of the problem, and in some cases apply, in a limited way, quantitative analysis techniques which sometimes produced intriguing results. Limited attempt at heuristic modeling was also made. The difficulties and possibilities of applying quantitative analysis to the new phenomenon are discussed.''

221. ———. ''Terrorism: Trends and Potentialities.'' Paper presented to the Joint National Meeting of the Operations Research Society of America and the Institute of Management Sciences, May 1-3, 1978, New York City. Published as ''International Terrorism: Trends and Potentialities.'' Santa Monica: RAND P-6117, May 1978.

The author's abstract reads: ''Although few terrorists have achieved their stated long range objectives, the use of terrorist tactics has brought them publicity and occasionally won them concessions. For typically short-sighted terrorists, these tactical successes are likely to be regarded as sufficient to preclude the abandonment of terrorist tactics. There is evidence of increasing sophistication on the part of terrorists in their weapons, in their tactics, and in their manipulation of the media. International coordination between terrorist groups seems to be increasing. Other potential developments include the emergence of a semi-permanent terrorist subculture dedicated to terrorism for its own sake, and the evolution of existing terrorist groups into quasi-political and perhaps international criminal syndicates using terrorist tactics for economic rather than political goals.''

222. ———. ''Trends in Terrorism.'' Paper presented to the 19th annual convention of the International Studies Association, February 22-25, 1978, Washington, D.C.

223. Jenkins, Brian M. and Johnson, Janera. ''International Terrorism: A Chronology, 1968-1974.'' Santa Monica: RAND Corporation R-1597-DOS/ARPA, March 1975.

Lists 507 incidents through April 1974 and gives an extensive list of terrorist groups.

224. ———. ''International Terrorism: A Chronology, 1974 Supplement.'' Santa Monica: RAND Corporation, R-1909-1-ARPA, February 1976.

Updates information listed in the previous RAND chronology, clarifying several incidents and adding more than one hundred others.

225. Johnson, Chalmers. ''Perspectives on Terrorism.'' Summary report of the Conference on International Terrorism, sponsored by the U.S. Department of State, March 25-26, 1976, Washington, D.C. Reprinted as FAR 25180-S.

A synthesis of the conventional wisdom about terrorism. Problems in the definition of terrorism, as well as in creating typologies, are noted. Johnson finds two types of causes—direct and permissive—breaking down the latter into categories of targets, technology, and toleration. The consequences of contemporary political violence for societies conclude the deliberations.

226. Johnson, Paul. "The Seven Deadly Sins of Terrorism." *New Republic*, September 15, 1979, pp. 19-21.

Terrorists deliberately suppress the moral instincts in humans and morally justify murder for its own sake, rejecting nonviolent politics. Terrorism assists the spread of totalitarianism, exploits the freedoms of liberal societies, and saps the will of civilization to defend itself.

227. Jones, David C. "The Terrorist Threat: Not a Passing Phenomenon." *TIG Brief*, January 17, 1975.

228. Jureidini, Paul. "Review of 'Terrorism: The Problem in Perspective' by Brian Crozier." Paper presented at the Conference on International Terrorism, U.S. Department of State, March 1976, Washington, D.C. Available as FAR 25924-N.

229. Kader, Omar. "Terrorism: Comparative Ideologies, Strategies and Tactics." Ph.D. dissertation, University of Southern California, in preparation.

230. Kahn, Jr., E. J. "How Do We Explain Them?" *New Yorker*, June 12, 1978, pp. 37-62.

A profile of Richard Lewis Clutterbuck, the renowned former British major-general who has written several books and articles on terrorism and insurgency.

231. Karanovic, Milivoje. "The Concept of Terrorism." *Jugoslovenska Revija za Krimologiju i Krivicno Pravo* 14 (April-June 1978): 219-234. Available in *International Summaries: A Collection of Selected Translations in Law Enforcement and Criminal Justice*, 3: 81-88, Washington, D.C.: U.S. Department of Justice, National Criminal Justice Reference Service, April 1979.

Discusses definitions and typologies of political terrorism.

232. Karber, Phillip A. "An Imbalance of Terror." Paper presented under the auspices of the National Institute of Social and Behavioral Science at the 137th annual meeting of the American Association for the Advancement of Science, December 1970.

233. ———. "Organizational Vulnerabilities of Terrorist Movements." Paper presented before the D.C. Political Science Association, May 1973, in Washington, D.C.

234. ———. ''Terrorism as Social Protest.'' Paper presented before the annual convention of the Southern Political Science Association, November 1971.

235. ———. ''Urban Terrorism: Baseline Data and a Conceptual Framework.'' *Social Science Quarterly* (December 1971): 521-533.
Notes some of the difficulties in data collection and proposes a new model of terrorism, which differs from counterinsurgency theories. Gives data purporting to show that urban guerrilla warfare does not exist and discusses Marighella's propaganda of the deed. As a symbolic act, terrorism can be viewed like other communication media, consisting of transmitter, intended recipient, message, and feedback.

236. Karpel, Craig S. ''The Victims of Terrorism Strike Back.'' *Penthouse* (August 1979): 71-180.

237. Kelley, C. M., *Terrorism: A Phenomenon of Sickness.* Claremont, Calif.: Claremont Men's College, 1974.

238. Kelley, R. J., *New Political Crimes and the Emergency of Revolutionary Nationalist Ideology.* Chicago: Rand-McNally, 1973.

239. Kissinger, Henry A. ''Hijacking, Terrorism and War.'' *Department of State Bulletin,* September 8, 1975, pp. 360-361.

240. Knauss, Peter R. and Strickland, D. A. ''Political Disintegration and Latent Terror.'' In Michael Stohl, ed., *The Politics of Terrorism*, pp. 77-117. New York: Dekker, 1979.
Explores the definitional and conceptual difficulties of political disintegration as a theoretical construct. Case studies are presented of London, the United States, Lebanon, Cyprus, and Algeria.

241. Knorr, Klaus. ''Is International Coercion Waning or Rising?'' *International Security* 1 (Spring 1977): 92-110.

242. Kupperman, Robert H. and Smith, Harvey A. ''Waiting for Terror.'' *Washington Review* 1 (January 1978): 50-61.

243. Kupperman, Robert H. and Trent, Darrell M. *Terrorism: Threat, Reality, Response.* Stanford: Hoover, 1979.
A collection of readings about technological responses to terrorism, written by major private researchers and governmental officials who have dealt with terrorism.

244. Laffin, John. "The Terrorist Industry: Murder Incorporated." *Spectator*, August 30, 1975.

245. Laqueur, Walter. "The Anatomy of Terrorism." In Jennifer Shaw, E. F. Gueritz, and A. E. Younger, eds., *Ten Years of Terrorism* pp. 7-21. New York: Crane, Russak, 1979.

246. ———. "Coming to Terms with Terror." *Times Literary Supplement*, April 2, 1976, p. 362.
Reviews books by Jenkins, Bell, and Niezing, observing that at the United Nations "among the opponents of anti-terrorist measures there was not a single democratically elected government."

247. ———. "The Continuing Failure of Terrorism." *Harper's* 253 (November 1976): 69-74.
Argues that terrorism occurs in cycles and that we are currently in a decline in a number of operations and campaigns. The reason why the public has not become aware of this is due to overconcentration of the media in certain areas and ambiguous use of the term, combining rebellion, street battles, rural guerrilla war, insurrection, coups, and other political violence under the same rubric. We will be unable to develop a comprehensive theory of terrorism's causes and must treat it on a case-by-case basis, rather than statistically. Arguments for and against concessions are offered.

248. ———. "Fehlgedeuteter Terrorismus." *Schweizer Monatshefte* 56 (October 1976): 567-576.

249. ———. "The Futility of Terrorism." *Harper's* (March 1976): 99-105.
Attacks several myths about terrorist behavior, including: political terror is a new and unprecedented phenomenon; terrorism appears whenever people have genuine, legitimate grievances—remove the grievances and terror will cease; terror is highly effective; the importance of terrorism will grow enormously in the years to come as the destructive power of its weapons increases; political terrorists are more intelligent and less cruel than ordinary criminals; and terrorists are poor, hungry, and desperate.

250. ———. "Guerrillas and Terrorists." *Commentary* (October 1974): 40-48.

251. ———. "Karl Heinzen: The Origins of Modern Terrorism." *Encounter* 49 (August 1977): 23-27.

252. ———. "Second Thoughts on Terrorism." *Washington Quarterly* (Autumn 1978): 104-109.

Reviews developments in global terrorism in the first months of 1978. Offers several criticisms of present-day theories of terrorism, many of which are telling but others which are off the mark, and ultimately leaves the reader little to build upon.

253. ———. "Terrorism Makes a Tremendous Noise." *Across the Board* 15 (January 1978): 57-67.

254. ———. ed. *The Terrorism Reader: A Historical Anthology.* New York: New American Library, 1978.
    A collection of readings by activists, critics, and observers of terrorism from Aristotle to the voices of today.

255. Larsson, Janerik. *Polistisk Terror i Sverige.* Goteborg: Sola, Seelig, 1968.

256. Lasswell, Harold D. "Terrorism and the Political Process." *Terrorism* 1 (1978): 255-264.
    Discusses sanctioning objectives and strategies: deterrence, withdrawal, rehabilitation, correction, prevention, and reconstruction. Distinguishes between the terrorist, proximate victim, and impact target.

257. Leff, Alexander, and Roos, John Victor. "The Transformation of Terrorism: Three Characteristics of the New Terrorism." *Stanford Journal of International Studies* 12 (Spring 1977): 179-184.
    A review of J. Bowyer Bell's *Transnational Terrorism*, Anthony M. Burton's *Urban Terrorism: Theory, Practice and Response,* and Richard Clutterbuck's *Living with Terrorism.*

258. Legum, Colin. "The Rise of Terrorism." *Current* 147 (January 1973): 3-9.

259. Leibstone, Marvin. "Undergrounds and the Uses of Terror." *Military Intelligence Magazine* (Summer-Fall 1975).

260. Leiden, Carl. "The Concept of Terror." Paper presented at the Conference on Terrorism, U.S. Department of State, October 1972. Washington, D.C. Reprinted as FAR 16462-S.
    Offers twelve points about related concepts and argues that terror is a psychological state of despair in which large numbers of individuals believe they are victims. This state is produced by a group through a series of usually violent acts that are intended to embarrass, challenge, or destroy some institution, government, or group.

261. Leiser, Burton M. "Terrorism, Guerrilla Warfare, and International Morality." *Stanford Journal of International Studies* 12 (Spring 1977): 39-66.

262. Lentner, Howard H. and Lewis, Thomas J. "Revolutionary Terrorism in Democratic Society." *Freedom at Issue* 7 (May-June 1971): 3-19.

263. Lenzer, Gertrud. "Women and Terrorism." Paper presented to the Conference on Psychopathology and Political Violence, November 16-17, 1979, at the University of Chicago.

264. Letman, Sloan T. "Some Sociological Aspects of Terror-Violence in a Colonial Setting." In M. Cherif Bassiouni, ed., *International Terrorism and Political Crimes*, pp. 33-42. Springfield, Ill.: Thomas, 1975.

265. Leurdijk, J. Henk. "Summary of Proceedings: Our Violent Future." In David Carlton and Carlo Schaerf, eds., *International Terrorism and World Security*, pp. 1-11. London: Croom Helm, 1975.

Gives the points of commonality of papers presented at the Fifth Course of ISODARCO at Urbino, Italy. Papers discussed terrorism, the arms race, European and Middle East security and peace teaching. The terrorism section notes problems of definitions, differing attitudes of governments, and possible measures of dealing with terrorism.

266. Levy, Sheldon G. "Terrorism." Paper presented at the Conference on Terrorism, U.S. Department of State, October 1972, Washington, D.C. Available as FAR 16463-S.

268. Lineberry, William P., ed. *The Struggle Against Terrorism.* New York: H. W. Wilson, 1977.

A collection of journalistic accounts of speeches on several aspects of international terrorism. All of the articles were originally published elsewhere.

269. Livingston, George D. "Political Terrorism: Past, Present, Future." *Law Enforcement Journal* 2 (Winter 1976): 34-39.

270. Livingston, Marius H.; Kress, Lee Bruce; and Wanek, Marie G., eds. *International Terrorism in the Contemporary World.* Westport, Conn.: Greenwood Press, 1978.

Proceedings of a conference, held April 26-28, 1976, at Glassboro State College in New Jersey, organized according to topics that discussed general trends in domestic and international terrorism throughout the world, specific types of incidents, such as hostage situations, potential threats to nuclear facilities, and the role of international law in coping with terrorist activities.

271. Louch, A. R. "Terrorism: The Immortality of Belief." Paper presented to the Conference on the Moral Implications of Terrorism: Justifications and Consequences, March 14-16, 1979, at UCLA.

272. Lucas, Colin. *The Structure of Terror: The Example of Javogues and the Loire*. London: Oxford University Press, 1972.

273. Mack, Andrew. "Non-Strategy of Urban Guerrilla Warfare." In J. Niezing, ed., *Urban Guerrilla: Studies on the Theory, Strategy, and Practice of Political Violence in Modern Societies*, pp. 22-45. Rotterdam, Netherlands: Rotterdam University Press, 1974.

No one theory of guerrilla warfare is applicable to all situations, and those who believe the opposite will be faced with failure. Illustrative material is provided from the United States, Northern Ireland, the Middle East, and Latin America.

274. Macomber, Jr., William B. "Deputy Under Secretary Macomber Discusses Terrorism in Interview on 'Today' Program." *Department of State Bulletin*, April 2, 1973, pp. 399-402.

275. Mallin, Jay. "Terror and the Military." Paper presented at the National Security Affairs Conference, July 1974, at the National War College.

Provides statistics showing the extent of the terrorist threat to vulnerable industrialized societies, notes four areas of particular concern to the military, and suggests what roles the military can play.

276. ———. "Terrorism as a Military Weapon." *Air University Review* (January 1977): 54-64. Revised version in Marius Livingston et al., eds., *International Terrorism in the Contemporary World*, pp. 389-401. Westport: Greenwood Press, 1978.

277. ———. "Terrorism as a Political Weapon." *Air University Review* 22 (July-August 1971): 45-52.

A shortened version of his introduction to *Terror and Urban Guerrillas* (see entry 1103). Mallin discusses the types of tactics used, their motivations, and examples of the Vietcong and Latin revolutionaries. Methods of combating terrorism are offered.

278. ———. "Terrorism in Revolutionary Warfare." *Strategic Review* (Fall 1974): 48-55.

Points out that revolutionaries have used terrorism to obtain attention and focuses on the activities of the Tupamaros. The actions of the armed forces demonstrated that the military can play a role when the police are overtaxed.

Mallin believes that the U.S. armed forces are inadequately trained for such a role.

279. Mann, Clarence J. "International Terrorism and the Overseas Business Community." In *International Terrorism:* Proceedings of an Intensive Panel at the 15th Annual Convention of the International Studies Association. Milwaukee: Institute of World Affairs, University of Wisconsin, 1974.

The author, assistant general counsel for international operations of Sears, Roebuck, and Company, argues that although multinational corporations are vulnerable targets for terrorists, they enjoy no special status in international law. The work of multinationals, which the author believes is necessary for economic development, is threatened by terrorist actions. Firms have dealt with the problem as a physical security issue. Mann suggests that they also attempt to undercut terrorism's benefits and eliminate safe havens by working with local governmental policy makers.

280. Marcus, Steven. "Culture and Terrorism." Paper presented to the Conference on Psychopathology and Political Violence, November 16-17, 1979, at the University of Chicago.

282. May, William G. "Terrorism as Strategy and Ecstasy." *Social Research* (Summer 1974): 277-298.

A discussion by a theologian of violence for its own sake and its interaction with the media.

283. McClure, Brooks. "Terrorism Today and Tomorrow: Prognosis and Treatment." In John D. Elliott and Leslie K. Gibson, eds., *Contemporary Terrorism: Selected Readings*, pp. 293-297. Gaithersburg, Md.: International Association of Chiefs of Police, 1978.

Gives an overview of the papers presented in the book. McClure concludes that taking a tough stance against terrorists—and never granting concessions—is the only solution to the problem.

284. McGuire, E. Patrick. "The Terrorist and the Corporation." *Across the Board* 14 (May 1977): 11-19.

285. McKnight, Gerald. *The Mind of the Terrorist.* London: Michael Joseph, 1974.

The most impressive aspect of this book is McKnight's ability to establish contacts with terrorists around the world. Unfortunately his interviews with them (including the URA, EOKA, IRA, and Tupamaros) do not proceed in a systematic manner, backed by a coherent set of theoretical propositions. He also assumes a good deal of background familiarity with terrorist history on the part of readers. Despite these two caveats, the book is well worth reading. Excerpted in *Palm Beach Post-Times*, May 25, 1975-May 27, 1975.

286. Mengel, Russell William. "Terrorism as a Transnational Phenomenon." Paper presented at the Seventh Security Assistance Symposium, U.S. Army Institute for Military Assistance, December 1974, at Fort Bragg, North Carolina.

287. Merari, Ariel. "A Classification of Terrorist Groups." *Terrorism* 1 (1978): 331-346.

Merari's 2 × 2 typology focuses on the targets of terrorists—foreigners or countrymen—as well as the locus of activity—domestic or abroad. He finds that xenofighters are more indiscriminate; foreign-based groups tend to perpetrate international terrorism and are more dependent upon foreign governmental support.

288. Methvin, Eugene H. "Analysis of Paul Wilkinson's Paper: 'A Fatality of Illusions: Dominant Images of International Terrorism.' " Paper presented to the Conference on International Terrorism, U.S. Department of State, March 25-26, 1976, Washington, D.C. Available as FAR 24508-S.

Notes that terrorists seem to have lost their grip on reality, having no moral reference points. Methvin suggests that rather than attempt a historical scholastic definition of the phenomenon, we should interview captured terrorists, noting their psyches as well as the "doctrine they are taught in Soviet terror schools."

289. ———. "History, Technology and Terrorism." Paper presented to the Conference on Terrorism and the Contemporary World, April 26-28, 1976, at Glassboro State College.

290. ———. "Objectivity and the Tactics of Terrorists." *Washington Star-News*, February 24, 1974.

291. Mickolus, Edward F. "Chronology of Transnational Terrorist Attacks upon American Business People, 1968-1976." *Terrorism* 1 (1978): 217-235.

Descriptions of each attack, during nine years of heightened terrorist activity, against U.S. corporate personnel and facilities.

292. ———. "Chronology of Transnational Attacks upon American Businessmen, 1968-1978." In Yonah Alexander and Robert A. Kilmarx, eds., *Political Terrorism and Business: The Threat and Response*, pp. 499-521. New York: Praeger, 1979.

Descriptions of attacks made during the last eleven years against American corporate facilities and personnel overseas.

293. ———. *Codebook: ITERATE (International Terrorism: Attributes of Terrorist Events)*. Ann Arbor, Mich.: Inter-University Consortium for Political and Social Research, University of Michigan, 1976. 47 pp.

The ITERATE project has collected data on 539 incidents of transnational terrorism from 1968 through 1974, described by approximately 150 variables. The codebook explains how to use the computer data base and explains methods of data collection and coding.

294. ———. "An Events Data Base for Studying Transnational Terrorism." In Richards J. Heuer, Jr., ed., *Quantitative Approaches to Political Intelligence: the CIA Experience*, pp. 127-163. Boulder, Colorado: Westview Press, 1978.

A revision of the paper presented to the Ralph Bunche Institute conference held in 1976. The author discusses the use of the ITERATE data set in intelligence work and prospects for its development.

295. ———. "International Terrorism: Review and Projection." Address to the Conference on Terrorism and the American Corporation, sponsored by Probe International, January 11-12, 1977 at Los Angeles, California.

An update of Mickolus's September 14-15, 1976 address to the Probe New York conference, which includes data on terrorist attacks worldwide and targeted against American businessmen from 1968 through 1976. Includes an extensive chronology.

296. ———. "Reflections on the Study of Terrorism." Paper presented to the Panel on Violence and Terror of the Conference on Complexity: A Challenge to the Adaptive Capacity of American Society, 1776-1976, sponsored by the Society for General Systems Research, March 24-26, 1977, Loyola College Conference Center, Columbia, Maryland.

Discusses the difficulties scholars have encountered in attempting to grapple with the phenomenon of contemporary terrorism. Solutions to these problems, such as a common data base, coordinated research agenda, and methods of increasing interdisciplinary communication, are explored.

297. ———. "Statistical Approaches to the Study of Terrorism." Paper presented to the Ralph Bunche Institute's conference on International Terrorism, June 9-11, 1976. In Seymour Maxwell Finger and Yonah Alexander, eds., *Terrorism: Interdisciplinary Perspectives*, pp. 209-269. New York: John Jay Press, 1977.

Discusses the work of other statisticians of terrorism, including Ted Gurr, Ernest Evans, and the RAND artificial intelligence project and how it might be used by researchers for diverse purposes. Some tabular presentations of data for events in the ITERATE data base are given, and a listing of descriptive variables is appended.

298. ———. "Transnational Terrorism." In Michael Stohl, ed., *The Politics of Terrorism*, pp. 147-190. New York: Dekker, 1979.

Uses data from the ITERATE project to show trends in types of events and repertoires of major terrorist groups. Dwells on problems of responding to such attacks in the long and short term.

299. ———. "Transnational Terrorism: Analysis of Terrorists, Events and Environments." Ph.D. dissertation, Yale University, in preparation.

Notes patterns in transnational terrorism, distinguishing it from international, domestic, and state terrorism. Data from the ITERATE project are used to give statistical analysis of trends in such behavior and evaluate suggested policies. The chronology, on which the ITERATE data set is based, will appear as *Transnational Terrorism: A Chronology of Events, 1968-1979* (Westport: Greenwood Press, 1980)

300. ———. "Trends in Transnational Terrorism." in Marius Livingston, Lee Bruce Kress and Marie Wanek, eds., *Terrorism in the Contemporary World*, pp. 44-73. Westport, Conn.: Greenwood Press, 1978.

Paper presented to the Glassboro State Conference on Terrorism in the Contemporary World on April 26-28, 1976. Provides data on the location, date, damage, perpetrators, victims, targets, and so forth of 1,298 incidents of transnational terrorism from 1968 to the present and comments about the future.

301. Mickolus, Edward F., and Heyman, Edward. "ITERATE: Monitoring Transnational Terrorism." Paper presented to the joint national meeting of the Operations Research Society of America and the Institute for Management Sciences, May 1-3, 1978, at New York City. Published in Yonah Alexander and John Gleason, eds., *Terrorism: Behavioral Perspectives.* New York: Pergamon, 1980.

Describes tentative findings of an ongoing project to apply quantitative techniques to the study of international terrorism. Problems that cropped up in a pilot data set on international terrorist incidents—ITERATE—and attempts to solve them in its successor are outlined. The possible applications of this data set are briefly explored.

302. ———. "Responding to Terrorism: Basic and Applied Research." In Stephen Sloan and Richard Shultz, eds., *Responding to the Terrorist Threat: Prevention and Control.* New York: Pergamon, 1980.

Reviews terrorism research that was undertaken during the 1970s for governments, private research firms, academic institutions, and security consulting companies.

303. Middendorff, Wolfgang. "The Personality of the Terrorist." *Kriminalistik* 30 (July 1976): 289-296, and (August 1976): 357-363. Available in *International Summaries: A Collection of Selected Translations in Law Enforcement and Criminal Justice,* 3: 89-97. Washington, D.C.: U.S. Department of Justice: National Criminal Justice Reference Service, April 1979.

304. Midlarsky, Manus I. and Hutchinson, Martha Crenshaw. "Why Violence Spreads: The Contagion of International Terrorism." Paper delivered to the annual meeting of the International Studies Association, March 21-24, 1979, at Toronto.

Uses statistical models to explain why international terrorism spread from Latin America to Western Europe. The paper was published in June 1980 by the *International Studies Quarterly,* along with a comment by Edward Heyman and Edward Mickolus "Observations on 'Why Violence Spreads.' "

305. Miksche, Ferdinand Otto. *Secret Forces: The Technique of Underground Movements.* 1950; reprint, Westport, Conn.: Greenwood Press.

306. Milbank, David L. "International and Transnational Terrorism: Diagnosis and Prognosis." Paper prepared for delivery to the State Department Conference on International Terrorism, March 25-26, 1976, at Washington, D.C.: Reprinted as FAR 24514-N.

Gives an overview of the past eight years of international terrorist activity, noting the trends in certain types of incidents, and discusses the probable causes of such behavior. The best summary of the literature on terrorism. Also mentions some possibilities for the future and doubts that surrogate warfare will become popular. The statistical appendixes, prepared by Milbank and Mickolus, give tabulations and graphs of trends in incidents, location, and American victimization.

307. ———. *Research Study: International and Transnational Terrorism: Diagnosis and Prognosis.* Washington, D.C.: Office of Political Research, Central Intelligence Agency, PR 76 10030, April 1976. Available from Document Expediting Project, Exchange and Gift Division, Library of Congress, Washington, D.C. 20540.

Assesses general trends in international and transnational terrorism during the past decade. Characteristics of groups, their activities, ideologies, and where they operate are noted, with statistical supplements. Future trends are explored. Reviewed by F. Clifton Berry, Jr., "Crime May Not Pay, But Terrorism Has—So Far," *Armed Forces Journal* 113 (August 1976): 18-19.

308. Miller, Abraham. "On Terrorism." *Public Administration Review* 37 (July-August 1977): 429-434.

A review of books by J. Bowyer Bell, Yonah Alexander, and Christopher Dobson. Miller argues that academic studies must be policy oriented and that although the books he cites are useful, they do not subject their insights to rigorous empirical testing.

309. Miller, James A. "Political Terrorism and Insurgency: An Interrogative Approach." In Seymour Maxwell Finger and Yonah Alexander, eds., *Terrorism: Interdisciplinary Perspectives*, pp. 64-91. New York: John Jay Press, 1977.

Miller refers to all forms of political violence in establishing his model. He attempts to employ a value-neutral definition of such acts, closely following Nieburg. Using the perspectives of the two antagonists, he notes twenty-nine factors of description, based upon the standard seven journalistic questions: who, what, when, where, why, how, and so what?

310. ———. "Political Violence Movements: An Interrogative, Integrative Systems Approach." Ph.D. dissertation, American University, 1976.

311. Minnery, J. and Truby, J. D. *Improvised Modified Firearms*. Boulder, Colo.: Paladin Press, 1975.

Illustrates hidden weapons, street guns, and guns used in espionage, by mobsters, and by civilian terrorists.

312. Minogue, Kenneth. "The Doctrine of Violence." *Times Literary Supplement*, November 7, 1975.

A review of Aron's *History and the Dialectic of Violence* (1975), Boulton's *The Making of Tania Hearst* (1975), Carr's *The Angry Brigade* (1975), Davis's *An Autobiography* (1975), and Clutterbuck's *Living with Terrorism* (1975).

313. Moodie, Michael. "Political Terrorism: A Unique Kind of Tyranny." Paper presented to the 19th annual convention of the International Studies Association, February 22-25, 1978, at Washington, D.C. Published in *Osterreichische Zeitschrift fur Aussenpolitik* 18 (1978): 27-38.

Gives an overview of academic research on the subject. Arguing that the work has been noncumulative because of idiosyncratic definitions by each researcher, Moodie offers his own conceptualization of the problem.

314. Moore, John R. "Future Warfare May Take the Form of Urban Terrorism" *Marine Corps Gazette* 63 (June 1979): 49-53.

Traces the shift from rural to urban guerrilla operations.

315. Morris, Robert. "Patty Hearst and the New Terror." *New Republic*, November 22, 1975, pp. 8-10.

Argues that the Hearst case has lessons and must be taken seriously. The article treats domestic and transnational terrorism, pointing out that terrorists may view the mass public as part of the system of oppression and may therefore consider them as legitimate targets.

316. Morton, Marian J. *Terrors of Ideological Politics.* Cleveland: Case Western Reserve University Press, 1972.

317. Moss, Robert. "International Terrorism and Western Societies." *International Journal* (Summer 1973): 418-430.

Among Moss's insights are: terrorism is going international; there will be more targets due to increased technology; three types of terrorists are (1) bomber Left; (2) violent protest movements and terrorist cells among religious, ethnic, and cultural minorities; and (3) ideological mercenaries. He discusses suggested methods for dealing with terrorists, including special police groups and international coordination of major nation efforts. The usefulness of his typology is doubtful, and few of his assertions about the causes of terrorism are backed by evidence.

318. ———. "Urban Guerrilla War." In Richard G. Head and Ervin J. Rokke, eds., *American Defense Policy*, 3d ed., pp. 242-259. Baltimore: Johns Hopkins Press, 1973. Reprinted with minor changes from *Adelphi Papers*, no. 79 (1971), and also in Jackwell Susman, ed. *Crime and Justice, 1971-1972: An AMS Anthology* (New York: AMS, 1974), pp. 405-427.

Notes four techniques of urban militancy: armed propaganda, kidnapping, riots and strikes, and subversion of the security forces. Moss sees terrorists as needing to be discriminate in their initial target selection, allowing them to win converts and erode public support for the state. Among the causes of terrorism suggested are internal migration and high rates of urbanization, relative deprivation, and the character of the terrorist. Problems of response are also treated.

319. ———. *The War for the Cities.* New York: Coward, McCann and Geoghegan, 1972. Published in England as *Urban Guerrillas: The New Face of Political Violence.* London: Temple Smith, 1971.

A series of case studies of urban attacks in contemporary societies, noting the apparent causes of the uprisings, the types of actions the groups took, and the responses of the governments involved.

320. "Multinationals Beware: You Are Terrorist's Target." *Business Insurance*, October 18, 1976, pp. 53-54.

321. Munger, Murl D. "The Growing Utility of Political Terrorism." Carlisle Barracks, Penn.: U.S. Army War College Strategic Studies Institute, March 7, 1977.

According to the author's abstract, "This memorandum considers the increasing use of terrorism to gain political objectives, which has been furthered by conditions unique to contemporary times. In the author's view, the world-wide coverage capabilities of the mass media, coupled with their willingness to report violent incidents, have provided the terrorist with a means of exposure to the world public that will permit him to articulate his motives and objectives. In addition . . .other trends which are contributing to the proliferation of terrorism: advancing weapons technology permits terrorist groups to possess extreme destructive power; the socio-psychological climate in world populace is conducive to the development of terrorism; and, little international cooperation in curbing terrorism has been achieved. He concludes that, since international cooperation to suppress terrorism is unlikely in the near future, it will be a factor in world affairs at least through the 1980's."

322. Nagel, W. H. "Devil's Advocate on the Question of Terrorism." *Etudes internationales de psycho-sociologie criminelle* 20-23 (1971-1972): 15-17.
    Nagel believes that sometimes terrorism is justified.

323. ———. "Terrorism." *Justitiele Verkenningen* 4 (1975): 150-156.
    A criminological and conceptual analysis of terrorism.

324. Nathan, J. A. "Terrorism and International Order." Paper presented to the annual meeting of the Midwest Political Science Association, April 20-22, 1978, at Chicago, Illinois.

325. ———. "Terrorism and the Moral Basis of the International System." Paper presented to the Conference on Moral Implications of Terrorism, March 14-16, 1979, at UCLA.

326. Novotny, Eric J. and Karber, Phillip A. "Organized Terror and Politics." *Short Essays in Political Science* (1973).

327. O'Ballance, Edgar. "Terrorism: The New Growth Form of Warfare" In Marius Livingston et al., eds. *International Terrorism in the Contemporary World*, pp. 415-420. Westport, Conn.: Greenwood Press, 1978.

328. Osmond, Russell Lowell. "Transnational Terrorism 1968-1974: A Quantitative Analysis." Ph.D. dissertation, Syracuse University, 1979.

329. ———. "Terrorism and Political Violence Theory: A Quantitative Examination." Paper presented to the Joint National Meeting of the Operations Research Society of America and the Institute of Management Sciences, May 1-3, 1978, at New York City.

The author's abstract reads: "Prevailing political violence theory was developed by political scientists before the dramatic increase in terrorist activities beginning in 1968. Various forms of terrorist behavior were included in that theory as a subset of political violence, but these were never systematically examined separately. An empirical scale of the intensity of terrorist behavior is presented and used to evaluate the usefulness of relying on existing political violence theory to understand the unprecedented recent increase in terrorism. A significant part of Ted Gurr's pioneering work on the development of political indicators is replicated. Results of the application of factor analysis and multiple regression techniques to the study of terrorism are discussed."

330. ———. "Transnational Terrorism and Political Violence: A Replication of Hypotheses." Ph.D. dissertation proposal, Syracuse University, November 1, 1977.

Osmond plans to use the ITERATE computer data to replicate the results of Gurr and the Feierabends on political violence.

331. Paine, Lauran. *The Terrorists*. London: Robert Hale, 1975.

332. Parry, Albert, *Terrorism from Robespierre to Arafat*. New York: Vanguard, 1976.

Traces the rise of terrorism from its uses by the state to the modern campaigns of the Tupamaros, IRA, JRA, and others. Reviewed by Robert A. Friedlander, "History as Demonology," *Saint Louis University Law Journal* 22 (1978): 233, 242, who faults Parry for finding Marxism behind every terrorist, not defining terms adequately, and showing little international legal sophistication.

333. Paul, Leslie. *The Age of Terror*. London: Faber, 1950, and Boston: Beacon Press, 1951.

334. Paust, Jordan J. "Definitional Approaches to Terrorism." Paper presented to the Conference on International Terrorism, sponsored by the Ralph Bunche Institute on the U.N. of the Graduate School and University Center of CUNY and the State University College at Oneonta of SUNY, June 9-11, 1976, published as "A Definitional Focus," in Seymour Maxwell Finger and Yonah Alexander, eds., *Terrorism: Interdisciplinary Focus*, pp. 18-29. New York: John Jay Press, 1977.

Paust considers terrorism as a strategy rather than as isolated events. He notes several factors that have been suggested in creating a definition: terror outcome, instrumental or immediate victims versus primary target, use of violence to produce terror, willful and intentional action, terror purpose, outcome of death or grievous bodily injury, damage to property, and acts calculated to endanger. He suggests noting participants and unintended targets, as well as resources of groups and the arena of the conflict. Finally, he urges the avoidance of "conclusionary definitions," which are used as epithets serving as a substitute for thinking.

335. Perenyi, Peter S. "State Department Conference on Terrorism: External Research Study XR/RNAS-21, Summary of Conference sponsored by the Bureau of Intelligence and Research and the Planning and Coordination Staff, December, 1972. Available as FAR 16636-S.

336. Perham, John. "The Computer: A Target." *Dun's* (January 1971): 34-36.

337. Peterson, R. W., and Chrisman, W. G. "International Terrorism Threat Analysis." Master's thesis, Naval Postgraduate School, 1977.

The authors, both lieutenant commanders in the U.S. Navy, surveyed experts in the study of terrorism to create rankings of incidents of international terrorism according to the degree of threat to U.S. interests.

338. ———. "Results from Expert Responses Concerning Perceptions of Terrorist Incident Threat." Monterey, Calif.: U.S. Naval Postgraduate School, National Security Affairs Department, 1977.

Summarizes responses from a group of experts from government, private enterprise, the military, law enforcement, academia, and policy research regarding the ranking of threats to the United States of specific incidents of international terrorism. A scale analogous to a Fahrenheit thermometer is used to create interval level data.

339. Peterson, William H. "The Economics of Terrorism." Address to the Wackenhut Corporation's Seminar on Terrorism, November 21, 1974.

340. Pfaff, William. "Reflections on Terrorism." *New Yorker*, September 18, 1978, pp. 134-142.

A historical approach to the subject, which notes that terrorism is not new and that philosophies that introduced similar justifications appeared in the 1880s, 1900s, and 1920s in forms as diverse as anarchism and fascism.

341. Pierre, Andrew J. "An Overview of the Causes of and Cures for International Terrorism Today." Paper presented to the International Studies Association Convention, February 20, 1975, at Washington, D.C.

Points out that terrorism is becoming increasingly important in world politics as modern technological society becomes more vulnerable and assists terrorists in gaining publicity. Perceptions of the morality of terrorism differ. Dealing with terrorism must involve prevention and deterrence, deal with root causes, and use international legal instruments.

342. ———. ''Summary of Comments at Conference on International Terrorism.'' Paper presented at the Conference on International Terrorism, U.S. Department of State, March 25-26, 1976, at Washington, D.C. FAR 24512-S.

An abstract of Pierre's winter 1976 *Orbis* article, in which he analyzes the world's responses to terrorism.

343. Pierson-Mathy, Paulette. ''Formes nouvelles de la lutte révolutionnaire et cooperation internationale dans le combat contre-révolutionnaire.'' In *Réflexions sur la définition et la répression du terrorisme*, pp. 59-94. Brussels: Editions de L'Université de Bruxelles, 1974.

344. Plastrik, S. ''On Terrorism.'' *Dissent* 21 (Spring 1974): 143.

A leftist attack upon the use of terrorism, notes that such actions are counterproductive in the long and short run. Plastrik argues that terrorism is based upon ''an absolute faith in some metaphysical ideal ('the revolution') and ''is matched by an absolute distrust of living people.''

345. Possony, Stefan T. ''The Genesis of Terrorists.'' *Defense and Foreign Affairs Digest* 1 (1978). Originally a lecture at the Conference on Terrorism and Countermeasures, September 26, 1977, at San Juan, Puerto Rico.

346. ———. ''Terrorism: A Global Concern.'' *Defense/Foreign Affairs Digest* (January 1973): 4-5.

347. ———. ''Terrorism and Marxist Ideology.'' Paper presented to the Conference on the Moral Implications of Terrorism, March 14-16, 1979, at UCLA.

348. Price, H. Edward. ''The Strategy and Tactics of Revolutionary Terrorism.'' Paper presented at the annual meeting of the Southern Sociological Society, April 1, 1975, at Washington, D.C. FAR document 22027. Published in *Comparative Studies in Society and History* 19 (January 1977): 52-66.

Price follows the distinctions established by Moss, Thornton, and Hutchinson and uses the examples of Uruguay, Northern Ireland, and Palestine in illustrating his theory of the uses of terrorism in independent states, colonial situations, and internal colonial situations.

349. Quester, George H. "World Tolerance for Terrorism." In Yair Evron, ed., *International Violence: Terrorism, Surprise and Control*, pp. 166-81. Jerusalem; Hebrew University of Jerusalem, Leonard Davis Institute for International Relations, 1979.

Discusses the consequences of giving in to terrorists' strategic demands.

350. Morente, Frederico Quintero. "Terrorism." *Military Review* (December 1965): 55-57.

351. Rackley, Frank M. "Measures of the Impact and Appeal of Terrorism for Religious Cults." Paper presented to the Conference on the Moral Implications of Terrorism, at UCLA, March 14-16, 1979.

353. Rapoport, David C. "Evaluation." Washington, D.C.: State Department Conference on International Terrorism, March 25-26, 1976. Reprinted as FAR 24838-S.

Rapoport begins with a number of suggestions useful for the logistics and substantive planning of any conference. He then discusses the importance of historical and societal factors in the terrorists' environment. Recently suggestions for the development of an international law distinguishing political belligerents, criminals, and those committing atrocities have been put forth.

354. ———. "The 'First' Terrorism Campaign." Paper presented to the annual convention of the Western Section of the International Studies Association, March 16-18, 1978.

355. ———. "Historical Religious Prototypes of Contemporary Terrorism." Paper presented to the Conference on Psychopathology and Political Violence, November 16-17, 1979, at University of Chicago.

356. ———. "Terrorism: The Jew as Perpetrator and Victim in the Great Revolt Against Rome." In press.

357. Rayne, Fred "Executive Protection and Terrorism." *Top Security* 1 (October 1975): 220-225.

The author interviewed several terrorist leaders and relates his insights regarding terrorist methods, selection of a victim, terrorist manuals, the dedication of terrorists, and the increase in international terrorism.

358. Reber, J. R. *Threat Analysis Methodology* Gaithersburg, Md.: International Association of Chiefs of Police, 1976.

359. Report of the Ad Hoc Commitee on International Terrorism. U.N. General Assembly Official Records. 28th session, supplement 28, A/9024.

360. Report of the Task Force on Disorders and Terrorism. Washington, D.C.: National Advisory Committee on Criminal Justice Standards and Goals, December, 1976. 661 pp.

An invaluable source book of suggestions on how law enforcement authorities should deal with terrorism. Its appendixes include a chronology of attacks within the United States, which is without equal, and an excellent annotated bibliography.

361. Roberts, Ken. "The Terror Trap." Carlisle Barracks, Penn.: U.S. Army War College, Strategic Studies Institute, Military Issues Research Memorandum AD AO14159, 1975.

Looks at the role of the superpowers in combating international terrorism. Due to the duality of Soviet policy in supporting freedom fighters but condemning other actions such as skyjackings of Soviet airliners, Roberts concludes that no progress will be made until the superpowers agree that it is in their common interest to work together to defeat terrorism.

362. Romaniecki, Leon. "The Soviet Union and International Terrorism." *Soviet Studies* 24, (University of Glasgow) (July 1974): 417-440.

A discussion of the Soviet Union's attitudes towards international law and the definition of aggression. The development of the Soviet view, based in part upon its relations with guerrilla groups and the world socialist movement, is outlined.

363. Romerstein, Herbert. "A Transnational Threat." *National Review*, November 25, 1977, pp. 1364-1366.

364. Rosenau, James N. "The Trader, the Tourist, and the Terrorist: Two Extremes and A Midpoint on the Same Transnational Continuum." Address to the 19th annual convention of the International Studies Association, February 22-25, 1978, at Washington, D.C.

365. Rothstein, Andrew. "Terrorism—Some Plain Words." *Labour Monthly* (September 1973): 413-417.

A discussion of ideology from Lenin to the IRA

366. Roucek, J. S. "Sociological Elements of a Theory of Terror and Violence." *American Journal of Economics and Sociology* 21 (April 1962): 165-172.

367. Rudolph, Jr., Edward W. *Terrorism and the Multinational Guerrilla.* Washington, D.C.: National War College, 1973.

368. Russell, Charles A. "Terrorism: An Overview 1970-1978." In Yonah Alexander and Robert A. Kilmarx, eds., *Political Terrorism and Business: The Threat and Response*, pp. 491-498. New York: Praeger, 1979.

369. Russell, Charles A.; Banker, Jr., Leon J.; and Miller, Bowman. "Out-Inventing the Terrorist." Paper presented at the Conference on Research Strategies for the Study of International Terrorism, May 30, 1977, at Evian, France. Reprinted in Yonah Alexander, David Carlton, and Paul Wilkinson, eds., *Terrorism: Theory and Practice* (New York: Praeger, 1978), and U.S. Senate Committee on Governmental Affairs "Report on an Act to Combat International Terrorism," 95th Cong. 2d sess., May 23, 1978, pp. 372-430.

An excellent discussion of three approaches to studying terrorism, with useful case materials.

370. Russell, Charles, and Miller, Bowman, *Transnational Terrorism: Terrorist Tactics and Techniques.* Gaithersburg, Md: International Association of Chiefs of Police, Clandestine Tactics and Technology, Group and Area Studies, 1977.

371. Ryter, Stephen L. "Terror: A Psychological Weapon." *The Review* (May-June 1966): 21, 145-150.

Defining terrorism as "a tactical psychological weapon, which seeks to dominate a community through fear," Ryter concentrates on domestic terrorism that does not involve foreigners and gives several examples of particularly horrifying incidents in Vietnam and Africa. He argues that the terrorist is attempting to be selective in his targeting and aims at creating fear in a general population. Those charged with protection of citizens cannot engage in counterterror, because such use destroys the system one wishes to preserve.

372. Salmon, Jean A. "Conclusions." In *Réflexions sur la définition et la répression du terrorisme*, pp. 271-275. Brussels: Editions de l'Université de Bruxelles, 1974.

373. Schaefer, Stephen. *The Political Criminal: The Problem of Morality and Crime.* New York: Free Press, 1974.

374. Schmitt, Karl. "Targets of Terrorists." Paper presented at the Conference on Terrorism, U.S. Department of State, October 1972, in Washington, D.C. Reprinted as FAR 16464-S.

Suggests that there are patterns to target selection. Those in power select targets of a pragmatic nature, whereas revolutionary terrorists aim at targets with a symbolic value, with some pragmatic aspects only secondary. Those engaged in colonial wars frequently attack their own people to coerce across class lines. The resort to terrorism is a sign of weakness in both groups.

375. Schreiber, Jan. *The Ultimate Weapon: Terrorists and World Order.* New York: Morrow, 1978. 218 pp.

376. Selzer, Michael. *Terrorist Chic: An Exploration of Violence in the Seventies.* New York: Hawthorne, 1979. 206 pp.
Reviewed by Norman Frankel, *Counterforce*, September 14, 1979.

377. Seminar on International Terrorism. Presented by Wackenhut Corporation, November 21-22, 1974, at Coral Gables, Florida.
Addresses included "U.S. Government Response to Terrorism," by Ambassador Lewis Hoffacker; "Kidnapping as a Revolutionary Tactic," by Carol E. Baumann; "The Economics of Terrorism," by William H. Peterson; "Psychology of Terror," by Frederick Hacker; "Problems of Protection," by James J. Rowley; "Private Sector Approach to Protection," by Jack Barbour; "The System and Its Impact," by Jeffrey Baker; "The Kidnap Victim," by J. Reginold Murphy; and "Countering the Enemy Electronically," by Howard G. Stewart.

378. Servier, Jean. *Le terrorisme.* Paris: Presses Universitaires, 1979.

379. Shaffer, Helen B. "Political Terrorism." In *Editorial Research Reports*, 1: 340-360, Washington: Congressional Quarterly, May 13, 1970.

380. Shaw, Eric D.; Hazelwood, Leo; Hayes, Richard E.; and Harris, Don R. "Analyzing Threats from Terrorism." In *The Role of Behavioral Science in Physical Security*, pp. 3-27. Special Publication 480-24. Washington: National Bureau of Standards, 1976.
A preliminary statement of how statistical analysis could and should be used in analyzing terrorism. Suggestions include the creation of indexes that forecast the likelihood of attacks from disturbed individuals and small terrorist groups, a profile of targets, an analysis of the length of time contagion effects can be expected to last, policy guidance for incident responses, and information on the impact of different outcomes of terrorism incidents.

381. Shaw, Jennifer; Gueritz, E. F.; and Younger, A. E., eds. *Ten Years of Terrorism: Collected Views.* New York: Crane, Russak, 1979.

Proceedings of a 1977 symposium held at the Royal United Services Institute for Defence Studies for experts from several Western European nations.

382. Shultz, Richard. "Conceptualizing Political Terrorism: A Typology and Application." Paper presented to the 19th annual convention of the International Studies Association, February 22-25, 1978, at Washington, D.C. Published in *Journal of International Affairs* 32 (Spring-Summer 1978): 7-16.

Shultz suggests that Wilkinson's types of terrorism can be studied by looking at the variables of causes, environment, goals, strategy, means, organization, and participation. He uses this research design to look at the Greek insurgency, the Malayan emergency, the Huk insurgency, and South Vietnam.

383. Sim, Richard. "Research Note: Institute for the Study of Conflict." *Terrorism* 1 (1978): 211-215.

The London-based group which publishes Conflict Studies, plans to widen its operations. It will start up a U.S. Committee in North America and open branch offices in Germany, France, and Latin America.

384. Singh, Baljit. "Political Terrorism: An Overview." Paper presented to the 34th annual meeting of the Midwest Political Science Association, May 1, 1976, at Chicago, Illinois. Available as FAR 27241-76.

Gives a brief history of terrorism, along with a useful compendium of hijacking statistics. Objectives of terrorists and an adaptation of the thoughts of Kautilya on the social order are discussed.

385. ———. "Political Terrorism: Third World Perspectives." Paper presented to the 18th annual convention of the International Studies Association, March 16-20, 1977 at St. Louis, Missouri.

386. Sixth Annual Security Assistance Symposium of the Foreign Area Officer Course. Civil Affairs and Security Assistance School, U.S. Army Institute for Military Assistance, Fort Bragg, North Carolina, May 28-30, 1974.

The report contains the results of workshop number 2 of the symposium, "Terrorism as Transnational Phenomena and Its Impact on Security Assistance Programs." The article provides a working definition of transnational terrorism and summarizes the principal conclusions of the workshop.

387. Sloan, Stephen. "Non-Territorial Terrorism: A Research Agenda and Problems." Paper presented to the annual convention of the American Political Science Association, September 1-4, 1977 at Washington, D.C. Available as FAR 29164-N.

Sloan discusses the work of his research group, which battled the definitional problem, coded 111 incidents (now 200) into machine-readable form, generated preliminary statistical results, conducted policy-relevant simulations, and made policy suggestions.

388. ———. ''Research on Terrorism: Problems and Prospects.'' Paper presented to the 19th annual convention of the International Studies Association, February 22-25, 1978 at Washington, D.C.

389. Sloan, Stephen, and Kearney, Richard. ''Non-Territorial Terrorism: An Empirical Approach to Policy Formation.'' *Conflict* 1 (1978): 131-144.

Using a data-base of around two hundred incidents, the authors note patterns in international terrorism.

390. ———. ''Terrorism Emerges as Deadly New Game.'' *Daily Oklahoman*, November 21-24, 1976.

A four-part series by two Oklahoma University faculty members on international terrorism, using statistics based upon 111 incidents.

391. Smart, I. M. H. ''The Power of Terror.'' *International Journal* (Spring 1975).

392. Smith, Colin. ''Portrait of a Terrorist: The World's Most Wanted Criminal.'' *Present Tense* 4 (Winter 1977): 52-57.

393. Smith, D. ''Scenario Reality: A New Brand of Terrorism.'' *Nation*, March 30, 1974, pp. 392-294.

394. Snitch, Thomas H. ''Decade of the Terrorist.'' *Intellect* (June 1978): 456-459.

395. ———. ''Political Assassinations 1968-1978: A Cross-National Assessment.'' Ph.D. dissertation, American University, in preparation.

Snitch seeks to replicate the work of those who studied political violence in the 1960s using large cross-national data sets. Several issues in events data analysis are addressed and the time sensitivity of the conclusions of the earlier studies are assessed.

396. Sobel, Lester A., ed. *Political Terrorism*. New York: Facts on File, 1975.

A detailed history of contemporary terrorism with excellent data on incidents.

397. ———. *Political Terrorism, Vol. 2: 1974-1978.* New York: Facts on File, 1978.
The updated version of Sobel's excellent earlier study, this survey of incidents, responses, and general topics in terrorism has added short feature articles on items of special interest.

398. Spegele, Roger. ''Terrorism in Unconventional Warfare.'' Master's thesis, University of California, 1964.

399. State Department Conference on Terrorism. Department of State External Research Study, XR/RNAS-21, December 29, 1972.
Summarizes conference sponsored by INR and the Planning Coordination Staff on October 24, 1972. Conferees generally agreed that almost any group under sufficient stress of unresolved grievances will resort to terrorism; terrorists may select either symbolic or pragmatic targets; terror is very difficult to eliminate—the best move a government can make is to reduce grievances; and regimes resorting to repression tend to defeat themselves.

400. Stenmeyer, W. ''The Ideological Criminal.'' *Congressional Record,* June 16, 1971, p. S9185.

401. Stephens, Maynard M. ''The Oil and Natural Gas Industries: A Potential Target of Terrorists.'' In Robert H. Kupperman and Darrell M. Trent, eds., *Terrorism,* pp. 200-223. Stanford: Hoover, 1979.

402. Stewart-Smith, Geoffrey. ''Terrorism: The New Growth Form of Warfare.'' *East-West Digest* 12 (June 1976): 476-481.
The author reports on the April 1976 international terrorism conference held at Glassboro, N.J., and offers the arguments oft-heard in the literature. Of interest is the author's allegation that ''no longer could there be any doubt that international terrorists were penetrating existing terrorist organizations in an attempt to gain control of them.''

403. Stiles, Dennis W. ''Sovereignty and the New Violence.'' *Air University Review* 27 (July-August 1976). Reprinted in John D. Elliott and Leslie K. Gibson, eds., *Contemporary Terrorism: Selected Readings,* pp. 261-267. (Gaithersburg, Md.: International Association of Chiefs of Police, 1978).
Stiles notes the developing power relationship between terrorists and society and is concerned with the terrorists' greater operational flexibility.

404. Stohl, Michael. "Myths and Realities of Political Terrorism." *The Politics of Terrorism*, pp. 1-19. New York: Dekker, 1979.

Stohl explores—and sometimes explodes—several widely held beliefs, including that terrorism is engaged in solely by antigovernmental forces, that it is intended to produce chaos, that it is engaged in by madmen, that it is criminal (not political), that all insurgency is terrorism, that governments always oppose terrorism, that it relates only to domestic conditions, and that it is a strategy of futility.

405. ———, ed. *The Politics of Terrorism*. New York: Dekker, 1979.

An introductory reader that gives statistics on domestic and international terrorist campaigns and reviews of regional experiences.

406. Strickler, Nina. "Anti-History and Terrorism: A Philosophical Dimension." In M. Cherif Bassiouni, ed., *International Terrorism and Political Crimes*, pp. 47-50. Springfield, Ill.: Thomas, 1975.

407. Strother, Robert S., and Methvin, Eugene H. "Terrorism on the Rampage." *Reader's Digest* (November 1975).

Discusses recent incidents, types of terrorists, and countermeasures.

408. Syrkin, Marie. "Political Terrorism." *Midstream* 18 (1972): 3-11.

409. Szabo, Denis, ed. *Dimensions of Victimization in the Context of Terroristic Acts*. Montreal: International Centre for Comparative Criminology, 1977.

Proceedings of a conference held June 3-5, 1977 in Santa Margherita Ligure, Italy. The conference notes several kinds of victims, including the immediate pawn in the game, the established authorities, the general public, the identified target, the international victim, and the reluctant terrorist. Victims' mechanisms of coping are identified as are implications for prevention and control of terrorism.

410. Targ, Harry R. "Societal Structure and Revolutionary Terrorism: A Preliminary Investigation." In Michael Stohl, ed., *The Politics of Terrorism*, pp. 119-143. New York: Dekker, 1979.

Explores the incidence of terrorism in preindustrial, postindustrial, and industrial nations.

411. Taylor, Edmund. *The Strategy of Terror*. Boston: Houghton Mifflin, 1942.

412. ———. "The Terrorists." *Horizon* 15 (Summer 1973): 58-65.

413. Taylor, Gordon Rattray. "Terrorism: How to Avoid the Future." In Marius Livingston et al., eds, *International Terrorism in the Contemporary World* pp. 462-468, Westport, Conn.: Greenwood Press, 1978.

414. Terekhov, Vladimir. "International Terrorism and the Fight Against It." *New Times* 11 (Moscow) (March 1974): 20-22.

415. "Terrorism." *Military Police Law Enforcement Journal* 3 (Fall 1976): entire issue.

416. "Terrorism." *Skeptic* 11 (January-February 1976): entire issue.
    Attempts to give an overview of current academic, government, and practitioner thinking on the use of and responses to terrorism. Articles include Irving Howe, "The Ultimate Price of Random Terror," Ron Ridenour, "Who Are the Terrorists and What Do They Want?" Walter Laqueur, "Can Terrorism Succeed?" Institute for the Study of Conflict, "Terrorism Can Be Stopped," and Sandra Stencel, "How to Protect Yourself from Terrorism."

417. "Terrorism and the Intellectuals." *Congressional Record* 119 (1973): 12660.

418. Thompson, W. Scott. "Political Violence and the 'Correlation of Forces.' " *Orbis* 19 (Winter 1976): 1270-1288.
    Attempting to avoid the use of an emotionally loaded term, Thompson refers to terrorism as "political violence." He is most concerned with the question of who benefits from the acts of terrorism and the disruption to Western societies that it causes. Mention is made of Soviet aid to various terrorist groups and liberation movements.

419. Thornton, Thomas Ferry. "Terror as a Weapon of Political Agitation." In Harry Eckstein, ed., *Internal War: Problems and Approaches*, pp. 71-99. New York: Free Press, 1964.
    An early treatment of revolutionary terrorism. Many concepts developed by Thornton have been employed by later authors. While Thornton limits himself to terrorism in internal warfare situations, his comments are also relevant to other types of terrorism, especially its transnational varieties.

420. Trick, Marcia McKnight. "Chronology of Incidents of Terroristic, Quasi-Terroristic, and Political Violence in the U.S.: January 1965 to March 1976." In *Report of the Task Force on Disorders and Terrorism*, pp. 507-595. Washington, D.C.: National Advisory Committee on Criminal Justice Standards and Goals, December 1976.

The chronology is the most comprehensive listing of attacks within the United States. It includes a brief description of the major clandestine groups operating in the United States, as well as statistical profiles of trends in terrorist behavior.

421. U.S. Department of Justice. *Terrorism—Its Tactics and Techniques—an FBI Special Study.* January 12, 1973.

The tactics and techniques employed by Palestinian terrorists, IRA, Canadian separatists, and various groups in Latin America are analyzed.

422. U.S. House of Representatives. Committee on Foreign Affairs. Subcommittee on the Near East and South Asia. ''International Terrorism: Hearings.'' 93d Cong, 2d sess., June 11-24, 1974.

Testimony by Hoffacker, Lefever, Methvin, Wolf, Falk, Lockwood, and Jenkins. Of great interest is the debate among witnesses over the State Department's no-ransom policy. Excellent arguments for both sides are presented. In addition to testimony, excerpts from Morf's *Terror in Quebec*, a Library of Congress brief on international terrorism, Hutchinson's ''Concepts of Revolutionary Terrorism,'' and other articles are presented.

423. ———. *Terrorism: A Staff Study* prepared by the Committee on Internal Security. 93d Cong., 2d sess., August 1, 1974.

424. ———. ''Terrorism.'' Part 1, Hearings before the Committee on Internal Security, 93d Cong., 2d sess., February-March 1974.

The testimony focused on political kidnappings and how terrorist activities affect U.S. internal security. Among those who spoke were a U.S. Public Health Service psychiatrist; David Hubbard, who has studied hijackers in Dallas; and the assistant director for research of the International Association of Chiefs of Police.

425. ———. ''Terrorism.'' Part 2, Hearings before the Committee on Internal Security, 93d Cong., 2d sess., May-June 1974.

Witnesses included Fred Rayne of Burns International Investigation; former Ambassador L. Burke Elbrick; and the deputy assistant secretary of state for security. Appendixes included Burns's executive protection handbook and several magazine article reprints.

426. ———. ''Terrorism.'' Part 3, Hearings before the Committee on Internal Security, 93d Cong., 2d sess., June-July 1974.

Speakers included two protection police officers, Braniff's security chief, a Uruguayan kidnapping witness, reporters, and the Air Transportation Association's security director.

427. ———. ''Terrorism.'' Part 4, Hearings before the Committee on Internal Security, 93d Cong., 2d sess., July-August 1974.

Among the witnesses were the assistant attorney general for legislative affairs; Richard W. Velde of the Law Enforcement Assistance Administration; three FBI representatives; the director of the National Institutes for Mental Health; and the author of a report dealing with the vulnerability of nuclear facilities.

428. U.S. Senate. Committee on the Judiciary. Subcommittee to Investigate the Administration of the Internal Security Act and Other Internal Security Laws. ''Terrorist Activity: International Terrorism,'' Part 4, 94th Cong., 1st sess., May 14, 1975.

Brian Crozier gave a typology of terrorists, and Ambassador Robert Fearey gave a background of the U.S. State Department's organization for combating terrorism, trends in hostage situations, and terrorist activities. Chronologies of incidents are included.

430. Van der Kaaden, J. J. ''Terrorism.'' *Institiele Verkenningen* 4 (1975): 138-150.

Surveys the types of incidents and history of terrorism.

431. Villemarest, P. F. de, with Faillant, Daniele. *Historie sécrête des organisations terroristes.* [Secret history of terrorist organizations] Geneva: Famot, 1976. 4 vol.

A review of history throughout the world, with sections on terrorism in each major region.

432. Von Baeyer-Katte, W. ''Terrorism.'' In C. D. Kernig, ed., *Marxism, Communism and Western Society*, 8:124. New York: Herder and Herder, 1973.

433. von Paczensky, Susanne, ed. *Women and Terror: Attempts to Explain the Participation of Women in Acts of Violence.* Hamburg: Rowohlt Tasenbuch, 1978.

434. Waciorski, Jerzy. *Le terrorisme politique.* Paris: A. Pedone, 1939.

435. Walter, Eugene Victor. ''Violence and the Process of Terror.'' *American Sociological Review* 29 (April 1964): 248-257.

''Process of terror'' is defined as being composed of three elements: violence, fear, and reactive behavior. Zones of terror are where the power relations do not follow the rules of an ordinary system of authority. Seiges and regimes of terror are conducted by revolutionaries and incumbents, respectively. Terror attempts to force the object toward an end, not destroy it; hence its violence must be somewhat limited. It differs from military terror, which seeks destruction. Nonviolent control through fear is intimidation, not terrorism, which uses violence defined as "immeasured or exaggerated harm to individuals, either not socially prescribed at all or else beyond established limits." Also discusses resistance, punishment, and war and provides a typology of states based on their use of violence.

436. Walzer, Michael. "The New Terrorists: Random Murder." *New Republic*, August 30, 1975, pp. 12-14.

Since the mid-twentieth century, terrorism has changed from selective assassination into random murder and represents a breakdown of the *political code*, roughly analogous to the laws of war.

437. ———. "Terrorism." In his *Just and Unjust Wars*, pp. 197-206. New York: Basic Books, 1977.

Walzer believes that terrorists must ultimately adhere to a political code, which establishes categories of innocents who are not to be attacked, in order for their self-esteem to be maintained. He attacks Sartre for his sweeping, and inconsistent, praise of Algerian terrorism on these grounds.

438. Walzer, Michael; Bell, J. Bowyer; and Morris, Roger. "Terrorism: A Debate." *New Republic*, December 27, 1975, pp. 12-15.

Walzer strongly argues for an across-the-board condemnation of terrorist acts. Bell argues that this point is logically sound but indignation alone does not lead to a sound policy of response. Morris, in a somewhat rambling piece, argues that terrorism does work and may work in the future for those who feel they have no alternatives. Walzer replies that it is absurd to demand that states that engage in forms of terrorism thereby legitimize terrorism by nonstate actors.

439. Wanek, Marie G. "Symposium Summary." In Marius Livingston, et al., eds., *International Terrorism in the Contemporary World*, pp. 1-18. Westport, Conn.: Greenwood Press, 1978.

440. Ward, Zelime. *Terrorism in Post-Industrial Nations* (University of Texas, 1979, ms.)

441. Waterman, Donald A., and Jenkins, Brian M. "Heuristic Modeling Using Rule-Based Computer Systems." Paper presented to the panel on Applications of Artificial Intelligence and Cognitive Psychology in International Relations of the 18th annual convention of the International Studies Association, March 16-20, 1977, at St. Louis, Missouri.

442. Watson, Francis M. *Political Terrorism: The Threat and the Response.* Washington, D.C.: Robert B. Luce, 1976.

A general survey of terrorism in the world. Chapter titles include "What is Terrorism?" "How Does It Work?" "Who Does It?" "Who Supports It?" "Where Can It Lead?" "What Can Be Done About It?" The appendix includes a chronology of attacks from 1968 through 1975 and a list of the major terrorist groups.

443. Weeks, Albert L. "Terrorism: The Deadly Tradition." *Freedom at Issue* 46 (May-June 1978): 3-11.

444. West, M. "Terror as an Historical Inheritance." *Esquire*, April 25, 1978.

445. Wilkinson, Paul. "The Concept of Terrorism and Its Relationship to Other Forms of Violence Such as Guerrilla War and Mass Insurrection." Paper presented to the Conference on Terrorism in the Contemporary World, April 26-28, 1976, at Glassboro State College.

446. ———. "A Fatality of Illusions: Dominant Images of International Terrorism." Paper presented at the Department of State Conference on International Terrorism in Retrospect of Prospect, March 25-26, 1976. Reprinted as FAR 24513-S.

Presents a useful discussion of the difficulties in attempting to define terrorism and distinguishes it from violence and force per se. The roles of ideology and criminality and the perceptions of the terrorist are emphasized to a greater extent than generally found. The author argues that only extreme measures will be successful against the nihilistic type of terrorist.

447. ———. "Terrorist Movements." In Yonah Alexander, David Carlton, and Paul Wilkinson, eds., *Terrorism: Theory and Practice*, pp. 99-117. Boulder: Westview, 1979.

Posits four types of terrorist movements—nationalists, ideologists, exiles, and world revolutionaries—and compares their tactics and successes.

448.———. "Theories of Terrorism." In Yonah Alexander, David Carlton and Paul Wilkinson, eds, *Terrorism: Theory and Practice*. Boulder: Westview, 1979.

449. ———. "Theories of Terrorism." In Yonah Alexander and Robert A. Kilmarx, eds., *Political Terrorism and Business: The Threat and Response.* New York: Holt, Rinehart, Winston, 1979.

450. ———. "Three Questions on Terrorism." *Government and Opposition*, (Summer 1973): 290-312.

Discusses the concept of terrorism, major forms of terrorism, and some contributory causes of terrorism.

451. ———. *Political Terrorism.* New York: Wiley, 1975.

Designed as a survey of the literature, discusses terrorism as an evaluative term, noting the debate over terrorists' morality. Sees terrorism as always indiscriminate. Gives a good presentation of the flaws in the other definitions of terrorism that have been forwarded. Discussion is presented on revolutionary and subrevolutionary terrorism with respect to righteous assassins, indigenous autocracy, foreign rule, totalitarianism, liberal democracies, and the international community. Countermeasures and partial steps toward a general theory complete the work.

452. Williams, Shahron G. "The Transnational Impact of Insurgency Terrorism: A Quantitative Approach." Ph.D. dissertation, City University of New York, 1978.

By use of statistical methods, such as multiple linear regression and time series models, the author establishes linkages (if not causal relationships) between the magnitude, duration, and intensity of all forms of insurgency terrorism and international intervention.

453. Winegarten, Renée. "Literary Terrorism." *Commentary* 57 (March 1974): 58-65.

Discusses the Jewish Sicarii, who killed imperial Roman leaders in broad daylight among crowds. Defines terrorism as a "systematic policy employed by the few to impose their outlook or their will through the intimidation of the passive many or the powerful antagonist." Notes seventeenth-century French anarchist Emile Henry, who argued that collective guilt justified his bombing of a café by stating, "there are no innocent people." Aesthetics of terrorism and Kafka, Greene, Koestler, Bloy, Yeats, and Shelley are discussed.

454. Wolf, John B. "An Analytical Framework for the Study and Control of Agitational Terrorism." *Police Journal* 49 (July-September 1976): 165-171. Available as FAR 25966-N.

455. ———. "Organization and Management Practices of Urban Terrorist Groups." *Terrorism* 1 (1978): 169-186.

In addition to discussing how terrorists go about communicating their message, Wolf notes management practices, cellular and columnar structures, personnel selection, and internal control measures.

456. ———. ''Terrorist Manipulation of the Democratic Process.'' In Marius Livingston et al., eds., *Terrorism in the Contemporary World*, Westport, Conn.: Greenwood Press, 1978., pp. 297-306.

457. ———. ''Update on Terrorism.'' Paper presented to the 23d National Conference of the Law Enforcement Intelligence Unit, April 26, 1978, at New Orleans.

458. ———. ''Urban Terrorist Operations.'' U.S. Department of State. FAR document 25970-N, 1976.

459. Wordemann, Franz. *Terrorismus: Motive, Tater, Strategien.* Munich: Piper Verlag, 1977.

460. Yarborough, William P. ''Terrorism: The Past as an Indicator of the Future.'' In Marius Livingston et al., eds., *International Terrorism in the Contemporary World*, pp. 454-461. Westport, Conn.: Greenwood Press, 1978.

461. Yost, Charles W. ''Forms and Masks of Terrorism.'' *Christian Science Monitor*, September 14, 1972.

462. Young, Robert. ''Revolutionary Terrorism, Crime and Morality.'' *Social Theory and Practice* 3 (Fall 1977): 287-302.
   Argues that terrorism should not be equated with crime and that the former is often more justified than is portrayed by the media.

463. Zahn, G. C. ''Terrorism for Peace and Justice.'' *Commonweal* October 23, 1970, pp. 84-85.

464. Zawodny, Janusz K. ''Infrastructure of Terrorist Groups.'' Paper presented to the Conference on Psychopathology and Political Violence, November 16-17, 1979, at the University of Chicago.

465. ———. ''The Internal Conflicts of Terrorist Organizations as Catalysts of External Violence.'' Paper presented to the annual convention of the Western Section of the International Studies Association, March 16-18, 1978. Published as ''Internal Organizational Problems and the Sources of Tensions of Terrorist Movements as Catalysts of Violence.'' *Terrorism* 1 (1978): 277-286.
   Command problems (security versus communications, clustering of ethnic groups under stress, role of women, and quality of membership) and

political problems (self-destructive potential of successful terrorist groups, inflated membership, and the role of leaders as givers of moral dispensation) may lead groups to more violent acts. An excellent piece of commonsense analysis, based upon the author's experiences with the World War II Polish underground.

466. Zinam, Oleg. "Terrorism and Violence in the Light of a Theory of Discontent and Frustration." In Marius Livingston et al., eds., *International Terrorism in the Contemporary World*, pp. 240-268. Westport, Conn.: Greenwood Press, 1978.

467. Zivic, J. "The Nonaligned and the Problem of International Terrorism." *Review of International Affairs* (Belgrade), January 20, 1973, pp. 6-8.

468. Zoppo, Ciro. "The Moral Factor in Interstate Politics and International Terrorism." Paper delivered to the Conference on Moral Implications of Terrorism, March 14-16, 1979 at UCLA.

TACTICS OF TERRORISTS

ASSASSINATIONS

469. Abrahamsen, David. *The Murdering Mind*. New York: Harper Colophon, 1973.

470. Agirre, Julen. *Operation Ogro: The Execution of Admiral Luis Carrero Blanco*. Translated by Barbara Probst Solomon. New York: Quadrangle, 1975.

Agirre, an émigré Basque journalist, interviews the four ETA members who assassinated Carrero. The book gives an almost day-to-day account of the year-long plans of the assassins and how the plan changed from the original kidnapping they had hoped for. Reviewed by Richard Eder, ''The Men in the Tunnel,'' *New York Times*, October 25, 1975, p. 27.

471. ''Assassination as a Weapon of Diplomacy.'' *Washington Post*, June 4, 1975, p. A18.

472. ''The Assassination Cult in Japan.'' *The China Weekly Review*, April 2, 1932, pp. 137-140.

473. ''Assassins' Victims.'' *Review of Reviews* 85 (November 1934): 15-17.

474. Barrett, R. T. ''Political Assassination in Japan.'' *Great Britain and the East*, March 10, 1938, p. 260.

475. Bell, J. Bowyer. ''Assassination in International Politics: Lord Moyne, Count Bernadotte and the Lehi.'' *International Studies Quarterly* 16 (March 1972): 59-82.

Looks at the history of assassination as a political strategy using LEHI attacks as illustrations. Bell believes that assassination is more humane, and therefore more moral, than conventional warfare.

476. Bernd, Joseph L. ''Assassination and Hypnosis: Political Influence or Conspiracy?'' Blacksburg, Va.: Virginia Polytechnic and State University, 1969.

477. Conrad, Thomas R. "Coercion, Assassination, Conspiracy: Pejorative Political Language." *Polity* 6 (1974): 418-423.

478. Cottrell, John. *Anatomy of an Assassination.* New York: Funk & Wagnalls, 1966.

479. Crotty, William J., ed. *Assassinations and the Political Order.* New York: Harper & Row, 1971.
A collection of writings that notes world patterns, public responses, political impacts, and motivations behind assassinations.

480. ———. "Presidential Assassinations." In James F. Short, ed., *Modern Criminals,* pp. 189-213. New Brunswick, N.J.: Transaction, 1973.
Argues that there are five types of assassination: anomic assassination, elite substitution, tyrannicide, terroristic assassination, and propaganda by deed. Discusses characteristics of the targets and of the assassins, suggesting that the latter gives a better explanation of such behavior. Public reaction and violence in America are also mentioned.

481. Danto, A. C. "A Logical Portrait of the Assassin" *Social Research* (Autumn 1974).
Views assassination as a type of political activity aiming at the alteration of policy and discusses similarities among assassins.

482. Demaret, Pierre, and Plume, Christian. *Target DeGaulle.* New York: Dial, 1975.
The story of thirty-one unsuccessful assassination attempts, with a history of the OAS providing a backdrop.

483. Dietze, Gottfried. "Will the Presidency Incite Assassination?" *Ethics* 76 (October 1965): 14-32.

484. Donovan, Robert J. *The Assassins.* New York: Popular Library, 1964.
Accounts of the lives of the eight men who have attempted assassination of U.S. presidents. A new chapter on the Kennedy case, which could be viewed as agreeing with conspiracy theories (although arguing Oswald acted alone), appears in the second edition. Unfortunately Donovan did not revise his chapter on the Secret Service.

485. Ellis, Albert, and Gullo, John. *Murder and Assassination.* New York: Lyle Stuart, 1971.

486. Feierabend, Ivo K.; Feierabend, Rosalind L.; Nesvold, Betty A.; and Jaggar, Franz M. "Political Violence and Assassination: A Cross-National Assessment." In William J. Crotty, ed., *Assassinations and the Political Order*, pp. 54-140. New York: Harper & Row, 1971.

Using data on eighty-four countries for 1948 through 1967, the authors establish where assassinations have occurred, pointing out certain patterns among nations.

487. Feierabend, Ivo; Feierabend, Rosalind; et. al. "Cross-National Comparative Study of Assassination." Mimeo. report prepared for the National Commission on the Causes and Prevention of Violence, Task Force I, vol. I, chap. 3.

488. Fine, Sidney. "Anarchism and the Assassination of McKinley." *American Historical Review* 60 (July 1955): 777-799.

489. Frank, Robert S. "Political Culture and Political Violence." Paper presented at the Conference on Terrorism in the Contemporary World, April 26-28, 1976, at Glassboro State College. FAR 25616-N. Published in Yonah Alexander and John M. Gleason, eds., *Terrorism: Behavioral Perspectives* (New York: Pergamon, 1980).

Using the Feierabends' data on assassinations, Frank uses factor analysis, correlations, and regression to find differences across nations in patterns of political violence.

490. Gales, Robert Robinson. "Notes: The Assassination of the President: Jurisdictional Problems." *Syracuse Law Review* 16 (Fall 1964): 69-81.

491. Galzerano, Ethel. "Dimensions of Political Trust and Belief in the Kennedy Assassination Conspiracy Theories." Ph.D. Dissertation, University of Missouri at Columbia in preparation.

492. Gross, Feliks. "Political Assassination." *Sociologia Internationalis* 10 (1972): 173-182. Reprinted as FAR 15641-N. In Marius Livingston, et al., eds., *International Terrorism in the Contemporary World*, pp. 307-315. Westport, Conn.: Greenwood Press, 1978.

493. Harris, Irving. "Who Would Kill a President? Little Brother." *Psychology Today* 10 (October 1976): 48-51, 103-104.

The study notes the psychological makeup of American presidential assassins. Its subtitle is, "A Survey of America's Political Assassins Points up Their Low Status in the Family Hierarchy, and Their Ambition to Take the Spotlight."

494. Hassel, Conrad V. "The Political Assassin." Quantico, Va.: Behavioral Science Unit, FBI Academy, n.d.

Hassel looked at ten individuals who attempted to assassinate U.S. presidents and found that socioeconomic variables gave no clues to their character. The assassins lacked a stable male authority figure during their developmental years, lacked meaningful relationships with the opposite sex, and suffered from delusions.

495. Hastings, Donald W. "The Psychiatry of Presidential Assassination." *Journal-Lancet* (March 1965).

Concludes that six of the eight men who attempted to assassinate U.S. presidents were psychotic. This is a series of four articles, studying two attacks per article: Jackson and Lincoln (March 1965): 93-100; Garfield and McKinley (April 1965): 157-162; the Roosevelts (May 1965): 189-192; and Truman and Kennedy (July 1965): 294-301.

496. Havens, Murray C. "Assassination in Australia." Unpublished manuscript prepared for the National Commission on the Causes and Prevention of Violence, 1968.

497. ———. "Assassination, Violence, and National Policy." Paper presented to the panel on Radical Alternatives for National Security Policy of the International Studies Association's Section on Military Studies' Third Biennial Conference, October 28-30, 1976, at Mershon Center, Ohio State University.

498. ———, et al. *Assassination and Terrorism: Their Modern Dimensions.* Sterling Swift, 1975.

499. Horowitz, Irving Louis. "Kennedy's Death: Myths and Realities" *Transaction* (July-August 1968). Reprinted in James F. Short, ed., *Modern Criminals*, pp. 171-179. (New Brunswick, N.J.: Transaction, 1973).

Attacks five major myths about the United States and assassination: (1). assassination has become a contagious and infectious American style; (2). the degree of violence has increased as the propensity to change has accelerated; (3). madmen and criminals will always be able to avail themselves of weapons, and therefore any legislation against carrying a gun penalizes only the innocent interested in self-protection; (4). individual responsibility should be assumed; (5). the assassination attempts on men of stature, such as Senator Kennedy, drastically affect the course of history.

500. Hurwood, Bernhardt J. *Society and the Assassin: A Background Book on Political Murder.* New York: Parent's Magazine Press, 1970.

501. Huth, Tom. "Portrait of Presidential Assassin: White, Short, Weak-Sighted Loner." *Washington Post*, (May 21, 1972), pp. Al, A22.

502. Hyams, Edward. *Killing No Murder.* London: Nelson, 1969. New York: Panther, 1970.

503. Jaszi, O. and Lewis, J. D. *Against the Tyrant: The Tradition and Theory of Tyrannicide.* Glencoe, Ill.: Free Press, 1957.
    Reviews theories legitimizing antistate violence and notes relationships between tyrannicide, terrorism, and anarchism.

504. Johnson, Francis. *Famous Assassinations of History from Philip of Macedon, 336 B.C., to Alexander of Serbia, 1903 A.D.* Chicago: A. C. McClurg and Co., 1903.

505. Kaplan, John. "The Assassins." *Stanford Law Review* 10 (May 1967): 1110-1151.

506. Kelly, Joseph B. "Assassination in War Time." *Military Law Review* 30 (October 1965): 101-111.

507. Kirkham, James F.; Levy, Sheldon G.; and Crotty, William J. *Assassination and Political Violence: A Staff Report to the National Commission on the Causes and Prevention of Violence.* New York: Bantam, 1970.

508. Knopf. "Sniping Incident: A New Pattern of Violence." *Law and Order* (May 1969): 28ff.

509. Leiden, Carl. "Assassination in the Middle East." *Trans-Action* 6 (May 1969): 20-23. Reprinted in James F. Short, ed., *Modern Criminals* pp. 161-170. (New Brunswick, N.J.: Transaction, 1973).
    Argues that there are six motives for assassination and gives examples of these in the Middle-East. Such motives are personal or family grievances, desire for political revenge, symbolic benefits to be derived from the death of the victim, practical need for removal, need for unofficial executions, and the need for a scapegoat.

510. Levy, Sheldon G. "Assassination and the Theory of Reduced Alternatives." *Peace Research Society (International) Papers* 17 (1970): 75-92.

511. ———. "Assassination—Levels, Motivations, and Attitudes." *Peace Research Society (International) Papers* 14 (1970): 47-82.

512. Lewis, Bernard. *The Assassins: A Radical Sect in Islam.* New York: Basic Books, 1968.

513. MacDonald, Arthur. "Assassins of Rulers." *Journal of the American Institute of Criminal Law and Criminology* 2 (November 1911): 505-520.

514. Marshall, John. "The Twentieth Century Vehme: Terror by Assassination." *Blackwood's Magazine* 257 (June 1945): 421-425.

515. Mazrui, Ali A. "Thoughts on Assassination in Africa." *Political Science Quarterly* 83 (March 1968): 40-58.

After definitional preliminaries, Mazrui discusses reasons why African assassinations tend to occur at the beginning of the year, why they occurred after independence rather than during colonial times, and assassination's relation to legitimacy, integration, hero worship and pan-Africanism.

516. McConnell, Brian. *The History of Assassination.* London: Frewin, 1969.

517. McKinley, James. *Assassination in America.* New York: Harper and Row, 1976.

518. McMillan, George. *The Making of an Assassin: The Life of James Earl Ray.* Boston: Little, Brown, 1976.

A detailed biography of the killer of Martin Luther King, Jr., arguing that Ray acted alone. Reviewed by Paul Valentine "The Murky Story of James Earl Ray: Exploring the Past of an Accused Murderer" *Washington Post*, October 15, 1976, p. B5.

519. Mindt, R. "Assassins and Murderers: A Comparison." *Monatsschrift fuer Krimonologie und Strafrechtsreform* 59 (February 1976): 2-17.

Mindt uses data on 215 political assassinations during the last two centuries to explore social class, education, mobility, criminal record, success, and offender's fate.

520. Padover, Saul K. "Patterns of Assassination in Occupied Territory." *Public Opinion Quarterly* (Winter 1943): 680-693.

Traces the historical roots of assassination from the early Greeks and Romans through feudal Europe, up to World War II. Pedover suggests what patterns may turn up in nations that participated in World War II.

521. Paine, Lauran. *The Assassins' World.* New York: Taplinger, 1975. 208 pp.

Discusses the practice of political murder in Asia, Latin America, and the Middle East.

522. Rapoport, David C. *Assassination and Terrorism*. Toronto: Canadian Broadcasting Corp., 1971. 88 pp.

The bulk of the book is a set of six radio addresses given on CBC. Rapoport uses historical examples to distinguish the philosophical, logistic, practical, and strategic aspect of assassination and terrorism. Appended is Nechaeyeff's *Revolutionary Catechism*.

523. Rothstein, David A. "The Presidential Assassination Syndrome." *Archives of General Psychiatry* 11 (1964): 245-254.

524. Schmitt, Karl M. "Assassination in Latin America." Unpublished manuscript, prepared for the National Commission on the Causes and Prevention of Violence, 1968.

525. Seikaly, Samir. "Prime Minister and Assassin: Butrus Ghali and Wardani." *Middle Eastern Studies* 13 (January 1977): 112-123.

526. Simon, Rita James. "Political Violence Directed at Public Office Holders: A Brief Analysis of the American Scene." Unpublished manuscript, prepared for the National Commission on the Causes and Prevention of Violence, 1968.

527. Soukup, James R. "Assassination in Japan." Unpublished manuscript, prepared for the National Commission on the Causes and Prevention of Violence, 1968.

528. Sparrow, Gerald. *The Great Assassins*. New York: Arco, 1969.

Vignettes on major assassinations throughout history.

529. Spragens, William C. "Political Impact of Assassination and Attempted Assassination." Paper presented to the Conference on Terrorism in the Contemporary World, April 26-28, 1976, at Glassboro State College. Available as FAR 25870-N.

Concentrates on the effects of recent assassinations in the United States, speculating on some of the major cases' unanswered questions.

530. Tischendorf, Alfred. "The Assassination of Chief Executives in Latin America." *South Atlantic Quarterly* 60 (Winter 1961): 80-88.

Discusses the twenty-eight assassinations of presidents that have occurred from 1806 through 1960 in Latin America. Tischendorf notes that pre-1930s security procedures were nonexistent, but that the majority of assassins have been promptly executed. Most of the assassinations occurred when the countries lacked political maturity or were going through periods of social or economic stress.

531. Tretiak, David. "Reflections on Political Assassinations in China." Unpublished manuscript, prepared for the National Commission on the Causes and Prevention of Violence, 1968.

532. Truby, J. David. *How Terrorists Kill: The Complete Terrorist Arsenal.* Boulder: Paladin, 1978.
   A discussion, profusely illustrated, of typical weapons used by terrorists.

533. U.S. House of Representatives. Committee on International Relations. Special Subcommittee on Investigations. "The Assassination of American Diplomats in Beirut, Lebanon, Hearing." 94th Cong. 2d sess., July 27, 1976.
   Testimony by Arthur R. Day, Victor H. Dikeos, and Sidney T. Telford of the U.S. Department of State on the killings of Ambassador Meloy and economic counselor Waring.

534. Westermeyer, J. "Assassination in Laos: Its Psychosocial Dimensions." *Archives of General Psychiatry* 28 (May 1974): 740-743.

535. Whittier, Charles H. "Assassination in Theory and Practice: A Historical Survey of the Religious and Philosophical Background of the Doctrine of Tyrannicide." Washington, D.C.: Library of Congress, Congressional Research Service, Government Division, Specialist in Humanities and Religion, April 12, 1978.
   A thorough discussion of the philosophical underpinnings of assassination and tyrannicide.

536. Wilson, Colin, *Order of Assassins: The Psychology of Murder.* London: Rupert Hart-Davis, 1972.
   The third book in Wilson's three-volume study of murder, this focuses on psychological theories of the motivations of assassins, citing much case material.

537. Wolf, John B. "Assassination Plot." Paper presented to the conference on Techniques for the Practitioner: Counter-Terrorism sponsored by the John Jay College of Criminal Justice, June 7, 1978, in New York City.

   For additional entries on assassinations, see items 1279, 1283, 1792, 1851, 1852, 1853, 1869, 1892, 1936, 1949, 1994, 1995, and 3101.

BOMBINGS

538. "Aids to the Detection of Explosives: A Brief Review of Equipment for Searching Out Letter Bombs and Other Explosive Devices." *Security Gazette* 17 (February 1975): 48, 49, 61.

Discusses the prices, uses, and where to obtain equipment such as hand-held probes, desk-top metal detectors, inspection mirrors, X-ray mail scanners, vapor detectors, and baggage systems.

539. Alexander, Yonah. "The Letter Bomb." Paper presented to the conference on Terror: The Man, the Mind and the Matter, October 15-16, 1976, at the John Jay School of Criminal Justice, New York City.

540. Anderson, Jack, and Whitten, Les. "Terrorists and Airports." *Washington Post*, February 10, 1974.

A discussion of security conditions at major international airports.

541. "Anti-Soviet Zionist Terrorism in the U.S." *Current Digest of the Soviet Press*, February 9, 1971, p. 68.

Five articles translated from *Pravda* and *Izvestia*, January 9-15, 1971. They condemn alleged acts of terrorism and harassment against Russian institutions and their staff members in the United States attributed to members of the Jewish Defense League protesting treatment of Soviet Jews.

542. Barracato, John S. "The Pathology of the Arsonist as Terrorist." Paper presented to the conference on Terror: The Man, the Mind and the Matter, October 15-16, 1976, at the John Jay School of Criminal Justice, New York City.

543. Bomb Scene Procedures: The Protective Response. Gaithersburg, Md.; International Association of Chiefs of Police, n.d.

544. Bomb Security Guidelines: The Prevention Response. Gaithersburg, Md.: International Association of Chiefs of Police, n.d.

545. "Bomb Threats." *Environment* (October 1972): 21.

546. Bomb Threats against U.S. Airports, 1974. Washington, D.C.: U.S. Department of Transportation, Federal Aviation Administration, Civil Aviation Security Service, 1975.

547. "Bomb Threats and Search Techniques." Washington, D.C.: Bureau of Alcohol, Tobacco and Firearms, U.S. Department of the Treasury, ATF P 7550.2, April 1975.

Discusses measures to be taken in the event of a phoned bomb threat, evacuation procedures, whom to call for what purposes, and other useful operational information.

548. "Bomb Threats on Decline; But Need of How to Handle is Still Vital." *Police Times: Voice of the American Federation of Police* (March 1975).

549. "A Bomber's Tactical Description of the Attack on a Military Installation." *Scanlan's* 1 (January 1971): 17ff

550. "Bombing Fallout." *Business Week*, November 22, 1969, p. 44.

551. "Bombing Incidents—1972." *FBI Law Enforcement Bulletin* (April 1973): 21.

552. Bombings in the U.S. Gaithersburg, Md.: International Association of Chiefs of Police, n.d.

553. Bond, Thomas C. "Fragging: A Study." *Army* 27 (April 1977): 45-47.

554. Brodie, Thomas G. *Bombs and Bombings: A Handbook to Detection, Disposal and Investigation for Police and Fire Departments.* Springfield, Ill.: Thomas, 1975.

555. Chase, L. J., ed. *Bomb Threats, Bombings and Civil Disturbances: A Guide for Facility Protection.* Corvallis, Ore.: Continuing Education Publications, 1971.

556. Clarke, W. A. and Warren, B. C. H. "Frustrate the Bomber by Using the Fluoroscope Letter-Bomb Detector." *Police Review*, January 3, 1975.

557. Clutterbuck, Richard. "Bombs in Britain." *Army Quarterly* 105 (January 1975): 15-21.

558. Dodd, Norman L. "Send for Felix." *Military Review* 58 (March 1978): 46-55.
Discusses the training given to members of the British Army bomb disposal squad working in Northern Ireland.

559. "Editorial: After a Bomb." *British Medical Journal*, January 25, 1975, pp. 172-173.

*560. Gilinsky, Victor. ''Bombs and Electricity.'' *Environment* 14 (September 1972): 10-17.

561. Howe, C. ''Prevalence of Bombing.'' *Nation*, March 30, 1970, pp. 361-363.

562. Iklé, Fred C. *The Social Impact of Bomb Destruction.* Norman: University of Oklahoma Press, 1958.

563. Incident Summary for the Month of May, 1975. Washington, D.C.: U.S. Department of Justice, FBI Bomb Data Program, 1975.

Incident summaries appear monthly and are generally obtainable from this program.

564. ''Is Your Industry a Bomb Target?'' *Industry Week*, June 27, 1970, p. 40.

565. Karber, Phillip A. ''Insurgency Without Revolution: Terrorist Bombings in the U.S.'' Paper presented before the annual convention of the American Sociological Association, September 1972.

566. ———. ''Newspaper Coverage of Domestic Bombings: Reporting Patterns of American Violence.'' *Bomb Incident Bulletins: Tab 02: Targets and Tactics* 1 (January 1973), pp. 17-23.

Uses a survey of eleven thousand U.S. newspapers to answer three questions: What are the characteristics of bomb incidents that elicit the most newspaper coverage? What characteristics of the newspaper itself affect the coverage of bomb incidents? How are bomb incidents portrayed in newspaper reports?

567. Karber, Phillip A., and Novotny, Eric J. ''Radical Bombings in the United States: What Happened to the 'Revolution?' '' *Bomb Incident Bulletins: Tab 02: Targets and Tactics* (Gaithersburg, Md.: International Association of Chiefs of Police, Research Division, January 1973), pp. 13-16.

Despite what appeared to be support for the Weathermen by seven thousand radicals, no campaign of revolutionary bombings was established. The authors attribute this to the lack of a synchronized campaign, organizational anarchy, and the lack of an above-ground mobilization base from which to recruit.

*Entries 560a through 599a follow entry 599.

568. Leibstone, Marvin, and Shriver, R. "Impact of Taggants in Explosives and Explosive Materials." Science Applications Inc., study prepared for the U.S. Congressional Office of Technology Assessment, Fall 1979.

Looks at the pros and cons of taggants as a deterrent in preventing bombings by terrorists and criminals.

569. Lenz, Robert R. *Explosives and Bomb Disposal Guide.* Springfield, Ill.: Thomas, 1973.

570. Lewald, Charles E. *Fundamentals of Incendiarism for Raiders and Saboteurs, and for Planning Measures.* Washington, D.C.: Research Analysis Corporation, 1956.

571. Lubkin, G. B. "Bomb Kills Physicist, Damages Equipment." *Psychology Today* 23 (October 1970): 73-74.

572. Lyons, H. A. "Terrorists' Bombing and the Psychological Sequelae." *Journal of the Ir. Medical Association*, January 12, 1974, pp. 15-19.

573. Mahoney, Harry T. "After a Terrorist Attack: Business as Usual." *Security Management* (March 1975): 16-19.

574. Maxwell, Neil. "How Do You Handle a Bomb Threat? Well, It's the Wrong Way: New Government 'Bomb Schools' Urge a Change in Tactics, Such as Fewer Evacuations." *Wall Street Journal*, January 29, 1971.

575. McAlister, R. "Intensive Care of Bomb-Blast Injuries." *Nursing Mirror*, November 14, 1974, pp. 66-68.

576. Novotny, Eric J., and Karber, Phillip A. "Terrorism Without Conspiracy: Radical Bombings and Organizational Effectiveness." Paper presented at the 1973 semiannual meeting of the National Capital Area Political Science Association, April 28, 1973, at University of Maryland.

577. Pike, Earl A. *Protection Against Bombs and Incendiaries: For Business, Industrial and Educational Institutions.* Springfield, Ill.: Thomas, 1973.

578. Railroad Sabotage Detection Research Final Technical Report, Fort Belvoir, Va.: Department of the Army, Engineer Research and Development Laboratories, 1965.

Presents a method of detection by monitoring acoustic or vibration signals introduced into the rail.

579. Secreted Explosive Detection by Bioluminescence. El Segundo, Calif.: RPC Corporation, 1972. 40 pp.

Demonstrates how to use luminescent organisms, which change their light emission when exposed to the presence of a hidden explosive's vapor.

580. Stoffel, John. *Explosives and Homemade Bombs.* Springfield, Ill.: Thomas, 1973. 324 pp.

581. Styles, George. "Bombs and Bomb Beaters." *International Defense Review* 9 (October 1976): 817-819.

582. ———. *Bombs Have No Pity.* London: William Luscombe, 1975.

The memoirs of the British Army bomb disposal teams in Northern Ireland between 1969 and 1972.

583. ———. "The Car Bomb." *Journal of the Forensic Science Society* (London) 15 (April 1975): 93-97.

584. ———. "Defeating the Terrorist Bomber." *International Defense Review* 10 (February 1977): 121-122.

585. ———. "Terrorism: The Global War of the Seventies." *International Defense Review* 4 (1976): 594-596.

Most of the article concentrates on the use of improvised explosive devices.

585a. "Terrorist Acts against U.N. Missions." *U.N. Monthly Chronicle* 8 (November 1971): 61-70.

586. U.S. House of Representatives. "Thefts and Losses of Military Weapons, Ammunition, and Explosives." Report of the Subcommittee on Investigations of the Committee on Armed Services. 94th Cong. 2d sess, April 14, 1976.

587. U.S. Senate. "Terroristic Activity: Terrorist Bombings and Law Enforcement Intelligence." Hearings before the Subcommittee to Investigate the Administration of the Internal Security Act and Other Internal Security Laws of the Committee on the Judiciary. 94th Cong., 1st sess., October 23, 1975, pt. 7.

588. Violence against Society. Washington, D.C.: U.S. Chamber of Commerce, 1971.

A transcript of a conference in which police experts on bombings told businessmen how to prevent attacks, what services are offered by the National Bomb Data Center, the use of the injunctive process against clear and present danger, and information on various statutes.

For additional readings on bombings, see the "Medical Treatments" discussion in the "Psychological Approaches" section, as well as entries 2357 and 3132.

HIJACKINGS

589. Aggarwala, Narinder. "Political Aspects of Hijacking." *International Conciliation* 585 (November 1971): 7-27.
An examination of the motivations for hijacking and the legal and political responses to the offense.

591. "Airlines Seek a Breakthrough: Preventions of Hijacking." *Science News*, August 31, 1968, pp. 204-205.
A discussion of Lockheed's magnetometer.

592. Arey, James A. *The Sky Pirates.* New York: Charles Scribner's Sons, 1972. 360 pp.
Arey is a member of the aviation community and has been able to obtain interviews with various pilots who have been hijacked, high-level administrators, and others. The first chapter is a translation of pilot-control tower chatter during an Arab hijacking on September 6, 1970. Long anecdotes detailing the motivations of other hijackers are also given. Many suggestions for prevention of hijacking are made. A complete chronology of incidents is appended.

593. Ashwood, Thomas M. "The Airline Response to Terrorism." In Yonah Alexander and Robert A. Kilmarx, eds., *Political Terrorism and Business: The Threat and Response*, pp. 226-243. New York: Praeger, 1979.

594. Asinof, Eliot. *The Fox is Crazy Too.* New York: Morrow, 1976. 308 pp.
Reviewed by Paul D. Zimmerman, "Life on the Lam" *Newsweek*, February 16, 1976, pp. 81A-B.
A life story of criminal Garrett Trapnell, who skyjacked a TWA 707 on January 28, 1972, and was shot by an FBI agent.

595. Atala, Charles, and Jacquenein, G. *La hijacking aerien ou la maîtresse illecite d'aeronef, hier, aujord'hui, Demain.* Montreal: Lemeac, Dossiers Interlex, 1973.

596. Baldwin, David A. "Bargaining with Airline Hijackers." In William Zartman, ed., *The 50% Solution* pp. 404-429. New York: Doubleday, 1976. Originally available as FAR 19182-N (January 1974).

Baldwin suggests how concepts developed by Thomas Schelling can be used in studying hijacking situations. He further refines these notions and probably makes a greater contribution to bargaining theory than he does to hijack prevention and response modes.

597. Bell, Robert G. "The U.S. Response to Terrorism against International Civil Aviation." *Orbis* (Winter 1976): 1326-1343.

While noting the American role in creating international legal instruments to combat terrorism against airliners, Bell also notes the FAA's program of training foreign airport security officials, various search procedures, and other methods of defense and prevention. He suggests that terrorism itself will not end with the elimination of the possibility of a specific type of terrorism, such as skyjacking. The terrorists will merely turn to the next target that is easy to attack. Terrorism can be eradicated only if its causes are attended to.

598. Blair, Ed, with Haas, Captain William R. *Odyssey of Terror.* Nashville: Broadman, 1977. 316 pp.

The story of the November 10, 1972, hijacking of Southern Airways flight 49.

599. Boltwood, Charles E.; Cooper, Michael R.; Fein, Victoria E.; and Washburn, Paul V. "Skyjacking, Airline Security, and Passenger Reactions: Toward a Complex Model for Prediction." *American Psychologist* 27 (June 1972): 539-545.

Assesses passengers' reactions to security proposals. Life imprisonment for hijackers and extended frisking authority for guards were rated highest of seven measures suggested, on scales of favorability, effectiveness, and convenience. Perceived effectiveness of a security procedure had a definite influence on a passenger's willingness to spend time on security procedures. Factor analysis was unable to locate an "overall concern for security" dimension. Eight factors isolated eight passenger subgroups who held differing opinions. Article summarized in M. R. Cooper, V. E. Fein, P. V. Washburn, and C. E. Boltwood, "Passenger Attitudes toward Airline Security and Threat of Skyjacking." *Proceedings of the 79th Annual Convention of the American Psychological Association*, pp. 407-408.

560a. Brockman, Richard. "Notes While Being Hijacked." *Atlantic.* (December 1976): 68-75.

561a. Burris, Joseph B. "A Study of Aerial Hijacking" Air Command and Staff College. Master's Thesis, May 1972.

562a. "Canada-Federal Republic of Germany-France-Italy-Japan-United Kingdom-United States: Declaration issued at the Conclusion of the Bonn Economic Summit Conference; Joint Statement on International Terrorism." *International Legal Materials* 17 (September 1978): 1281-1285.

563a. Chauncey, Robert. "Deterrence: Certainty, Severity, and Skyjacking." *Criminology* 12 (February 1975); 447-473.

A longitudinal comparison of the effects of antihijacking methods used from 1962 to 1973. Increasing the certainty of punishment is more effective than increasing the severity of it.

564a. Clark, Lorne S. "The Struggle to Cure Hijacking." *International Perspectives* (January-February 1973): 47-51.

565a. Clyne, Peter. *An Anatomy of Skyjacking.* London: Abelard-Schuman, 1973. 200 pp.

Studies of the trials of three Arab terrorists who attacked an El Al Airliner in 1969 and of Kozo Okamoto, a member of the JRA Lod Airport massacre team. Clyne is concerned with security precautions, deterrents, capital punishment, terrorist motivations, and negotiation strategies. Classifies skyjackings as being of five types: criminal extortions, bluffs, unorthodox means of transportation, lunacies, and acts of terror. Advocates ad hoc approach to negotiations, with agreements being honored.

566a. Codd, Michael. "The TWA Croatian Case." Address to the Conference on Terrorism and the Media, sponsored by the Ralph Bunche Institute and the Institute for Studies in International Terrorism, November 17, 1977, at New York City.

567a. Dailey, James T. "Development of a Behavioral Profile for Air Pirates." *Villanova Law Review* 18 (1973).

568a. Dailey, John, and Pickrel, Evan. "Federal Aviation Administration's Behavioral Research Program for Defense Against Hijackings." *Aviation, Space, and Environmental Medicine* (April 1975): 423-427.

569a. Eliot, Chris. "Security in the Air." *Aerospace International* (February-March 1978): 13.

570a. Elten, Jorg Andrees. "This is a Hijacking." *Reader's Digest* 99 (July 1971): 213-217.
Concentrates on mistakes made in PFLP operations.

571a. "FAA Studies Ways to End Hijackings." *American Aviation*, March 17, 1969, p. 24.
A discussion of the FAA attempt to create a profile of the hijacker, as well as methods for detecting weapons. Such measures are to be considered part of the philosophy of prevention on the ground.

572a. Fenello, Michael J. "Technical Prevention of Air Piracy." *International Conciliation* 585 (November 1971): 28-41.
A survey of some of the techniques, physical and psychological, tried in the United States.

573a. Forsberg, O. "IFALPA Position Report on Hijacking." *Air Line Pilot* 39 (July 1970): 42-46.
The statement by O. Forsberg, president of the IFALPA, noted that the group was against security guards on aircraft, called for review of security measures at major airports, and requested the use of news media to obtain support of the public against air piracy.

574a. Fourth Semi-Annual Report to Congress on the Effectiveness of the Civil Aviation Security Program, January 1-June 30, 1976. Washington, D.C.: Department of Transportation, Federal Aviation Administration, Civil Aviation Security Service, September 20, 1976. 34pp.
Argues that the measures have been successful in deterring hijackers as well as capturing several potential offenders, and uses fifteen statistical tables and graphs to support its claims.

575a. Gablonski, Edward. *Terror from the Sky: Airwar.* Garden City, N.Y.: Doubleday, 1971.

576a. Harris, F. Gentry. "Requirements for a Comprehensive Study of Skyjacking and Related Phenomena." Paper presented at the 1973 Annual Meeting of the American Psychological Association.

577a. Haugen, William J. and Poates, John T. "USAR Aircraft Hijacking: An Analysis of Policies and Procedures." Maxwell AFB, Alabama, Air University, May 1974. Distribution limited to USG agencies; proprietary information; other requests should be referred to director, Air University Library.

Examines the formulation of the civil aviation security system since it has provided the basis for and the initial direction of military antiskyjacking policy. Military and selected civilian hijack cases are analyzed to determine the modes of operation of skyjackings and its threat to USAF craft. Concludes that policy should include no concessions, no bargains, and no take-offs.

578a. Hawkins, G. ''Skyjacking.'' *Australian Journal of Forensic Sciences* 7 (June 1975): 157-168.

Points out the diversity of types of skyjackers and suggests various methods of control and prevention under the categories of technical and security measures and legal and political safeguards.

579a. "Hijack Reference Data." Washington, D.C.: Federal Aviation Administration, Task Force on Deterrence of Air Piracy, June 10, 1970.

A foreword is provided by H. L. Reighard, deputy federal air surgeon. The booklet contains charts and analyses of trends and events involving U.S. aviation.

580a. Hijacking: Selected Readings. Bibliographic List No. 5. Washington, D.C.: Department of Transportation, Office of Administrative Operations, Library Services Division, July 1971. 53 pp.

Covers articles (mostly found in newspapers and news weeklies) written between February 1969 and December 1970 on skyjacking. Most items are annotated, and a useful index is appended.

581a. Hijacking: Selected References. Bibliographic List No. 18. Washington, D.C.: Federal Aviation Administration, June 1969. 22 pp.

Annotates 206 items, mostly newspaper articles, covering 1961-1969.

582a. "Hijacking: Why Governments Must Act." *Aeronautical Journal* 74 (February 1970): 143-145.

The Royal Aeronautical Society was the site of an Air Law Group discussion on which papers were presented on the legal background, BALPA, IFALPA, and GAPAN presentations of the pilots' point of view, insurance, and international organization.

583a. Hotz, Robert. ''More On Hijacking.'' *Aviation Week and Space Technology*, November 10, 1969, p. 11.

Cuba's hostile treatment of hijackers may serve as a deterrent to future attacks. Unfortunately Arab support to Palestinian terrorists (particularly in the form of Syria's commeration of a hijacking by issuing a postage stamp) continues.

584a. "How the Airlines Hope to Stop the Hijackers." *Popular Mechanics* 133 (May 1970): 83-85.

585a. Hubbard, David G. *The Skyjacker—His Flights of Fantasy.* New York: Macmillan, 1971. 262 pp. (New York: Collier, 1973).
Psychological profiles of 16 U.S. skyjackers. Also provides a general hijacker description and list of all worldwide hijack attempts from 1930 through July 1970. Believes that there is no such thing as a politically motivated skyjacking and that all of them may be explained by needs to escape physical gravity and social bonds.

586a. The International Civil Aviation Organization and Arab Terrorist Operations: A Record of Resolutions. Jerusalem: Ministry for Foreign Affairs, 1973.

587a. "International Hijacking and Terrorism." *Department of State Bulletin*, June 4, 1973, pp. 828-829.

588a. Johnson, Arthur, and Barham "Hijacking: Why Governments Must Act." *Aeronautical Journal* 74 (1970): 143ff

589a. Jost, Walter. *Refzeichen: Haifa.* Zurich: Schweizer Verlaghaus AG, 1972.
A detailed memoir of the hijacking of the Swissair plane involved in the 1970 Dawson Field incident.

590a. Journal of Air Law and Commerce 37 (Spring 1971): 229-233.
Gives statistics on airline hijackings.

591a. Landes, William M. "An Economic Study of the U.S. Aircraft Hijacking, 1961-1976." *Journal of Law and Economics* 21 (April 1978): 1-32.

592a. Landry, James E. "Airport Security." *Aviation Week and Space Technology*, May 14, 1973, p. 7.
Landry, general counsel for the Air Transport Association of America, argues that customs security officers, with high visibility, have served as a deterrent to skyjackers and that their forces should not have been reduced. He suggests a new international approach to the problem. Rather than sanctions against states that grant safe haven, he proposes fact finding.

593a. Lee, Dean Andrew. "Hijacking." Unpublished manuscript, Soochow University, n.d.

594a. Master List of All Hijacking Attempts, Worldwide, Air Carrier, and General Aviation. Washington, D.C.: Department of Transportation, Federal Aviation Administration, Office of Aviation Medicine, updated periodically.

595a. McArthur, W. J.; Dean, P. J.; Carroll, J. R.; Holliday, T.; and Stokes, R. E. "Handling the Hijacker." *Aerospace Medicine* 43 (October 1972): 1118-1121.

The authors give a psychological classification of hijackers and different methods for dealing with them. One should attempt to calm the hijackers and avoid provoking anxiety. A short training program for crew is outlined.

596a. Mialek, J. R. "Short-Range Ammunition: A Possible Anti-Hijacking Device." *Journal of Forensic Sciences* 21 (October 1976): 856-861.

Special short-range ammunition resembles a normal cartridge but contains a pouch holding a lead shot and cannot penetrate aircraft walls at ranges greater than six feet. The bullets did not exit human cadavers under any conditions. The applications of this ammunition to hijackers are suggested.

597a. Oberg, Duane C. "The Air Force and the Aerial Pirate." Air Command and Staff College Master's thesis, 1973.

598a. O'Donnell, John J. "Air Crimes: Perspective from the Cockpit." *Villanova Law Review* 18 (1973).

599a. ———. "Statement before the Subcommittee on Foreign Assistance of the Senate Committee on Foreign Relations, International Terrorism and Aviation Security," September 14, 1977.

O'Donnell, president of the Air Line Pilots Association, International, points out why hijacking became a favorite tactic of terrorists in the early 1970s and what must be done in the airline security field to prevent such incidents.

600. ———. "Suspension of Service: Pilot's Answer to Hijacking." *Air Line Pilot* (July 1972): 7.

601. Oren, Uri. *Nine-nine Days in Damascus: The Story of Professor Shlomo Samueloff and the Hijack of TWA Flight 840 to Damascus.* London: Weidenfeld and Nicolson, 1970. 194 pp.

Memoirs of a hijack victim held long after the PFLP released non-Jewish passengers.

602. Perret, Robert-Louis. "Punishment of Aerial Piracy: A New Development." *Interavia* 6 (1976): 545.

603. Phalen, Tom. and Fergin, Gregory G. "Terrorism: A Hijacking and a Coup." *Department of State Newsletter* 197 (January 1978): 8-14.

Phalen recounts his experiences as a hostage on a JAL flight hijacked by the Japanese Red Army, and Fergin recalls events at the airport during the coup.

604. Phillips, David. *Skyjack: The Story of Air Piracy.* London: Harrap, 1973. 288 pp.

The discussion is primarily aimed at discovering what methods have proven successful in deterrence. As is usual with this literature, Phillips gives many anecdotes and long quotations from aviation officials. He devotes time to parajackers, something missing in other works.

605. Ramon, Zvia. "A Study of the Offense of Skyjacking." Master's thesis, John Jay College of Criminal Justice, 1973.

606. Reighard, H. L. "FAA Goal: Stop In-Flight Crime at the Gate." *Air Line Pilot* 39 (1970): 18-20.

607. Report of the President's Science Advisory Committee Sub Panel on Hijacking. Washington, D.C.: President's Science Advisory Committee, March 1973.

608. Rich, Elizabeth. *Flying Scared: Why We Are Being Skyjacked and How to Put a Stop to It.* New York: Stein and Day, 1972. 194 pp.

Written by an airline hostess. Some of the incident descriptions are unique to the book and may be of use as a data source.

609. Rogers, William P. "U.S. and Cuba Reach Agreement on Hijacking." *Department of State Bulletin*, March 5, 1973, pp. 260-262.

610. Rosenfield, Stanley B. "Air Piracy: Is it Time to Relax Our Standards?" *New England Law Review* 9 (Fall 1973): 81ff

611. Ross, I. "Take This Plane to Havana." *Reader's Digest* 94 (May 1969): 113-117.

Governments are searching to discover methods of detection at the gate.

612. Rountree, William M. "U.S. Pledges Continued Efforts for Aviation Security." *Department of State Bulletin*, September 10, 1972, pp. 356-358.

613. "Security in Air Transport: Achievements and Expectations." *Interavia* (1975): 178.

614. "A Select Bibliography on Aerial Piracy." United Nations List No. 6, November 20, 1972.

615. Shaffer, Helen B. "Control of Skyjacking." *Editorial Research Reports* 1 (January 1973): 67-84.
   Gives a brief survey of the hijacking problem.

616. Shepard, N. "Israel and the Air Gangsters." *New Statesman*, February 27, 1970, p. 280.

617. Sloan, Stephen, and Kearney, Richard. "An Analysis of a Simulated Terrorist Incident." *Police Chief* 44 (June 1977): 57-59.
   An analysis of a simulated air hijacking held during a seminar on terrorism at the University of Oklahoma.

618. Smith, R. C. "Handling Disturbed Passengers." Technical Summary of Flight Safety Foundation Air Safety Seminar, 1971. pp. 121-126.

619. Snow, Peter, and Phillips, David. *The Arab Hijack War.* New York: Ballantine, 1970. 176 pp.
   A detailed account of the negotiations between the Bern Five and the PFLP after the mass hijacking in September 1970. The history of the Jordanian civil war sparked by this incident is given as well.

620. ————. *Leila's Hijack War.* London: Pan, 1970.

621. Stokes. R. E. "Hijacking." Paper presented at the Human Factors Symposium, April 1970, at Toronto, Canada.

622. Strategic Survey 1972. London: International Institute for Strategic Studies, 1973.
   Presents statistics on ransom skyjackings, trends in overall skyjackings, success of attacks, and casualties.

623. "A Survey of Security Equipment for Airport Use." *Interavia* (1975): 179-182.

624. Turi, Robert T.; Friel, Charles M.; Sheldon, Robert B.; and Matthews, John P. "Descriptive Study of Aircraft Hijacking." *Criminal Justice Monograph* 3 (Sam Houston State University, Huntsville, Texas: Institute of Contemporary Corrections and the Behavioral Sciences, 1972).
   Presents statistics on the number of incidents, types of aircraft and weapons, and composite profiles of skyjackers, twenty of whom were interviewed.

625. Turner, James S. G. "Piracy in the Air." *Naval War College Review* 22 (September 1969): 86-116.

626. U.S. Department of State. *Foreign Policy Briefs*, December 30, 1968. Discusses aircraft hijacking up to that date.

627. U.S. Foreign Policy for the 1970's: Shaping a Durable Peace. A Report to the Congress by Richard Nixon, President of the U.S., May 3, 1973, pp. 221-223, on International Hijacking and Terrorism.

628. U.S. House of Representatives. Committee on Foreign Affairs. Subcommittee on Inter-America Affairs "Air Piracy in the Caribbean Area." 90th Cong. 2d sess., 1968.

629. ———. Committee on Interstate and Foreign Commerce." Preliminary Report on Aircraft Piracy." 91st Cong., 1st sess., 1969.

630. ———. Subcommittee on Aviation. Committee on Public Works and Transportation. "Hearings on HR 13261 to amend the Federal Aviation Act of 1958, Relating to Aircraft Piracy, to Provide a Method for Combating Terrorism, and for Other Purposes." 95th Cong., 2d sess., July 18, 19, 20, 25, 1978.

631. U.S. Senate. Committee on Finance. "Skyjacking." Hearings on H.R. 19444, October 6, 1970, 91st Cong., 2d sess., 1970.

632. "What Makes a Skyjacker?" *Science Digest* 71 (1972): 21-22.

633. Whelton, Charles, *Skyjack.* New York: Tower, 1970.

634. White, Edward T. "Terrorism in Civil Aviation—A Perennial World Problem?" (Air Command and Staff College, Maxwell Air Force Base, Alabama, May, 1974 also submitted to the Graduate Faculty of Auburn University in Political Science). Available as FAR 21141-G AD 920 510L.

White argues that international agreements have not stopped terrorism against aviation and suggests that the only solution may be a negotiated settlement of the Middle East question.

635. Wright, Jim. "A Congressman Speaks: Airline Hijacking: A Time for Cautious Optimism." *Airways* 4 (June 1970): 20-25.

Notes problems involved in stopping skyjacking and suggested solutions.

For additional readings, see the "Hijacking" section in the "Legal Responses" category, as well as entries 424, 711, 1650, 1748, 1816, and 3211.

HOSTAGE INCIDENTS

636. Abell, F. *Prisoners of War in Britain, 1756-1815*. London: Oxford University Press, 1914.

637. "Aftermath of the Kidnappings." *Nation*, March 9, 1974, p. 292.
    An editorial that worries about calls for greater police and FBI intelligence activities against terrorist groups. Claims that control of handguns might be as effective in halting kidnaps as search procedures were in stopping hijackings.

638. Alix, Ernest Kahler. *Ransom Kidnapping in America, 1874-1974: The Creation of a Capital Crime*. Carbondale: Southern Illinois University Press, 1978.
    Looks at the perceived threat of kidnapping to society and notes the sociohistorical trends of legislation banning it.

639. Alves, M. M. "Kidnapped Diplomats: Greek Tragedy on a Latin Stage." *Commonweal*, June 26, 1970, pp. 311-314.

640. Arenberg, Gerald. *Hostage*. Washington, D.C.: American Police Academy, 1976. 34pp.
    Arenberg uses international and domestic case material to illustrate his points about the types of attackers, victim behavior, police negotiation strategies, and how a response team should be organized.

641. Aston, Clive C. "Hostage Taking: An Overview." In *An Age of Terror*. New York: Macmillan, 1979.

642. ———. "Political Hostage Taking in Western Europe." In Stephen Sloan and Richard Shultz, eds., *Responding to the Terrorist Threat: Prevention and Control*. New York: Pergamon, 1980.

643. Austria. Federal Chancellery. "The Events of September 28 and 29, 1973: A Documentary Report." Vienna, 1973.
    Describes an incident in which a train carrying Soviet Jews emigrating to Israel was seized by Arab terrorists in Austrian territory and subsequent negotiations that led to their release.

644. Background Documentation Relating to the Assassinations of Ambassador Cleo A. Noel, Jr. and George Curtis Moore. Washington, D.C.: U.S. Department of State, 1973.

Includes a list of twenty-five "significant terrorist incidents involving U.S. Foreign Service personnel" from November 1963 to January 1973, including the deaths of ten officials.

645. Baumann, Carol Elder. *The Diplomatic Kidnappings: A Revolutionary Tactic of Urban Terrorism.* The Hague: Nijhoff, 1973.

Discusses the theory of guerrilla warfare in Latin America; problems of asylum and state responsibility for the protection of diplomats; treaties on terrorism; and cases of "diplonappings." Essentially a work on international law, Baumann is silent on what to do about other kinds of transnational kidnappings (of businessmen or tourists, for example). Argues that the costs should be maximized and benefits of kidnapping minimized through concerted international action, including no granting of asylum.

646. ———. "The Diplomatic Kidnappings: An Overview." In *International Terrorism: Proceedings of an Intensive Panel at the 15th Annual Convention of International Studies Association*, pp. 30-44. Milwaukee; Institute of World Affairs, University of Wisconsin, 1974.

Baumann looks at "diplonappings" in the contexts of urban terrorism and international law. Governments quickly moved to halt such attacks, which present threats to the principles of diplomatic inviolability, state responsibility for protection, political asylum, and the right of extradition. Baumann suggests a dual policy of maximizing risks and minimizing rewards will deter hostage-takers. However, such a policy must be adopted worldwide to be effective.

647. Beall, Marshall D. "Hostage Negotiations." *Military Police Law Enforcement Journal* 3 (Fall 1976). Reprinted in John D. Elliott and Leslie K. Gibson, eds., *Contemporary Terrorism: Selected Readings*, pp. 223-232. Gaithersburg: International Association of Chiefs of Police, 1978.

Notes the uses of hostages throughout history and points out that hostage-takers today are criminals, psychopaths or politically motivated individuals. A typology of events in a hostage situation is offered to allow policemen to understand ongoing events in such crises.

648. Bennett, James P., and Saaty, Thomas L. *Terrorism: Patterns for Negotiations: Three Case Studies Through Hierarchies and Holarchies* (Wharton School, University of Pennsylvania, August 1977). Available as "Terrorism: Patterns for Negotiation; A Case Study Using Hierarchies and Holarchies," in Robert H. Kupperman and Darrell M. Trent, eds., *Terrorism*, pp. 244-285. (Stanford, Calif.: Hoover, 1979).

The authors attempt to create value hierarchies during crisis situations as a tool in establishing negotiating strategy.

649. Biderman, A. D. "Cultural Models on Captivity Relationships." Washington, D.C.: Air Force Office of Scientific Research, AFOSR-452, February 1961.

650. ———. *Death as a Criterion in the Study of Extreme Captivity Situations.* Washington, D.C.: Air Force Office of Scientific Research, AFOSR-453, February 1961.

651. ———. *Necessary, Permissible, and Obligatory Discourse with Captor Personnel.* Washington, D.C.: Bureau of Social Science Research, Inc., prepared for the U.S. Air Force, Office of Scientific Research, Office of Aerospace Research, 1965.

652. ———. "The Objectives of Training for the Event of Capture." Multilith. Air Force Personnel and Training Research Center, Intelligence Methods Branch, January 5, 1956.

653. Blacksten, Ric, and Engler, Richard. "Hostage Studies." Arlington, Va.: Ketron Concept Paper, Ketron, January 8, 1974.
   A game theoretic approach to hostage situations such as kidnapping and skyjacking. A very promising attempt to apply this type of analysis.

654. Bolz, Jr., Francis A. "Hostage Confrontation and Rescue." In Robert H. Kupperman and Darrell M. Trent *Terrorism*, pp. 393-404. Stanford: Hoover, 1979.

655. ———. "Strategies in Negotiation." Paper presented to the conference on Terror: The Man, the Mind and the Matter, October 15-16, 1976, at the John Jay School of Criminal Justice, New York City.

656. Bondy, C. "Rehabilitating the Internee." *Public Opinion Quarterly* 7 (1948): 629-632.

657. Bongert, Y.; Kellens, G.; Leaute, J.; Schaub, S.; Grebing, G.; Lafon, J.; and Le Taillanter, R. *Taking Hostages.* Paris: Neret, 1975. 84 pp.
   A collection of six short papers on the psychological and sociological dimensions of seizing hostages and society's reactions.

658. Book, Don. "Hostage Defense Measures: A Training Program." Master's thesis, Sam Houston State University, 1977.

659. Cassidy, William L. *Political Kidnapping: An Introductory Overview.* Boulder: Sycamore, 1978. 47 pp.

Cassidy develops a typology of kidnappings and looks at the operational phases of such incidents.

660. Cherry, William A. "Countermeasures against the Barricaded Gunman: Theory and Techniques." *Law and Order* 22 (October 1974): 12-14.

Cherry suggests that officers should not assume that all barricade situations need involve shootouts and that another method should be tried, involving isolation of the gunman. Hostages complicate the initial problem, and the merits of five strategies of response are discussed: acquiese totally, refuse to negotiate, stall, attempt to modify the individual's demands, do not bargain in good faith. The importance of training, intelligence gathering, and special equipment is also cited.

661. Clutterbuck, Richard. *Kidnap and Ransom: The Response.* London: Faber and Faber, 1978.

662. Codd, Michael J.; Cottell, Louis C.; and Schryver, Harold. "Recommended Guidelines—Incidents Involving Hostages." Special Operations Division, City of New York Police Department, n.d.

The pamphlet discusses, in great detail, how NYPD officers should respond to a hostage situation, who is in command, what types of equipment and individuals should be deployed where and when, and what types of bargaining techniques will be used.

663. "Contribution a l'étude du phénomène de la prise d'otages, livre I." [Contributions to a study of the phenomenon of Hostage-Taking, Volume I.] Paris: French Ministry of the Interior, n.d.

664. Cook, Don. "Hostage Defense Measures: A Training Program." Master's thesis, Sam Houston State University, 1977.

665. Cooper, H. H. A. "Pacta sunt servanda: Good Faith Negotiations with Hostage Takers." Gaithersburg, Md.: International Association of Chiefs of Police Training Program, 1977.

Cooper argues that the state must carry out its part of bargains with terrorists, criminals, and other hostage-takers, marshaling numerous arguments to support his case. He correctly notes the lack of empirical evidence in this area.

666. "Countersniper, Barricaded Suspect and Hostage Tactics." Los Angeles Police Department, n.d.

667. Crelinsten, Ronald D., and Szabo, Denis. *Hostage-Taking.* Lexington, Mass.: Lexington Books, 1979.

The book is based upon an international seminar held in May 1976 in Santa Margherita, Italy, and looks at several temporal phases and possible types of hostage incidents. Experiences in several Western European countries are highlighted.

668. Crelinsten, Ronald D., and Laberge-Altmejd, Danielle, eds. *Hostage-Taking: Problems of Prevention and Control.* Montreal: International Centre for Comparative Criminology, 1976.

669. Culley, John A. "Defusing Human Bombs—Hostage Negotiations." *FBI Law Enforcement Bulletin* (October 1974): 10-14.

670. Cullinane, Maurice J. "Terrorism: A New Era of Criminality." *Terrorism* 1 (1978): 119-124.
Looks at the successful countermeasures used during the Hanafi siege and argues that prolonged negotiations rather than immediate assault are more effective.

671. Curle, A. "Transitional Communities and Social Reconnection: A Follow-up Study of the Civil Resettlement of British Prisoners of War." *Human Relations* 1 Part I: pp. 42-68, Part II: pp. 240-288.

672. Dearlove, A. R. "Enforced Leisure: A Study of Activities of Officer Prisoners of War." *British Medical Journal* 1 (1945): 406-409.

673. Dor-Shav, Netta. "Nazi Concentration Camp Survivors: Twenty-five Years Later." Paper presented to the symposium on the Effects of Institutional Coercion by Law, Government, and Violence, of the 84th annual convention of the American Psychological Association, September 3-7, 1976, at Washington, D.C.

674. Dortzbach, Karl, and Dortzbach, Debbie. *Kidnapped.* New York: Harper and Row, 1975. 179 pp.
The memoirs of a missionary nurse who was kidnapped by the Eritrean Liberation Front on May 27, 1974, and of her husband who was involved in the negotiations. Her response was a revitalized faith in God and a friendship with the peasants she was kept with. Unfortunately, "the names of the Eritreans and of some missionaries in the story have been changed."

675. Elbrick, C. Burke. "The Diplomatic Kidnappings: A Case Study." In *International Terrorism: Proceedings of an Intensive Panel at the 15th Annual Convention of the International Studies Association*, pp.45-56. Milwaukee: Institute of World Affairs, University of Wisconsin, 1974.

Elbrick discusses his experience as a hostage in Brazil, two months after he became the U.S. ambassador. He was ultimately released in exchange for fifteen political prisoners.

676. Ellsberg, Daniel. "The Theory and Practice of Blackmail." Santa Monica: RAND Corporation, P-3883, July 1968.

A pioneering study, using insights from bargaining models and game theory.

677. "Expert's Advice: Negotiate with Terrorists, Don't Shoot Them." *Chicago Tribune*, June 18, 1974, sec. 1, p. 12.

An interview with Dr. Frederick Hacker, a professor of law and psychiatry, who argues that terrorists never act as individuals but always according to a group code. He believes that police should not be in charge of combating terrorism. Rather a national or international team of negotiators should be formed. Hacker believes kidnappers want their hostages to live because a dead hostage is no bargaining lever. One should always attempt to negotiate, giving the terrorists "a feeling of equality because you have recognized them."

678. "Extortion." *Assets Protection* 1 (Summer 1975): entire issue.

Articles by Shaw, Hubbard, Vandiver, and Pizer on how to analyze and respond to such threats.

679. Fariello, Antonio. "The Phenomenon of Hostage-Taking: The Italian Experience." In Ronald Crelinsten and Denis Szabo, *Hostage-Taking*, pp.97-103. Lexington, Mass.: Lexington Books, 1979.

680. Fawcett, J. E. S. "Kidnappings Versus Government Protection." *World Today* 26 (September 1970): 359-362.

Looks at the historical concept of diplomatic protection and notes that recent kidnappings have had common objectives, chosen political targets and had the indirect collaboration of third countries.

681. FitzGerald, Bruce D. "The Analytical Foundations of Extortionate Terrorism." *Terrorism* 1 (1978): 347-362.

FitzGerald uses game theory to explore when extortionate terrorism will be used, when will it succeed or fail, what constitutes an optimal threat, when unsuccessful threats should be carried out or abandoned, and how a victim should respond. Ordinal preferences must be aided by von Neumann-Morgenstern utilities to answer compromise questions. Long-term variables of credibility and resolve must be added to complete the picture.

682. Fitzhugh, David. "Terrorism and Diplomacy." *Foreign Service Journal* 54 (February 1977): 14-17.

A discussion of the no-concessions policy as it affects U.S. foreign service officers.

683. Fly, Claude. *No Hope But God.* New York: Hawthorn Books, 1973.

Fly's memoirs of being a prisoner of the Tupamaros for seven months. Appended is his "Christian Checklist," a list of biblical readings that helped him through his ordeal.

684. Frackers, Willem. "Organizational Aspects of Hostage-Taking Prevention and Control in the Netherlands." In Ronald D. Crelinsten and Denis Szabo, *Hostage-Taking,* pp. 105-118. Lexington, Mass.: Lexington Books, 1979.

685. Friedman, P. "The Effects of Imprisonment." *Acta Medica Orientalia* 7 (1948): 163-167.

686. Friggens, Paul. "Claude Fly's Seven Month Nightmare." *Reader's Digest* 99 (September 1970): 64-70.

Summary of Fly's *No Hope But God.* (see entry 683).

687. Goodwin, James E. "Repatriation of Prisoners of War: Forcible and Non-Forcible." Carlisle Barracks, Penn.: U.S. Army War College, 1960.

688. Haldane, David. "An Interview with Dr. Frederick Hacker." *Penthouse* 9 (November 1977).

Hacker has participated in several negotiation sessions with terrorist hostage-takers.

689. Hamer, John. "Protection of Diplomats." *Editorial Research Reports,* (October 3, 1973), pp. 759-776.

Hamer's major categories include: Growing Threat to World Diplomats, Fear for Officials' Safety and Disrupted Relations, Violent Attacks on Diplomats Here and Abroad, Rash of Political Kidnappings by Terrorist Groups, Inability of Nations to Unite Against Terrorism, Tradition of Diplomatic Inviolability, New Search for Guaranteed Protection.

690. Hassel, Conrad V. "The Hostage Situation: Exploring the Motivation and the Cause." *Police Chief* 42 (September 1975): 55-58.

691. Hawes. T. H. "Returned Prisoners of War." *Lancet* 1 (1945): 643.

692. Hayter, William. "The Politics of Kidnapping." *Interplay* 4 (January 1971): 14-16.

The taking of foreign diplomats as hostages by revolutionary guerrilla groups in various countries is discussed.

693. Higgins, L. L. "Executive Terrorism and Hostage Taking." *Police Times* 11 (December 1976): 20-21.

694. Hoover, J. Edgar. "The Extremist-Terrorist Demand: A Death Sentence for Industry?" *Finance* (May 1971).

695. "Hostage Negotiation." In *Training Key Number 234.* Gaithersburg, Md.: Professional Standards Division of the International Association of Chiefs of Police, 1976.

696. "Hostage-Negotiation Response." In *Training Key Number 235.* Gaithersburg, Md: Professional Standards Division of the International Association of Chiefs of Police, 1976.

697. Hostage Taking: Problems of Prevention and Control. Montreal: International Centre for Comparative Criminology, October 1976.

698. Howard, Bruce. "Living with Terrorism." *Washington Post.* July 18, 1976, pp. C-1, C-4.

Howard points out the decline in morale in the Foreign Service due to the U.S. negotiations policy, as well as the treatment of kidnap victims when they return home. Interviews with many victims bolster his arguments, and suggestions for improvement in the department's policies are forwarded.

699. Hughes, Edward. "Terror on Train 734: Hostages Taken by South Moluccan Guerrillas." *Reader's Digest* 109 (August 1976): 64-69.

700. Jackson, Geoffrey. *Surviving the Long Night: An Autobiographical Account of a Political Kidnapping.* New York: Vanguard, 1974. 226 pp.

Jackson's memoirs of his nine-month kidnapping by the Tupamaros. Published in the United Kingdom as *People's Prison* (London: Faber and Faber, 1973), 221 pp.

701. Jenkins, Brian M. "Do What They Ask. And Don't Worry. They May Kill Me But They Are Not Evil Men." *New York Times* March 10, 1975.

A summary of the RAND findings on hostage survival.

702. ———. "Hostage Survival: Some Preliminary Observations." Santa Monica: RAND Corporation, 1975. Draft presented to USIA International Terrorism Seminar, August 11, 1975, Washington, D.C.

Gives updates of previous RAND statistics on hostage situations; makes many suggestions on how to avoid being kidnapped and how to behave in the event of being seized. Studies psychology of hostages.

703. ———. "Hostage Survival: Some Preliminary Observations." Santa Monica: RAND Corporation, April 1976. Reprinted as FAR 25050-N.

A summary of the findings of RAND's study of individuals who have been held hostage by political terrorists. Aspects of capture, captivity, and the postrelease experience are discussed

704. ———. "Hostages and Their Captors: Friends and Lovers." Santa Monica: RAND Corporation, P-5519, October 1975. Reprinted as FAR 23873-N.

A rewrite of his October 3, 1975, *New York Times* article.

705. ———. "Should Corporations Be Prevented from Paying Ransom?" Sana Monica: RAND Corporation, P-5291, September 1974.

Based upon written testimony submitted to the Judiciary and Criminal Justice Committees of the California State Assembly, August 5, 1974. In discussing proposed bills preventing ransom payment, Jenkins suggested that they would not deter and may in fact become an obstacle to effective deterrence. He suggested that they could be easily circumvented and could raise complicated lawsuits. They could damage the image of the United States and American firms and might shift the risk from corporations to private families.

706. ———. "Terrorism and Kidnapping." Santa Monica: RAND Corporation, P-5255, June 1974. 10 pp.

Discusses theory of terrorism, its utility and its effectiveness seen from the terrorists' point of view, the reason for its apparent increase in recent years, and some recent and possible future trends. Notes kidnapping by terrorist groups, some of the motives for kidnapping, and the reasons why kidnapping is still a very unpopular crime in this country.

707. Jenkins, Brian; Johnson, Janera; and Ronfeldt, David. "Numbered Lives: Some Statistical Observations from Seventy-seven International Hostage Episodes." *Conflict* 1 (Fall 1978).

A reprint of a RAND study which uses simple two-way frequency tables to study types of victims, responses, and other variables.

708. Jenkins, Brian; Johnson, Janera; and Ronfeldt, David. "Numbered Lives: Some Statistical Observations from Seventy-seven International Hostage Episodes." Santa Monica: RAND Corporation, P-5905, July 1977.

709. Karrass, Chester. *Give and Take.* New York: Crowell, 1974.
A primer on negotiation strategies.

710. "Kidnappings for Ransom." Washington, D.C.: U.S. Department of Justice, Federal Bureau of Investigation, n.d.
This flyer gives suggestions on procedures to follow if there is an actual kidnapping, as well as preincident suggestions for businessmen, parents, children, and school officials.

711. Kobetz, Richard W. "Hostage Incidents: The New Police Priority." *Police Chief* (May 1975).

712. Kupperman, Robert H.; Wilcox, Richard H.; and Smith, Harvey A. "Crisis Management: Some Opportunities." In Robert H. Kupperman and Darrell M. Trent, *Terrorism*, pp. 224-243. Stanford: Hoover, 1979.

713. Kwok, M. L., and Peterson, R. E. "Political Kidnapping: 1968-1973." *Journal of Contemporary Revolutions* 6 (Fall-Winter 1974-1975).

714. Lang, Daniel. "A Reporter at Large: The Bank Drama." *New Yorker,* November 25, 1974, pp. 56-126.
Describes the takeover, including hostages, of a Swedish bank. Delves into psychological relationships between the criminals and the hostages.

715. Laushway, Lynda. "Trust—The Key to Hostage Incidents?" *Liaison* 2 (February 1976): 1-4, 13.

716. MacPherson, Myra. "The Hostage-Takers: An Epidemic of People Gone Mad." *Washington Post,* February 20, 1977, p. A-4.
The United States experienced ten incidents of hostage-taking within twelve days. The author interviewed several prominent psychologists about the types of people who take hostages, finding that they are criminals, terrorists, or mentally unstable individuals. The role of the media in imitation of tactics as well as giving hostage-takers clues regarding the tactics that will be used against them is discussed, as well as methods for hostage survival.

717. Maher, G. F. *Hostage: A Police Approach to a Contemporary Crisis.* Springfield, Ill.: Thomas, 1977. 100 pp.

A comprehensive overview of tactical plans, training, equipment, theory, and practical application of negotiation techniques for hostage, barricade, and suicide situations.

718. Mangham, W. D. "Kidnapping for Political Ends." In *Seaford House Papers*. London: Royal College of Defence Studies. 1971.

719. McClure, Brooks. "Hostage Survival." In Marius Livingston et al., eds., *International Terrorism in the Contemporary World*, pp. 276-281. Westport, Conn.: Greenwood Press, 1978.

Discusses methods of surviving as a political hostage, drawing upon the experiences of previous victims of diplomatic kidnapping.

720. ———. "Hostage Survival." *Conflict* 1 (Fall 1977).

A series of pointers on the psychology of being a hostage and how several political kidnap victims have coped with the experience.

721. McHenry, Donald. "Terrorism and Hostage Negotiations." (New York: Carnegie Endowment for International Peace).

722. Means, John. "Political Kidnappings and Terrorism." *North American Review* 255 (Winter 1970): 16-19.

Asserts that there is no evidence of an international conspiracy. Kidnappings have been successful in getting prisoners released. Mentions that Tupamaros train high school students by having them kidnap random targets for a few hours. The progovernment "death squadrons" who attack suspected Brazilian terrorists are mentioned in Means's use of Brazil as the classic model. The extreme heterogeneity in ideology of terrorists is stressed.

723. Messick, Hank and Goldblatt, Burt. *Kidnapping: The Illustrated History*. New York: Dial, 1974. 206 pp.

Accounts of the major kidnappings in the last century and mentions a few incidents of note in antiquity. The treatment of international incidents is poor, in one place incorrectly equating the Laun and Samuelson incidents. The authors also argue that the kidnapping of Eichmann by the Israelis is equivalent to the 1972 Munich massacre.

724. Mickolus, Edward. "Negotiating for Hostages: A Policy Dilemma." *Orbis* 19 (Winter 1976): 1309-1325. Reprinted in John D. Elliott and Leslie K. Gibson, eds., *Contemporary Terrorism: Selected Readings*, pp. 207-221. Gaithersburg: International Association of Chiefs of Police, 1978.

Discusses the policy debate on how to deal with terrorists' taking hostages and forwarding demands for their release. The no-ransom position is contrasted with the flexible response option. Statistics on nationality of hostages, terrorists, targets of demands, location of incidents, and yearly trends are provided.

725. Middendorff, W. "New Developments in the Taking of Hostages and Kidnapping—A Summary." Washington, D.C.: National Criminal Justice Reference Service translation, 1975.

Discusses West German views of the priorities to be considered in established hostage negotiation policies. Death of a hostage is a rare occurence, and authorities must also note protection of the public and apprehending the offenders. A review of the views of others on the subject is given.

726. ———. "New Developments in the Taking of Hostages and Kidnapping: West Germany, Part 2." *Polizeiblatt* 37. (November 1974): 166-170.

Gives a typology of kidnappers, presents thirty-five cases of such offenses in Europe and the United States, and discusses offender personality types. Arguments favoring a harsher approach by West German police are discussed. In German.

727. ———. "Taking Hostages and Kidnapping." *Kriminalistik* (December 1972).

728. ———. "The Victimology of The Taking of Hostages." *Kriminalistik* (April 1974).

729. Miller, Abraham H. "Hostage Negotiations and the Concept of Transference." In Yonah Alexander, David Carlton and Paul Wilkinson, eds., *Terrorism: Theory and Practice*, pp. 137-158. Boulder: Westview, 1979.

Miller reviews the common wisdom about the Stockholm syndrome and suggests that its evocation is dependent upon the identities of the terrorists and victims, their interaction, and time.

730. ———. "Hostages as Victims: Research and Policy Issues." Paper presented to the International Studies Association annual convention, March 21, 1979, at Toronto.

731. ———. "Negotiations for Hostages." Paper presented to the 18th annual convention of the International Studies Association, March 16-20, 1977, at St. Louis, Missouri. Published as "Negotiations for Hostages: Implications from the Police Experience." *Terrorism*. 1 (1978): 125-146.

An account of the Hanafi siege.

732. ———. "Negotiations for Hostages: Implications from the Police Experience." Washington, D.C.: Law Enforcement Assistance Administration, National Institute of Law Enforcement and Criminal Justice, May 1977.

Using the Hanafi Muslim seizures in Washington as illustrative, Miller forwards arguments against the strict no-concessions policy articulated by the U.S. Department of State. Use is made of ITERATE data to suggest that the bargaining situation is a ritual and that certain concessions can be granted to terrorists that will save face for them and lead to the safe release of hostages.

733. ———. University of Cincinnati. *Proposal of the LEAA Fellowship Program to Study Social Control Responses to Terrorism.* September 1976-August 1977.

Part 4 outlines Miller's quantitative approach to the subject, noting specifics of hostage negotiation incidents. The author hopes to be able to make policy recommendations to agents of social control, as well as to establish a data base of incidents of terrorism.

734. ———. "SWAT (Special Weapons and Tactics)—The Practical Link in Hostage Negotiations." In Yonah Alexander and Robert A. Kilmarx, eds., *Political Terrorism and Business: The Threat and Response*, pp. 331-356. New York: Praeger, 1979.

735. Miller, Judith. "Bargain with Terrorists?" *New York Times Magazine*, July 18, 1976, pp. 7, 38-42.

Reviews arguments forwarded by Brian Jenkins in his studies of hostage negotiations policies. Problems of deterrence, morale, and prevention are discussed using case histories. Summarizing Foreign Service morale, Miller quotes the following: "What good is a 'hang tough' posture during a kidnapping," said a Foreign Service committee representative, "if the Department is unwilling to be firm on pressure for punishment? They're perfectly willing to sacrifice us in the name of deterrence, but unwilling to rock the diplomatic boat afterward."

736. Miron, Murray S., and Goldstein, A. P. *Hostage.* Kalamazoo: Behaviordelia, 1978. 190 pp.

The authors look at the characteristics of hostage-takers, which in turn will affect choice of negotiators and how to handle the situation.

737. Monroe, James L. *Prisoners of War and Political Hostages: A Select Bibliography.* Springfield, Va.: Monroe Corporation, prepared for the Air Force Office of Scientific Research, October 1973. 45 pp.

A comprehensive compilation of articles, books, and government reports on the topic, although shying away from cases of diplomatic kidnappings. Unfortunately the list is not annotated. Topics include prisoners of war and political hostages, from the Korean War to the present, using the categories of behavioral studies, legal analyses, military documents, historical reports, journalistic studies, and related bibliographies. Foreign scientific and press reports are only partially covered.

738. Morgan, J. P. "Confrontation Management." St. Petersburg, Fla.: Public Safety Agency, n.d.

739. Murphy, J. Reginold. "The Kidnap Victim." Address to the Wackenhut Corporation's seminar on terrorism, November 22, 1974.

740. ———. "Political Terrorism: Means to an End?" *Encore* (September 1974): 22.

Murphy was kidnapped shortly after the Patricia Hearst-SLA incident by an individual claiming to represent the right-wing American Revolutionary Army.

741. Murphy, John F. "The Threat and Use of Force Against Internationally Protected Persons and Diplomatic Facilities." Paper presented to the Conference on International Terrorism, sponsored by the Ralph Bunche Institute, June 9-11, 1976, at New York City.

Unfortunately most national penal legislation refers only to attacks within their borders. Thus the doctrine of diplomatic inviolability should grow to cover persons, property, and premises outside such borders. Murphy discusses a new convention, pointing out that the political offense exception is not eliminated by it. The paper closes with useful recommendations on security and hostage negotiations policies.

742. Myers, Robert P. "Hostage Defense Measures." Paper presented to the Conference on Terrorism in the Contemporary World, April 26-28, 1976, at Glassboro State College.

Myers, the assistant coordinator for combating terrorism in the U.S. Department of State, outlines the response of the U.S. government to terroristic attacks, drawing particular attention to the U.S. position regarding bargaining with terrorists.

743. Najmuddin, Dilshad. "Kidnapping of Diplomatic Personnel." *Police Chief* 40 (February 1973): 18-23.

Gives case studies of such incidents, suggesting that compromises not be made and that the host nation centralize the efforts of its security agencies in securing the hostage's release.

744. Needham, James P. "Neutralization of Prison Hostage Situations: A Model." Master's thesis, Sam Houston State University, 1976. Available from the Sam Houston State University Library, as well as the Defense Documentation Center.

The author, a major in the U.S. Army's Military Policy Corps, surveyed police departments of fifty major American cities and the department of corrections of fifty states in an attempt to create a model of management considerations that will allow prison administrators to develop their own hostage plans. Needham wishes to apply the police model of hostage situations to prison scenarios.

745. Newman, Samuel A. *How to Survive as a Prisoner of War.* Washington Crossing, Pa.: Washington Crossing Foundation, 1969. 183 pp.

746. O'Leary, V., et al. *Peaceful Resolution of Prison Conflict: Negotiations as a Means of Dealing with Prison Conflict.* Hackensack, N.J.: Council on Crime and Delinquency, 1973.

747. "Patient Sieges: Dealing with Hostage-Takers." *Assets Protection* 1 (1976): 21-27.

Discusses the tactical aspects of the negotiations that took place in the Herrema, Beilen, and London Spaghetti House incidents. The New York Police Department model of phases of negotiations, types of strategies, characteristics of good teams and good negotiators, and the role of mediators are used.

748. Pepper, Curtis Bill. *Kidnapped! Seventeen Days of Terror.* New York: Harmony, 1978. 150 pp.

In 1978 Italy logged thirty-six kidnappings with political and criminal motives. This, the story of a 1977 kidnapping in Milan, is an attempt to place the welter of abductions in cultural perspective.

749. Peterson, Richard E. "Political Kidnapping: A New Risk in International Business." *Interfaces* 8 (February 1978): 46-53.

Using statistics based upon a congressional study of kidnappings, Peterson shows outcomes from various types of responses to terrorist demands.

750. Platero, Dalila. "To Be Prepared Not to Be Prepared." *Assets Protection* 1 (1976): 16-20.

Platero puts the response to kidnapping of the male into the larger context of family relations, noting the changes that the wife's role will undergo and some mechanisms for coping with such stress.

751. Political Kidnappings, 1968-73. A staff study prepared by the Committee on Internal Security of the United States House of Representatives. 93rd Cong., 1st sess., August 1, 1973. 54 pp.

Gives a brief introduction to the problem of kidnappings, along with a chronology of the major attempts and characteristics of the groups responsible for them.

752. Rabe, Robert. "Terrorism and Hostage Negotiation." Paper presented to the panel on Violence and Terror of the Conference on Complexity: A Challenge to the Adaptive Capacity of American Society, sponsored by the Society for General Systems Research, March 24-26, 1977, at Columbia, Maryland.

The deputy chief of police of Washington, D.C., reflects the impact of the New York Police Department model of hostage scenarios in stressing containment of the situation and buying time. He points to problems of protecting the perpetrator's rights while not allowing him to exploit them to the extent of harming society.

753. Rabinowitz, Dorothy. "The Hostage Mentality." *Commentary* 63 (June 1972).

754. Radford, R. A. "The Economic Organization of a POW camp." *Economica* 11 (1945): 189-201.

755. Salewski, Wolfgang. "Conduct and Negotiations in Hostage Situations." *Schriftenreihe der Polizei-Fuhrungsakademie* 4 (1977): 58-65. Available in *International Summaries: A Collection of Selected Translations in Law Enforcement and Criminal Justice*, 3:98-104. Washington, D.C.: U.S. Department of Justice, National Criminal Justice Reference Service, April 1979.

756. Samuels, Jon M. "Kidnap/Hostage Negotiation and Parallel Actions." In *Hostage Situations: Tactics and Countermeasures*, pp. 1-8. Gaithersburg, Md.: Research Division, Technical Research Unit, International Association of Chiefs of Police, n.d.

Samuels outlines the characteristics of an effective negotiator and makes suggestions as to how negotiations should be handled, citing the advantages of the authorities in such a situation. Strategies for dealing with mental cases, criminals, and revolutionaries are compared, and special sections deal with how to behave as a hostage and how to prepare ransom packages or engage in armed assaults.

757. ———. "A Practical Guide to Hostage Survival" *Hostage Situations: Tactics and Coutermeasures*, pp. 9-14. Gaithersburg, Md.: Research Division, Technical Research Unit, International Association of Chiefs of Police, n.d.

Samuels discusses the victim's views of the kidnapping and points out that one's reactions of shock, fear, and humiliation are common. He gives special attention to the possible phases of the attack, including the initial shock, travel en route to the place of imprisonment, the experience of being imprisoned, strategies of escape, and the postrelease experience and debriefing.

758. Schlossberg, Harvey, and Freerman, Lucy. *Psychologist with a Gun.* New York: Coward, McCann and Geoghegan, 1974.

The author is a psychologist-detective attached to the New York Police Department who recounts his insights regarding hostage negotiation; however, the bulk of the book is devoted to evaluation and counseling of police officers.

759. Sharp, John C. *In Japanese Hands: A List of Books Dealing with Prisoner of War and Internment Camps in the Far East 1941-1945.* Birmingham, England, 1952.

760. Simon, Douglas W. "Policy Recommendation Exercises." *International Studies Notes* 2 (Spring 1975): 19-21.

Presents a one-move political game involving a scenario that confronts the policy maker with a Black September barricade-and-hostage situation and a list of demands.

761. Simon, Douglas W.; Rhone, Richard S.; and Perillo, Michael. "Simulation of the Seizure of Heads of State." Mimeographed. Madison, N.J.: Drew University Department of Political Science, January 1977.

A summary of two all-manual simulation runs of the Black September takeover of a summit meeting between the United States and the Soviet Union.

762. Sloan, Stephen; Kearney, Richard; and Wise, Charles. "Learning About Terrorism: Analysis, Simulations, and Future Directions." *Terrorism* 1 (1978): 315-329.

A summary of the work of the Oklahoma Study Group on International Terrorism.

763. Sponsler, T. H. "International Kidnapping." *International Lawyer* 5 (January 1971): 25-52.

764. Stech, Frank J. "Terrorism and Threat Communication." Mimeographed. Bethesda: Analytic Support Center, Mathtech, May 31, 1978.

Discusses several researchable areas on the tactics of negotiations, including use of positive or negative sanctions, threats versus promises, and difficulties in establishing communication channels.

765. Stechel, Ira. "Terrorist Kidnapping of Diplomatic Personnel." *Cornell International Law Journal* 5 (Spring 1972): 189-217.

766. Stratton, John. "The Terrorist Act of Hostage-Taking: Considerations for Law Enforcement." *Journal of Police Science and Administration* 2 (1978).

767. ———. "The Terrorist Act of Hostage-Taking: A View of Violence and the Perpetrators." *Journal of Police Science and Administration* 1 (1978): 6-8.

768. "Task Force on Kidnapping." *External Affairs* 23 (1971): 6-11.
   A transcript of an interview by the editors of *Canada Today* with Claude Roquet and Allen Rowe on the operations of the special task force created by the Canadian Department of External Affairs following the kidnapping of James Cross, senior British trade commissioner in Montreal, by members of the Quebec Liberation Front.

769. "Terrorism: The Companies in the Guerrillas' Sights." *Economist*, June 1, 1974, pp. 42-43.

770. Tuchman, Barbara. "Perdicaris Alive or Raisuli Dead." *American Heritage* 10 (August 1959).
   The story of Teddy Roosevelt's response to the kidnapping of a (supposed) U.S. citizen by bandits in Tangiers. Raisuli wanted French pressure on the Moroccan sultan and achieved this by U.K. and U.S. pressure on France. Raisuli also managed to kidnap Waler Heruis of the *London* and *New York Times* on June 18, 1903, and released him in exchange for political prisoners on June 30.

771. U.S. Department of Justice. "Hostage Situations: Bibliography." Quantico, Va.: FBI Academy, 1973.
   Approximately one hundred citations on hostage situations, airline hijackings, bank takeovers, and prevention of incidents.

772. ———. "Hostage Situations." Quantico, Va.: Learning Resources Center, FBI Academy, January 1975.
   This updated bibliography includes 426 citations to books, periodicals, newspaper reports, and government documents.

773. U.S. House of Representatives. Committee on Armed Services. *Problems of Prisoners of War and Their Families.* 91st Cong., 2d sess., March 6, 1970.

774. ———. Committee on Foreign Affairs. "American Prisoners of War in Southeast Asia, 1970, Hearings." 91st Cong., 2d sess., April-May 1970.

775. ———. Committee on Foreign Affairs. Subcommittee on Inter-American Affairs. "Safety of US Diplomats: Hearings April 27, 1970." 91st Cong., 2d sess., 1971.

Kidnappings and attempted kidnappings of diplomats in various Latin American nations. Hearings on problems raised by terrorist attacks on U.S. diplomatic personnel abroad. Brief review of proposal in OAS for uniform treatment of kidnappers seeking asylum.

776. ———. Committee on Interstate and Foreign Commerce. "Aircraft Piracy." H.R. Rep. No. 91-33, 91st Cong., 1st sess., 1969.

777. U.S. Senate "Terroristic Activity: Hostage Defense Measures." Hearings before the Subcommittee to Investigate the Administration of the Internal Security Act and Other Internal Security Laws of the Committee of the Judiciary. 94th Cong., 1st sess., July 25, 1975, pt. 5.

Brooks McClure covered types of hostage situations, terrorist activities, and hostage survival measures.

778. Vaders, Gerard. *Stranger on a Train: The Diary of a Hostage.* Netherlands, 1976.

One of the survivors of the December 1975 Moluccan siege recounts his experience. Vaders had been selected for execution by the terrorists but was passed by when the terrorists came to view him as a human being rather than a symbol.

779. Vayrynen, Raimo. "Some Aspects of Theory and Strategy of Kidnapping." *Instant Research on Peace and Violence* 1 (1971): 3-21.

780. Vouin, R. "Hostage Taking" *Etudes internationales de psycho-sociologies criminelle* 24-25 (1973): 67-71.

Developments in French law give kidnappers several options and provide incentives for freeing hostages quickly and safely.

781. West, L. J. et. al. "Unclassified Bibliography: Prisoners of War, Civilian Internees, and Political Prisoners." Multilithed. University of Oklahoma School of Medicine, Department of Psychiatry and Neurology, n.d.

782. "What to Do When the Kidnapper Strikes." *Burroughs Clearing House* (July 1972): 25.

783. Wohlstetter, Roberta. "Kidnapping to Win Friends and Influence People." *Survey* (Autumn 1974): 1-40. Also paper No. 45, California Seminar on Arms Control and Foreign Policy, September 1974.

Notes the details of a mass kidnapping engineered by Raul Castro and the Twenty-sixth of July rebels in 1958. Also mentions the May 18, 1904, kidnapping of Perdicaris by Raisuli and his bandit gang in Tangiers. Compares these kidnappings but fails to show what relevance they have to what the author admits are the new kinds of kidnap situations we face today.

784. Wolf, John B. "Hostage Negotiations." Paper prepared for the New Jersey Department of Corrections, Corrections Officers Training Academy and Staff Development Center, Jamesburg, April 14, 1977.

785. Xerin, J. "Torture and Hostage-Taking" *Revue de science criminelle et de droit pénal comparé* 1 (1973): 175-180.
The author calls for increased work in criminal law on political crime.

For additional readings, see the "Psychological Approaches" section, plus entries 45, 377, 422, 428, 1281, 1650, 1675, 1676, 1706, 1717, 1857, 1863, 1902, 1961, 1968, 2093, 2175, and 2396.

POTENTIAL NUCLEAR THREATS

786. Adelson, Alan M. "Please Don't Steal the Atomic Bomb." *Esquire* 44 (May 1969): 130-133.
Based upon many interviews with AEC officials, Lumb committee members, and private contractors, Adelson points out several gaping holes in our private safeguards program. The article is now somewhat outdated.

787. Advisory Panel on Safeguarding Special Nuclear Material. *Report to the AEC.* Washington, D.C., March 10, 1967

788. Allen, Perry H. "The Threat of Nuclear Blackmail: What Are the Chances of Stealing or Hijacking Fissionable Materials for Extortion or Sabotage?" *American Legion Magazine* 98 (May 1975): 8-11.

789. American National Standards Institute. *Industrial Security for Nuclear Power Plants.* ANSI Standard N18.17 Subcommittee ANS-3, American Nuclear Society, n.d.

790. Anderson, Jack. "An Appalling Lack of Nuclear Safeguards." *Washington Post*, March 27, 1977, p. C-7.
Anderson cites a secret report prepared by the Congressional Office of Technology Assessment, "Nuclear Proliferation and Safeguards," which argues that "a well trained commando (unit) of about 8 to 20 attackers using an imaginative plan and aid by insiders could heist a bomb." Methods for dealing with these difficulties are suggested.

791. ———. ''Will Nuclear Weapons Fall into the Hands of Terrorists?'' *Parade*, September 29, 1974, pp. 12ff.

792. Anderson, Marion. ''Fallout on the Freeway: The Hazards of Transporting Wastes in Michigan.'' Ann Arbor: Public Interest Research Group in Michigan, January 18, 1974.

793. ''Austria Seeks 'Atom Guerrilla.' '' *Washington Post*, April 23, 1974.

794. ''Austrian Police Search for Radioactive Package.'' *London Times*, April 24, 1974.

795. Avenhaus, R., and Gupta, D. ''Effective Application of Safeguards, Manpower and Other Techniques in Fuel Cycles.'' *Safeguards Techniques: Proceedings of a Symposium on Progress in Safeguards Techniques Organized by the International Atomic Energy Agency and held in Karlsruhe, July 6-10, 1970.* Vienna: International Atomic Energy Agency, 1970.

796. Ayers III, Russell W. ''Policing Plutonium: The Civil Liberties Fallout.'' *Harvard Civil Rights-Civil Liberties Law Review* 10 (1975).

797. ''Backyard A-Bombs.'' *Time*, November 27, 1972, p. 14.
    A note on Mason Willrich's comments before the American Nuclear Society and the Atomic Industrial Forum in Washington, D.C., in which he warned of the dangers of increases in amount and access to nuclear material. The AEC argued that a team of experts would be needed to construct a bomb, but it is still spending several million dollars annually for special nuclear materials protection.

798. Bair, W. J.; Richmond, C. R.; and Wachholz, B. W. ''A Radiobiological Assessment of the Spatial Distribution of Radiation Dose from Inhaled Plutonium.'' Washington, D.C.: U.S. Atomic Energy Commission, 1974.

799. Bair, W. J., and Thompson, R. C. ''Plutonium: Biomedical Research.'' *Science*, February 22, 1974. pp. 715-722.

800. Barnaby, Frank. ''Safeguards: With or Without Strings?'' *New Scientist and Science Journal*, February 25, 1971, pp. 430-432.

801. Bartels, W. C., and McDowell, S. C. T. ''Progress in Development of Technology for Nuclear Materials Safeguards.'' Paper presented at the annual meeting of the American Nuclear Society, June 26, 1974, at Philadelphia.

802. Beres, Louis René. ''Countering Nuclear Terrorism: Deterrence and Situation Management.'' Paper presented to the annual meeting of the International Studies Association, March 21, 1979, at Toronto.

After arguing that terrorists could easily acquire nuclear capabilities and that terrorists do not respond to standard forms of deterrence, Beres evidences a lack of understanding of the limitations of the international legal system. He then argues that present nuclear safeguards are hardware, rather than behaviorally oriented and suggests methods to remedy this deficiency.

803. ———. ''Hic Sunt Dracones: The Nuclear Threat of International Terrorism.'' *Terrorism.* In press.

804. ———. ''International Terrorism and World Order: The Nuclear Threat.'' *Stanford Journal of International Studies* 12 (Spring 1977): 131-146.

805. ———. ''The Nuclear Threat of Terrorism.'' Paper presented at the annual meeting of the North American Peace Science Conference, November 1975, at Cambridge, Massachusetts. Reprinted as FAR 23645-N.

806. ———. ''The Nuclear Threat of Terrorism.'' *International Journal of Group Tensions* 6 (1976): 53-66.

807. ———. ''The Nuclear Threat of Terrorism.'' *International Studies Notes.* In press.

808. ———. ''Preventin'g Nuclear Terrorism'' Paper presented to the 19th annual convention of the International Studies Association, February 22-25, 1978, at Washington, D.C.

809. ———. *Terrorism and Global Security: The Nuclear Threat.* Boulder: Westview, 1979, 225 pp.

Beres offers a behavioral, rather than physical security, approach to problems of security.

810. ———. ''Terrorism and International Security: The Nuclear Threat.'' *Chitty's Law Journal* 26 (March 1978): 73-89.

811. ———. ''Terrorism and the Nuclear Threat in the Middle East.'' *Current History* 70 (January 1976): 27-29.

Beres worries that Palestinian terrorist groups are sufficiently willing to engage in indiscriminate attacks against virtually any population group to be attracted to a high-risk attack upon a nuclear installation or to engage otherwise in nuclear terrorism. The growing links between international terrorists lead the author to believe that this increases their overall capability to acquire and successfully use nuclear weapons.

812. ———. "The Threat of Palestinian Nuclear Terrorism in the Middle East." *International Problems* 15 (Fall 1976): 48-56.

813. Berkowitz, Bernard J., et. al. *Superviolence: The Civil Threat of Mass Destruction Weapons.* Santa Barbara: ADCON Corporation, 1972.

814. Bernstein, Barton J. "The Quest for Security; American Foreign Policy and International Control of Atomic Energy, 1942-1946." *Journal of American History* 60 (March 1974): 1003-1044.

815. Bible, A. "A 1972 Look at Cargo Security: Everyone's Business." *Traffic World*, March 20, 1972.

816. Bigart, Homer. "Engineers Pursue Lost Radium Hunt." *New York Times*, August 19, 1966, pp. 35, 40.

817. ———. "Second Shipment of Radium Is Lost." *New York Times*, September 9, 1966.

818. Bigney, Russell E.; Crancer, John W.; Hamlin, Thomas M.; Hetrick, Bradley; and Munger, Murl D. "Exploration of the Nature of Future Warfare." AD-A001, 439 5/4. Carlisle Barracks, Pa.: Army War College, June 1974.
    Looking at present trends in economics, politics, and technology, as well as anticipated psychosociological drives, the authors believe that conflict in the next century will take the forms of terrorism, insurgency, minor war, major war, and total war.

819. Blair, Bruce. "A Proposal for Analyzing the Terrorist Threat to U.S. Nuclear Programs." Unpublished manuscript, Yale University, 1976.
    Blair, a former Strategic Air Command officer, points out that the nuclear armed terrorist question has been improperly specified. Rather than worry solely about the theft of special nuclear material, we should ask whether terrorists can acquire the ability to detonate a nuclear weapon. Weaknesses in the security systems of U.S military facilities are outlined, as are research strategies for determining terrorist motivations and objectives.

820. Blair, Bruce G., and Brewer, Garry D. "The Terrorist Threat to U.S. Nuclear Programs." Technical Report No. 2, School of Organization and Management, Yale University, October 1976. Published as "The Terrorist

Threat to World Nuclear Programs.'' *Journal of Conflict Resolution* 21 (September 1977): 379-403.

The authors believe that there is no doctrine or adequate institutional focus for preventing terrorism. Looking at terrorist threats to the intercontinental ballistic missile system, they formulate recommendations for improvement.

821. Bloomfield, Lincoln P. ''Nuclear Spread and World Order.'' *Foreign Affairs* 53 (July 1975): 743-755.

822. Boskey, Bennett, and Willrich, Mason, eds. *Nuclear Proliferation: Prospects for Control.* New York: Dunellen, 1970.

823. Brady, D. ''Nuclear Safeguards Policy: A Case Study in Regulation.'' Manhattan, Kan.: Kansas State University, KSU/DS-16, October 1971.

824. Brady, David, and Rappoport, Leon. ''Policy-Capturing in the Field: The Nuclear Safeguards Problem.'' *Organizational Behavior and Human Performance* 9 (April 1973).

The authors interviewed individuals most influential in formulating safeguards policy, such as AEC staff, industry officials, and Joint Committee on Atomic Energy members, and found significant differences among them in the amount of safeguards stringency they perceive in present programs and prefer in future ones.

825. Brobst, William A. ''Transportation Accidents: How Probable?'' *Nuclear News* 16 (May 1973): 48-54.

826. ———. ''Where, Oh, Where Did My Atoms Go?'' Remarks by the chief, Transportation Branch, Division of Waste Management and Transportation, U.S. Atomic Energy Commission, at the 13th annual meeting of the Institute of Nuclear Materials Management, 1972, at Boston.

827. Brown, Herbert H. ''Nuclear Facilities and Materials.'' In Alona E. Evans and John F. Murphy, eds., *Legal Aspects of International Terrorism.* Washington, D.C.: American Society of International Law, 1977.

828. Buchanan, J. R., ed. ''Safeguards against the Theft or Diversion of Nuclear Materials.'' *Nuclear Safety* 15 (September-October 1974): 513-619.

829. Burnham, S., *The Threat to Licensed Nuclear Facilities.* MITRE Technical Report, MTR-7022. McLean, Va.: MITRE Corporation, September 1975. Prepared for authorized distribution only.

A report for the Nuclear Regulatory Commission, which notes what types of groups—terrorist, criminal, or other—may attempt to attack nuclear facilities.

830. California: Nuclear Blackmail or Nuclear Threat Emergency Response Plan. Sacramento, Calif.: California Office of Emergency Services, 1976.

831. Calogero, Francesco. Review of *Nuclear Theft* and *The Curve of Binding Energy. Survival* 17 (March-April 1975): 91-93.
Calogero agrees with the warnings of the three authors, pointing out that the proliferation of those with the knowledge of how to make a bomb is another serious problem. He wonders if blackmail threats have already been made and are being hushed up by governmental authorities.

832. Cargo Theft and Organized Crime: A Deskbook for Management and Law Enforcement. Washington, D.C.: U.S. Department of Justice and U.S. Department of Transportation, DOTP 5200.6, October 1972.

833. "Cesium Sources Stolen, Found; Damaged Reported." *Nuclear News* (February 1975): 59.

834. Cherico, P. "Security Requirements and Standards for Nuclear Power Plants." *Security Management* 18 (January 1975): 22-24.
A discussion of the old AEC requirements on physical security plans, security guards, alarm systems, and general security systems. Projected requirements reagrding materials and plant protection, personnel selection, training, and access control are mentioned.

835. Chester, C. V. "Estimates of Threats to the Public from Terrorist Acts Against Nuclear Facilities." *Nuclear Safety* 17 (November-December 1976): 659-665.

836. Clark, Robert P. "Coping with Nuclear Terrorism: The Assessment of Countermeasures." Washington, D.C.: Brookings Institution Guest Scholar Program, 1977.
Discusses three major evaluative techniques commonly used in assessing countermeasures: political-budgetary, rational choice, and adaptive. Each method had its advantages and limitations, and an optimal strategy would employ a mix of the three.

837. Coates, James, and Randolph, Eleanor. "7,152 lbs. of Atom Bomb Materials 'Lost.' " *Chicago Tribune*, July 23, 1979.

The second of a series of four articles on nuclear terrorism, this report summarizes several cases of lost nuclear materials at U.S. and other facilities.

838. Code of Federal Regulations. Title 10. Energy. 10 CFR 50—*Licensing of Production and Utilization Facilities.* Revision of July 30, 1974, for export of production and utilization facilities, 39 CFR 40249.

10 CFR 70—*Special Nuclear Material.* 10 CFR 71—*Packaging of Radioactive Material for Transport and Transportation of Radioactive Material Under Certain Condition.* 10 CFR 73—*Physical Protection of Special Nuclear Material.* 10 CFR 110—*Unclassified Activities in Foreign Atomic Energy Programs.*

839. Cohen, Bernard L. "The Hazards in Plutonium Dispersal." Oak Ridge, Tenn.: Institute for Energy Analysis, 1975.

840. Coleman, Jerry Peter. "International Safeguards against Non-Government Nuclear Theft: A Study of Legal Inadequacies." *International Lawyer* 10 (Summer 1976): 493-513.

841. Comey, D. D. "Perfect Trojan Horse; Threat of Nuclear Terrorism." *Bulletin of the Atomic Scientist* 32 (June 1976): pp. 33-34.

842. Costanzi, F. A. et al. "Diverter Preference and Vulnerability Index: New Measures for Safeguards in the Fuel Cycle." Manhattan, Kan.: Kansas State University, KSU/DS14, 1972.

843. Crowson, Delmar L. "Progress and Prospects for Nuclear Materials Safeguards. IAEA SM 133/60, Vienna, 1970.

Author heads AEC's Office of Safeguards and Materials Management. Notes that audits for plutonium-239 loss average within +0.18 to 0.51 percent, with 0.2 percent "not unusual."

844. Crowson, D. L. "Safeguards and Nuclear Materials Management in the USA." *International Conference on Constructive Uses of Atomic Energy, Joint Session of the American Nuclear Society and the Atomic Industrial Forum.* Washington, D.C., 1968.

845. Curry, Robert V. "Plutonium-Safeguards and Physical Security." Remarks made before the Atomic Industrial Forum Topical Conference, March 6, 1975, at Kansas City.

846. Day, Jr., Samuel H. "We Re-Set the Clock." *Bulletin of the Atomic Scientists* (September 1974).

847. DeNike, Douglas. "Nuclear Safety and Human Malice." Mimeographed. University of Southern California School of Medicine, 1972.

848. ———. "Radioactive Malevolence." *Science and Public Affairs* (February 1974): 16-20.
One of the rare articles that considers military, as well as terrorist, attacks upon nuclear installations and predicts the postattack problems of such a disaster.

849. ———. "The Vulnerability to Antisocial Interventions of Nuclear Power Plants and Their Auxiliary Activities." Testimony before the Los Angeles Department of Water and Power, August 1, 1974.

850. "Details of Criminal Investigations of Large-Valued Thefts Related to Nuclear Materials." U.S. National Science Foundation, Research Applied to National Needs, June 1972.

851. Dolphin, G. W. et al. "Radiological Problems in the Protection of Persons Exposed to Plutonium." Harwell, England: National Radiological Protection Board of the United Kingdom, 1974.

852. Donnelly, Warren H. "Some Notes on Congress and Nuclear Safeguards." Paper presented for the Workshop on Plutonium, Safeguards, and the Breeder, Session on Safeguards and the Public, sponsored by the Atomic Industrial Forum, October 23, 1974.

853. Doub, William O., and Duker, Joseph M. "Making Nuclear Energy Safe and Secure." *Foreign Affairs* 53 (July 1975).

854. Drew, Elizabeth. "A Reporter in Washington, D.C., Summer Notes, 1." *New Yorker*, October 18, 1976, pp. 90, 151-157.
This section of Drew's article chronicles her attendance at a Congressional hearing on nuclear exports and problems of diversion safeguards.

855. Dumas, L. J. "National Security and the Arms Race." In David Carlton and Carlo Schaerf, eds., *International Terrorism and World Security*, pp. 158-164. London: Croom Helm, 1975.
Discusses the possibilities of nuclear accidents, accidental wars, diversion of special nuclear material, and the alteration of the defense-offense balance due to technology. Examples are provided of each.

856. "Effects of the Possible Use of Nuclear Weapons and the Security and Economic Implications for States of the Acquisition and Further

Development of These Weapons." New York: Department of Political and Security Council Affairs, A/6868, United Nations, 1968.

857. Environmental Survey of Transportation of Radioactive Materials to and from Nuclear Power Plants. Washington, D.C.: U.S. AEC, Directorate of Regulatory Standards, 1972.

858. "Estimates of Security Personnel Required to Protect Nuclear Fuel Cycle Components against Theft of Special Nuclear Materials and Sabotage." International Research and Technology Corporation, Final Report for U.S. Nuclear Regulatory Commission, August 21, 1975.

859. Everything You Always Wanted to Know about Shipping High-Level Nuclear Wastes. U.S. AEC, Division of Waste Management and Transportation, WASH—1264, August 1974.

860. "Exports of Nuclear Materials and Technology, Hearings." U.S. Senate. Committee on Banking, Housing and Urban Affairs. Subcommittee on International Finance. 93rd Cong., 2nd sess., July 12, 15, 1974.

861. "FBI Fears Rise of A Threats." *Los Angeles Times*, January 4, 1975.

862. Feiveson, Harold A. "Latent Proliferation: The International Security Implications of Civilian Nuclear Power." Ph.D. dissertation, Princeton University, 1972.

863. Feld, Bernard. "The Menace of a Fission Power Economy." *Science and Public Affairs* 30 (April 1974): 32-34.

864. Flood, Michael. "Nuclear Sabotage." *Washington Post*, January 9, 1977, pp. C1, C4,. Excerpted from *Bulletin of the Atomic Scientists* 32 (October 1976): 29-36.
    Flood summarizes the conventional wisdom on the issue, siding with those who believe that a facility could be taken over. He avoids becoming embroiled in the dispute over whether terrorists can make a bomb.

865. Ford, D. F., et al. *The Nuclear Fuel Cycle: A Survey of the Public Health, Environmental, and National Security Effects of Nuclear Power.* Cambridge, Mass., 1974.

866. Foster, G.; Evans, J.; Shriver, R.; and Leibstone, Marvin. "Unauthorized Reenablement of Nuclear Weapons." Paper prepared for the Department of Energy, December 1978.
    Looks at how terrorists would be able to steal and use a nuclear weapon.

867. "Four Nuclear Safety Dilemmas." *Defense Monitor* 4 (February 1975): 8-12.

Unfortunately the article does not go into great detail about nuclear terrorists, seizure by allies, unauthorized use, and nuclear accidents. Several suggestions, primarily assuming the possibility of harms derived from forward-deployed tactical nuclear weapons, are made.

868. Frank, Forrest R. "International Convention against Nuclear Theft." *Bulletin of the Atomic Scientists* 31 (December 1975): 51.

869. ———. "Nuclear Terrorism and the Escalation of International Conflict." *Naval War College Review* 29 (Fall 1976): 12-27.

Frank believes that terrorist use of a nuclear device might lead to a serious international crisis and then to war. The threat of nuclear terrorism will be solved only when terrorism in general is halted. Until then, he suggests several unilateral, bilateral, and multilateral steps to be taken to minimize escalation between states.

870. Fuller, John G. *We Almost Lost Detroit*, Pleasantville, N.Y.: Reader's Digest, 1975.

The story of the near-disaster at the Enrico Fermi atomic reactor on October 5, 1966.

871. Geesaman, Donald P. "Plutonium and the Energy Decision." *Bulletin of the Atomic Scientists* 27 (September 1971): 33-35.

872. Geesaman, Donald P., and Abrahamson, Dean E. "The Dilemma of Fission Power." *Bulletin of the Atomic Scientists* 30 (November 1974): 37-41.

873. Gilinsky, Victor. "Fast Breeder Reactors and the Spread of Plutonium." Santa Monica: RAND Corporation, RM-5148-PP, March 1967.

874. Gillette, Robert. "Nuclear Safeguards: Holes in the Fences." *Science*, December 14, 1973, pp. 1112-1114.

875. ———. "Plutonium (I): Questions of Health in a New Industry." *Science*, September 20, 1974, pp. 1027-1032.

876. ———. "Plutonium (II): Watching and Waiting for Adverse Effects." *Science*, September 27, 1974, pp. 1140-1143.

877. "Going Nuclear." *Congressional Record* 120 (1974): E 4380.

878. Gravel, Mike. "A Question of Nuclear Sabotage." *Congressional Record*, Senate, S4023, March 15, 1972.

879. Greenberg, Martin H. and Norton, Augustus R., eds. *Studies in Nuclear Terrorism*. Boston: G. K. Hall, 1979.
A collection of articles that have appeared in journals or been presented at international conferences.

880. Haefele, W., et al. "Safeguards System Studies and Fuel Cycle Analysis." In Ruth Farmakes, ed., *Proceedings of the International Conference on the Constructive Uses of Atomic Energy, November 10-15, 1968*, pp. 161-179, Washington, D.C.: American Nuclear Society, 1969.

881. Hall, D. "Adaptability to Nuclear Explosives." Prepared for delivery to the Symposium on Implementing Nuclear Safeguards, October 25, 1971, at Kansas State University.

882. Hofmann, Paul. "Sixty-seven U.N. Inspectors Pursue 'Lost' Nuclear Material." *New York Times*, June 20, 1975.
Gives background on IAEA, its staff, ideological position, and basic functions.

883. Holdren, John P. "Bootleg Bombs: Letters to the Editor." *Physics Today* (April 1974).

884. Holton, Gerald. "Reflections on Modern Terrorism." *Terrorism* 1 (1978): 265-276. Also in *Jerusalem Journal of International Relations* 3 (Fall 1977): 96-104.
Holton believes that terrorism by groups and by states will merge in the future, with high-technology attacks as a by-product.

885. Hosmer, Craig. "Remarks at 11th Annual Meeting, Institute of Nuclear Materials Management, May 25, 1970." Reprinted in *Congressional Record*, House, H5621, June 16, 1970.

886. Hutchinson, Martha Crenshaw. "Defining Future Threats: Terrorist and Nuclear Proliferation." Paper presented to the Conference on International Terrorism, sponsored by the Ralph Bunche Institute, June 9-11, 1976, at New York City. In Seymour Maxwell Finger and Yonah Alexander, eds., *Terrorism: Interdisciplinary Perspectives* (New York: John Jay Press, 1977).
A reworking of her International Studies Association address, this paper surveys virtually all of the unclassified literature on this question. Various

incidents, capabilities, and intentions of terrorists and problems of bargaining and deterrence are discussed.

887. ———. ''Defining Future Threat: Terrorists and Nuclear Proliferation.'' Paper presented to the International Symposium on Terrorism in the Contemporary World, April 26-28, 1976, at Glassboro State College. Reprinted as FAR 25656-N.

888. ———. ''Terrorism and the Diffusion of Nuclear Power.'' Paper prepared for delivery to the 17th Annual Convention of the International Studies Association, February 25-29, 1976, at Toronto, Canada. Reprinted as FAR 25657-N.
      A review of the literature on the possibilities of nuclear terrorism, noting some previous hoaxes, IAEA safeguards problems, and suggested remedies. The author notes the characteristics of a group that could engage in this form of terrorism, as well as their possible motivations. The role of macrolevel international relations theory, as well as rethinking of deterrence concepts in relation to terrorism, is noted.

889. Imai, Ryukichi, ''Nuclear Safeguards.'' 86 *Adelphi Papers* (London: International Institute of Strategic Studies, March 1972).

890. Improvements Needed in the Program for the Protection of Special Nuclear Material. Report to the U.S. Congress. Washington, D.C.: U.S. General Accounting Office, 1973.

891. "Indian Uranium Being Smuggled." *London Times*, October 8, 1974.

892. "Industrial Sabotage in Nuclear Power Plants." *Nuclear Safety* 2 (March-April 1970): 107.

893. "Industry Inundated by Proposed New Safeguards Rules." *Nuclear Industry* (February 1973): 45-47.

894. Inglis, David Rittenhouse. *Nuclear Energy: Its Physics and Its Social Challenge*. Reading, Mass.: Addison-Wesley, 1973.

895. Ingram, Timothy H. ''Nuclear Hijacking: Now within Grasp of Any Bright Lunatic.'' *Washington Monthly* (December 1972): 20-28.

896. Inman, Guy. ''Research and Development for Safeguards.'' Washington, D.C.: U.S. Atomic Energy Commission, 1968.

897. Institute of Nuclear Materials Management. *Nuclear Materials: Safeguards in Transportation.* Final Report, 1970.

898. International Atomic Energy Agency. *Safeguards Techniques: Proceedings of a Symposium in Karlsruhe, July 6-10, 1970.* Vienna: International Atomic Energy Agency, 1970.

899. International Research and Technology Corporation. *Estimates of Security Personnel Required to Protect Nuclear Fuel Cycle Components Against Theft of Special Nuclear Materials and Sabotage.* Washington, D.C.: Nuclear Regulatory Commission. August 21, 1975.

900. Jaeger, Thomas. *Principles of Radiation Protection Engineering.* Translated by Lawrence Dresner. New York: McGraw-Hill, 1965.

901. Jenkins, Brian Michael. ''The Impact of Nuclear Terrorism.'' Santa Monica: The RAND Corporation, September 1978.
  Jenkins assumes that a nuclear device will have been detonated by the 1990s. Discusses the effects of such an action upon calls for nuclear disarmament, the debate over nuclear energy, antiterrorist cooperation, and strategic doctrine.

902. ———. ''New Vulnerabilites and the Acquisition of New Weapons by Non-Government Groups.'' Paper presented at the 1976 Conference on International Terrorism, U.S. Department of State, at Washington, D.C. Available as FAR 27311-N.

903. ———. ''The Potential for Nuclear Terrorism.'' Address to the Conference on Nuclear Arms Proliferation and Nuclear Terrorism at the Arms Control Association, May 8, 1977, at Washington, D.C. Reprinted in Santa Monica: The RAND Corporation, May 1977, P-5876.
  Although a nuclear terrorist incident could occur, Jenkins finds that it is impossible to predict when it will occur or who will engage in such behavior.

904. ———. ''Terrorism and the Nuclear Safeguards Issue.'' Santa Monica: RAND Corporation, P-5611, March 1976. Reprinted as FAR 25034-N. Transcript of testimony before the U.S. House of Representatives, Interior and Insular Affairs Subcommittee on Energy and the Environment, February 26, 1976.
  Jenkins points out that the public often confuses nuclear safety with nuclear safeguards and uses the latter to voice its uncertainty and anxiety. He notes that there are many possible threats, including alarming hoaxes, acts of

low-level symbolic sabotage, occupation or seizure of nuclear facilities, acts of serious sabotage aimed at causing widespread casualties and damage, thefts of nuclear material, armed attacks on nuclear weapons storage sites, thefts of nuclear weapons, the dispersal of radioactive contaminants, the manufacture of homemade nuclear weapons, and the detonation or threatened detonation of such devices. He feels that terrorists want a lot of people watching, not dead, and will probably not explode a device but use it to induce fear and achieve maximum publicity. Actions of groups opposing nuclear power are also explored.

905. ———. ''Will Terrorists Go Nuclear?'' Testimony given before the Committee on Energy and Diminishing Materials of the California State Assembly, November 19, 1975. Santa Monica, Ca.: California Seminar on Foreign Policy and Arms Control, January 1976.

An early version of his House of Representatives testimony, in which he argues that the pattern of terrorist incidents suggests that they are aiming at publicity, not for hundreds of thousands of terminally ill, vengeance-seeking individuals who are suffering due to a nuclear action with long-term effects. He notes that large groups may worry about adverse public opinion and repression, whereas smaller groups would feel less constrained. However, smaller groups would have fewer resources to employ for the perpetration of such an action. He ends with suggestions about future trends, paralleling those of skyjackings and kidnappings: an early period of imitation of events by other groups, with a later decline in frequency of incidents as security measures are strengthened and publicity declines due to the incident's becoming a commonplace event.

906. Jenkins, Brian, and Krofcheck, Joseph. ''The Potential Nuclear Non-State Adversary.'' Report prepared for the Congress of the U.S., Office of Technology Assessment, May 1977.

907. Jenkins, Brian M., and Rubin, Alfred P. ''New Vulnerabilities and the Acquisition of New Weapons by Nongovernment Groups.'' In Alona Evans and John F. Murphy, eds., *Legal Aspects of International Terrorism.* Washington, D.C.: American Society of International Law, 1977.

908. Joslin, Charles. ''Nuclear Genie: Keeping It Safely Bottled up Is a Costly Business.'' *Barron's*, September 23, 1973, pp. 19-21.

909. Karber, Phillip A., et al. ''Draft Working Paper B: Analysis of the Terrorist Threat to the Commercial Nuclear Industry: Summary of Findings.'' Vienna, Va.: BDM Corporation, BDM/W-15-176-TR, 1975.

910. Karber, Phillip A., et al. "Draft Working Paper C: Analysis of the Terrorist Threat to the Commercial Nuclear Industry: Supporting Appendices." Vienna, Va.: BDM Corporation, BDM/W-75-176-TR, 1975.

911. Karber, Phillip A.; Mengel, R. William; and Novotny, Eric J. "A Behavioral Analysis of the Terrorist Threat to Nuclear Installations." Unpublished manuscript prepared for the U.S. Atomic Energy Commission, Sandia Laboratories, July 1974.

912. Karber, Phillip A.; Mengel, R. William; Greisman, H. C.; Newman, G. S.; Novotny, Eric J.; and Whitley, A. G. *Analysis of the Terrorist Threat to the Commercial Nuclear Industry.* Report submitted to the Special Safeguards Study, Nuclear Regulatory Commission, in response to Contract No. AT (49-24)-0131. Vienna, Va.: BDM/75-176-TR. 414 pp.

The study centers around seven questions regarding the motives and types of resources relevant to various attacks upon nuclear installations. BDM used various statistical and intuitive methods to attempt to formulate answers.

913. Kinderman, E. M. "Plutonium: Home Made Bombs?" Paper presented to the Conference on Nuclear Public Information, Information-3, organized by the Atomic Industrial Forum, March 5-8, 1972. Reprinted in U.S. Senate, Committee on Government Operations, *Peaceful Nuclear Exports and Weapons Proliferation*, pp. 25-26. Washington, D.C.: Government Printing Office, 1975.

914. Klevens, Edward H. "The Plutonium Connection and a Small Case of Blackmail." *American Journal of Physics* 44 (April 1976): 406-407.

Klevens reviews two films about the possibilities of clandestine manufacture of a nuclear device.

915. Kouts, Herbert. "Technical Progress in Nuclear Materials Safeguards." *Transactions of the American Nuclear Society* 13 (November 1970).

916. Krakowiecki, Marie. "Regulation of Site Security for Nuclear Plants to Toughen." *Business Insurance*, September 20, 1976, pp. 9-10.

917. Kratzer, Myron B. "A New Era for International Safeguards." *Nuclear News* (February 1971): 40-43.

918. Krieger, David. "Nuclear Power: A Trojan Horse for Terrorists." In B. Jasani, ed., *Nuclear Proliferation Problems*, pp. 187-200. Cambridge: MIT Press for the Stockholm International Peace Research Institute, 1974.

919. ———. "Terrorists and Nuclear Technology: The Danger is Great; the Question Is Not Whether the Worst Will Happen, but Where and How." *Bulletin of Atomic Scientists* (June 1975): 28-34.

Krieger looks at how terrorists might acquire nuclear materials or weapons, how they could use them, and how to minimize these possibilities. He mentions stealing, buying, or constructing a weapon, as well as the possibilities of radiation dispersal devices, sabotage of nuclear facilities, and transported materials.

920. ———. "What Happens If . . .? Terrorists, Revolutionaries, and Nuclear Weapons." *Annals of the American Academy of Political and Social Science* 430 (March 1977): 44-57.

921. Kriegsman, William E. "Safeguards Objectives and Regulations in Perspective." Remarks before the Atomic Industrial Forum Topical Conference, March 20, 1974, at New Orleans.

922. Kupperman, Robert. "Nuclear Terrorism: Armchair Pastime or Genuine Threat?" *Jerusalem Journal of International Relations* 3 (Summer 1978): 19-26.

923. Kurve, Mavin. "Mystery of Uranium Smuggling Deepens." *Times of India*, May 7, 1974.

924. Lapp, Ralph E. "Nuclear Weapon Systems" *Bulletin of the Atomic Scientists* (March 1961).

925. ———. "The Ultimate Blackmail." *New York Times Magazine*, February 4, 1973, p. 13.

926. Larson, Clarence E. "Nuclear Materials Safeguards: A Joint Industry Government Mission." *Proceedings of the AEC Symposium on Safeguards Research and Development, Los Alamos Scientific Laboratory, UCLA, October 27-29, 1969.* Springfield, Va.: Clearinghouse for Federal Scientific and Technical Information, WASH 1147, 1969.

Warns of a "likely" future nuclear black market that would rapidly grow once a source of supply is identified. Cites an "unavoidable" industry loss rate of 1 to 2 percent and feels that we may be unable to solve all special nuclear materials safeguarding problems.

927. Larus, J. *Nuclear Weapons Safety and the Common Defense.* Columbus: Ohio State University Press, 1967.

928. Lawrence, Robert M., and Larus, Joel, eds. *Nuclear Proliferation, Phase II.* Lawrence, Kan.: University of Kansas Press, 1973.

929. Leachman, Robert B. "Diversion Safeguards: Political and Scientific Effectiveness in Nuclear Materials Control." Final Report for Grant No. GI-9 of the National Science Foundation. Manhattan, Kan.: Kansas State University, June 1972.

930. ———. "Preventive Criminology Applied to Fissionable Materials." Washington, D.C.: U.S. National Science Foundation, Research Applied to National Needs, 1972.

931. Leachman, Robert B., and Althoff, Phillip, eds. *Preventing Nuclear Theft: Guidelines for Industry and Government: Security Measures Conferences.* New York: Praeger, 1972. 377 pp.

    Contents: "Safeguards Overview"; "National Safeguards System"; "International Safeguards Systems"; "Thefts, Criminology, and Jurisdiction"; "The Fuel Cycle and Measurements"; "Optimizing Inspections." Papers and summaries of discussions presented at the Symposium on Implementing Nuclear Safeguards, sponsored by the Diversion Safeguards Program at Kansas State University, October 25-27, 1971.

932. Lieberman, J. *The Scorpion and the Tarantula: The Struggle to Control Atomic Weapons.* Boston: Houghton Mifflin, 1970.

933. Leibstone, Marvin; Evans, J.; and Bott, D. "Analysis of Small Group Encounter Experience." Science Applications, Inc., study prepared for the Nuclear Regulatory Commission, May 1978.

    Looks at incidents of attacks on secured facilities or attempts to hijack protected road shipments.

934. Lovatt, James E. *Nuclear Materials Management and Control.* New York: Gordon and Breach, 1972.

935. Lumb, Ralph F. "The Safeguards Issue." Nuclear Surveillance and Auditing Corporation, 1973.

936. Mabry, Jr., Robert Caldwell. "Nuclear Theft: Real and Imagined Dangers." Master's thesis, Monterey: Naval Postgraduate School, 1976.

937. Matson, Eric K. *Terrorists Armed with Nuclear Weapons.* Research Study Report No. 1810-76, Air Command and Staff College, Air University, May 1976. Available as FAR 25273-N AD BO11 885L.

938. McCullough, C. Rogers. ''An Appraisal of Industrial Sabotage in Nuclear Power Plants.'' Southern Nuclear Engineering, Inc., SNE UC-80, July 1968.

939. McCullough, C. Rogers; Turner, Stanley E.; Lyerly, Ray L. ''An Appraisal of the Potential Hazard of Industrial Sabotage in Nuclear Power Plants.'' TID4500 *Reactor Technology* (July 1968).

940. McPhee, John. *The Curve of Binding Energy.* New York: Farrar, Straus and Giroux, 1974. 170 pp.
      Includes interviews with Theodore Taylor on how terrorists might make nuclear weapons. Much of it is an account of Taylor's career and his other interests. Parts of the book appeared in the *New Yorker*, December 3, 10, 17, 1973.

941. McWhinney, Jr., Robert T. ''Safeguards: Regulatory Requirements.'' Remarks made before the Atomic Industrial Forum Workshop on Plutonium, Safeguards and the Breeder, October 9, 1974, at Knoxville, Tennessee.

942. Medical Research Council. *The Toxicity of Plutonium.* London: HM Stationery Office, 1975.

943. Meguire, Patrick G., and Kramer, Joel J. *Psychological Deterrents to Nuclear Theft: A Preliminary Literature Review and Bibliography.* Gaithersburg: National Bureau of Standards, NBSIR 76-1007, March 1976.

944. Meidl, J. H. *Explosive and Toxic Hazardous Materials.* Beverly Hills: Glencoe, 1970.

945. Mengel, Russell William. ''The Impact of Nuclear Terrorism on the Military's Role in Society.'' In Marius Livingston et al., eds., *International Terrorism in the Contemporary World*, pp. 402-414, Westport, Conn.: Greenwood Press, 1978.

946. ———. ''Mass Destruction Terrorism: A Double Edge Sword.'' Paper presented to the panel on Violence and Terror of the Conference on Complexity: A Challenge to the Adaptive Capacity of American Society, sponsored by the Society for General Systems Research, March 24-26, 1977, at Columbia, Maryland.
      Mengel argues that the number of incidents of terrorism is not increasing, but the amount of damage and injury caused by any one attack is, which has ramifications for chemical, biological and nuclear incidents. He finds the escalation of terrorism to be a four-stage process, which involves stresses upon

group cohesion. Technical aspects of sophisticated attacks, as well as group laziness, further inhibit the willingness to undertake such ventures. Society is faced with a complex mix of constraints against government preemptive action and response, including civil rights considerations and the "back-burner" position of potential threats in setting national priorities. However, society could benefit from an attempt to quantify our knowledge and use a general systems approach to planning and response.

947. ————. *Terrorism and New Technologies of Destruction: An Overview of the Potential Risk*. Report prepared for the National Advisory Committee Task Force on Disorder and Terrorism. Vienna, Va.: BDM Corporation, W-76-044-TR, May 25, 1976.

According to the report's foreword, "This Report initially examines the technologies available to terrorists, focusing on the employment of nuclear, chemical and biological weaponry. To achieve realistic and balanced appraisal of the potentialities of terrorists and their capacity to engage in high technology terrorism, each technology as well as the likely motivations, targets, resources and modes of employment are discussed. The latter segments of the Report address control and response mechanisms relevant to local, State and Federal organizations. A brief review of current mechanisms is presented, followed by recommendations across a range of topics including: Planning; resources and training; decision-making; local-state-Federal relationships; intelligence; legislative; civil liberties and economies."

948. Meyer, W.; Loyalka, S. K.; Nelson, W. E.; Williams, R. W. "The Homemade Nuclear Bomb Syndrome." *Nuclear Safety* (July-August 1977).

949. Moonman, Eric. "War May Be the Least of Our Worries over the Bomb." *Times* (London), July 24, 1974, p. 16.

950. Morgan, K. Z., and Turner, J. E., eds. *Principles of Radiation Protection*. New York: Wiley, 1967.

951. Mullen, Robert K. *The International Clandestine Nuclear Threat.* Santa Barbara: Mission Research Corporation, June 1975.

952. ————. "Mass Destruction and Terrorism." *Journal of International Affairs* 32 (Spring-Summer, 1978): 63-89.

Discusses the specific characteristics of various types of chemical and biological weapons, as well as nuclear materials. While Mullen agrees that it is possible for a group to construct an atomic/biological/chemical weapon, dissemination of the agent is more difficult than often believed. Further, it remains to be demonstrated why a terrorist group would be willing to pay the massive costs in popular support that use of a mass destruction weapon would entail.

953. ———. "Nuclear Threats." Paper prepared for delivery to the 19th annual convention of the International Studies Association, February 22-25, 1978, at Washington, D.C.

954. "Mystery Radiation Hits Another Train." *Los Angeles Times*, April 20, 1974.

955. Norman, Lloyd. "Our Nuclear Weapons Sites: Next Target of Terrorists?" *Army* 27 (June 1977): 28-31.
    Argues that although the sophistication of nuclear weapons has increased, their security has not.

956. Norton, Augustus R. "Nuclear Terrorism and the Middle East." *Military Review* 56 (April 1976): 3-11.

957. ———. "Terrorists, Atoms and the Future: Understanding the Threat." *Naval War College Review* (May-June 1979): 30-50. Adapted from the introduction to Augustus Norton and Martin Greenberg, eds., *Studies in Nuclear Terrorism* (Boston: G. K. Hall, 1979).
    Norton believes that terrorists will not soon use nuclear weapons.

958. ———. *Understanding the Nuclear Terrorism Problem*. Gaithersburg, Md.: International Association of Chiefs of Police, 1979.

959. "Nova: The Plutonium Connection." Transcript reprinted in *Congressional Record*, March 11, 1975, pp. S3620ff.
    A television program of how an MIT student was able to design a nuclear device from publicly available reference works.

960. Novick, S. "Basement H-Bombs." *Scientist and Citizen* (December, 1968.

961. Novotny, Eric J., and Whitley, A. Grant. "Draft Working Paper D: A Select Bibliography on the Terrorist Threat to the Commercial Nuclear Industry." Vienna, Va.: BDM Corporation, BDM/W-75-176-TR, 1975.
    A thorough bibliography on this aspect of possible future terrorism.

962. Nuclear Power Growth 1974-2000. Washington, D.C.: U.S. Atomic Energy Commission, Office of Planning and Analysis, February 1974, WASH-1139.

963. "Nuclear Theft and Terrorism: Discussion Group Report." In *Sixteenth Strategy for Peace Conference Report*, pp. 33-40. Muscatine, Iowa: Stanley Foundation, October 9-12, 1975, at Warrenton, Virginia.

The discussion group, chaired by Ted Taylor, considered five possibilities: theft of nuclear weapons; theft of nuclear materials from military or civilian programs for the purpose of clandestine construction of nuclear explosives; theft of plutonium for radioactivity dispersal; sabotage of nuclear power plants or nuclear waste-storage facilities to release enough radioactive materials to be a serious threat to populated areas; theft of nuclear materials for sale to a black market, or for extortion, but not for explicit destructive use. Technical, political, and social measures to be taken to reduce these threats are suggested.

964. *Operational Accidents and Radiation Exposure Experience Within USAEC 1943-1967.* Washington, D.C.: U.S. Atomic Energy Commission, Division of Operational Safety, 1968.

965. "Peaceful Nuclear Exports and Weapons Proliferation: A Compendium." U.S. Senate. Committee on Government Operations. 94th Cong., 1st sess., April 1975.

966. Pendley, Robert, and Scheinman, Lawrence. "International Safeguarding as Institutionalized Collective Behavior." *International Organization* 29 (Summer 1975).

967. Perry, H. A. "The Threat of Nuclear Blackmail: What Are the Chances of Stealing or Hijacking Fissionable Materials for Extortion or Sabotage?" *American Legion Magazine* 98 (May 1975): 8-11.

968. Physical Protection of Classified Matter and Information. Washington, D.C.: U.S. Atomic Energy Commission, Division of Security, June 26, 1969.

969. Phillips, James G. "Energy Report/Safeguards, Recycling, Broaden Nuclear Power Debate." *National Journal Reports* 7 (1975): 419-429.

970. Phillips, John Aristotle. "The Fundamentals of Atomic Bomb Design — An Assessment of the Problems and Possibilities Confronting a Terrorist Group or Non-Nuclear Nations Attempting to Design a Crude Pu-239 Fission Bomb." Junior thesis, Princeton University, 1976.

Phillips's term paper has attracted much interest on the part of the press and has also led to attempts by France and Pakistan to acquire copies of the paper. Most of the piece is written in technical terms beyond the grasp of the average reader.

971. Phillips, John Aristotle, and Michaelis, David. *Mushroom: The Story of the A-Bomb Kid.* New York: Morrow, 1978. 287 pp.

About the Princeton student who became famous when he designed a workable atomic bomb in order to fulfill his academic requirements for a physics course and to demonstrate that if he, at most an average student, could design such a bomb, almost anyone else could.

972. Ponte, Lowell. ''Atomizing the World.'' *Skeptic* 14 (1976).

973. ———. ''Better Do As We Say: This Is an Atom Bomb and We're Not Fooling'' *Penthouse* (February 1972).

974. ———. ''Who is Arming the New Terrorists?'' *Playgirl* (April 1977): 34-124.

The question goes unanswered. Rather Ponte centers on the three primary weapons of ''techno-terrorism'': nuclear, chemical, and biological weapons. Much of the article is impressionistic, but among the items that will not be found elsewhere in the literature is: ''In 1965, a newly-nuclear People's Republic of China secretly offered 2 crude atomic bombs to a unit of Al-Fatah Arab terrorists in Syria. With the help of spies in Al-Fatah the CIA intercepted the offer and threatened China with direct nuclear retaliation. The offer was withdrawn.'' Another example of ''monkey-wrench politics'' was in 1970: ''Chicago police captured members of a group calling itself The Order of the Rising Sun. Neo-Nazi and racist-supremicist in nature, the group had already prepared a 'large batch' of typhoid germs and had plans to dump them into the water supplies of Chicago, St. Louis, and other Midwestern cities.''

975. Proceedings of the AEC Symposium on Safeguards Research and Development. Los Alamos, N.M., 1969. Available from National Technical Information Service (NTIS), Springfield, Va.

976. Proceedings of the Rocky Flats Symposium on Safety in Plutonium Handling Facilities. Sponsored by the AEC, April 13-16, 1971. Available from NTIS, Springfield, Virginia.

977. Protecting Special Nuclear Material in Transit: Improvements Made and Existing Problems. Report to the Joint Committee on Atomic Energy, U.S. Congress. Washington, D.C.: U.S. General Accounting Office, 1974.

978. Public Law 93-377. Act to Amend the Atomic Energy Act of 1954, as amended, and the Atomic Weapons Rewards Act of 1966, and for other purposes.

979. Public Law 93-438. The Energy Reorganization Act of 1974.

980. Public Law 93-485. An Act to Amend the Atomic Energy Act of 1954, as amended, to Enable Congress to Concur in or Disapprove International Agreements for Cooperation in Regard to Certain Nuclear Technology.

981. Public Law 93-500. An Act to Amend and Extend the Export Administration Act of 1974.

982. Quester, George. "What's New on Nuclear Proliferation?" Paper prepared for the 1975 Aspen Workshop on Arms Control. Reprinted in U.S. Congress, House Committee on International Relations, Subcommittee on International Security and Scientific Affairs "Nuclear Proliferation: Future US Foreign Policy Implications." Hearings. 94th Cong., 1st sess., 1975.
   Quester introduces the concept of microproliferation to discuss nuclear terrorism.

983. "Radioactive Needle Sought after Theft Suspect Is Arrested." *Los Angeles Times*, November 2, 1974.

984. "Radioactive Plates Stolen from Lab." *Los Angeles Times*, October 1974.

985. "Radioactive Spray Used in Vendetta." *Washington Post*, April 18, 1974.

986. Ramey, J. T. "Providing for Public Safety in the Nuclear Industry—The Engineerng Approach." Paper presented to the National Academy of Engineering Symposium on Public Safety, 1970 at Washington, D.C., National Academy of Sciences.

987. Randall, Nan. "If the Unthinkable Happened Here . . ." *Washington Post*, January 29, 1978, pp. C1, C4.
   A former program director of SANE discusses the probable physical effects of a nuclear attack on Washington by the Soviets, as well as the explosion of a fifteen-kiloton terrorist bomb placed in front of the White House.

988. Rapoport, Daniel. "The Government Is up in the Air over Combating Mass Terrorism." *National Journal*, November 26, 1977, pp. 1853-1856.

989. Rappoport, L., and Pettinelli, J. D. "Social Psychological Studies of the Safeguards Problem." Paper presented at the Symposium on Implementing Nuclear Safeguards, October 25, 1971, at Kansas State University.

990. ———. "Social Psychological Studies of the Safeguards Problem." U.S. National Science Foundation, Research Applied to National Needs. 1972.

991. Rasmussen, Norman C. "Rasmussen on Nuclear Safety." *IEEE Spectrum* (August 1975): 45-55.

992. Ray, Dixy Lee. "The Importance of Nuclear Safeguards." Remarks before the Fourth International Symposium on Transportation and Packaging of Radioactive Materials, September 24, 1974, at Miami.

993. Recommendations for the Physical Protection of Nuclear Materials. Vienna, Va.: International Atomic Energy Agency, 1972.

994. Reford, Robert W. "Problems of Nuclear Proliferation" *Behind the Headlines* 34 (May 1975): 22 pp.

995. Rosenbaum, David M. "Nuclear Terror." *International Security* 1 (Winter 1977): 140-161. Reprinted in John D. Elliott and Leslie K. Gibson, eds., *Contemporary Terrorism: Selected Readings* pp. 129-147. (Gaithersburg: International Association of Chiefs of Police, 1978).

A shortened version of the MITRE study, suggesting that nations, criminals, and terrorists may be attracted to nuclear terrorism. Rosenbaum suggests ways in which the Soviet Union and People's Republic of China would be vulnerable to such attacks and evaluates suggestions that have been forwarded on preventing the problem.

996. Rosenbaum, D. M.; Googin, J. N.; Jefferson, R. M.; Kleitman, D. J.; and Sullivan, W. C. "Special Safeguards Study," Unpublished unclassified portions of the study were released by Senator Abraham Ribicoff and appeared in the *Congressional Record*, April 30, 1974, p. S6621.

997. Rossides, E. T. "What Is US Customs Doing to Stop Cargo Theft?" *Traffic World*, March 20, 1972.

998. Rotblat, Joseph. "Controlling Weapons-Grade Fissile Material." *Bulletin of the Atomic Scientists* 33 (June 1977): 37-43.

999. Safeguards Dictionary. Washington, D.C.: U.S. Atomic Energy Commission, Brookhaven National Laboratory, Office of Safeguards and Material Management, 1971, WASH-1173.

1000. Safeguards Systems Analysis of Nuclear Fuel Cycles. Washington D.C.: U.S. Atomic Energy Commission, Office of Safeguards and Materials Management, October 1969.

1001. Safeguards Techniques: Proceedings of a Symposium on Progress in Safeguards Techniques Organized by the International Atomic Energy Agency and Held in Karlsruhe, July 6-10, 1970. Vienna, Austria: IAEA, 1970.

1002. Sagan, L. A. "Human Costs of Nuclear Power." *Science* 177 (1972).: 487.

1003. Sanders, Benjamin. *Safeguards against Nuclear Proliferation.* Cambridge, Mass.: MIT Press, and Stockholm, Almqvist and Wiksell, 1975. 114 pp. Written for the Stockholm International Peace Research Institute.

1004. Scheinman, Lawrence. "Safeguarding Nuclear Materials." *Bulletin of the Atomic Scientists* (April 1974): 34-36.

Scheinman singles out three parts to the problem of nuclear diversion: detection, prevention, and recovery. The first is currently handled by the IAEA, whereas the latter two tasks remain in the hands of single nation-states. He argues that the nuclear-weapon states should be subject to the highest standards of diversion safeguards, since their security systems would be of the greatest interest to potential terrorists. He suggests that these problems should be addressed in an international organization context and that multinational physical facilities should be considered.

1005. Schlesinger, James R. "Expectations and Responsibilities of the Nuclear Industry." Remarks before the American Nuclear Society annual meeting, October 20, 1971. Reprinted in *Congressional Record*, October 28, 1971, p. H10125.

1006. "Security Review of Certain NATO Installations." *Congressional Record*, April 29, 1975, pp. S7184-S7190.

1007. Shapley, Deborah. "Plutonium: Reactor Proliferation Threatens a Nuclear Black Market." *Science*, April 9, 1971, pp. 143-146.

Notes that it takes only 5 kilograms of plutonium to make a Nagasaki-sized bomb. The few losses of special nuclear materials have included: in late 1969, the experimental SEFOR reactor in Strickler, Arkansas, was found deficient in "a few kgs." of plutonium; a Nuclear Materials Enrichment Corporation plant in Apollo, Pennsylvania, discovered about 6 percent of its materials had gone unaccounted for over a six-year period; in Bradwell,

England, two reactor plant workers dropped twenty fuel rods over the plant fence and left them, apparently to be picked up. The theft was intercepted. Mentions the weaknesses of IAEA; low budgets, inspections do not cover non-NPT members, inspections do not cover military facilities, no police power. Mentions Lumb panel (AEC 1967 Ad Hoc Advisory Panel on Safe-guarding SNM) recommendations as well as AEC classified study by Wright, Long, and Co., on the threat of nuclear hijacking by the mafia and organized crime.

1008. "Smuggled Uranium." *Environment.* (December 1974).

1009. Special Safeguards Study: Scopes of Work. Washington, D.C.: U.S. Nuclear Regulatory Commission, Office of Special Studies, NUREG-75/060, June 1975.

1010. Speth, J. Gustave; Tamplin, Arthur R.; and Cochran, Thomas B. "The Plutonium Decision: A Report on the Risks of Plutonium Recycle." Washington, D.C.: Natural Resources Defense Council, 1974.

1011. Staff, Chauncey. "Social Benefit versus Technological Risk." *Science* 165 (1969), p. 1232.

1012. Stevenson, Adlai E. "Nuclear Reactors: America Must Act." *Foreign Affairs* 53 (October 1974).

1013. Stockton, Bayard, and Janke, Peter. *Nuclear Power, Protest and Violence.* London: Institute for the Study of Conflict, Conflict Studies, No. 102, 1978. 20 pp.

1014. "Suspicion Falls on Nepal as Uranium Gang's HQ." *London Times*, May 2, 1974.

1015. Tamplin, Arthur R., and Cochran, Thomas B. "Radiation Standards for Hot Particles: A Report on the Inadequacy of Existing Radiation Protection Standards Relating to Internal Exposure of Man to Insoluble Particles of Plutonium and Other Alpha-Emitting Hot Particles." Washington, D.C.: Natural Resources Defense Council, 1974.

1016. Tamplin, A. R. and Gofman, J. W. *Population Control Through Nuclear Pollution.* Chicago: Nelson-Hall, 1970.

1017. Taylor, L. S. "Radiation Protection Trends in the U.S." *Health Physics* 30 (July 1970).

1018. Taylor, Theodore B. "International Safeguards of Non-military Nuclear Technology, Part II, The Need for Nuclear Safeguards" *International Research and Technology Nuclear Journal* 1 (February 1969): 1-15.

Discusses examples of nuclear threats, including a small organization enforcing nuclear disarmament, assassination of government leaders, and international black market.

1019. ———. "The Need for a Major AEC Program to Provide for Physical Security of Special Nuclear Materials." Washington D.C.: International Research and Technology Corporation, 1971.

1020. ———. *Preliminary Survey of Non-National Nuclear Threats.* International Research and Technology Corporation under subcontract to Stanford Research Institute, US Army Research Office, September 17, 1968.

1021. ———. "Resources Required to Make Fission Explosives." *Utility of SSNM for Unauthorized Purposes. Appendix II.* Arlington, Va.: International Research and Technology Corporation, June 17, 1975.

1022. Taylor, Theodore B. and Colligan, Douglas. "Nuclear Terrorism: A Threat of the Future." *Science Digest* (August 1974): 12-17.

Taylor points out examples of large MUFs, along with the famous Miami bomb hoax. The dangers of bombs and dispersal devices, and the ease with which they could be manufactured, are pointed out. Flaws in security measures are mentioned, and action is called for.

1023. Taylor, Theodore B.; Van Cleave, W. R.; and Kinderman, E. M. "Preliminary Survey of Non-National Nuclear Threats." Stanford Research Institute Technical Note SSC-TN-5205-83, September 1968.

Creates a set of 150 classification categories, each with from two to several dozen elements, which can be used to describe 1,070 possible nuclear threat incidents.

1024. "The Threat of Nuclear Theft and Sabotage." *Congressional Record,* April 30, 1974, pp. S6621-6630.

1025. Trucking Security Manual. National Association of Transportation Security Advisors, n.d.

1026. Tucker, James Guy. "The Transportation of Radioactive Materials: Federal Preemption vs. State Regulation." *State Government* 47 (Spring 1974).

1027. Turner, S. E. et al. ''Industrial Sabotage in Nuclear Power Plants.'' *Nuclear Safety* (March-April, 1970).

1028. U.S. Atomic Energy Commission. *Environmental Survey of Transportation of Radioactive Materials to and from Nuclear Power Plants.* Washington D.C.: AEC Directorate of Regulatory Standards, December 1972.

1029. ———. *Physical Protection of Classified Matter and Information,* AEC Manual Appendix and revisions-2401. Washington, D.C.: AEC Division of Security, June 26, 1969.

1030. ———. *Reactor Safety Study: An Assessment of Accident Risks in US Commercial Nuclear Power Plants.* [Rasmussen Study] August 1974, WASH-1400.
    This multivolume work includes Summary Report; Appendix I: ''Accident Definition and Use of Event Trees''; Appendix II, vol. I: ''Fault Tree Methodology''; Appendix II, volume II: ''PWR Fault Trees''; Appendix II, Volume III: ''BWR Fault Trees''; Appendix III: ''Failure Data''; Appendix IV: ''Common Failure Modes''; Appendix V: ''Quantitative Results of Accident Sequences''; Appendix VI: ''Calculation of Reactor Accident Consequences''; Appendix VII: ''Release of Radioactivity in Reactor Accidents''; Appendix VIII: ''Physical Processes in Reactor Meltdown Accidents''; Appendix IX: ''Safety Design Rationale for Nuclear Power Plants''; Appendix X: ''Design Adequacy.''

1031. ———. *Safeguards Research and Development; Proceedings of a Symposium, October 27-29, 1969.* Springfield, Va.: Clearinghouse for Federal Scientific and Technical Information, WASH, 1147, 1970.

1032. U.S. Comptroller-General. ''Improvements Needed in the Program for the Protection of Special Nuclear Material; Report to the Congress.'' Washington, D.C.: General Accounting Office, November 7, 1973.

1033. U.S. Senate. Committee on Banking, Housing and Urban Affairs. Subcommittee on International Finance. ''Exports of Nuclear Materials and Technology, Hearings.'' July 12, 15, 1974.

1034. ———. Committee on Government Operations. *Peaceful Nuclear Exports and Weapons Proliferation.* (Washington, D.C.: Government Printing Office, 1975.

1035. U.S. Statutes of General Interest to Security Officer in the Atomic Energy Program. Washington, D.C.: U.S. Atomic Energy Commission, Division of Security, January 1970.

1036. "Utility of Strategic Special Nuclear Materials for Unauthorized Purposes." *Preliminary Report of a Study for the Nuclear Regulatory Commission.* Arlington, Va.: International Research and Technology Corporation, June 19, 1975

1037. Walske, Carl. "Safeguards—The Industry's Role and Views." Paper presented at the Atomic Industrial Forum's Workshop on Plutonium, Safeguards, and the Breeder, October 1974, at Knoxville, Tennessee.

1038. Weinberg, Alvin M. "Social Institutions and Nuclear Energy." *Science*, July 7, 1972, pp. 27-34.

1039. Wick, O. J., ed. *Plutonium Handbook: A Guide to the Technology.* New York: Gordon and Breach, 1967.

1040. Wildhorn, Sorrel, and Kakalik, James S. "Thoughts on Comparing Guard Force Concepts for the Protection of Nuclear Plants and Materials." Santa Monica: RAND Corporation, November 17, 1975.

1041. Willrich, Mason, ed. *Civil Nuclear Power and International Security.* New York: Praeger, 1971. 124 pp.

Essays on the nature of the problem, the military potential of civil nuclear power, international safeguards, and the international political context.

1042. ———, ed. *International Safeguards and Nuclear Industry.* Baltimore: Johns Hopkins University Press, 1973. 307 pp.

A collection of studies for the American Society of International Law on safeguards and the possibilities of governmental and nongovernmental diversion of nuclear materials. Appendixes include material about the IAEA.

1043. ———. "Nongovernmental Nuclear Weapon Proliferation." In B. Jasani, ed., *Nuclear Proliferation Problems*, pp. 168-186. Cambridge: MIT Press for the Stockholm International Peace Research Institute, 1974.

1044. ———. "Terrorists Keep Out." *Bulletin of the Atomic Scientists* 31 (May 1975): 12-16.

Based on an address Willrich presented to the 15th Annual Conference of UPI Editors and Publishers. Defines terrorism as "threats or acts of violence planned, attempted or carried out by an individual or group with a specific political intent in mind." Notes the AEC response to the Willrich and Taylor Ford Foundation report. Argues that safeguards should aim at prevention of theft, with detection a supplementary function.

1045. Willrich, Mason, and Taylor, Theodore B. ''Nuclear Theft.'' *Survival* 16 (July-August 1974): 186-191.

An extract from chapter 6 of *Nuclear Theft: Risks and Safeguards*, it discusses reasons for theft by one person acting alone, by a criminal group, by a terrorist group, diversion of material by a political faction within a nation, nuclear black market, and the scope of the risk, reasons for same, and options open to each.

1046. ———. *Nuclear Theft: Risks and Safeguards*. Cambridge, Massachusetts: Ballinger 1974. 252 pp.

Concludes that nuclear weapons are relatively easy to make assuming the requisite materials are available; the use of nuclear energy to generate electric power will result in very large flows, in various fuel cycles, of materials that can be used to make nuclear weapons; without effective safeguards to prevent nuclear theft, the development of nuclear power will create substantial risks to security and safety. The U.S. system of safeguards is incomplete. Although regulatory actions have strengthened requirements substantially, some basic issues pertaining to physical protection measures have not yet been resolved; a system of safeguards can be developed that will keep the risks of theft of nuclear weapon materials from the nuclear power industry at very low levels. Gives much technical information about the different types of civilian nuclear power installations, projections of U.S. and foreign facilities, and detailed AEC safeguards requirements.

1047. Wohlstetter, Roberta. ''Terror on a Grand Scale.'' *Survival* 28 (May-June 1976): 98-104.

Points out that the analysis of the possible motives of nuclear-armed terrorists has been rather thin. She notes that few terrorists have engaged in mass-destruction actions by chemical and biological weapons, which may say something about their willingness to use nuclear weapons. It is also noted that terrorists do not mention their using nuclear weapons—only concerned scientists have so far made that suggestion.

1048. Woods, G. D. ''The Possible Criminal Use of Atomic or Biochemical Materials.'' *Australian and New Zealand Journal of Criminology* 8 (June 1975): 113-123.

The entire article, save one paragraph, is devoted to possible nuclear terrorism. Gaps in security are pointed out, government responses—tactical and strategic—to these threats are presented, and a new energy policy is suggested.

1049. ''Workable International Safeguards: Opinions Differ Widely on How IAEA National Systems Shape Up.'' *Nuclear Industry* 19 (November-December 1972): 52-55.

1050. Zoppo, Ciro. "The Nuclear Genie in the Mideast." *New Outlook* (February 1975). Reprint series of Santa Monica's California Seminar on Arms Control and Foreign Policy, December 1974, paper no. 47. Available upon request at no charge.

1051. ———. "Toward a U.S. Policy on Nuclear Technology Transfer to Developing Countries." Santa Monica: California Seminar on Arms Control and Foreign Policy, July 1971, paper no. 2.

For additional readings, see entries 427, 1164, 1787, and 1805.

TERRORIST AND
GUERRILLA PHILOSOPHIES

1052. Ali, Tariq, ed. *The New Revolutionaries: A Handbook of the International Radical Left.* New York: William Morrow, 1969. 319 pp.

A series of writings by major student anarchists and leftists throughout the world.

1053. Ashley, Karen; Ayers, Bill; Dohrn, Bernardine; Jacobs, John; Jones, Jeff; Long, Gerry; Machbinger, Howie; Mellen, Jim; Robbins, Terry; Rudd, Mark; and Tappis, Steve. "You Don't Need a Weatherman to Tell You Which Way the Wind Blows." In *Debate within SDS: RYM II Vs. Weatherman.* Detroit: Radical Education Project, 1970. Microfilm copy at Boston University Library Special Collections.

1054. Bakunin, Michael, and Nechayev, Sergei. *The Revolutionary Catechism.* Available in a number of collections of readings.

Outlines the philosophy of the terrorist, as told by a major theorist and a major practitioner in nineteenth-century Russia.

1056. Baumann, Michael Bommi. *How It Began* FRG, 1978.

One of the original Baader-Mainhof Gang, now apparently retired, remembers.

1057. Bayo, Alberto. *150 Questions to a Guerrilla.* Translated by R. I. Madigan and Angel de Lumus Medina. Boulder, Colo.: Panther, 1963. Also Montgomery, Ala.: Air University, n.d.

A former guerrilla during the Spanish Civil War who also maintained close ties to Castro gives many practical suggestions for the conduct of unconventional warfare.

1058. Berkman, Alexander. *Prison Memoirs of an Anarachist.* New York: Schocken, 1970.

First published in 1913, this is a major work on anarchist justifications of terrorism.

1059. Burton, Anthony M. *Urban Terrorism: Theory, Practice and Response.* New York: Free Press; London: Leo Cooper, 1975. 260 pp.

Discusses philosophical and historical roots, case studies of the Tupamaros, IRA, and separatists, and muses about the future in Europe.

1060. Caute, David. *Frantz Fanon*. New York: Viking, 1970. 116 pp.
Reviewed by Bernard S. Morris, *American Political Science Review* 70 (December 1976): 1258-1259.

1061. Cohen, Guela. *Woman of Violence: Memoirs of a Young Terrorist, 1943-1948*. Translated by Hille Halkin. New York: Holt, Rinehart, and Winston, 1966. 275 pp.
Cohen was a member of the Stern Gang, responsible for clandestine radio broadcasts. Imprisoned for a time, she escaped to continue her work. The account ends on Israel's Independence Day, 1948.

1062. Cranston, Maurice William, *The New Left: Six Critical Essays on Ché Guevara, Jean-Paul Sartre, Herbert Marcuse, Frantz Fanon, Black Power, R. D. Laing*. New York: Library Press, 1971. 208 pp.

1063. Deakin, Thomas J. "The Legacy of Carlos Marighella." *FBI Law Enforcement Bulletin* 43 (October 1974): 9-15. Also available from Washington, D.C.: National Criminal Justice Reference Service Microfiche Program, 1974.
A discussion of major urban terrorist groups, their tactics, philosophies, and organizational structures, focusing on the Weathermen, Black Panthers, and Symbionese Liberation Army.

1064. Debray, Regis. *Prison Writings*. Translated by Rosemary Sheed. New York: Random House, 1973.

1065. ———. "Revolution in the Revolution? Armed Struggle and Political Struggle in Latin America." *Monthly Review* 19 (July-August 1967): 128 pp.

1066. Derber, M. "Terrorism and the Movement." *Monthly Review* 22 (February 1971): 36ff.
A confrontation of the beliefs of the Old and New Lefts as they relate to revolution in the United States.

1067. Devlin, Bernadette. *The Price of My Soul*. New York: Knopf, 1969.

1068. Elliott, John D. "Writer-Theoreticians of Urban Guerrilla Warfare." *Short Essays in Political Science* (March 1975).

1069. Fallaci, Oriana. "A Leader of Fedayeen: 'We Want a War Like the Vietnam War': Interview with George Habash." *Life*, June 12, 1970, pp. 32-34.

1070. Fanon, Frantz. *The Wretched of the Earth.* New York: Grove Press, Harmondsworth: Penguin, 1967.

A psychological study of the effects of colonialism upon the oppressed and the problems of the revolutionary's psyche.

1071. Ferreira, J. C. *Carlos Marighella.* Havana: Tricontinental 1970.

1072. Figner, Vera. *Zapechatlenniy Trud* [Remembered toil]. 2 vol. 2d rev. ed. Moscow, 1928. Vol. 1 partly translated as *Das Attentat auf den Zaren Alexander II.* Berlin, 1926.

Memoirs of one of the early Russian terrorists.

1073. Gendzier, Irene L. *Frantz Fanon: A Critical Study.* New York: Vintage, 1974.

1074. Gerassi, John, ed. *Towards Revolution.* London: Weidenfeld and Nicolson, 1971.

Includes interviews with and articles by leading theorists and practitioners of terrorism.

1075. ———. *Venceremos: The Speeches and Writing of Che Guevara.* London: Panther, 1968. 606 pp.

1076. Giesmar, Peter. *Fanon.* New York: Dial, 1971. 214 pp.

Reviewed by Bernard S. Morris, *American Political Science Review* 70 (December 1976): 1258-1259.

1077. Goehlert, Robert. "Anarchism: A Bibliography of Articles: 1900-1975." *Political Theory* 4 (1976).

1078. Green, G. *Terrorism: Is It Revolutionary?* New York: Outlook, 1970.

The Old Left looks at the terrorism of the New Left.

1079. Gregor, A. J. "Terror and Violence in Fascist Thought." Paper given to the Conference on Moral Implications of Terrorism: Justifications and Consequences, UCLA, March 14-16, 1979.

1080. Grivas-Dighenes, George. *Guerrilla Warfare and EOKA's Struggle —A Politico-Military Study.* London: Longmans, 1964.

1082. Guevara, Ernesto Ché. *Episodes of the Revolutionary War.* New York: International Publishers, 1968, 144 pp.

1083. ———. *Guerrilla Warfare.* New York: Random House, 1969.

1084. Guillen, Abraham. *Desafio al Pentagano.* Montevideo: Ediciones Andes, 1969.

1085. Hachey, Thomas, ed. *Voices of Revolution: Rebels and Rhetoric.* New York: Dryden Press, 1973.

1086. Hacker, A. "Dostoyevsky's Disciples: Man and Sheep in Political Theory." *Journal of Politics* 18 (1955): 590-613.

1087. Halliday, F. "An Interview with Ghassan Kannafani on the PFLP and the September Attack." *New Left Review* 67 (May-July 1971): 47-57.

1088. *Handbook for Volunteers of the IRA, Notes on Guerrilla Warfare.* Issued by General Headquarters, 1956. Boulder, Colo., Paladin, n.d.

1089. Hodges, Donald C., ed. *Philosophy of the Urban Guerrilla: The Revolutionary Writings of Abraham Guillen.* New York: Morrow, 1973. 316 pp.

Guillen provided one of the first alternative philosophical models to Guevara's stress on rural attacks. In this volume, he covers such topics as revolution and materialism, interimperialist rivalries, rebellion of the third world, capitalism versus socialism, problems in revolutionary strategy, and revolution in Latin America.

1091. Hook, Sidney, "The Ideology of Violence." *Encounter* 34 (April 1970): 26-38.

Hook argues that one cannot divorce questions of violence from their political context. He believes that the politics of protest approach justifies violence in every case and drowns out the voices of moderation. He attacks other apologies for the use of violence for polarizing communities.

1054. Huberman, Leo, and Sweezy, Paul M., eds. *Regis Debray and the Latin American Revolution.* New York: Monthly Review Press, 1968, 138 pp.

1093. "Interview with Naif Hawatmeh: Definitions of a Battle." *Tricontinental* 31 (July-August 1972): pp. 94-110.

1094. James, Daniel, ed. *The Complete Bolivian Diaries of Ché Guevara and Other Captured Documents.* New York: Stein and Day, 1968. 330 pp.

1095. Kadi, Leila S., ed. *Basic Political Documents of the Armed Palestinian Resistance Movement.* Beirut: Palestine Liberation Organization Research Center, 1969.

1096. Kahane, Rabbi Meir. *Never Again! A Program for Survival.* Los Angeles: Nash, 1971. 287 pp.

Kahane explains the motivations of the Jewish Defense League.

1097. Kenworthy, Eldon. "Latin American Revolutionary Theory: Is It Back to the Paris Commune?" *Journal of International Affairs* 25 (1971): 164-170. Reprinted as FAR 15260-N.

1098. Khaled, Leila. *My People Shall Live: The Autobiography of a Revolutionary.* London: Hodder and Stoughton, 1973. New York: Bantam, 1974. 223 pp.

Memoirs of the PFLP's most famous skyjacker. The rhetoric at times becomes unintentionally humorous.

1099. Klimov, M. "Terror." In *Entsiklopediya Gosudarstva i Prava*, 3: 1173-1178 Moscow, 1927.

1100. Kravchinski, S. M. *La Russia Sotteranea.* new ed. Milan, 1896. Translated as *Underground Russia.* New York, 1883.

Memoirs of an early Russian terrorist.

1101. Kutner, Luis. "A Philosophical Perspective on Rebellion." In M. Cherif Bassiouni, ed. *International Terrorism and Political Crimes*, Springfield, Ill.: Thomas, 1975. pp. 51-66.

1102. Lawrence, T. E. *Seven Pillars of Wisdom.* Reprint ed., New York: Dell, 1962.

1103. Mallin, Jay, ed. *Terror and Urban Guerrillas: A Study of Tactics and Documents*, Coral Gables, Fla.: University of Miami Press, 1971.

An anthology of works from several of the recognized modern leaders and developers of doctrine for urban warfare and terrorism. Lenin's ideas on terrorism and its role in an overall revolution; 1965 Viet Cong Directive on VC attitude on terrorism; writings by Yasir Arafat and William Khoury; George Prosser on principles of city fighting; Carlos Marighella's *Minimanual* on the role of the urban guerrilla; "One Hundred and Fifty Questions for a Guerrilla" by Alberto Bayo Giroud, who trained Castro's guerrillas. Many operational comments, such as how to make many types of bombs, are provided.

1104. Mao Tse-Tung. *Basic Tactics.* New York: Praeger, 1966.

1105. ———. *On Guerrilla Warfare.* New York: Praeger, 1961.

1106. Miller, Bowman H., and Russell, Charles A. "The Evolution of Revolutionary Warfare: From Mao to Marighella and Meinhof." In Robert H. Kupperman and Darrell M. Trent, eds., *Terrorism*, pp. 185-199. Stanford: Hoover, 1979.

1107. Marighella, Carlos. *For the Liberation of Brazil*. Harmondsworth: Penguin, 1972.

1108. ———. "Minimanual of the Urban Guerrilla." *Survival* 13 (1971): 95ff.
Excerpts from the famous guerrilla how-to manual.

1109. ———. "Minimanual of the Urban Guerrilla." *Tricontinental (Havana)* 16 (January-February 1970): 15-56. Reprinted in Jay Mallin, ed., *Terror and Urban Guerrillas* (Coral Gables, Fla.: University of Miami Press, 1971), pp. 70-115. Also appeared as Joint Publications Research Service, JPRS 50349, April 20, 1970. Can be ordered from Clearinghouse for Federal Scientific and Technical Information, Springfield, Va. 22151.
The major urban guerrilla manual of the 1970s. Encourages assassination, stating, "Execution is the killing of a North American spy, of an agent of the dictatorship, of a police torturer, of a fascist personality in the government involved in crimes and persecution against patriots, of a stool pigeon, informer, police agent, or police provocateur."

1110. Martic, Milos. *Insurrection: Five Schools of Revolutionary Thought*. New York: Dunellen, 1975.

1111. Martin, Guy. "Fanon's Relevance to Contemporary African Political Thought." *Ufahamu* 4 (Winter 1974): 11-34.

1112. Masters, Anthony. *Bakunin: The Father of Anarchism*. New York: E. P. Dutton, 1974.

1114. Mirsky, Zinovy. "Terrorism: Who's Responsible?" *New Times* 2 (1979): 18-20.
The Leninists do not believe that they are responsible for the Western world's terrorism and argue that Lenin himself opposed terrorism. They suggest that it stems from the crisis of capitalism and that intelligence agencies are behind it.

1115. Momboisse, Raymond D. *Blueprint of Revolution: The Rebel, The Party, The Techniques of Revolt*. Springfield, Ill.: Thomas, 1970. 336 pp.
Looks at the nature and pattern of revolutions, their leaders and revolutionary parties. Recruitment, training, security, and operations are discussed.

1117. Most, Johann. *The Beast of Property.* New Haven, Conn.: International Workingman's Association Group, 1883.

1118. ———. *Science of Revolutionary War: Manual for Instruction in the Use and Preparation of Nitro-Glycerine, Dynamite, Gun-Cotton, Fulminating Mercury, Bombs, Fuses, and Poisons, etc., etc.,* New York: International Zeitung Verein, 1884.

1119. Nechayev, Sergey. "Catechism of the Revolutionist." In Michael Confino, ed., *Daughter of a Revolutionary.* London: Alcove Press, 1974.
   The classic statement of a major terrorist figure of the nineteenth century.

1120. Niezing, J. *Urban Guerrilla: Studies on the Theory, Strategy, and Practice of Political Violence in Modern Societies.* Rotterdam: Rotterdam University Press, 1974. 154 pp.
   A series of readings discussing problems facing the urban guerrilla, including mass support, recruitment, psychological approaches to terrorism, and ideology versus "actionism."

1121. Nomad, Max. *Apostles of Revolution.* Boston: Little, Brown, 1939.

1122. Parrilli, R. E. F. "Effects of Castrismo and Guevarismo on Leftist Thought in Latin America." *Revista de Derecho Puertorriqueno* 12 (1972): 69ff.

1123. Powell, W. *The Anarchist Cookbook.* New York: Lyle Stuart, 1971. 160 pp.
   The major how-to book of U.S. urban terrorists.

1124. "Prairie Fire: Publication Advocating Domestic Insurrection." *Congressional Record* 120 (1974): E5719.

1125. "Programma Ispolnitelnago Komiteta, 1879g [Program of the executive committee, 1879]." Reprinted in Sbornik Programm i Programmnikh Statey Partii, "Narodny Voli" (Geneva, 1903), pp. 3-8.
   The program of early Russian anarchists. Paragraph 2, section D defines terrorism by noting that "terroristic activity, consisting in destroying the most harmful person in the government, in defending the party against espionage, in punishing the perpetrators of the notable cases of violence and arbitrariness on the part of the government and the administration, aims to undermine the prestige of the government's power, to demonstrate steadily the possibility of struggle against the government, to arouse in this manner the revolutionary spirit of the people and their confidence in the success of the cause, and finally, to give shape and direction to the forces fit and trained to carry on the fight."

1126. Rapoport, David C. "The Politics of Atrocity." Paper presented to the Conference on International Terrorism, sponsored by the Ralph Bunche Institute on the U.N. of the Graduate School and University Center of CUNY and the State University College at Oneonta of SUNY, June 9-11, 1976.

Looking at the philosophy of anarchism, Rapoport discovers that anarchists believe: society is full of latent hostilities, brought on by the unfulfilled promise of heaven on earth; society muffles these hostilities by its social mores; society undermines its own conventions by explaining them historically rather than necessarily; the quickest method to destroy social norms is through terrorism. Problems the anarchists have in determining the nearness of their goal are pointed out, and the escape into terrorism as a personal therapeutic rather than a political tool is viewed as the result.

1127. Riessner, Will, ed. *Leon Trotsky: Against Individual Terrorism.* New York: Pathfinder, 1974.

1128. Savinkov, Boris V. *Vospominaniya Terrorista.* Kharkov, 1926. Translated by J. Shaplen as *Memoirs of a Terrorist.* 1931. Reprint ed., New York: Kraus Reprint, 1970.

1129. Segre, D. V., and Adler, J. H. "The Ecology of Terrorism." *Encounter* 40 (February 1973): 17-24. Reprinted in *Survival* (Summer 1973).

States, "There used to be a belief that some cultures are prone to terrorism and others immune, but this is now felt to be both false and pernicious." Mentions increasing numbers of hijackings per year, inability of international society to deal with guerrilla warfare outside of international law, convenience of political indulgence, and lenient punishment. Includes "A Modest Proposal" by Sebastian Haffner and "They Are among Us" from the *Economist*. Haffner suggests making hijack-proof planes, with inaccessible pilot cabins and anaesthetic gas ducts in the passenger compartments; mentions minimal critical mass needed to operate—a combination of popular support and technological ability; laments the standardization of the global village, which makes it easier for terrorism's export. "The test for civilized society is to hang on"—*Economist*; analogized football team sociology to terrorism's dynamics; terrorists' unpredictability comes from their multiple targets, limited numbers, and the variety of their cultural roots; concludes that terrorism is contagious, and no one environment breeds it.

1130. Shigenobu, Fusako. *My Love, My Revolution.* (1974)

The leader of the Japanese Red Army explains her political development.

1131. Shukairy, Ahmad. *Liberation—Not Negotiation.* Beirut: Palestine Liberation Organization Research Center, 1966.

1132. Sinclair, Andrew. *Guevara*. London: Fontant/Collins, 1970. 94 pp.

1133. Spiridovich, A. I. *Partiya Sotsialistov-Revolutsionerov i Eya Predshestvenniki 1886-1916*. 2d. ed. Petrograd, 1918. Translated by V. Lazarevski as *Histoire du Terrorisme Russe, 1886-1917*. Paris, 1930.

1134. Stanage, S. M. *Reason and Violence: Philosophical Investigations*. Totowa, N.J.: Littlefield, Adams and Company, 1974.

Stanage looks at the philosophical and historical roots of violence and the relationships between violent individuals and victims.

1135. Stern, Susan. *With the Weatherman: The Personal Journal of a Revolutionary Woman*. New York: Doubleday, 1975.

Briefly noted by Joseph McLellan, *Washington Post Book World*, September 21, 1975. Stern provides the first diary of a member of the most violent U.S. terrorist group of the early 1970s.

1136. Stirner, Max (Johann Caspar Schmidt). *Der Einzige and sein Eigentum [The ego and its own]*. Berlin, 1845. Translated by S. T. Byington. London: Fifield, 1907. New York: Boni and Liveright, n.d.

Stirner was one of the original philosphers of terrorism, basing his views on ultraindividualism, arguing that there is no such thing as natural law and that the ego is the only certainty. The state, no matter of what type, must be annihilated.

1137. "A Strategy for the Liberation of Palestine." Mimeographed. Amman: Popular Front for the Liberation of Palestine Information Department, 1969.

1139. Talmon, J. L. "The Legacy of Georges Sorel: Marxism, Violence, Fascism." *Encounter* 34 (February 1970): 47-60.

1140. "Terrorism and Marxism." *Monthly Review* 24 (November 1972): 1-6.

1141. Terrorism in Cyprus: The Captured Documents. Transcribed extracts issued by authority of the Secretary of State for the Colonies. London: H. M. Stationery Office, 1956.

1142. Trotsky, Leon. *Against Individual Terrorism*. New York: Pathfinder, 1974.

1143. ———. *The Defense of Terrorism—Terrorism and Communism, A Reply to Karl Kautsky*. London: George Allen and Unwin, 1935.

1144. ———. *Terrorism and Communism*. Ann Arbor: University of Michigan Press, 1961.

1145. Tucker, Gerald E. "Machiavelli and Fanon: Ethics, Violence and Action." *Journal of Modern African Studies* 16 (September 1978): 397-416.

1146. Vallieres, Pierre. *White Niggers of America: The Precocious Autobiography of a Quebec Terrorist*. New York: Monthly Review Press, 1971.
The author was the intellectual leader of the FLQ.

1148. Weinberg, Leonard. "Fascism and Terrorism: Theory and Practice."
Paper given to the Conference on Moral Implications of Terrorism: Justification and Consequences. March 14-16, 1979, at UCLA.

1149. Yaari, Ehud. "Al Fatah's Political Thinking." *New Outlook* 11 (November-December 1968): 20-33.
Ideology and activities of Al Fatah.

For additional readings, see entries 60, 523, 1197, 1238, 1262, 1268, 1292, 1319, 1342, 1474, 1520, 1521, 1544, 1587, 1633, 1665, 1679, 1680, 1774, 1794, 1800, 1818, 1837, 1870, 1889, 1898, 1899, 1944, 2256.

LINKS OF
TERRORIST GROUPS

1150. Alexander, Yonah. "International Network of Terrorism." Paper presented to the 18th annual convention of the International Studies Association, March 16-20, 1977, at St. Louis, Missouri.

1151. ———. "Network of International Terrorism." In Yonah Alexander, David Carlton, and Paul Wilkinson, eds., *Terrorism: Theory and Practice.* Boulder: Westview, 1978.

1152. ———. "Terrorism: Transnational Interconnections." Paper presented to the 19th annual International Studies Association Convention, February 22-25, 1978, at Washington, D.C.

1153. Alexander, Yonah, and Kilmarx, Robert A. "International Network of Terrorist Movements." In *Political Terrorism and Business: The Threat and Response*, pp. 64-105. New York: Praeger, 1979.

1154. Anable, David. "Terrorism: How a Handful of Radical States Keeps it in Business." *Christian Science Monitor*, March 15, 1977.
   One of the best articles available on state support to terrorist groups, bringing together much material scattered throughout the literature.

1155. ———. "Terrorism: Loose Net Links Diverse Groups; No Central Plot."*Christian Science Monitor*, March 14, 1977.
   The first of a two-part series on international connections of terrorist groups, mentioning the confederation centered around Carlos and the PFLP, as well as the Latin American cooperative arrangements.

1156. ———. "Terrorism: Loose Net Links Diverse Groups: No Central Plot." In John D. Elliott and Leslie K. Gibson, eds., *Contemporary Terrorism: Selected Readings*, International Association of Chiefs of Police, pp. 247-259. Gaithersburg, 1978.
   An excellent detailing of the links among terrorist groups as well as aid furnished to them by sympathetic states.

1157. Barron, John. *KGB: The Secret Work of Soviet Secret Agents.* New York: Bantam, 1974. 624 pp.

A detailed account of many KGB operations conducted since its inception. While focusing on activities of Soviet agents (a list of two thousand KGB agents is appended), material can also be found on Soviet and bloc support by funding, training, and arming of various terrorist groups, including the IRA, the MAR of Mexico, Turkish and Latin American guerrillas, and Al Fatah.

1158. Bell, J. Bowyer. "Arms Transfers, Conflict, and Violence at the Sub-State Level." Paper presented to the Conference on Implications of the Military Build-up in Non-Industrial States, International Security Studies Program, May 6-8, 1976, at Fletcher School of Law and Diplomacy, Tufts University. Not to be quoted or cited without permission. A revision of his keynote address to the Conference on Terrorism in the Contemporary World, April 26-28, 1976, at Glassboro State College.

Suggests that groups can be divided into nationalists and those stressing economic and social programs. The problems of the IRA in dealing with sophisticated weapons are discussed. Arms transfers to the Irgun and Israel are also described, as are those to the MPLA and actors in the current Lebanese conflict.

1159. "The Boss of the Terrorist Support Networks." *Le Point* (Paris), June 21, 1976, pp. 7-13.

A discussion of the Curiel apparatus, its cover, how it operates, and the groups it has supported. The author suggests that Curiel is in the pay of the Soviets, who use him to find out what the next major terrorist operations will be.

1160. Bunn, Gordon. "Kill, Carlos, Kill. Run, Carlos, Run." *Oui* (May 1976).

Claims that the Venezuelan terrorist Carlos has connections with the intelligence services of Cuba, Libya, and the Soviet Union.

1161. Burnham, James. "Entering the Terrorist Age? The Protracted Conflict" *National Review* (March 1974): 252.

Discusses the links among many terrorist groups, their sources of funding, and their activities. Does not limit himself to mentioning the PFLP-JRA link, as many others do, but also goes into Trotskyites, IRA links, mafia aid, and government terrorism.

1162. Clutterbuck, Richard. "Terrorist International" *Army Quarterly and Defense Journal* (London) (January 1974): 154-159.

Mentions linkages among major groups; suggests that small groups that receive huge ransoms will not be able to spend them quickly and will thus be able to finance other groups; gives a few other interesting, possibly testable propositions.

1163. Copeland, Miles. *Beyond Cloak and Dagger: Inside the CIA.* New York: Pinnacle Books, 1975.

Discusses the problems that intelligence organizations face in combating international terrorists. Among these are the fact that there is no single organization that is to be penetrated, they are not merely agents of foreign powers, and ordinary means of prevention cannot be readily applied.

1164. Demaris, Ovid. *Brothers in Blood: The International Terrorist Network.* New York: Scribner's, 1977. 441 pp.

A study of the Carlos group, Palestinian terrorists, Baader-Meinhof Gang, IRA, and the possibilities of nuclear terrorism. Demaris has brought together a wealth of historical material on Middle Eastern politics, showing its relevance to contemporary political violence.

1165. Dobson, Christopher, and Payne, Ronald. *The Carlos Complex: A Study in Terror.* New York: G. P. Putnam's Sons, 1977. 254 pp.

1166. Eisenberg, Denis, and Landau, Eli. *Carlos: Terror International.* London: Corgi, 1976. 285 pp.

A sensationalistic treatment of Carlos's exploits.

1167. Fisk, Robert. "The Role Libya Sees for Itself in the Irish Struggle." *London Times*, April 21, 1975, p. 14.

Points out Qaddafi's ties with Republicans and Loyalists.

1168. Francis, Samuel T. "The Terrorist International and Western Europe." Washington, D.C.: Heritage Foundation, Backgrounder No. 47, December 21, 1977. Updated April 18, 1978.

The author brings a conservative approach to the question but nonetheless notes the existence of right-wing terrorism. Much time is spent on the links between the Western European and Palestinian terrorist groups. Francis also devotes attention to aid given by governments, especially from the Soviet bloc, to terrorists.

1169. "Guerrillas of Uruguay, Chile, Bolivia, and Argentina Link Up." *Washington Post*, February 15, 1974.

Notes the announcement of the creation of the Revolutionary Coordinating Junta, created by the Tupamaros, Leftist Revolutionary Movement of Chile, People's Revolutionary Army of Argentina, and Bolivia's National Liberation Army.

1170. Haggman, Bertil. ''10.000 veluddannede terrorister.'' [Ten thousand well-trained terrorists] *Jyllands-Posten, Arhus*, December 11, 1977.

The first of a three-part series on the links of transnational terrorist groups. The author points to connections among Latin groups, Palestinians, and Euroterrorists and notes the aid given them by sympathetic states. An abridged version of this series appeared in the January 1978 edition of *Counterforce*.

1171. ———. ''Terrorister slar til i fae-lesskab.'' [Terrorists strike in fellowship] *Jyllands-Posten, Arhus*, December 18, 1977.

A detailed accounting of the specific instances of links among terrorist groups, from the provision of funds, safe haven, arms, and training, to joint operations.

1172. Hertel, Ingo. ''Guerrillas formieren sich in Westeuropa: Internationale Koordinierung.'' *Frankfurter Allgemeine Zeitung*, September 5, 1975, p. 3.

1173. Holley, Charles. ''Why Libya Exports Chaos: The Anatomy of an International Terror Network.'' *Atlas World Press Review* 15 (November 1976): 6-8.

1174. Kaufmann, Jacques. *L'internationale terroriste*. Paris: Plon, 1977. 321 pp.

1175. Kwitny, Jonathan. ''Thriving Black Market Puts Military Weapons into Amateurs' Hands.'' *Wall Street Journal*, January 11, 1977, p. 1.

The last article in a series on terrorism, focusing on the transfer of rifles, machine guns, and portable rockets to revolutionaries.

1176. Landau, Eli, and Eisenberg, Dennis. *Carlos: terroriste international* Translated by Eva Adrien de Theas. Montreal: Stanke, 1976. 288 pp.

1177. "Latin America's Terrorist International." *Economist Foreign Report*, March 23, 1977. pp. 1-4.

An account of the Revolutionary Coordinating Junta, Latin links with non-Latin terrorist groups, and Cuban support to guerrillas.

1178. Ledeen, Michael. ''The Doomsday Army.'' *Playboy* 24 (February 1977): 36-37.

In addition to the exploits of Carlos, the Rome correspondent for the *New Republic* discusses Qaddafi's funding of Italian groups.

1179. Lewis, Flora. ''Western Europe's Militant Minorities Find Common Cause in Secret Meeting.'' *New York Times*, July 8, 1975, p. 4.

Notes a secret meeting held in Trieste in 1974 of minority groups in Europe who point to their domination of a particular region of land but are effectively powerless in their nation. They argue for a new type of political unit, differing from EEC or nation-states. ETA is singled out for its operational code and ties to other groups. The meeting included Basques, Croats, Bretons, Irish, Catalans, Galicians, Welsh, Scots, Corsicans, Sardinians, Flemings, Friesians, Piedmontese, and Occitanians.

1180. Mosbey, John C. *The Prison-Terrorist Link*. Cerberus, Inc., 1977. 33 pp.

1181. Okumura, Satoshi. ''Clandestine Organization of International Terrorism Exposed: Unmasking of Curiel Apparat Revealed Another Being in the Shadow.'' *Keizei Orai* (Tokyo) (December 1978).

Beginning with an account of the discovery of Japanese Red Army links to the Curiel organization, Okumura traces Curiel's funding to the KGB, which he believes is attempting to use the Apparat as a method of keeping tabs on terrorists.

1182. Pons, Philippe. ''The Paris Connection.'' *Le Monde*, September 15-16, 1974, p. 15.

On Japanese Red Army activity; mentions some actions, notes strict discipline of the group, names certain leaders, discusses the conduct of their operations.

1183. Revesz, Laslo. *Christian Peace Conference: Church Funds for Terrorists*. London: Institute for the Study of Conflict, 1978.

The study refers to the allocation by the World Council of Churches of 45,000 pounds sterling to the Patriotic Front guerrillas accused of the June 1978 massacre of British missionaries. The author believes that the Soviet-sponsored CPC regards itself as the vanguard for the World Council.

1184. Russell, Charles A. ''Transnational Terrorism,'' *Air University Review* 27 (January-February 1976): 26-35.

Notes recent actions of terrorists, their growing international links, how they came together, what agreements are involved, how other groups are tangentially related.

1185. Smith, Colin. *Carlos: Portrait of a Terrorist*. London: Sphere Books, 1976. 304 pp.

A useful study of Carlos's background and major operations.

1186. Sterling, Claire. "The Terrorist Network." *Atlantic* 242 (November 1978): 37-47.

Centers on cooperation among Western European terrorists, primarily the Red Brigades and Baader-Meinhof Gang. Mention is also made of contacts with Palestinian and Latin American organizations.

1187. Tinnin, David. "Terror, Inc." *Playboy* 24 (May 1977): 152-182.

Tinnin concentrates on the network that supposedly revolves around Carlos and the PFLP, citing some of their major exploits. Among the interesting items is that there are several Carlos's, that the Israelis had managed to infiltrate agents into Entebbe Airport, and that Abu Daoud was only the logistics coordinator for the Olympics raid. Tinnin argues that the KGB is quietly in the background, promoting many of these attacks on the West.

1188. Tobon, Nydia. *Carlos: Terrorist or Guerrilla?* Barcelona: Ediciones Grijalbo, 1978. 217 pp.

1189. "Trading in Terror, Carlos Becomes the World's Most Wanted Criminal." *People Weekly*, October 11, 1976, pp. 24-27.

A superficial treatment of Carlos's exploits, reporting that he has funneled "arms and logistical support to terrorists in Northern Ireland, Japan, and Latin America, as well as to Basques, Bretons and Corsicans." The article also notes the $1.5 million paid him by Colonel Qaddafi for the OPEC raid.

1190. "U.S.S.R: 'Greatest Subversive Center in the World.' " *Human Events*, May 31, 1975, p. 5.

Testimony of Brian Crozier on May 14, 1975, to Senate Internal Security subcommittee. Similar to his introduction to 1973-1974 edition of the *Annual of Power and Conflict.*

1191. U.S. Senate. Judiciary Committee. "Terrorist Activity: Interlock between Communism and Terrorism, Part 9." Hearings before the Subcommittee on Internal Security. 94th Cong., 2d sess., 1976, May 7, 1976.

1192. Weinraub, Bernard. "Libyans Arm and Train World Terrorists." *New York Times*, July 16, 1976, pp. A1, A6.

Presents material on Libyan aid in the form of weapons, forged passports, cash, documents, and contacts for numerous groups, including the IRA, Carlos's groups, Black September, ELF, and groups in Yemen, Somalia, Syria, Tunisia, Morocco, Panama, and the Philippines.

1193. Wolf, John B. "The International Terrorist Coalition and Its Impact upon the Multinational Corporation." Paper presented to the 8th annual conference of the International Association of Airport and Seaport Police, May 24, 1977, at Boston.

1194. Yonay, Ehud. "The PLO Underground in California." *New West*, February 26, 1979, pp. 22-31.
Offers an impressive detailing of Palestinian activities in the United States, paying particular attention to funding of overseas terrorist groups. An annex lists Palestinian attacks on American targets and suggests that Sirhan Sirhan may have been a Fatah agent.

For additional readings, see entries, 1294, 1671, 1778, 1787, 1968, and 1997.

TERRORISM BY GEOGRAPHIC AREA

NORTH AMERICA

Canada

1195. Beaton, L. "Crisis in Quebec." *Round Table* 241 (January 1971): 147-152.

1196. Beauregard. "Who Inspired the FLQ Terrorists?" *Atlas* 19 (December 1970): 24.

1197. Bergeron, Leandre. *The History of Quebec: A Patriot's Handbook.* Translated by Baila Marcus. Toronto: New Canada Press, 1971.
    An FLQ analysis of the situation in Canada.

1198. Breton, Raymond. "The Socio-Political Dynamics of the October Events." In Dale C. Thomson, ed., *Quebec Society and Politics: Views from the Inside*, pp. 213-238. Toronto: McClelland and Stewart, 1973.

1199. Cook, Ramsey. "The French-Canadian Question." *Political Quarterly* 36 (January-March 1965).

1200. Daniels, D. *Quebec, Canada and the October Crisis.* Montreal: Black Rose, 1973.

1201. Desbarats, Peter. "In Our Weeks of Anguish: A Journal of October." *Saturday Night* 85 (Canada) (December 1970): 19-25.
    The activities of the FLQ during 1970, with special focus on the October kidnappings.

1202. "Fertile Soil for Terror." *Canada and World* 36 (1970): 16-19.

1203. Frank, Joseph and Kelly, Micheal. "Etude préliminaire sur la violence collective en Ontario et au Québec, 1963-1973." *Canadian Journal of Political Science* 10 (March 1977): 145-157.

Surprisingly the authors find that there were more acts of political violence in Ontario than in Quebec, often believed to be the center of Canadian violence.

1204. Godin, Gerald. "Notes on Terrorism." *Canadian Forum* (November 1971): 26-27.

1205. Green, L. C. "Terrorism: The Canadian Perspective." In Yonah Alexander, ed., *International Terrorism: National, Regional, and Global Perspectives*, pp. 3-29, New York: AMS Press, 1976.

Green takes an international lawyer's perspective, noting the positions Canada has taken in various international forums, as well as its attempts to work out bilateral agreements to halt specific types of terrorist actions.

1206. Grosman, Brian A. "Dissent and Disorder in Canada." In *Report of the Task Force on Disorders and Terrorism*, pp. 479-496. Washington, D.C.: National Advisory Committee on Criminal Justice Standards and Goals, December 1976.

1207. Hagy, J. W. "Quebec Separatists: The First Twelve Years." In N. Sheffe, ed., *Issues for the Seventies*. Toronto: McGraw-Hill, 1971.

1208. Holt, Simma. *Terror in the Name of God: The Story of the Sons of Freedom Doukhobors*. Toronto: McClelland and Stewart, 1964.

An attack on the actions of an immigrant religious group in Canada, which has carried out antiauthority operations.

1209. Lacoursiere, Jacques. *Alarme citoyens*. Ottawa: Les Editions la Presse, Guy Lalumiere & Associes, 1972. 438 pp.

A study of the FLQ, with particular attention being paid to the Cross-Laporte kidnap case. Numerous photographs are included.

1210. Latouche, Daniel. "Violence, politique et crise dans la Société Québecoise." In Laurier Lapierre et al., eds., *Essays on the Left: Essays in Honour of T. C. Douglas*, pp. 175-199. Toronto: McClelland and Stewart, 1971.

1211. Laurendeau, Marc. *Les Québeçois violents: Un ouvrage sur les causes et la rentabilité de la violence d'inspiration politique au Québec.* Montreal: Les Editions du Boreal Express, 1974.

1212. Masse, Gilles. "L'évolution du terrorisme au Québec, 1963-1972." Unpublished manuscript. Montreal.

1213. McKinsey, Lauren S. "Dimensions of National Political Integration and Disintegration: The Case of Quebec Separatism, 1960-1975." *Comparative Political Studies* 9 (October 1976): 335-360.

1214. Milner, H. "The Implication of the Vallieres Declaration." *Our Generation* 8 (1972): 27-35.

1215. Milner, Sheilagh Modgins, and Miller, Henry. *The Decolonization of Quebec: An Analysis of Left Wing Nationalism.* Toronto: McClelland and Stewart, 1973.

1216. Mitchell, Thomas H. "Violence and Politics in Canada." Paper presented to the Fifth Biennial Meeting of the Association for Canadian Studies in the United States, September 30, 1979 at Meridian House, Washington, D.C.

Argues that Canada has not been the mythical peaceful kingdom and has had collective political violence comparable to the levels reached in many other industrialized democracies. Mitchell presents empirical evidence to illustrate this point and exhaustively reviews the political science literature on political violence in Canada, presenting an extensive bibliography.

1217. Moore, Brian. *The Revolution Script.* New York: Holt, Rinehart & Winton, 1971. 261 pp.

Account of James Cross's kidnapping by the Quebec Liberation Front, based upon interviews and public sources. Designed to be read as a novel, with much of the interpersonal relationships of the terrorists fictionalized. Nonetheless, many data on the kidnappings of Cross and Laporte are presented.

1218. Morf, Gustave. *Terror in Quebec: Case Studies of the FLQ.* Toronto: Clarke, Irvin and Company, 1970. 177 pp.

History of the FLQ since 1963. Biographies of its leaders and personality sketch of Pierre Vallieres. The author, a Canadian psychologist, conducted hundreds of interviews with incarcerated members of the FLQ.

1219. Pelletier, Gerard. *La crise d'Octobre.* Montreal: Editions du Jour, 1971.

A review of the Cross-LaPorte kidnappings in Canada in 1970.

1220. Radwanski, George, and Windeyer, Kendal. *No Mandate But Terror.* Richmond Hill, Ontario: Simon and Schuster, 1970.

1221. Redlick, Amy Sands. "Transnational Factors Affecting Quebec Separatist Terrorism." Paper presented to the 17th annual convention of the International Studies Association, February 25-29, 1976, at Toronto, Canada.

ISA abstract states: "Although the underlying reasons for the mid-1960s violence in Quebec were unique to Quebec—centuries of deprivation being quickly overturned by the processes of industrialization, urbanization, and secularization—some precipitating force may have come from the international flows of concepts, information, and tactics, as well as from other transnational groups. This analysis will describe many of these external, foreign factors which may have influenced the Quebec separatists/terrorists of the 1960's. Some specific trends concerning the role of transnational flows of ideas, concepts, and information in an unstable situation should emerge and help to mold some general hypotheses dealing with this type of phenomenon."

1222. ———. *"The Impact of Transnational Interactions on Separatism: A Case Study of the Quebec Separatist Movement."* Ph.D. dissertation, Tufts University, in preparation.

1223. Regush, Nicholas M. *Pierre Vallieres: The Revolutionary Process in Quebec.* Vancouver: Fitzhenry and Whiteside, 1973. New York: Dial Press, 1973.

1224. Reid, Malcolm. *The Shouting Signpainters: Literary and Political Account of Quebec Revolutionary Nationalism.* Toronto: McClelland and Stewart, 1972.

1225. Reilly, Wayne G. "Canada, Quebec and Theories of Internal War." *American Review of Canadian Studies* 3 (Autumn 1973): 67-75.

1226. Rioux, Marcel. *Quebec in Question.* Translated by James Boake. Toronto: James Lewis and Samuel, 1971.

1227. Rotstein, Abraham, ed. *Power Corrupted: The October Crisis and the Repression of Quebec.* Toronto: New Press, 1971.

1228. Ryan, Claude. *Le devoir et la crise d'Octobre 70.* Ottawa: Lemeac, 1971.

1229. ———. "The French-Canadian Dilemma." *Foreign Affairs* (April 1965).

1230. Savoie, Claude. *La veritable histoire du FLQ.* Montreal: Les Editions du Jour, 1963.

1231. Saywell, John. *Quebec 70: A Documentary Narrative.* Toronto: University of Toronto Press, 1971. 152 pp.

Notes the political and social underpinnings of the 1970 incidents in Quebec. Discusses the kidnappings of Laporte and Cross and subsequent events. Includes interviews with government members and FLQ terrorists, the FLQ manifesto, and various other FLQ publications.

1232. Singer, Howard L. "Institutionalization of Protest: The Quebec Separatist Movement." Department of Political Science, Ph.D. dissertation, New York University, 1976.

1233. Smith, Denis. *Bleeding Hearts . . .Bleeding Country: Canada and the Quebec Crisis.* Edmonton, Alberta: M. G. Hurtig, 1971.

1234. Stewart, James. *The FLQ: Years of Terrorism.* Richmond Hill: 1970.
A general account of FLQ campaigns, compiled by the *Montreal Star.*

1235. Stewart, J. and Reid, R. R. *The FLQ: Seven Years of Terrorism.* Markham: Simon and Schuster, 1970.

1236. Torrance, Judy. "The Response of Canadian Governments to Violence." *Canadian Journal of Political Science* 10 (September 1977): 473-496.

1237. Trait, Jean-Claude. *FLQ 70: Offensive D'autonne.* Ottawa: Les Editions de l'Homme Ltee, 1970. 230 pp.
A day-by-day, sometimes minute-by-minute, account of the kidnap cases of Cross and Laporte, with photographs of the principals and texts of the FLQ communiqué issued during negotiations.

1238. Vallieres, Pierre. *The Assassination of Pierre Laporte.* Translated by Ralph Wells. Toronto: James Lorimer, 1977. 192 pp.
A leader of the FLQ questions the response of the police during and after the incident.

1239. White, C. A. "Terrorism: Idealism or Sickness." *Canada and World* 39 (1974): 14-15.

1240. Woodcock, George. "Anarchism and Violence." In Abraham Rothstein, ed., *Power Corrupted: The October Crisis and the Repression of Quebec.* Toronto: Free Press, 1971.

1241. Woodcock, George, and Avakunovec, J. *The Doukhobors.* Toronto: Oxford, University Press, 1968.

For additional readings, see entries, 421, 422, 768, 1146, 1276, 2112, 2988, and 2994.

United States

1242. Adelson, Alan. *SDS: A Profile.* New York: Charles Scribner's Sons, 1972.

1243. Atthowe, Patricia. "Terrorism: The FALN's Undeclared War." *Defense and Foreign Affairs Digest* (1978): 48-45.

After briefly reviewing FALN attacks in the United States, Atthowe argues that FALN "acts as an agent provocateur for the Soviet-Cuban cabal." She also believes that the U.S. government's response to terrorism has been crippled by congressional restrictions.

1244. Baker, Marilyn. "U.S. Terrorist Groups and Revolutionary Activities." Address to the Wackenhut Corporation's seminar on terrorism, November 22, 1974.

1245. Belcher, Jerry, and West, Don. *Patty/Tania.* New York, 1976. 347 pp.

1246. Bennett, R. K. "Brotherhood of the Bomb." *Reader's Digest* (December 1970): 102ff.

1247. ———. "Terrorists among Us: An Intelligence Report." *Reader's Digest* (October 1971): 115ff.

1248. Boulton, David. *The Making of Tania Hearst.* London: New English Library, 1975.

1249. Brissenden, P. F. *The IWW: A Study of American Syndicalism.* New York: Columbia, 1920.

1250. Broehl, Jr., Wayne G. *The Molly Maguires.* Cambridge: Harvard University Press, 1964.

1251. Brown, Richard Maxwell. *Strain of Violence: Historical Studies of American Violence and Vigilantism.* New York: Oxford University Press, 1975. 397 pp.

1252. Bugliosi, Vincent with Gentry Curt. *Helter Skelter: The True Story of the Manson Murders.* New York: W. W. Norton, 1974.

1253. Burrows, William E. *Vigilante.* New York: Harcourt Brace Jovanovich, 1976.

1254. Castillo, Pedro. ''Ethnic and Racial Minorities and the Role of Violence in the Civil Rights Movement in the United States.'' Paper presented to the Conference on Terrorism in the Contemporary World, April 26-28, 1976, at Glassboro State College.

1255. Chalmers, David M. *Hooded Americanism.* Garden City: Doubleday, 1965.

1256. Daniels, Stuart. ''The Weathermen.'' *Government and Opposition* 9 (Autumn 1974): 430-459.

1257. *Domestic Terrorist Matters.* Washington, D.C.: FBI, 1974.

1258. Francis, Samuel T. and Poole, William T. ''Terrorism in America: The Developing Internal Security Crisis.'' 59 *Backgrounder* (Washington, D.C.: Heritage Foundation, June 2, 1978), 23 pp.

The authors note the major domestic U.S. groups, citing ties with international terrorists and foreign governments. Difficulties that U.S. federal agencies and local law enforcement officials have had in combating terrorism, especially regarding congressionally-imposed restraints, are discussed.

1259. Gilmore, William J. ''Psycho-History and Violence: The Manson Family.'' Paper presented to the Conference on Terrorism in the Contemporary World, April 26-28, 1976, at Glassboro State College.

Gilmore interviewed many individuals involved in the Manson attacks, including some of the participants, and presents demographic characteristics of the group's members, exploding many myths.

1260. Gleason, John M. ''A Poisson Model of Incidents of International Terrorism in the U.S.'' Paper presented to the joint national meeting of the Operations Research Society of America and the Institute of Management Sciences, May 1-3, 1978, at New York City.

Looking at international terrorist incidents in the United States from 1968 through 1974, Gleason establishes that the Poisson is a good model to predict their occurrence.

1261. Greisman, Harvey C. ''Terrorism in the U.S.: A Social Impact Projection.'' Paper presented at the annual meeting of the American Sociological Association, August-September 1976, at New York City. Reprinted as FAR 26275-N

1262. Heath, G. Louis. *Vandals in the Bomb Factory: A History and Literature of the Students for a Democratic Society.* Metuchen, N.J.: Scarecrow, 1976.

1263. Hoge, Thomas A. "Are Terrorists Stalking America's Bicentennial?" *American Legion Magazine* (March 1976): 18-21, 42-43.

Despite its title, the article focuses on the activities of the major international groups.

1264. Homer, Frederic D. "Terror in the United States: Three Perspectives." In Michael Stohl, ed., *The Politics of Terrorism*, pp. 373-405. New York: Dekker, 1979.

Homer looks at interpretations of the United States as a violent, pluralistic, and democratic society and explores the range of possible general responses to terrorism, outlining their benefits and drawbacks.

1265. Hopkins, Charles W. "The Deradicalization of the Black Panther Party: 1967-1973." Ph.D. dissertation, University of North Carolina, 1978.

1266. Horn, Stanley F. *Invisible Empire: The Story of the Ku Klux Klan, 1866-1871.* Boston: Houghton Mifflin, 1939.

1267. Howe, Irving. "Political Terrorism: Hysteria on the Left." *New York Times Magazine*, April 12, 1970, p. 25.

1268. "Interview: Meir Kahane: A Candid Conversation with the Militant Leader of the Jewish Defense League." *Playboy* 19 (October 1977): 69-78.

The introduction lists many acts of JDL harassment. Kahane explains JDL motivations.

1269. Jacobs, Harold, ed. *Weatherman*. Berkeley: Ramparts, 1970.

1270. Johnpoll, Bernard K. "Perspectives on Political Terrorism in the United States." In Yonah Alexander, ed., *International Terrorism: National, Regional, and Global Perspectives*, pp. 30-45. New York: AMS, 1976.

Discusses the history of U.S. labor terrorism, the Molly Maguires, the Klans, Johann Most's philosophies, the Weathermen, and the SLA. He concludes that such movements have never accomplished the stated aims of their founders, are generally counterproductive, serving the interests of the ruling elite, and are not revolutionary instruments.

1271. ———. "Terrorism and the Mass Media in the U.S." Paper presented to the Conference on International Terrorism, sponsored by the Ralph Bunche Institute, June 9-11, 1976, at New York City. Published in Seymour Maxwell Finger and Yonah Alexander, eds., *Terrorism: Interdisciplinary Perspectives*, pp. 157-165. (New York: John Day, 1977).

Notes the criteria used by mass media editors in determining inclusion of items: news is timely, a unique event, an adventurous event, has entertainment value, and affects the lives of its readers. Johnpoll lionizes the role of the press, effectively arguing that the press has no responsibility to educate the public but rather to serve the market. The press is seen as a business establishment and must react to public demand rather than higher goals. Terrorism is seen as a juridical question, and ''the press has no effect on terrorist behavior . . . There is nothing the mass media can or should do about violence.''

1272. ———. ''Terrorism and the Media.'' Paper presented to the 18th annual convention of the International Studies Association, March 16-20, 1977, at St. Louis, Missouri.

1273. Jones, J. H. *The Minutemen*. Garden City: Doubleday, 1968.

1274. Lerner, M. ''Anarchism and the American Counter-Culture.'' *Government and Opposition* 5 (1970): 430-455.

1275. Lewis, Gordon K. *Notes on the Puerto Rican Revolution: An Essay on American Dominance and Caribbean Resistance*. New York: Monthly Review, 1975. 288 pp.
     Reviewed by William Kennedy, ''Rumblings of Revolution,'' *Washington Post Book World*, August 24, 1975.

1276. Lipset, S. ''On the Politics of Conscience and Extreme Commitment.'' *Encounter* (August 1971): 66ff.
     Compares the activities of the Canadian and U.S. terrorist groups.

1277. Lutton, Wayne C. ''Terrorist Underground in America.'' *Journal of the American Christian College* (July-August 1976).

1278. Maurer, Marvin. ''The Ku Klux Klan and the National Liberation Front: Terrorism Applied to Achieve Diverse Goals.'' In Marius Livingston et al., eds., *International Terrorism in the Contemporary World*, pp. 131-152, Westport, Conn.: Greenwood Press, 1978.

1279. McKinley, James. ''Inside Sirhan.'' *Playboy* 25 (April 1978): 96-98, 206-214.
     McKinley interviewed the cellmate of Sirhan Sirhan, the assassin of Senator Robert F. Kennedy. Sirhan had attempted to recruit the former criminal as an aide in stealing nuclear materials for Libyan leader Qaddafi.

1280. McLellan, Vin, and Avery, Paul. *The Voices of Guns: The Definitive and Dramatic Story of the Twenty-two Month Career of the SLA.* New York: G. P. Putnam's, 1976. 544 pp.

A history of the Symbionese Liberation Army, from its birth in the California prisons to the November 6, 1973, murder of Dr. Marcus Foster, to the kidnapping, conversion, and trial of Patty Hearst. The authors argue that Hearst was a victim of ''coercive persuasion,'' MIT Professor Edgar Schein's term for brainwashing within a pressure group. Reviewed by Ross Thomas, ''Tania and Her Friends,'' *Washington Post Book World*, February 6, 1977, p. F-7.

1281. Mullaney, Patrick, ''The Kiritsis Case.'' Address to the conference on Terrorism and the Media, sponsored by the Ralph Bunche Institute and the Institute for Studies in International Terrorism, November 17, 1977, at New York City.

1282. O'Brien, Paul L. ''Fledgling Revolt: USA.'' Carlisle Barracks, Penn.: Army War College, January 3, 1972.

O'Brien looks at the activities and international connections of the Students for a Democratic Society and other antiwar groups of the late 1960s. He notes their antimilitary activities and their effects on the U.S. military.

1283. ''The Official Transcript of Sirhan's Testimony.'' In *The Lost Significance of Sirhan's Case.* Los Angeles: Organization of Arab Students, 1969.

1284. Oppenheimer, Martin. *Urban Guerrilla.* Penguin: Harmondsworth, Middlesex, England, 1969. New York: Quadrangle. 189 pp.

A radical American sociologist looks at the prospects for various types of revolutions in the U.S. Scenarios are projected for three types of black uprisings, and comparisons are made with historical parallels. Problems inherent in strategies of violence are outlined, and nonviolent alternatives are advocated.

1285. Overstreet, Harry and Bonaro. *The Strange Tactics of Extremism.* New York: Norton, 1964. 315 pp.

Reviewed by Thomas M. Kuchel, in *American Political Science Review* 59 (June 1965): 454-456.

1286. Payne, Les, and Findley, Tim. *The Life and Death of the SLA.* New York: Ballantine, 1976. 369 pp.

1287. Perasall, R. B., ed. *Symbionese Liberation Army—Documents and Communications.* Amsterdam: Rodopi N. V. Keizergracht, 1974.

1288. Popov, Milorad I. "The American Extreme Left: A Decade of Conflict." *Conflict Studies* 29 (December 1972): 19 pp.

1289. Powers, Thomas. *Diana: The Making of a Terrorist.* Boston: Houghton-Mifflin, 1971. 225 pp.
The life of the Weatherwoman who died in an accidental explosion in a terrorist bomb factory.

1290. ———. *The War at Home.* New York: Grossman, 1973. 348 pp.
A history of the protest against the U.S. involvement in the Vietnam War.

1291. Randel, William Pierce. *The Ku Klux Klan: A Century of Infamy.* Philadelphia: Chilton, 1965.

1292. Raskin, Jonah, ed. *The Weather Eye: Communiques from the Weather Underground, May 1970-May 1974.* New York, 1974. 124 pp.

1293. Reisz, John B. "A Theory on Terrorist Activity in America and Its Effect on the United States Army." Master's thesis, U.S. Army Command and General Staff College, 1979.

1294. Rose, Gregory F. "The Terrorists Are Coming." *Politics Today* 5 (July-August 1978): 22-54.
Argues that U.S. terrorists have established close links with foreign terrorists and intelligence organizations. Rose believes that U.S. and foreign terrorists are soon going to engage in a campaign of violence on U.S. soil and that domestic law enforcement and intelligence agencies are ill equipped to cope with such a situation.

1295. Rose, Thomas, ed. *Violence in America: A Historical and Contemporary Reader.* New York: Vintage, 1970. 381 pp.

1296. Rosenbaum, H. Jon, comp. *Vigilante Politics.* Philadelphia: University of Pennsylvania Press, 1976.
The work is devoted to the creation of a theory of "establishment violence." and focuses on incidents in U.S. history.

1297. Sale, Kirkpatrick. *SDS.* New York: Random House, 1973.

1298. Sanders, Ed. *The Family: The Story of Charles Manson's Dune Buggy Attack Battalion.* New York: E. P. Dutton, 1971. 383 pp.

1299. Schang, Gabrielle, and Rosenbaum, Ron. ''Now the Urban Guerrillas Have a Real Problem; They're Trying to Make It in the Magazine Business.'' *More* 6 (November 1976): 16-21.
    Problems of the Weathermen in publishing *Osawatomie*.

1300. Search and Destroy: A Report by the Commission of Inquiry into the Black Panthers. New York: Metropolitan Applied Research Center, 1973.
    The commission looked into a police raid that the publishers characterized as ''a harrowing indictment of officially endorsed lawlessness, racism, and violence.''

1301. Sederberg, Peter C. ''The Phenomenology of Vigilantism in Contemporary America: An Interpretation.'' *Terrorism* (1978): 287-305.
    Sederberg creates a 2 × 2 table of vigilantism, noting the axes of official-private participation and spontaneous-organized orchestration. He finds that ''the main objective . . .is the preservation of social stability in the face of innovative behavior.'' He also gives a glimpse of the vigilante personality.

1302. ''The Symbionese Liberation Army in Los Angeles: A Report by the Police Commission to Mayor Tom Bradley.'' Los Angeles Police Department, 1974.

1303. ''Terrorism in California.'' *Criminal Justice Digest* 2 (July 1974): 1-8.
    Groups mentioned include the United Prisoners Union, the Polar Bear Party, the Black Guerrilla Family, Black Liberation Army, Republic of New Africa, Weatherman, Black September and the Manson clan.

1304. Thayer, George. *The Farther Shores of Politics: The American Political Fringe Today.* New York: Simon and Schuster, 1967. 616 pp.
    A discussion of the fringe groups of the United States as of 1967. This is the most comprehensive survey of violent and nonviolent extremists and is based upon hundreds of interviews of members, police, and those who study these groups.

1305. Tierney, John J., Jr. ''Terror at Home: The American Revolution and Irregular Warfare.'' *Stanford Journal of International Studies* 12 (Spring 1977): 1-20.

1306. Trelease, Allen W. *White Terror: The Ku Klux Klan Conspiracy and Southern Reconstruction.* New York: Harper and Row, 1971. 557 pp.

1307. U.S. House of Representatives. Committee on Internal Security. ''The Symbionese Liberation Army: A Study.'' 93d Cong., 2d sess., February 18, 1974.

1308. U.S. Senate. Committee on the Judiciary. Subcommittee to Investigate the Administration of the Internal Security Act and Other Internal Security Laws. ''Hearings: State Department Bombing by Weatherman Underground.'' 94th Cong., 1st sess., January 31, 1975.

1309. ———. Committee of the Judiciary. Subcommittee to Investigate the Administration of the Internal Security Act and Other Internal Security Laws. ''Terroristic Activity: The Cuban Connection in Puerto Rico: Castro's Hand in Puerto Rican and U.S. Terrorism.'' 94th Cong., 1st sess., July 30, 1975, pt. 6.

1310. ———. Committee on the Judiciary. Subcommittee to Investigate the Administration of the Internal Security Act and Other Internal Security Laws. ''Terroristic Activity: Inside the Weatherman Movement, Hearings.'' 93d Cong., 2d sess., October 18, 1974, pt. 2.

1311. ———. Committee on the Judiciary. Subcommittee to Investigate the Administration of the Internal Security Act and Other Internal Security Laws. ''Terroristic Activity: Terrorism in the Miami Area.'' 94th Cong., 2d sess., May 6, 1976, pt. 8, pp. 607-662.
   Testimony of Lieutenant Thomas Lyons and Detective Raul J. Diaz, of the Dade County Public Safety Department, on Cuban terrorism.

1312. ———. Committee on the Judiciary. Subcommittee to Investigate the Administration of the Internal Security Act and Other Internal Security Laws. ''Trotskyite Terrorist International: Hearings.'' July 24, 1975.
   Documents and testimony relating to the Socialist Workers party and related groups.

1313. ———. Committee on the Judiciary. Subcommittee to Investigate the Administration of the Internal Security Act and Other Internal Security Laws. ''The Weather Underground: Report.'' 94th Cong, 1st sess., January 1975.

1314. Vestermark, Seymour D. ''Extremist Groups in the U.S.'' Gaithersburg: International Association of Chiefs of Police, 1975.

1315. Wolf, John B. "Domestic Terrorist Movements." In Yonah Alexander and Robert A. Kilmarx, eds., *Political Terrorism and Business: The Threat and Response*, pp. 18-63. New York: Praeger, 1979.

1316. ———. "Terrorism and Terrorist Groups in the US." Paper presented to the International Association of Bomb Technicians and Investigators, October 3, 1977, at Hyannis, Massachusetts.

For additional readings, see entries 273, 420, 421, 567, 731, 1053, 1063, 1096, 1123-1124, 1135, 1687, 1777, 1892, 1925, 3173, 3175, 3404, 3476, 3502, 3508, 3559, 3583, 3585, 3596, 3605, 3628, and 3629.

LATIN AMERICA

General Treatments

1317. Alleman, Fritz R. "Terrorism in Latin America—Motives and Forms." Translated by Helga Bennett for *International Summaries: A Collection of Selected Translations in Law Enforcement and Criminal Justice*, 3: 19-25. Washington, D.C.: U.S. Department of Justice: National Criminal Justice Reference Service, April 1979.
A brief survey of terrorism in selected Latin American nations.

1318. Anderson, Thomas P. "Political Violence and Cultural Patterns in Central America." In Marius Livingston et al., eds., *International Terrorism in the Contemporary World*, pp. 153-359. Westport, Conn.: Greenwood Press, 1978.

1319. Blackburn, Robin, ed. *Strategy for Revolution: Essays on Latin America by Regis Debray*. New York: Monthly Review, 1970.

1320. Butler, Ross E. "Terrorism in Latin America." In Yonah Alexander, ed., *International Terrorism: National, Regional, and Global Perspectives*, pp. 46-61. New York: AMS, 1976.
Butler notes the importance of the writings of Guillen, as well as Guevara and Marighella, upon the tactical and strategic thinking of Latin terrorists, illustrating his points with studies of the Tupamaros and Argentine ERP.

1321. Cobo, Juan. "The Roots of 'Violencia.' " *New Times* (Moscow), August 5, 1970, pp. 25-27.
Violence and the guerrilla revolutionary movement in Latin America.

1322. Cozean, Krymis, Hitt, and Arensberg *Cuban Guerrilla Training Centers and Radio Havana: A Selected Bibliography.* Washington D.C.: Center for Research in Social Systems, CINFAC R-1098, October, 1978.

1323. Craig, Alexander. "Urban Guerrilla in Latin America." *Survey* 17 (Summer 1971): 112-128. Also available as FAR 14752-N.

1324. Darragh, Shaun M. "The Urban Guerrilla of Carlos Marighella." *Infantry* 63 (1973): 23-26.

1325. Davis, Jack. *Political Violence in Latin America.* London: International Institute for Strategic Studies, 1972.

1326. Col. De Rocquigny "Urban Terrorism." *Military Review* 38 (1969): 93-99. Reprinted from *Révue militaire d'information* (February 1968).

Analyzes urban terrorism in the broader context of psychological warfare, finding that terrorism can often be counterproductive.

1327. Duff, Ernest A., and McCamant, John F. *Violence and Repression in Latin America: A Quantitative and Historical Analysis.* New York: Free Press, 1975.

1328. Einaudi, Luigi R. "Latin American Student Radicalism: A Different Type of Struggle." Santa Monica: RAND Corporation, P-3897, July 1968.

1329. Estep, Raymond. "Guerrilla Warfare in Latin America, 1968-1975." Maxwell Air Force Base, Ala.: Directorate of Documentary Research, Air University Institute for Professional Development. AU-202-75-IPD, June 1975. Reprinted as FAR 2291-G.

Discusses the rise and fortunes of major guerrilla movements in Peru, Guatemala, Venezuela, Colombia, Bolivia, Brazil, Uruguay, Argentina, Mexico, Chile, and Nicaragua.

1330. Freysinger, Robert C. *"The Problems of Resistance of the Contemporary Christian Radical Movement."* Ph.D. dissertation, University of Massachusetts, 1977.

1331. Garner, William R. "Toward A Theory of Violence and Anomie in Latin American Politics: The Psychological Variables." Paper presented at the annual meeting of the Midwest Association of Latin American Studies, October 1972, at Southern Illinois University. Reprinted as FAR 16575-N.

1332. Goodsell, James N. "Terrorism in Latin America." *Commentator* (March 1966): 9.

1333. ———. "Urban Guerrillas in Latin America." *Commentator* 14 (1970): pp. 7-8.

1334. Gott, Richard. "The Future of Guerrilla Warfare: What Lessons from Latin America." *Current* 130 (1971): 55-59.

1335. ———. *Guerrilla Movements in Latin America.* Garden City: Doubleday, 1971. 629 pp.

An often rambling account, sympathetic to the guerrillas. Gott spent much time traveling with many of these groups.

1336. Halperin, Ernst. "From Peron to Somoza: The New Terrorism." *Washington Quarterly* (Autumn 1978): 110-114.

The epicenter of terrorism in Latin America has moved from the southern cone to Central America, where several groups, particularly the FSLN, stand a better chance of success. The successful terrorist will be one who attacks an unpopular regime in a country whose people are willing to accept violence as a legitimate means of political expression, who projects a favorable image, and whose aims are realistic.

1337. ———. "Terrorism in Latin America." *Washington Papers* 4 480033 (Beverly Hills, California: Sage Professional Papers Series, 1976).

1338. Harris, Richard. *Death of a Revolutionary: Ché Guevara's Last Mission.* New York: Norton, 1970.

1339. Hennessy, A. "The New Radicalism in Latin America." *Journal of Contemporary History* 7 (January-April 1972): 1-26.

Hennessy compares present-day Latin revolutionaries with old-line communist groups. He notes the roles of the university and churches. He believes that the shift from rural to urban operations can be traced to Guevara's defeat in Bolivia and suggests that Marighella's writings will serve as the urban guerrilla's intellectual model.

1340. Herreros, Aureliano Yanes. "El Anarquismo Como Doctrina y Movimiento." *Rivista de Estudios Politicos* 1 (1978): 99-114.

1341. Hoagland, John H. "Changing Patterns of Insurgency and American Response." *Journal of International Affairs* 25 (1971): 120-141.

Notes the differences between rural and urban guerrilla warfare in Latin America. Due to the clandestine nature of such activities, the development of recognizable alternative leaders is impaired.

1342. Hodges, Donald. *The Legacy of Ché Guevara: A Documentary Study.* London: Thames and Hudson, 1977. 216 pp.

1343. Horowitz, Irving Louis; Castro, José de; and Gerassi, John, eds. *Latin American Radicalism 1969.* London: Jonathan Cape, 1969. 656 pp.
A documentary report on Left and nationalist movements.

1344. Jaquett, J. S. "Women in Revolutionary Movements in Latin America." *Journal of Marriage and the Family* 35 (May 1973): 344-354.

1345. Kling, Merle. "Violence and Politics in Latin America." In Irving Louis Horowitz, José de Castro, and John Gerassi, eds. *Latin American Radicalism.* New York: Random House, 1969.
Taking note of the extent and numerous types of political violence in Latin America, Kling argues that it is recurring, chronic, and rule conforming rather than an aberration.

1346. Kohl, James, and Litt, John. *Urban Guerrilla Warfare in Latin America.* Cambridge: MIT Press, 1974. 425 pp.
Presents three case studies (Brazil, Uruguay, and Argentina) of urban attacks in Latin America. Listings of the major groups in these areas and chronologies of their activities are provided. Appended is Marighella's *Minimanual*, as well as a chapter from Gilio's book on the Tupamaros.

1347. Lamberg, Robert F. "La Guerrilla Urbana: Condiciones y Perspectivas de la 'Segunda Ola' Guerrilla." *Foro Internacional* 11 (1971): 431-443.
The use of urban guerrilla warfare in Latin America, its advantages and disadvantages, are outlined. Types of individuals attracted to this form of expression are discussed. Movements in Brazil, Argentina, and Uruguay receive extensive notice.

1348. ———. "Latin America's Urban Guerrillas." *Swiss Review of World Affairs* 20 (1970): 18-19.
Reviews the activities of groups in Uruguay, Guatemala, Brazil, and Argentina.

1349. Max, Alphonse. *Guerrillas in Latin America.* The Hague: International Documentation and Information Centre, 1971.

1350. Vega, Luis Mercier. *Guerrillas in Latin America: The Techniques of the Counterstate.* New York: Praeger, 1969. 246 pp.

1351. Moreira, Alves Marcio. *A Grain of Mustard Seed.* Garden City, N.Y.: Doubleday Anchor, 1973.

1352. Moreno, Francisco José, and Mitrani, Barbara, eds. *Conflict and Violence in Latin American Politics.* New York: Cornell University Press, 1971, 452 pp.

1353. Moss, Robert. "Urban Guerrillas in Latin America." *Conflict Studies* 8 (October 1970): 1-15.

1354. Neely, Alan P. "Protestant Antecedents of the Latin American Theology of Liberation." Ph.D. dissertation, American University, 1977.

1355. Riding, Alan. "The Death of the Latin American Guerrilla Movement." *World*, July 3, 1973, pp. 29-32.

1356. Roberts, Kenneth E, and Munger, Murl D. "Urban Guerrillas in the Americas." Carlisle Barracks, Penn.: Army War College Strategic Studies Institute, December 30, 1976.

1357. Ronfeldt, David E., and Einaudi, Luigi R. "Prospects for Violence." In Luigi R. Einaudi, ed., *Beyond Cuba: Latin America Takes Charge of Its Future.* New York: Crane, Rusak, 1974.

1358. Russell, Charles A., and Hildner, Robert E. "Urban Insurgency in Latin America: Its Implications for the Future." *Air University Review* 22 (1971): 55-64.

1359. Russell, Charles A.; Miller, James A.; and Hildner, Robert E. "The Urban Guerrilla in Latin America: A Select Bibliography." *Latin American Research Review* 9 (Spring 1974): 37-79.

Generally aims at military and political aspects of urban guerrilla actions. Ideological disputes within the groups that did not result in changes in strategy, tactics, or outlook were not included.

1360. Sloan, John W. "Political Terrorism in Latin America: A Critical Analysis." In Michael Stohl, ed., *The Politics of Terrorism*, pp. 301-322. New York: Dekker, 1979.

Looks at enforcement and agitational terrorism in Argentina, Uruguay, and Brazil.

1361. "Terrorism in Latin America." *Atlas* 20 (1971): 18-21,

1362. Trebat, T. J. "Internal Violence and the International System: The Experience in Latin America." *Notre Dame Lawyer* 46 (1971).

1363. West, Gerald T. "Political Violence and Terrorism in Latin America: Yesterday, Today, and Tomorrow." Paper presented to the International Symposium on Terrorism in the Contemporary World, April 26-28, 1976, at Glassboro State College. Reprinted as FAR 25651-N.

For additional readings, see entries 273, 277, 421, 775, 1122, 1155, 1157, 1169, 1170, 1177, 1186, 1189, 2396, and 3407.

Argentina

1364. David, Pedro R. "Profile of Violence in Argentina: 1955 to 1976." In *Report of the Task Force on Disorders and Terrorism*, pp. 474-478. Washington, D.C.: National Advisory Committee on Criminal Justice Standards and Goals, December 1976.

Presents a short history of Argentine politics, noting rises and falls of domestic violence with regular and irregular changes of government. The role of Perón in quietly promoting the student radicals during his exile is noted, as are developments before and after his death.

1365. Heyman, Edward. "Background to Human Rights Violations in Argentina." Washington, D.C.: Library of Congress, Congressional Research Service, Foreign Affairs and National Defense Division, July 29, 1977.

Treats terrorists as nonofficial violators of human rights. Heyman deals wih the ERP, Montoneros, and AAA, placing them in their cultural and historical context.

1366. Janke, Peter. "Terrorism in Argentina." *Journal of the Royal United Services Institute* (September 1974).

1367. Johnson, Kenneth F. "Guerrilla Politics in Argentina." *Conflict Studies* 63 (1975): 21 pp.

1368. ———. "A War of Eponyms: Exploring the Psychology of Argentina's Guerrilla Politics." Paper presented to the Southwest Social Science convention, March 1975, at San Antonio.

1369. Megalis, Elaine. "Murder in Argentina." *Christian Century*, November 9, 1977, pp. 1030-1033.

1370. McCrary, Ernest. "Coping with Terrorism in Argentina." *Business Week*, March 9, 1974. pp. 40-42.

1371. Piacentini, Pablo. "Terror in Argentina." *Index on Censorship* 6 (March-April 1977): 3-7.

Criticizes the crackdown by the government against press freedoms in Argentina, as well as citing instances of what he believes are officially accepted (if not sanctioned) kidnappings and assassinations of media personalities.

1372. Price, Joedd. "The Ezeiza Massacre: Contemporary Violence and Reform Movements in Latin America." Paper presented to the Conference on Terrorism in the Contemporary World, April 26-28, 1976, at Glassboro State College.

1373. Rock, David. "Revolt and Repression in Argentina." *World Today*, 33 (June 1977): 214-222.

1374. Russell, Charles A.; Schenkel, James F.; and Miller, James A. "Urban Guerrillas in Argentina: A Select Bibliography." *Latin American Research Review* 9 (Fall 1974): 53-89.

Concentrates on the politics and programs of the five major guerrilla groups operating since 1968. Other citations include chronologies and information on international links. The bibliography is almost solely devoted to newspaper articles.

1375. "Victor Samuelson-Ransom (Argentina)." *Congressional Record* 120 (1974): E4088.

For additional readings, see entries 1169, 1320, 1329, and 3267.

Uruguay

1376. Alsina, Geronimo. "The War and the Tupamaros." *Bulletin Tricontinental* (August 1972).

1377. Beque, Carlos. "Robin Hoods of Uruguay: A Strategy for Revolution." *Atlas* 18 (1969): 45-47.

1378. Cardillo, L. M. "The Tupamaros: A Case of Power Duality in Uruguayan Politics." Unpublished manuscript, Fletcher School of Law and Diplomacy, 1975.

1379. Clutterbuck, Richard L. "Two Typical Guerrilla Movements: The IRA and the Tupamaros." *Canadian Defense Quarterly* 24 (1972): 17-29.

1380. Connolly, Stephen, and Druehl, Gregory. "The Tupamaros: The New Focus in Latin America." *Journal of Contemporary Revolutions* 3 (Summer 1971): 59-68.

1381. Costa, Omar. *Los Tupamaros.* Mexico, D.F.: Coleccion Ancho Mundo, 1971.

1382. Costa-Gavras, and Solina, Franco. *State of Siege.* Screenplay translated by Brooke Leveque; documents translated by Raymond Rosenthal. New York: Ballantine, 1973.
    A fictionalized, and often misleading, account of the Mitrione kidnapping and murder.

1383. D'Oliviera, S. L. "Uruguay and the Tupamaro Myth." *Military Review* 53 (April 1973): 25-36.

1384. Ruiz, Oscar Duenas, and de Duenas, Mirna Rugnon. *Tupamaros, Libertad o Muerte.* Bogotá, Colombia: Ediciones Mundo Andino, 1971.

1385. Falcoff, Mark. "The Uruguay That Never Was: A Historian Looks at Costa Gavras' *State of Siege.*" Paper presented at the annual meeting of the Pacific Coast Council of Latin American Studies, October 1974, at UCLA. Reprinted as FAR 20717-N.

1386. Foland, Frances M. "Uruguay's Urban Guerrillas." *New York Institute of Current World Affairs Newsletter* (October 1971): Also Available as FAR 14919-N.

1387. Generals and Tupamaros: The Struggle for Power in Uruguay, 1969-1973. London: Latin America Review of Books, 1974.
    History of the Tupamaros, reprinted from *Latin América*, a weekly journal.

1388. Gerassi, Marysa N. "Uruguay's Urban Guerrillas." *Nation* 209 (1969): 309.

1389. Gilio, Maria Esther. *The Tupamaro Guerrillas.* New York: Saturday Review Press, 1972. 204 pp. Also published as *The Tupamaros.* London: Secker and Warburg, 1972.

1390. Labrousse, Alain. *The Tupamaros: Urban Guerrillas in Uruguay.* Harmondsworth: Penguin, 1973. 168 pp.

Discusses Tupamaro origins, history, and aims, furnishing guerrilla documents.

1391. Martinez, Anzorena G. *Los Tupamaros.* Mendoza, Argentina: Editorial la Tecla, n.d.

1392. Max, Alphonse. *Tupamaros: A Pattern for Urban Guerrilla Warfare in Latin America.* The Hague: International Documentation and Information Centre, 1970.

1393. Mayans, Ernesto, ed. *Tupamaros, Antologia Documental.* Cuernavaca, Mexico: Centro Intercultural de Documentation, 1971. 492 pp.

Perhaps the best collection of materials on and by the Tupamaros. This book includes a sixty-three-page chronology of the group's actions from May 1962 through March 1971. Its bibliography lists approximately 250 sources in a number of languages.

1394. Mercader, Antonio, and de Vera, Jorge. *Tupamaros: Estrategia y Accion.* Montevideo: Editorial Alfa, 1971.

1395. Miller, James Arnold. "The Tupamaro Insurgents of Uruguay." In Bard E. O'Neill, D. J. Alberts, and Stephen J. Rossetti, eds., *Political Violence and Insurgency: A Comparative Approach*, pp. 199-283. Arvada, Colo.: Phoenix, 1974.

1396. Moss, Robert. "Urban Guerrillas in Uruguay." *Problems of Communism* (September-October 1971).

1397. ———. "Uruguay: Terrorism Versus Democracy." *Conflict Studies* 14 (August 1971).

1398. Nunez, Carlos. *The Tupamaros: Urban Guerrillas of Uruguay.* New York: Times Change Press, 1970. 48 pp.

1399. Porzecanski, Arturo C. *Uruguay's Tupamaros: The Urban Guerrilla.* New York: Praeger, 1973.

Covers the period 1962-1972, noting tactics, strategy, ideology, motivations, objectives, organization, and the group's effects upon the Uruguayan government.

1400. Rizowy, Charles. "The Effects of Support Withdrawal on Uruguay's Political System: The Tupamaros Urban Guerrilla Warfare: 1960-1973." Ph.D. dissertation, University of Chicago, in preparation.

1401. Suarez, Carlos, and Sarmiento, Ruben Anaya. *Los Tupamaros.* Mexico, D.F.: Editorial Extemporaneous, 1971.

1402. La Subversion: Las Fuerzas Armadas al Pueblo Oriental. Montevideo: Junta de Comandantes en Jefe, Republica Oriental del Uruguay, 1977. 777 pp.
  A discussion of continental and national subversive movements, focusing on the Tupamaros and Cuban support for such groups.

1403. "Taps for the Tupamaros." *Reader' Digest* (November 1972).

1404. The Tupamaros: Urban Guerrilla Warfare in Uruguay. New York: Liberated Guardian, n.d.

1405. Wilson, Carlos. *The Tupamaros: The Unmentionables.* Boston: Branden, 1973.

  For additional readings, see entries 278, 285, 332, 348, 683, 686, 700, 1059, 1169, 1320, 1329, 1677, 2054, and 2994.

Other Latin Countries

1406. Alves, Marcio Moreira. "Bresil: Etat terroriste et guérilla urbaine." *Politique aujord'hui* (Paris) (July-August 1971).

1407. Bejar, Hector. *Peru 1965: Notes on a Guerrilla Experience.* Translated by William Rose. New York: Monthly Review, 1970.

1408. Biocca, E. *Strategy of Terror: The Brazilian Model.* Bari, Italy: De Donato Editore, Lungomare Nazario Sauro, 1974. 252 pp.
  Biocca blames political violence on state terror.

1409. Callahan, Edward F. "Terror in Venezuela." *Military Review* 49 (February 1969): 49-56.
  Looks at governmental countermeasures that led to the failure of urban terrorist activity from 1960 to 1964. Concentrates on the problems a government faces in responding to terrorism.

1410. Chaplin, David. "Peru's Postponed Revolution." *World Politics* (April 1968).

1411. DeGramont, A. "How One Pleasant, Scholarly Young Man from Brazil Became a Kidnapping, Gun-Toting, Bombing Revolutionary." *New York Times Magazine*, November 15, 1970.

1412. Dubois, Jules. *Freedom Is My Beat*. New York: Bobbs-Merrill, 1959.
    Chapter 25 gives an account of the June 1958 kidnapping of U.S. servicemen and businessmen by rebels led by Raul Castro.

1413. Evans, Robert Derval. "Brazil: The Road Back from Terrorism." *Conflict Studies* 47 (July 1974); 20 pp.

1414. Johnson, Kenneth F. "Guatemala: From Terrorism to Terror." *Conflict Studies* 23 (May 1972): 4-17.
    Compares the left-wing violence of the guerrillas who attacked Peralta's government in the 1960s and the response of the succeeding rightist Mendez Montenegro government. Strategy and tactics of domestic and state terrorism are outlined.

1415. ———. "On the Guatemalan Political Violence." *Politics and Society* 4 (Fall 1973): 55ff.

1416. Maullin, Richard. *Soldiers, Guerrillas and Politics in Colombia.* Lexington, Mass.: Lexington Books, 1973. 168 pp.

1417. Mena, Lucila Ines. "Bibliografia Anotada Sobre el Ciclo de la Violencia en la Literatura Colombiana." *Latin American Research Review* 13 (1978): 95-107.

1418. Morley, Morris, and Petras, Betty. "Chile: Terror for Capital's Sake." *New Politics* 11 (Winter 1974): 36-50.

1419. Pearson, Neale J. "Guerrilla Warfare in Brazil." Paper presented at the annual meeting of the Midwest Association of Latin American Studies, October 1972, at Southern Illinois University. Reprinted as FAR 16493-N.

1420. Ronfeldt, David F. "The Mexican Army and Political Order since 1940." RAND P-5089, Santa Monica, Calif.: The RAND Corporation, September 1973.
    The army since 1940 has been heavily involved in national development, although not to the same extent as have armies in other Latin nations. Ronfeldt initially looks at the military's "residual" political roles, then goes on to discuss internal and external forces that may change these roles.

1421. Sandstrom, Harold M. "West Indian Black Power Ideology." Paper presented to the Conference on Terrorism in the Contemporary World, April 26-28, 1976, at Glassboro State College.

1422. Truskier, Andy. "Politics of Violence: The Urban Guerrilla in Brazil." *Ramparts* 9 (October 1970): 30-34, 39.
Interviews with four members of Brazilian revolutionary guerrilla groups.

For additional readings, see entries 204, 530, 675, 783, 1063, 1169, 1192, 2028, 3267, and 3295.

EUROPE

General Treatments

1423. Altavilla, E. *Criminal Europe*. Milan: Rizzoli, 1978.

1424. Aston, Clive C. "Crisis Management and the Impact of Terrorism on the International Political Order of Western Europe." Ph.D. dissertation, London University.

1425. Bell, J. Bowyer. "The Gun in Europe: Bombs in the Trevi Fountain." *New Republic*, November 22, 1975, pp. 10-12.
Argues that Europe has now become a breeder of domestic terrorists and not merely a battleground for transnational attacks. But what is of note is that Europe can continue under such a threat. Governments must be extremely careful in how they react to terrorist campaigns.

1426. ———. "Terror: An Overview." Paper presented to the Conference on Terrorism in the Contemporary World, Glassboro State College, April 26-28, 1976, at Glassboro. Reprinted as FAR 25660-N.

1427. Bouman, Pieter Jan. *Vrijheidshelden en Terroristen: Dvijf Eeuwen Geweld in Europa*. Amsterdam: Elsevier, 1977. 192 pp.

1428. Corrado, Raymond R. "Ethnic and Student Terrorism in Western Europe." In Michael Stohl, ed., *The Politics of Terrorism*, pp. 191-257. New York: Dekker, 1979.
Presents two case studies of the background history, and present-day actions of the Irish Republican Army and Baader-Meinhof Gang, which, unfortunately, are riddled with minor factual errors.

1429. Crozier, Brian. "Terrorism: The Problem in Perspective." London: Institute for the Study of Conflict, February-March 1976. Reprinted as FAR 25042-N.

1430. Goodman, Jr., Raymond W.; Hoffman, Jerome E.; McClanahan, James R.; and Tompkins, Thomas C. *A Compendium of European Theater Terrorist Groups.* Air Command and Staff College, Air University Research Study Report No. 1030-76, May 1976. 213 pp. Available as FAR 25272-N AD B011 879L.

An encyclopedic survey of terrorist groups in Europe and the Middle East. The study discusses the origins, political orientation, size, organizational structure, personalities, modus operandi, weapons, and significant operations of the major threats to U.S. facilities.

1431. Iviansky, Ze'ev. "Individual Terror: Concept and Typology." *Journal of Contemporary History* 12 (January 1977): 43-63.

1432. Kopkind, Andrew. "Euro-terror." *New Times,* June 12, 1978, pp. 29-65.

1433. Laqueur, Walter. "Interpretations of Terrorism: Fact, Fiction and Political Science." *Journal of Contemporary History* 12 (1977): 1-42.

1434. Mueller-Borchert, H. J. *Guerrilla Warfare in Industrial Nations: Goals, Starting Points and Prospects of Success.* Hamburg: Hoffmann und Campe Verlag, 1973. 182 pp.

1435. Ronchey, Alberto; Vogel, Hans-Jochen; Barcher, Karl Dietrich; Revel, Jean-Francois; Rabehl, Bernd; Dahrendorf, Ralf; and O'Brien, Conor Cruise. "A Discussion on Terrorism." *Washington Quarterly* (Autumn 1978): 118-130.

The discussants are Europeans working in academe, government, and the press.

1436. Sjaastad, Anders C. "Deterrence of Terrorism and Attacks Against Off-Shore Oil Installations in Northern Europe." In Yair Envon, ed., *International Violence: Terrorism, Surprise and Control,* pp. 182-202. Jerusalem: Hebrew University of Jerusalem, Leonard Davis Institute for International Relations, 1979.

Discusses several scenarios, including threats against NATO access to oil.

1437. Tiltman, H. Hessell. *The Terror in Europe.* New York: Frederick A.Stokes Company. 1932.

1438. Vedovato, Giuseppe. "Il Terrorismo Europeo." *Rivista di Studi Politici Internazionali* 45 (April-June 1978): 283-284.

1439. Wigne, J. S. *Terreur in de Politiek: Politieke Geheime Genootschappen in Deze Tijd.* The Hague: Kruseman, 1967.

For additional readings, see entries 192, 652, 1168, 1170, 1172, and 3237.

Ireland

1440. Alexander, Joyce M. "A Metagame Analysis of the Conflict in Northern Ireland." Paper presented at the Annual Conference of the Peace Science Society-International, April 1975, Ottawa, Canada. Reprinted as FAR 22190-P.

1441. ———. "Northern Ireland: An Operations Research Approach to Conflict Resolution." Paper presented to the Seminar on Conflict Analysis sponsored by the State Department and Arms Control and Disarmament Agency, June 1975. Reprinted as FAR 22189-G.

1442. Barritt, D. P. and Carter, C. F. *The Northern Ireland Problem.* New York: Oxford University Press, 1972.

1443. Barry, Tom B. *Guerrilla Days in Ireland.* New York: Devin-Adair, 1956.

1444. Beaslai, Piaras. *Michael Collins and the Making of a New Ireland.* Dublin: Talbot, 1927.

1445. ———. *Michael Collins, Soldier and Statesman.* Dublin: Talbot, 1937.

1446. Beckett, J.C. "Northern Ireland." *Journal of Contemporary History* 6 (1971): 121-134.

1447. Beeson, T. R. "British and the IRA." *Christian Century*, January 28, 1976, pp. 60-62.

1148. Bell, Geoffrey, *The Protestants of Ulster.* London: Pluto, 1976. 159 pp.

1449. Bell, J. Bowyer. "The Chroniclers of Violence in Northern Ireland: The First Wave Interpreted." *Review of Politics* 34 (October 1974): 521-543.

1450. ———. "The Chroniclers of Violence in Northern Ireland: A Tragedy in Endless Acts." *Review of Politics* 38 (October 1976): 510-533.
An updating of Bell's reviews of the literature on the Irish troubles.

1451. ———. "Comments on a Paper Presented by Dr. Brian Jenkins." Conference on International Terrorism, U.S. Department of State, March 25-26, 1976. Reprinted as FAR 24505-S.

Discusses the problems in weapons acquisition and use of the Belfast Brigade of the Provisional IRA. He doubts that the use of sophisticated devices will rise because "revolutionaries, like most, prefer the easy life, opt for the conventional response, and regard innovation, especially if it requires a training course, with suspicion."

1452. ———. "The Escalation of Insurgency: The Experience of the Provisional IRA (1969-1971)." *Review of Politics* 35 (July 1973): 398-411. Republished as "The Escalation of Insurgency" *An Phoblacht* (Dublin), Iml 5, Uimh 8, Feabhra 22 (1974): 4-5, 89.

1453. ———. "The Secret Army." Paper presented to the Conference on Terror: The Man, the Mind and the Matter, October 15-16, 1976, at the John Jay School of Criminal Justice, New York City.

1454. ———. *The Secret Army: A History of the IRA*. London: Anthony Blond; Cambridge: MIT, 1974. 434 pp.

Reviewed by Leonard W. Doob, *Key Reporter* 40 (Spring 1975): 7.

1455. ———. "Societal Lessons and Patterns: The Irish Case." In Robin Higham, ed., *Civil War in the Twentieth Century*, pp. 217-228. Lexington: University of Kentucky Press, 1974.

1456. ———. "Strategy, Tactics, and Terror: An Irish Perspective, 1969-1974." In Yonah Alexander, ed., *International Terrorism*, pp. 65-89. New York: Praeger, 1976.

1457. Bennett, Richard Lawrence. *The Black and Tans*. Boston: Houghton Mifflin, 1960.

1458. Biggs-Davison, John. "Thoughts on the Ulster Discontents." *Contemporary Review* 233 (August 1978): 67-74.

1459. Birrell, Derek. "Relative Deprivation as a Factor in Conflict in Northern Ireland." *Sociological Review* 20 (August 1972): 317-343.

Demonstrates that the Catholics have an objective case of relative deprivation and that their perceptions closely parallel this objective condition. Possible causes of their increased political activity are suggested.

1460. Boulton, David. *The Ulster Volunteer Force, 1966-1973*. Dublin: Gill and Macmillan, Torc Books, 1973. 188 pp.

1461. Bowden, Tom. *The Breakdown of Public Security: The Case of Ireland (1916-1921) and Palestine (1936-1939)*. New York: Sage, 1977. 342 pp.

1462. ———. "The IRA and the Changing Tactics of Terrorism." *Political Quarterly* (London) 47 (October-December 1976): 425-437.

Looks at the historical roots of the two current wings of the IRA, pointing out that the reason Collins won was his attention to obtaining public support, a failing of the Provos. The campaign of 1939 is compared with that of 1973's "Hot Autumn" in London. A useful chronology of bombing attacks in 1939 is included.

1463. Brady, Edward Marl. *Ireland's Secret Service in England*. Dublin: Talbot, n.d.

1464. Breen, Dan. *My Fight for Irish Freedom*. Dublin: Talbot Press, 1924.

1465. Canavan, Francis. "The Prospects for a United Ireland." Paper presented at the annual meeting of the New England Political Science Association, April 1975, at University of Hartford. Reprinted as FAR 22489-P.

1466. Carlton, Charles. *Bigotry and Blood: Documents on the Ulster Troubles*. Chicago: Nelson-Hall, 1977. 160 pp.

1467. Carty, James. *Ireland from the Great Famine to the Treaty*. Dublin: C. J. Fallon, 1951.

1468. Charters, David A. "Intelligence and Psychological Warfare Operations in Northern Ireland." *Journal of the Royal United Services Institute for Defense Studies* 122 (September 1977): 22-27.

1469. Clark, Dennis. "Northern Ireland's Legacy of Conflict." Paper presented at the annual meeting of the American Association for the Advancement of Science, December 1971, at Philadelphia. Reprinted as FAR 15417-N.

1470. ———. "Terrorism in Ireland: Renewal of a Tradition." In Marius Livingston et al., eds., *International Terrorism in the Contemporary World*, pp. 77-83. London: Greenwood Press, 1978.

After noting that Ireland's troubles must be viewed in the context of British repression, Clark suggests some areas in which present-day IRA tactics and strategy differ from that of its historic forebears.

1471. ———. "Which Way the IRA?" *Commonweal* 13 (1973): 294-297.

1472. Clutterbuck, Richard. *Britain in Agony.* London: Faber and Faber, 1978. 335 pp.

1473. ———. "Intimidation of Witnesses and Juries." *Army Quarterly* 104 (April 1974): 285-294.

Uses of internment camps and other detaining procedures to prevent intimidation by Irish Republican Army terrorists.

1474. Collins, Michael. *The Path to Freedom.* Dublin: Talbot, 1922.

1475. Coogan, Tim Pat. *The IRA.* New York: Praeger, 1970. 373 pp. London: Pall Mall, 1970.

Noted briefly in *Foreign Affairs* (January 1972). Coogan, an Irish journalist, traces the history of the Irish Republican underground, noting that although the group has historically been an action-oriented separatist movement, it has suffered ideological divisions.

1476. ———. *Ireland since the Rising.* New York: Praeger, 1966.

1477. Cronin, Sean. *"IRA Ideology and the Roots of Conflict in Northern Ireland. 1956-1962.* Ph.D. dissertation, New School, in preparation.

1478. Crozier, Brian. *Ulster: Politics and Terrorism.* London: Institute for the Study of Conflict, 1973. 20 pp.

The causes of the Northern Ireland conflict are discussed, with constitutional and security issues throughout its history being outlined. The appendix gives information on the Provisional and Official wings of the Irish Republican Army, the Ulster Defense Association, and the Ulster Volunteer Force.

1479. Curran, Joseph M. "Ulster Repartition: A Possible Answer?" Paper presented at the annual meeting of the Southern Historical Association, November 1975 at Washington, D.C. Reprinted as FAR 23503-N.

1480. Curran, Mary E. "The Rationality of Mass Violence: Agrarian Crime in Pre-Famine Ireland." Paper presented to the panel on Violence and Terror of the conference on Complexity: A Challenge to the Adaptive Capacity of American Society, sponsored by the Society for General Systems Research, March 24-26, 1977, at Columbia, Maryland.

A summary of Curran's Columbia dissertation, for which she combed police records of mid-nineteenth century Ireland in an attempt to find patterns in agrarian violence. She finally used Mancur Olson's collective goods formulations to explain that violence, rather than being directed against the landlords who caused their poverty, was channeled by peasants against other peasants to compel general compliance with measures that would be in the general interest but that allowed "free riders." Such mechanisms of terrorism to ensure obedience by a group's members are widespread among contemporary terrorist organizations.

1481. Darby, John. *Conflict in Northern Ireland: The Development of a Polarized Community.* Dublin: Gill and Macmillan; New York: Barnes and Noble, 1976. 268 pp.

1482. Denieffe, Joseph. *A Personal Narrative of the Irish Revolutionary Brotherhood.* Cambridge: Houghton Mifflin, 1906.

1483. Desmond, Shaw. *The Drama of Sinn Fein.* London: W. Collins Sons, 1923.

1484. Dillon, Martin, and Lehane, Denis. *Political Murder in Northern Ireland.* Harmondsworth: Penguin, 1973. 317 pp.
Two Belfast reporters suggest that the campaign of political murders is not the work of psychopaths and is seen by some as legitimate acts of war.

1485. Dilnot, F. "Ireland Under Sinn Fein." *Outlook* (January 1919).

1486. Dodd, Norman L. "The Corporals' War: Internal Security Operations in Northern Ireland." *Military Review* 56 (July 1976): 58-68.

1487. "Editorial: Ulster Catharsis." *Lancet*, March 2, 1974. pp. 343-344.

1488. Enloe, Cynthia H. "Police and Military in Ulster: Peacekeeping or Peace-Subverting Forces?" *Journal of Peace Research* 15 (1978): 253-258.

1489. Evelegh, Robin. *Peacekeeping in a Democratic Society: The Lessons of Northern Ireland.* London: Hurst, 1978.
Reviewed by Bart Milner, "Who Orders Soldiers to Shoot Suspects?" *Irish Times*, March 8, 1979.

1490. Fisk, Robert. "The Effect of Social and Political Crime on the Police and British Army in Northern Ireland." In Marius Livingston, et al., eds., *International Terrorism in the Contemporary World*, pp. 84-93. Westport, Conn.: Greenwood Press, 1978.

1491. Fitzgibbon, Constantine. *Red Hand: The Ulster Colony.* Garden City: Doubleday, 1972.

1492. Foley, Gerry. *Ireland in Rebellion.* New York: Pathfinder, 1972.

1493. ———. *Problems of the Irish Revolution: Can the IRA Meet the Challenge.* New York: Pathfinder, 1972.

1494. Furmanski, Louis S. *"The Essence of Conflict: A Theoretical Inquiry into Conflict Analysis: The Case of Northern Ireland."* Ph.D. dissertation, Purdue University, in preparation.

1495. Gleason, James Joseph. *Bloody Sunday.* London: Davies, 1962. 212 pp.
    An account of the founding of Ireland due to IRA terrorism.

1496. Goodhart, Philip. *The Climate of Collapse: The Terrorist Threat to Britain and Her Allies.* Petersham, Surrey: Foreign Affairs Publishing Co., Ltd., June 1975. 15 pp.
    The author is joint secretary of the Conservative 1922 Committee. He argues that the United Kingdom must be firm, not hesitant or querulous on subject of terrorism. Reviewed in *London Times*, June 16, 1975.

1497. Griffiths, H. "Community Development: Some More Lessons from the Recent Past in Northern Ireland." *Community Development Journal* 10 (January 1975).

1498. Hachey, Thomas. "Just and Unjust Wars: The IRA's Perspective." Paper delivered to the Conference on Moral Implications of Terrorism, March 14-16, 1979, at UCLA.

1499. Hall, R. A. "Violence and Its Effects on the Community." *Medical Legal Journal* 43 (1975): 89-100.
    The IRA's effect upon Northern Ireland's social organization is followed by a discussion of forensic science's response to terrorist explosives.

1500. Hamilton, Iain. "The Irish Tangle." *Conflict Studies* 6 (1970).

1501. Harding, John W. "Ireland's Reign of Terror and Why." *Current History* (September 1920).

1502. Holt, Edgar. *Protest in Arms, The Irish Troubles, 1916-1923.* New York: Coward-McCann, 1960.

1503. Howard, A. J. "Urban Guerrilla Warfare in a Democratic Society." *Medicine, Science and the Law* 12 (October 1972): 231-243.
    The roots of violence in society, focusing on its effects for Northern Irish forensic scientists.

1504. Hull, Roger H. *The Irish Triangle: Conflict in Northern Ireland.* Princeton: Princeton University Press, 1976. 312 pp.

Reviewed briefly by Michael Reisman, *American Journal of International Law* 71 (April 1977): 375-376.

1505. Janke, Peter, and Price, D. L. "Ulster: Consensus and Coercion." *Conflict Studies* 50 (1974).

1506. Johnson, Paul. "The Resources of Civilisation." *New Statesman,* October 31, 1975. p. 531.

Suggests the death penalty for IRA bombers, whom the author characterizes as an "organization of psychopathic murderers." He argues that the United Nations has been ineffective and that "civilized powers" should act together.

1507. Krumpach, Robert. "Terrorism in Northern Ireland: An Overview." Translated by Charles Orme for *International Summaries: A Collection of Selected Translations in Law Enforcement and Criminal Justice,* 3: 27-36, Washington, D.C.: U.S. Department of Justice, National Criminal Justice Reference Service, April 1979.

Reviews the history of the current situation, terrorist tactics, police activities, and the political environment.

1508. Lebow, Richard Ned. "Civil War in Ireland: A Tragedy in Endless Acts?" *Journal of International Affairs* 27 (1973): 247-260.

1509. ———. "The Origins of Sectarian Assassination: The Case of Belfast." *Journal of International Affairs* 32 (Spring-Summer 1978): 43-61.

1510. Lee, A. M. "Insurgent and 'Peacekeeping' Violence in Northern Ireland." *Social Problems* 20 (1973): 532-546.

1511. Lieberson, Goddard. *The Irish Uprising, 1916-1922.* New York: Hinkhouse, 1964.

1512. London Sunday Times Insight Team. *Northern Ireland: A Report on the Conflict.* New York: Vintage, 1972.

1513. Lowry, D. "Ill-Treatment, Brutality, and Torture: Some Thoughts upon the 'Treatment' of Irish Political Prisoners." *DePaul Law Review* 22 (1973): 553ff.

1514. Lynch, William J. "The Orange and the Green: Literature's Look into the Northern Ireland Conflict." Paper presented at the annual meeting of the

American Association for the Advancement of Science, December 1971, at Philadelphia. Reprinted as FAR 15344-N.

1515. MacDonald, Michael Douglas. "Origins of Political Violence in Northern Ireland." Ph. D. dissertation, University of California, in preparation.

1516. Macdonald, W. "Underground Ireland." *Nation* (June 1960).

1517. MacEvin, Gary. *Northern Ireland: Captive of History.* New York: Holt, Rinehart, and Winston, 1974.

1518. MacNamara, Donal E. J. "Political Terrorism: Crime or Tactic (The Case of the IRA)." Paper presented at the annual meeting of the American Society of Criminology, October 30-November 2, 1975, at Toronto.

1519. MacNeill, J. G. S. "Agent Provocateur in Ireland." *Contemporary* (November 1918).

1520. MacStiofain [pseud.], Sean. *Revolutionary in Ireland.* Farnborough, U.K.: Gordon Cremonesi, 1975. 372 pp.

Reviewed by Peter Driscoll, "Messages from an IRA Leader in the Name of Reuniting Ireland." *Washington Post,* July 31, 1975, p. E8. An autobiography of the chief of staff on the IRA Provisionals and the main instigator of the split between the Officials and the Provisionals. He argues strongly for using violence as a political tool. Author's real name is John Edward Drayton Stephenson.

1521. McGuire, Maria. *To Take Arms: My Years with the IRA Provisionals.* New York: Viking, 1973. London: Macmillan, 1973. 159 pp.

Memoirs of IRA membership. McGuire left the IRA in August 1972, objecting to the indiscriminate bombing campaign.

1522. Mealing, Elisha Thorpe. "Ulster, Some Causes and Effects of Low Intensity Operations, 1969-1972." Carlisle Barracks, Penn.: Army War College, December 23, 1972.

Looks at the causes of the conflict, and the effects of British troops in peacekeeping operations during 1969-1972. The author interviewed participants as well as monitored news releases and the literature.

1523. Miller, Martin S. "The Irish Revolutionary Leadership 1916-1923: A Case Study of Intra-Elite Conflict." Ph.D. dissertation, City University of New York, in preparation.

1524. Moodie, Michael. ''The Patriot Game: The Politics of Violence in Northern Ireland.'' In Marius Livingston et al., eds., *International Terrorism in the Contemporary World*, pp. 94-110. Westport, Conn.: Greenwood Press, 1978.

Moodie discusses the Irish Troubles during 1974 through early 1976, focusing on the IRA's use of violence when it perceived the British as not granting political concessions quickly enough and not carrying out their part of agreements.

1525. ———. ''Terrorism in Ireland.'' Paper presented to the Conference on Terrorism in the Contemporary World, April 26-28, 1976, at Glassboro State College.

1526. Moodie, Michael L., and Bray, Frank T. J. ''British Policy Options in Northern Ireland.'' *Fletcher Forum* 1 (Fall 1976): 3-14.

1527. Moss, Robert, and Hamilton, Iain. ''The Spreading Irish Conflict.'' *Conflict Studies* 17 (1971).

1528. Oberschall, Anthony. ''Conflict and Conflict Regulation in Northern Ireland.'' Paper presented at the annual meeting of the American Sociological Association, August 1973, at New York City. Reprinted as FAR 18029-N.

1529. O'Brien, Conor Cruise. *Herod: Reflections on Political Violence.* London: Hutchinson, 1978. 236 pp.

1530. ———. ''Liberty and Terrorism.'' *International Security* 2 (Fall 1977): 56-67.

1531. ———. ''Liberty and Terror.'' Cyril Foster Lecture, Oxford University, May 1977.

1532. O'Broin, Leon. *Dublin Castle and the 1916 Rising.* Dublin: Helicon, 1966.

1533. O'Callaghan, Sean. *The Easter Lily: The Story of the IRA.* New York: Roy, 1938.

1534. ———. *Execution.* London: Frederick Muller, 1974.

1535. O'Day, Alan. ''Northern Ireland, Terrorism, and the British State.'' In Yonah Alexander, David Carlton, and Paul Wilkinson, eds., *Terrorism: Theory and Practice*, pp. 121-135. Boulder: Westview, 1979.

O'Day surveys the history of Irish terrorism, giving particular attention to Parnellism.

1536. O'Farrell, Patrick. *Ireland's English Question.* New York: Schocken, 1971.

1537. O'Flaherty, Liam. *The Terrorist.* London: Archer, 1923.
An account of the IRA's activities.

1538. O'Leary, John. *Recollections of Fenians and Fenianism.* London: D. Appleton, 1896.

1539. O'Sullivan, P. M. *Patriot Graves: Resistance in Ireland.* Chicago: Follett, 1972.

1540. Phillips, Walter Alison. *The Revolution in Ireland, 1906-1923.* London: Longmans and Green, 1927.

1541. Pollard, H. B. C. *The Secret Societies of Ireland.* London: Philip Allan, 1922.

1542. Power, Paul F. "Civil Protest in Northern Ireland: Functions and Dysfunctions." Paper presented at the Midwest Regional Meetings of the International Studies Association and the Peace Research Society (International), May 1972, at Toronto, Canada. Reprinted as FAR 15872-N.

1543. ———. "Violence, Consent and the Northern Ireland Problem." *Journal of Commonwealth and Comparative Politics* 14 (July 1976): 119-140. Reprinted as FAR 26308-N.

1544. Provisional IRA. *Freedom Struggle.* Irish Republican Publicity Bureau, June 30, 1973. 101 pp.
A pamphlet by the IRA spelling out their views. An appendix lists their dead.

1545. Reed, David. "Northern Ireland: The Endless War." *Reader's Digest* 107 (July 1975): 85-93.

1546. Report to the Commission to Consider Legal Procedures to Deal with Terrorist Activities in Northern Ireland. London: HMSO, 1972.

1547. Report of the Committee of Privy Counsellors Appointed to Consider Authorized Procedures for the Interrogation of Persons Suspected of Terrorism. London: HMSO, 1972.

1548. Rose, Richard. *Northern Ireland: Time of Choice.* Washington, D.C.: American Enterprise Institute for Public Policy Research, 1976. 175 pp.

Reviewed briefly by Michael Reisman, *American Journal of International Law* 71 (April 1977): 375-376.

1549. Schmitt, David. *Violence in Northern Ireland: Ethnic Conflict and Radicalization in an International Setting.* Morristown, N.J.: General Learning Press, 1974.

1550. Scott, Malcolm. *"Conflict Regulation vs. Mobilization: The Dilemma of Northern Ireland."* Ph.D. dissertation, Columbia University, 1976.

1551. Skidelsky, Robert. ''The Irish Problem: An Historical Perspective.'' In Yonah Alexander, David Carlton, and Paul Wilkinson, eds., *Terrorism: Theory and Practice.* Boulder: Westview, 1979.

1552. Stewart, Anthony T. Q. *The Ulster Crisis.* London: Faber, 1967.

1553. Sullivan, Eileen. ''Violence in Northern Ireland.'' Paper presented to the Conference on Terrorism in the Contemporary World, Glassboro State College, April 26-28, 1976.

1554. Tansil, Charles Callan. *America and the Fight for Irish Freedom.* New York: Devin-Adair, 1957.

1555. Taylor, Rex. *Michael Collins.* London: Hutchinson, 1958.

1556. Thayer, George. *The British Political Fringe.* London: Anthony Blond, 1965.

A survey of the radical Left, Right, and idiosyncratic fringe groups in Britain, including separatist movements and violence-prone organizations.

1557. Ulster: Consensus and Coercion. London: Institute for the Study of Conflict, 1973. 24 pp.

1558. U.S. House of Representatives. Committee on Foreign Affairs. Subcommittee on Europe. ''Northern Ireland: Hearings'' 92d Cong., 2d sess., 1972.

1559. Voris, W. H. Van. *Violence in Ulster: An Oral Documentary.* Amherst: University of Massachusetts Press, 1975. 326 pp.

An American scholar interviewed hundreds of Ulstermen in the research for this book.

1560. ''Which Way the IRA?'' *Commonweal*, January 5, 1973, p. 294.

1561. Williams, Desmond. *The Irish Struggle.* London: Routledge and Kegan, 1966.

1562. Winchester, Simon. *In Holy Terror.* London: Faber and Faber, 1974.
A journalist's view of the Irish Troubles.

1563. ———. *Northern Ireland in Crisis.* New York: Holmes and Meier, 1974.

1564. Wolpin, Kenneth I. "An Economic Analysis of Crime and Punishment in England and Wales, 1894-1967." *Journal of Political Economy* 86 (October 1978): 815-840.

1565. Wright, Steve. "An Approach toward the Development of Empirical Statistical Techniques for the Holistic Analysis of Substate Conflicts: Analysis of the Northern Irish Conflict, 1969-1976." In Yonah Alexander and John M. Gleason, eds., *Terrorism: Behavioral Perspectives.* New York: Pergamon, 1980.

1566. Younger, Calton. *Ireland's Civil War.* New York: Taplinger, 1969.

For additional readings, see entries 12, 34, 35, 70, 136, 139, 192, 204, 273, 285, 332, 348, 421, 747, 1059, 1067, 1088, 1157, 1558, 1161, 1162, 1164, 1167, 1189, 1192, 1379, 1428, 1958, 2112, 2967, 2990, 3060, 3064, 3173, 3194, 3195, 3205, 3265, 3266.

Italy

1567. Aglietta, A. *Diary of a Jury Member at the Red Brigades Trial.* Milan: Libri Edizioni, 1979.

1568. Allum, Percy. "Political Terrorism in Italy." *Contemporary Review* 233 (August 1978): 75-84.

1569. Ballardin, G. *To Die for ENEL.* Milan: SuperCo, 1979.

1570. Basaglia, F. and Fornari, F. *Violence.* Florence: Vallecchi, 1978.

1571. Bell, J. Bowyer. "Violence and Italian Politics." *Conflict* 1 (Fall 1977).

1572. Bertini, B.; Franchi, P.; and Spagnoli, U. *Extremism, Terrorism and Democratic Order.* Rome: Editori Riuniti, 1978.

1573. Bianchi, A.; Granato, F.; and Zingarelli, D. *Marginality and Freedom of Deviants*. Milan: Franco Angeli, 1978.

1574. Blackstone Associates. "Italy: Threat Assessment." *Terrorism* 2 (1979): 283-296. Reprint of Blackstone Reports, *Risk Assessment for Italy* (Washington, D.C.: Blackstone Associates, 1978).

The firm looks at the effectiveness of the Italian police in fighting terrorism, notes the near-term prospects of Italian terrorists, and points out several political indicators that may give a clue to the future actions—particularly targeting of foreign firms—of these groups.

1575. Bocca, Giorgio. *Italian Terrorism 1970/1978*. Milan: Rizzoli, 1978. 158 pp.

1576. ———. *Moro: An Italian Tragedy: Letters, Documents, Polemics*. Rome: Tascabili Bompiani, 1978. 145 pp.

1577. Bozzi, A. *The Uncomfortable Inmate: A Manual from Prison*. Milan: Feltrinelli, 1972.

1578. Bufalini, P. *Terrorism and Democracy*. Rome: Editori Riuniti, 1978.

1579. Cantore, Romano; Rossella, C.; and Valentini, C. *Dall-interno della Guerriglia* [From within the guerrilla]. Milan: Mondadori, 1978. 207 pp.

1580. Caserta, John. *The Red Brigades: Italy's Agony*. New York: Manor, 1978. 240 pp.

1581. Consiglio Regionale Piedmonto. *A Region against Terrorism: 1969-1978 Facts and History*. Savigliano: Nuove Arti Grafiche S.p.A., 1979.

1582. Dispot, L. *The Machine of Terror: Genealogy of Terrorism*. Venice: Marsilio, 1978.

1583. Ferrarotti, F. *At the Roots of Violence*. Milan: Rizzoli, 1979.

1584. Feustel, Sandy. "Terrorism: Not Just an Italian Problem." *European Community* (May-June 1978): 19-22.

1585. Fiorillo, Ernesto. "Terrorism in Italy: Analysis of a Problem." *Terrorism* 2 (1979): 261-270.

Using statistics from recent Italian terrorism, the author jumps to a consideration of terrorism in general and suggests that univariate explanations of the causes of terrorism are too limited. He argues that superprisons will not stop terrorism and that what is called for is a complete restructuring of society.

1586. Hahn, Karl Josef. ''Italien nach dem Mord an Aldo Moro.'' *Politische Studien* 29 (July-August 1978): 379-384.

1587. Jovinelli, S.; Novelli, S.; and Ventimiglia, E. *Letters from the Movement, Dear Comrades . . . Greeting Not with Fists Because Now I Do Not Know What It Means.* Rome: Napoleone, 1978.

1588. Kopkind, Andrew. ''Euro-Terror: Fear Sears the Soul.'' *New Times,* June 12, 1978, pp. 28-36, 61-66.
An impressionistic account of the woes of Italy and Germany.

1589. Ledeen, Michael. ''Aldo Moro's Legacy.'' *New Republic,* May 13, 1978, pp. 24-25.

1590. ———. ''Inside the Red Brigades: An Exclusive Report.'' *New York,* May 1, 1978. pp. 36-39.

1591. Manzini, G. *Indagine su un Brigatista Rosso: La Storia di Walter Alasia.* [Investigation of a Red Brigades member: Story of Walter Alasia] Turin: Einaudi, 1978.

1592. Minucci, A. *Terrorism and Italian Crisis: The Interview with Jochen Kreimer.* Rome: Editori Riuniti, 1978.

1593. Monicelli, Mino. *L'ultrasinistra in Italia.* [The Italian ultraleft] Rome-Bari: Laterza, 1978. 237 pp.

1594. Mori, A. M. *The Silence of Women and the Moro Case.* Cosenza: Lerici, 1978.

1595. Nese, Marco. *Terrorism.* Rome: La Tipografica, 1978.

1596. Neuberg, A. *Armed Insurrection.* Milan: Feltrinelli, 1970.

1597. Orlando, Federico. *P 38.* Milan: Editoriale Nuova, 1978. 253 pp.

1598. ''Osservazioni sul decreto legge contro il Terrorismo, trasmesse al Parlamento a cura di Magistratura democratica.'' *Foro Italiano* 5 (1978): 156-160.

1599. Parenti, F. *Together to Kill: The Psychology of Group Violence.* Rome: Armando, 1978.

1600. Pellicani, A. *The Professional Revolutionaries.* Florence: Vallecchi, 1975.

1601. Petacco, A. *The Anarchist Who Came from America.* Verona: Mondadori, 1970.

1602. "Phenomenological and Dynamic Aspects of Terrorism in Italy." *Terrorism* 2 (1979): 159-170.

A statistical study by an anonymous Italian terrorism expert who looks at differences among the major Italian terrorist groups in terms of targeting, ideology, clandestinity, and future prospects.

1603. Pisano, Vittorfranco S. *Contemporary Italian Terrorism: Analysis and Countermeasures.* Washington D.C.: Library of Congress Law Library. 1979. 190 pp.

Discussions include the history of Italian intelligence, left-wing terrorism, rightist terrorism, and current measures to counter terrorism.

1604. ———. "The Origins of Italian Terrorism." *New America* (January 1979).

1605. ———. "A Survey of Terrorism of the Left in Italy: 1970-78." *Terrorism* 2 (1979): 171-212.

The author looks at the post-World War II history of Italy, seeing this as the background for terrorism by the Left in the 1970s. He explores the development, tactics, ideology, personnel, and future of the Red Brigades, Partisan Action Groups, October 22 Group, Armed Proletarian Nuclei, and Front Line and tests four hypotheses on foreign and domestic links of leftist Italian terrorists.

1606. ———. *Terrorism in Italy.* Washington: Heritage Foundation, 1978. 12 pp.

1607. Possony, Stefan T. "Giangiacomo Feltrinelli: The Millionaire Dinamitero." *Terrorism* 2 (1979): 213-230.

Argues that through his leftist publishing empire of the 1950s and 1960s, Feltrinelli helped foster urban guerrilla ideas throughout Europe, spawning the urban terrorist movements of the 1970s.

1608. Proletarian Armed Groups. Quaderno di Controinformazione, Italy, 1975.

1609. Ronchey, Alberto. "Guns and Gray Matter: Terrorism in Italy." *Foreign Affairs* (Spring 1979): pp. 921-40.

An Italian political columnist surveys the growth of terrorism in Italy, concentrating upon its domestic political effects.

1610. ——. "Terror in Italy: After Moro's Murder." *Dissent* 25 (Fall 1978): 383-385.

1611. ——. "Terror in Italy: Between Red and Black." *Dissent* 25 (Spring 1978): 150-156.

1612. Russell, Charles A. "Terrorist Incidents—Italy 1978." *Terrorism* 2 (1979): 297-300.

A statistical compendium on terrorism in Italy, based upon a very small sampling of that nation's terrorism problem.

1613. Saint-Just, L. A. L. de. *Terror and Freedom*. Rome: Editori Riuniti, 1971.

1614. Sciascia, L. *The Moro Affair*. Palermo: Sellino, 1978.

1615. Selva, Gustavo, and Marcucci, E. *The Martyrdom of Aldo Moro*. Bologna: Capelli, 1978. 187 pp.

1616. Sezione Problemi dello Stato Comitato Regionale Ligure PCI. *Terrorism and New Extremism*. Genoa: G. Del Cielo, 1979.

1617. Silj, Alessandro. *Brigate Rosse-Stato*. [Red Brigades-State: The conflict as shown in the daily press] Florence: Vallecchi, 1978. 243 pp.

1618. ——. "*Mai Piu Senza Fucile!*" *Alle Origini dei NAP e delle BR*. Rome: Vallecchi, 1977. Translated by Salvator Attanasio, *Never Again Without a Rifle: The Origins of Italian Terrorism* (Karz, 1979). Reviewed by Ciro Elliott Zoppo, " 'Never Again without a Rifle,' By Alessandro Silj: A Review of a Book and a Situation," *Terrorism* 2 (1979): 271-281.

Silj uses the biographies of dead and jailed members of the Red Brigades and Armed Proletarian Nuclei to study the motivations and ideologies of Italy's two major leftist terrorist groups. Zoppo agrees that the organizations are incorrect in believing that they will force the state to engage in system-wide repression, and finds that in fact the police have been successful in selectively rooting out the major terrorists. However, major cultural and societal problems in Italy will continue to provide these groups with new recruits.

1619. Soccorso Rosso Napoletano. Brigate Rosse. [The Red Brigades; what they have done, what they have said, what has been said about them] Milan: Feltrinelli, 1976. 294 pp.

1620. ———. *I Nap: Storia Politica dei Nuclei Armati Proletari e Requisitoria del Tribunale di Napoli*. [The Armed Proletarian Nuclei] Milan and Naples: Collettivo Editoriale Libri Rossi, 1976. 249 pp.

1621. Sossi, M. *Within the Red Brigades Prison*. Novara: Editoriale Nuova, Instituto Geografico de Agostini, 1979.

1622. Sterling, Claire. "Italy: The Feltrinelli Case." *Atlantic Monthly* 230 (July 1972): 10-18.

1623. Tessandori, Vincenzo. *BR: Imputazione: Banda Armata, Cronaca e Documenti delle Brigate Rosse*. [Red Brigades: charge; armed group] Rome: Garzanti, 1977. 414 pp.

1624. Vedovato, Giuseppe. "Aldo Moro." *Rivista di Studi Politici Internazionali* 45 (April-June 1978): 163-168.

1625. ———. "Terrorismo: Italia e Mondo Esterno." *Rivista di Studi Politici Internazionali* 45 (April-June 1978): 277-278.

1626. Verri, P. *Armed Conflict, Fighters and Humanitarian Rights*. Rome: Scuola Carabinieri, 1973.

1627. Weinberg, Leonard. "Political Violence During the 1976 Italian Election Campaign." Paper presented at the annual meeting of the Western Political Science Association, March-April 1977, at Phoenix. Available as FAR 26907-N.

1628. ———. "Patterns of Neo-Fascist Violence in Italian Politics." *Terrorism* 2 (1979): 231-259.
Comparing the 1919-1922 fascist political violence to contemporary neofascist violence, Weinberg finds that the former was directed primarily against peasants and socialist local governments, whereas the latter has attacked leftist students and institutions. Fascist violence was rural and urban, whereas neofascist violence has been almost strictly urban.

1629. Whetten, Lawrence L. ''Italian Terrorism: Record Figures and Political Dilemmas.'' *Terrorism* 1 (1978): 377-395.

A discussion of contemporary Italian politics, the role of the PCI, and the growth of left- and right-wing terrorism by students.

1630. Weiser, Theodor. ''Italy: The Terrorist War on the State.'' *Swiss Review of World Affairs* (December 1978): 11-13.

For additional readings, see entries 204, 679, 748, 1178, 1186, and 3267.

West Germany

1631. Althammer, Walter. *Gegen den Terror: Texte/Dokumente.* Bonn: Aktuell, 1978, 236 pp.

1632. Der Baader-Meinhof Report. *Aus Akten des Bundesdriminalamtes, der "Sonderkommission Bonn" und des Bundesamts fur Verfassungsschutz.* v. Hase and Koehler Verlag Mainz, 1972.

1633. Baumann, Michael. *Terror or Love? The Personal Account of a West German Urban Guerrilla.* 1979.

Excerpts were printed as ''What a German Urban Guerrilla Learned,'' *New York Times*, April 11, 1979, p. A25.

1634. Becker, Jillian. *Hitler's Children: The Story of the Baader-Meinhof Terrorist Gang.* Philadelphia: J. B. Lippincott, 1977. 322 pp.

1635. Bergedorfer Gespraechskreis. *Terrorismus in der demokratischen Gesellschaft.* Hamburg, 1978.

1636. Berner, Georg. '' 'Radikalenerlass' und Rechtsprechung.'' *Politische Studien* 28 (May-June 1977): 287-304.

1637. Binder, Sepp. *Terrorismus.* Bonn, 1978.

1638. Blei, Herman. ''Terrorism, Domestic and International: The West German Experience.'' In *Report of the Task Force on Disorders and Terrorism*, pp. 497-506. Washington, D.C.: National Advisory Committee on Criminal Justice Standards and Goals, December 1976.

The personal backgrounds of the major members of the BMG, Second of June Movement, and Socialist Patients Collective form the context for a discussion of these groups' attacks. The German legal responses in three areas are studied, with detailing of specific provisions in penal codes.

1639. Bradshaw, Jon. ''A Dream of Terror.'' *Esquire Fortnightly*, July 18, 1978, pp. 24-50.

Bradshaw engaged in scores of interviews with individuals who in some way dealt with the Baader-Meinhof Gang members over the years, and paints character sketches of the group.

1640. Bundeskriminalamt. Sonderkommission Bonn und Bundesamt fur Verfassungschutz. *Aus den Akten . . ., Der Baader-Meinhof Report: Dokumente-Analysen-Zusammenhange.* Mainz, 1972. 245 pp.

1641. Cattani, Alfred. ''Recht gegen Terror.'' *Schweizer Monatshefte* 57 (June 1977): 168.

1642. Corves, Erich. ''Terrorism and Criminal Justice Operations in the FRG.'' In Ronald D. Crelinsten, Danielle Laberge-Altmejd, and Denis Szabo, eds., *Terrorism and Criminal Justice: An International Perspective.* Lexington, Mass.: Lexington Books, 1978.

1643. Crijnen, A. J. *De Baader-Meinhof Groep.* Utrecht: Uitgeverij Hot Spectrum, 1975. 125 pp.

An account by a noted Dutch journalist of the history, aims, ideology, membership and recent activities of the BMG.

1644. De Wit, John, and Ponsaers, Paul. ''On Facts and How to Use Them.'' *Terrorism* 1 (1978): 363-375.

The authors argue that the Springer-dominated major papers of the FRG twisted the debate on radical student reaction to the Buback slaying by focusing on prototypes of terrorists versus those who support society. The views of French anarchist Michel Foucault and Marxist J. Baudrillard are discussed in this context.

1645. Dornberg, John. ''West Germany's Embattled Democracy: The Antiterrorist Menace from the Right.'' *Saturday Review*, June 10, 1978, pp. 18-21.

1646. Einsele, Helga, and Low-Beer, Nele. ''Political Socialization and Conditions of Custody.'' In *International Summaries: A Collection of Selected Translations in Law Enforcement and Criminal Justice*, 3: 63-69. Washington, D.C.: U.S. Department of Justice, National Criminal Justice Reference Service, April 1979.

A study of women's emancipation and political terrorism in West Germany.

1647. Elliott, John D. ''Action and Reaction: West Germany and the Baader-Meinhof Guerrillas.'' *Strategic Review* 4 (Winter 1976): 60-67.

Uses Eastonian categories to discuss the threat to the German political system and how Germany was able to survive. Data are collected from press reports from Germany and the *New York Times*.

1648. ———. "Terrorism in West Germany." Ph.D. dissertation, George Washington University, in preparation.

Elliott will consider the political response of the FRG to the terrorist threat at three levels: the national, land, and international.

1649. ———. *West Germany's Political Response to Contemporary Terrorism*. Gaithersburg, Md.: International Association of Chiefs of Police, 1978.

1650. **"The Events and Decisions Connected with the Kidnapping of Hanns Martin Schleyer and the Hijacking of the Lufthansa Jet 'Landshut.' "** In *International Summaries: A Collection of Selected Translations in Law Enforcement and Criminal Justice*, 3: 3-15. Washington, D.C.: U.S. Department of Justice: National Criminal Justice Reference Service, April 1979.

An English-language summary of a press release from the FRG government.

1651. Fetscher, Irving. *Terrorismus und Reaktion*. Cologne: Europaische Verlaganstalt, 1977. Translated as "Terrorism and Reaction" by Sybille Jobin for *International Summaries: A Collection of Selected Translations in Law Enforcement and Criminal Justice*, 3: 45-51. Washington, D.C.: U.S. Department of Justice: National Criminal Justice Reference Service, April 1979.

Looks at the fallacious thinking of West German terrorists, public response, and antiterrorist measures.

1652. Funke, Manfred, ed. *Terrorismus: Untersuchungen zur Struktur and Strategie revolutionarerer Gewaltpolitik*. Bonn: Schriftenreihe der Bundeszentrale fur politische Bildung, 1977. 391 pp.

A collection of readings concentrating on terrorism in Germany.

1653. Geissler, H., ed. *Der Weg in die Gewalt*. Munich, 1978.

1654. Gemmer, Karlheinz. "Problems, Means and Methods of Police Action in the Federal Republic of Germany." In Ronald Crelinsten and Dennis Szabo, eds., *Hostage-Taking*, pp. 119-126. Lexington, Mass.: Lexington Books, 1979.

1655. German Federal Republic. Bundestag. Wissenschaftliche Dienste. *Terrorismus und Gewalt: Auswahbibliographie mit Annotationen*. Bonn: Deutscher Bundestag, 1975.

1656. Horchem, Hans Josef. *Extremisten in einer selbstbewussten Demokratie.* West Germany, 1976.

1657. ———. ''Right-wing Extremism in Western Germany.'' *Conflict Studies* 65 (1975): 11 pp.

1658. ———. ''Urban Guerrilla in West Germany: Origins and Prospects.'' Paper presented at the Conference on International Terrorism, U.S. Department of State, March 1976. Reprinted as FAR 25048-S.

1659. ———. ''West Germany's Red Army Anarchists.'' *Conflict Studies* 46 (June 1974): 13 pp.

1660. ''Interview with Dr. Wilfried Rasch.'' In ''Terrorism: the World at Bay.'' Television report produced by WHYY-Television, Philadelphia, and aired over the Public Broadcasting Service March 21, 1978. A transcript is available through World Publications, PTV, Kent, Ohio.

Rasch interviewed several incarcerated members of the Baader-Meinhof Gang.

1661. Kramer, Jane. ''A Reporter in Europe: Hamburg.'' *New Yorker*, March 20, 1978, pp. 44-87.

Kramer concludes that although it appears that the first generation of Baader-Meinhof terrorists was reacting to the German past, such simple explanations do not hold for their antecedents.

1662. Lasky, Melvin J. ''Ulrike and Andreas: The Bonnie and Clyde of West Germany's Radical Subculture May Have Failed to Make a Revolution, but They Have Bruised the Body Politic.'' *New York Times Magazine*, May 11, 1975, pp. 14ff.

Gives an account of the New Left roots of the Baader-Meinhof Gang, their movement toward violence, some of their attacks, and the current legal status of the group members. Lasky focuses on their individual personalities rather than the gang's existence as an organization.

1663. ———. ''Ulrike Meinhof and the Baader-Meinhof Gang.'' *Encounter* (June 1975): 9-14.

Lasky chronicles the Baader-Meinhof Gang's actions, including their prison escapes. The group's actions established that a liberal-industrial society is highly vulnerable to armed fanatics.

1664. Luebbe, H. *Endstation Terror.* Stuttgart, 1978.

1665. Mahler, Horst. ''Terrorism in West Germany: Interview with Horst Mahler.'' *Socialist Review* 39 (May-June 1978): 118-123.

1666. Mehnert, Klaus. *Twilight of the Young: The Radical Movements of the 1960s and Their Legacy.* New York: Holt, Rinehart and Winston, 1976. 420 pp.

While focusing primarily on student movements, Mehnert gives some consideration of the West German terrorist situation.

1667. Menges, Constantine C. "Germany: Terrorism, the Universities, and Democracy." *Freedom at Issue* 46 (May-June 1978): 12-13.

1668. Moons, Eric J. H. "Political and Judicial Approach to Terrorism and Anarchistic Criminality in the Federal Republic of Germany." *Revue de droit pénal et de criminologie* 5 (May 1978): 503-543. Available in *International Summaries: A Collection of Selected Translations in Law Enforcement and Criminal Justice*, 3: 123-129. Washington, D.C.: U.S. Department of Justice, National Criminal Justice Reference Service, April 1979.

Concentrates on the West German reaction to Baader-Meinhof terrorism.

1669. Oestreicher, P. "Roots of Terrorism—West Germany: Special Case." *Round Table* 269 (1978): 75-80.

1670. Pate, Clarence W. "The Psychology of the Left-Wing Radical Terror in Post-World War II Germany: The Baader-Meinhof Group." Paper presented to the Conference on Terrorism in the Contemporary World, April 26-28, 1976, at Glassboro State College.

1671. Portner, Dieter. *Bundeswehr und Linksextremismus.* Munich: Gunter Olzog Verlag, 1976. 210 pp.

A thorough chronicle of the activities of German leftist and anarchist groups, citing their literature, links with other groups, foreign ties, and other characteristics.

1672. Possony, Stefan T. and Bouchey, L. Francis. *International Terrorism: The Communist Connection; with a Case Study of the West German Terrorist Ulrike Meinhof.* New York: American Council for World Freedom, 1978. 172 pp.

1673. Rasch, W. "Creation of Confinement Conditions for Politically Motivated Offenders in West Germany." *Montasschrift fuer Kriminologie und Strafrechtsreform* 59 (June 1976): 61-69.

Concern has been raised regarding how to establish maximum security imprisonment that does not lead to sensory and perceptual deprivation.

1674. Rauball,R. *Baader-Meinhof Group.* Berlin: Walter de Gruyter, 1972. 265 pp.

A discussion of the first generation of West German terrorists.

1675. Rupprecht, Reinhard. ''Security Problems in Connection with the Olympic Games, 1972, in Munich.'' Mimeographed. Munich, n.d.

1676. Schreiber, Manfred. ''After Action Report of Terrorist Activities, 20th Olympic Games, Munich, West Germany.'' Mimeographed. Munich, n.d.

1677. Schubert, Alex. *Stadtguerilla: Tumpamaros in Uruguay—Rote Armee Fraktion in der Bundesrepublik.* Berlin. 1974. 124 pp.

1678. Schwagerl, H. J. ''Dangers of Political Extremism in West Germany.'' *Kriminalistik* 30 (November 1976): 497-500.
   Surveys the political and social conditions in West Germany that serve as a backdrop for violence by the Left and Right. Statistics from the government are presented.

1679. Stumper, A. ''Remarks on the Baader-Meinhof Affair.'' *Revue de Droit pénal et de criminologie* (October 1973): 33-44.
   The author believes that the BMG acted due to alienation and nihilistic motives rather than from a coherent political philosophy.

1680. Textes des prisonniers de la Fraction armée rouge et dernières lettres d'Ulrike Meinhof. Paris: Maspero, 1977.

1681. Tophoven, Rolf. *Politik durch Gewalt: Guerilla und Terrorismus heute.* Bonn, 1976. 173 pp.

1682. von Thadden, Adolf. *Die Schreibtischtater, Das geistige Umfled des Terrorism.* Hanover: Greiffen-Verlag, 1977.

1683. Wagenlehner, Gunther. ''Motivation for Political Terrorism in Germany.'' In Marius Livingston et al., eds., *International Terrorism in the Contemporary World,* pp. 195-203. Westport, Conn.: Greenwood Press, 1978.

1684. Wassermann, R. *Terrorism Against a Constitutional State.* Darmstadt: Hermann Luchterhand, 1976. 266 pp.
   A criminological analysis of the major FRG terrorist groups.

1685. Weiss, Peter. ''Joe McCarthy Is Alive and Well and Living in West Germany: Terror and Counter-Terror in the Federal Republic.'' *New York University Journal of International Law and Politics* 9 (Spring 1976): 61-90.

1686. White Paper on German Terrorism from Schleyer to Mogadishu. Rome: Giarrapico, 1978.

1687. Wolf, John B. ''Prisons, Courts and Terrorism: The American and West German Experience.'' *Police Journal* (July 1977).

Points out that lawyers have misused the penal system to allow them to aid terrorist planning, recruit prisoners into the gang, and so forth. Several recommendations are given.

For additional entries, see 204, 1056, 1106, 1164, 1186, 1428, 3173, and 3267.

Other European Countries

1688. Barker, Dudley. *Grivas: Portrait of a Terrorist.* London: Cresset, 1959. 202 pp.

1689. Bassand, Michel. ''Le Separatisme Jurassien.'' Paper presented at the 9th World Congress of the International Political Science Association, Montreal, Canada, August 1973. Reprinted as FAR document 17982-N.

1690. Broido, Vera. *Apostles Into Terrorists: Women and the Revolutionary Movement in the Russia of Alexander II.* New York: Viking, 1977. London: Temple Smith, 1978. 238 pp.

A discussion of the role of women in the Russian anarchist movement of 1860-1880.

1691. Byford-Jones, W. *Grivas and the Story of EOKA.* London: Robert Hale, 1959. 192 pp.

1692. Carr, Gordon. *The Angry Brigade.* London: Gollancz, 1975, 207 pp. Reviewed briefly in *Economist*, August 2, 1975, p. 103.

This is the first full-length account of the history of England's first urban guerrilla group. Carr brings out how life in the counterculture can dehumanize and break down inhibitions about the use of violence.

1693. Clissold, Stephen, ed. *A Short History of Yugoslavia: From Early Times to 1966.* Cambridge University Press, 1966.

Includes some material on Croatian terrorists.

1694. Esman, Milton J., ed. *Ethnic Conflict in the Western World.* Ithaca: Cornell University Press, 1977.

Attempts to determine why Scots, Welsh, Quebeçois, Bretons, Basques, and other ethnic minorities reasserted their demands in the late 1960s, at times resorting to violence.

1695. Foley, Charles, and Scobie, W. I. *The Struggle for Cyprus.* Stanford: Hoover Institution Press, 1975.

1696. Goren, Roberta. *"Soviet Attitude and Policy to International Terrorism, 1967-1977."* Ph.D. dissertation, University of London, in preparation.

1697. Greer, Donald. *The Incidence of Terror during the French Revolution.* Cambridge: Harvard University Press, 1935.

1698. Haggman, Bertil. "Sweden's Maoist 'Subversives'—A Case Study." *Conflict Studies* 58 (1975).

1699. Hendel, Samuel. "Terror in the USSR." Paper presented to the Conference on Terrorism in the Contemporary World, April 26-28, 1976, at Glassboro State College.

1700. Hewsen, Robert H. "Who Speaks Today of the Armenians?" In Marius Livingston et al., eds., *International Terrorism in the Contemporary World*, pp. 444-446. Westport, Conn.: Greenwood Press, 1978.

1701. Jacob, James Edwin. "The Basques and Occitans of France: A Comparative Study in Ethnic Militancy." Ph.D. dissertation, Cornell University, 1979.

1702. Joesten, Joachim. *The Red Hand: The Sinister Account of the Terrorist Arm of the French Right-Wing "Ultras" in Algeria and on the Continent.* New York: Abelard-Schuman, 1962.

1703. Jurjevic, M. *Ustasha under the Southern Cross.* Melbourne: Jurjevic, 1973. 71 pp.

1704. Londres, Albert. *Les Comitadjiis; ou, le terrorisme dans les Balkans.* Paris, 1923.

1705. Longuet, Jean, and Silber, Georges. *Terroristes et policiers.* Paris, 1909.

1706. Mathewson, William. "The Terrorists: Bitterness Surrounding Dutch Train Hijacking Lingers a Year Later." *Wall Street Journal*, January 6, 1977, pp. 1, 18.

A detailed study of the two takeovers in December 1975, the negotiations, and the postincident treatment of the hostages.

1707. Meysels, Lucien O. "Terrorism: Austria Comes of Age?" *Gazette: Austria's English-Language Magazine* (January 1978): 7.

A listing of terrorist incidents in the 1970s, concentrating on recent events.

1708. Preston, Paul. "Walking the Terrorist Tightrope." *Contemporary Review* 234 (March 1979): 119-123.

Argues that ETA terrorists threaten Spanish democracy.

1709. Reilly, Donald E. "Urban Guerrillas in Turkey: Causes and Consequences." Carlisle Barracks, Penn. Army War College, March 6, 1972.

Concentrates on political developments in Turkey, documents on guerrilla strategy, and types of terrorist actions.

1710. Rudolph, Joseph R. "Sub-System Accommodation and the Politics of Ethno-Nationalism: The Proposed Regional Assemblies for Wales, Scotland, Flanders, and French-Speaking Belgium." Paper presented at the annual convention of the Midwest Political Science Association, May 1975, at Chicago. Reprinted as FAR 22371-P.

1711. Shipley, Peter. *Revolutionaries in Modern Britain.* London: Bodley Head, 1976. 255 pp.

1712. Stafford, David. "Anarchists in Britain Today." *Government and Opposition* 5 (1970).

1713. ———. "Anarchists in Britain Today." *Government and Opposition* 6 (1971): 345-353.

1714. Stephens, Robert. *Cyprus: A Place of Arms.* London: Pall Mall Press, 1966.

1715. Tomasic, Dinko. "The Ustasha Movement." In *Slavonic Encyclopedia*, pp. 1337-1341. New York: Kennicat Press, 1949.

1716. U.S. Senate. Committee on Foreign Relations. "With Respect to the Release of Abu Daoud." Senate Report 95-1, 95th Cong., 1st sess., 1977.

1717. Van Drevan, Waldo P. "Came the Dawn: South Moluccan Terror in the Netherlands." *Counterforce* 1 (September-October 1977): 15-21.

A richly detailed description of the May 1977 attacks in the Netherlands by the South Moluccan exile youths.

1718. Zwerin, Michael. *A Case for the Balkanization of Practically Everyone . . . The New Nationalism.* London: Wildwood House 1976. 188 pp.

Discusses the growing separatist sentiments among Occitanians, Basques, Welsh, Romanis, Bretons, Mohawks, Catalans, and Lapps.

For additional readings, see entries 12, 35, 136, 139, 204, 285, 382, 470, 482, 643, 699, 747, 778, 1080, 1141, 1157, 1179, 1189, 3173, 3192, 3393, and 3623.

AFRICA

1719. Bell, J. Bowyer. "Endemic Insurgency and International Order, The Eritrean Experience." *Orbis* 17 (Summer 1974): 427-450.

1720. Boyce, F. "The Internationalizing of Internal War: Ethiopia, the Arabs, and the Case of Eritrea." *Journal of International and Comparative Studies* 5 (1972): 51-73.

1721. Campbell, John Franklin. "Rumblings along the Red Sea: The Eritrean Question." *Foreign Affairs* 48 (April 1970): 537-548.

Discusses the history of the problems in the area, Ethiopian relations with Arab countries, tactics of the Eritrean Liberation Front, and ELF relations with other nations.

1722. Clarke, John Henrik. "The Nineteenth Century Origins of Terrorism Against African People." Paper presented to the Conference on Terrorism in the Contemporary World, April 26-28, 1976, at Glassboro State College.

1723. Dorabji, Elena Venturini. "South African National Congress: Change from Non-Violence to Sabotage between 1952 and 1964." Ph.D. dissertation, University of California, 1979.

1724. Gibson, Richard. *African Liberation Movements: Contemporary Struggles Against White Minority Rule.* New York: Oxford University Press, 1972.

A survey of the activities, personnel, ideology, and hopes of the major African guerrilla groups. While a bit dated, the book still offers useful insights into the behavior of guerrillas.

1725. Horrell, Muriel. *Terrorism in Southern Africa.* Johannesburg: South African Institute of Race Relations, 1968.

1726. Jacobs, Walter Darnell; Peterson, Carl A.; and Yarborough, William P. *"Terrorism in Southern Africa: Portents and Prospects."* New York: American African Affairs Association, 1973. 35 pp. Available as FAR 18845-N.

1727. Leakey, L. S. B. *Mau Mau and the Kikuyu.* New York: John Day, 1952.

1728. Maier, F. X. *Revolution and Terrorism in Mozambique.* New York: American African Affairs Association, 1974. 60 pp. Available as FAR 19320-N.

1729. Majdalany, Fred. *State of Emergency: The Full Story of Mau Mau.* Boston: Houghton Mifflin, 1963.

1730. Mathews, A. S. "Terrors of Terrorism." *South African Law Journal* 91 (August 1974): 381ff. Terrorism and legal definitions in South Africa.

1731. Mojekwu, Christopher C. "The Linkages between Protest, Rebellion, and Terrorism." Paper presented to the Conference on Terrorism in the Contemporary World, April 26-28, 1976, at Glassboro State College. Published as "From Protest to Terror-Violence: The African Experience," in Marius Livingston et al., eds., *International Terrorism in the Contemporary World*, pp. 177-181. Westport, Conn.: Greenwood Press, 1978.

Mojekwu, a former high official in the breakaway Biafran government, uses case examples from African experience.

1732. Morris, Michael. *Terrorism: The First Full Account in Detail of Terrorism and Insurgency in Southern Africa.* Capetown: Timmins, 1971.

1733. N'Diaye, J. P. "Pourquoi Khartoum?" *Jeune Afrique*, March 17, 1973, pp. 2-5.

1734. Nzuwah, Mariyawanda. "A Bibliography of Contemporary Publications on Southern Africa from 1970." *Journal of Southern African Affairs* 3 (April 1978): 235ff.

1735. Pew, Mary Jean. "South Africa and Terrorism." *Worldview* (February 1968): 6-8.

1736. Répression, violence et terreur: Rébellions au Congo. Brussels: Centre de Recherche et d'Information Socio-Politiques, 1969.

1737. Sherman, Richard. "Eritrea in Revolution." Ph.D. dissertation, Brandeis University, in preparation.

1738. Sundiata, Ibrahim K. "Integrative and Disintegrative Terror: The Case of Equatorial Guinea." In Marius Livingston et al., eds., *International Terrorism in the Contemporary World*, pp. 182-194. Westport, Conn.: Greenwood Press, 1978.

1739. ———. "Terror as a Means of Political Integration in the African Context." Paper presented to the Conference on Terrorism in the Contemporary World, April 26-28, 1976, at Glassboro State College.

1740. Teixeria, Bernardo. *The Fabric of Terror: Three Days in Angola.* New York: Devin-Adair, 1965.

1741. Venter, A. J. *The Terror Fighters.* Capetown: Purnell, 1969.

1742. Welfling, Mary B. "Terrorism in Sub-Sahara Africa." In Michael Stohl, ed., *The Politics of Terrorism*, pp. 259-300. New York: Dekker, 1979.
    Looks at terrorism in colonial and independent black Africa, noting the comparative rarity of dissident violence. Unfortunately little attention is paid to state terrorism, particularly in Uganda.

    For additional entries, see 34, 35, 515, 644, 674, 1158, 1183, 1192, 1752, 2068, 3200, and 3295.

ASIA

1743. Bose, Nemai Sadhan. "Morality of the Use of Violence: A Conceptual Dichotomy in the Indian Perspective." Paper delivered to the Conference on Moral Implications of Terrorism, March 14-16, 1979, at UCLA.

1744. Boyd, Jr., James A. "The Japanese Red Army." Research Report No. 0200-78. Air Command and Staff College, Air University, April 1978. Available as FAR 29106-N AD B028 137L.

1745. Cary, James. "The Terrorist Organizations Are Growing and Threatening." *Yomiuri* (Tokyo), October 23, 1974.

1746. Davies, Dave. "The Ustasha in Australia." Sidney: Communist Party of Australia, April 1972.

Gives a history of the Croatian separatists in Australia, linking them to the Nazi occupation of Yugoslavia and numerous terrorist actions in urban areas of Australia. It purports to link members of the Liberal party to what are viewed as far right fascists.

1747. Hula, Richard C. "Political Violence and Terrorism in Bengal." Paper presented at the annual meeting of the Southwest Region of the International Studies Association, March 30-April 2, 1977, at Dallas, Texas. Published in Michael Stohl, ed., *The Politics of Terrorism*, pp. 351-372. New York: Dekker, 1979.

Surveys two hundred years of colonial and nationalist violence in India.

1748. "Hijackings by Japan's Red Army." *Japan Quarterly* (January-March 1978): 8-11.

1749. Kato, Shuichi. "Socio-Psychological Background of Terror in Japan Today." Paper presented to the Conference on Terrorism in the Contemporary World, April 26-28, 1976, at Glassboro State College.

1750. Khaleque, Abdul. *Terrorism's Menace: How to Combat It.* Jalpaiguri, A. Wadubat: Jalpaiguri Kohinoor Printing Works, 1932.

1751. Khan, Mohammad I. "The Role of Violence in Gandhi's India: 1919-1947." Paper presented to the Conference on Terrorism in the Contemporary World, April 26-28, 1976, at Glassboro State College.

1752. Khapoya, Vincent B. "African and Vietnamese Liberation Movements: A Comparative Study." Paper presented at the Conference on African Responses in Southern Africa from 1652 to the present, January 1976, at Northride, California. Reprinted as FAR 24429-N.

1753. Kirk, Donald. "The Khmer Rouge: Revolutionaries or Terrorists?" Paper presented at the SEADAG Ad Hoc Seminar on Communist Movements and Regimes in Indochina, Asia House, September-October 1974. Available as FAR 20332-N.

1754. Kuriyama, Yoshihiro. "Terrorism at Tel Aviv Airport and a 'New Left' Group in Japan." *Asian Survey* 13 (March 1973): 336-346.

Discusses the roots of the URA in the New Left movement of the 1960s in Japan. The merger of the Red Army Faction with the Tokyo-Yokohama Joint Struggle against the Japan-U.S. Security Treaty, and its consequences, is noted, as well as the ideology and activities of the group.

1755. Lambrick, H. T. trans. *The Terrorist*. London: Ernest Benn, Ltd., 1972. 246 pp.

An account of the Hur group in Sind, now part of Pakistan, but during the time of operations, a province of British India. The story notes the attacks led by Sainrakhio in the mid-1940s. The author was involved in countering these terrorist operations during the period.

1756. Laushey, David M. *Bengal Terrorism and the Marxist Left*. Calcutta: Firma K. L. Mukhopadhyay, 1975.

1758. Mallin, Jay. *Terror in Viet Nam*. Princeton: D. Van Nostrand, 1966. 114 pp.

1760. Military Assistance Command. *Vietnam Terrorist Incident Reporting System (TIRS)*. Saigon: Military Assistance Command, Vietnam, n.d.

1761. Mitchell, Edward J. "Some Econometrics of the Huk Rebellion." *American Political Science Review* 63 (December 1969): 1159-1171.

1762. Muller, Christian. "Japanese Radicals as Transnational Terrorists." *Swiss Review of World Affairs* (April 1979).

An update of the history of the Japanese Red Army and its associates.

1763. Muros, R. F. "Communist Terrorism in Malaya." *U.S. Naval Institute Proceedings* (October 1961).

1764. Noble, Lela Garner. "The Moro National Liberation Front in the Philippines." *Pacific Affairs* 49 (Fall 1976): 405-424.

Discusses the MNLF's origins from other groups, its regional strengths, organizational structure and leadership, tactics, and prospects. A postscript notes their skyjacking activities in 1976.

1765. Otsuka, Bunsei. "Rengo Sekigun: Sono Seiritsu Kara Hokai Made." [The URA: its founding to its disintegration] *Skokun* 4 (May 1972).

1765a. Pike, Douglas. "The Kind of War That Is Vietnam: People's War with Terror as the Tool." *Air Force and Space Digest* (June 1970).

1766. Rappoport, Leon H. "Failed Violence: Aspects of American Experience in Vietnam." Paper presented to the International Symposium on Terrorism in the Contemporary World, April 26-28, 1976, at Glassboro State College. Reprinted as FAR 25652-N.

1767. Rees, David. "North Korea's Growth as a Subversive Center." *Conflict Studies* 28 (London: Institute for the Study of Conflict).

1768. Reynolds, J. A. C. "Terrorist Activity in Malaya." *Marine Corps Gazette* (November 1961).

1769. Seymour, W. N. "Terrorism in Malaya." *Army Quarterly* (April 1949).

1770. Shimbori, Michiya. "The Sociology of a Student Movement—A Japanese Case Study." *Daedalus* (Winter 1968).

1771. Shuja, Sharif M. "Political Violence in Southeast Asia: A Critical Analysis of Some Models." *Pakistan Horizon* (1977): 48-64.

1772. Shultz, Richard T. "The Limits of Terrorism in Insurgency Warfare: The Case of the Vietcong." *Polity* 11 (Fall 1978): 67-91. FAR 26226-N.

1773. ———. "A Study of the Selective Use of Political Terrorism in the Theory and Process of Revolutionary Warfare: The National Liberation Front of South Vietnam." Paper presented to the Southwest Asian Studies Association Conference, Houston, October 1975, at Houston, Texas. Published in *International Behavioral Scientist* (July 1976).

1774. Steinhoff, Patricia G. "Portrait of a Terrorist: An Interview with Kozo Okamoto." *Asian Survey* 16 (September 1976): 830-845.

Steinhoff interviewed the surviving member of the Lod Airport attack squad, as well as his father. This study is without parallel in exploring some of the motivations of the individual, the role of suicide in Japanese and Western societies, the role of violence in the Japanese student leftist movement, and how they combined to lead the trio to their actions. Noteworthy background material on the logistics of the operation is also included.

1775. "Subject: 'Japanese Red Army.' " Distributed by the Embassy of Japan to the United States, 1975.

An excellent summary of the organizational origins of the Japanese Red Army, the United Red Army, the Red Army Faction, and related groups, their actions, and personnel.

1776. Takagi, Masayuki. "Rengo Sekigun to Shin Sayoku undo." [The URA and the new left movement] *Asahi Journal*, April 14, 1972.

1777. Taylor, Robert W.; and Kim, Byong-Suh. ''Violence and Change in Postindustrial Societies: Student Protest in America and Japan in the 1960s.'' In Marius Livingston et al., eds. *International Terrorism in the Contemporary World*, pp. 204-222. Westport, Conn.: Greenwood Press, 1978.

1778. ''Terror: Behind the 'Red Army.' '' *Asia Week*, November 26, 1976, pp. 26-31.

Focuses on the activities of Fusako Shigenobu, rumors of her death in Tal Zaatar, and JRA links to groups in the Middle East, Europe, and Japan. Aspects of JRA training, organizational dynamics, and operational code are outlined. Speculation is made as to the reasons for the change noted in JRA activity since 1974.

1779. Terror in East Pakistan. Karachi Publications, 1971.

1780. ''Tokushu: Rengo Sekigun Jiken no imi suru mono—ningen, kakumei, skukusei.'' [Special: The meaning of the URA incident—man, revolution, and purge] *Asahi Journal*, April 14, 1972, pp. 4-17.

For additional readings, see entries 34, 204, 277, 285, 332, 382, 472, 474, 534, 603, 1103, 1130, 1161, 1181, 1182, 1189, 1192, 1278, 3267, 3272, 3273, 3316, and 3406.

MIDDLE EAST

1781. ''Accessories to Terror: The Responsibility of Arab Governments for the Organization of Terrorist Activities.'' *Middle East Information Series.* Jerusalem: Ministry for Foreign Affairs, Division of Information, Israel Information Centre, July 1973.

Outlines Arab governmental aid to terrorist groups in training, aiding, and giving safe haven to various groups. Presents a chronology of Arab terrorists' activities in foreign nations from 1968 through 1973.

1782. The ''Activities'' of the Hagana, Irgun and Stern Bands. New York: Palestine Liberation Organization, n.d.

1783. Aines, Ronald C. ''The Jewish Underground against the British Mandate in Palestine.'' Master's thesis, Union College, 1973.

1784. Aksentijevic, M. ''Reflections on the Palestinian Resistance.'' *Middle East Information Series* 25 (1973-1974): 17-22.

1785. Alexander, Yonah. ''The Religionation of the Middle East Conflict by Some Moslem Groups Outside the Area.'' *International Problems* 11 (December 1972): 16-22.

1786. ———. *The Role of Communications in the Middle East Conflict: Ideological and Religious Aspects.* New York: Praeger, 1973.

1787. ———. ''Terrorism in the Middle East: A New Phase?'' *Washington Quarterly* 1 (Autumn 1978): 115-117.
   Notes the linkages among various Palestinian terrorist groups, including a working arrangement between the PFLP and FSLN, proxy operations in Israel by Europeans, aid to the IRA, and Soviet support. Also notes Faruk Qaddumi's interest in Fatah's obtaining nuclear weapons.

1788. Alter, Robert. ''The Masada Complex.'' *Commentary* (July 1973).

1789. ''Another Black September.'' *To the Point*, September 27, 1974, pp. 7-8.

1790. Ariel, Dan. *Explosion!* Tel Aviv: Olive, 1972.

1791. Aronson, Shlomo. ''Strategies of Middle Eastern Terrorism.'' Paper presented to the annual convention of the Western Section of the International Studies Association, March 16-18, 1978.

1792. ''The Assassination of Lord Moyne.'' *Jewish Agency's Digest of Press and Events*, November 11, 1944, pp. 1-3.

1793. Avineri, Shlomo, ed. *Israel and the Palestinians: Reflections on the Clash of Two National Movements.* New York: St. Martin's Press, 1971. 168 pp.
   Reviewed by Amos Perlmutter, *American Political Science Review* 70 (December 1976): 1321-1322.

1794. Avner. [pseud.] *Memoirs of an Assassin.* Translated by Burgo Partridge. New York: Thomas Yoseloff, 1959. 200 pp.
   An account of Irgun activities in Palestine and the United Kingdom, along with the mailing of letter bombs in Italy, as related by an Irgun member. The translator, in his introduction, attempts to assess the reliability of Avner's statements.

1795. al-Ayyubi, H. ''Guide to Researchers: Fateh's Political and Military Ideas.'' *Shu'un Filastiniya* 29 (January 1974): 116-126.

1796. ———. "Palestine Resistance in the Phase of Flexible and Dynamic Defence." *Shu'un Filastiniya* 19 (March 1973): 28-34.

1797. al-Azm, Sadiq Jalal. *Dirasa Naqdiya li Fikr al-Muqawama al-Filastiniya.* [A critical study of the thought of the Palestinian Resistance] Beirut: Dar al-Auda, 1973.

1798. Bassiouni, M. Cherif. "Self-Determination and the Palestinians." *Proceedings of the American Society of International Law* 65 (1971).

1799. Bassiouni, M. Cherif, and Fisher, E. "An Arab-Israeli Conflict: Real and Apparent Issues, an Insight into Its Future from the Lessons of the Past." *St. John's Law Review* 44 (1970): 399-465.

1800. Begin, Menachem. *The Revolt: Story of the Irgun.* Translated by Samuel Katz, member of the Command of the Irgun Zvai Leumi. Tel Aviv: Hadar Publishing Company, 1964. 386 pp. Los Angeles: Nash, 1972.

Memoirs of an important Irgun leader, frequently polemical in tone, giving a case study of the motivations and modus operandi of a terrorist group.

1801. Beit-Hallahmi, B. "Some Psycho-Social-Cultural Factors in the Arab-Israeli Conflict: A Review of the Literature." *Journal of Conflict Resolution* 16 (July 1972): 269-280.

1802. Belack, Carl N. "Transnational Terrorism and World Politics: A Case Study of the Palestine Arab Resistance Movement." Ph.D. dissertation, Columbia University, in preparation.

1803. Bell, J. Bowyer. "Arafat's Man in the Mirror: The Myth of the Fedayeen." *New Middle East* (London) 19 (April 1970): 19-24.

1804. ———. "Bab el Mandeb, Strategic Troublespot." *Orbis* 16 (Winter 1973): 975-989.

1805. ———. "Israel's Nuclear Option." *Middle East Journal* 26 (Autumn 1972): 379-388.

1806. ———. *Terror out of Zion: Irgun, LEHI, and the Palestine Underground, 1929-1949.* New York: St. Martin's Press, 1977. 359 pp.

1807. Ben-Dor, Gabriel. "The Strategy of Terrorism in the Arab-Israel Conflict: The Case of the Palestinian Guerrillas." In Yair Evron, ed., *International Violence: Terrorism, Surprise and Control*, pp. 126-165. Jerusalem:

Hebrew University of Jerusalem, Leonard Davis Institute for International Relations, 1979.

A survey of the strengths and ideologies of the major Palestinian groups, with an appended chronology of major terrorist attacks.

1808. Benjamin, Charles M. "The Kurdish Non-State Nation." Paper presented at the annual meeting of the International Studies Association, February 1975, at Washington, D.C. Reprinted as FAR 22464-N.

1809. Bishop, Vaughn F. "The Role of Political Terrorism in the Palestinian Resistance Movement: June 1967-October 1973." In Michael Stohl, ed., *The Politics of Terrorism*, pp. 323-350. New York: Dekker, 1979.

Bishop, after a lengthy discussion of the problem of definition, looks at the causes and tactics of Arab terrorism.

1810. Black September. Beirut: Palestine Liberation Organization Research Center, 1973.

1812. Blick, Edward. "Arab Terrorism and Israeli Retaliation: Some Moral, Psychological and Political Reflections." Paper delivered to the Conference on Moral Implications of Terrorism, March 14-16, 1979, at UCLA.

1813. Borisov, J. *Palestine Underground: The Story of Jewish Resistance.* New York: Judea Publishing Co., 1947.

1814. Borodin, Nikolai. "The Palestinian Resistance Movement: A Soviet View." *New Middle East* (December 1972): 27-28.

A Soviet writer explains the Russian attitude toward the Palestinian movement in the light of the Munich massacre.

1815. Bowen, Roderic. "Report on Procedures for the Arrest, Interrogation and Detention of Suspected Terrorists in Aden." London: Great Britain Foreign Office, November 14, 1966.

1816. Brandon, Henry. "Jordan: The Forgotten Crisis (1): Were We Masterful." *Foreign Policy* 10 (Spring 1973): 158-170.

Discusses the events that led up to the 1970 Jordanian civil war. New material on U.S. decision making during the PFLP multiple skyjacking is presented.

1817. Calvert. Peter. "The Diminishing Returns of Political Violence." *New Middle East* (London) 56 (May 1973): 25-27.

1818. Carre, Oliver. *L'Idéologie Palestinienne de résistance.* Paris: Colin, 1972.

1819. Carreras, Fernand. *L'Accord FLN-OAS, des négotiations sécrêtes cessez-le-feu.* Paris: R. Laffont, 1967.

1820. Caspard, J. "Palestine: Who's Who among the Guerrillas." *New Middle East* (London) (March 1970): 12-16.

1821. Chaliand, Gerard. "Le double combat du PFLP." *Le monde diplomatique* (July 1970).

1822. ———. *The Palestinian Resistance.* Middlesex: Penguin, 1972.
A look at Al-Fatah and rival guerrilla organizations now operating in Palestine, showing how these groups have gained in power and influence since the June 1967 war.

1823. ———. *The Palestinian Resistance Movement (in Early 1969).* (Beirut, Lebanon: Fifth of June Society, 1969.
Describes training, background, and ideologies of several groups through interviews with commando leaders and rank-and-file members.

1824. ———. "Terrorisme et Politique." *Le monde diplomatique* 230 (May 1973): 24.

1825. "Chronology: Activities of Arab Guerrillas Since 1968." *Congressional Record* 119 (1973): 43427.

1826. "Chronology of Zionist and Israeli Terrorism." *Palestine Digest* 2: pp. 3-8.

1826a. Clark, Michael K. *Algeria in Turmoil.* New York: Praeger, 1959.

1827. Cleveland, Raymond H.; Heifner, Charles T.; Cudd, George S.; Dome, Martin; and Fruehauf, Benjamin F. "A Global Perspective on Transnational Terrorism: A Case Study of Libya." Maxwell Air Force Base, Ala.: Research Report, Air War College, Air University, April 1977.
Authors' abstract notes: "After a brief review of the history of terrorist groups and their activity, Libya is presented as a representative example of those countries which lend support to terrorists on a global scale. The many facets of that support are examined, including a look at the unique economic, political, and sociological elements of Libya. Special attention is given to Libya's charismatic leader, Colonel Mu'ammar Qaddafi. Next follows a dis-

cussion of counterstrategies that are currently used to oppose terrorism, both by unilateral and alliance actions. Finally, a broad spectrum of counteractions are proposed. . . . Three specific approaches are . . .the recommended course of action for the U.S."

1828. Colebrook, Joan. "Israel—With Terrorists." *Commentary* 58 (July 1974): 30-39.
Argues that increasingly sophisticated acts of terrorism, backed politically and economically by great powers, will eventually be as devastating as conventional warfare.

1829. Cooley, John K. "China and the Palestinians." *Journal of Palestinian Studies* 1 (1972): 19-34.

1830. ———. *Green March, Black September: The Story of the Palestinian Arabs.* London: Frank Cass, 1973. 263 pp. Portland, Ore.: International Scholarly Book Services, 1973.
Cooley is the Beirut correspondent for the *Christian Science Monitor* and ABC. He found the BSO to have no central leadership and to have shunned publicity. Cooley wishes to show that the key to peace in the Middle East is a settlement of the Palestinian problem. He outlines the history of the situation, traces the fortunes of the guerrillas, and notes the wide range of Israeli opinion. A bibliography including works by PLO, PFLP, and PDFLP spokesmen is presented. A good source book on who is who and what they believe, with an attempt to show the Arab case in a favorable light.

1831. ———. "Moscow Faces a Palestinian Dilemma." *Mid East* 11 (1970): 32-35.

1832. Curtis, Michael; Neyer, Joseph; Waxman, Chaim I.; and Pollack, Allen. *The Palestinians: People, History, Politics* (New Brunswick, N.J.: Transaction, 1975. 277 pp.
Discusses the history and political goals of the Palestinian people. Of note is its chronology of Arab terrorist acts, the political program of the Palestine National Council, and its selection of readings on Israeli views of the problem.

1833. Davis, M. *Jews Fight Too!* New York: Jordan, 1945.

1834. DeSaussure, Hamilton. "Foreword to Symposium on Terrorism in the Middle East." *Akron Law Review* 7 (1974): 373ff.

1835. Desjardins, Thierry. *Le Martyre du Liban.* Paris: Librairie Plon—SAS Production, 1976.
A reporter for *Figaro* views the Lebanese civil war.

1836. Dhaher, Ahmed. "The PLO." Ph.D. dissertation, University of West Virginia, in preparation.

1837. Denoyan, Gilbert. *El Fath Parle: Les Palestiniens contre Israel.* Paris: Editions Albin Michel, 1970.

1838. Dinstein, Yoram. "Terrorism and Wars of Liberation: An Israeli Perspective of the Arab-Israeli Conflict." In M. Cherif Bassiouni, ed., *International Terrorism and Political Crimes,* pp. 155-172. Springfield, Ill.: Thomas, 1975.

1839. ———. "Terrorism and Wars of Liberation Applied to the Arab-Israeli Conflict: An Israeli Perspective." Paper presented to the Conference on Terrorism in the Contemporary World, April 26-28, 1976, at Glassboro State College.

1840. Dobson, Christopher. *Black September: Its Short, Violent History.* New York: Macmillan, 1974. 179 pp.
    The author does a good job of collecting data on the various major incidents of Palestinian terrorism since 1968. He mentions more names connected with the movement than most other books do. He attributes terrorist actions to a flaw in Arab national character.

1841. Domenach, J. M. "Terrorism." *Al-Haq* 2 (May 1973): 72-75.

1842. Dorsey, Jr., W. H. "Arab Commandos." *New Republic,* November 22, 1969. pp. 19-22.

1843. Duchemin, Jacques. *Histoire du FLN.* Paris: La Table Ronde, 1962. 331 pp.
    An early history of the FLN, including its French operations.

1844. Ellenberg, Edward S. "The PLO and Its Place in Violence and Terror." In Marius Livingston et al., eds., *International Terrorism in the Contemporary World,* pp. 165-176. Westport, Conn.: Greenwood Press, 1978.

1845. El-Rayyes, Riad, and Nahas, Dunia, eds. *Guerrillas for Palestine: A Study of the Palestinian Commando Organization.* Beirut: An-Nahar Press Services, 1974.

1846. al-Fattal, R. K. "Palestine Liberation Movement." *Islamic Review* 57 (June 1969): 33-36.

1847. Feuer, G. ''Les accords passé par les gouvernements de Jordanie et du Liban avec les organisations palestiniennes.'' *Annuaire François de droit international* (1970): 177.

1848. Fisher, E. M. and Bassiouni, M. Cherif. *Storm over the Arab World.* Chicago: Follett, 1972.

1849. Fishman, Gideon. ''Criminological Aspects of International Terrorism: The Dynamics of the Palestinian Movement.'' In Marc Riedel and Terence P. Thornberry, eds., *Crime and Delinquency: Dimensions of Deviance*, pp. 103-113. New York: Praeger, 1974.

Fishman mentions frustration-aggression experienced simultaneously and collectively within society. He argues that the terrorist modus operandi since 1967 has changed. He presents a simple typology based upon incident location, victim, offender, and responsibility assumed or denied, discusses recruitment changes in groups, and suggests some possible testable propositions. Mentions four mechanisms for neutralization of the violent act: denial of the victim, denial of responsibility, condemnation of the condemner, and appeal to higher loyalties. Places the problem of international terrorism in the context of labeling of deviants theory and concludes that what is needed are ''successful degradation ceremonies.''

1850. Franjieh, S. ''How Revolutionary Is the Palestinian Resistance? A Marxist Interpretation.'' *Journal of Palestine Studies* 1 (1972): 52-60.

1851. Frank, Gerold. *The Deed.* New York: Simon and Schuster, 1963. 319 pp.

A journalist who covered the trial gives an account of the assassination of Lord Moyne by two young members of the Stern Gang.

1852. ———. ''The Moyne Case: A Tragic History.'' *Commentary* (December 1945): 64-71.

1853. Franzius, Enno. *History of the Order of Assassins.* New York: Funk and Wagnalls, 1969.

1854. Friendly, Sr., A. ''The Middle East: The Fedayeen.'' *Atlantic Monthly* 224 (September 1969): 12-20.

1855. Ganahl, Joseph. *Time, Trial, and Terror: An Analysis of the Palestinian Guerrilla Revolution.* Air War College Professional Study, 1975. 87 pp.

1856. Gaspard, J. ''Palestine: Who's Who among the Guerrillas.'' *New Middle East* 18 (March 1970): 12-16.

Concentrates on the ideological differences between Fatah, the PFLP, and the PDFLP. Contrasts in the makeup of the rank and file are also noted. He speculates on what the guerrillas will do next if convinced that their regular crimes are unable to defeat Israel militarily.

1857. Ghareeb, E. "Munich and Beyond." *Arab Palestinian Resistance* 4 (October 1972): 39-43.

1858. Ghilan, M. "Is There a Black September?" *Israel and Palestine* 16-17 (December 1972-January 1973): 1-2.

1859. Gimlin, Hoyt. "Arab Guerrillas." *Editorial Research Reports*, April 25, 1969.

1860. Golan, Galia. "The Soviet Union and the PLO." *Adelphi Papers* 131 (Winter 1976): Available as FAR 26780-N.

1861. Goldberg, Yona. *Haganah or Terror.* New York: Hechalutz, 1947.

1862. Grant, Z. B. "Commando Revolution: A Hundred Years' War in the Middle East?" *New Republic*, January 24, 1970, pp. 9-11.

1863. Groussard, Serge. *The Blood of Israel: The Massacre of the Israeli Athletes, the Olympics, 1972.* Translated by Harold J. Salemson. New York: Morrow, 1975. 464 pp.
Reviewed by Peter Jennings, "A Minute-by-Minute Reliving of the 1972 Munich Massacre," *Washington Post*, July 19, 1975, p. C2. A detailed description of the negotiations betwen the BSO and the German authorities is the book's strongest point. The author appears to hold the Germans responsible for not saving the hostages.

1864. Haddad, W. "Jordan's Civil War of 1970-71 in Historical Perspective." *Illinois Quarterly* 34 (September 1971): 43-53.

1866. Harkabi, Yehoshafat. *The Arabs' Position in Their Conflict with Israel.* Jerusalem: Israel Universities Press, 1972.

1867. ———. "Fedayeen Action and Arab Strategy." *Midstream* 15 (May 1969): 14-22.

1868. Harrington, M. "The New Left and the Arab-Israeli Conflict." *Current* 118 (May 1970): 23-27.

1869. al-Hasan, B., et al. ''Political Assassination and the Revolution: A Panel.'' *Dirasat 'Arabiya* 8 (January 1972): 2-6, 151-166. In Arabic.

1870. al-Hasan, H. ''Fateh between Theory and Practice: The Theoretical Framework.'' *Shu'un Filastiniya* 7 (March 1972): 9-21. In Arabic.

1871. Heller, Mark A. *''Foreign Occupation and Political Elites: A Study of the Palestinians.''* Ph.D. dissertation, Harvard University, 1976.

1872. Henissart, Paul. *Wolves in the City.* New York: Simon and Schuster, 1970. 508 pp. also London: Rupert Hart-Davis, 1971.
   A history of the Algerian war for independence.

1873. Heradstveit, Daniel. ''A Profile of the Palestine Guerrillas.'' *Co-operation and Conflict* 7 (1972): 13-36.

1874. ———. ''The Role of International Terrorism in the Middle East Conflict and Its Implications for Conflict Resolution.'' In David Carlton and Carlo Schaerf, eds., *International Terrorism and World Security*, pp. 93-103. London: Croom Helm, 1975.
   Discusses differences between conflict resolution, conflict management, and ''conflict rancorous,'' as well as the roles of perceptions and behavior.

1875. Hermann, K. ''Reason from the Barrel of a Gun; In Action with Arab Commandos.'' *Atlas* 19 (1970): 23-25.

1876. Himber, Robert; Bedell, Ross; and Danish, Paul. ''Terror in Beriut [sic]: An Inside Look at the PLO'' *Soldier of Fortune* 2 (Winter 1977): 16-21, 72.
   A discussion of how the UNWRA is used as a front to obtain money for Palestinian terrorism.

1877. Hirsch, Valia. ''The Truth about the Terrorists.'' *Today* 1 (January 1945): 10-12.

1878. Hirst, David. *The Gun and the Olive Branch: The Roots of Violence in the Middle East.* London: Faber and Faber, 1977. 367 pp.

1879. Horowitz, Irving Louis. *Israeli Ecstasies/Jewish Agonies.* New York: Oxford University Press, 1974. 272 pp.
   Last chapter discusses contemporary terrorist threats.

1880. Hottinger, A. ''The Fedayeen in Jordan.'' *Swiss Review of World Affairs* 20 (September 1970): 15-19.

1881. "How American Radicals See the Resistance Dilemma." *Journal of Palestine Studies* 1 (Summer 1972): 3-26.

1882. Howley, Dennis C. *The U.N. and the Palestinians.* New York: Exposition Press, 1975. 168 pp.

Discusses the history of the Palestinian community and its emergence as a political force. Of interest to students of terrorism is the appendix, which lists the major guerrilla groups operating in the area.

1883. Hudson, Michael C. "Developments and Setbacks in the Palestinian Resistance Movement." *Journal of Palestine Studies* 1 (Spring 1972): 64-84.

1884. Hurni, Ferdinand. "Terrorism and the Struggle for Palestine." *Swiss Review of World Affairs* 28 (February 1979): 14-23.

1885. Hussain, Mehmood. *The PLO: A Study in Ideology and Tactics.* New York: International Publications Service, 1975.

1886. Hutchinson, Martha Crenshaw. "Revolutionary Terrorism: The FLN in Algeria." (Ph.D. dissertation, available through University microfilms, Ann Arbor, Michigan.)

1887. ——. *Revolutionary Terrorism: the FLN in Algeria, 1954-1962.* Stanford: Hoover, 1978.

1888. The ICAO and Arab Terrorist Operations: A Record of Resolutions. Jerusalem: Ministry for Foreign Affairs, 1973.

1889. Ittayem, Mashur. *"The Palestine National Struggle: The PFLP and the Transformation of Ideology."* Ph.D. dissertation, American University, 1977.

1890. Abou Iyad: Palestinien sans patrie; entretiens avec Eric Rouleau. Paris: Fayolle, 1978. 360 pp.

1891. Jabber, Fuad. "The Arab Regimes and the Palestinian Revolution, 1967-71." *Journal of Palestine Studies* 2 (1973): 79-101.

1892. Jansen, Godfrey. *Why Robert Kennedy Was Killed: The Story of Two Victims.* New York: Third Press, 1970. 280 pp.

Attempts to give the impression that Sirhan's actions on behalf of the Palestinians were not the work of a solitary, crazed individual. A chapter is also devoted to the terrorist acts of Leila Khaled.

1893. Jureidini, Paul A. *Case Studies of Insurgency and Revolutionary Warfare: Algeria, 1954-1962.* Washington, D.C.: American University, 1963.

1894.———. *The Palestinian Revolution: Its Organizations, Ideologies, and Dynamics.* Washington, D.C.: Center for Research in Social Systems, 1970.

1895. ———. "The Palestinian Revolution: Its Organization, Ideologies, and Dynamics." Washington, D.C.: American Institutes for Research, 1972.

1896. ———. "The Relationship of the Palestinian Guerrilla Movement with the Government of Jordan: 1967-70." Ph.D. dissertation, American University, 1975.

1897. Jureidini, Paul A., and Hazen, William E. *The Palestinian Movement in Politics.* Lexington, Mass.: D.C. Heath, 1976. 139 pp.

A current treatment of the major Palestinian groups, noting the strains within the PLO, and the political philosophies of the mainstream groups as contrasted with the Rejection Front, with a chronology of major Arab terrorist attacks.

1898. Katz, Doris. *The Lady Was a Terrorist: During Israel's War of Liberation.* Introduction by Konrad Bercovici. New York: Shiloni, 1953. 192 pp.

Katz, writing for an American audience, works for Shelach, the Organization for the Rehabilitation of Fighters in Israel's War of Liberation, which acts as an apologist group for the historical deeds of the Irgun.

1899. Katz, Samuel. *Days of Fire.* Garden City, N.Y.: Doubleday, 1968.

The author, an Irgun leader, gives backgrounds of major principals, chronologies of events, bibliographies, and detailed accounts of Irgun actions.

1900. Kazziha, Walid. *Revolutionary Transformation in the Arab World: Habash and His Comrades from Nationalism to Marxism.* New York: St. Martin's Press, 1975. 118 pp.

Reviewed by William B. Quandt, *American Political Science Review* 71 (September 1977): 1238-1239.

Quandt views the book as a useful history of the movement, which has spawned the South Yemen regime, as well as the PFLP and PDFLP. Kazziha was a member of the movement for eight years and writes from experience rather than with theoretical rigor.

1901. Kelidar, Abbas. "The Palestine Guerrilla Movement." *World Today* 29 (October 1973): 412-420.

1902. "Khartoum-Mocking the Dead." *Congressional Record* 120 (1974): S 11701.

1903. al-Khashaf. *Arab Terrorism, American Style.* Gaithersburg, Md.: International Association of Chiefs of Police, 1974.

1904. Kiernan, Thomas. *Arafat: The Man and the Myth.* New York: Norton, 1976. 281 pp.

A biography of the leader of the PLO, based upon interviews with Arafat and scores of individuals who have dealt with him. Reviewed by Judith Miller, "You Say Shalom, I Say Salaam," *Washington Post-Book World*, September 26, 1976, who argues that the book is too hostile to Arafat to be of scholarly use.

1905. Kimche, Jon. "Israel and the Palestinians." In *The Arab-Israeli Dispute.* London: Institute for the Study of Conflict Special Report, 1971.

Discusses the difference between the Irgun and contemporary Palestinian terrorists, operating from an outside base and with little support within Israel.

1906. Krosney, Herbert. "The PLO's Moscow Connection." *New York*, September 24, 1979, pp. 64-72.

The author, a Canadian Broadcasting Company producer, interviewed two Palestinian guerrillas who claimed to have had Soviet training. A general description of the guerrillas' course of study, as well as the political environment of this training, is presented.

1907. Kuroda, Yasumasa. "Young Palestinian Commandos in Political Socialization Perspective." *Middle East Journal* 26 (Summer 1972): 253-270.

Data for this study on political socialization of stateless persons come from a survey conducted in Jordan in 1970. Factor analysis and canonical analysis are used in the study of commando membership, political activity, political efficacy, social background, and political learning.

1908. Kurtzer, Daniel C. "Palestine Guerrilla and Israeli Counter-Guerrilla Warfare: The Radicalization of the Palestine Community to Violence." Ph.D. dissertation, Columbia University, in preparation.

1909. Laffin, John. *Fedayeen: The Arab-Israeli Dilemma.* London: Cassell, 1973. 160 pp.

1910. Lajeikin, V. "Criminal Policy of the Israeli Extremists." *International Affairs* (Moscow) 1 (January 1972): 41-47.

1911. Laqueur, Walter. *Confrontation: The Middle East and World Politics.* New York: Bantam, 1974.

Laqueur notes the reactions of various Middle Eastern nations to the activities of the Black September organization as part of his general survey of the region's politics.

1912. Legum, Colin. "Who Are the Terrorists?" *Beirut Daily Star,* December 3, 1972, pp. 4-7.

1913. Leibstone, Marvin. "Palestinian Terror, Past, Present, and Future: Some Observations." Paper prepared for the International Association of Chiefs of Police, January 1979.

Leibstone looks at the Middle Eastern political situation, describes the use of terrorism by the major Palestinian groups, and discusses its effects upon world stability.

1914. ———. "World Terror: The PLO." Paper presented to the OACSI, U.S. Army, 1975 in Washington, D.C.

1915. L'Heureux, Richard J. "Syria and the Palestinian Resistance Movement 1965-1975." Wright-Patterson Air Force Base, Ohio: Air Force Institute of Technology, May 11, 1976.

1916. "Libya's Foreign Adventures." *Conflict Studies* 41 (London: Institute for the Study of Conflict).

1917. Little, S. "Fedayeen: Palestinian Commandos." *Military Review* 50 (November 1970): 49-55.

1918. Little, Thomas. "The Nature of the Palestinian Resistance Movement." *Asian Affairs* 57 (1970): 157-169.

1919. ———. "New Arab Extremists: A View from the Arab World." *Conflict Studies* 4 (May 1970): 5-22.

Notes the historical, contemporary, economic, and political contexts of the Palestinian question, pointing out the extent of Soviet and Western influence. The appendix lists the names, ideology, and leadership of the major terrorist groups in the area.

1920. Lofty, Medhat Samy. "Comments from a Member of the Office of the Ministry of Justice, Egypt." Presented at the panel on Approaches to the Problem of International Terrorism of the World Peace through Law Convention, October 14, 1975, at Washington, D.C.

1921. Lundsten, Mary E. "Old Wine, Recycled Bottles: A Synthetic Approach to Social Conflict in Palestine." Paper presented at the annual meeting of the International Studies Association, February 1976, at Toronto, Canada. Reprinted as FAR 24736-N.

1922. Ma'oz, Moshe. *Soviet and Chinese Relations with the Palestinian Guerrilla Organizations.* Jerusalem: Hebrew University of Jerusalem, March 1974.

1923. Mardor, Munya. *Haganah.* New York: New American Library, 1966.

1924. Mark, Clyde F. "Palestinians and Palestine." Washington, D.C.: Library of Congress, Congressional Research Service, Major Issues System, Foreign Affairs and National Defense Division, October 15, 1976.

A background paper on the Palestinian question, discussing the plight of the refugees, the role of the PLO, Israeli viewpoints, and U.S. policy. Congressional hearings and legislation are listed, along with a short bibliography and chronology of incidents occurring between January 1974 and September 1976.

1925. Matekalo, I. *Mysteries of International Terrorism.* Paris: Julliard, 1973. 221 pp.

A discussion of terrorism by the Black Panthers, Black September, and the Dev Genc.

1926. McWilliams, Carey. "Algerian Terrorism." *Nation*, November 12, 1960, pp 4-5.

1927. Mecklin, John M. "Fire and Steel for Palestine." *Fortune* (July 1970): 84-89.

1928. Medwed, Howard. "Third Thoughts on Entebbe." *Bulletin of the Atomic Scientists* (November 1976): 8-9.

A discussion of some of the ramifications of the self-help justification for the Entebbe raid.

1929. Medzini, Roni. "China and the Palestinians." *New Middle East* 32 (1971): 34-40.

1930. Mertz, R. "Why George Habash Turned Marxist." *Mid East* 10 (1970); 31-36.

1931. Monteil, Vincent. *Secret Dossier on Israeli Terrorism.* Paris: Guy Authier, 1978. 450 pp.

A pro-Palestinian view of the Israeli response to terrorism, including a discussion of the Mossad-Black September assassination duels. In French.

1932. Morgan, William D. "The U.S.S.R. and the Palestinian Question." Industrial College of the Armed Forces, report no. 194, February 28, 1975. FAR document 21732.

Morgan sees the policy of the Soviets as reacting to events rather than a long-range preplanned strategy. From a disinterested position to active support for the PLO, the Soviets have reacted pragmatically. Future possibilities based upon discernible trends are outlined.

1933. Morland, Barange, and Martinez. *Histoire de l'organisation de l'armée secrète.* Paris: Julliard, 1964.

Names given are pseudonyms of police officers.

1934. Moshe, Ben, ed. "Issues and Analysis: Arab Terror vs. Pioneering." Jerusalem: World Zionist Organization, n.d.

1935. Moughrabi, Fouad. "The Refusal Front: A Study of the High Risk Politics in the Palestine Resistance Movement." Paper presented to the 17th annual convention of the International Studies Association, February 25-29, 1976, at Toronto, Canada.

ISA abstract states: "The Palestine Resistance Movement contains at least two distinct patterns of political behavior, one pragmatic and flexible, the other committed to armed struggle and a no-compromise position. This paper discusses the latter, 'high risk politics,' as a function of personality and situational variables."

1936. "The Moyne Case: A Tragic History." *Commentary* 2 (December 1945): 64-71.

1937. Mroue, K. "The Arab Liberation Movement." *World Marxist Review* 15 (October 1972): 121-123.

1938. ———. "Arab National Liberation Movement." *World Marxist Review* 16 (February 1973): 65-72.

1939. Nakleh, Emile A. "The Anatomy of Violence: Theoretical Reflections of Palestinian Resistance." *Middle East Journal* 25 (Spring 1971): 180-200.

Examines the Palestinian resistance movement in the framework of traditional concepts of political theory, such as justice, legalism, individual obligation and responsibility, political community building, and search for excellence through individual creativeness.

1940. Nassar, Jamal. ''The Palestine Liberation Organization.'' Ph.D. dissertation, University of Cincinnati, in preparation.

1941. Nasser Terror Gangs: The Story of the Fedayun. Jerusalem: Ministry for Foreign Affairs, 1956.

1942. Nolin, Thierry. *La Haganah: L'armée sécrète d'Israel.* Paris: Ballard, 1971.

1943. Norden, Eric. ''The Politics of Death.'' *Penthouse* (August 1973): 52ff.
Gives headquarters, leadership, membership, background, and activities of eight terrorist groups.

1944. OAS parle. Paris: Julliard, 1964.
A collection of Secret Army Organization documents.

1945. O'Ballance, Edgar. *Arab Guerrilla Power, 1967-1972.* London: Faber and Faber, 1973. Hamden, Conn.: Archon, 1974. 246 pp.
Notes the rise and fall of the fortunes of the numerous Arab guerrilla groups in recent memory. Discusses more than a score of terrorist bands operating in the area.

1946. ———. ''Guerrilla Activities in the Middle East.'' Paper presented to the Conference on Terrorism in the Contemporary World, April 26-28, 1976, at Glassboro State College. Published as ''Terrorism in the Middle East,'' in Marius Livingston, et. al., eds., *International Terrorism in the Contemporary World*, pp. 160-164. Westport, Conn.: Greenwood Press, 1978.

1946a. ———. ''Some Arab Guerrilla Problems.'' *Military Review* 52 (October 1973): 27-34.

1947. Ofer, Yehuda. *Operation Thunder: The Entebbe Raid: The Israelis' Own Story.* Translated by Julian Meltzer. Harmondsworth: Penguin, 1976. 141 pp. Published in Hebrew as *Operation Jonathan: Liberation from Entebbe* (Tel Aviv: Massada, 1976).

1948. Olson, Robert. ''International Terrorism: Turkey.'' Paper delivered to the 7th annual meeting of the Middle East Studies Association, November 8-10, 1973 at Milwaukee, Wisconsin.

1949. O'Neil, Paul. ''A Charming Assassin Who Loved the Good Life.'' *Life* 2 (April 1979): 101-108.

O'Neil claims that the Israeli Mossad intelligence service killed Black September leader Ali Hassan Salameh by a radio-controlled explosive hidden in a Volkswagen parked on the street where he lived.

1950. O'Neill, Bard. *Armed Struggle in Palestine: An Analysis of the Palestinian Guerrilla Movement.* Boulder, Colo.: Westview, 1978. 350 pp.

O'Neill finds that a Palestinian state under the PLO may not be a real threat to Israeli security.

1951. ———. ''Israel and the Fedayeen: Persistence or Transformation.'' *Strategic Review* 4 (Spring 1976).

1952. ———. ''Israel's Counter-insurgency and the Fedayeen.'' *Army Quarterly* 53 (July 1973): 452-460.

1953. ———. *Revolutionary Warfare in the Middle East: The Israelis versus the Fedayeen.* Boulder, Colo.: Paladin, 1974. 140 pp.

Appendix B has tables of incidents and casualties.

1954. ———. ''Towards a Typology of Political Terrorism: The Palestinian Resistance Movement.'' Paper presented to the 19th annual convention of the International Studies Association, February 22-25, 1978, at Washington, D.C. Published in *Journal of International Affairs* 32 (Spring-Summer 1978): 17-42.

The author borrows concepts devised by Richard Shultz in a companion paper to analyze the different orientations toward terrorism of the Palestinian formations. The paper is very well researched and is attuned to the subtle distinctions between the groups, which are too often fuzzed over by popular treatments.

1955. ''Palestinian Atrocities.'' *Congressional Record* 120 (1974): E5361.

1956. Peeke, John Louis. ''Jewish-Zionist Terrorism and the Establishment of Israel.'' Master's thesis, Naval Postgraduate School, 1977.

An excellent historical account of the operations of the Haganah, Irgun, and LEHI during the Israeli struggle for independence.

1957. Peretz, Don. ''Arab Palestine: Phoenix or Phantom?'' *Foreign Affairs* 48 (January 1970: 322-333.

Palestinian Arab nationalism and guerrilla activities against Israel. Discusses the historic problems that have faced the Palestinians, their relations with Arab governments, and Israeli Arab opinion.

1958. Perlmutter, Philip. ''Israeli, Irish and Arab Terrorism.'' *Christian Century*, May 14, 1975, pp. 486-487.

1959. "The Permanent War: Arabs vs. Israelis." *Trans-action* 7 (1970).
Includes articles by R. Rosenzweig, G. Tamarin, D. Peretz, F. Khouri, Y. Harkabi, A. Perlmutter, and S. Avineri.

1960. "PLO Activities Since July 1970." *Congressional Record* 120 (1974): E6577.

1961. "PLO and the 1972 Olympic Massacre." *Congressional Record* 120 (1974): E6692.

1962. Politics in Uniform: A Study of the Military in the Arab World and Israel. Compiled by An-Nahar Arab Report Research Staff. Lebanon: Co-operative Printing Company, S.A.L., 1972. Chapter 10 on PLO.

1963. Prlja, A. ''The Crisis of the Palestinian Movement.'' *Review of International Affairs*, November 20, 1971, pp. 20-22.

1964. Pryce-Jones, David. *The Face of Defeat: Palestine Refugees and Guerrillas.* New York: Holt, Rinehart, and Winston; London: Widenfeld and Nicolson, 1972.
Presents a compilation of his newspaper articles and other writings to give readers an introduction to the frustrations experienced by the Palestinians.

1965. Quandt, W. B. ''Palestinian and Algerian Revolutionary Elites: A Comparative Study of Structures and Strategies.'' Paper delivered at the 1972 Annual Convention of the American Political Science Association, September, 1972, Washington, D.C.

1966. Quandt, William B; Jabber, Fuad; and Lesch, Ann Mosely. *The Politics of Palestinian Nationalism.* Berkeley: University of California Press, 1973. 234 pp.

1967. Rayfield, Gordon. ''The Role of Terror in the Middle East.'' Ph.D. dissertation, City University of New York, in preparation.

1968. The Red Devils. Riyadh, Saudi Arabia, 1976.
Traces the lives of Carlos and his four accomplices in the December 1975 OPEC raid and gives an account of their activities after Carlos killed a French intelligence agent and Lebanese police informer in Paris in 1974. It claims Carlos is hiding in Malta under secret protection.

1969. Reed, David. "The Arch-Terrorist Who Went Scot-Free." *Reader's Digest* 111 (September 1977): 114-118.

1970. ———. "Fedayeen: Israel's Fanatic Foe." *Readers' Digest* (October 1970): 168-173.

1971. Reisner, Neil. "The Popular Front for the Liberation of Palestine." In David Wallechinsky and Irving Wallace, *The People's Almanac #2*, pp. 1314-1315. New York: Morrow, 1978.
    A chronicle of the history and attacks made by the PFLP.

1972. "Rescue at Entebbe." *Readers Digest* (October 1976): 122-128.

1973. Riedel, Bruce. *The Palestine Liberation Organization.* FAR document 22114-P, 1975. 30 pp.

1974. Romaniecki, Leon. *The Arab Terrorists in the Middle East and the Soviet Union.* Jerusalem: Soviet and East European Research Center of the Hebrew University of Jerusalem, 1973.

1975. Ross, Philip. "The Illustrated Story of the Great Israeli Rescue." *New York*, August 2, 1976, pp. 26-38.
    A retelling of the Entebbe episode, with drawings by Julian Allen. The map of the airport is the best published.

1976. Rothstein, Raphael. "Undercover Terror: The Other Mid-East War." *World*, January 30, 1973, pp. 21-22.

1977. Rouleau, E. "Palestinians in Purgatory." *Worldview* 16 (1973): 28-35.

1978. Sarhan, A. "The Swiss Attitude toward the Arab-Israeli Conflict in the Light of the Sentencing of the Palestinian Fedayin." *Revue egyptienne de droit international* 25 (1970): 215-224. In Arabic.

1979. The Savage Kinship: A Chronology of the Use of Violence for Political Ends in Arab Countries. Jerusalem: Carta, 1973.

1980. Sayigh, Rosemary. *Palestinians, From Peasants to Revolutionaries: A People's History Recorded from Interviews with Camp Palestinians in Lebanon.* London: Zed, 1979. 206 pp.

1981. Schiff, Zeev, and Rothstein, Raphael. *Fedayeen: Guerrillas against Israel.* New York: David McKay, 1972. 246 pp.
    A primarily Israeli view of the actions of Fatah and other groups.

1982. Schmidt, Dana Adams. *Armageddon in the Middle East.* Arab versus Israeli through the October War: The New York Times Survey Series. New York: John Day, 1974. 269 pp.

1983. "Scope and Limit of a Fedayeen Consensus." *Wiener Library Bulletin* (1970-1971): 1.

1984. Sharabi, Hisham. *Palestine Guerrillas: Their Credibility and Effectiveness.* Supplementary Papers, Center for Strategic and International Studies, Georgetown University, and Beirut, Institute for Palestine Studies, 1970.

1985. "Since Jordan: The Palestinian Fedayeen." *Conflict Studies* 38 (September 1973): 3-18.

An analysis of international, regional, and internal factors affecting the fedayeen since the 1970 Jordanian battles. The fedayeen were unable to resolve ideological and organizational fissures, their relations with Arab states and Communists, and their lack of territory. The movement's command structure, and particular groups, are discussed.

1986. Slater, Leonard. *The Pledge.* New York: Simon and Schuster, 1970. 343 pp.

Based on interviews, the author presents the history of the underground effort to arm the Haganah in its quest to establish a Jewish homeland. Their difficulties in Palestine with the Irgun, as well as Arab terrorists such as the Helpers and Young Chivalry, are briefly noted.

1987. Sloan, Stephen, and Wise, Charles. "International Terrorism." *Anti-Defamation League Bulletin* (1977): 3-8.

Gives a brief overview of the major Palestinian groups, branding them all as terrorists.

1988. Stetler, Russell, ed. *Palestine: The Arab-Israeli Conflict.* Palo Alto, Calif.: Ramparts Press, 1974.

1989. Suleiman, M. "Attitudes of the Arab Elite toward Palestine and Israel." *American Political Science Review* 67 (July 1972): 482-489.

1990. ———. "Mass Media and the June Conflict." *Arab World* 14 (1969): 59-65.

1991. Tabbora, Lina. *Suvivre dans Beyrouth.* Paris: Olivier Orban, 1977.

1992. Tekoah, Yosef. Letter dated November 20, 1972, from the Permanent Representative of Israel to the U.N. addressed to the Secretary-General. (UNGA: A/c. 1/L.872, 27th Session, 6th Committee, Agenda item 92: Measures to Prevent International Terrorism which Endangers or Takes Innocent Human Lives or Jeopardizes Fundamental Freedoms, and Study of the Underlying Causes of Those Forms of Terrorism and Acts of Violence Which Lie in Misery, Frustration, Grievance and Despair, and Which Cause Some People to Sacrifice Human Lives, Including Their Own, in an Attempt to Effect Radical Changes, November 20, 1972.

1993. Textes de la révolution palestinienne, 1968-1974: presentes et traduits par Bichara et Naim Khader. Paris: Sindbad, 1975. 350 pp.

1994. Tinnin, David B. *Hit Team.* Boston: Little, Brown; and London: Weidenfeld and Nicolson, 1976.

The activities of the Israeli intelligence bureau's counterterrorism squad are reviewed. After the Munich Olympics massacre, the team was able to kill twelve of thirteen targets. The error in Oslo is explored in detail, bolstered by the public record, official documents, and interviews with trial witnesses.

1995. ———. "The Wrath of God." *Playboy* 23 (August 1976): 70-180.

1996. Tophoven, Rolf. *Fedayin.* Munich: Bernard and Graefe Verlag fur Wehrwessen, 1975.

1997. ———. "The Palestinians and the Network of International Terrorism." Translated by Helga Bennett. In *International Summaries: A Collection of Selected Translations in Law Enforcement and Criminal Justice*, 3: 37-44. Washington, D.C.: U.S. Department of Justice: National Criminal Justice Reference Service, April 1979.

A review of the types of aid given by Palestinians to specific terrorist groups.

1998. Turki, Fawaz. *The Disinherited: Journal of a Palestine Exile.* New York: Monthly Review Press, 1972.

1999. U.S. Senate. Committee on Foreign Relations. "Terrorist Attack at Istanbul Airport, Report to Accompany S. Res. 524." 94th Cong., 2d sess., Report No. 94-1235, September 16, 1976.

2000. Vallaud, Pierre. *Le Liban au bout du fusil.* Paris: Hachette, 1976.

A discussion of the Lebanese civil war and the role of the Palestinians.

2001. Vatikiotis, P. J. *Conflict in the Middle East.* London: Allen and Unwin, 1971.

2002. ———. ed. *Revolution in the Middle East and Other Case Studies.* London: Allen and Unwin, 1972.

2003. Verges, Jacques M. *Pour les fidayine.* Paris: Les Editions de Minuit, 1969.

2004. Vieille, Paul. *Petrole et violence; terreur blanche et résistance en Iran, sous la direction de Paul Vieille et Abol Hassan Banisadr.* Paris: Editions Anthropos, 1974.

2005. Violence and Dialogue in the Middle East: The Palestine Entity and Other Case Studies. A summary record of the 24th annual conference of the Middle East Institute, October 2-3, 1970, at Washington, D.C.

2006. George E. Wales, ''Algerian Terrorism.'' *Naval War College Review* (October 1961): 26-42.

2007. ———. ''Algerian Terrorism.'' *Naval War College Review* 22 (1969): 26ff.

2008. Who Are the Terrorists? Aspects of Zionist and Israeli Terrorism. Monograph Series 33. Beirut: Institute for Palestine Studies and the Arab Women's Information Committee, 1972.

2009. Wilson, Barbara. *Palestinian Guerrilla Movements.* Washington, D.C.: American University, Center for Research in Social Systems, 1969.

2010. Wolf, John B. ''Black September: A Description of an International Terrorist Organization and an Assessment of Its Implications for Urban Law Enforcement Agencies of the United States.'' Master's thesis, John Jay College of Criminal Justice, 1974.

2011. ———. ''Black September: Militant Palestiniasm.'' *Current History* 64 (January 1973): 5-8.
    Presents the history of Palestinian liberation organizations from the early development of Al Fatah to the Black September Organization. Argues that the situation will not end unless the Arab refugees' plight is solved. Presents excellent data on BSO leadership.

2012. ———. ''The Palestinian Resistance Movement.'' *Current History* 60 (January 1971): 26-31.

2013. ———. ''Responses to Terrorism: Self-Defense or Reprisal?'' *International Problems* 12 (July 1973): 28-33.

2014. Woods, Jr., Stephen R. ''The Palestinian Guerrilla Organizations: Revolution or Terror as an End.'' Carlisle Barracks, Penn.: Army War College, May 1, 1973.

Attempts to determine whether the Palestinians have given up hope of defeating the Israelis and have turned to nihilism as a way of life.

2016. Yaari, Ehud. ''The Decline of al-Fatah.'' *Midstream* 17 (May 1971): 3-12.

2017. ———. *Strike Terror: The Story of Fatah.* New York: Sabra Books, 1970.

2018. Yahalom, Dan. *File on Arab Terrorism.* Jerusalem: Carta, 1973.

2019. Yahalom, Yivtah. *Arab Terror.* Tel Aviv: World Labour Zionist Movement, 1969.

2020. Yalin-Mar, N. ''A Letter to a Black September Fighter.'' *Middle East International* 22 (April 1973): 14-16.

2021. Yaniv, A. *P.L.O.: A Profile.* Jerusalem: Israel Universities Study Group for Middle East Affairs, 1974.

2022. Yodfat, Y. A. ''Moscow Reconsiders Fatah.'' *New Middle East* 13 (October 1969): 15-18.

For additional readings, see ''self-help'' section, as well as entries 12, 34, 136, 139, 192, 204, 273, 348, 421, 475, 512, 525, 533, 589, 601, 619, 620, 811, 812, 956, 1069, 1087, 1093, 1095, 1098, 1103, 1131, 1137, 1149, 1155, 1157, 1158, 1161, 1162, 1164, 1165, 1166, 1168, 1170, 1173, 1178, 1186, 1187, 1189, 1192, 1194, 1430, 1675, 1676, 1702, 1716, 1733, 2994, 3295, 3316, 3393, and 3400.

STATE TERRORISM

2023. Alesevich, Eugene. "Police Terrorism." In Marius Livingston, et al., eds., *International Terrorism in the Contemporary World*, pp. 269-275. Westport, Conn.: Greenwood Press, 1978.

2024. Amnesty International. *Report on Torture.* New York. Farrar, Straus, and Giroux, 1975. 285 pp.
    A. I. is remarkably impartial in its report and does not single out any particular nation on the basis of its official political ideologies. Rather it has attempted to locate and evaluate evidence of torture being practiced by all of the world's governments. It is quick to point out that a nation's exclusion does not mean lack of torture and could mean more efficient suppression of damaging information. Discussions of the effects of torture and legal remedies are also forwarded. The report centers on torture as an aspect of state terrorism, and perhaps due to lack of reliable evidence, gives only brief mention of torture conducted by groups not holding governmental power.

2025. Andics, Helmut. *Rule of Terror: Russia under Lenin and Stalin.* New York: Holt, Rinehart, and Winston, 1969. 208 pp.

2026. Arens, Richard. "Terrorism from Above: Genocide." Paper presented to the Conference on Psychopathology and Political Violence, November 16-17, 1979, at the University of Chicago.

2027. Bergmen, R. A. M. "Who Is Old? Death Rate in Japanese Concentration Camp as Criterion of Age." *Journal of Gerontology* 3 (1948): 14-17.

2028. Bicudo, Helio. *My Testimony on the Death Squad.* São Paulo, Brazil: São Paulo Justice and Peace Commission, October 1976.
    The author was a district attorney named as a special prosecutor to prepare indictments against death squad murderers in São Paulo. Ties with the police and military forces are given special attention. Reviewed by Bruce Handler, "Death Squads Tied to Brazil's Regime," *Washington Post*, December 26, 1976, pp. A-38—A-39.

2029. Brown, Richard Maxwell. ''The History of Extralegal Violence in Support of Community Values.'' In Thomas Rose, ed., *Violence in America: A Historical and Contemporary Reader*, pp. 86-95. New York: Vintage, 1970.

2030. ———. *Strain of Violence: Historical Studies in American Violence and Vigilantism.* New York: Oxford University Press, 1975.
   Reviewed by J. W. Ely, *Columbia Law Review* 76 (1976): 361.

2031. Chambard, Claude. *The Maquis: A History of the French Resistance Movement.* Indianapolis: Bobbs-Merrill, 1976.
   The battle between the Nazi government-by-terror and French undergrounds is the object of study.

2032. Conquest, Robert. *The Great Terror.* New York: Macmillan, 1973. 844 pp.
   The definitive study of Stalin's purges in the 1930s.

2033. Crozier, Brian. *Since Stalin.* New York: Coward-McCann, 1970. Published in England as *The Future of Communist Power* (London: Eyre and Spottiswoode, 1970).

2034. Dadrian, Vahakn N. ''The Common Features of the Armenian and Jewish Cases of Genocide: A Comparative Victimological Perspective.'' In Israel Drapkin and Emilio Viano, eds., *Victimology: A New Focus*, pp. 99-120, Lexington, Mass.: Lexington Books, 1975. Available as FAR 22820-P.

2035. ———. ''Factors of Anger and Aggression in Genocide in Turkey.'' *Journal of Human Relations* 19 (1971): 394-417.

2036. ———. ''The Structural-Functional Components of Genocide: A Victimological Approach to the Armenian Case.'' In Israel Drapkin and Emilio Viano, eds., *Victimology*, pp. 123-136. Lexington, Mass.: Lexington Books, 1974. Available as FAR 22821-P.

2037. Dallin, Alexander, and Breslauer, George W. *Political Terror in Communist Systems.* Stanford, Calif.: Stanford University Press, 1970. 172 pp.
   Notes the function of terrorism in many stages of political control, including takeover, mobilization, and postmobilization. Reviewed by Carl J. Friedrich, *Problems of Communism* (November 1970): 46-48, who prefers to allow for psychic states of terror that may be induced by imaginary dangers, as well as real dangers considered by the authors. He argues that totalitarian states do not exist without terror but that they may come to develop more sophisti-

cated types of terror. Terror's functions in the takeover, mobilization, and postmobilization stages of a nation's political development are discussed.

2038. ———. "Political Terror in the Post-Mobilization Stage." In Chalmers Johnson, ed., *Change in Communist Systems*. Stanford: Stanford University Press, 1970.

2039. Dror, Yehezkel. *Crazy States: A Counter-Conventional Strategic Issue*. Lexington, Mass.: D. C. Heath, 1971. 118 pp.

Despite the introduction of jargon, Dror presents a fascinating piece on entities that have shown many of the behavioral patterns of terrorist groups. His consideration of their strategies, capabilities, methods of responding to them and the probable response to them makes this neglected book important reading for those seeking formal treatment of terrorist behavior.

2040. Federn, E. "The Terror as a System: The Concentration Camp." *Psychiatry Quarterly Supplement* 22 (1948).

2041. Friedrich, Carl J. ed. *Totalitarianism*. New York: Grosset & Dunlap, 1963.

2042. Glicksman, William M. "Violence and Terror: The Nazi-German Conception of Killing and Murder." In Marius Livingston et al., eds., *International Terrorism in the Contemporary World*, pp. 423-429. Westport, Conn.: Greenwood Press, 1978.

2043. Gross, Feliks. "Politics of Violence: Terror and Political Assassination in Eastern Europe and Russia." Unpublished manuscript prepared for the National Commission on the Causes and Prevention of Violence, 1968.

2044. ———. *Violence in Politics: Terror and Political Assassination in Eastern Europe and Russia*. The Hague: Mouton, 1972. 139 pp.

Gives a history of terrorism in the area, discusses types and functions of such terror, and muses about sociological theories on the causal and driving mechanisms of terror. The appendixes include the writing of the region's early advocates of terrorism.

2045. Hamilton, Lawrence C. "Dynamics of Insurgent Violence: Preliminary Findings." In Yonah Alexander and John Gleason, eds., *Terrorism: Behavioral Perspectives*. New York: Pergamon Press, 1980.

Using path and factor analysis, Hamilton explores three competing theories of the relationship between terrorism and state oppression.

2046. Hendel, Samuel. ''The Price of Terror in the U.S.S.R.'' In Marius Livingston et al., eds., *International Terrorism in the Contemporary World*, pp. 122-130. Westport, Conn.: Greenwood Press, 1978.

2047. Hinkle, Jr., L. E., and Wolff, H. G. ''The Methods of Interrogation and Indoctrination Used by Communist State Police.'' *Bulletin of the New York Academy of Medicine* 33 (1957): 600-615.

2048. Katsh, Abraham I. ''Terror, Holocaust and the Will to Live (Nazi Germany).'' Paper presented at the Conference on Terrorism in the Contemporary World: An International Symposium, April 26-28, 1976, at Glassboro State College. FAR 25655-N. Published in Marius Livingston, et al., eds., *International Terrorism in the Contemporary World*, pp. 430-435. Westport, Conn.: Greenwood Press, 1978.

2049. Korbonski, Stefan. ''Terror and Counter-Terror in Nazi Occupied Poland, 1939-1945.'' Paper presented to the conference on Terror: The Man, the Mind and the Matter, October 15-16, 1976, at the John Jay School of Criminal Justice, New York City.

2050. Kren, George M. ''Another Aspect of War: The Holocaust, A Generation After.'' *Military Affairs* (December 1976).

2051. ———. ''The SS: A Social and Psychohistorical Analysis.'' Paper presented to the International Symposium on Terrorism in the Contemporary World, April 26-28, 1976, at Glassboro State College. FAR 25617-N. Published in Marius Livingston, et al., eds., *International Terrorism in the Contemporary World*, pp. 436-443. Westport, Conn.: Greenwood Press, 1978.

2052. Kren, George M., and Rappoport, L. ''S.S. Atrocities: A Psychohistorical Perspective.'' *History of Childhood Quarterly* 3 (Summer 1975).

2053. ———. ''The Waffen SS.'' *Armed Forces and Society* (November 1976).

2054. Langguth, A. J. *Hidden Terrors*. New York: Pantheon, 1978. 339 pp.
    Reviewed by Laurence Stern, *Washington Post Book World*, May 28, 1978. Langguth points to police-state tortures in Latin America as well as leftist terrorism. His central point of reference is the kidnap-murder of Daniel Mitrione, a police chief from Indiana who became a public safety adviser in Uruguay during the time of the Tupamaros.

2055. Levy, Sheldon G. "Predictors of Response to Oppressive Government." Paper presented to the 84th annual convention of the American Psychological Association, September 3-7, 1976, at Washington, D.C.

Author's abstract: "Hypotheses that systemic punishment, past political activity and level of dogmatism are central predictors to the endorsement of responses to hypothetical examples of governmental injustice were tested on a mail sample of 445 Detroit adults. Factor analyses of responses to 10 hypothetic situations indicated a 2-dimensional response space consisting of the legal vs. the illegal response."

2056. Levytsky, Boris. *The Uses of Terror: The Soviet Secret Service 1917-1970.* Translated by H. A. Piehler. London: Sidgwick and Jackson, 1971. 349 pp.

A history of the Cheka, GPU, and NKVD and the uses to which they have been put by the Soviet state.

2057. Loomis, Stanley. *Paris in the Terror, June 1793-1794.* Philadelphia: Lippincott, 1964. 415 pp.

2058. Mallison, Sally V., and Mallison, W. Thomas. "The Control of State Terror Through the Application of the International Humanitarian Law of Armed Conflict." Paper presented at the Conference on Terrorism in the Contemporary World, April 26-28, 1976, at Glassboro State College. Reprinted as FAR 25497-N.

2059. Merleau-Ponty, Maurice. *Humanism and Terror: An Essay on the Communist Problem.* Translated and with notes by John O'Neill. Boston: Beacon Press, 1969. 189 pp.

2060. Moore, Jr., Barrington. *Terror and Progress in the U.S.S.R.* Cambridge: Harvard University Press, 1954.

2061. Nowell, George W. "Vigilantism: Terrorism in Support of the Establishment." *Stanford Journal of International Studies* 12 (Spring 1977): 185ff.

2062. O'Higgins, Paul. "Unlawful Seizure of Persons by States." In M. Cherif Bassiouni, ed. *International Terrorism and Political Crimes*, pp. 336-342. Springfield, Ill.: Thomas, 1975.

2063. Payne, Robert. *The Terrorist: The Story of the Forerunners of Stalin.* New York: Funk and Wagnalls, 1957.

2064. ———. *Zero: Story of Terrorism*. New York: John Day, 1950.

2065. Rosenbaum, H. John, and Sederberg, Peter C. "Vigilantism: An Analysis of Establishment Violence." *Comparative Politics* 6 (1974): 541-570.

2066. Solzhenitsyn, Alexander. *Gulag Archipelago 1918-1956: An Experiment in Literary Investigation*. New York: Harper and Row, 1973. 660 pp.

The celebrated account of Soviet treatment of dissidents.

2067. A Summary of Interviews with Former Inmates of Soviet Labor Camps. New York: International Public Opinion Research, 1952.

2068. Walter, Eugene Victor. *Terror and Resistance: A Study of Political Violence*. New York: Oxford University Press. 385 pp.

A sociological approach to terrorism spelling out Walter's theories of the causes and driving mechanisms of terrorism. Case material from Africa is presented in support of his arguments.

For additional entries, see 332 and 1699.

RESPONSES

GENERAL

2069. Anable, David. "Tackling the International Problem." *Current History* 180 (February 1976): 51-60.

2070. Becker, Louise Giovane; Browne, Marjorie Ann; Cavanaugh, Suzanne; and Kaiser, Frederick M. *Terrorism: Information as a Tool for Control.* Library of Congress: Congressional Research Service, July 28, 1978. 237 pp.

A summary of proceedings and compilation of papers presented at a CRS forum held on April 19, 1978. Participants discussed the overall terrorist threat, legislative initiatives, government policies and procedures, control of information, and implications for democratic societies.

2071. Bell, J. Bowyer. "Dealing with Terrorist Acts." *Intellect* 104 (May 1976): 551ff.

2072. ———. *A Time of Terror: How Democratic Societies Respond to Revolutionary Violence.* New York: Basic Books, 1978. 292 pp.

2073. Bleiberg, Robert M. "Grace in Adversity: Corporate Enterprise Faces Heavy Radical Attack." *Barrons*, May 17, 1976, p. 7.

2074. Blishchenko, I. P. "International Violence as a Special Problem of the Fight against Crime." *International Review of Criminal Policy* 32 (1976): 8-13.

Discusses international conventions against terrorist acts involving airplanes, assassination, and bombing, noting general provisions.

2075. Bourne, Robin. "Terrorist Incident Management and Jurisdictional Issues: A Canadian Perspective." *Terrorism* 1 (1978): 307-313.

A member of the Department of the Solicitor General outlines Canadian organization and procedures for crisis response, focusing on the "lead minister" concept.

2076. Browne, Jeffrey T. "International Terrorism: The American Response." Washington, D.C.: School of International Service, American University, December 1973.

2077. Buckley, William F. "Capital Punishment for Terrorism." *Washington Star-News*, February 12, 1974.

2079. Burnham, James. "Antiterror Problems." *National Review*, March 29, 1974, p. 365.

Argues that many people and governments may not oppose all terrorist actions and that countermeasures may require antidemocratic principles that infringe upon civil rights.

2080. ———. "Assessing the Terrorism Trade Off." *National Review*, January 5, 1973, p. 22.

2082. "Cabinet Committee to Combat Terrorism; The President's Memorandum to the Secretary of State on the Establishment of the Committee, September 25, 1972." *Weekly Compilation of Presidential Documents*, October 2, 1972, p. 1452.

2083. Cathey, Paul. "Business—The Easily-Reached Prime Target for Terrorists." *Chilton's Iron Age*, April 4, 1977, pp. 19-23.

Surveys the views of several heads of private security consultant firms, as well as political-economic research groups, regarding the increasing attractiveness of American targets.

2084. Chapman, Brian. *The Police State.* London: Pall Mall, 1970.

Analyzes the agencies of the police state and suggests the existence of phases of their development.

2085. Clutterbuck, Richard. "Business: Fending off Attack." *Atlas* (January 1978): 35-36.

2086. ———. "Terrorism: A Soldier's View." In *Ten Years of Terrorism: Collected Views*, pp. 56-75. New York: Crane, Russak, 1979.

2087. Coates, Joseph F. "Logical and Pathological Legal and Political Responses to Urban Terrorism in the U.S." Paper presented at the annual meeting of the American Political Science Association, 1972, at Washington, D.C.

2088. "Crime Prevention and Terrorism at a Conference of Scandinavian Police Chiefs." *Svensk Polis* 6-7 (1975): 2-11.

Extracts from speeches given at the Eleventh Conference of Scandinavian Police Chiefs at Stockholm, May 1975, by Swedish, Danish, Norwegian, and Finnish representatives.

2089. "Crime without Punishment." *Parade*, March 16, 1975.

2090. Daniker, Gustav. *Antiterror-Strategie: Fakten, Folgerungen, Forderungen, Neue Wege Der Terroristenbekampfung.* Stuttgart: Verlag Huber Frauenfeld, 1978. 325 pp.

2091. Dean, Ben. "Organizational Response to Terrorist Victimization: A Case Study of the Hanafi Hostage-Takings." In Ronald D. Crelinsten, ed., *Dimensions of Victimization in the Context of Terroristic Acts*, pp. 119-127. Montreal: International Center for Comparative Criminology, 1977.

2092. Donner, Frank. "The Terrorist as Scapegoat: Intelligence on the Attack." *Nation*, May 20, 1978, pp. 590-594.

Argues that fear of domestic terrorism is being misused as a rationalization for expanding internal security activities.

2093. "Editorial." *Foreign Service Journal* (June 1970).

Examines various proposals for combating terrorism. Argues that governments should agree not to pay ransoms in the form of money or prisoner release and should not pressure other governments to take steps they would not use on behalf of their own nationals.

2094. Ellenberg, Edward S. *International Terrorism vs. Democracy.* Cologne, 1972.

2095. ———. *Western Democracies vs. Terrorism: A Study of Ineffectiveness.* Cologne, 1974.

2096. Elliott, John D. "Contemporary Terrorism and the Police Response." *Police Chief* (February 1978): 40-43.

Delves into problems faced by democratic societies in dealing with terrorists at large, in the courts, and in prison. Illustrative material from the 1977 West German experience is presented.

2097. ———. "Reactions of Organized Societies to Contemporary Terrorism." Paper presented to the 18th annual convention of the International Studies Association, March 16-20, 1977, at St. Louis, Missouri.

2098. Evans, Ernest. "The American Policy Response to International Terrorism." Ph.D. dissertation, Massachusetts Institute of Technology, 1977.

Evaluates the U.S. multilateral, bilateral, and unilateral approaches to terrorism, making many suggestions for policy improvements.

2099. ———. "American Policy Response to Transnational Terrorism: Problems of Deterrence." Paper presented to the Conference on International Terrorism, sponsored by the Ralph Bunche Institute on the U.N. of the Graduate School and University Center of CUNY and the State University College at Oneonta of SUNY, June 9-11, 1976. Published in Seymour Maxwell Finger and Yonah Alexander, eds., *Terrorism: Interdisciplinary Perspectives*, New York: John Jay Press, 1977, pp. 106-117.

Deterrence is viewed as an attempt to have costs and risks of a situation outweigh the benefits of an act by one's opponent. The development of the U.S. hard-line deterrent approach since the Elbrick kidnapping is outlined. Evans suggests that kidnappers want neither money nor prisoner release and that the current policy is irrelevant rather than effective. Other motivations of terrorists are suggested. Cosmetic concession may have a deterrent impact, and Evans suggests aiming at giving negative publicity.

2100. ———. *Calling a Truce to Terror; The American Response to International Terrorism.* Westport, Conn.: Greenwood Press, 1979, 180 pgs. Reviewed by Edward Mickolus American Political Science Review (September 1980).

2101. ———. "The Failure of U.S. Policy." *Counterforce* 1 (February 1977): 9.

Summarizes the findings of his dissertation, arguing that the United States did not treat terrorism as a political question. We had assumed that there was an international consensus on terrorism and had also failed to note the uses of negotiation situations, the goals of which had been spelled out by Habash and Marighella in writings and interviews.

2102. Farhi, David. "The Limits to Dissent: Facing the Dilemmas Posed by Terrorism." Aspen, Colo.: Occasional Papers of the Aspen Institute for Humanistic Studies, July 12, 1977.

2103. Fitzpatrick, T. K. "The Semantics of Terror." *Security Register* 1: 21-23.

2104. Flew, Antony. "Torture: Could the End Justify the Means?" *Crucible* (January 1974): 12-23.

2105. Fooner, M. "New Era of Criminality: Terrorism, Technology in Crime: Major Hazards Facing Society." *New York State Division of Criminal Justice Services Newsletter* 3 (April-May 1974): 6, 7, 15.

Discusses the use of computers for criminal activity, as well as recent trends in terrorism. He believes that Interpol would be effective in combating terrorism.

2106. "Foreign Terrorism Spreading to U.S.? Interview with Armin Meyer, Government Coordinator for Combatting Terrorism." *U.S. News and World Report*, July 16, 1973, pp. 37-40.

Mentions expansion of Execution Protection Service duties to protect embassy staffs and their families under P.L. 92539 (1972). U.S. curbing of skyjacking has been impressive—thirty-two attempts, sixteen successful in 1972, only one (unsuccessful) attempt in first half of 1973. U.S. government will not pay ransoms, but U.S. corporations "have to make their own decisions on the matter."

2107. Fowler, Norman. "How to Meet the Terrorist Threat." *Daily Telegraph*, September 4, 1974.

2108. Fox, K. O. "Capital Punishment and Terrorist Murder: The Continuing Debate." *Army Quarterly and Defence Journal* 106 (April 1976): 189-193.

2109. Friedlander, Robert A. "Coping with Terrorism: What Is To Be Done?" In Yonah Alexander, David Carlton, and Paul Wilkinson, eds., *Terrorism: Theory and Practice*, pp. 231-245. Boulder, Colo.: Westview, 1979.

2110. Gavzer, Gernard. "The Search for a Way to Combat Terrorists." *Parade*, May 20, 1979, pp. 8-11.

The author interviewed terrorists and government officials in the Middle East, Western Europe, and North America. He argues, along the lines of William Colby, that the key is better intelligence, improved security procedures, widespread public support, and international cooperation.

2111. Geijer, Lennart. "Victim Compensation or Indemnification." In Ronald D. Crelinsten, ed., *Dimensions of Victimization in the Context of Terroristic Acts*. Montreal: International Center for Comparative Criminology, 1977.

2112. Gellner, John. *Bayonets in the Streets: Urban Guerrillas at Home and Abroad*. Don Mills, Ontario: Collier-Macmillan, 1974. 196 pp.; New York: Free Press, 1974.

On the IRA, FLQ, and the October 1970 incidents. Reviewed briefly in *Economist*, August 2, 1975, p. 103, which argues that Gellner is attempting to justify the use of the War Measures Act in Quebec in 1970. Gellner also advocates creation of an internal security force such as the French Compagnie Republicaine de Securité.

2113. Godfrey, David. ''The Response of the Banking Community.'' In Yonah Alexander and Robert A. Kilmarx, eds. *Political Terrorism and Business: The Threat and Response*, pp. 244-264. New York: Praeger, 1979.

2114. Govea, Roger. ''Terrorism and the American Response.'' Paper presented to the 19th annual convention of the International Studies Association, February 22-25, 1978, at Washington, D.C.
Notes several approaches to responding to terrorism and points out that many misconceptions pervade the study of terrorism.

2115. Graves, C. Allen. ''The U.S. Government's Response to Terrorism.'' In Yonah Alexander and Robert A. Kilmarx, eds., *Political Terrorism and Business: The Threat and Response*, pp. 293-306. New York: Praeger, 1979.

2116. Green, H. P. ''Q-Clearance: The Development of a Personnel Security Program.'' *Bulletin of the Atomic Scientists* (May 1964).

2117. Greer, Herb. ''Grim Argument.'' *Encounter* 46 (1976): 50ff.
Surveys the legal status of the terrorist and argues for the death penalty.

2118. Gregory, Frank. ''Protest and Violence: The Police Response; A Comparative Analysis of Democratic Methods.'' *Conflict Studies* 75 (September 1976): 14 pp.
Attempts to explore the reasons why democratic nations need not become authoritarian in their response to riots, terrorism, and other forms of political violence. His arguments are augmented by case studies of the police responses in France, Italy, West Germany, Japan, the United Kingdom, and the United States.

2119. Greisman, H. C. ''Terrorism and the Closure of Society: A Social Impact Projection.'' *Technological Forecasting and Social Change* 14 (July 1979): 135-146.
In looking at the United States, the author concludes that a maximally efficient attack on terrorism would also create a garrison state.

2120. Gremminger, Steven. ''Federal Government and Terrorism.'' Paper presented to the Conference on Moral Implications of Terrorism, March 14-16, 1979, at UCLA.

2121. ———. ''Governmental Response to Terrorism: Terrorism and Criminality.'' Paper presented to the Conference on Psychopathology and Political Violence, November 16-17, 1979, at the University of Chicago.

2122. Grey, Lord. ''Political Problems of Terrorism and Society.'' In Jennifer Shaw, E. F. Gueritz, and A. E. Younger, eds., *Ten Years of Terrorism*, pp. 39-55. New York: Crane, Russak, 1979.

2123. Grondona, Mariano. ''Reconciling Internal Security and Human Rights.'' *International Security* 3 (Summer 1978): 3-16.

2124. Gude, Edward W. ''Dealing with Worldwide Terror.'' *Society* 10 (January 1973): 9ff.

2125. ———. ''Some Rough Notes on Response to Terrorism.'' Paper presented at the Conference on Terrorism. U.S. Department of State, October 1972, Washington, D.C. Available as FAR 16419-S.

2126. Gurr, Ted Robert. ''Some Characteristics of Contemporary Political Terrorism.'' Paper presented to the panel on Political Terrorism of the annual meeting of the Southwest Region of the International Studies Association, March 30-April 2, 1977, at Dallas, Texas.

2127. Hadley, Arthur T. ''America's Vulnerability to Terrorism: Carter Sides with the Optimists in Government Dispute.'' *Washington Post*, December 4, 1977, pp. C1, C5.

   Discusses the merits of Presidential Review Memorandum-30, which established a National Security Council working group on terrorism. Gaps in the U.S. ability to respond to terrorist attacks, the likelihood of selection of American targets by terrorists, and disagreements with the U.S. policy-making communities are explored.

2127a. Heyman, Edward; Mickolus, Edward; and Schlotter, James. ''Responding to Terrorism: Basic and Applied Research.'' In Stephen Sloan and Richard Shultz, eds., *Responding to the Terrorist Threat: Security and Crisis Management*. New York: Pergamon, 1980.

   A review of the literature of prevention and response.

2128. Highan, Robin, ed. *Bayonets in the Streets: The Use of Troops in Civil Disturbances*. Lawrence: University of Kansas Press, 1969.

2129. Hoenack, Stephen A.; Kudrie, Robert T.; and Sjoquist, David L. ''The Deterrent Effect of Capital Punishment: A Question of Identification.'' *Policy Analysis* (1978).

2130. Hoffacker, Lewis. "Prevention and Control: The Response of the U.S. Government." Paper presented to the International Studies Association Convention, February 20, 1975, at Washington, D.C.

The head of the State Department's Office for Combatting Terrorism explains the working of the Cabinet Committee for Combatting Terrorism and its working group, which were established by the president in September 1972.

2131. ———. "The U.S. Government Response to Terrorism: A Global Approach." *Department of State Bulletin*, March 18, 1974, pp. 274-278. Also published in *International Terrorism: Proceedings of an Intensive Panel at the 15th annual convention of the International Studies Association*, pp. 85-96. 1974.

Hoffacker explains U.S. policy of responding to terrorism and claims that there does not appear to be any prospect of a diminution of the causes of terrorism. He notes the workings of the Cabinet Committee to Combat Terrorism, made up of representatives of the departments of State, Transportation, Treasury and Defense, the attorney general's office, the U.S. Mission to the United Nations, the Central Intelligence Agency, the Federal Bureau of Investigation, and the Press Assistant of National Security and Domestic Affairs.

2132. ———. "The U.S. Government Response to Terrorism; A Global Approach." In M. Cherif Bassiouni, ed., *International Terrorism and Political Crimes*, pp. 537-545.Springfield, Ill.: Thomas, 1975.

2133. Horchem, Hans Josef. "The German Government Response to Terrorism." In Yonah Alexander and Robert A. Kilmarx, eds., *Political Terrorism and Business: The Threat and Response*, pp. 428-447. New York: Praeger, 1979.

2134. Horowitz, Irving Louis. "Can Democracy Cope with Terrorism?" *Civil Liberties Review* 4 (May-June 1977): 29-37.

2135. ———. "Terrorism and Civil Liberties." Paper presented to the Conference on International Terrorism, sponsored by the Ralph Bunche Institute, June 9-11, 1976, at New York City. Published as "Transnational Terrorism, Civil Liberties, and Social Science," in Seymour Maxwell Finger and Yonah Alexander, eds., *Terrorism: Interdisciplinary Perspectives*, pp. 283-297. New York; John Jay Press, 1977.

Horowitz essentially calls for a moratorium on academic studies of terrorism, warning of a terrorist-studies industry, with grave implications for civil liberties.

2137. "Interrogation Procedure: Lord Gardiner's Report." *International Commission of Jurists Report* (June 1972): 17-22.

Procedures recommended by the minority report, British Committee on Privy Counsellors, concerning interrogation of persons suspected of terrorism in Northern Ireland.

2138. Janke, Peter. ''The Response to Terrorism.'' In Jennifer Shaw, E. F. Gueritz, and A. E. Younger, eds., *Ten Years of Terrorism*, pp. 22-38. New York: Crane, Russak, 1979.

2139. Jaszi, Peter A. ''Law Enforcement Planning for Extraordinary Violence.'' Paper presented to the panel on Violence and Terror of the Conference on Complexity: A Challenge to the Adaptive Capacity of American Society, sponsored by the Society for General Systems Research, March 24-26, 1977, at Columbia, Maryland.

Jaszi begins with a series of dilemmas for officials dealing with acts of terrorism and quasi-terrorism and argues that we should engage in more contingency planning, which involves five phases: problem identification, definition of objectives, preliminary specification of operating procedures, solicitation of outside views and comments, and final specification of operating procedures. One must consider all possible types of terrorist attacks and note the differences between threats and violent acts. Objectives will include ''the detection of offenses, prevention or minimization of harm to persons and property, apprehension of offenders, and collection of evidence relevant to future prosecutions and investigations.'' Other goals, which are specifically relevant to terrorist behavior, include considerations of effects of governmental responses upon imitative violence by observers who are potential terrorists, as well as the impression the public receives of authority. Goals may have to be ranked, which should include consideration of general societal values as well as organizational interests.

2140. Jenkins, Brian Michael. ''Testimony before the Subcommittee on Foreign Assistance of the Senate Committee on Foreign Relations.'' September 14, 1977, 11 pp.

Argues that the U.S. government is not properly organized to respond effectively to terrorist incidents and makes several suggestions for improvement.

2141. ———. ''Upgrading the Fight against Terrorism.'' *Washington Post*, March 27, 1977, pp. C-1, C-4.

Takes exception to the musings of Walter Laqueur and argues that terrorism is on the increase. Notes several trends, such as growing intergroup linkages, greater technical and technological sophistication, and difficulty of defense, all of which point to increases in terrorism. He outlines the problems the U.S. government currently faces in responding to terrorism and suggests a new governmental organization that would be above bureaucratic jurisdictional battles and that might be able to employ Entebbe-style commandos and improved intelligence services.

2142. Jenkins, Brian; Tanham, George; Wainstein, Eleanor; and Sullivan, Gerald. "U.S. Preparation for Future Low-Level Conflict: A Report of a Discussion, October 19-20, 1976, at the Rand Corporation, Washington, D.C." Santa Monica: RAND Corporation, P-5830, July 1977.

2143. Kasurak, P. "Coping with Urban Guerrillas: Democracy's Dilemma." *Canadian Defense Quarterly* 3 (1974): 41-46.

2144. Kerstetter, W. A. "Practical Problems of Law Enforcement." In Alona Evans and John F. Murphy, eds., *Legal Aspects of International Terrorism.* Washington, D.C.: American Society of International Law, 1977.

2145. Klieman, Aaron S. "Emergency Politics: The Growth of Crisis Government." *Conflict Studies* 70 (April 1976).
    Topics discussed include types of response to crises, threat to civil liberties, the Philippines under martial law, India's state of emergency, and democratic safeguards neutralized.

2146. Kupperman, Robert. "Changing Weapons and New Technology of Terrorism." Paper presented to the 19th annual convention of the International Studies Association, February 22-25, 1978, at Washington, D.C.
    ACDA's chief scientist suggests three main areas in which governments can effectively respond to terrorism.

2147. ———. "Facing Tomorrow's Terrorist Incident Today." Washington, D.C.: Law Enforcement Assistance Administration, October 1977.
    The chief scientist of ACDA argues that we must have effective intelligence collection, development of counterterrorist technology, and development of contingency plans in meeting the terrorist threat.

2148. ———. "Terrorism: Challenges and Responses." Address to the Conference on Terrorism and the Media, sponsored by the Ralph Bunche Institute and the Institute for Studies in International Terrorism, November 17, 1977, at New York City.

2149. ———. "The Threat: Some Technological Considerations." In Yonah Alexander and Robert A. Kilmarx, eds., *Political Terrorism and Business: The Threat and Response,* pp. 1-17. New York: Praeger, 1979.
    A companion piece in the same book is entitled, "Countermeasures: Some Technological Considerations" (pp. 170-186).

2150. ———. ''Treating the Symptoms of Terrorism: Some Principles of Good Hygiene.'' *Terrorism* 1 (1977): 35-49.

Argues that governments may have to reconsider the ''no substantive bargaining with terrorists'' policy in the event of an incident of intermediate terrorism. Kupperman calls for a new debate upon operational imperatives of crisis management and offers some advice on preparedness measures.

2151. Legum, Colin. ''How to Curb International Terrorism.'' *Current History* 147 (1973): 3-9.

2152. Leiser, Burton. ''In Defense of Capital Punishment.'' *Barrister* 1 (1974): 10.

Argues that the death penalty for terrorists has deterrent and prophylactic value.

2153. Luttwak, Edward. ''National Controls.'' Paper presented to the panel on Terrorism and Controls of the 18th annual convention of the International Studies Association, March 16-20, 1977, at St. Louis, Missouri.

2154. Methvin, Eugene H. ''Domestic Intelligence Is Our Only Curb on Terrorism.'' *Human Events*, February 7, 1976, pp. 10-12.

2155. Milaccio, Vincent. ''Terrorist Surveillance and Control.'' Paper presented to the conference on Terror: The Man, the Mind and the Matter, October 15-16, 1976, at the John Jay School of Criminal Justice, New York City.

2156. Moodie, Michael. ''Political Terrorism: A Unique Kind of Tyranny.'' *Osterreichische Zeitschrift fur Aussenpolitik* 18 (1978): 27-38.

Moodie believes that societies must not play into terrorists' hands by overreacting, even at the cost of some lives.

2157. Moss, Robert. *Counter Terrorism*. London: Economist Brief Books, number 29, 1972.

2158. Neale, William D. ''Oldest Weapon in the Arsenal: Terror'' *Army* (August 1973).

Neale believes that sheer force alone will not halt terrorism and that the legitimate grievances must be alleviated.

2159. Nixon, Richard M. ''Action to Combat Terrorism: Statement by the President, September 27, 1972.'' *Weekly Compilation of Presidential Documents*, October 2, 1972, pp. 1459-1460.

2160. O'Ballance, Edgar. "Israeli Counter-Guerrilla Measures." *Journal of the United Services Institute for Defence Studies* 117 (March 1972): 47-52.

2161. "Opening Statement by the Honorable Robert A. Fearey, Special Assistant to the Secretary and Coordinator for Combating Terrorism, Department of State before the Senate Internal Security Subcommittee." May 14, 1975.

Explains functions of CCT and State Department regarding terrorism. Examines some trends in terrorism: decline in Arab attacks against non-Israeli targets; fewer safe-haven-providing nations: "no diminution of terrorist violence against Israel and in most countries that have domestic terrorism problems"; discussion of why terrorists have not as yet resorted to mass murder.

2162. Paskins, Barrie. "What's Wrong with Torture?" *British Journal of International Studies* 2 (July 1976): 138-148.

Paskins attempts to define the core meaning of torture. Notes the various moral positions on its use and that a discussion of this topic merits consideration. He attacks standard positions in light of the just-war tradition. The case of a nuclear bomber is illustrated.

2163. Paust, Jordan J. "Private Measures of Sanction." In Alona Evans and John F. Murphy, eds., *Legal Aspects of International Terrorism.* Washington, D.C.: American Society of International Law, 1977.

2164. ———. "Response to Terrorism: A Prologue to Decision Concerning Private Measures of Sanction." *Stanford Journal of International Studies* 12 (1979): 79.

2165. "Perspectives on Benefit-Risk Decision Making." Washington, D.C.: National Academy of Engineering, Committee on Public Engineering Policy.

2166. Phillips, Charles D. "Counterterror Campaign: The Road to Success or Failure." Carlisle Barracks, Penn. Army War College, October 17, 1975.

2167. Pierre, Andrew J. "Summary of Comments at Conference on International Terrorism." Washington D.C.: Department of State, S/CCT, March 25, 1976.

Gives a broad overview of the problem of terrorism, noting international law, security, and political responses to terrorism in the form of prevention as well as deterrence. Suggestions regarding incarceration of terrorists, sanctions against nations granting safe haven, and the need for international cooperation among like-minded nations are made.

2168. Possony, Stefan T. ''Coping with Terrorism.'' *Defense/Foreign Affairs Digest* (February 1973): 6-7.

2169. Quainton, Anthony C. E. ''Governmental Response to Terrorism: Policy and Decision-Making.'' Paper presented to the Conference on Psychopathology and Political Violence, November 16-17, 1979, at the University of Chicago.

2170. ———. ''Moral Quandaries of U.S. Policy.'' Address to the Conference on Moral Implications of Terrorism: Justifications and Consequences, March 14-16, 1979, at UCLA.

2171. Quester, George. ''Eliminating the Terrorist Opportunity.'' Paper presented to the Conference on Moral Implications of Terrorism, March 14-16, 1979, at UCLA.

2172. Rabe, Robert. ''The Police Response to Terrorism.'' In Yonah Alexander and Robert A. Kilmarx, eds., *Political Terrorism and Business: The Threat and Response*, pp. 307-330. New York: Praeger, 1979.

2173. Radliffe, Julian. ''The Insurance Companies' Response to Terrorism.'' In Yonah Alexander and Robert A. Kilmarx, eds., *Political Terrorism and Business: The Threat and Response*, pp. 265-276. New York: Praeger, 1979.

2174. Rapoport, David C. ''New Rules Could Curb Terrorists.'' *Los Angeles Times*, December 8, 1974, p. 12.
   Traces code of conduct of groups in past thirty years, noting that targets have increased. Calls for more competent media coverage.

2175. ''Remarks by Benjamin O. Davis, Jr., Assistant Secretary of Transportation for Environment, Safety, and Consumer Affairs, before the D.C. Chapter of the American Society of Traffic and Transportation, at the Embers Restaurant, Washington, D.C.'' *Department of Transportation News*, June 11, 1973.

2176. Roberts, Kenneth E. ''Terrorism and the Military Response.'' Military Issues Research Memorandum ACN 75039. Carlisle Barracks, Penn.: Strategic Studies Institute, U.S. Army War College, October 14, 1975.
   A concise analysis of the problems faced by the U.S. military in responding to international terrorism. A host of considerations not found elsewhere in the literature are raised.

2177. Russell, Charles A.; Banker Jr., Leon J.; and Miller, Bowman H., "Out-Inventing the Terrorist." In Yonah Alexander, David Carlton, and Paul Wilkinson, eds., *Terrorism: Theory and Practice*, pp. 3-42. Boulder, Colo.: Westview, 1979.

2178. Sabetta, Anne R. "Transnational Terror: Causes and Implications for Response." *Stanford Journal of International Studies* 12 (Spring 1977): 147-156.

2179. Shultz, Richard. "Responding to the Terrorist Threat: The State of the Operational Art." Paper presented to the annual convention of the International Studies Association, March 1979, in Washington, D.C.

Although somewhat dated, this is an excellent survey of methods for combating terrorism. Schultz looks at the response of businesses (focusing on physical security and executive protection), airlines' hostage-negotiation teams, quick response teams, nuclear installations, law enforcement networks, research organizations, and the international legal community.

2180. ———. "Responding to Terrorism: Prevention and Control." *International Studies Notes* 6 (Spring 1979): 3-4.

A summary of papers presented at the 1979 annual convention of the International Studies Association.

2181. Shultz, Richard, and Sloan, Stephen, eds. *Responding to the Terrorist Threat: Security and Crisis Management.* New York: Pergamon, 1980.

This collection of original articles looks at various methods for combating terrorism, from academic studies of the causes of terrorism to practical measures of executive and public protection.

2182. Silver, Morris. "Political Revolution and Repression: An Economic Approach." *Public Choice* 17 (Spring 1974): 63-71.

2183. Simpson, Howard R. "Terror." *U.S. Naval Institute Proceedings* 96 (April 1970): 64-69.

Terrorism as a political weapon: effects on security, political control, and national purposes.

2184. Sloan, Stephen. "International Terrorism: Academic Quest, Operational Art and Policy Implications." *Journal of International Affairs* 32 (Spring-Summer 1978): 1-6.

2185. ———. "Simulating Terrorism: Behavioral, Tactical, Administrative, Policy and Issue Dimensions." Paper presented to the International Studies Association annual convention, March 21, 1979, at Toronto.

2186. ———. "Simulating Terrorism: From Operational Techniques to Question of Policy." *International Studies Notes* 5 (Winter 1978): 3-8.

Describes how the Oklahoma terrorism simulations are conducted and draws conclusions from several runnings.

2187. Spargur, Robert E. *A Study of Terrorism and How to Reduce It.* Maxwell Air Force Base, Ala.: Air University, 1975. 63 pp.

2188. Speck, D. H. "Growing Problem of Terrorism." *Journal of California Law Enforcement* 10 (January 1976): 88-92.

Looks at how law enforcement could counter the trends in international and domestic terrorism seen in 1974 and 1975.

2189. Tanter, Raymond, and Kaufman, Lisa. "Terror and Reprisal: Process and Choice." In Yair Evron, ed., *International Violence: Terrorism, Surprise and Control,* pp. 203-230. Jerusalem: Hebrew University of Jerusalem, Leonard Davis Institute for International Relations, 1979.

The authors use quantitative methods similar to Blechman's 1972 study of Israeli reprisals and use decision trees to explore the policy consequences of several empirical findings.

2190. "Terrorism." Radio, TV Reports, Inc., WRC-TV, NBC Network, *Not for Women Only.* March 14, 1974. Full text of program.

Interview conducted by Barbara Walters with Ambassador Louis Hoffacker, Dr. Frederick Hacker, and Congressman Richard Ichord. Discussion of proposed antiransom bill and professional negotiations team.

2191. Terrorism: A Statement of the Problem. Fort Lauderdale, Fla.: Audio Intelligence Devices, December 1975.

2192. Thornton, T. P. "Terrorism and the Death Penalty." *America,* December 11, 1976, pp. 410-412.

2193. "Thwarting Terrorism: International Terrorism Has Emerged in Its Full Odious Degeneracy." *Alternative* 10 (October 1976): 22-24.

2194. Trent, Darrell M. "A National Policy to Combat Terrorism." *Policy Review* (Summer 1979): 1-13.

Trent questions U.S. preparedness in dealing with future threats. He makes several suggestions regarding the coordination of responsibility among the Federal Emergency Management Agency, the Emergency Management Committee, and several other federal agencies.

2195. "U.S. Efforts to Combat Terrorism." *Public Information Series* P-520. Washington, D.C.: Bureau of Public Affairs, U.S. Department of State, January 2, 1973.

2196. U.S. House of Representatives. Committee on the Judiciary. Subcommittee on Civil and Constitutional Rights. "Federal Capabilities in Crisis Management and Terrorism." 95th Cong., 2d sess., 1979.

2197. Vacca, Roberto. "A Systems Approach to the Problem of Avoidance, Prevention and Resistance to Terrorism." Paper presented to the Conference on Terrorism in the Contemporary World, April 26-28, 1976, at Glassboro State College.

2198. Van Dalen, H. "Terror as a Political Weapon." *Military Police Law Enforcement Journal* 2 (Spring 1975): 21-26.
    Points out that terrorists' unpredictability leads to excessive fear in the public, with resultant hostility toward governments unable to protect their citizens. The author suggests removing the conditions that cause dissent in a democracy and attempting to co-opt the terrorists.

2199. van den Haag, Ernest. "Crime, Punishment, and Deterrence." *Society* 14 (March-April 1977): 11-23.

2200. Van Dine, Steve; Conrad, John P.; and Dinitz, Simon. "The Incapacitation of the Chronic Thug." *Journal of Criminal Law and Criminology* 70 (Spring 1979): 125ff.

2201. Watson, Jr., Frank M. *Political Terrorism: How to Combat It.* New York: McKay, 1976.

2202. Waugh, William J. "International Terrorism: Theories of Response and National Policies." Ph.D. dissertation, University of Mississippi, in preparation.
    Develops an events typology based upon the geographical and political relationship of the events to the responding governments. The success of policies, particularly as they relate to hostage safety, is explored.

2203. Weiler, Gershon. "A Case for Capital Punishment (for Arab Terrorism in Israel)"; "A case against capital punishment" by Leon Sheleff Shaskolsky; "A new high in ethnocentrism (commenting on the article by Gershon Weiler)" by Daniel Amit, *New Outlook* 17 (October 1974): 46-58.

2204. Wilkinson, Paul. *Terrorism and the Liberal State.* London: Macmillan, 1977. 257 pp.

Wilkinson begins with a discussion of the political philosophy behind the liberal state and the role of violence and force in establishing legitimate order. This is followed by a discussion of the threat of internal terrorism and problems of responding to it. The book concludes with speculations on the future of international terrorism.

2205. ———. "Terrorism versus Liberal Democracy—The Problems of Response." *Conflict Studies* 67 (January 1976).

Discussion includes the undeclared war against society, terrorism's underlying causes, the risks of the soft-line approach, the case for the death penalty, and problems of mobilizing public opinion.

2206. ———. "Pros and Cons of Hanging Terrorists." *Police* 8 (February 1976): 24-25.

Capital punishment, if mandated by the public, would be necessary, although it could lead to massive terrorist reprisals.

2207. Wolf, John B. "The American Corporation and Terrorism: The Threat and the Response." Paper presented to the monthly meeting of the Society of Investigators of Greater Newark, New Jersey, April 14, 1977.

2208. ———. "An Analytical Framework for the Study and Control of Agitational Terrorism." *Police Journal* 49 (July-September 1976): 165-171. Reprinted as FAR 25966-N.

2209. ———. "Anti-Terrorism: Operations and Controls." Paper presented to the conference on Counter-Terrorism sponsored by the John Jay College of Criminal Justice, June 6, 1978, at New York City.

2210. ———. "Anti-Terrorism: Operations and Controls in a Free Society." Washington, D.C.: USIA Availability List, November 15, 1977.

2211. ———. "Controlling Political Terrorism in a Free Society." *Orbis* 19 (Winter 1976): 1289-1308. Reprinted as FAR 25968-N.

Wolf suggests public education and creation of uniform penal codes and hostage policies; notes problems of coordinating state and federal hostage policies; and advocates a discretionary death penalty, improved court management, ransom laws, a responsible media, computerized information systems, and the creation of a Counterterrorist Assessment and Response Group.

2212. ———. "Police Intelligence Focus for Anti-Terrorist Operations." Paper presented to the Sixth International Training Conference of the International Association of Bomb Technicians and Investigators, May 26, 1978, at Dallas.

2213. ———. ''Target Analysis: The Essential Component of the Corporate Response to Terrorism.'' Paper presented to the Conference on Terrorism and U.S. Business, sponsored by the Georgetown Center for Strategic and International Studies, December 14, 1977, in Washington, D.C.

2214. ———. ''Terrorist Manipulation of the Democratic Process.'' *Police Journal* 48 (April-June 1975): 102-112.

Discusses terrorist motivations and how they manipulate democratic governments by the concern for limiting civil rights. This limits police responses to the early stages of terrorist campaigns.

For additional readings, see entries 360, 377, 1651, 1654, and 1815.

PHYSICAL SECURITY

2215. Adkins, Jr., Elmer H. ''Protection of American Industrial Dignitaries and Facilities Overseas.'' *Security Management* 18 (July 1974): 14, 16, 55.

Stresses the importance of good relations with the host government and its police forces. However, the corporation should establish its own terrorist contingency plans, maintain careful intelligence on the situation, and inspect all facilities.

2216. Adkins, L. ''Terrorism—How to Manage a Crisis.'' *Dun's Review* (January 1978): 96.

2217. Allbach, D. M. ''Countering Special-Threat Situations.'' *Military Police Law Enforcement Journal* 2 (Summer 1975): 34-40.

Such types of incidents include snipers, barricade scenarios, terrorist attacks, and other hostage situations. The composition and objectives of a negotiation team are discussed, as well as the organization, equipment, training, and operational tactics of special reaction teams.

2218. Basic Guidelines for the Executive. Denver: Williams and Associates, 1979. 44 pp.

A concise framework for security at the office, home, or in transit.

2219. Berman, Claire. ''The Growing Spectre of Executive Kidnapping.'' *TWA Ambassador* (August 1976): 22-25.

Discusses the rise of kidnappings of business officials and ambassadors and notes the rise of security service corporations. Some of the techniques for avoiding kidnapping are mentioned.

2220. Clutterbuck, Richard. *Living with Terrorism*. London: Faber and Faber, 1975. New Rochelle: Arlington House, 1976. 160 pp.

Reviewed by K. Minogue, "The Doctrine of Violence," *Times Literary Supplement*, November 7, 1975, p. 1318; Brian M. Jenkins, *Survival* 18 (September-October 1976): 240; and *Economist*, August 2, 1975, p. 103. Clutterbuck argues against repressive counterterrorism, which could break down society's support of the government.

2221. "Countering Terrorism: Security Tips for Businessmen Going Abroad." U.S. Department of State, Office of Security, January 1977.

A useful checklist of considerations to make in planning to live and work in hostile environments.

2222. Cunningham, William C., and Gross, Philip J., eds. *Prevention of Terrorism: Security Guidelines for Business and Other Organizations.* McLean; Hallcrest, June 1978, 98 pp.

2223. Cunnliff, Robert E., and McCoy, Kenneth B. *Safeguards against Terrorism: A Handbook for U.S. Military Personnel and Families.* Air University, 1973. 52 pp.

2224. Davis, Albert. "The Industry Response to Terrorism." In Yonah Alexander and Robert A. Kilmarx, eds., *Political Terrorism and Business: The Threat and Response.* New York: Praeger, 1979.

2225. Deane-Drummond, Anthony. *Riot Control.* London: Royal United Services Institute for Defense Studies, 1975. 150 pp.[approx.]

Chapters include the historical background, crowds and riots, motivation, government, police and the military, selected riots and their lessons, the revolutionary background, riot control equipment. Reviewed by Joseph Hanlon, "Will Weapons, Spies and Teacher Restrictions Prevent Riots?" *New Scientist*, April 19, 1975.

2226. Department of Defense Guidance Document on Protection of MAAG/MSN/MILGP/ Personnel and Installations Against Terrorism. Fort Bragg, N.C.: U.S. Army Institute for Military Assistance, April 1975. 116 pp.

A series of checklists and discussions of measures to take to deter terrorist attacks and what to do if attacked. A helpful annotated bibliography is appended.

2227. Draft DOD Handbook 2000.12, Subject: Protection of Department of Defense Personnel Abroad against Terrorist Acts. n.d.

2228. Dwyer, Tom. "Meeting the Terrorist Threat: Air Force Security Police Training in Dealing with Terrorists." *Airman* 19 (December 1975): 36-39.

2229. "Executive Protection." *Security Register* 1: 15-19.

Subtitle: "An Examination of the Philosophy and History of Terrorism, Terrorist Strategy and Tactics, and a Discussion of Why the Concept of Executive Protection Must Be Expanded to Counter the New Terrorism."

2230. Executive Protection Handbook. Miami: Burns International Investigation Bureau, 1974. 24 pp.

Gives security tips to business personnel going overseas on how to avoid becoming the victims of terrorist attacks.

2231. Fitzpatrick, T. K. "Movement Security: The Case for Armor." *Assets Protection Journal* 1 (1976): 3-10.

Points out that many kidnappings and assassination attempts occur when executives are in transit. He argues that armor can aid the executive in escaping from the scene but should not be viewed as giving total protection against a sustained attack.

2232. Fulton, Arthur B. "Countermeasures to Combat Terrorism at Major Events." Case study prepared for the 18th Session of the Senior Seminar in Foreign Policy, U.S. Department of State, 19, 1975-1976. Reprinted as FAR 25070-S.

2233. Fuqua, Paul, and Wilson, Jerry V. *Terrorism: The Executive's Guide to Survival.* Houston: Gulf, 1978.

2234. General Security Tips for U.S. Businessmen Abroad. U.S. Department of State, Office of Security, October 6, 1973. 5 pp.

Discusses precautionary measures, travel precautions, security measures for home and family, and suggested behavior in case of kidnapping.

2235. Grodsky, M. "Protection of Dignitaries." *International Police Academy Review* 6 (October 1972): 1-6.

Principles and special problems regarding visiting dignitaries are outlined. The International Police Academy's special course in VIP security is mentioned.

2236. Healy, R. J. *Design for Security.* New York: Wiley, 1968.

A how-to book on architectural security, preventive design against bombings and lootings, and so forth.

2237. Hernon, Frederick E. "Executive Terrorism: Guidelines for Avoiding Kidnapping for Ransom." *Magazine of Bank Administration* 53 (January 1977): 18-21.

2238. "How to Better Safeguard Your Bank's Executives from Kidnapping." *Bank Security Report* 5 (March 1976): 3-4.

A commonsense checklist of items that should be on file in handling the incident, as well as preventive measures that can easily be taken.

2239. Jimlstad, L. "Preventive Measures against Terrorists by the Swedish Police." *Svensk Polis* 4 (1975): 1-6.

Swedish legislation, police equipment, and cooperation with its neighbors against terrorists.

2240. Kelly, James. "The Corporate Security Crisis: A Preventative and Protective Response." Paper presented to the conference on Terror: The Man, the Mind and the Matter, held at the John Jay School of Criminal Justice, October 15-16, 1976, at New York City.

2241. Kimble, Joseph P. *Operational Guideline: Community Tensions and Civil Disturbances.* Gaithersburg, Md.: International Association of Chiefs of Police, July 1967.

2242. Kirk, Donald. "Foiling Kidnappers." *New York Times Magazine,* February 19, 1978, pp. 14-42.

The security service provided by Fred Rayne's firm to multinational corporate executives is discussed.

2243. Kobetz, Richard, and Cooper, H. H. A. *Target Terrorism: Providing Protective Services.* Gaithersburg, Md.: International Association of Chiefs of Police, 1978.

The authors explore contingency planning, threat analysis, and how to prepare for potential terrorist attacks.

2244. Kramer, ed., Joel J., "The Role of Behavioral Science in Physical Security: Proceedings of the Annual Symposium held at the Defense Nuclear Agency, Washington, D.C., on April 29-30, 1976." Also available from National Bureau of Standards, February 1977.

2245. LaBruzza, L. P. "Security and Evasive Driving." *International Police Academy Review* (October 1970).

Points to patterns in previous kidnappings and suggests countermeasures.

2246. Leibstone, Marvin; Evans, J.; and Shriver, R. "Countering Terrorism on Military Installations." Science Applications, Inc., study prepared for the U.S. Army, July 1978.

Looks at crisis management, education, and training, personnel and equipment capabilities, targets, and intelligence.

2247. Marshall. "An Analytic Model for the Fluxgate Magnetometer." *IEEE Transactions on Magnetics* 3 (1967).

2248. McClure, Brooks. "Corporate Vulnerability and How to Assess It." In Yonah Alexander and Robert A. Kilmarx, eds., *Political Terrorism and Business: The Threat and Response*, pp. 138-169. New York: Praeger, 1979.

2249. Moore, Kenneth C. *Airport, Aircraft and Airline Security.* Los Angeles: Security World, 1976. 374 pp.
    A discussion of the state of the art in airline security.

2250. "Plan for Terrorism, Security Chiefs Told." *Business Insurance*, November 14, 1977. p. 34.

2251. Prevention of Terrorism: Security Guidelines for Business and Other Organizations. McLean, Va.: Hallcrest, 1978.
    Suggests strategies for protection at home, in the office, and in transit, giving an overview of terrorism and an annotated bibliography on terrorism.

2252. Prevention of Terroristic Crimes: Security Guidelines for Business, Industry, and Other Organizations. Report prepared by the Private Security Advisory Council, Law Enforcement Assistance Administration, U.S. Department of Justice, May 1976. 42 pp.
    Offers tips on personal and corporate security in the office, at home, and while traveling.

2253. Reynolds, O. "Blind Man's-Buff: Tactics in Anti-Terrorist Operations." *Army Quarterly* (October 1968): 95-101.

2254. Russell, Charles A., and Miller, Bowman H. "Terrorism, Tactics and the Corporate Target." In Yonah Alexander and Robert A. Kilmarx, eds., *Political Terrorism and Business: The Threat and Response*, pp. 106-119. New York: Praeger, 1979.
    A companion chapter is entitled "Terrorist Tactics and the Executive Target" (pp. 120-137).

2255. "Security Suggestions for U.S. Businessmen Abroad." Washington, D.C.: U.S. Department of State, Office of Security, 1976.

2256. Shaw, Paul. "Executive Protection." *Security Register* 1 (1974): 15-19.
    Shaw traces the history of the terrorist philosophy, from its roots in nineteenth-century anarchism, its borrowings from Mao, Giap, Fanon, and

Marighella, to its flowering in the actions of the Tupamaros. He warns that security officers must be aware of weak spots that would allow terrorist actions aimed at obtaining supplies and/or money, hurting the establishment and obtaining maximum publicity.

2257. "Sniper Suppression and Building Clearance." Portland, Ore.: Police Bureau Training Division, 1968.

2258. Swan, Richard A. "Special Threat Situation Team Training." *Military Police Law Enforcement Journal* 1 (Spring 1974).

2259. U.S. Department of the Army. Office of the Provost Marshal General. "Industrial Defense Plan Against Civil Disturbances, Bombings, Sabotage." Washington, D.C., 1970.

2260. U.S. Department of State. Office of Security. "Counter Terrorist Briefing." Presented to USIA International Terrorism Seminar, August 11, 1975, at Washington, D.C.
  Gives a brief chronology of some major attacks against official U.S. personnel. Most of the paper contains detailed instructions on how to avoid kidnapping, what to do if you receive a bomb threat, essentials of residence security, guarding against letter bombs, and so forth.

2262. Wolf, John B. "Police Intelligence: Focus for Counter-Terrorist Operations." *Police Journal* 49 (January-March 1976): 19-27. Reprinted as FAR 25965-N.

2263. ———. "The Police Intelligence System." Washington, D.C.: U.S. Department of State FAR document 25967-N, October 1975.

  Also see entries 425, 426, 543, 544, 554, 555, 556, 569, 574, 577, 578, 579, 584, 589, 789, 834, 845, 858, 890, 899, 916, 977, 993, 1006, 1025, 1029, 1032, 1035, 1040, and 1673.

INTERNATIONAL LEGAL APPROACHES

General

2264. Abu-Lughad, Ibrahim. "Unconventional Violence and International Law." *American Journal of International Law* 67 (November 1973): 100-104.

2265. Akehurst, Michael. "Arab-Israeli Conflict and International Law." *New Zealand Universities Law Review* 5 (1973): 231ff.

2266. Alexander, Yonah; Browne, Marjorie Ann; and Nanes, Allan S., eds. *Control of Terrorism: International Documents.* New York: Crane, Russak, 1979. 240 pp.

Multilateral treaties and U.N. resolutions are included along with draft treaty texts.

2267. American Bar Association. Section on International Law. "Council Resolution on International Terrorism." *International Legal News* 2 (1973): Reprinted in *Vista* 8 (April 1973): 53, 56.

2268. "Approaches to the Problems of International Terrorism Symposium." *Journal of International Law and Economics* 10 (1976).

2269. Barber, Charles T. "Sanctions against Modern Transnational Crimes." Paper presented at the Conference on New Directions in International Relations Teaching and Research, May 1976, at Indiana University. Available as FAR 25331-N. Published as "Sanctions against Transnational Terrorism." In Yonah Alexander, David Carlton, and Paul Wilkinson, eds., *Terrorism: Theory and Practice.* Boulder, Colo.: Westview, 1979.

2270. Bassiouni, M. Cherif. "Criminological Policy." In Alona Evans and John F. Murphy, eds., *Legal Aspects of International Terrorism.* Washington, D.C.: American Society of International Law, 1977.

2271. ———. "An International Control Scheme for the Prosecution of International Terrorists: An Introduction." In Alona Evans and John F. Murphy, eds., *Legal Aspects of International Terrorism.* Washington, D.C.: American Society of International Law, 1977.

2272. "International Legal Controls." Paper presented to the Conference on Terrorism in the Contemporary World, April 26-28, 1976, at Glassboro State College.

2273. ———, ed. *International Terrorism and Political Crimes.* Springfield, Ill.: Thomas, 1975. 594 pp.

Most of the volume is a collection of papers presented at the Conference on Terrorism and Political Crimes held at the International Institute for Advanced Criminal Sciences, Siracuse, Italy, June 4-16, 1973. The book's appendixes include most of the major conventions on terrorism.

2274. ———. "Methodological Options for International Legal Control of Terrorism." *Akron Law Review* 7 (1974).

2275. ———. ''Methodological Options for International Legal Control of Terrorism.'' In *International Terrorism and Political Crimes*, pp. 485-492. Springfield, Ill.: Thomas, 1975.

2276. ———. ''Perspectives on World Order and Disorder.'' Address to the Conference on Terrorism in the Contemporary World, April 26-28, 1976, at Glassboro State College.

2277. "Symposium on International Control of Terrorism." *ISBA Globe* 11 (1973).

2278. Baudouin, Jean-Louis; Fortin, Jacques; and Szabo, Denis. *Terrorisme et justice; Entre la liberte et l'ordre: Le crime politique*. Montreal: Editions du Jour, 1970. 175 pp.

Three professors of law and criminology at the University of Montreal discuss the history and development of Canadian legal doctrine regarding political crime. Concepts of treason, sedition, state responsibility for protection of its citizens, and situations of national emergency are given special treatment. These concepts are compared with those of the United States, Soviet Union, France, the United Kingdom, Nazi Germany, and Fascist Italy.

2279. Baxter, Richard R. ''A Skeptical Look at the Concept of Terrorism.'' *Akron Law Review* 7 (1974).

2280. Canadian Council of International Law. *International Terrorism*. Proceedings of the Third Annual Conference, October 18-19, 1974, at the University of Ottawa.

2281. Caradon, Lord; Bathurst, Maurice; and Van Straubenzee, William R. ''International Law and International Terrorism.'' In *Ten Years of Terrorism: Collected Views*, pp. 147-169. New York: Crane, Russak, 1979.

2282. Child, Richard B. ''Concepts of Political Prisonerhood.'' *New England Journal on Prison Law* 1 (Spring 1974): 1-33.

2283. Corves, Erich. ''International Cooperation in the Field of International Political Terrorism.'' *Terrorism* 1 (1978): 199-210.

Takes a legal approach to the problem, suggesting five types of cooperative acts needed.

2284. Coussirat-Cloustere, V., and Eisemann, P. M. ''Enlèvement de personnes privées et le droit international.'' *Revue générale de droit international public* 76 (April-June 1972): 346ff.

2285. Crozier, Brian. ''Political Crime.'' *Encyclopaedia Britannica Yearbook 1975-76.*

Argues that the motivation for a crime is irrelevant, and that those committing political crimes should not be treated as political prisoners.

2286. Dautricourt, J. Y. ''International Criminal Court: The Past and the Evolution of Its Failure.'' Paper presented to the Conference on Terrorism in the Contemporary World, April 26-28, 1976, at Glassboro State College.

2287. Davis, Eric. ''Le terrorisme en droit international.'' In *Réflexions sur la définition et la répression du terrorisme*, pp. 105-174. Brussels: Editions de L'Université de Bruxelles, 1974.

2288. Derriennic, Jean Pierre. ''The Nature of Terrorism and the Effective Response.'' *International Perspectives* 7 (May-June 1975).

2289. Dimitrijevie, Vojin. ''Aktuelna Pravna Pitanja Medunarodnog Teorizma.'' *Jugoslavenska Reija za Medunarodno Pravo* 21 (1974): 55ff.

A discussion of international legal aspects of terrorism.

2290. ''Documents on Terrorism.'' *Terrorism* 1 (1977): 97-108.

This section of the journal is similar to *International Legal Materials.* Listed are section 620A of the U.S. Foreign Assistance Act of 1961, the Export Administration Amendments of 1977, U.S. Senate Resolution 48 on the Abu Daoud case, the European Convention on the Suppression of Terrorism, correspondence and U.S. resolutions on the drafting of an international convention against the taking of hostages, and a resolution adopted by the participants in the Round Table on the Protection of Victims of Violence, held in Geneva, February 9-10, 1976, at the Henry Dunant Institute.

2291. Dugard, John. ''International Terrorism: Problems of Definition.'' *International Affairs* (Great Britain) 50 (January 1974): 67-81.

An abridged version appeared in the 1973 *American Society of International Law Proceedings.*

2292. ———. ''Towards the Definition of International Terrorism.'' *American Journal of International Law* 67 (November 1973): pp. 94-100.

2293. Evans, Alona E. ''Apprehension and Prosecution of Offenders: Some Current Problems.'' In Alona Evans and John F. Murphy, eds., *Legal Aspects of International Terrorism*. Washington, D.C.: American Society of International Law, 1977.

2294. ———. Remarks before panel on Approaches to the Problem of International Terrorism, 6th Conference on the Law of the World, October 13, 1975, at Washington, D.C.

2295. ———. "Terrorism and Political Crimes in International Law." *Proceedings, 67th Annual Meeting of the American Society of International Law* (April 12-14, 1973), pp. 87-110.

2296. Evans, Alona E., and Murphy, John F., eds. *Legal Aspects of International Terrorism.* Washington, D.C.: American Society of International Law, 1977.

The final report of the ASIL research under State Department contract no. 1722-520057.

2297. ———. *Legal Aspects of International Terrorism.* Lexington, Mass.: Lexington Books, 1978. 690 pp.

An extremely useful compendium of domestic and international law on several current issues in international terrorism.

2298. Fields, Jr., Louis. "Terrorism: Summary of Applicable U.S. and International Law." In Yonah Alexander and Robert A. Kilmarx, eds., *Political Terrorism and Business: The Threat and Response*, pp. 277-292. New York: Praeger, 1979.

The State Department's expert on the international legal attempt to combat terrorism reviews the major international conventions on terrorism, as well as noteworthy U.S. federal law.

2299. Franck, Thomas M. "International Legal Action Concerning Terrorism." *Terrorism* 1 (1978): 187-197.

Appended is Franck's proposed "Draft Convention of the Duty of States Not to Encourage International Terrorism by Complying with Terrorist Demands."

2300. Franck, Thomas M., and Lockwood, Jr., Bert B. "Preliminary Thoughts towards an International Convention on Terrorism." *American Journal of International Law* 68 (January 1974): 69-90.

2301. ———. "Terrorism: What Is It? What Is It For? Should It be Suppressed, Regulated, Condoned or Encouraged? Some Preliminary Thoughts Towards an International Convention on Terrorism." Paper presented at the annual meeting of the American Political Science Association, September 1973, at New Orleans. Available as FAR 18148-N.

2302. Friedlander, Robert A. "Coping with Terrorism: What Is to Be Done?" *Ohio Northern University Law Review* 5 (1978): 432-443.

Points out some gaps and loopholes in existing international law that could easily be corrected.

2303. ———. "The Origins of International Terrorism: A Micro Legal-Historical Perspective." *Israel Yearbook on Human Rights* 6 (1976): 49-61.

A survey of terrorism before World War II and international legal efforts to deal with it.

2304. ———. "Restrictions on Terrorism: What Is Being Done?" Paper presented to the conference on Terror: The Man, the Mind and the Matter, October 15-16, 1976, at the John Jay School of Criminal Justice, New York City.

2305. ———. "Sowing the Wind: Rebellion and Terror-Violence in Theory and Practice." *Denver Journal of International Law and Policy* 6 (Spring 1976): 83-93.

Discusses the morality of those who use terrorism for political purposes and what liberal democratic societies can do to combat them.

2306. ———. "Terrorism." *Barrister* 2 (Summer 1975): 10ff.

2307. ———. "Terrorism and International Law: What Is Being Done?" *Rutgers-Camden Law Journal* 8 (Spring 1977): 383-392.

Presents a brief, current survey of the international legal response to terrorism, arguing that the problem is fundamentally a legal question.

2308. ———. "Terrorism and Political Violence: Do the Ends Justify the Means?" In Marius Livingston et al., eds., *International Terrorism in the Contemporary World*, pp.316-324. Westport, Conn.: Greenwood Press, 1978. Revised and published in *Chitty's Law Journal* 24 (September 1976): 240-245.

A useful review of international legal responses to terrorism.

2309. ———, comp. *Terrorism: Documents of International and Local Control*. Dobbs Ferry, N.Y.: Oceana, 1978. 2 vols.

Examines international and domestic legislation against terrorism and notes sociopolitical factors limiting the response. Past and present proposals to extend the battle against terrorism are outlined.

2310. ———. "Terrorism: What's behind Our Passive Acceptance of Trans-national Mugging?" *Barrister* 2 (Summer 1975): 10-71.

This is perhaps the strongest statement against any form of nongovernmental terrorism to be found. Friedlander admits that international law has failed to halt terrorism and suggests tough measures.

2311. Future International Efforts to Ensure the Prosecution and Punishment of Acts of International Terrorism: The Use of Treaties. Procedural Aspects of International Law Institute, December 1976.

2312. Glaser, S. "Terrorisme international et ses divers aspects." *Revue internationale de droit comparé* 25 (1973): 825ff.

2313. Green, Leslie C. "International Law and the Suppression of Terrorism." In G. W. Bartholomew, ed., *Malaya Law Review Legal Essays* (1975).

2314. ———. *The Nature and Control of International Terrorism*. University of Alberta, Canada, 1974. 56 pp.

Discusses different types of international terrorism, such as hijackings, kidnappings, and bombings, and notes that the nationality of the terrorist, victim, and location of the incident are important factors. Problems associated with international measures, such as actions by the United Nations, creation of international criminal courts, antiterrorism conventions, and other legal steps are discussed.

2315. Gross, Leo. "International Terrorism and International Criminal Jurisdiction." *American Journal of International Law* 67 (July 1973): 508-511.

Compares the proposals in the League of Nations and U.N. draft conventions on terrorism with those put forward by the Foundation for the Establishment of an International Criminal Court.

2316. Hall, Wilfred George Carlton. *Political Crime: A Critical Essay on the Law and Its Administration in Cases of a Certain Type*. London: Allen and Unwin, 1923. 96 pp.

An early exposition of British law regarding various types of acts against the state, noting the definition of the act, types of evidence necessary to convict, punishments for the action, and certain precedents.

2317. Hargrove, John Lawrence. "Proposal by the American Society of International Law for a Research Project on Legal Aspects of International Terrorism." Submitted to the Department of State in Response to solicitation RFP-ST-75-28, March 24, 1975.

The study will set out definitions, compile and analyze existing national legal measures and practices, as well as international measures for same, and make recommendations.

2318. Harvard Research in International Law. "Draft Convention on Piracy with Comments." *American Journal of International Law Supplement* 26 (1932): 739ff.

2319. ———. "Jurisdiction in Respect to Crime." *American Journal of International Law Supplement* 29 (1935): 445ff.

2320. Hulsman, L. H. C. "Violence, Terrorism and Norms of Criminal Law." *Delikt en Delinkwent* (June 1973): 299-303.
   Notes similarities between terrorism, the philosophy of criminal law, and mechanisms of sanction.

2321. "International Terrorism." *Digest of United States Practice in International Law.* Washington, D.C.: U.S. Government Printing Office, 1973.
   This section notes documents and incidents relating to international and domestic terrorism.

2322. Jaszi, Peter. "Victim Interests in Anti-Terrorist Legal and Law Enforcement Policy." In Ronald D. Crelinsten, ed., *Dimensions of Victimization in the Context of Terroristic Acts*, pp. 133-146. Montreal: International Center for Comparative Criminology, 1977.

2323. Juillard, Patrick. "Les enlèvements de diplomates." In *Annuaire français de droit international* 17: 205-231. Paris: Centre National de la Recherche Scientifique, 1972.

2324. Keller. "Political Terrorism." *Law and Order* (May 1973): 25ff.

2325. Kittrie, Nicholas N. "The Control of Terrorism." Paper presented to the conference on Terror: The Man, the Mind and the Matter, October 15-16, 1976, at the John Jay School of Criminal Justice, New York City.

2326. ———. "A New Look at Political Offenses and Terrorism." In Marius Livingston et al., eds., *International Terrorism in the Contemporary World*, pp. 354-375. Westport, Conn.: Greenwood Press, 1978.

2327. ———. "Political Crime and Terrorism." Paper presented to the Conference on Terrorism in the Contemporary World, April 26-28, 1976, at Glassboro State College.

2328. ———. "Reconciling the Irreconcilable: The Quest for International Agreement over Political Crime and Terrorism." *Yearbook of World Affairs* (1978): 208-236.

2329. Kos-Rabcewicz Zubkowski, L. "The Creation of an International Criminal Court." In M. Cherif Bassiouni, ed., *International Terrorism and Political Crimes*, pp. 519-536. Springfield, Ill.: Thomas, 1975.

2330. ———. "Essential Features of an International Criminal Court." In Marius Livingston et al., eds., *International Terrorism in the Contemporary World*, pp. 333-340. Westport, Conn.: Greenwood Press, 1978.

2331. ———. "Towards a Feasible International Criminal Court." Paper presented to the Conference on Terrorism in the Contemporary World, April 26-28, 1976, at Glassboro State College.

2332. Lador-Lederer, J. J. "A Legal Approach to International Terrorism." *Israel Law Review* 9 (1974): 194-200.

2333. Leach, E. *Custom, Law and Terrorist Violence.* 1977.

2334. Leber, J. R. "International Terrorism: Criminal or Political." *Towson State Journal of International Affairs* 7 (1973).

2335. Legros, Pierre. "La notion de terrorisme en droit comparé." In *Réflexions sur la définition et la répression du terrorisme*, pp. 229-239. Brussels: Editions de l'Université de Bruxelles, 1974.

2336. Lockwood, Bert. "The Utility of International Law in Dealing with International Terrorism." Paper presented to the International Studies Association Convention, February 20, 1975, at Washington, D.C.

2337. Makhovskii, A. "Zakhvat Grazhdanskogo Vozdushnogo Sydna v Svete Mezhdunarodnogo Prava." *Sovetskoe Gosudarstvo i Pravo* 8 (1971): 59ff.

2338. Mallison, William T. "Comment: Juridical Control of Terrorism." *Akron Law Review* 7 (1974).

2339. Mallison, Jr., W. T., and Mallison, S. V. "The Concept of Public Purpose Terror in International Law." *Journal of Palestine Studies* (Winter 1975): 36-51.
    Zionist terror receives mention.

2340. ———. "The Concept of Public Purpose Terror in International Law: Doctrines and Sanctions to Reduce the Destruction of Human and Material Values." *Howard Law Journal* 18 (1973): 12-28.

2341. ———. "The Concept of Public Purpose Terror in International Law: Doctrines and Sanctions to Reduce the Destruction of Human and Material Values." In M. Cherif Bassiouni, ed., *International Terrorism and Political Crimes*, pp. 67-85. Springfield, Ill.: Thomas, 1975.

2342. ———. "An International Law Appraisal of the Juridical Characteristics of the Resistance of the People of Palestine: The Struggle for Human Rights." In M. Cherif Bassiouni, ed., *International Terrorism and Political Crimes*, pp. 173-190. Springfield, Ill.: Thomas, 1975.

2343. Mann, Clarence. J. "Personnel and Property of Transnational Business Operations." In Alona Evans and John F. Murphy, eds., *Legal Aspects of International Terrorism*. Washington, D.C.: American Society of International Law, 1977.

2344. Markus. "Is There a Diplomatic Solution to Terrorism?" *Barrister* 2 (Fall 1975).

2345. McHugh, Lois. "International Terrorism: Legal Documentation." Washington, D.C.: Library of Congress, Congressional Research Service, Foreign Affairs and National Defense Division, January 20, 1978.

2346. Mertens, M. Pierre. "L'introuvable acte de terrorisme." In *Réflexions sur la définition et la répression du terrorisme*, pp. 27-58. Brussels: Editions de l'Université de Bruxelles, 1974.

2347. Meyer, Alex. "Luftpiraterie als Rechtsproblem." [Aerial hijacking as a legal problem] *Zeitschrift fur Luftrecht und Weltraumrechtsfragen* (1969): 77ff.

2348. Mickolus, Edward. "Multilateral Legal Efforts to Combat Terrorism: Diagnosis and Prognosis." *Ohio Northern University Law Review* 6 (1979): 13-51.

A discussion of the regional and multilateral legal conventions to combat terrorism, with a chart showing their ratification status.

2349. Milte, Kerry. "Terrorism and International Order." *Australian and New Zealand Journal of Criminology* 8 (June 1975): 101-111.
Sections discuss definitions of terrorism, maximum disruption through amplification, terrorism as seen existentially, terrorism and national liberation, and the prevention of terrorism.

2350. Moore, John Norton. "Towards Legal Restraints on International Terrorism." *Proceedings of the American Society of International Law* (1973): 88-94.
Author is counselor on international law in the Department of State.

2351. Murphy, John F. "International Legal Controls of International Terrorism: Performance and Prospects." *Illinois Bar Journal* 63 (April 1974).
Panel discussion at the 1973 annual meeting of the Illinois Bar Association.

2352. ———. "International Terrorism: From Definition to Measures Towards Suppression." *International Terrorism:* Proceedings of an Intensive Panel at the 15th annual Convention of the International Studies Association, pp. 14-29. Milwaukee: Institute of World Affairs, University of Wisconsin, Milwaukee, 1974.
Murphy argues that it is not necessary to settle the definitional dispute between those who view individual versus state terrorism as most important and suggests that the world community should work toward outlawing specific types of acts that are unacceptable, no matter what the motivation. He surveys the work of the United Nations and International Civil Aviation Organization, notes flaws, and suggests alternative approaches.

2353. ———. "Professor Gross's Comments on International Terrorism and International Criminal Jurisdiction." *American Journal of International Law* 68 (April 1974): 306.

2354. ———. "A Progress Report on a Study Project of 'Legal Aspects of International Terrorism' Being Conducted by the American Society of International Law." Paper presented to the Conference on Terrorism in the Contemporary World, April 26-28, 1976, at Glassboro State College.

2355. Nyhart, J. D., and Kessler, J. C. "Ocean Vessels and Offshore Structures." In Alona Evans and John F. Murphy, eds., *Legal Aspects of*

International Terrorism. Washington, D.C.: American Society of International Law, 1977.

2356. Palmer, Bruce. "Codification of Terrorism as an International Crime." In M. Cherif Bassiouni, ed., *International Terrorism and Political Crimes*, pp. 507-518. Springfield, Ill.: Thomas, 1975.

2357. Panzera, A. F. "Postal Terrorism and International Law." *Revista di Diritto Internazionale* 48 (1975): 762-765.
A history of letter bombs and a review of the provisions of the Universal Postal Convention of 1974.

2358. Paust, Jordan J. "An Approach to Decision with Regard to Terrorism." *Akron Law Review* 7 (1974).

2359. ———. "Selected Terroristic Claims Arising from the Arab-Israeli Context." *Akron Law Review* 7 (1974).

2360. ———. "Some thoughts on 'Preliminary Thoughts' on Terrorism." *American Journal of International Law* 68 (July 1974): 502-503.

2361. ———. "A Survey of Possible Legal Responses to International Terrorism: Prevention, Punishment, and Cooperative Action." *Georgia Journal of International and Comparative Law* 5 (1975): 431-469.
Much of the opening discussion on definitions of terrorism and legal prescriptions against it is taken from the author's earlier *Military Law Review* article. Of interest are his suggestions for combating terrorism, including educational programs for international lawyers as well as the general public, data sharing and intelligence, investigation and prosecution, prevention of the export of terrorism, self-help, and international organization sanctions.

2362. Peleg, Ilan. "Transnational Terrorism: A Growing Challenge in the Emerging World." Paper presented to the 19th annual convention of the International Studies Association, February 22-25, 1978, at Washington, D.C.
An overview of recent international legal debate on responding to terrorism.

2363. Pierre, Andrew J. "Coping with International Terrorism." *Survival* 18 (March-April 1976): 60-67. A shortened version is in *Orbis* 19 (Winter 1976): 1251-1269.
Pierre sees terrorists as motivated by a number of causes, including achieving transcendent political goals, receiving publicity, undermining support and authority of the state, and obtaining funds for the poor or to buy arms.

He discusses international legal measures that have been mentioned to prevent terrorism in general, as well as skyjacking and kidnapping conventions. He concludes that terrorism is a political question requiring political solutions, including prevention and deterrent measures.

2364. ———. "The Politics of International Terrorism." *Orbis* 19 (Winter 1976): 1251-1269.

Notes the problems of getting multilateral conventions accepted by world bodies. He makes suggestions regarding the prevention and deterrence of international terrorist attacks.

2365. "Protocol Concerning Measures to be Taken Against the Anarchist Movement, St. Petersburg, March 1-14, 1904." In Georg Friedrich von Martens, ed., *Nouveau recueil genéral de traites et autres actes relatifs aux rapports de droit international*, 10: 81. Leipzig: Dieterien, 1909-1939.

2366. Radovanovic, Ljubomir. "The Problem of International Terrorism." *Review of International Affairs* (Belgrade) 23 (October 1972): 6-8.

Discusses the problems faced by international conferences on terrorism, pointing out that many wish to make a distinction between legitimate freedom fighters and terrorists. The question of asylum further complicates the issues.

2367. Réflexions sur la définition et la répression du terrorisme. Brussels: Editions de l'Université de Bruxelles, 1974. 292 pp.

Reviewed briefly by Benjamin B. Ferencz, *American Journal of International Law* 69 (April 1975): 473-474.

2368. "The Role of International Law in Combatting Terrorism." *Current Foreign Policy* (January 1973).

2369. Rosen, Steven J., and Frank, Robert. "Measures Against International Terrorism." In David Carlton and Carlo Schaerf, eds., *International Terrorism and World Security*, pp. 60-68. London: Croom Helm, 1975.

Argues that concerted action has not been taken on international terrorism because the perspectives of governments differ radically. Discusses various conventions that have been adopted.

2370. Rovine, Arthur. "The Contemporary International Legal Attack on Terrorism." *Israel Year Book on Human Rights* 3 (1973).

2371. Rubin, Alfred P. "International Terrorism and International Law." Paper presented to the Conference on International Terrorism, sponsored by the Ralph Bunche Institute on the U.N. of the Graduate School and University

Center of CUNY and the State University College at Oneonta of SUNY, June 9-11, 1976. Published in Seymour Maxwell Finger and Yonah Alexander, eds., *Terrorism: Interdisciplinary Perspectives*, pp. 121-127. New York: John Jay Press, 1977.

Suggests that we have laws, but must enforce them. Rubin wonders if a definition of international terrorism is theoretically possible. What constitutes a common crime? Defining terrorism in the United States is irrelevant for purposes of municipal law, as it can be treated as common crime, but the crossing of borders is important, as it then entails the heralded political offense exception. There may be some areas for cooperation in suppressing certain acts that transcend ideology of governments.

2372. Saldana, I. "Le terrorisme." *Revue international de droit pénal* 13 (1936): 26-37.

2373. Schafer, S. *The Political Criminal: The Problem of Morality and Crime.* 1974.

2374. Schloesing, E. "La répression international du terrorisme." *Revue politique et parlementaire* 841 (April 1973): 50-61.

2375. DeSchutter, Bart. "Problems of Jurisdiction in the International Control and Repression of Terrorism." In M. Cherif Bassiouni, ed., *International Terrorism and Political Crimes*, pp. 377-390. Springfield, Ill.: Thomas, 1975.

2376. ———. "Prospective Study of the Mechanisms to Repress Terrorism." In *Réflexions sur la définition et la répression du terrorisme*, pp. 253-266. Brussels: Editions de l'Université de Bruxelles, 1974.

2377. Sliwowski, George. "Legal Aspects of Terrorism." In David Carlton and Carlo Schaerf, eds., *International Terrorism and World Security*, pp. 69-77. London: Croom Helm, 1975.

Discusses some of the conventions proposed in international conferences for the suppression of terrorism and why many of them have been defeated or watered down.

2378. Smith, Monique, and Slone, John. "International Conventions on Terrorism: A Selected Review." *International Summaries: A Collection of Selected Translations in Law Enforcement and Criminal Justice*, 3: 165-172, Washington, D.C.: U.S. Department of Justice, National Criminal Justice Reference Service, April 1979.

A compilation of the major points of selected international legal conventions against terrorism.

2379. Sotille, Antoine. "Le terrorisme international." *Académie de droit international: recueil des cours* 65 (1938): 87-184.

2380. Sundberg, Jacob W. F. "The Case for an International Criminal Court." *Journal of Air Law and Commerce* 37 (1971): 211-227.

Argues that an international criminal court would impose the same penalties for the same crime, whatever the individual's nationality or motivation.

2381. ———. "Piracy and Terrorism." In M. Cherif Bassiouni and Ved Nanda, eds., *A Treatise on International Criminal Law* (1973).

2382. "Terrorism." Work Paper of the Abidjan World Conference on World Peace Through Law, August 26-31, 1973, in Abidjan, Ivory Coast.

2383. "Terrorism and Political Crimes in International Law." *American Journal of International Law* 67 (November 1973): 87-111.

2384. Tiewul, S. A. "Terrorism: A Step Towards International Control." *Harvard International Law Journal* 14 (1973): 585ff.

2385. Tran-Tam. "Crimes of Terrorism and International Criminal Law." In M. Cherif Bassiouni and V. Nanda, eds., *A Treatise on International Criminal Law*, pp. 490, 1973.

2386. ———. "Terrorisme et le droit pénal international contemporain." *Revue de droit international de science diplomatiques et politiques* 45 (1967): 11-25.

2387. "Treaty on the Non-Proliferation of Nuclear Weapons: Review Conference, May 1975." *International Atomic Energy Agency Bulletin* 17 (April 1975): 2-61.

2388. Vasilijevic, V. A. "Essai de détermination du terrorisme en tant que crime international." *Jugoslavenska Revija za Medunarodno Pravo* 20 (1973): 169ff. In Serbo-Croat, with a summary in French.

2389. Vinci, Piero. "Some Considerations of Contemporary Terrorism." *Terrorism* 2 (1979): 149-157.

Italy's former U.N. ambassador discusses problems of definition and response in dealing with terrorism on the international and internal levels.

2390. Wilkinson, Paul. "Terrorism: The International Response." *World Today* 34 (January 1978): 5-13.

Conventions and treaties against terrorism will fail as long as several states remain sympathetic to various terrorist formations. For the present, effective unilateral measures, including an enhanced intelligence capability, are necessary.

2391. Woetzel, Robert K. "Detente in Action: A Convention on International Crimes." In Marius Livingston et al., eds., *International Terrorism in the Contemporary World*, pp. 341-345. Westport, Conn.: Greenwood Press, 1978.

2392. ———. "International Criminal Jurisdiction." Paper presented to the Conference on Terrorism in the Contemporary World, April 26-28, 1976, at Glassboro State College.

2393. ———. "The Potential Role of an International Criminal Court." In *International Terrorism: Proceedings of an Intensive Panel at the 15th Annual Convention of the International Studies Association*, pp. 73-84. Milwaukee: Institute of World Affairs, University of Wisconsin, 1974.

International crimes would include: crimes against peace, war crimes against humanity, hijacking, kidnapping, terrorism, international traffic in illicit hard drugs, slavery, piracy, and international pollution or spoliation. Discusses draft convention suggested by the Foundation for the Establishment of an International Criminal Court. Mentions many instances of terrorism by individuals.

2394. "World Code Urged for Punishing Terrorists." *Christian Science Monitor*, January 22, 1975.

2395. Zlataric, Bogdan. "History of International Terrorism and its Legal Control." In M. Cherif Bassiouni, ed., *International Terrorism and Political Crimes*, pp. 474-484. Springfield, Ill.: Thomas, 1975.

Also see entry 55.

The Law of War

2396. "Amerique Latine: Intégration, guérilla et droits de l'homme." *Bulletin de la Commission Internationale de Juristes* 32 (December 1967): 26-33.

Focusing on Latin American incidents, this article notes problems in dealing with kidnapping and other incidents of urban guerrilla campaigns.

2397. Bailey, Sydney D. *Prohibitions and Restraints in War*. London: Oxford University Press, 1972. 194 pp.

2398. Baxter, Richard R. "The Geneva Conventions of 1949 and Wars of National Liberation." In M. Cherif Bassiouni, ed., *International Terrorism and Political Crimes*, pp. 120-132. Springfield, Ill.: Thomas, 1975.

2399. Bond, James. "Applications of the Law of War to Internal Conflicts." *Georgia Journal of International and Comparative Law* 3 (1973): 345ff.
    Includes a section, "Claim to Use Terror Tactics," and interpretations of article 3 of the Geneva Convention.

2400. ———. *The Rules of Riot: Internal Conflict and the Law of War.* Princeton, N.J.: Princeton University Press, 1974. 280 pp.
    Problems of the international law of war as it relates to guerrilla operations are discussed.

2401. Bowett, O. "Reprisals Involving Recourse to Armed Force."*American Journal of International Law* (January 1972): 1-36.

2402. Brownlie, Ian. "International Law and the Activities of Armed Bands." *International and Comparative Law Quarterly* 7 (1958): 712ff.

2403. Bundu, A. C. "Recognition of Revolutionary Authorities: Law and Practice of States." *International and Comparative Law Quarterly* 27 (January 1978): 18-45.

2404. Eide, A. "International Law, Dominance, and the Use of Force." *Journal of Peace Research* 11 (1974): 1-20.

2405. Falk, Richard A. "Terror, Liberation Movements, and the Processes of Social Change." *American Journal of International Law* 63 (1969): 423ff.

2406. Friedmann, Wolfgang. "Terrorist and Subversive Activities." *American Journal of International Law* 50 (1956): 475ff.

2407. Galyean, T. E. "Acts of Terrorism and Combat by Irregular Forces: An Insurance 'War Risk'." *California Western International Law Journal* 4 (1974): 314ff.

2408. Khan, Ranmatullah. "Guerrilla Warfare and International Law." *International Studies* (New Delhi) 9 (October 1967).

2409. Lahey, Kathleen A., and Sang, Lewis M. "Control of Terrorism Through a Broader Interpretation of Article 3 of the Four Geneva Conventions of 1949." In M. Cherif Bassiouni, ed., *International Terrorism and Political Crimes*, pp. 191-200. Springfield, Ill.: Thomas, 1975.

2410. "The Law of Limited International Conflict." Washington, D.C.: Institute of World Polity, Georgetown University, April 1965.

Surveys trends in law governing conflict short of conventional war and recommends U.S. positions on these issues.

2411. Lawrence, W. "The Status under International Law of Recent Guerrilla Movements in Latin America." *International Lawyer* 7 (1973): 405ff.

2412. Mallison, Sally V., and Mallison, W. Thomas. "The Control of State Terror Through the Application of the International Humanitarian Law of Armed Conflict." Paper presented at the Conference on Terrorism in the Contemporary World, April 26-28, 1976, at Glassboro State College. FAR 25497-N. Published in Marius Livingston et al., eds., *International Terrorism in the Contemporary World*, pp. 325-332. Westport, Conn.: Greenwood Press, 1978.

2413. Mallison, William T., and Mallison, Sally V. "An International Law Appraisal of the Juridical Characteristics of the Resistance of the People of Palestine: The Struggle for Human Rights." In M. Cherif Bassiouni, ed., *International Terrorism and Political Crimes*, pp. 173-190. Springfield, Ill.: Thomas, 1975.

2414. ———. "The Juridical Characteristics of the Palestinian Resistance: An Appraisal in International Law." *Journal of Palestine Studies* 2 (Winter 1973): 64-78.

2415. Meron, Theodor. "Some Legal Aspects of Arab Terrorists' Claim to Privileged Combatancy." *Nordisk Tidaskrift for International Ret* 50 (1970): 47-85.

Gives an analysis of recent national trials of terrorists in Belgium, Greece, Israel, Malaysia, the Netherlands, and Switzerland.

2416. ———. *Some Legal Aspects of Arab Terrorists' Claims to Privileged Combatancy.* New York: Sabra, 1970.

2417. Meyrowitz, H. "Status des guérilleros dan le droit international." *Journal du droit international* 100 (October-December 1973): 875ff.

2418. Novogrod, John C. "Internal Strife, Self-Determination and World Order." In M. Cherif Bassiouni, ed., *International Terrorism and Political Crimes*, pp. 98-119. Springfield, Ill.: Thomas, 1975.

2419. Paust, Jordan J. "Terrorism and the International Law of War." *Military Law Review* 64 (1974): 1-36.

Surveys international legal protections for noncombatants and combatants. The author shows a historical buildup of community expectations against the use of terrorism and suggests areas in which law remains to be made.

2420. Reisman, William Michael. "Private Armies in a Global War System: Prologue to Decision." *Virginia Journal of International Law* 14 (1973): 1ff.

2421. Rostow, Eugene B. "Illegality of the Arab Attack on Israel of October 6, 1973." *American Journal of International Law* 69 (1975): 272ff.

2422. Santos, M. Barbero. "Delitos de Bandolerismo, Rebelion Militar y Terrorismo Regulados por ed Decreto de 21 Septiembre de 1960." *La Justicia* (Mexico) 33 (January 1974): 43ff.

2423. Schwarzenberger, Georg. "Terrorists, Hijackers, Guerrilleros and Mercenaries." *Current Legal Problems* 24 (1971): 257-282. Also in *University of Toledo Law Review* (1971): 71ff.

2424. "A Study of the Applicability of the Laws of War to Guerrillas and Those Individuals Who Advocate Guerrilla Warfare and Subversion." Washington, D.C.: U.S. Army, Office of the Judge Advocate General, 1972.

2425. Synge, T. M. "The Problem of Prisoners in Future Warfare." *Royal United Service Institute* 77 (1932): 120-123.

2426. Taulbee, J. L. "Retaliation and Irregular Warfare in Contemporary International Law." *International Lawyer* (Chicago) 7 (January 1973): 195-204.

2427. Tharp, Jr., Paul S. "The Laws of War as a Potential Legal Regime for the Control of Terrorist Activities." *Journal of International Affairs* 32 (Spring-Summer 1978): 91-100.
    Tharp begins with a historical development of exceptions to extradition treaties, noting that the "political offenses exception" makes this rule of law difficult to apply against terrorists. The private criminal law approach is similarly found wanting. He offers a law of war approach in which certain targets, actions, and weapons would be out of bounds, in return for more humane treatment of captured offenders. Problems with this approach are discussed.

2428. Tollefson, M. "Enemy Prisoners of War." *Iowa Law Review* 32 (November 1946): 51-77.

2429. Toman, Jiri. "Terrorism and the Regulation of Armed Conflicts." In M. Cherif Bassiouni, ed., *International Terrorism and Political Crimes*, pp. 133-154. Springfield, Ill.: Thomas, 1975.

2450. Veuthey, Michel. "A Survey of International Humanitarian Law in Noninternational Armed Conflicts: 1949-1974." In M. Cherif Bassiouni, ed., *International Terrorism and Political Crimes*, pp. 86-97. Springfield, Ill.: Thomas, 1975.

2451. Woetzel, Robert K. "International Crimes by Governmental and Nongovernmental Forces: Kidnapping, Hijacking, Terrorism, War Crimes and Crimes Against Humanity: An Impartial Solution." Paper presented at the annual meeting of the International Studies Association, March 1974, at St. Louis, Missouri. Available as FAR 19778-N.

Extradition Law

2452. "The Abu Daoud Affair." *Journal of International Law and Economics* 2 (1977): 539-582.

2453. Bassiouni, M. Cherif. "Ideologically Motivated Offenses and the Political Offense Exceptions in Extradition: A Proposed Judicial Standard for an Unruly Problem." *De Paul Law Review* 19 (1969): 217ff.

2454. ———. "International Extradition: An American Experience and a Proposed Formula." *Revue internationale de droit penal* 39 (1968).

2455. ———. "International Extradition in the American Practice and World Public Order." *Tennessee Law Review* 36 (1969).

2456. ———. "The Political Offense Exception in Extradition Law and Practice." In his *International Terrorism and Political Crimes*, pp. 398-447. Springfield, Ill.:Thomas, 1975.

2457. ———. "Unlawful Seizures of Persons by States as Alternatives to Extradition." In his *International Terrorism and Political Crimes*, pp. 343-368. Springfield, Ill.: Thomas, 1975.

2458. Cantrell, Charles L. "The Political Offense Exemption in International Extradition: A Comparison of the United States, Great Britain, and the Republic of Ireland." *Marquette Law Review* 60 (Spring 1977): 777-824.

2459. Carbonneau, Thomas E. "The Provisional Arrest and Subsequent Release of Abu Daoud by French Authorities." *Virginia Journal of International Law* 17 (Spring 1977): 495-513.

Uses the Daoud case to illustrate political and legal obstacles to the extradition and punishment of terrorists.

2460. Cardozo, M. H. "When Extradition Fails, Is Abduction a Solution?" *American Journal of International Law* 55 (1961): 127-135.

2461. Cochard, Renata. "Terrorism and Extradition in Belgian Law." In *Réflexions sur la définition et la répression du terrorisme*, pp. 207-228. Brussels: Editions de l'Université de Bruxelles, 1974. Translated from the French in *International Summaries: A Collection of Selected Translations in Law Enforcement and Criminal Justice*, 3: 139-146. Washington, D.C.: U.S. Department of Justice, National Criminal Justice Reference Service, April 1979.

2462. "Constitutional and International Law: International Kidnapping —Government Illegality as a Challenge to Jurisdiction." *Tulane Law Review* 50 (1975): 169ff.

2463. Costello, Declan. "International Terrorism and the Development of the Principle 'aut dedere aut judicare.' " Paper presented to the Seventh Conference on the Law of the World, World Peace Through Law Center, 1975, at Washington, D.C. Published in *Journal of International Law and Economics* 10 (1975).

2464. Deere, Lora L. "Political Offenses in the Law and Practice of Extradition." *American Journal of International Law* 27 (1933): 247ff.

2465. Evans, Alona E. "Jurisdiction, Fugitive Offender, Forcible Abduction, Ker-Frisbie Rule, Treaties, Extradition." *American Journal of International Law* 69 (1975): 406.

2466. ———. "The Realities of Extradition and Prosecution." Paper presented to the Conference on International Terrorism, sponsored by the Ralph Bunche Institute on the U.N. of the Graduate School and University Center of CUNY and the State University College at Oneonta of SUNY, June 9-11, 1976.

Discusses the major conventions regarding skyjacking and how they relate to questions of extradition, prosecution, and deportation, giving statistics on the number of skyjackers in 460 incidents of this decade and the number extradited. More than one-half of those skyjackers returned to the

United States by Cuba were returned before the 1973 note of agreement by those two countries, leading her to infer that the agreement is not a deterrent to skyjacking.

2467. ———. "Reflections upon the Political Offenses in International Practice." *American Journal of International Law* 57 (1963).

2468. "Extraterritorial Jurisdiction and Jurisdiction Following Forcible Abduction: A New Israeli Precedent in International Law." *Michigan Law Review* 72 (1974): 1087ff.

2469. Garcia-Mora, Manuel R. "Crimes against Humanity and the Principle of Non-extradition of Political Offenses." *Michigan Law Review* 62 (1964).

2470. ———. "The Nature of Political Offenses: A Knotty Problem of Extradition Law." *Virginia Law Review* 48 (1962).

2471. ———. "The Present Status of Political Offenses in the Law of Extradition and Asylum." *University of Pittsburgh Law Review* 14 (1953).

2472. Green, Leslie C. "The Nature of Political Offenses." *Solicitor Quarterly* 3 (1964).

2473. Harvard Research in International Law. "Draft Convention on Extradition and Comments." *American Journal of International Law* 29 (1935): 16f.

2474. Khan, Muhammed Zafrulla. "Asylum—Article 14 of the Universal Declaration." *Journal of the International Commission of Jurists* 8 (1967).

2475. Marchant, Daniel. "Abductions Effected Outside National Territory." *Bulletin of the International Commission of Jurists* 7 (Winter 1966): 243-268.

2476. Rapoport, Sandra E. "Between Minimal Courage and Maximum Cowardice: A Legal Analysis of the Release of Abu Daoud." *Brooklyn Journal of International Law* 3 (Spring 1977): 195-209.

2477. Shearer, I. A. *Extradition in International Law*. Dobbs Ferry: Oceana; Manchester: Manchester University Press, 1971. 283 pp.
Reviewed by Alona E. Evans, *American Journal of International Law* 67 (July 1973): 600-602.

2478. Silver, Isadore. "Toward a Theory of the Political Defense." *Catholic Lawyer* 18 (1972): 206-236.

2479. "Treaty on Extradition and Protection Against Anarchism, Mexico City, January 28, 1902." In Georg Friedrich von Martens, ed. 6, 3 ser. *Nouveau recueil genéral de traites et autres actes relatifs aux rapports de droit international*, p. 185. Leipzig: Dieterich, 1909-1939.

2480. "Tribunal de Apelaciones en lo Penal y Juzgado de Crimen de 3er Turno, Extradicion. Delitos Politicos. Terrorismo, Tratado de Derecho Penal Internacional de Montevideo de 1889. Delitos Contra la Seguridad del Estado. Concepto de Delito Conexo." In *Anuario Uruguayo de Derecho Internacional, 1962*, pp. 269-323. Montevideo: Republica Oriental del Uruguay, 1962.

2481. Vogler, Theo. "Perspectives on Extradition and Terrorism." In M. Cherif Bassiouni, ed., *International Terrorism and Political Crimes*, pp. 391-397. Springfield, Ill.: Thomas, 1975.

2482. Weis, P. "Asylum and Terrorism." *International Commission of Jurists Review* (December 1977): 37-43.

Also see entries 1716 and 1969.

Domestic Legislation against Terrorism

2483. "Act for the Protection of Foreign Officials and Official Guests of the U.S." U.S. Department of State, December 6, 1972.
A circular diplomatic note from the department to all foreign missions in the United States explaining the provisions of the act.

2484. "Airport Searches: Fourth Amendment Anomalies." *New York University Law Review* 48 (November 1973): 1043-1062.
48(November 1973): 1043-1062.
Courts have upheld such searches on questionable constitutional grounds.

2485. "Airport Security: Piracy within the Terminal." *Valparaiso University Law Review* 8 (Fall 1973): 85-106.
A discussion of the constitutionality of airport searches of passengers and baggage.

2486. "Airport Security Searches and the Fourth Amendment." *Columbia Law Review* 71 (1971): 1039-1058.

2487. **"Antihijacking Act of 1974: A Step beyond the Hague Convention."** *South Texas Law Journal* 16 (1975): 356ff.

2488. **"Antiskyjacking System: A Matter of Search-or-Seizure."** *Notre Dame Lawyer* 48 (1973): 1261ff.

2489. Archinard, André. "La Suisse et les infractions non aerliennes commises a bord des aeronefs civils." *ASDA Bulletin SVIR*, no. 3 (1968): 3-9; no. 1 (1969): 2-10; no. 2 (1969): 1-12.

2490. Bishop, Jr., Joseph W. "Can Democracy Defend Itself against Terrorism?" *Commentary* 65 (May 1978): 55-62.
    An examination of the emergency measures employed in Northern Ireland and a discussion of possible abuse of these powers.

2491. Boschi, M. "Tendencies in Court Decisions Concerned with the Illegal Capture of Aircraft: Italy." *Rivista di Polizia* 28 (August-September 1975): 497-517.
    A comparison of U.S. and Italian antihijacking law.

2492. **"Brazilian Hijacking Law (October 20, 1969): Decree-law 975 of 20 October 1969 Defining Crimes of Smuggling and Transportation of Terrorists and Subversives in Aircraft."** *International Legal Materials* 9 (1970): 180-184.

2493. Brodsky. " 'Terry' and the Pirates: Constitutionality of Airport Searches and Seizures." *Kentucky Law Journal* 62 (1974)

2495. **"Contact Ban between Prisoners and the Outside World: Information about a Law to Fight Terrorism."** In *International Summaries: A Collection of Selected Translations in Law Enforcement and Criminal Justice*, 3: 147-153. Washington, D.C.: U.S. Department of Justice, National Criminal Justice Reference Service, April 1979.
    This pamphlet was published by the FRG Ministry of Justice in 1978 to explain the background and provisions of the contact ban law promulgated in October 1977.

2496. Crelinsten, Ronald D.; Laberge-Altmejd, Danielle; and Szabo, Denis. *Terrorism and Criminal Justice.* Lexington, Mass.: Lexington Books, D. C. Heath, 1978.

2497. **"Criminal Law Reform: Bonn Hits at Urban Terrorists."** *German International* 19 (January 1975): 16-17.

2498. "Cuban Hijacking Law (September 16, 1969)." *International Legal Materials* 8 (1969): 1175-1177.

2499. Dershowitz, Alan. "Legal and Jurisprudential Aspects of Terrorism." Paper delivered at a panel on Terrorism: International and Comparative Perspectives, Association of American Law Schools, December 29, 1975, at Washington, D.C.

2500. ――――. "Terrorism and Preventive Detention: The Case of Israel." *Commentary* 50 (December 1970): 3-14.

2501. de Schutter, Bart. "Prevention, Legislation and Research Pertaining to Terrorism in Belgium." In Ronald D. Crelinsten, Danielle Laberge-Altmejd, and Denis Szabo, eds., *Terrorism and Criminal Justice: An International Perspective*. Lexington, Mass.: Lexington Books, 1978.

2502. ――――. "Problems of Jurisdiction in the International Control and Repression of Terrorism." In M. Cherif Bassiouni, ed., *International Terrorism and Political Crimes*, pp. 377-390. Springfield, Ill.: Thomas, 1975.

2503. Elwin, G. "Swedish Anti-Terrorist Legislation." *Contemporary Crises* (July 1977): 289-301.
The emergency law of 1973 is analyzed and criticized because of its treatment of foreigners and politically active persons.

2504. Evans, Alona E. "Report on Aircraft Hijacking in the U.S.: Law and Practice." *Criminal Law Bulletin* 10 (September 1974): 589-604.
The motives behind the 152 successful U.S. hijackings betwen 1961 and 1972 are examined, and legal problems are reviewed.

2505. Fenello, Michael J. "Individual Rights vs. Skyjack Deterrence: An Airline Man's View." *Villanova Law Review* 18 (1973).

2506. Fields, Rona M. "Torture and Institutional Coercion: Northern Ireland—A Case Study." Paper presented at the annual meeting of the American Sociological Association, August-September 1976, at New York City. Reprinted as FAR 26240-N.

2507. Gaynes, Jeffrey B. "Bringing the Terrorist to Justice: A Domestic Law Approach." *Cornell International Law Journal* 11 (Winter 1978): 71-84.

2508. German Information Center. "A Comparative Survey of the Anti-Terrorist Legislation in the Federal Republic of Germany, France, England,

and Sweden, and an Overview of the Legal Situation in the U.S." *Relay from Bonn*, January 16, 1978.

2509. Gora, J. M. "The Fourth Amendment at the Airport: Arriving, Departing or Cancelled?" *Villanova Law Review* 18 (1973): 1036.

2510. Herold, M. "Fight against terrorism in the FRG." *Revue internationale de criminologie et de police technique* 27 (January-March 1974): 27-29.
Possible roles and activities of the police and public are discussed.

2511. Ingraham, Barton. *Political Crime in Europe: A Comparative Study of France, Germany, and England.* Berkeley: University of California Press, 1979.
Ingraham defines political crime as "all acts which officials treat as if they were political and criminal, regardless of their real nature and of the motivations of their perpetrators."

2512. Jenkins, Brian M. "Combatting International Terrorism: The Role of Congress." (Santa Monica: RAND Corporation, P-5808, January 1977).
Discusses the apparent rise in international terrorism in the past few years, noting statistical trends in terms of incidents and casualties, as well as pointing out unquantified aspects, such as shock and publicity, of terrorist actions. Jenkins makes many points for Congress to consider in establishing a U.S. response. Among the topics for consideration are the unilateral versus international approach, mass destruction, military capabilities, nuclear safeguards, arms transfers, human rights, U.S. business abroad, the United States as a theater for terrorism, how to organize the government response, and the role of intelligence.

2513. Johnston, L. D. "Aviation Crimes Act of 1972." *New Zealand University Law Review* 5 (1973): 305ff.

2514. Leaute, Jacques. "Terrorist Incidents and Legislation in France." In Ronald D. Crelinsten, Danielle Laberge-Altmejd, and Denis Szabo, eds., *Terrorism and Criminal Justice: An International Perspective.* Lexington, Mass.: Lexington Books, Heath, 1978.

2515. Legros, Pierre. "The Idea of Terrorism in Comparative Law." In *International Summaries: A Collection of Selected Translations in Law Enforcement and Criminal Justice*, 3:115-122. Washington, D.C.: U.S. Department of Justice, National Criminal Justice Reference Service, April 1979, pp. 115-122.
Looks at several definitions of terrorism in codified municipal laws.

2516. Lowry, David R. "Draconian Powers: The New British Approach to Pretrial Detention of Suspected Terrorists." *Columbia Human Rights Law Review* 9 (Spring-Summer 1977): 185-222.

2517. Luzzi, Aldo. "Terrorist Criminality." *Polizia Moderna* 4 (April 1978): 20-23. Available in *International Summaries: A Collection of Selected Translations in Law Enforcement and Criminal Justice*, 3: 130-137. Washington, D.C.: U.S. Department of Justice, National Criminal Justice Reference Service, April 1979.

A study of terrorism in Italy, concentrating on the development of statutes to cope with terrorism.

2519. McCollum, J. R. "Warrantless Searches under Anti-Hijacking Program." *Baylor Law Review* 26 (Fall 1974): 604-615.

Searches for miniaturized explosives are deemed unwarranted and unnecessary.

2520. Nanes, Allen S. "International Terrorism." Washington, D.C.: Library of Congress, Congressional Research Service, Major Issuues System, Foreign Affairs and National Defense Division, Issue Brief Number IB74042, October 18, 1976.

An update of the April 4, 1974, CRS issue brief, giving a description of U.S. legislation on terrorism, lists of congressional hearings, a chronology from September 1969 to October 1976 of incidents, and a brief bibliography.

2521. ———. "International Terrorism." Washington, D.C.: Library of Congress, Congressional Research Service, Major Issues System, Issue Brief IB74042, May 11, 1977.

This update of previous CRS compilations lists major congressional and United Nations work in combating terrorism and provides an extensive chronology of major terrorist attacks.

2522. Prevention of Terrorism (Temporary Provisions) Act of 1974. United Kingdom, 1974.

For purposes of the legislation, terrorism is "the use of violence for political ends, and includes any use of violence for the purpose of putting the public or any section of the public in fear."

2523. Radvanyi, Miklos. *Anti-Terrorist Legislation in the FRG.* Washington, D.C.: Library of Congress Law Library, 1979. 140 pp.

The discussion includes sections on the German system of government, a history of emergency legislation, the role of civil servants, recent amendments to criminal codes, and FRG participation in international legal efforts.

2524. Rauch, Elmar. ''The Compatibility of the Detention of Terrorists Order (Northern Ireland) with the European Convention for the Protection of Human Rights.'' *New York University Journal of International Law and Politics* 6 (Spring 1973): 1-27.

2525. Sharp, J. M. ''Canada and the Hijacking of Aircraft.'' *Manitoba Law Journal* 5 (1973): 451ff.

2526. Street, H. ''Prevention of Terrorism (Temporary Provisions) Act 1974.'' *Criminal Law Review* (April 1975): 192-199.
    An analysis of antiterrorist legislation enacted by the United Kingdom to control terrorism in Northern Ireland.

2527. Sundberg, Jacob W. F. ''Antiterrorist Legislation in Sweden.'' In Marius Livingston et al., eds., *International Terrorism in the Contemporary World*, pp. 111-121. Westport, Conn.: Greenwood Press, 1978.

2528. ''The Terrorism Act of South Africa.'' *Bulletin of the International Commission of Jurists* (June 1968): 28-34.

2530. ''United Kingdom: Suppression of Terrorism Act 1978.'' *International Legal Materials* 17 (September 1978): 1130-1135.

2531. U.S. House of Representatives. Committee on International Relations. ''International Terrorism: Legislative Initiatives, Hearings and Markup, September 12-October 5, 1978.''

2532. ——. Committee on Interstate and Foreign Commerce. Subcommittee on Transportation and Aeronautics. ''Hearings on Implementation of the Tokyo Convention, HR 14301.'' 91st Cong, 1st sess., ser. 91-26, November 4, 1969.

2533. ——. Committee on the Judiciary. ''Implementing International Conventions against Terrorism: Report Together with Dissenting Views to Accompany HR 15552.'' 94th Cong., 2d sess., report no. 94-1614, 1976.

2534. U.S. Senate. Committee on Foreign Relations. *Combatting International and Domestic Terrorism: Hearing.* June 8, 1978.

2535. ——. Committee on the Judiciary. ''Implementing International Conventions against Terrorism: Report to Accompany S. 3646.'' 94th Cong., 2d sess., report no. 94-1273, 1976.

2536. Wright, J. K. "Hijacking Risks and Airport Frisks: Reconciling Airline Security with the Fourth Amendment." *Criminal Law Bulletin* 9 (July-August 1973): 491-517.

The right to privacy should be upheld, and limitations should be placed upon searches and evidentiary use of property seized.

2537. Yamamoto, Soji. "The Japanese Enactment for the Suppression of Unlawful Seizure of Aircraft and International Law." *Japanese Annual of International Law* 15 (1971): 70-80.

Also see entries 563, 978, 979, 980, 981, 1035, 1668, 2290, and 2298.

State Responsibility for Terrorist Acts

2538. Akehurst, Michael. "State Responsibility for the Wrongful Acts of Rebels—An Aspect of the Southern Rhodesian Problem." British *Yearbook of International Law* 43 (1968-1969).

2539. Eagleton, Clyde. "The Responsibility of the State for the Protection of Foreign Officials." *American Journal of International Law* 19 (April 1925).

2540. Eustathiades, C. "La cour pénal internationale pour la répression du terrorisme et le problème de la responsabilité internationale des états." *Revue générale de droit international Public* 43 (1936): 384-415.

2541. FitzGerald, Gerald. "Concerted Actions against States Found in Default of Their International Obligations in Respect of Unlawful Interference with International Civil Aviation." *Canadian Yearbook of International Law* 261 (1972).

2542. Friedlander, Robert A. "Reflections on Terrorist Havens." *Naval War College Review* 32 (March-April 1979): 59-67.

Surveys the international legal agreements designed to combat terrorism and notes that the U.S. response to safe havens has been weak when compared with a stance it could have taken.

2543. Garcia-Mora, Manuel R. *International Responsibility for Hostile Acts of Private Persons Against Foreign States.* The Hague: Martinus Nijhoff, 1962.

2544. Goldie, L. F. E. "State Responsibility and International Terror." Paper presented to the Conference on Terrorism in the Contemporary World, April 26-28, 1976, at Glassboro State College.

2545. Heinz III, H. John. "Testimony before the Foreign Relations Committee, Subcommittee on Foreign Assistance, on the Problem of Terrorism." September 14, 1977.

Heinz proposed S483, a bill designed to stop state aid to and abetting of terrorist groups.

2546. Javits, Jacob K. "International Terrorism: Apathy Exacerbates the Problem." *Terrorism* 1 (1978): 111-117.

The senator argues in favor of S2236, a bill to establish sanctions against states aiding terrorists.

2547. Karkashian, John E. "Statement before the Subcommittee on Foreign Assistance of the Senate Foreign Relations Committee." September 14, 1977.

The acting director of the State Department's Office for Combatting Terrorism explains what the U.S. government response to terrorism has been and what can be done to inhibit states wishing to aid terrorist groups.

2548. Ketelsen, Doris. "Moskaus Haltung zum internationalen Terrorismus." [Moscow and international terrorism] *Osteuropa* 28 (November 1978): 965-977.

2549. Kutner, Luis. "Constructive Notice: A Proposal to End International Terrorism." *New York Law Forum* 19 (Fall 1973): 325-350.

Suggests that heads of state be liable for actions of terrorists that they could reasonably have been aware of.

2550. Lauterpacht, Hans. "Revolutionary Activities by Private Persons against Foreign States." *American Journal of International Law* 22 (1928): 105-130.

2551. Lillich, Richard. "Sanctuary and Safe-Haven for Terrorists: The Relevancy of International Law." Procedural Aspects of International Law Institute study for the Department of State under contract no. 1724-620225, 1977.

2552. ———. "State Responsibility for Injuries to Aliens Occasioned by Terrorist Activities." Procedural Aspects of International Law Institute study for the Department of State under contract no. 1724-6200411, 1977.

2553. ———. "Statement before the Subcommittee on Foreign Assistance of the Senate Committee on Foreign Relations, Concerning Legal Responses to International Terrorism." September 14, 1977.

Lillich discusses international legal approaches to the question of state aid to terrorist groups, suggesting that the doctrine of state responsibility applies. Several suggestions for U.S. unilateral initiatives are made.

2554. Lillich, Richard B., and Carbonneau, Thomas E. "The 1976 Terrorism Amendment to the Foreign Assistance Act of 1961." *Journal of International Law and Economics* 11 (1976): 223-236. Available as FAR 27310-N.

The authors discuss draft proposals forwarded in the House and Senate to deny military assistance to states that grant sanctuary from prosecution to any individual committing an act of international terrorism. Differences between the bills, including the use of the term "aids and abets," concurrent resolutions, and arguments for and against congressional action in general, and initiatives specifically in this area, are outlined.

2555. Lillich, Richard B., and Paxman, John M. "State Responsibility for Injuries to Aliens Occasioned by Terrorist Activities." *American University Law Review* (Winter 1977): 217-313.

The responsibilities to prevent acts of local and nonlocal terrorism, as well as to punish offenders, are discussed in terms of a useful continuum of state involvement in the case.

2556. Paust, Jordan. "Responses to Terrorism: A Prologue to Decision Concerning Measures of Sanction." *Stanford Journal of International Studies* 12 (Spring 1977): 79-130.

2557. Preuss, Lawrence. "Kidnapping of Fugitives from Justice on Foreign Territory." *American Journal of International Law* 29 (1935): 502-507.

Mentions *Ker v. Illinois* (1886), in which the U.S. Supreme Court held that no constitutional right of his had been violated when a U.S. agent technically kidnapped him in Peru. The article arose from numerous kidnappings of political refugees conducted by Nazi Germany.

2558. Ribicoff, Abraham. "Diplomacy Is Not Enough." *Air Line Pilot* 47 (September 1978): 6-8.

Ribicoff's speech to the ALPA executive board meeting presented statistics on terrorism and hijacking. The senator believes that a list of unsafe airports should be publicly available and that nations aiding terrorists should be punished.

2559. "State Responsibility to Deter, Prevent or Suppress Skyjacking Activities in Their Territory." United Nations: A/Res/2645 (XXV), November 25, 1970.

2560. Stevenson, John R. ''International Law and the Export of Terrorism.'' *Record of the Association of the Bar of the City of New York* 29 (December 1972): 716-729.

Argues that it is counterproductive to attempt to define terrorism and that we should identify specific categories of offenses that can be controlled internationally. Discusses conventions on hijacking, kidnapping of diplomats, and export of terrorism to states not parties to the conflict. A good, brief summary of each of the major conventions.

2561. ———. ''International Law and the Export of Terrorism.'' *Department of State Bulletin*, December 4, 1972, pp. 645-652.

Covers hijacking and other crimes against civil aircraft, kidnapping and assassination of foreign officials, and the export of terrorism to countries not involved in the conflicts that led to the acts.

2562. Slomanson. ''ICJ Damages: Tort Remedy for Failure to Punish or Extradite Terrorists.'' *California Western International Law Journal* 5 (1974); 121ff.

2563. U.S. House of Representatives. Committee on International Relations. Subcommittee on International Security and Scientific Affairs. ''International Terrorism: Legislative Initiatives, Hearings and Markup.'' 95th Cong., 2d sess., September 12, 14, 20, 28, October 5, 1978.

Testimony by representatives from the departments of State and Justice, FAA, ACDA, and FBI.

2564. U.S. Senate. Committee on Foreign Relations. ''Combating International and Domestic Terrorism.'' Hearing on S.2236. 95th Cong., 2d sess., June 8, 1978.

2565. ———. Committee on Foreign Relations. ''Countering International Terrorism: Report to Accompany S. Con. Res. 72.'' 95th Cong., 2d sess., report no. 95-936, 1978.

2566. ———. Committee on Foreign Relations. Subcommittee on Foreign Assistance. ''International Terrorism.'' Hearing. 95th Cong., 1st sess., September 14, 1977.

The hearings centered on congressional proposals to impose sanctions against states that aid and abet international terrorism. Testimony and supporting documents were presented by representatives of the Department of State, Air Line Pilots Association, the Rand Corporation, the Senate, and the University of Virginia Law School. A CIA summary of terrorism in 1976 is reprinted.

2567. ———. Committee on Governmental Affairs. "An Act to Combat International Terrorism." 95th Cong., January 23-30, February 22, March 22-23, 1978.

Complete texts of the hearings on the Ribicoff bill, S2236, the Omnibus Anti-Terrorism Act, as well as supporting documentation supplied by leading academics, research institutes, and government officials.

2568. ———. Committee on Governmental Affairs. "An Act to Combat International Terrorism." Report to Accompany S.2236. 95th Cong., 2d sess., report no. 95-908, May 23, 1978.

A report by the committee on the hearings and conclusions regarding the Ribicoff-sponsored antiterrorism act. Appendixes were written by Brian Jenkins, Charles Russell, Robert Kupperman, and Frank Ochberg.

2569. "The Use of Sanctions to Assure Members Comply with Anti-Skyjacking Conventions: A U.S. Proposal." International Civil Aviation Organization, Legal Committee Working Draft No. 776, October 9, 1970.

2570. Vucinic, Milan. "The Responsibility of States for Acts of International Terrorism." *Review of International Affairs* 23 (1972): 11-12.

Also see entries 418, 1154, 1157, 1159, 1160, 1173, 1181, 1187, 1190, 1192, 1672, 1767, 1781, 1787, 1827, and 1906.

Measures of Self-Help in Combating Terrorism

2571. Alexander, Yonah. "The Entebbe Raid and Next Time." Paper presented to the Conference on Terror: The Man, the Mind and the Matter, October 15-16, 1976, at the John Jay School of Criminal Justice, New York City.

2572. Alexander, Yonah, and Levine, Herbert M. "Prepare for the Next Entebbe." *Chitty's Law Journal* 25 (September 1977): 240-242.

2573. Beaumont, Roger A. "Military Elite Forces: Surrogate War, Terrorism, and the New Battlefield." *Parameters: Journal of the U.S. Army War College* 9 (March 1979): 17-29.

2574. Ben-Porat, Yeshayahu; Haber, Eitan; and Schiff, Zeev. *Entebbe Rescue*. New York: Dell, 1976. 347 pp.

A popular treatment of the Entebbe raid, originally published in Israel.

2575. ———. *Entebbe*, Paris: 1976.

Reviewed in "Israel Considered Joint Entebbe Raid," *Washington Post*, December 1, 1976, p. A-9. The authors, Israeli journalists with access to newly declassified documents, argue that former Israeli ambassador to France Asher Ben Nathan was sent to Paris during the hostage negotiations to discuss a joint raid with the French with France's interior minister, Michael Poniatowsky. By the time Ben Nathan met with him on July 2, the Israelis had decided to make a unilateral strike against the terrorists.

2576. Blum, Yehuda Z. "The Beirut Raid and the International Double Standard: A Reply to Professor Richard A. Falk." *American Journal of International Law* 64 (1970): 73ff. Reprinted in John Norton Moore, ed., *The Arab-Israeli Conflict* (Princeton University Press, 1974), vol. 2.

Using the 1951 Draft Code on Offenses against the Peace and Security of Mankind and the 1965 Declaration of the Inadmissibility of Intervention in the Domestic Affairs of States and the Protection of Their Independence and Sovereignty, Blum argues that states that foment acts of terrorism against another state are in violation of international law. He points to Arab state support of the Palestinians' attacks as a major example of this illegal practice. He also argues that Israel has the right to retaliate against these state supporters whenever it is attacked by terrorists because a state of war exists.

2577. "Control of Terrorism in International Life: Cooperation and Self-Help." Seminar in *Proceedings of the American Society of International Law*. 71st annual meeting, April 21-23, 1977, at San Francisco, California.

2578. Cooper, H. H. A. "Hostage Rescue Operations: Denouement at Algeria and Mogadishu Compared." *Chitty's Law Journal* 26 (March 1978): 91-103.

2579. Dan, Uri. *Operation Entebbe* (Israel, 1976).

The first of the books to come out about the Israeli raid on Uganda's Entebbe Airport in July 1976.

2580. DelGrosso, C. S., and Short, John C. "A Concept for Antiterrorist Operations." *Marine Corps Gazette* 63 (June 1979): 54-59.

The authors offer an eight-step guide for these tactics: isolate the objective area, negotiate, conduct intelligence operations, select time and location for attack, rehearse, assemble, distract the enemy, and attack. In comparing the capabilities of the U.S. armed services, the Marines are judged to possess "the organic capability to perform an antiterrorist mission with minimal augmentation and, therefore, minimal degradation in the all-important command and control areas."

2581. Eaker, Ira C. "Israel Solves a Hijacking." *Air Force Times*, July 26, 1976, pp. 13-14.

2582. Falk, Richard A. "The Beirut Raid and the International Law of Retaliation." *American Journal of International Law* 63 (July 1969): 415-443. Reprinted in Morton A. Kaplan, ed., *Great Issues of International Politics* (Chicago: Aldine, 1970).

Falk argues that the Israeli raid did not follow certain established norms regarding the permissibility of retaliation. Among these considerations are attempts at pacific resolution, proportionality, military targeting, providing an immediate explanation before relevant international organs, and establishing a link between those who attacked the retaliator and those retaliated against.

2583. Foxley-Norris, Christopher. "Entebbe and After." *Army Quarterly* 106 (October 1976): 397-401.

2584. Friedlander, Robert A. "The Mayaguez in Retrospect: Humanitarian Intervention or Showing the Flag?" *Saint Louis University Law Journal* 22 (1978): 601-613.

After examining the positions of both sides on the permissibility of humanitarian intervention, the author suggests that it is not a doctrine but a last-clear-chance exception to other international legal norms.

2585. Getlein, Frank. "Working Both Ends of the Street: U.N. Reaction to Israeli Entebbe Raid." *Commonweal*, July 30, 1976, pp. 485-486.

2586. Green, L. C. "Humanitarian Intervention—1976 Version." *Chitty's Law Journal* 24 (September 1976), 217-225.

Discusses the international legal interpretation of the Israeli response to the PFLP's hijacking of an Air France plane to Entebbe.

2587. Hamrick, Tom. "The Black Berets." *Army* (May 1977): 28-33.

The author, clearly enamoured of the group, discusses the training and capabilities of the Ranger team given the task of rescuing Americans held hostage by terrorists.

2588. Hastings, Max. *Yoni, Hero of Entebbe.* New York: Dial, 1979. 248 pp.

2589. Hayden, Thomas. "Antiterrorist Contingency Readiness." *United States Naval Institute Proceedings* 105 (March 1979): 100-103.

The author suggests that a Navy/Marine Corps strike team could augment FBI and police efforts to deal with terrorist incidents.

2590. Knisbacher. "The Entebbe Operation: A Legal Analysis of Israel's Rescue Action." *Journal of International Law and Economics* 12 (1977).

2591. Moynihan, Daniel P. "The Totalitarian Terrorists." *New York*, July 26, 1976, pp. 38-40. Reprinted in John D. Elliott and Leslie K. Gibson, eds., *Contemporary Terrorism: Selected Readings* (Gaithersburg, Md.: International Association of Chiefs of Police, 1978), pp. 159-163.

Moynihan lauds the Israeli attack at Entebbe Airport and calls for other nations to have the courage to support such responses.

2592. Murphy, John F. "State Self-Help and Problems of Public International Law." In Alona Evans and John F. Murphy, eds., *Legal Aspects of International Terrorism*. Washington, D.C.: American Society of International Law, 1977.

2593. Pedersen, Fred C. "Controlling International Terrorism: An Analysis of Unilateral Force and Proposals for Multilateral Cooperation." *University of Toledo Law Review* 8 (Fall 1976): 209-250.

2594. Salter, Leonard M. "Commando Coup at Entebbe: Humanitarian Intervention or Barbaric Aggression?" *International Lawyer* 11 (Spring 1977): 331-338.

Argues that "there are solid grounds in law and history . . .for contending that hot pursuit is a matter of self-defense where the neutral state (Uganda) has allowed its territory to be used as refuge by military elements of one of the combatant parties."

2595. "Seminar on the Control of Terrorism in International Life: Cooperation and Self-Help." Held during the 71st annual meeting of the American Society of International Law, April 21-23, 1977, at San Francisco, California.

The moderator was Alona E. Evans, Wellesley College. Discussants included M. Cherif Bassiouni of DePaul University College of Law, Harry Almond of the Office of General Counsel, U.S. Department of Defense, L. F. E. Goldie, Division of Legal Affairs, U.N. Secretariat, and John F. Murphy, University of Kansas School of Law. Reporters were James Hatten and Edwin L. Cassady, Staff Judge Advocate's Office, the Presidio.

2596. Sheehan, Jeffrey A. "The Entebbe Raid: The Principle of Self-Help in International Law as Justification for State Use of Armed Force." *Fletcher Forum: A Journal of Graduate Studies in International Affairs* 1 (Spring 1977): 135-153.

2597. Stevenson, William. *90 Minutes at Entebbe*. New York: Bantam, 1976. 216 pp.

The first of the American books published shortly after the Israeli rescue operation at Uganda's Entebbe Airport in July 1976. The author asserts that three of the hijackers were captured and taken to Israel; some of the hostages who had been released before the raid and flown to Europe were hypnotized there by Israeli intelligence agents to obtain details of their capture; British intelligence sources in Kenya supplied information that contributed to Israel's decision to stage the raid; an Israeli missile ship was dispatched off the East African coast to serve as a communications center because of Israeli fears that plans of the raid would be discovered; President Amin's plane was followed by an Israeli Phantom jet while officials debated and then dropped a plan to capture him; fifty Israeli agents flew to Kenya to assure that the Nairobi Airport could be used by the raiders to refuel their planes on the way home. Reviewed by Robert E. Tamasson, *New York Times*, July 26, 1976, p. 4.

2598. Thompson, Sir Robert; Fuchs, N. L.; Kloppenberg, R. E.; Stokreef, J.; and Wegener, Ulrich. "Terrorism and Security Force Requirements." In *Ten Years of Terrorism*, pp. 128-146. New York: Crane, Russak, 1979.

2599. Tinnin, David. "The Hit Team, Part 1." *London Sunday Times Magazine*, September 12, 1976, pp. 38-52.

Excerpts from Tinnin's book. Discusses how the teams were set up and some of their initial operations.

2600. ———. "Terror against Terror: The Hit Team Takes Israel's Revenge." *London Sunday Times Magazine*, September 19, 1976, pp. 44-54.

Excerpts from Tinnin's book. Notes the last operations of the group, including their Norwegian error.

2601. ———. with Halevy, David. "Strike Teams." *Playboy* 26 (February 1979): 90-197.

Tinnin compares the antiterrorist strike forces of the United States and its allies, discussing doctrine, specific tactics, and weapons.

2602. Tophoven, Rolf. "International Terrorism: Challenge and Defensive Measures." In *International Summaries: A Collection of Selected Translations in Law Enforcement and Criminal Justice*, 3: 105-112. Washington, D.C.: U.S. Department of Justice, National Criminal Justice Reference Service, April 1979.

A study of the lessons of the Israeli raid on Entebbe, as they apply to the West German experience.

2603. Wahl, Jonathan. "Responses to Terrorism: Self-Defense or Reprisal?" *International Problems* 5 (1973): 28-33.

2604. Wall, J. M. "Rescue at Entebbe." *Christian Century*, July 21, 1976, p. 651.

2605. Winkates, James E. "Hostage Rescue: An Appraisal of the Son Tay, Mayaguez, and Entebbe Missions." Paper presented to the 19th annual convention of the International Studies Association, February 22-25, 1978, at Washington, D.C. Published as "Hostage Rescue in Hostile Environments: Lessons Learned from the Son Tay, Mayaguez, and Entebbe Missions." In Yonah Alexander and Robert A. Kilmarx, eds., *Political Terrorism and Business: The Threat and Response* (New York: Praeger, 1979), pp. 357-427.

2606. Wise, Charles, and Sloan, Stephen. "Countering Terrorism: The U.S. and Israeli Approach." *Middle East Review* (Spring 1977): 55-59.

U.S. policy is basically defensive in nature, whereas the Israelis also employ an offensive policy, assassinating terrorists in the field. A few suggestions are made on how the United States could borrow some of the underlying philosophy of the Israeli method while retaining its ethicolegal principles.

Also see entries 161, 1928, 1947, 1971, and 1975.

Hijacking

General Legal Observations

2607. Agrawala, S. K. *Aircraft Hijacking and International Law.* Bombay: Tripathi; New York: Oceana, 1973. 242 pp.

2608. "Aircraft Hijacking: Criminal and Civil Aspects." *University of Florida Law Review* 22 (1969): 72ff.

2609. "Anti-Hijacking Proposals Proliferate." *Aviation Week and Space Technology*, September 21, 1970, p. 27.

2610. "Are the Skies Really Friendly? Proposed Theories of Relief for the Injured Hijacked Passenger." *Southwestern University Law Review* 5 (1974): 430ff.

2611. Baccelli, Guido Rinaldi. "Pirateria Aerea: Realta Effettiva e Disciplina Giuridica." *Diritto Aereo* 9 (1970): 150ff.

2612. Barrie, G. N. "Crimes Committed Aboard Aircraft." *South African Law Journal* 83 (1968): 203-208.

2613. Bekes, Imre. "The Legal Problems of Hijacking and Taking of Hostages." In Marius Livingston et al., eds., *International Terrorism in the Contemporary World*, pp. 346-353. Westport, Conn.: Greenwood Press, 1978.

Bekes, professor of criminal law at the University of Budapest, gives a Hungarian perspective on the international legal approach to hijacking.

2614. Beristain, A. "Terrorism and Aircraft Hijackings." *International Journal of Criminology and Penology* 2 (1974): 327ff.

2615. Bidinger, Jerome R., and Bninski, Roman A. "A Legal Response to Terrorist Hijacking and Insurance Liability (Problems in the Application of the War Risk Exclusion Clauses Commonly Found in All-risk Aviation Hull Insurance Policies, in Cases of Damages Resulting from International Terrorist Hijackings: Implications of the Decision in Pan American World Airways, Inc., versus Aetna Casualty and Surety Company, et.al." *Law and Policy in International Business* 6 (Fall 1974): 1167-1210.

2616. Boyle, Robert P. "International Act to Combat Aircraft Hijacking." *Lawyer of the Americas* 4 (1972): 460-473.

2617. Bradford, A. Lee. "Legal Ramifications of Hijacking Airplanes." *American Bar Association Journal* 48 (November 1962): 1034-1039.

Discusses the legal problems faced by all participants in a skyjacking.

2618. M. Bravo, Navarro. "Apoderamiento Ilicito de Aeronaves en Vuelo." *Revista Espanola de Derecho Internacional* 22 (1969): 788ff.

2619. Breton, J. M. "Piraterie aerienne et droit international public." *Revue générale de droit international Public* 75 (1971): 392-445.

2620. Brower, Charles N. "Aircraft Hijacking and Sabotage: Initiative or Inertia?" *Department of State Bulletin*, June 18, 1973, pp. 872-875.

2621. ———. "International Enforcement of Air Security—U.S. Initiatives." *Villanova Law Review* 18 (1973).

2622. Butler, Charles F. "The Path to International Legislation Against Hijacking." In Edward McWhinney, ed., *Aerial Piracy and International Law*, pp. 27-54. Leiden: Sijthoff, 1971.

2623. Carbone, Sergio M. "Repressione della c.d. Pirateria Aerea nei Rapporti Internazionali." *Revista di Diritto Internazionale Privato e Processuale* (1971): 534ff.

2624. Cardman, Frank A. "A View on Aircraft Piracy and Sabotage." Paper delivered at the Inter-American Aviation Law Conference, April 28, 1971, at University of Miami (Florida) School of Law.

2625. Chaturvedi, S. C. "Hijacking and the Law." *Indian Journal of International Law* 11 (1971): 89-105.

2626. Cheng, Bin. "Crimes on Board Aircraft." *Current Legal Problems* 12 (1959): 177ff.

2627. Chung, David Y. "Some Legal Aspects of Aircraft Hijacking in International Law." Ph.D. dissertation, University of Tennessee, 1976.

2628. Crelinsten, Ronald D., and Laberge-Altmejd, Danielle, eds. *The Impact of Terrorism and Skyjacking on the Operations of the Criminal Justice System.* Montreal: International Centre for Comparative Criminology, Final Report on Basic Issue Seminar, 1976.

2629. Davis, Jr., Benjamin O. "The Government's Response to Hijacking." *Villanova Law Review* 18 (1973).

2630. "Deterring Airport Terrorist Attacks and Compensating the Victims." *University of Pennsylvania Law Review* 125 (May 1977): 1134-1165.

2631. Dinstein, Yoram. "Criminal Jurisdiction over Aircraft Hijacking." *Israel Law Review* 7 (1972): 195-206.

2632. Dowd, D. W. "Introduction: Symposium on Skyjacking Problems and Potential Solutions." *Villanova Law Review* 18 (1973).

2633. Emanuelli, C. "Legal Aspects of Aerial Terrorism: The Piecemeal vs. the Comprehensive Approach." *Journal of International Law and Economics* 10 (1975): 503ff.

2634. Emanuelli, Claude. *Les moyens de prévention et de sanction en cas d'action illicite contre l'aviation civile internationale.* Paris: Editions Pedone, 1974. 159 pp.
    Argues that law must draw the distinction between terrorist activities (including sabotage) and actions by individuals who are seeking asylum and skyjack solely for transportation.

2635. Evans, Alona E. "Aircraft and Aviation Facilities." In Alona E. Evans and John F. Murphy, eds., *Legal Aspects of International Terrorism.* Washington, D.C.: American Society of International Law, 1977.

2636. ———. "Aircraft Hijacking: Its Cause and Cure." *American Journal Of International Law* 63 (October 1969): 695-710.
   Gives data on the history of air hijacking during the past two decades, noting the dramatic increase in it in the last two years. Methods of control being suggested at the same time are mentioned: control on the ground by searches, in-flight guards, private organization intervention against nations giving asylum, criminal sanctions against hijacking, and possible international controls.

2637. ———. "Aircraft Hijacking: What Is Being Done." *American Journal of International Law* 67 (October 1973): 641-671. Reprinted in M. Cherif Bassiouni, ed., *International Terrorism and Political Crimes* (Springfield, Ill.: Thomas, 1975), pp. 219-247.
   Presents statistics on the frequency of skyjackings and notes the change in the types of hijackings and responses to it. Existing skyjack laws, their enforcement, and future, as well as legal problems involving skyjackings, complete the article.

2638. ———. "Aircraft Hijacking: What Is to Be Done?" *American Journal of International Law* 66 (1972): 819-822.

2639. ———. "The Law and Aircraft Hijacking." *Syracuse Journal of International Law and Commerce* 2 (1973): 265-274.

2640. ———. "A Proposed Method of Control." *Journal of Air Law and Commerce* 37 (1971): 171-181.
   Notes that problems of carrier liability in hijackings are coming to the fore.

2641. Feller, S. Z. "Comment on Criminal Jurisdiction over Aircraft Hijacking." *Israel Law Review* 7 (1972): 207-214.

2642. Fenston, John, and de Saussure, Hamilton. "Conflict in the Competence and Jurisdiction of Courts of Different States to Deal with Crimes Committed on Board Aircraft and Persons Involved Therein." *McGill Law Journal* 56 (1952): 66ff.

2643. Fenwick, C. G. " 'Piracy' in the Caribbean." *American Journal of International Law* 55 (1961): 426-428.

2644. Fick, Ronald L.; Gordon, Jon I.; and Patterson, John C. "Aircraft Hijacking: Criminal and Civil Aspects." *University of Florida Law Review* 22 (1969): 72ff.

2645. FitzGerald, Gerald F. "Development of International Rules Concerning Offences and Certain Other Acts Committed on Board Aircraft." *Canadian Yearbook of International Law* 1 (1963): 230-251.

2646. ———. "The London Draft Convention on Acts of Unlawful Interference Against International Civil Aviation." In Edward W. McWhinney, ed., *Aerial Piracy and International Law*, pp. 36-54. Leiden: A. W. Sijthoff, 1971.

2647. ———. "Recent Proposals for Concerted Action against States in Respect of Unlawful Interference with International Civil Aviation." *Journal of Air Law and Commerce* 40 (1974): 161ff.

2648. ———. "Toward Legal Suppression of Acts against Civil Aviation." *International Conciliation* 585 (November 1971): 42-78.

An extended discussion of the Tokyo, Hague, and Montreal conventions by the ICAO's legal adviser.

2649. Friedlander, Robert A. "Banishing Fear from the Skies: A Statutory Proposal." *Duquesne Law Review* 16 (1977-1978): 283-305.

Makes several proposals designed to clarify jurisdictional questions left open by antihijacking conventions.

2650. ———. "Review of Edward McWhinney, *The Illegal Diversion of Aircraft and International Law*, Nancy Douglas Joyner, *Aerial Highjacking as an International Crime*, and Claude Emanuelli, *Les moyens de prévention et de sanction en cas d'action illicite contre l'aviation civile internationale*." *De Paul Law Review*. In press.

Concentrates on the authors' differing views of the value of multilateral conventions.

2651. Gertler, Z. J. "Amendments to the Chicago Convention: Lessons from Proposals That Failed." *Journal of Air Law and Commerce* 40 (1974): 225ff.

2652. Gist, Francis J. "The Aircraft Hijacker and International Law." Master's thesis, McGill University, 1968.

2653. Glasser, S. "Quelques observations sur le détournement d'aeronefs." *Revue générale de droit international public* 76 (1972): 12ff.

2654. Green, L. C. "Extradition versus Asylum for Aerial Hijackers." *Israel Law Review* 10 (1975).

2655. ———. "Hijacking and the Right of Asylum." In Edward McWhinney, ed., *Aerial Piracy and International Law*. New York: Oceana, 1971.

2656. ———. "Hijacking, Extradition and Asylum." *Chitty's Law Journal* 22 (1974): 135ff.

2657. ———. *Law and Society*. Leiden: A. W. Sitjhoff, 1975; Dobbs Ferry: Oceana, 1975.
Includes a chapter, "Hijacking, Extradition and Asylum."

2658. Hammarskjold, Kurt. "Air Piracy as an International Crime: Suggestions for International Action." *International Review of Criminal Policy* 32 (1976): 14-20.
What has been done; what should be done. Nations not abiding by the present treaties should do so.

2659. Hirsch, Arthur I., and Fuller, David. "Aircraft Piracy and Extradition." *New York Law Forum* 16 (Spring 1970): 392-419.

2660. Horlick, Gary N. "The Developing Law of Air Hijacking." *Harvard International Law Journal* 12 (1971): 33-70.

2661. ———. "The Public and Private International Response to Aircraft Hijacking." *Vanderbilt Journal of Transnational Law* 6 (1972): 144ff.

2662. Ivanov, V. "Against Air Pirates." *Izvestiya*, January 16, 1973.

2663. Jacobson, Peter M. "From Piracy on the High Seas to Piracy in the High Skies: A Study of Aircraft Hijacking." *Cornell International Law Journal* 5 (1972): 161-187.

2664. Joyner, Nancy Douglas. *Aerial Hijacking as an International Crime*. Dobbs Ferry, N.Y.: Oceana, 1974. 344 pp.
Reviewed by Alona E. Evans, *American Journal of International Law* 71 (April 1977): 370-372. Joyner looks at the development of the concept of piracy, its application to aerial offenses, and the degree of compliance by states that have joined international conventions against hijacking. Joyner uses probit analysis to assess the predictive capacity of several variables upon a nation's enforcement of hijacking laws. An extensive bibliography and texts of conventions are appended.

2665. Juglart, M. de. "Infranctions commises a bord aeronefs dans la doctrine internationale." *Revue française de droit aerien* 14 (1960): 123ff.

2666. Kaminski, G. " 'Luftpiraterie': die rechtliche beurteilung der an Bord von Luftfahrzeugen begangenen Straftaten unter besonderer der 'Luftpiraterie.' " *Osterreichische Zeitschrift fur Aussenpolitik* 10 (1970): 78ff.

2667. Khan, Ranmatullah. "Hijacking and International Law." *Africa Quarterly* 10 (1971): 398-403.

2668. Knauth, Arnold W. "Status of Aircraft with Reference to Criminal Law for Aircraft." *Report of the Forty-eighth Conference of the International Law Association*, pp. 277-305. London and New York, 1958.

2669. Kojanec, G. "Hijacking of Aircraft in Recent International Law." *Communita Internazionale* 26 (April 1971): 266-281.
A discussion of several international treaties.

2670. Kolosov, Y. "Legal Questions of the Security of Civil Aviation." *International Affairs* (Moscow) (April 1974): 42-46.

2671. Lee, Andrew. "International Suppression of Hijacking." In M. Cherif Bassiouni, ed., *International Terrorism and Political Crimes*, pp. 248-256. Springfield, Ill.: Thomas, 1975.

2672. "Leningrad Trial of Would-Be Hijackers." *Current Digest of the Soviet Press*, February 2, 1971, pp. 4-5.

2673. Lester. "Crimes on Aircraft." *New Law Journal* 117 (1967): 497ff.

2674. Lissitzyn, Oliver. "Hijacking, International Law, and Human Rights." In Edward McWhinney, ed., *Aerial Piracy and International Law*, pp. 116-123. New York: Oceana, 1971.

2675. ———. "In-Flight Crime and U.S. Legislation." *American Journal of International Law* 67 (April 1973): 306-313.

2676. ———. "International Control of Aerial Hijacking: The Role of Values and Interests." *Proceedings of the American Society of International Law* (1971): 80-86.

2677. ———. "The Treatment of Aerial Intruders in Recent Practice and International Law." *American Journal of International Law* 47 (1953): 559ff.

2678. Lownefeld, Andreas F. *Aviation Law: Cases and Materials.* New York: Matthew Bender, 1972.

Chapter 7 is devoted to aerial hijacking, giving texts and analyses of international conventions. The 1972 Document Supplement has texts of U.S. and U.N. documents, along with several foreign statutes and hijacking statistics.

2679. Loy, Frank E. "Department of Transportation Reviews Problem of Aircraft Hijacking and Proposals for International Action." *Department of State Bulletin* 60 (1969): 212.

2680. ——. "Some International Approaches to Dealing with Hijacking of Aircraft." *International Lawyer* 4 (1970): 444-452.

2681. "Luftpiraterie als Rechtsproblem." [Air piracy as a legal problem] *Zeitschrift fur Luftrecht und Weltraumrechtsfragen*, April 1, 1969, pp. 77-80.

Argues that all proposed technical measures are too risky for practical implementation and that legal sanctions are the only plausible response. The Aircraft Piracy Amendment to the Federal Aviation Administration Act provides for capital punishment or twenty years imprisonment for hijacking, and a $10,000 fine for interference with aircraft personnel. Mexican, Swiss, and German legal measures are discussed, as is a U.N. resolution calling for the creation of an international punitive code.

2682. "Die Luftpiraterie in Rechtlicher Sicht." [Air piracy from the legal standpoint] *Zeitschrift fur Luftrecht und Weltraumrechtsfragen*, July 1, 1969, pp. 151-155.

Discusses the legal consequences of aerial hijacking as reflected in Swiss law and the Tokyo Convention. Swiss law allows prosecution of hijackers for several misdemeanors and felonies, such as endangering human life, deprivation of property, threats, coercion, deprivation of freedom, and public disturbance. Air piracy in the context of war is considered.

2683. Lynn, Robert H. "Hijacking as a Political Crime: Who Should Judge?" *California Western International Law Journal* 2 (1971).

2684. Malawer, Stuart S. "U.S. Foreign Policy and International Law: The Jordanian Civil War and Air Piracy." *International Problems* 10 (1971): 31-40.

2685. Malik, Sushman. "Legal Aspects of the Problem of Unlawful Seizure of Aircraft." *Indian Journal of International Law* 9 (1969): 61-75.

2686. Malmborg, K. E. "Malmborg Sees Advance in Hijack Conventions." *Virginia Law Weekly, DICTA* 24 (1972): 1.

2687. ———. "New Developments in the Law of International Aviation: The Control of Aerial Hijacking." *Proceedings of the American Society of International Law* (1971): 75-80.

2688. Mankiewicz, R. H. "Les aeronefs internationant." *1962 annuaire français de droit international.*

2689. ———. Aspects du problêmes du droit pénal de l'aviation internationale." *1953 annuaire français de droit international*, p. 112ff.

2690. ———. "Le droit pénal de l'aviation." *McGill Law Journal* 4 (1957): 13ff.

2691. Mankiewicz, René . "La problématique de la 'piraterie aerienne.' " *Etudes internationales* 8 (March 1977): 100ff.

2692. Mapelli y Lopez, E. "Consideraciones sobre la Extorsion de Aeronaves." *Il Diritto Aereo* 8 (1969): 261ff.

2693. ———. *Illegal Seizure of Aircraft.* Madrid: Editorial Tecnos SA 1973. 237pp.

2694. Martin, Peter. "The Unlawful Seizure of Aircraft." *Law Society's Gazette* 66 (1969): 714ff.

2695. McClintock, Michael C. "Skyjacking: Its Domestic Civil and Criminal Ramifications." *Journal of Air Law and Commerce* 39 (January 1973): 29-80.

2696. McKeithen, R. L. Smith. "Prospects for the Prevention of Aircraft Hijacking Through Law." *Columbia Journal of Transnational Law* 9 (1970): 60-80.

2697. McMahon, John P. "Air Hijacking: Extradition as a Deterrent." *Georgetown Law Journal* 58 (June 1970): 1135-1152.

2698. McNeil, Mark S. "Aerial Hijacking and the Protection of Diplomats." *Harvard International Law Journal* 14 (1973): 595ff.

2699. McWhinney, Edward. *The Illegal Diversion of Aircraft and International Law.* Leiden: Sijthoff, 1975. 123pp.

Argues that hijacking involves a number of issues and that the multiplicity of motivations of skyjackers requires pluralistic solutions rather than the monolithic approach seen so far. Ten problems of illegal diversion that still call for resolution are identified.

2700. ———. "International Legal Problem-Solving and the Practical Dilemma of Hijacking." In *Aerial Piracy and International Law*, pp. 15-26. New York: Oceana, 1971.

2701. ———. "New Developments in the Law of International Aviation: The Control of Aerial Hijacking." *American Journal of International Law* 55 (1971): 71ff.

2702. Meyer, Alex. "Un nouveau problème juridique: La piraterie aerienne." [A new juridical problem: air piracy]" *Revue Française de droit aerien* 23 (July-September 1969): 261-298.

Looks at domestic legislation of several nations, as well as international treaties, aimed at combating crimes committed on board aircraft.

2703. ———. "Versicherungs- und Haftungs-Fragen bei Luftpiraterie." In his *Internationale Luftfahrtabkommen*, pp. 220-234 (1972). Also available in *Zeitschrift fur Luftrecht und Weltraumrechtsfragen* (1970): 293ff.

2704. Minor, W. W. "Skyjacking Crime Control Models." *Journal of Criminal Law and Criminology* 66 (March 1975): 94-105.

We are moving from deterrence to a prevention model.

2706. Perret, Robert Louis. "Punishment of Aerial Piracy: A New Development." *Interavia* 31 (June 1976).

2707. Peterson, Edward A. "Jurisdiction-Construction of Statute-Aircraft Piracy." *Journal of Air Law and Commerce* 30 (1964): 292-295.

2708. du Pontavice, E. "La piraterie aerienne: nation et effets." [Air piracy: concept and effects] *Revue générale de l'air et de l'espace* 32 (July-September 1969): 276-339.

The author studies the concept of air piracy and the applicability of maritime law. He finds that municipal law is inexact on the concept of air piracy, and outlines French internal law in this regard. He considers such aspects as passengers and freight and third parties.

2709. ———. "Seeking a Definition for Piracy in the Air." *ITA Bulletin*, March 30, 1970, pp. 321-324.

A shorter version of the above article.

2710. Poulantzas, Nicholas M. "Hijacking or Air Piracy?" *Nederlands Juristenblad* 20 (1970): 566-574.

2711. ———. "Hijacking v. Piracy: A Substantial Misunderstanding, Not a Quarrel over Semantics." *Revue héllenique de droit international* 23 (1970): 80-90.

2712. Pourcelet, Michael. "La capture illicité d'aeronefs/hijacking." [The illegal capture of aircraft hijackings]. *Revue générale de l'air et de l'espace* 32 (1969): 269-275.

The author notes the various aspects of hijacking, using the 1970 attack on an El Al B707 for illustration. Hijackings can have negative effects on the tourist industry. The Tokyo Convention is discussed, along with methods of enforcement.

2713. ———. "Comment: Hijacking. The Limitations of the International Treaty Approach." In Edward McWhinney, ed., *Aerial Piracy and International Law*, pp. 55-58. Leiden: Sijthoff, 1971.

2714. Pradelle, P. de la. "Les détournements d'aeronefs et le droit international." [Aircraft diversion and international law] *Revue générale de l'air et de l'espace* 32 (1969): 249-260.

Hijackers can be motivated by politics, criminal gain, or psychotic reasons. Crews should tailor their responses to these differences. In general, such takeovers are viewed as piracy by the International Law Association and cannot be justified by "protected persons" claims.

2715. Rafat, Amir. "Control of Aircraft Hijacking: The Law of International Civil Aviation." *World Affairs* 134 (Fall 1971): 143-156.

2716. Reeves, W. H. "Political Hijacking: What Law Applies in Peace and War." *Vanderbilt Law Review* 22 (1969): 1117ff.

2717. Rein, Bert. "A Government Perspective." *Journal of Air Law and Commerce* 37 (1971): 183-193.

2718. Rhinelander, John B. "The International Law of Aerial Piracy: New Proposals for the New Dimension." In Edward McWhinney, ed., *Aerial Piracy and International Law*, pp. 59-96. Leiden: Sijthoff, 1971.

2719. Rousseau, C. "Algérie et Congo-Kinshasa: Enlévement en avion de M. Moise Tschombe au-dessus des Baleares et détention de l'ancien chef du gouvernement congolais par les autorités algériennes, 30 Juin 1967." [Algeria and Congo-Kinshasa: The hijacking of Moise Tschombe's plane and his detention by Algerian authorities, June 30, 1967] *Revue générale de droit international public* 1 (1968): 145ff.

2720. Roww, A. C. de. *Skyjacking and the Sabotaging of Aerial Navigation.* Groningen: H. D. Tjeenk, 1973.
Discusses the legal problems and responses to aerial sabotage and hijacking.

2721. Ruppenthal, Karl M. "World Law and the Hijackers." *Nation* February 3, 1969, pp. 144-146.
Gives a brief history of skyjacking and notes the provisions of the Tokyo Convention.

2722. Salinas, Luis Tapia. "La Politica Aeria Internacional y la 'Pirateria Aerea.' " *Revista de Politica Internacional* 150 (March-April 1977): 97-110.

2723. Sampaio de Lacerda, J. C. "La Piraterie Aerienne, ses Aspects Actuels et Futurs." *Revue française de droit aerien* 24 (1970): 281ff.

2724. Samuels, Alec. "The Legal Problems: An Introduction." *Journal of Air Law and Commerce* 37 (1971): 163-170.
Introduces a journal symposium on air hijacking by outlining problems involving jurisdiction, prosecution, punishment, and extradition.

2725. Sarkav, A. K. "The International Air Law and Safety of Civil Aviation." *Indian Journal of International Law* 12 (April 1972): 200-208.
A brief history of air law from the 1919 convention through the Tokyo, Hague, and Montreal treaties. Some statistics on recent hijackings are provided.

2726. "Searching for Hijackers: Constitutionality, Costs and Alternatives." *University of Chicago Law Review* 40 (Winter 1973).

2727. "Seeking a Definition for Piracy in the Air." *ITA Bulletin*, March 30, 1970, pp. 321-324.

2728. Sheehan, William M. "Hijacking and World Law." *World Federalist: U.S. Edition* 16 (1970): 14-19.

2729. Shelhoup, Kamal G. "Extradition and Political Asylum as Applied to Aircraft Piracy." Ph.D dissertation, Claremont Graduate School, 1979.

2730. Shepard, Ira M. "Air Piracy: The Role of the International Federation of Airline Pilots Associations." *Cornell International Law Journal* 3 (1970): 79-91.

2731. Shubber, Sami. "Is Hijacking of Aircraft Piracy in International Law?" *British Yearbook of International Law* 43 (1968-1969): 193-204.

2732. Smith, Chester L. "The Probable Necessity of an International Prison in Solving Aircraft Hijacking." *International Lawyer* 5 (April 1971): 269-278.

As many skyjackings occur to secure the release of imprisoned former skyjackers, Smith suggests that an international prison be established so that a government that has sentenced terrorists will not have its planes put in jeopardy by those seeking to secure the release of the prisoners.

2733. Steelman, H. "International Terrorism Vis-à-Vis Air-hijacking." *Southwestern University Law Review* 9 (1977): 85-110.

An overview of hijacking incidents and legal responses.

2734. Stephen, John E. " 'Going South'—Air Piracy and Unlawful Interference with Air Commerce." *International Lawyer* 4 (1970): 433-443.

Surveys domestic, bilateral, and international law on hijacking.

2735. Sundberg, Jacob W. F. " 'Abu Thalaat' La guerre contre l'aviation civile internationale." *Revue de droit pénal et de criminologie* (October 1971).

2736. ———. "Flygkapningar—om utlandska brott och inlandsk politik." *1970 Svensk Juristtidning*.

2737. ———. "Lawful and Unlawful Seizure of Aircraft." *Terrorism* 1 (1978): 423-440.

Discusses Swedish case law relevant to questions of skyjacking. Among Swedish and foreign cases mentioned are the Tannous and Halasseh case, the Tshombe skyjacking, Flamourides' case, Tsironis's case, the Hashim hijacking, the Rebrina hijacking, and the Norrmalmstorg robbery.

2738. ———. "Piracy: Sea and Air." In *Report of the 54th Conference of the International Law Association*, pp. 755-771. The Hague, 1970, and London, 1971.

2739. ———. "La piraterie aerienne." *1970 Revue internationale de droit pénal* pp. 165ff.

2740. ———. "Thinking the Unthinkable or the Case of Dr. Tsironis." In M. Cherif Bassiouni, ed., *International Terrorism and Political Crimes*, pp. 448-459. Springfield, Ill.: Thomas, 1975.

2741. ———. "Unlawful Seizure of Aircraft." *Arkiv for Luftrett* (Oslo) 6 (1974): 44-54.

2742. "Symposium on the Unlawful Seizure of Aircraft: Approaches to the Legal Problems." *Journal of Air Law and Commerce* 37 (1971): 162-233.

2743. Toothman. "Legal Problems of Skyjacking." *American Bar Association Institute on International and Comparative Law* (1969): 251ff.

2744. U.S. House of Representatives. *Anti-Hijacking Act of 1974, House Report 93-885.* 1974.
   Additional related publications include Senate report no. 93-13 and House conference report no. 93-1194.

2745. ———. Committee on Interstate and Foreign Commerce. Subcommittee on Transportation and Aeronautics. "The Anti-Hijacking Act of 1973: Hearings." February 27-28, March 1, 6-9, 1973.

2746. ———. Committee on Commerce. "Amending the Federal Aviation Act of 1958 to Provide a More Effective Program to Prevent Air Piracy." Senate Report No. 93-13, 93d Cong., 1st sess., 1973.

2747. ———. Committee on Commerce. Subcommittee on Aviation. "The Administration's Emergency Anti-Hijacking Regulations: Hearings." 1973.

2748. ———. Committee on Commerce. Subcommittee on Aviation. "Anti-Hijacking Act of 1971: Hearings." March 6, June 29, August 13, 1972.

2749. ———. Committee on Foreign Relations. "Aircraft Hijacking Convention: Hearings." June 7, July 20, 1971.

2750. ———. Committee on the Judiciary. "Aircraft Piracy Amendments of 1973." Senate Report No. 93-722, 1974.

2751. "U.S. to Ask Denial of Asylum to Hijackers." *Aviation Week and Space Technology*, February 10, 1969, pp. 27-28.
   A discussion of the possibility of including a protocol to the Tokyo Convention that would alter extradition law to include air piracy as an extraditable offense.

2752. Valay, M. E. "Le déroutement des aeronefs." [The diversion of aircraft] *Revue générale de l'air et de l'espace* 32 (1969): 340-351.

Looks at aerial hijacking, especially in the Americas, but also points out that these crimes have occurred in Athens, Egypt, Damascus, and Algeria, generally for political reasons. The crime is difficult to qualify legally (as mutiny, barratry, piracy, or act of war), but various international methods to combat it have been suggested.

2753. Valladao, Haroldo. "Piracy: Sea and Air." In *Report of the Fifty-fourth Conference of the International Law Association*, pp. 735-754. The Hague, 1970, London, 1971.

2754. ———. "Piraterie aerienne: nouveau delit international." [Air piracy: A new international crime] Paper presented to the conference on Freedom of the Skies, McGill University, November 1967. Published in *Revue générale de l'air et de l'espace* 32 (1969): 261-268, and in Edward McWhinney and Bradley, eds., *The Freedom of the Air*, pp. 226ff. 1968.

Valladao discusses aerial piracy as defined by the 1958 FAA act and mentions other types of acts that facilitate that commission of other crimes, such as smuggling, prisoner escape, and the use of clandestine airports.

2755. ———. "Punition internationale de l'actuelle piraterie aerienne." In Edward McWhinney, ed., *Aerial Piracy and International Law*, pp. 97-115. Leiden: Sitjhoff, 1971.

2756. VanPanhuys, Harold F. "Aircraft Hijacking and International Law." *Columbia Journal of Transnational Law* 9 (1970): 1-22.

2757. Vasiljevic, T. "Mésures a l'égard de la piraterie aerienne en yougoslavie (état actual)." *Revue de droit pénal et de criminologie* 52 (December 1971-January 1972): 463ff.

2758. Volpe, John A., and Stewart, Jr., John T. "Aircraft Hijacking: Some Domestic and International Responses." *Kentucky Law Journal* 59 (Winter 1971): 372-405.

2759. Wilberforce, Sir R. "Crime in Aircraft." *Journal of the Royal Aeronautical Society* 67 (1963): 175ff.

2760. Wilson, R. A. "Terrorism, Air Piracy and Hijacking." *Australian Journal of Forensic Sciences* 7 (June 1975): 169-174.

Discusses developments in terrorist activities, the involvement of the International Criminal Police Organization, and Australian and international legislation governing the response to terrorist attacks.

2761. Wurfel, Seymour W. "Aircraft Piracy: Crime or Fun?" *William and Mary Law Review* 70 (Spring 1969): 820-873.

Lists each incident of skyjacking from 1961 and notes the legal aspects of piracy, jure gentium, international conventions, U.S. piracy law, aircraft piracy statutes, extradition problems, and possible solutions.

2762. Zotiades, George B. "The International Criminal Prosecution of Person Charged with an Unlawful Seizure of Aircraft." *Revue héllenique de droit international* 23 (1970): 12-37.

2763. Zussman, Ben Yakir. " 'The Leningrad Trial' in the Light of the International Law of Hijacking." *Hapraklit* 27 (1971): 563.

For further reading, see section on "Hijacking as a Terrorist Tactic," as well as entries 1888, 2347, and 2466.

The Tokyo Convention

2764. Boyle, Robert P. "Hijacking Airplanes: An Additional Note." *American Bar Association Journal* 49 (1963).

Discusses the "Convention on Offenses and Certain Other Acts Occurring on Board Aircraft."

2765. ———. "Jurisdiction over Crimes Committed in Flight: An International Convention." *American Criminal Law Quarterly* 3 (Winter 1965): 68ff.

2766. Convention on Offenses and Certain Other Acts Committed on Board Aircraft. September 14, 1963, Tokyo Convention. Reproduced in U.S. Department of State, *U.S. Treaties and Other International Agreements*, part 3 (1969), 20: 2941-2958. Reprinted in UNSG Report A/c.6/418 Annex II; ICAO Doc. 8364.

Signed by United States in 1969. Requires states to return hijacked aircraft to the control of their lawful commanders and to facilitate continuation of air journeys interrupted by violence. Provides rules for the exercise of jurisdiction over offenses committed aboard aircraft during flight. The convention does not have provisions for apprehension of hijackers beyond existing extradition laws of individual states.

2767. DeNaro, Jacob. "Inflight Crimes, The Tokyo Convention and Federal Judicial Jurisdiction." *Journal of Air Law and Commerce* 35 (1969): 171-203.

2768. FitzGerald, Gerald F. "Offences and Certain Other Acts Committed on Board Aircraft: The Tokyo Convention of 1963." *Canadian Yearbook of International Law* 2 (1964): 191-204.

2769. Hirano, R. "Convention on Offences and Certain Other Acts Committed on Board Aircraft of 1963." *Japanese Annual of International Law* 8 (1964): 44-52.

2770. International Civil Aviation Organization. Subcommittee of the Legal Committee on the Subject of Unlawful Seizure of Aircraft. *Reports and Documentation.* First and Second Session, Doc. No. 8838-LC/157, 1963.

2771. Johnson, Lyndon B. "Convention on Offenses and Certain Other Acts Committed on Board Aircraft: Removal of Injunction of Secrecy." *Congressional Record*, September 25, 1968, p. S11450.

2772. Lopez Gutierrez, Juan J. "Should the Tokyo Convention of 1963 Be Ratified?" *Journal of Air Law and Commerce* 31 (1965): 1-21.

2773. Mendelsohn, A. I. "In-Flight Crime: The International and Domestic Picture under the Tokyo Convention." *Virginia Law Review* 53 (1967): 509-563.

2774. Pulsifer, Roy, and Boyle, Robert. "The Tokyo Convention on Offences and Certain Other Acts Committed on Board Aircraft." *Journal of Air Law and Commerce* 20 (1964): 305-354.

2775. Robinson. "Changing Concepts of Sabotage: A Challenge to the Status of U.S. Carriers in International Civil Aviation?" *Journal of Air Law and Commerce* 34 (1968): 533ff.

2777. Samuels, Alec. "Crimes Committed on Board Aircraft: Tokyo Convention Act, 1967." *British Yearbook of International Law* 42 (1967): 271-277.

2778. "Tokyo Convention." *International Criminal Police Review* 186 (1965): 81-86.

The Hague Convention

2779. Abramovsky, Abraham. "Multilateral Conventions for the Suppression of Unlawful Seizure and Interference with Aircraft, Part I: The Hague Convention." *Columbia Journal of Transnational Law* 13 (1974): 381ff.

2780. Cheng, Bin. Paper delivered to the Symposium on the Hague Convention on Hijacking of Aircraft—The Legal Aspects, Air Law Group of the Royal Aeronautical Society, November 1, 1971.

2781. Convention for the Suppression of Unlawful Seizure of Aircraft.
1970. Reproduced in U.S. Department of State. *U.S. Treaties and Other International Agreements* 22, pt. 2 (1971): 1641-1684, ICAO Doc. 8920.

Signed at the Hague on December 15, 1970, and came into force on October 14, 1971, when the necesary ten ratifications by signatory states had been reached. The United States signed it in 1971. It requires states to prosecute or extradite suspected air hijackers found in their territory.

2782. Crivellaro, A. ''Ancora sulla Cosiddetta Pirateria Aerea: il Testo Definitivo della Convenzione dell'Aga.'' *Giurisprudenza Italiana* (1972): 3ff.

2783. ———. ''Il Progetto di Convenzione dell 'OACI Relativo Alla Cattura Illecita de Aeromobili.'' *Giurisprudenza Italiana* (1971).

2784. "Draft Proposals on Unlawful Seizure of Aircraft." *International Legal Materials* 8 (March 1969): 245-257.

A reproduction of ICAO documents LC/SC SA, Report, February 21, 1969.

2785. Guillaume. ''La convention de la Hague des 16 Décembre 1970.'' *Annuaire français de droit international* (1970).

Summarizes the December 16, 1970, meeting in the Hague of seventy-four members of the International Civil Aviation Organization, which led to the drafting of a convention closing loopholes in air piracy law.

2786. International Civil Aviation Organization. International Conference on Air Law—Convention for the Suppression of Unlawful Seizure of Aircraft. The Hague. *Volume I: Minutes.* Doc. 8979-LC/165-1, December 1970.

2787. ———. International Conference on Air Law—Convention for the Suppression of Unlawful Seizure of Aircraft. The Hague. *Volume II: Documents.* Doc. 8979-LC/165-2, December 1970.

2788. ———. Legal Committee. 17th Session. ''Minutes and Documents Relating to the Subject of Unlawful Seizure of Aircraft.'' Doc. 8877-LC/161, February 9-March 11, 1970.

2789. ———. Legal Committee, 18th Session. London. *Volume I: Minutes.* Doc. 8936-LC/164-1, September 29-October 22, 1970.

2790. ———. Legal Committee, 18th Session. London. *Volume 2: Documents.* Doc. 8936-LC/164-2, September 29-October 22, 1970.

2791. ———. "Resolutions Adopted by the Assembly and Index to Documentation." 17th Session (Extraordinary). Doc. 8895 A17-RES, June 16-30, 1970.

2792. Mankiewicz, R. H. "The 1970 Hague Convention." *Journal of Air Law and Commerce* 37 (1971): 195-210.
A review of how the Hague Convention was designed to cover gaps in the Tokyo Convention.

2793. "New Developments in the Law of International Civil Aviation: The Control of Aerial Hijacking—Panel Discussion." *Proceedings of the American Society of International Law* 65 (1971): 71ff.

2794. November, Celine Y. "Aircraft Piracy: The Hague Hijacking Convention." *International Lawyer* 6 (1972): 642-656.
Discusses how the Hague Convention was meant to handle gaps in the Tokyo agreement. Issues relating to jurisdiction, extradition, and implementation are reviewed.

2795. "Piracy: Sea and Air." *Report of the Fifty-fourth Conference of the International Law Association*, The Hague, August 23-29, 1970, pp. 705-754. London, 1971.

2796. Poulantzas, Nicholas M. "The Hague Convention for the Suppression of Unlawful Seizure of Aircraft (December 16, 1970)." *Nederlands Tijdschrift voor International Recht* 18 (1971): 25-75.

2797. Ragski, J. "Konwencga Haska o Zwalczanin Bezprawnego Zawladniecia Statkami Powietrznymi." *Panstwo i Prawo* (1971): 708ff.

2798. Rein, Bert. "A Government Perspective." *Journal of Air Law and Commerce* 37 (1971): 183-193.
Rein, a State Department officer, reviews the U.S. government's response to hijacking, notes that different measures will have deterrent effects on different types of hijackers, depending on motivations, and outlines U.S. hopes at the Hague Conference.

2799. Report of the Subcommittee on Unlawful Seizure of Aircraft. ICAO Doc. LC/SC SA. 1969.
The proceedings of the Hague Convention.

2800. Schmidt-Rantsch. "Die Internationale Luftrechtskonferenz in Den Haag und das Abkommen zur Bekampfund der widerrechtlicen Inbesitznahme von Luftfahrzeugen." *ZfLW* 63 (1971).

2801. Shubber, Sami. "Aircraft Hijacking under the Hague Convention: A New Regime?" *International and Comparative Law Quarterly* 22 (1973): 687ff.

2802. ———. "Aircraft Hijacking under the Hague Convention upon Asylum." *Harvard International Law Journal* 16 (1975): 93ff.

2803. Sundberg, Jacob W. F. "The Wisdom of Treaty Making: A Glance at the Machinery behind the Production of Law-Making Treaties and a Case Study of the Hague Hijacking Conference of 1970."*Scandinavian Studies in Law* (1972): 285-306.
    Gives behind-the-scenes details of the bargaining that went on at the Hague Conference.

2804. U.S. Senate. Committee on Foreign Relations. "Aircraft Hijacking Convention: The Convention for the Suppression of Unlawful Seizure of Aircraft, signed at the Hague, December 16, 1970." Hearings before the Committee on Executive A. 92d. Cong., 1st sess., June 7, July 20, 1971.

2805. "Unlawful Interference with Aircraft." *Report of the Fifty-fourth Conference of the International Law Association*, August 23-29, 1970, at the Hague, pp. 336-404. London, 1971.

2806. White, Gillian M. E. "The Hague Convention for the Suppression of Unlawful Seizure of Aircraft." *International Commission of Jurists Review* 6 (April-June 1971): 38-45.

2807. Yevseyev, P., and Kolosov, Y. "Air Bandits Outlawed." *International Affairs* (Moscow), November 8, 1971, pp. 83ff.
    Discusses the U.N. General Assembly resolution 2645 (XXV) and the 1970 Hague Convention.

The Montreal Convention

2808. Abramovsky, Abraham. "Multilateral Conventions for the Suppression of Unlawful Seizure and Interference with Aircraft Part 2: The Montreal Convention." *Columbia Journal of Transnational Law* 14 (1975): 268ff.

2809. "Air Law—Warsaw Convention and Montreal Agreement: Hijacking Victims May Recover Damages from Airline." *New York University Journal of International Law and Politics* 6 (1973): 555ff.

2810. Brower, Charles N. "Department Urges Senate Advice and Consent to Ratification of Montreal Convention on Aviation Sabotage." *Department of State Bulletin*, October 16, 1972, 444-448.

2811. Convention for the Suppression of Unlawful Acts against the Safety of Civil Aviation. 1971. Reproduced in U.S. Department of State, *U.S. Treaties and Other International Agreements*, 24, pt 1. (1973), pp. 565-602. Reprinted in UNSG Report A/C.6/418 Annex III; ICAO Doc. 8966.

Adopted on September 23, 1971, in Montreal, came into force the following month. The United States signed it in November 1971. The convention requires extradition or prosecution of persons who sabotage or otherwise destroy aircraft or who endanger the safe flight of an aircraft by damaging it or destroying or damaging air navigation facilities.

2812. Documentation Related to the Assembly of the ICAO Assembly: Seventeenth Session, Extraordinary, Montreal, June 16-30, 1970.

Reports from the conference include: Minutes of the Plenary Meetings (Doc. 8893, A17-Min. P/1-7); Report of the Executive Committee (Doc. 8892, A17-Ex); Report of Committee B (Doc. 8891, A17-Committee B); Resolutions adopted by the Assembly, 17th Session, Extraordinary (Doc. 8895, A17-RES).

2813. International Civil Aviation Organization. *International Conference on Air Law Volume I: Minutes*. Montreal, Doc. No. 9081-LC/170-1, September 1971.

2814. ———. *International Conference on Air Law, Volume II: Documents*. Montreal, Doc. No. 9081-LC/170-2, September 1971.

2815. ———. *Legal Committee, 20th Session (Special) Volume II: Documents*. Montreal, Doc. 9050-LC/169-2, January 9-30, 1973.

2816. Malmborg, K. E. "New Developments in the Law of International Aviation: The Control of Aerial Hijacking." *Proceedings of the American Society of International Law* (1971): 75ff.

2817. "Reports and Documents: Subcommittee of the Legal Committee on the Subject of Unlawful Seizure of Aircraft." International Civil Aviation Organization, 1st sess. February 10-21, 1969, and 2d sess., September 23-October 3, 1969, Montreal, Canada. Doc. 8838-LC/157.

2818. Rogers, William P. "ICAO Resolution on Air Piracy Welcomed." *Department of State Bulletin*, July 24, 1972, p. 125.

2819. "Sovereign Rights Position Snags Strong Anti-Hijacking Proposal." *Aviation Week*, September 18, 1972, p. 25.

2820. Thomas, C. S., and Kirby, M. J. "Convention for the Suppression of Unlawful Acts Against the Safety of Civil Aviation." *International and Comparative Law Quarterly* 22 (June 1973).

Other International Legal Conventions

League of Nations Antiterrorist Actions

2821. "Agreement Concerning Mutual Defense against Undesirable Foreigners (Quito, August 10, 1935)." In Manley O. Hudson, ed., *International Legislation*, 7: 166-167. Washington, D.C.: Carnegie Endowment for International Peace, 1931-1950.

2822. Caloyanni, M. A. "The Proposals of M. Laval to the League of Nations for the Establishment of an International Permanent Tribunal in Criminal Matters." *Transactions of the Grotius Society* 21 (1936).

2823. ———. "Le terrorisme et la création d'une cour répressive internationale." *Revue de droit international* 15 (1935): 46ff.

2824. ———. *Convention for the Prevention and Punishment of Terrorism.* Drafted by the League of Nations, November 16, 1937. Reproduced in Manley O. Hudson, ed., *International Legislation* (Washington, D.C.: Carnegie Endowment for International Peace, 1941), 7: 862-878. Also in *League of Nations Off. J.* 19 (1938): 23ff, and see 27 UNGAOR Annex I, Agenda Item 92, UN Doc. A/c 6/418 (1972) Doc. C94, M, 47, 1938, V, pp. 5-17.

Signed by twenty-four countries but ratified by only one state and thus never came into force. Defined acts of terrorism very broadly and did not differentiate between international and civil conflict or between such conflicts that would spread to third countries.

2825. "The Convention for the Prevention and Punishment of Terrorism." *British Yearbook of International Law* 19 (1938): 214-216.

2826. de Vabres, H. Donnedieu. "La répression internationale du terrorisme; les conventions de Génève." *Revue de droit international et de legislation comparée* 19 (1938): 37-74.

2827. Kuhn, Arthur K. "The Complaint of Yugoslavia against Hungary with Reference to the Assassination of King Alexander." *American Journal of International Law* 29 (1935): 87-92.

Discusses state responsibility for suppressing terrorists within its borders who conspire to engage in political activities of a hostile nature outside its borders.

2828. League of Nations. "International Repression of Terrorism Draft Convention." ser. 1938 V.2 (Proceedings in V.3). League of Nations Publications, V. Legal, 1938.

The 1937 volume also has the draft convention, as well as the Report of the Committee for the International Repression of Terrorism.

2829. Mosler, H. "Die Konferenz zur internationalen Bekampfung des Terrorismus (November 1937)." *Zeitschrift fur auslandisches offentliches Recht und Volkerrecht* 8 (1938): 99ff.

2830. Pella, Vespasian V. "La répression des crimes contre la personalité de l'état." *Recueil des cours de l'académie de droit international de la Haye* 3 (1930): 677-831.

2831. ———. "La répression du terrorisme et la création d'une cour internationale." *Revue de Droit International Prive* 5, 6 (1939): 785, 120.

2832. "Precedents in the Aborted League of Nations 1937 Treaty Outlawing Terrorism." United Nations: A/C. 6/418 Annex 1, November 2, 1972.

2833. Roux, J. A. "Le projet de convention internationale pour la répression des crimes présentant un danger public." *Revue international de droit pénal* 12 (1935): 99-130.

2834. von Gretshaninow, A. "Der Plan eines internationalen Abkommens betreffend die Bekampfung politischen Verbrechen un die Errichtung eines internationalen Strafgerichtshofs." *Zeitschrift fur auslandisches offentliches Recht und Volkerrecht* 5 (1935).

Organization of American States Convention

2835. Brach, Richard S. "The Inter-American Convention on the Kidnapping of Diplomats." *Columbia Journal of Transnational Law* 10 (1971): 392-412.

2836. "Convention to Prevent and Punish the Acts of Terrorism Taking the Form of Crimes against Persons and Related Extortion That are of International Significance." 1971. OAS official documents OAS/SER.A/17 SEPF. Treaties Serial No. 37 (341.2-SEPF-7960). Also in *American Journal of International Law* 65 (October 1971): 898-901. Reprinted in UNSG Report A/C. 6/418 Annex V. (Done at Washington, February 2, 1971) 10 *Interna-*

tional Legal Materials (March 1971), pp. 255-258. Reproduced from OAS document AG/doc, 88 rev. 1, corr 1 of February 2, 1971.

2837. "Implementing International Conventions Against Terrorism." U.S. House of Representatives, 94th Cong., 2d sess., report no. 94-1614, September 18, 1976.

A discussion of bills needed to implement certain international conventions, including the 1971 OAS convention and the U.N. convention on the protection of diplomats.

2838. "Inter-American Juridical Committee: Draft Convention on Terrorism and Kidnapping of Persons for Purposes of Extortion." September 26, 1970. Statement of Reasons for the Draft Convention on Terrorism and Kidnapping (October 5, 1970). *International Legal Materials* 119 (November 1970): 117-182, 1250-1273. Reproduced from the official English translation published in the OAS doc. CP/doc.54/70 rev. 1, November 4, 1970.

2839. Jova, J. J. "OAS Asked to Consider Problem of Kidnapping." *Department of State Bulletin*, May 25, 1970, p. 662.

2840. Lapeyre, Edison Gonzalez. *Aspectos Juridicos del Terrorismo.* Montevideo: Amalio M. Fernandez, 1972. 125 pp.

Notes the history of attempts to define, control, and punish terrorist activities. Principles of Uruguayan, Latin American, and U.N. conventional law, and their development through time, are outlined. Texts of resolutions and conventions of various international organizations dealing with this aspect of the law are provided.

2841. ———. "Secuestro de Diplomaticos y Consules." *Revista Uruguaya de Derecho Internacional* 1 (1972): 161ff.

2842. Melo, Artemio Luis. "Inviolabilidad Diplomatica y el Caso del Embajador Von Spreti." *Revista de Derecho Internacional y Ciencias Diplomaticas* 19 (1970): 147-156.

2843. Murphy, James. "The Role of International Law in the Prevention of Terrorist Kidnapping of Diplomatic Personnel." In M. Cherif Bassiouni, ed., *International Terrorism and Political Crimes*, pp. 285-313. Springfield, Ill.: Thomas, 1975.

Reviews the historical development of diplomatic privileges and immunities and discusses the OAS and U.N. conventions on internationally protected persons.

2844. Poulantzas, Nicholas M. "Some Problems of International Law Connected with Urban Guerrilla Warfare: The Kidnapping of Members of Diplomatic Missions, Consular Offices and Other Foreign Personnel." *Annales d'études internationales* 3 (1972): 137-167.

2845. Wilson, Clifton E. "Personal Immunities of Diplomatic Agents." In his *Diplomatic Privileges and Immunities*, pp. 46-77. Tucson: University of Arizona, 1967.

A discussion of legal issues related to protection, assault and attack, arrest and detention, and violations of dignity (racial discrimination). Gives data on terrorist incidents prior to 1968.

Also see entry 775.

United Nations Antiterrorist Actions

2846. Aerial Hijacking or Interference with Civil Air Travel. G.A. Res. 2645 (XXV). 25 U.N. GAOR, Supp. (No. 99). U.N. Doc. A/8176 (1970).

A November 1970 General Assembly resolution calling for states to extradite or prosecute offenders and requesting adoption of the Tokyo Convention.

2847. Bennett, Jr., W. Tapley. "U.S. Initiatives in the U.N. to Combat International Terrorism." *International Lawyer* 7 (October 1973): 755ff.

2848. ———. "U.S. Outlines Principles for Work of Ad Hoc Committee on Terrorism." *Department of State Bulletin*, September 3, 1973, pp. 337-339.

2849. ———. "U.S. Votes against U.N. General Assembly Resolution Calling for Study of Terrorism." *Department of State Bulletin*, January 22, 1973, pp. 81-94.

2850. Bloomfield, Louis M., and FitzGerald, Gerald F. *Crimes against Internationally Protected Persons: Prevention and Punishment: An Analysis of the U.N. Convention.* New York: Praeger, 1975. 290 pp.

Discusses the legislative history of the UNGA convention of December 14, 1973. Its place in the international law relating to such persons is discussed, and twenty-three appendixes present the texts of important conventions and U.N. resolutions.

2851. "Causes and Preventions of International Terrorism." United Nations Study A/C 6/418, Corr 1 Add 1, November 2, 1972. "Comments of Member States on the Question of the Protection and Inviolability of Diplomatic Agents and Other Persons Entitled to Special Protection Under International Law." United Nations: A/8710/Add.1, 1972.

2852. Convention on the Prevention and Punishment of Crimes Against Internationally Protected Persons, Including Diplomatic Agents. GA Res. 3166, 28 U.N. GAOR Supp. (No. 30), U.N. Doc. A/9030 (1973). *Department of State Bulletin* 70 pp. 91-95, 1973.

Adopted by the U.N. General Assembly on December 14, 1973, and states that those who kidnap, murder, and attack diplomats and other internationally protected persons are to be neither extradited nor prosecuted.

2853. "Convention on the Prevention and Punishment of Crimes against Diplomatic Agents and Other Internationally Protected Persons: An Analysis." *Virginia Journal of International Law* 14 (1974): 703ff.

2854. "Coping with Terrorism: The Democracies Must Act Jointly Outside the U.N." *Atlas World Press Review* 23 (September 1976): 11-14.

An interview with three foreign journalists: Gitta Bauer of Springer Foreign News Service, Brian Saxton of the BBC's U.N. desk, and George Wolff, U.N. correspondent for Agence France-Presse.

2855. "Draft Convention for the Prevention and Punishment of Certain Acts of International Terrorism." *Department of State Bulletin* October 16, 1972, pp. 431-433. Also U.N. Doc. A/C.6/L.850 (1972).

2856. Evans, Ernest. "American Policy Response to International Terrorism: Problems of Multilateral Deterrence." Paper presented at the Conference on Terrorism in the Contemporary World, April 26-28, 1976, at Glassboro State College. Available as FAR 25286-N. Published in Marius Livingston, et al., eds., *International Terrorism in the Contemporary World*, pp. 376-385. Westport, Conn.: Greenwood Press, 1978.

A content analysis of speeches made at the United Nations on international terrorism.

2857. Finger, Seymour Maxwell. "Can the United Nations Deal Effectively with International Terrorism?" Paper presented to the Joint National Meeting of the Operations Research Society of America and the Institute of Management Sciences, May 1-3, 1978, at New York City.

A 1972 U.S. draft antiterrorism convention was defeated by Arab and African opposition. A West German proposal on hostages is being discussed by a special committee and has better chances of passage.

2858. ———. "Terrorism: United Nations Perspectives." Paper presented to the 18th annual convention of the International Studies Association, March 16-20, 1977, at St. Louis, Missouri.

2859. ———. "The United Nations Response to Terrorism." In Yonah Alexander and Robert A. Kilmarx, eds., *Political Terrorism and Business: The Threat and Response*, pp. 428-490. New York: Praeger, 1979.

2860. Forcible Diversion of Civil Aircraft in Flight. G.A. Res. 2551 (XXIV), 24, U.N. GAOR, Supp. (No. 105), UN Doc. A/7845 (1969).

A December U.N. General Assembly resolution urging national legislation prohibiting and penalizing illegal seizure of aircraft and supporting International Civil Aviation Organization efforts toward drafting a convention.

2861. "General Assembly Resolution on Terrorism: Final Text and Member Votes." U.N. A/Res/3034 (XXVII), December 18, 1972.

2862. Green, L. C. "Double Standards in the United Nations: The Legalisation of Terrorism." *Archiv des Volkerrechts* 18 (1979): 129-148.

2863. ———. "The Legalization of Terrorism." In Yonah Alexander, David Carlton, and Paul Wilkinson, eds., *Terrorism: Theory and Practice*, pp. 175-197. Boulder: Westview, 1979.

Green laments the U.N. response to terrorism, arguing that its concentration on struggles for self-determination and independence has given carte blanche to liberation groups to employ any methods they deem necessary.

2864. Hoveyda, Fereydoun. "The Problem of International Terrorism at the United Nations." *Terrorism* 1 (1977): 71-83.

The permanent representative of Iran to the United Nations describes the early efforts of the secretary-general to inscribe an item on terrorism on the General Assembly's agenda and how matters have slowly progressed from there.

2865. "International Law Commission: Draft Articles on the Prevention and Punishment of Crimes against Diplomatic Agents and Other Internationally Protected Persons." *International Legal Materials: Current Documents* 11 (September 1972).

2866. "International Law Commission: Question of the Protection and Inviolability of Diplomatic Agents and Other Persons Entitled to Special Protection under International Law." *International Legal Materials: Current Documents* 11 (May 1972).

2867. Jack, Homer A. "Hostages, Hijacking and the Security Council." *America*, September 4, 1976, pp. 94-97. Reprinted as "Can the U.N. Act?" in William P. Lineberry, ed., *The Struggle Against Terrorism*, pp. 163-173. New York: Wilson, 1977.

A discussion of the ineffectual legal response in the United Nations to terrorism, including a summary of the Entebbe raid debate in the Security council.

2868. Jack, H. A. "Terrorism: Another U.N. Failure." *America* October 20, 1973, pp. 282-285.

2869. Korey, William. "Moral Bankruptcy at the U.N." *Midstream* 19 (1973): 34-42.
Concerning failure of the 1972 General Assembly to take meaningful action on international terrorism.

2870. Lagoni, Rainer. "The U.N. and International Terrorism." *Europa-Archiv* 6 (1977): pp. 171-180. Available in *International Summaries: A Collection of Selected Translations in Law Enforcement and Criminal Justice*, 3: 154-164. Washington, D.C.: U.S. Department of Justice, National Criminal Justice Reference Service, April 1979.

2871. Lee, Edward G., and April, Serge. "Behind-the-Scenes Negotiation of Treaty to Protect Diplomats." *International Perspectives* (May-June 1975): 3-7.

2872. "Legal Committee Report on the Terrorism Issue." United Nations: A/8069, December 16, 1972.

2873. "Legal Committee's Chairman Reports on Consultations with the Members." United Nations: AC. 6/L. 866/Con 1, November 9, 1972.

2874. Mueller, Gerhard O. W. "United Nations Activities and Transnational Violence." Paper presented to the conference on Terror: The Man, the Mind and the Matter, October 15-16, 1976, at the John Jay School of Criminal Justice, New York City.

2875. Murphy, James. "The Role of International Law in the Prevention of Terrorist Kidnapping of Diplomatic Personnel." In M. Cherif Bassiouni, ed., *International Terrorism and Political Crimes*, pp. 285-313. Springfield, Ill.: Thomas, 1975.

2876. ———. "Protected Persons and Diplomatic Facilities." In Alona Evans and John F. Murphy, eds., *Legal Aspects of International Terrorism*. Washington, D.C.: American Society of International Law, 1977.

2877. ———. "The Trend towards Anarchy in the U.N." *American Bar Association Journal* (March 1968).

2878. ———. "United Nations Proposals on the Control and Repression of Terrorism." In M. Cherif Bassiouni, ed., *International Terrorism and Political Crimes*, pp. 493-506. Springfield, Ill.: Thomas, 1975.

A discussion of the still-born U.S. draft convention of 1972, which the author believes failed due to the acrimonious atmosphere that prevailed after the Munich Olympics attack. Technical changes to the convention's wording might have been able to save it.

2879. Murphy, John F.; Goldie, L. F. E.; Almond, Harry; and Johnson, Chalmers. "Discussion: Control of Terrorism in International Life: Cooperation and Self-Help." *Proceedings of the Seventy-first Annual Meeting of the American Society of International Law, San Francisco, April 21-23, 1977*, pp. 17-32.

Murphy identifies obstacles to international response, Goldie discusses U.N. gestures, Almond notes the Department of Defense response, and Johnson summarizes the findings of the 1976 State Department conference on international terrorism.

2880. Nixon, Richard M.; Rogers, William P.; and Scali, John. "U.S. Calls for Firm International Stand Against Terrorism Extortion and Blackmail; Statements, March 2, 1973." *Department of State Bulletin*, March 26, 1973, p. 353.

2881. Paust, Jordan J. " 'Non-Protected' Persons or Things." In Alona Evans and John F. Murphy, eds., *Legal Aspects of International Terrorism*. Washington, D.C.: American Society of International Law, 1977.

2882. Pauw, Wilfried De. "La question de terrorisme devant la XXVII assemblé des nations uniés: Résolutie betreffende het internationaal terrorisme." In *Réflexions sur la définition et la répression du terrorisme*, pp. 175-190. Brussels: Editions de l'Université de Bruxelles, 1974.

2883. Phelps, Phelps. "U.N. Fails to Curb Worldwide Terrorism." *Human Events*, October 12, 1974, p. 12.

Cites UNA-USA figures on costs of terrorism; gives a brief history of U.N. Ad Hoc Committee's creation and lack of outputs; makes proposals that include antiterrorist squads prepared for action whenever an incident occurs, an international Western treaty suspending air services to safe-haven nations, and altering media coverage of terrorists.

2884. Poulantzas, N. "Some Problems of International Law Connected with Urban Guerilla Warfare: The Kidnapping of Members of Diplomatic Missions, Consular Offices and Other Foreign Personnel." *Annals of International Studies* 3 (1972): 137ff.

2885. Przetacznik, Franciszek. ''Convention on the Special Protection of Officials of Foreign States and International Organizations.'' *Revue belge de droit international* 9 (1973): 455ff.

2886. ———. ''Prevention and Punishment of Crimes against Internationally Protected Persons.'' *Indian Journal of International Law* 13 (January-March 1973): 65ff.

2887. ———. ''Special Protection of Diplomatic Agents.'' *Revue de droit international, de sciences diplomatiques et politiques* 50 (October-December 1972): 270ff.

2888. ''Questions Relating to International Terrorism.'' *Yearbook of the United Nations* (1972).

2889. Rozakis, Christos L. ''Terrorism and the Internationally Protected Persons in the Light of the ILC Draft Articles.'' *International and Comparative Law Quarterly*, 4th ser. 23 (January 1974): 32-72.

2890. *Safety of International Civil Aviation.* GA Res. 32/8 (XXXII), 32 UN GAOR, Supp., UN Doc. A/RES/32/8 (1977).
   A text of the November 3, 1977, General Assembly condemnation of hijacking, which calls for adoption of the ICAO convention.

2891. Smith, Dale O. ''Why Subsidize Terror?'' *National Defense: Peace Through Preparedness* 59 (May-June 1975): 457-459.
   Suggests that the Arabs ''foot the bill'' of UNWRA and take care of the Palestinians, with the United States dropping all of its contributions.

2892. Suy, Erik. ''La question du terrorisme devant la XXVII assemblée des nations uniés: Besluiten uit de Discussies in de Zesde Commissie.'' In *Réflexions sur la définition et la répression du terrorisme.* Brussels: Editions de L'Université de Bruxelles.

2893. Swift, Richard N. ''Transnational Terrorism: Recent Developments at the U.N.'' Paper presented to the 19th annual convention of the International Studies Association, February 22-25, 1978, at Washington, D.C.

2894. ''Terrorism: The Proposed U.S. Draft Convention.'' *Georgia Journal of International and Comparative Law* 3 (Spring 1973): 430-447.
   Introduces the draft resolution presented at the September 1972 U.N. General Assembly.

2895. **"United Nations Analytic Study Prepared by the Secretary-General of Observations of States Submitted in Accordance with General Assembly Resolution 3034 xxvii."** A/Ac. 160/2, June 1973.

2896. **"U.N. Draft Code of Offenses Against the Peace and Security of Mankind."** Paris: A/2693, GAOR 9, Sess. Suppl. 9, 1954.

2897. **"U.N. Draft Resolution on Terrorism Submitted by the United States."** UN: A/C. 6/L., 850, September 25, 1972.

2898. **"U.N. Failure to Act on Terrorism."** *Congressional Record* 120 (1974): H11670.

2899. **U.N. General Assembly.** *Report of the Ad Hoc Committee on International Terrorism.* GAOR 28th sess., supplement no. 28 (A/9028), 1973.

2900. **U.S. House of Representatives.** Committee on the Judiciary, Subcommittee on Criminal Justice. "International Protected Persons Bills: Unsworn Declarations Bills, Hearings on HR 12942, 13709, 11106, and 11217." 94th Cong., 2d sess., June 30, 1976, serial no. 45.

2901. **Williams, Maureen, and Chatterjee, S. J.** "Suggesting Remedies for International Terrorism: Use of Available International Means." *International Relations* 5 (November 1976): 1069-1093.
   Attempts to define and combat terrorism by international conventions are viewed as ineffective. The Security Council is suggested as a more appropriate vehicle.

2902. **Wood, M. C.** "Convention on the Prevention and Punishment of Crimes against Internationally Protected Persons, Including Diplomatic Agents." *International and Comparative Law Quarterly* 22 (1974): 791ff.

2903. **Yafe, R.** "The U.N. and the Terrorist Menace." *Israel Horizons* 20 (September-October 1972): 9-10, 21.
   Also see entries 56 and 359.

Inter-European Legal Conventions

2904. **Alberich, Julio Cola.** "Las Medidas Europeas Contra el Terrorismo." *Revista de Politica Internacional* 150 (March-April 1977): 363-364.

2905. **"Convencion Contra el Terrorismo, Firmada en Estrasburgo por el Consejo de Europa."** *Revista de Politica Internacional* 150 (March-April 1977): 364-369.

2906. "**Convenzione Europea Sulla Repressione del Terrorismo (Strasburgo, 10 Novembre 1976).**" *Revista di Studi Politici Internazionali* 44 (April-July 1977): 320-324.

2907. "**European Convention on the Suppression of Terrorism, Opened for Signature January 27, 1977.**" Reprinted in *International Legal Materials* 15 (1976): 1272ff.

2908. Golsong, H. "European Convention for the Suppression of Terrorism: Provocation or Instrument of Peace?" *Instantanes criminologiques* 30 (1976): 33-35.

A discussion of the seventeen-nation Council of Europe agreement. The convention attempts to define which crimes will not be under the "political offenses" exception to extradition.

DISASTER RESPONSE

2909. Allport, Gordon W., et al. "Personality under Social Catastrophe." *Character and Personality* 10 (1941): 1-8. Reprinted in Clyde Kluckholn, *Personality in Nature, Society and Culture.* New York: Knopf, 1948.

2910. Baker, George W., and Chapman, Dwight W., eds. *Man and Society in Disaster.* New York: Basic Books, 1962.

2911. Barton, Allan H. *Communities in Disaster: A Social Analysis of Collective Stress Situations.* Garden City, N.Y.: Doubleday, 1970.

2912. ——. *Social Organization under Stress: A Sociological Review of Disaster Studies.* Washington, D.C.: National Academy of Sciences, 1963.

2913. Berkol, Faruk N. "Natural Disasters: A Neglected Variable in National Development Strategies." *International Social Science Journal* 28 (1976): 730-735.

2914. Bluhm, Hilde O. "How Did They Survive? Mechanisms of Defense in Nazi Concentration Camps." In Bernard Rosenberg et. al., *Mass Society in Crisis.* New York: Macmillan, 1964.

2915. Boder, D. P. "The Impact of Catastrophe. I. Assessment and Evaluation." *Journal of Psychology* 38 (1954): 3-50.

2916. Bristow, Allen P. *Police Disaster Operations.* Springfield, Ill.: Thomas, 1973. 240 pp.

2917. Bucher, Rue. "Blame and Hostility in Disaster." *American Journal of Sociology* 62 (March 1957): 467-475.

Analyzed the reactions of residents of Elizabeth, N.J., in 1951-1952 when three airplanes crashed within three months. Argues that scapegoating or blaming of individuals will occur when the situation is sufficiently defined to assess responsibility, and the people responsible violated moral standards and will not take action to remedy the situation if left to their own volition.

2918. Cornell, James. *The Great International Disaster Book.* New York: Scribners, 1976. 382 pp.

2919. Drabeck, Thomas E., and Quarantelli, Enrico L. "Scapegoats, Villains, and Disasters." *Transaction* (March 1967). Reprinted in James F. Short, ed., *Modern Criminals.* New Brunswick, N.J.: Transaction, 1973. pp. 215-229.

Discusses three theories of scapegoating: that it is irrational, in which people can work off their frustration; that it is rational and seeks to prevent future occurrences; and that it at times gets in the way of prevention by attacking individuals rather than the system responsible for the conditions allowing disasters.

2920. Dwyer, W. A. "Disaster Planning Can Save Lives." *Journal of the Medical Society of New Jersey* 69 (November 1972): 953-955.

2921. Dynes, Russell, and Quarantelli, Enrico L. "What Looting in Civil Disturbances Really Means." *Transaction* (May 1968). Reprinted in James F. Short, ed., *Modern Criminals.* New Brunswick, N.J.: Transaction, 1973. pp. 231-246.

Argues that those who loot in disasters are outsiders, whereas looters in civil disturbances are locals. In disasters, property rights are redefined, so what is needed to help save lives becomes public property. In civil disturbances, the entire system of allocation of rewards is being called into question. The authors argue that looting, as defined, is quite rare in disasters.

2922. Eddy, Paul; Potter, Elaine; and Page, Bruce. *Destination Disaster: From the Tri-Motor to the DC-10: The Risk of Flying.* New York: Quadrangle, 1976. 412 pp.

Reviewed by Robert Buckhorn "Coffin in the Sky," *Washington Post Book World*, October 17, 1976, p. N-3. A British account of the crash of Turkish Airlines flight 981, March 3, 1974, which resulted in the deaths of all 346 persons on aboard.

2923. Elder, Bob, and Elder, Sarah. *Crash.* New York: Atheneum, 1977. 253 pp.

Reviewed by Robert J. Serling, "A Tragedy of Errors," *Washington Post Book World*, March 27, 1977, p. E7. The authors deal with the crash in the Florida Everglades of an Eastern Airlines Lockheed 1011 on December 29, 1972, the first fatal accident involving a wide-body jetliner. The details of how the crash came about are explored.

2924. Fritz, Charles E. "Disaster." In Robert K. Merton and Robert A. Nisbet, *Contemporary Social Problems: An Introduction to the Sociology of Deviant Behavior and Social Disorganization*, pp. 651-694. New York: Harcourt, Brace and World, 1961.

A review of the early literature on social responses to many forms of disaster.

2925. Fritz, Charles, and Mathewson, J. H. *Convergence Behavior in Disasters*. Washington, D.C.: National Academy of Sciences, 1957.

2926. Fuller, John G. *The Poison That Fell from the Sky*. New York: Berkeley, 1977. 166 pp.

An anecdotal indictment of the corporate response to the Seveso, Italy, tragedy, in which an accident at a chemical plant in Switzerland created a dioxin cloud that poisoned a town. Hazards connected with similar chemicals are outlined.

2927. Grosser, George H.; Wechsler, Henry; and Greenblatt, Milton, eds. *The Threat of Impending Disaster: Contributions to the Psychology of Stress*. Cambridge, Mass.: MIT Press, 1964. 335 pp.

2928. Hirshleifer, Jack. "Some Thoughts on the Social Structure after a Bombing Disaster." *World Politics* 8 (1956): 206-227.

2929. Janis, Irving L., et al. *The Problem of Panic*. Washington, D.C.: Committee on Disaster Studies, NRC-NAS, Office of Civil Defense, TB-19-2, June 1955.

2930. Johnston, Moira. *The Last Nine Minutes: The Story of Flight 981*. New York: Morrow, 1976. 317 pp.

Reviewed by Robert Buckhorn, "Coffin in the Sky," *Washington Post Book World*, October 17, 1976, p. N3. A detailed account of the crash of a Turkish Airlines DC10 on March 3, 1974, which killed 346 persons.

2931. Kolata, Gina Bari. "Catastrophe Theory: The Emperor Has No Clothes." *Science*, April 15, 1977, pp. 287, 350-351.

Kolata discusses some of the criticisms that have only recently been leveled against the inappropriate applications of catastrophe theory and dwells on the possible reasons for this late development.

2932. Leonard, V. A. *Police Pre-Disaster Preparation.* Springfield, Ill.: Thomas, 1973. 344 pp.

2933. Logan, Leonard, et al. *A Study of the Effect of Catastrophe on Social Disorganization.* Chevy Chase, Md.: Operations Research Office: Technical Memorandum no. ORO-T-194, July 22, 1952.

2934. Nash, Jay Robert. *Darkest Hours.* New York: Wallaby, 1977. 775 pp.
Reviewed briefly in *Washington Post Book World*, November 6, 1977. The book contains 630 pages of encyclopedic references on catastrophes, as well as 145 pages, arranged by category, of chronologies of disasters.

2935. Newton, Douglas, ed. *Disaster, Disaster, Disaster, Catastrophes Which Change Laws.* New York: Franklin Watts, 1961.

2936. Quarantelli, E. L., and Dynes, R. R. ''When Disaster Strikes.'' *Psychology Today* 5 (1972): 66-70.

2937. Rado, S. ''Emergency Behavior.'' In *Psychoanalysis and Behavior: Collected Papers.* New York: Grune and Stratton, 1956.

2938. Richardson, J. W., ed. *Disaster Planning.* Proceedings of a Symposium, October 10-11, 1974, at the Royal Naval Hospital, Haslar, Gosport, Harts. Bristol: John Wright and Sons, 1975.

2939. Schultz, D. P. *Panic Behavior.* New York: Random House, 1964.

2940. Shaw, Adam. *Sound of Impact: The Legacy of TWA Flight 514.* New York: Viking, 1977. 247 pp.
Shaw deals with the personal lives of the ninety-two persons who died in the crash of a B727 that hit a mountain while approaching Dulles Airport on December 1, 1977. Reviewed by Robert J. Serling, ''A Tragedy of Errors,'' *Washington Post Book World*, March 27, 1977, p. E-7.

2941. Stern, Gerald M. *The Buffalo Creek Disaster: The Story of the Survivors' Unprecedented Lawsuit.* New York: Random House, 1976. 274 pp.
The lawyer in a disaster that killed 125 and left 4,000 homeless discusses the legal proceedings that he led after the event. This may be useful in projecting future societal responses to disaster victims, as well as aiding

governments and corporations in disaster insurance planning. Reviewed briefly by Coleman McCarthy, "Coal Country Tragedy with a Hopeful Ending" *Washington Post*, May 4, 1976, p. p. B4.

2942. Veltford, Helen Rank, and Lee, George E. "The Coconut Grove Fire: A Study of Scapegoating." *Clinical Supplement to the Journal of Abnormal and Social Psychology* 38 (April 1943): 138-154.

Discusses the Cocoanut Grove fire of November 28, 1942, in which 498 persons were killed.

2943. Wolfenstein, M. *Disaster: A Psychological Essay*. Glencoe, Ill.: Free Press, 1957.

2944. Wooley, Frank M. "Natural Disasters" and "Man-Made Disasters." In David Wallechinsky and Irving Wallace, eds., *The People's Almanac* pp. 543-569. Garden City, N.Y.: Doubleday, 1975.

These two articles note major disasters throughout history and what societal responses have been.

See also entries 870 and 3140.

MEDIA AND TERRORISM

2945. Alexander, Yonah. ''Communications Aspects of International Terrorism.'' *International Problems* 16 (Spring 1977): 55-60. A summary of a paper presented at the annual convention of the International Studies Association, February 25-29, 1976, at Toronto. FAR 25352-N.

Citing case examples, Alexander points out that terrorists use the media to obtain worldwide exposure for their causes. He also finds that the media lead to an exportation of violent techniques. The essential tension that faces the media is protection of the public's right to know versus aiding the terrorists by publicizing their message.

2946. ———. ''Terrorism in the Mass Media in the Middle East.'' In Seymour Maxwell Finger and Yonah Alexander, eds., *Terrorism: Interdisciplinary Perspectives* pp. 166-206. New York: John Jay Press, 1977.

Discusses the mass media's coverage of international terrorism and its consequences, as well as the strategic significance of communications between domestic and foreign terrorist groups. Terrorists, especially in the Middle East, manipulate the media to enhance their effectiveness (to create an emotional state of extreme fear) and draw the attention of the whole world and influence their responses.

2947. ———. ''Terrorism and the Media: Some Considerations.'' Paper presented to the 19th annual meeting of the International Studies Association, February 29, 1978, at Washington, D.C. Published in Yonah Alexander, David Carlton, and Paul Wilkinson, eds., *Terrorism: Theory and Practice* Boulder: Westview, 1979. pp. 159-174.

Makes several suggestions for improved coverage.

2948. ———. ''Terrorism and the Media.'' Paper presented to the Joint National Meeting of the Operations Research Society of America and the Institute of Management Sciences, May 1-3, 1978, at New York City.

The author's abstract reads: ''On the one hand, extensive coverage by the media is a major reward for terrorists; establishment of communication channels willingly or unwillingly become tools in the terrorist strategy; and advertising terrorism increases the effectiveness of its message through repetition and imitation. Balanced against this concern is the vital importance of protecting 'the people's right to know' and of a free press in open societies. How then should the media and public policy weigh these two concerns?''

2949. ———. ''Terrorism, the Media and the Police.'' *Journal of International Affairs* 32 (Spring-Summer, 1978): 101-113.

Terrorists use the media to spread fear, increase public awareness of their cause, and, inadvertently, export the knowledge of their techniques. Media coverage during incidents can interfere with police operations (by providing the terrorists with intelligence), contribute to impaired decision making, and harass relatives of victims by interviews. However, press coverage can also serve to ventilate terrorist hostilities, satisfy the public's appetite for information, and give the impression of competent governmental crisis management.

2950. Andel, A. M. von. ''Media en Gijzeling.'' [Media and the taking of hostages] *Algemeen Politieblad*, August 2, 1975, pp. 384-386.

A summary of a conference of criminologists and members of the Dutch Ministry of Justice, Parliament, the police, and news media on the role of the media in hostage situations. It was suggested that the media show restraint to avoid harming hostages and not divulge information unknown to the kidnappers.

2951. Arlen, Michael J. ''Reflections on Terrorism and the Media.'' *More* 7 (June 1977): 12-21.

The moral quandaries facing television news editors dealing with hostage situations are explored.

2952. Bremen, Phil. ''Television's Dilemma: Stay on the Air or Bail Out?'' *Quill* (March 1977): 10-11.

A discussion of the media's role in the handling of terrorist incidents.

2953. Catton, Jr., William R. ''Militants and the Media: Partners in Terrorism.'' *Indiana Law Journal* 53 (Summer 1978): 703-715.

2954. Cooper, H. H. A. ''Terrorism and the Media.'' In Yonah Alexander and Seymour Maxwell Finger, eds., *Terrorism: Interdisciplinary Perspectives*, pp. 141-156. New York: John Jay Press, 1977.

2955. ———. ''Terrorism and the Media.'' *Chitty's Law Journal* 24 (September 1976): 226-232.

An excellent survey of the arguments surrounding the role of the media in terrorist events. Cooper calls for responsible reporting by journalists rather than government-imposed silence.

2956. Crozier, Brian. *Television and Conflict.* London: ISC Special Report, November 1978.

2957. Cullinane, Maurice J. "The Hanafi Case." Address to the Conference on Terrorism and the Media, sponsored by the Ralph Bunche Institute and the Institute for Studies in International Terrorism, November 17, 1977, at New York City.

2958. Czerniejewski, Halina J. "Guidelines for the Coverage of Terrorism." *Quill* (July-August 1977): 21-23.

2959. "Debate on Coverage of Terrorism Comes up with Few Solutions." *RTNDA Communicator* (April 1977).

2960. Drummond, William J., and Zycher, Augustine. "Arafat's Press Agents" *Harper's* (March 1976): 24.
     The authors argue that the press has badly mishandled the coverage of terrorist incidents, and that "they know how to do it, but they cannot do it."

2961. Epstein, Edward C. "The Uses of 'Terrorism': A Study in Media Bias." *Stanford Journal of International Studies* 12 (Spring 1977): 66-78.

2962. Evans, Jack, and Leibstone, Marvin. "Terrorism: Is the Media a Victim?" *Radioactive* (July 1977): 10-11.
     One of a series of articles written for media commentators explaining the dynamics of terrorism and hostage negotiation tactics.

2963. Fenyvesi, Charles. "Looking into the Muzzle of Terrorists." *Quill* (July-August 1977): 16-18.

2964. "From Triumph to Tragedy in TV Coverage of Munich Olympics." *Broadcasting*, September 11, 1972, pp. 22-23.

2965. Gruen, George E. "Public Opinion and Terrorism." Paper presented to the Conference on International Terrorism, sponsored by the Ralph Bunche Institute, New York City, June 9-11, 1976.
     Discusses the effects of the press on the American public's attitudes toward the PLO, using two Yankelovich polls and a survey of editorials in the fifty largest U.S. newspapers as his data base. He concludes that the news has tended to oversimplify, equating the Palestinians with the PLO.

2966. Halloran, James D. "Mass Communication: Symptom or Cause of Violence?" *International Social Science Journal* 30 (1978): 816-833.

2967. Heron, Paddy. ''Television's Role in Reporting Ulster Violence.'' *Harrangue: A Political and Social Review* (Belfast) 2 (Summer 1974).

2968. Hickey, Neil. ''Terrorism and Television, Part 1.'' *TV Guide*, July 31-August 6, 1976, pp. 2-6. Reprinted as ''Gaining the Media's Attention.'' In William P. Lineberry, ed., *The Struggle Against Terrorism*. New York: H. W. Wilson, 1977.

Through a series of interviews, Hickey explores questions of media contagion, self-censorship in a competitive environment, terrorist escalation to break self-censorship, the extent of the public's right to know and the media's right to report, and steps the media can take.

2969. ———. ''Terrorism and Television: The Medium in the Middle, Part 2.'' *TV Guide*, August 7-13, 1976, pp. 10-13.

Hickey interviews a number of experts on how the media should respond to acts of terrorism. Among suggested solutions: do not report ''how to'' aspects of the incident, downplay or omit names of those claiming credit, omit live coverage, emphasize the inhuman aspect of the action, refrain from interviewing terrorist leaders on camera, give air time to terrorist acts only in proportion to their objective news value, emphasize statistics showing the terrorists' low probability of success, and provide other outlets for dissident opinion.

2970. Hottellet, Richard C. ''Terrorism and the Media.'' Address to the Conference on Terrorism and the Media, sponsored by the Ralph Bunche Institute and the Institute for Studies in International Terrorism, November 17, 1977, at New York City.

2971. Jaehnig, Walter B. ''Journalists and Terrorism: Captives of the Libertarian Tradition.'' *Indiana Law Journal* 53 (Summer 1978): 717-744.

2973. Kelly, Micheal J., and Mitchell, Thomas H. ''Transnational Terrorism and the Western Elite Press.'' Paper presented to the annual meeting of the Canadian Political Science Association, May 30, 1979, at Saskatoon, Saskatchewan.

The authors conducted an excellent content analysis of *New York Times* and *London Times* treatment of terrorist events, finding that many incidents go unmentioned, Latin America is poorly covered, the sensational—and casualty-producing—attacks are heavily covered. Palestinians are the most effective in garnering publicity, and the causes for the actions are rarely reported.

2974. Leibstone, Marvin. ''Terrorism and the Media.'' Paper prepared for the International Association of Chiefs of Police, November 1978.

Makes several suggestions for journalists covering political violence.

2975. ———. ''Terrorism and the Media.'' Paper presented to the Conference on Moral Implications of Terrorism, March 14-16, 1979, at UCLA.

2976. Mark, Robert. ''Kidnapping, Terrorism and the Media in Britain.'' In *Ten Years of Terrorism*, pp. 76-86. New York: Crane, Russak, 1979.

London's former police commissioner traces the development of the media's treatment of criminal and political terrorist actions, generally giving them high marks for cooperating with the police.

2977. ''The Media and Terrorism.'' Seminar cosponsored by the Chicago Sun-Times and Chicago Daily News. Chicago: Field Enterprises, April 1977.

2978. Methvin, Eugene. ''Modern Terrorism and the Rise of Megamedia in 'The Global Village.' '' Unpublished manuscript, March 1976.

2979. Monday, Mark. ''What's Wrong with our Aim.'' *Quill* (July-August 1977): 19-20.

A discussion of the media's treatment of terrorist incidents.

2980. Mosse, Hilde L. ''Terrorism and the Mass Media.'' Paper presented at the Conference on Terrorism in the Contemporary World, April 26-28, 1976, at Glassboro State College. Available as FAR document 25375-N. Published as ''The Media and Terrorism'' in Marius Livingston, ed., *International Terrorism in the Contemporary World*. Westport, Conn.: Greenwood Press, 1978, pp. 282-286.

2981. Paust, Jordan J. ''International Law and Control of the Media: Terror, Repression and the Alternatives.'' *Indiana Law Journal* 53 (1978): 621f.

2982. Pandiani, John A. ''Crime Time TV: If All We Knew Is What We Saw.'' *Contemporary Crises: Crime, Law and Social Policy* 2 (October 1978): 437-458.

2983. Rabe, Robert. ''Terrorism and the Media.'' Address delivered to the Washington, D.C., Chapter of the Radio-Television News Directors Association, March 24, 1977.

The deputy police chief of Washington and the head of its hostage negotiations group chided the media for its irresponsible handling of hostage incidents. He argued that the First Amendment freedom of the Press is not an absolute and must be tempered by reason. The media should set guidelines and priorities that put human life ahead of ratings and should not impede police operations by tying up phone lines, interviewing suspects, reporting police movements, and trying to make news. The media must see that they are part of the problem before anything can be done.

2984. Redlick, Amy Sands. "The Transnational Flow of Information as a Cause of Terrorism." In Yonah Alexander, David Carlton, and Paul Wilkinson, eds., *Terrorism: Theory and Practice*, pp. 73-95. Boulder: Westview, 1979.

Looks at the penetrability of societies by volatile information, focusing on Western (particularly North American) experiences.

2985. "Relations with the News Media." Standards 6.25, 7.10, and 8.7, "News and Entertainment Media Responsibility for the Prevention of Extraordinary Violence" Standard 10.2, "News Media Self-Regulation in Contemporaneous Coverage of Terrorism and Disorder" Standard 10.8, and "Followup Reporting of Extraordinary Violence by News Media" Standard 10.12 in *Report of the Task Force on Disorders and Terrorism*. Washington, D.C.: National Advisory Committee on Criminal Justice Standards and Goals, 1976.

2986. "Responsibility of News Media Not to Encourage Terrorism." *Congressional Record* 121 (1975): H8965.

2987. Salomone, Franco. "Terrorism and the Mass Media." In M. Cherif Bassiouni, ed., *International Terrorism and Political Crimes*, pp. 43-46. Springfield, Ill.: Thomas, 1975.

2988. Siegal, Arthur. "Canadian Newspaper Coverage of the FLQ Crisis: A Study of the Impact of the Press on Politics." Ph.D. dissertation, McGill University, 1974.

2989. Sommer, Michael. *Terrorism and the Media*. Forthcoming.

2990. Terraine, John; Bell, Martin; Walsh, Robin. "Terrorism and the Media." In *Ten Years of Terrorism*, pp. 87-108. New York: Crane, Russak, 1979.

Discusses problems the British media face in dealing with terrorism, particularly in Northern Ireland, and the balance of values that must be met.

2991. "Terrorism and the Media: Special Issue." *Terrorism: An International Journal* 2 (1979): entire issue.

Included in the issue are edited proceedings of two conferences: Terrorism: Police and Press Problems and Terrorism and the Media.

2992. Terry, Herbert A. "Television and Terrorism: Professionalism Not Quite the Answer." *Indiana Law Journal* 53 (Summer 1978): 745-777.

2993. Weisman, John. "When Hostages' Lives Are at Stake: Should a TV Reporter Push on or Pull Back?" *TV Guide*, August 26, 1978. pp. 4-9.

Various police officials, reporters, and academics discuss the pros and cons of media coverage of hostage situations.

2994. Yong, Torado. "International Terrorism and Public Opinion Policy Processes." *Co-Existence* 8 (July 1971): 147-159.

By looking at the cases of the FLQ kidnapping of Cross, Palestinian hijacking, and the Tupamaros' kidnapping of Fly, Yong hopes to offer a solution to the problem of information legitimacy.

See also entries 566, 1271, 1272, 1645, 1786, 3383, 3596, 3622, and events data section.

PSYCHOLOGICAL AND MEDICAL APPROACHES TO TERRORISM

2995. Abel, T. ''The Sociology of Concentration Camps.'' *Social Forces* 30 (1951): 150-155.

2996. Abelson, Robert P.; Aronson, Elliott; McGuire, William J.; Newcomb, T. M.; Rosenberg, Milton J.; Tannenbaum, Percy H., eds. *Theories of Cognitive Consistency: A Sourcebook.* Chicago: Rand McNally, 1968.

2997. Adams, J. S. ''Reduction of Cognitive Dissonance by Seeking Consonant Information.'' *Journal of Abnormal and Social Psychology* 62 (1961): 74-78.

2998. Adler, H. G. ''Ideas toward a Sociology of the Concentration Camp.'' *American Journal of Sociology* 63 (1958): 513-522.

2999. Ansbacher, H. L. ''Attitudes of German Prisoners of War: A Study of the Dynamics of National Socialistic Followership.'' *Psychology Monographs* 62 (1948): 42.

3000. Arntzen, F. I. ''Psychological Observations of Prisoners of War.'' *American Journal of Psychiatry* 104 (1948): 446-447.

3001. Artz, C. P. ''Our Responsibility to Trauma.'' *Journal of the American College of Emergency Physicians* 4 (1975): 520ff.

3002. Axelrod, Robert, ed. *Structure of Decision: The Cognitive Maps of Political Elites.* Princeton: Princeton University Press, 1976. 404 pp.

3003. Bach-y-Rita, George, and Veno, Arthur. ''Habitual Violence: A Profile of Sixty-two Men.'' *American Journal of Psychiatry* 131 (September 1974): 1015-1017.
    A group of sixty-two violent prison inmates were found to have a high incidence of self-destructive behavior and childhood pathology, suggesting deprivation and neurological impairment.

3004. Bachet, M. "Persistent Hallucinatory Phenomena of Captivity Psychoses." *Bulletin of Medicine* (Paris) 59: 247-253.

3005. Baekeland, F. "Exercise Deprivation: Sleep and Psychological Reactions." *Archives of General Psychiatry* 22 (April 1970): 365-369.

3006. Balliner, W. F.; Rutherford, R. B.; Zuidema, G. D. *The Management of Trauma.* 2d ed. Philadelphia: W. B. Saunders, 1973.

3007. Balloch, J.; Braswell, L. R.; Rayner, J. R.; and Killian, L. M. "Studies of Military Assistance in Civilian Disaster: England and the U.S." Committee on Disaster Studies, National Academy of Sciences-National Research Council, August 20, 1953.

3008. Barag, G. "Belated Reactions in Former Concentration Camp Inmates." *Harefuah* 50 (1956): 228-229.

3009. Behling, C. F. "Effects of Commitment and Certainty upon Exposure to Supportive and Nonsupportive Information." *Journal of Personality and Social Psychology* 19 (1971): 152-159.

3010. Belz, Mary, et al. "Is There a Treatment for Terror?" *Psychology Today* (October 1977): 54ff.

3011. Bell, J. Bowyer. "The Profile of a Terrorist: A Cautionary Tale." In *International Terrorism: Proceedings of an Intensive Panel at the 15th Annual Convention of the International Studies Association, March 23, 1974,* St. Louis, Missouri.
  Based upon hundreds of field interviews, Bell believes that there is no one terrorist type valid across cultures and locations and that few generalizations on terrorist behavior can be made.

3012. Berkowitz, Leonard. "The Study of Urban Violence: Some Implications of Laboratory Studies of Frustration and Aggression." *American Behavioral Scientist* 2 (November 1968): 14ff.
  Reviews studies on violence and environment in animals and argues for their generalizability regarding civil disorder.

3013. Berkowitz, Leonard, and Cottingham, D. R. "The Interest Value and Relevance of Fear-Arousing Communications." *Journal of Abnormal and Social Psychology* 60 (1960): 37-43.

3014. Bettelheim, Bruno. "Individual and Mass Behavior in Extreme Situations." *Journal of Abnormal and Social Psychology* 38 (1943): 417-452.

3015. Bexton, W. H. *Some Effects of Perceptual Isolation on Human Subjects.* Ph.D. dissertation, McGill University, 1953.

3016. Bickman, L. "The Effect of Another Bystander's Ability to Help on Bystander Intervention in an Emergency." *Journal of Experimental Social Psychology* 7 (1971): 367-379.

3017. ———. "Social Influence and Diffusion of Responsibility in an Emergency." *Journal of Experimental Social Psychology* 8 (1972): 438-445.

3018. Biderman, A. D. "Communist Attempts to Elicit False Confessions from Air Force Prisoners of War." *Bulletin of the New York Academy of Medicine* 33 (1957): 616-625.

3019. ———. *Communist Techniques of Coercive Interrogation.* Lackland Air Force Base, Tex.: Air Force Personnel and Training Research Center, AFPTRC Development Report TN-56-132, December 1956.

3020. ———. "Effects of Communist Indoctrination Attempts: Some Comments Based on an Air Force Prisoner-of-War Study." *Social Problems* 6 (1959): 304-313.

3021. ———. "Social Psychological Needs and 'Involuntary' Behavior as Illustrated by Compliance in Interrogation." *Sociometry* 23 (June 1960): 120-147.

3022. Biller, Owen A. "Suicide Related to the Assassination of President John F. Kennedy." *Suicide and Life-Threatening Behavior* 7 (Spring 1977): 40-44.

3023. Bing, R., and Vischer, A. L. "Some Remarks on the Psychology of Internment, Based on the Observation of Prisoners of War in Switzerland." *Lancet* 196 (1919): 696-697.

3024. Black, E. A., ed. *The Study of Injured Patients: A Trauma Conference Report.* DHEW NIH Publication No. 74-603, February 1973.

3025. Blake, R. R.; Berkowitz, H.; Bellamy, R.; and Mouton, Jane S. "Volunteering as an Avoidance Act." *Journal of Abnormal and Social Psychology* 53 (1956): 154-157.

3026. Blakely, J. *The Care of Radiation Casualties.* Springfield, Ill.: Thomas, 1968.

3027. Blakemore, W. E.; Fitts, Jr., W. T., eds. *Management of the Injured Patient.* New York: Harper and Row, 1969.

3028. Bloch, H. A. ''The Personality of Inmates of Concentration Camps.'' *American Journal of Sociology* 52 (1946-1947): 335-341.

3029. Bluhm, Hilde O. ''How Did They Survive? Mechanisms of Defense in Nazi Concentration Camps.'' *American Journal of Psychotherapy* 2 (1948): 3-32.

3030. Bohler, J., and Krosl, W. ''A Comprehensive System of Trauma Services: The Austrian Experience.'' *Modern Medicine* 40 (1972): 57ff.

3031. Bower, W. F., and Hughes, C. W. *Surgical Philosophy in Mass Casualty Management.* Springfield, Ill.: Thomas, 1960.

3032. Brock, T. C. ''Effects of Prior Dishonesty on Post-Decisional Dissonance.'' *Journal of Abnormal and Social Psychology* 66 (1963): 325-331.

3033. Brown, J. S., and Jacobs, A. ''Fear in Motivation and Acquisition.'' *Journal of Experimental Psychology* 39 (1949): 747-759.

3034. Cave, E. F.; Burke, J. F.; and Boyd, R. J. *Trauma Management.* Chicago: Year Book Medical Publishers, 1974.

3035. Citrome, P. ''Conclusions d'une enquête sur le suicide dans les camps de concentration.'' [Conclusions of a study on suicide in concentration camps] *Cahiers international sociology* 12: 147-149.

3036. Clemesdon, D. J. ''Blast Injury.'' *Physiology Review* 36 (1956): 336ff.

3037. Cocharne, A. L. ''Notes on the Psychology of Prisoners of War'' *British Medical Journal (Supplement)* 1 (1946): 282-284.

3038. Cohen, A. R. ''The Effects of Individual and Situational Structure on Threat-Oriented Reactions to Power.'' Ph.D. dissertation, University of Michigan, 1953.

3039. Cohen, B. M., and Cooper, M. Z. *A Follow-up Study of World War II Prisoners of War.* Washington, D.C.: Veterans Administration Medical Monograph, U.S. Government Printing Office, 1954.

3040. Cohen, E. A. *Human Behavior in the Concentration Camp*. New York: Norton, 1953.

3041. Coleman, Lee S. "Perspectives on the Medical Research of Violence." *American Journal of Orthopsychiatry* 44 (October 1974): 675-687.

3042. Cooper, H. H. A. "What Is a Terrorist: A Psychological Perspective." *Legal Medical Quarterly* 1 (1977): 16-32.
    Addresses many phenomenological questions regarding the life and attitudes of terrorists. His insights are based upon logic rather than rigorous empirical testing.

3043. Corning, P. A. "The Biological Bases of Behavior and Some Implications for Political Science." *World Politics* 23 (April 1971): 321-370.

3044. Crawford, Thomas J., and Naditch, Murray. "Relative Deprivation, Powerlessness, and Militancy: The Psychology of Social Protest." *Psychiatry* 33 (May 1970): 208-223.

3045. Cressy, D. L., and Krassowski, W. "Inmate Organization and Anomie in American Prisons and Soviet Labor Camps." *Social Problems* 5 (1958): 217-230.

3046. Davies, James Chowning. "Aggression, Violence, Revolution and War." In Jeanne N. Knutson, ed., *Handbook of Political Psychology*. San Francisco: Jossey-Bass, 1973.

3047. Diggory, J. C. "Some Consequences of Proximity to a Disease Threat." *Sociometry* 19 (1956): 47-53.

3048. Disaster and Emergency Medical Services for Infants and Children. Evanston: American Academy of Pediatrics, 1972.

3049. Dowling, Joseph A. "Psycho-History and Violence: Personality and Historical Factors." Paper presented to the Conference on Terrorism in the Contemporary World. April 26-28, 1976, at Glassboro State College. Published as "Prolegomena to a Psychohistorical Study of Terrorism." In Marius Livingston et al., eds., *International Terrorism in the Contemporary World*. Westport, Conn.: Greenwood Press, 1978, pp. 223-230.
    A look at the history of terrorism, citing common factors in the philosophies of various anarchists.

3050. Downton, James V. *Rebel Leadership: Commitment and Charisma in the Revolutionary Process.* New York: Free Press, 1973. 306 pp.

A sociopsychological study of the leaders of extremist movements, including an "end of the world" group, the Bolsheviks, and the Nazis.

3051. Druckman, Daniel. "Human Factors in International Negotiations: Social-Psychological Aspects of International Conflict." 02-020 *Sage Professional Papers on International Studies.* Beverly Hills: Sage, n.d.

3052. Early Care of the Injury Patient. Report of the Committee on Trauma, American College of Surgeons. Philadelphia: W. B. Saunders, 1972.

3053. Edelman, Murray. "Political Symbols, Myths and Language as Factors in Terrorism." Paper presented to the Conference on Terrorism in the Contemporary World, April 26-28, 1976, at Glassboro State College.

3054. Eitinger, Leo. "The Stress of Captivity." In Ronald D. Crelinsten, ed., *Dimensions of Victimization in the Context of Terroristic Acts*, pp. 71-85. Montreal: International Center for Comparative Criminology, 1977.

3055. Eitinger, Leo, and Strom, Axel. *Morality and Morbidity after Excessive Stress.* New York: Columbia, 1976. 154 pp.

The authors studied concentration camp victims to assess the long-term consequences of stress.

3056. Evseeff, G. S., and Wisniewski, E. M. "A Psychiatric Study of a Violent Mass Murder." *Journal of Forensic Sciences* 17 (July 1972): 371-376.

The authors studied an individual who was beaten, abandoned, and sexually abused during his childhood. These traumas apparently led to "homicidal-proneness," in which he killed his family.

3057. Farber, M. L. "Imprisonment as a Psychological Situation." Ph.D. dissertation, State University of Iowa, 1940.

3058. Federn, E. "The Endurance of Torture." *Complex* 1 (1951): 34-41.

3059. Fenyvesi, Charles. "Living with a Fearful Memory." *Psychology Today* (October 1977): 61ff.

3060. Fields, Rona M. "Psychological Genocide: The Children of Northern Ireland." *History of Childhood Quarterly* 3 (Fall 1975): 201-224. Reprinted as FAR 26242-N. Revised as "Psychological Genocide." Paper presented at the Annual Meeting of the American Sociological Association, New York City, August-September 1976. Reprinted as FAR 26243-N.

3061. ———. ''Psychological Sequelae of Terrorization.'' In Yonah Alexander and John Gleason, eds., *Terrorism: Behavioral Perspectives*. New York: Pergamon, 1980.

3062. ———. ''A Society on the Run: A Psychology of Northern Ireland.'' Report. Department of Sociology, Clark University, 1976. Available as FAR 26487-N.

3063. ———. *Society under Siege: A Psychology of Northern Ireland*. Philadelphia: Temple University Press, 1977, 267 pp.

3064. ———. ''Torture and Institutional Coercion: Northern Ireland: A Case Study.'' Paper presented at the Annual Meeting of the American Sociological Association, August-September 1976, at New York City. Reprinted as FAR 26240-N.

3065. Flint, Jr., T., and Cain, H. D. *Emergency Treatment and Management*. 4th ed. Philadelphia: W. B. Saunders, 1972.

3066. Forcey, Linda R. ''Personality in Politics: The Commitment of a Suicide'' Ph.D. dissertation, State University of New York at Binghamton, 1978.

3067. Forman, Paul B. ''Panic Theory.'' *Sociology and Social Research* 37 (1953): 295-304.

3068. Fox, C. L. ''The Role of Alkaline Sodium Salt Solutions in the Treatment of Severe Burns.'' *Annals of the New York Academy of Sciences* 150 (1968): 823ff.

3069. ———. ''Silver Sulfadiazine: A New Topical Therapy for Therapy of Pseudomonas Infection Burns.'' *Archives of Surgery* 96 (1968): 184ff.

3070. Frank, J. D. ''Emotional Reaction of American Soldiers to Unfamiliar Disease.'' *American Psychiatry* 102 (March 1946): 631-640.

3071. ———. ''Some Psychological Determinants of Violence and Its Control.'' *Australian and New Zealand Journal of Psychiatry* 6 (September 1972): 158-164.

3072. Freedman, Lawrence Z. ''Why Does Terrorism Terrorize? A Psychiatric Perspective.'' Paper presented to the Conference on Psychopathology and Political Violence, November 16-17, 1979, at the University of Chicago.

3073. Friedman, P. "Some Aspects of Concentration Camp Psychology." *American Journal of Psychiatry* 105 (1949): 601-605.

3074. Fromm-Reichmann, Freida. "Psychiatric Aspects of Anxiety." In Maurice R. Stein, ed., *Identity and Anxiety.* New York: Free Press, 1960.

3075. Frye, Roland L., and Stritch, Thomas M. "Effects of Timed vs. Non-Timed Discussion upon Measures of Influence and Change in Small Groups." *Journal of Social Psychology* 63 (1964): 139-143.

The authors demonstrate that the lack of time in stressful situations leads to early group agreement.

3076. "Game Plan for Trauma Care." *Emergency Medicine* 9 (1977): 72ff.

3077. Gardner, Edith R. "Coerced Confessions of Prisoners of War: How Is the Nation to Cope with False Confessions Which Have Been Coerced?" *George Washington Law Review* 24 (1956): 528-563.

3078. Gault, W. B. "Some Remarks on Slaughter." *American Journal of Psychiatry* 128 (October 1971): 450-454.

3079. Geen, R. G., and Stoner, D. "Context Effects in Observed Violence." *Journal of Personal and Social Psychology* 25 (January 1973): 145-50.

3080. ———. "Reactions to Aggression-Related Stimuli Following Reinforcement of Aggression." *Journal of Psychology* 83 (January 1973): 75-102.

Individuals whose aggressive responses were reinforced verbally showed greater aggressiveness when shown aggression-provoking verbs than those who had not been reinforced. However, there was no difference between the groups regarding words having weaker aggressive connotations.

3081. George, Alexander L. "Adaptation to Stress in Political Decision Making: The Individual, the Small Group, and Organizational Contexts." In George V. Coehlho, David A. Hamburg, and John E. Adams, eds., *Coping and Adaptation*, pp. 176-245. New York: Basic Books, 1974.

3082. Gissane, W. "The Care of the Injured: The Development and Purpose of an Accident Hospital." *Annals of the Royal College of Surgeons of England* 41 (1967): 335ff.

3083. Glass, Albert J. "The Psychological Aspects of Emergency Situations." *Police* (June 1972): 18ff.

3084. Goldstein, J., and Strauss, H. ''Changes in Recall Salience of Concentration Camp Experience: A Case Study.'' New School for Social Research, Project MG-213, n.d.

3085. Gordon, D. S. ''Missile Wounds of the Head and Spine.'' *British Medical Journal* 1 (1975): 614ff.

3086. Grah, R. C., and Coppel, D. L. ''Intensive Care of Patients with Bomb Blast and Gunshot Injuries.'' *British Medical Journal* 1 (1975): 502ff.

3087. Greenberg, Bradley S., and Wotring, Edward C. ''Television Violence and Its Potential for Aggressive Driving Behavior.'' *Journal of Broadcasting* 18 (Fall 1974): 473-480.

3088. Greene, W., and Cockburn, A. ''Case of the Paranoid Hijacker.'' *Esquire* (July 1975): 10.

3089. Greenson, R. R. ''The Psychology of Apathy.'' *Psychoanalytic Quarterly* 18 (1949): 290-302.

3090. Grodzins, Morton. *Loyal and Disloyal: Social Boundaries of Patriotism and Treason.* Chicago: University of Chicago Press, 1946.

3091. Gross, Feliks. ''Social Causation of Individual Political Violence.'' Paper presented to the Conference on Terrorism in the Contemporary World, April 26-28, 1976, at Glassboro State College.

3092. Group for the Advancement of Psychiatry. ''Psychiatric Aspects of the Prevention of Nuclear War.'' Formulated by the Committee on Social Issues. Report No. 57. New York City, 1964.

3093. Gutman, David. ''The Fascination of the Terrorist.'' Paper presented to the 18th annual convention of the International Studies Association, March 16-20, 1977, at St. Louis, Missouri.

3094. ———. ''Killers and Consumers: The Terrorist and His Audience.'' Mimeographed. Northwestern University Medical School, n.d. (approx. 1977).

3095. Guttmacher, Manfred S. *The Mind of the Murderer.* New York: Farrar, Strauss, and Cudahy, 1960. 244 pp.
    A psychiatric typology of murderers.

3096. Hacker, Frederick J. "Pathology: Personal and Political." Paper presented to the Conference on Psychopathology and Political Violence, November 16-17, 1979, at the University of Chicago.

3097. ———. "Psychology of Terror." Address to the Wackenhut Corporation's seminar on terrorism, November 21, 1974.

3098. ———. "The Psychology of the Terrorists' Victim and Hostage." Panel held at the Second annual convention of the International Society of Political Psychology, May 24-26, 1979, Washington, D.C.

3099. Hampden-Turner, C. *Radical Man: The Process of Psycho-Social Development.* Cambridge: Schenkman, 1970.

3100. Hart, R. J.; Lee, J. O.; Boyles, D. J.; et al. "The Summerland Disaster." *British Medical Journal* 1 (1975): 256ff.

3101. Hassel, Conrad V. "Political Assassin." *Journal of Police Science and Administration* 2 (December 1974): 399-403.
    A somatotypical, demographic, and psychological analysis of assassins.

3102. ———. "Terror: The Crime of the Privileged—An Examination and Prognosis." Paper presented at the International Conference on Terrorism, June 1, 1977, at Evian, France. Reprinted in *Terrorism* 1 (1977): 1-16.
    Hassel takes a psychological approach to the problem, stressing maturation processes in Western societies, mental illness (especially paranoia in terrorist leadership), and the participation of women in terrorist movements.

3103. *Health Aspects of Chemical and Biological Weapons.* Geneva: World Health Organization, 1970.

3104. Healy, R. J. *Emergency and Disaster Planning.* New York: Wiley, 1969.

3105. Heilman, M. E. "Threats and Promises: Reputational Consequences and Transfer of Credibility." *Journal of Experimental Social Psychology* 10 (1974): 310-324.

3106. Heilman, M. E., and Toffler, B. "Reacting to Reactance: An Interpretation of the Need for Freedom." *Journal of Experimental Social Psychology* 12 (1976): 519-529.

3107. Hinkle, Jr., L. E. "Notes on the Physical State of the Prisoner of War as It May Affect Brain Function." Washington, D.C.: Bureau of Social Science Research, 1963.

3108. Holden, Constance. "Study of Terrorism Emerging as an International Endeavor." *Science*, January 5, 1979, pp. 33-35.

A summary of the International Scientific Conference on Terrorism, held in West Berlin in November 1978. Among the insights offered were those of David Hubbard and F. Gentry Harris, psychologists who suggested that most terrorists suffer from faulty vestibular functions of the middle ear, which correlate with a history of learning to walk late, dizzy spells, visual problems, and general clumsiness. Adolphe Jonas suggested that inconsistent mothering also has a part to play.

3109. Horowitz, Irving Louis. "An Inventory of the Terrorist as Political Deviant." Paper presented at the Conference on Terrorism, U.S. Department of State, October 1972. Reprinted as FAR 16461.

3110. ———. "Political Terrorism and Personal Deviance." *Department of State External Research Study* SR/RNAS-5, February 15, 1973.

Discusses the profile of the terrorist, nature of terror, Marxism and terrorism, and alternative responses.

3111. Hubbard, David G. "Bringing Skyjackers Down to Earth: Views of a Psychiatrist." *Time*, October 4, 1971, pp. 64-65.

3112. ———. "Extortion Threats: The Possibility of Analysis." *Assets Protection* 1 (Summer 1975): 17-19.

Hubbard notes his experience with skyjackers' threats in showing that psychiatric and linguistic data can be helpful during incidents.

3113. ———. "A Glimmer of Hope: A Psychiatric Perspective." In M. Cherif Bassiouni, ed., *International Terrorism and Political Crimes*, pp. 27-32. Springfield, Ill.: Thomas, 1975.

3114. ———. "Organic Factors Underlying the Psychology of Terror." In Yonah Alexander and John Gleason, eds., *Terrorism: Behavioral Perspectives*. New York: Pergamon, 1980.

3115. ———. "A Story of Inadequacy: Hierarchical Authority vs. the Terrorist." In Yonah Alexander and Robert A. Kilmarx, eds., *Political Terrorism and Business: The Threat and Response*, pp. 187-200. New York: Praeger, 1979.

3116. Hulsman, Louk. "Terrorism and Victims." In Ronald D. Crelinsten, ed., *Dimensions of Victimization in the Context of Terroristic Acts*, pp. 149-163. Montreal: International Center for Comparative Criminology, 1977.

3117. Ilfeld, Jr., F. W. "Overview of the Causes and Prevention of Violence." *Archives of General Psychiatry* 20 (June 1969): 675-689.

3118. Jackman, N. R. "Survival in the Concentration Camp." *Human Organization* 17 (1958): 23-26.

3119. Jacobson, Edith. "Observations on the Psychological Effects of Imprisonment on Female Political Prisoners." In K. R. Eissler, *Searchlights on Delinquency*. New York: International University Press, 1949.

3120. Janis, Irving. *Air War and Emotional Stress*. New York: McGraw-Hill, 1951.

3121. ———. "Group Identification under Conditions of External Danger." In D. Cartwright and A. Zander, eds., *Group Dynamics: Research and Theory*. New York: Harper and Row, 1968.

3122. ———. "Psychological Effects of Warnings." In George W. Baker and Dwight W. Chapman, eds., *Man and Society in Disaster*. New York: Basic Books, 1962.

3123. Janis, Irving L., and Mann, Leon. *Decision Making: A Psychological Analysis of Conflict, Choice, and Commitment*. New York: Free Press, 1977. 488 pp.

3124. Jeffrey, M., and Bradford, E. J. G. "Neurosis in Escaped Prisoners of War." *British Journal of Medical Psychology* 20 (1945-1946): 422-435.

3125. Jelenko, C., and Frey, C. F. *Emergency Medical Services: An Overview*. Bowie., Md.: Robert J. Brady, 1976.

3126. Johnson, C. R. *Conflict and Accommodation between Selected Groups of Military Prisoners of War and the Dominant Group in the World War with Special Reference to Certain Origins of These Processes: A Study in the Social Psychology of Prisoner of War Life*. Los Angeles: University of Southern California Press, 1938.

3127. Johnson, Roger. "The Dynamics of Individual and Group Aggression." Paper presented to the Conference on Terrorism in the Contemporary World, April 26-28, 1976, at Glassboro State College.

3128. Jones, Edward E., and Nisbett, Richard E. "The Actor and the Observer: Divergent Perceptions of the Causes of Behavior." In Edward E. Jones et al, eds., *Attribution: Perceiving the Causes of Behavior.* Morristown: General Learning Press, 1972.

The authors argue that actors attribute the causes of their behavior to situational characteristics, while observers attribute behavior of characteristics of the actor.

3129. Jones, M. "Rehabilitation of Forces Neurosis Patients (Prisoners of War) to Civilian Life." *British Medical Journal (Supplement)* 1 (1946): 533-534.

3130. Jones, M., and Tanner, J. M. "Clinical Characteristics, Treatment, and Rehabilitation of Repatriated Prisoners of War with Neurosis." *Journal of Neurology, Neurosurgery and Psychiatry* 2 (1948): 53-60.

3131. Kaplan, Abraham. "The Psychodynamics of Terrorism." *Terrorism* (1978): 237-254. Revised version in Yonah Alexander and John Gleason, eds., *Terrorism: Behavioral Perspectives.* New York: Pergamon, 1980.

Discusses the terrorist, victim, target, and two types of audiences and notes the pursuit of absolute ends, lack of self-esteem, renewal of the sense of masculinity, reaction formation to positive feelings toward the target, and symbol-magic.

3132. Karber, Phillip A. "The Psychological Dimensions of Bombing Motivations." *Bomb Incident Bulletins: Tab 02: Targets and Tactics* (Gaithersburg, Md.: International Association of Chiefs of Police, Research Division, June 1973), pp. 24-32.

Uses the rationality of the bomber and his justification to create a 3 x 2 typology of motivations: experimentation, revenge, criminal, vandalism, protest, and terrorist.

3133. ———. "Some Psychological Effects of Terrorism as Protest." Paper presented before the annual convention of the American Psychological Association, August 1973.

3134. Katz, C. J. "Experiences in a Prison Camp as a Background for Therapy." *Mental Hygiene* 34 (1950): 90-96.

3135. Kelly, George A. ''Revolutionary Warfare and Psychological Action.'' *Military Review* 9 (October 1970): 4-13.

3136. Kelman, Herbert C. ''Violence without Moral Restraint: Reflections on the Dehumanization of Victims and Victimizers.'' *Journal of Social Issues* 29 (1973): 25-61.

Kelman's 1973 Kurt Lewin Memorial Address. He discusses the problem of sanctioned massacres, which are generally conducted by nation-states but which could be extended to include the campaigns of terrorists. Factors that reduce the strength of restraining forces against violence include authorization, routinization, and dehumanization. Suggestions are made to alter these processes.

3137. Kennedy, T. L., and Johnston, G. W. ''Civilian Bomb Injuries.'' *British Medical Journal* 1 (1975): 382ff.

3138. Kent, G. *The Effects of Threats.* Columbus: Ohio State University Press, 1967.

3139. Kerr, A. G., and Byrne, J. E. T. ''Blast Injuries of the Ear.'' *British Medical Journal* 1 (1975): 559ff.

3140. Killian, L. ''The Significance of Multiple-Group Membership in Disaster.'' *American Journal of Sociology* 57 (1952): 309-314.

3141. Kirman, B. H. ''Mental Disorder in Released Prisoners of War.'' *Journal of Ment. Sci.* 92 (1946): 803-813.

3142. Knutson, Jeanne N. ''The Psychodynamics of the Terrorists' Behavior.'' Panel held at the second annual convention of the International Society of Political Psychology, May 24-26, 1979, at Washington, D.C.

3144. Kraut, Robert E. ''Verbal and Nonverbal Cues in the Perception of Lying.'' Paper presented to the symposium on Lying and Impression Management, 84th annual convention of the American Psychological Association, September 3-7, 1976, at Washington, D.C.

3145. Laborit, Henri. ''The Biological and Sociological Mechanisms of Aggression.'' *International Social Science Journal* 30 (1978): 727-749.

3146. Landfield, A. W. ''A Movement Interpretation of Threat.'' *Journal of Abnormal and Social Psychology* 49 (1954): 529-532.

3147. Laskin, Eva. "Several Methods of Preparing Individuals to Resist Social Pressure to Conform." Ph.D. dissertation, Yale University, 1955.

3148. Lasswell, Harold. "The Study of the Ill as a Method of Research into Political Personalities." *American Political Science Review* 23 (November 1929): 996-1001.

3149. Latane, B., and Darley, J. M. "Social Determinants of Bystander Intervention in Emergencies." In J. Macauley and Leonard Berkowitz, eds., *Altruism and Helping Behavior*. New York: Academic Press, 1970.

3150. L'Etang, H. *The Pathology of Leadership*. New York: Hawthorn, 1970.

3151. Howard Leventhal, et al. "Effects of Fear and Specificity of Recommendation Upon Attitudes and Behavior." *Journal of Personality and Social Psychology* 2 (1965): 20-29.

3152. Levy, Sheldon G. "Terrorism." Paper presented to the Conference on Terrorism, U.S. Department of State, October 1972. Reprinted as FAR 19463.

Discusses some possible contributions of social psychology to many aspects of terrorism. The work of Zajonc on repetition's increasing support; Freud on identification with the aggressor; Brody, North, and Holsti on threat and ambiguous stress; and studies of prisoners of war are mentioned. The importance of dissonance reduction in the population is part of the strategy of terrorists, as well as those seeking to counter terrorist successes.

3153. Lichter, S. Robert. "Psychopolitical Models of Student Radicals: A Methodological Critique and West German Case Study." Ph.D. dissertation, Harvard University, 1977.

3154. Liebert, R. *Radical and Militant Youth: A Psychiatrist's Report*. New York: Praeger, 1971.

3155. Lilly, J. C. "Mental Effects of Reduction of Ordinary Levels of Physical Stimuli on Intact, Healthy Persons." *Psychiatric Research Report of the American Psychiatric Association* 5 (1956): 1-28.

3156. Lincoln, A., and Leirnger, G. "Observers' Evaluations of the Victim and the Attacker in an Aggressive Incident." *Journal of Personality and Social Psychology* 22 (May 1972): 202-210.

3157. Lion, J. R. *Evaluation and Management of the Violent Patient.* (Springfield, Ill.: Thomas, 1972).

3158. Livingstone, R. H., and Wilson, R. I. "Gunshot Wounds of the Limbs." *British Medical Journal* 1 (1975): 667ff.

3159. Lowenthal, Leo. "Crisis of the Individual: Terror's Atomization of Man." *Commentary* (1946): 1-8.

3160. Luby, E., and Gottlieb, J. "Sleep Deprivation." In S. Arieti, ed., *American Handbook of Psychiatry,* vol. 3. New York: Basic Books, 1966.

3161. Lunden, W. A. "Captivity Psychosis among Prisoners of War." *Journal of Criminal Law, Criminology, and Police Science* 39 (1949): pp. 721-733.

3162. Lupsha, Peter. "Explanation of Political Violence: Some Psychological Theories."*Politics and Society* 2 (1971): 88-104.

3163. Lyons, H. A. "Violence in Belfast: A Review of the Psychological Effects." *Community Health* (Bristol) 5 (November-December 1973): 163-168.

3164. ———. "Violence in Belfast: A Review of the Psychological Effects." *Public Health* 87 (September 1973): 231-238.

3165. MacKinnon, D. W. "Violation of Prohibitions." In Henry Murray, ed., *Explorations in Personality.* New York: Oxford University Press, 1938.

3166. Marcus, Anthony M. "Some Psychiatric and Sociological Aspects of Violence." *International Journal of Group Tensions* 4 (June 1974): 254-268.

3167. Margolin, Joseph. "Psychological Perspectives." Paper presented to the Conference on International Terrorism, sponsored by the Ralph Bunche Institute, June 9-11, 1976, at New York City. Published in Seymour Maxwell Finger and Yonah Alexander, eds., *Terrorism: Interdisciplinary Perspectives* (New York: John Jay Press, 1977). pp. 270-282.

Review of work that might be adapted to the study of terrorism. Despite their deviance from standard societal norms of behavior, terrorists nonetheless are viewed as subject to the same constraints on action as those engaging in more acceptable modes of expression.

3168. McCaughey, W.; Coppel, D. O.; and Dundee, J. W. "Blast Injuries to the Lungs: A Report of Two Cases." *Anaesthesia* 28 (1973): 2ff.

3169. McVey, Ronald. "The Terrorist Mind." Paper presented to the conference on Terror: The Man, the Mind and the Matter, October 15-16, 1976, at the John Jay School of Criminal Justice, New York City.

3170. Meier, Norman C.; Mennenga, G. H.; and Stoltz, H. J. "An Experimental Approach to the Study of Mob Behavior," *Journal of Abnormal Psychology* 34 (1964): 506-524.

3171. "Mentality of the War Prisoner." *Lancet* 2 (1918): 675-676.

3172. "Mentality of the War Prisoner." *Scientific American* 87 (1919): 105.

3173. Middendorff, Wolf, "Personality of Terrorism, Especially Women as Terrorists, Parts 1 and 2." *Kriminalistik* 7-8 (July-August 1976): 289-296, 357-363.
    A history of terrorism in Russia, Eire, the United States, and West Germany.

3174. Milgram, Stanley. "Research on Victimization." In Ronald D. Crelinsten, ed., *Dimensions of Victimization in the Context of Terroristic Acts*, pp. 177-180. Montreal: International Center for Comparative Criminology, 1977.

3175. Miron, Murray. "Psycholinguistic Analysis of the SLA." *Assets Protection* 1 (1976).

3176. Mitscherlich, A. "Introduction to Panel on Protest and Revolution." *International Journal of Psychoanalysis* 50 (1969): 103-108.

3177. Moffitt, J. Weldon, and Stagner, Ross. "Perceptual Rigidity and Closure as a Function of Anxiety." *Journal of Abnormal and Social Psychology* 52 (1956): 354-357.
    The authors demonstrate experimentally that threat-induced anxiety decreases the willingness to consider new approaches and increases the unwillingness to shift focus to new cues.

3178. Moore, R. "Psychiatric Sequelae of the Belfast Riots." *British Journal of Psychiatry* 120 (April 1972): 471.

3179. Morgen, A. "Aggressiveness, Aggression and Terrorism." *Etudes internationales de psycho-sociologie criminelle* 20-23 (1971-1972).
    Argues that terrorism can be prevented by reducing society's use of aggression.

3180. Moseley, H. F. ed. *Accident Surgery*. New York: Appleton-Century-Crofts, 1962.

3181. Moyer, Kenneth E. ''Possible Physiological Mechanisms Underlying the Individual's Acts of Terror.'' Paper presented to the Conference on Terrorism in the Contemporary World, April 26-28, 1976, at Glassboro State College.

3182. Moylan, J. A.; Detmer, D. E.; Rose, J.; et al. ''Evaluation of the Quality of Hospital Care for Major Trauma.'' *Journal of Trauma* 16 (1976): 517ff.

3183. Murray, Edward J. *Motivation and Emotion*. Englewood Cliffs, N.J.: Prentice-Hall, 1964.

3184. Nelson, Stephen D. ''Nature/Nurture Revisited I.'' *Journal of Conflict Resolution* 18 (June 1974): 285-335.

3185. ———. ''Nature/Nurture Revisited II: Social, Political, and Technological Implications of Biological Approaches to Human Conflict.'' *Journal of Conflict Resolution* 19 (December 1975): 734-761.

3186. Neurath, P. M. ''Social Life in the German Concentration Camps: Dachau and Buchenwald.'' Ph.D. dissertation, Columbia University, 1952.

3187. Newman, P. H. ''The Prisoner of War Mentality: Its Effect after Repatriation.''*British Medical Journal* 1 (1944): 8-10.

3188. Niremberski, M. ''Psychological Investigation of a Group of Internees at Belsen Camp.'' *Journal of Ment. Sci.* 92 (1946): 60-74.

3189. Nisbett, Robert E., and Valins, S. ''Perceiving the Causes of One's Own Behavior.'' In E. E. Jones, et. al. *Attribution: Perceiving the Causes of Behavior*. Morristown, N.J.: General Learning Press, 1971.

3190. ''Notes from a Trauma Team.'' *Emergency Medicine* 8 (1976): pp. 153ff.

3191. Ochberg, Frank. ''Preparing for Terrorist Victimization.'' In Yonah Alexander and Robert A. Kilmarx, eds., *Political Terrorism and Business: The Threat and Response*, pp. 201-218. New York: Praeger, 1979.

3192. ———. "The Victim of Terrorism: Psychiatric Considerations." Paper presented to the Fourth International Seminar on Terrorism, sponsored by the Centre International de Criminologie Comparee, June 1, 1977, at Evian, France. Reprinted in U.S. Senate. Committee on Governmental Affairs, "Report on an Act to Combat International Terrorism" (Report 95-908. 95th Cong., 2d sess., May 23, 1978), pp. 335-371. Published in *Terrorism* 1 (1978): 147-168.

A discussion of victim responses to hostage situations, using material from the case of one of the December 1975 Moluccan train siege hostages.

3193. ———. ed. *Victims of Terrorism*. Boulder: Westview, 1979. 200 pp.

Ochberg studied the behavior, reactions, and residual problems of hostages.

3194. Odling-Smee, W. "Victims of Belfast's Violence" *Nursing Times*, September 6, 1973, pp. 1143-1146.

3195. O'Malley, P. P. "Attempted Suicide before and after the Communal Violence in Belfast, August 1969, A Preliminary Study." *Journal Ir. Medical Association*, March 4, 1972, pp. 109-113.

3196. Palmer, J. D. "The Many Clocks of Man." In G. Nelson and J. Ray, ed., *Biologic Readings for Today's Students*. New York: Wiley, 1971.

3197. Paul, O., and Schatz, M. "On Sudden Death." *Circulation* 43 (1971): 7.

3198. Pepitone, Albert. "The Social Psychology of Violence." *International Journal of Group Tensions* 2 (1972): 19-32.

3199. Pepitone, A., and Kleiner, R. "The Effects of Threat and Frustration on Group Cohesiveness." *Journal of Abnormal and Social Psychology* 54 (1957): 192-199.

3200. Pereira, Orlindo Gourveia. "Effects of Violence on Military Personnel in the Portuguese Colonies." Paper presented to the symposium on the Effects of Institutional Coercion by Law, Government, and Violence, of the 84th annual convention of the American Psychological Association, September 3-7, 1976, at Washington, D.C.

3201. Perry, D. G., and Perry, L. C. "Denial of Suffering in the Victim as a Stimulus to Violence in Aggressive Boys." *Child Development* 45 (March 1974): 55-62.

3202. Petzel, T. P., and Michaels, E. J. ''Perception of Violence as a Function of Levels of Hostility.'' *Journal of Consulting Clinical Psychology* 41 (August 1973): 35-36.

3203. Pieczenik, Steve R. ''The Social Psychological Constraints of the Terrorist Event.'' Panel held at the second annual convention of the International Society of Political Psychology, May 24-26, 1979, at Washington, D.C.

3204. Pisano, R., and Taylor, S. P. ''Reduction of Physical Aggression: The Effects of Four Strategies.'' *Journal of Personality and Social Psychology* 19 (1971): 237-242.

3205. Plunkett, G. L. ''The Northern Ireland Situation.'' Paper presented to the symposium on the Effects of Institutional Coercion by Law, Government, and Violence, of the 84th annual convention of the American Psychological Association, September 3-7, 1976, at Washington, D.C.

3206. Proceedings: American Medical Association's Conference on Emergency Medical Services. Chicago, April 6, 1967.

3207. ''Psychiatric Problems of Repatriated Prisoners: Proceedings, Section of Psychiatry, Royal Society of Medicine.'' *British Medical Journal (Supplement)* 1 (1946): 402-403.

3208. 'Psyching Out Terrorists.'' *Medical World News*, June 27, 1977.

3209. ''Psycholojournalist Explains 'Emotion Behind the Motion.' '' *Editor and Publisher*, January 18, 1975, p. 37.
      Mentions NIMH studies of terrorism and disaster.

3210. Quarantelli, Enrico L. 'The Nature and Conditions of Panic.'' *American Journal of Sociology* 60 (November 1954): 267-275.

3211. Reighard, M.D., H. L. ''Hijacker Motivations.'' Paper presented to the 18th International Congress of Aerospace Medicine, September 15, 1969, at Amsterdam. Available in *Hijack Reference Data* (Washington, D.C.: Federal Aviation Administration, Task Force on Air Piracy, 1970).

3212. The Relevance for the Social Sciences of Knowledge Derived from Studies of Stressful Captivity. Washington, D.C.: Bureau of Social Science Research, 1961.

3213. Rogge, O. J. *Why Men Confess.* New York: Thomas Nelson, 1959.

3214. Rogow, A. "Some Psychiatric Aspects of Political Science and Political Life." In G. Abearian and J. Soule, eds., *Social Psychology and Political Behavior*. Columbus: Merrill, 1971.

3215. Rosenblatt, Paul C. "Origins and Effects of Group Ethnocentrism and Nationalism." *Journal of Conflict Resolution* 8 (1964): 131-146.

Rosenblatt discovers that increased threat increases the need to be defended, to justify one's loyalties, ethnocentrism, nationalism, hostility toward perceived sources of threat, and perceived in-group commonality.

3216. Roth, Walton. "Psychosomatic Implications of Confinement by Terrorists." In Ronald D. Crelinsten, ed., *Dimensions of Victimization in the Context of Terroristic Acts*, pp. 41-60. Montreal: International Center for Comparative Criminology, 1977.

3217. Ruge, Mari Holmboe. "Image and Reality in Simulated International Systems." In J. A. Laponce and Paul Smoker, eds., *Experimentation and Simulation in Political Science*, pp. 293-314. Toronto: University of Toronto Press, 1972.

Ruge finds that decision making is determined more by subjective, actor-related factors than by structural characteristics of the situation.

3218. Russell, Charles A., and Miller, Bowman H. "Profile of a Terrorist." *Military Review* 58 (August 1977): 21-34. Reprinted in *Terrorism* 1 (1977): 17-34.

A well-detailed study of the demographics of terrorism, which concludes from a survey of eighteen major groups that terrorists tend to be males in their early twenties, with some college, who have lived in an urban environment, and were recruited for the terrorist organization in college. Most are middle class and unmarried, sporting political philosophies that are a blend of Marxism-Leninism, anarchism and nationalism.

3219. Rutherford, W. H. "Disaster Procedures." *British Medical Journal* 1 (1975): 443ff.

3221. Scharff, W. H., and Schlottman, R. S. "The Effects of Verbal Reports of Violence on Aggression." *Journal of Psychology* 84 (July 1973): 283-290.

3222. Schein, M., and Singer, M. T. "Projective Test Responses of Prisoners of War Following Repatriation." *Psychiatry* 21 (1958): 375-385.

3223. Schlossberg, Harvey. "Developing a Terrorist Profile." Paper presented to the conference on Terror: The Man, the Mind and the Matter,

October 15-16, 1976, at the John Jay School of Criminal Justice, New York City.

3224. Schoenberg, Bernard; Gerber, Irwin; Wiener, Alfred; Kutscher, Austin H.; Peretz, David; and Carr, Arthur C., eds. *Bereavement: Its Psychosocial Aspects.* New York: Columbia, 1976. 375 pp.

3225. Scott, J. P. "The Control of Violence." *Conditional Reflex* 6 (April-June 1971): 63-66.

3226. Scott, P. D. "Victims of Violence." *Nursing Times,* July 4, 1974, pp. 1036-1037.

3227. Segal, E. "Medical Psychological Observations in the Time of Disaster." *Higena Ruhanit* 5 (1945-1948): 103-108.

3228. Segal, H. A. "Initial Psychiatric Findings of Recently Repatriated Prisoners of War."*American Journal of Psychiatry* 3 (1954): 358-363.

3229. Segal, J. *Factors Related to the Collaboration and Resistance Behavior of US Army POWs in Korea.* Washington, D.C.: Human Engineering Research Office, 1956.

3230. Sewell, Alan F. "Political Crime: A Psychologist's Perspective." In M. Cherif Bassiouni, ed., *International Terrorism and Political Crimes,* pp. 11-26. Springfield, Ill.: Thomas, 1975.

3231. Shoham, S. G. et al. "Interaction in Violence." *Human Relations* 27 (1974): 417ff.

3232. Shuval, Judith T. "Some Persistent Effects of Trauma: Five Years after the Nazi Concentration Camps." *Social Problems* 5 (1957-1958): 230-243.

3233. Silverstein, Martin Elliot. "Emergency Medical Preparedness." In Yonah Alexander and Robert A. Kilmarx, eds., *Political Terrorism and Business: The Threat and Response,* pp. 219-225. New York: Praeger, 1979. Also available in *Terrorism* (1977): 51-69.

Silverstein devises a model of on-site treatment of victims of terrorism that allows a greater probability of successful recovery than evacuation. His medical rescue system is based upon a common injury model, a common physiological response model, and a common resuscitation model. A detailed checklist for the treatment of victims is appended, as is a bibliography on trauma.

3234. ———. ''The Medical Survival of Victims of Terrorism.'' In Robert H. Kupperman and Darrell M. Trent, eds., *Terrorism*, pp. 349-392. Stanford: Hoover, 1979.

3235. Sinha, A. K. P. ''Experimental Induction of Anxiety by Conditions of Uncertainty.'' Ph.D. dissertation, University of Michigan, 1950.

3236. Slomich, Sidney J., and Kantor, Robert E. ''Social Psychopathology of Political Assassination.'' *Bulletin of the Atomic Scientists* 25 (March 1969): 9-12.

3237. Slote, Walter H. ''Case Analysis of a Revolutionary.'' In Frank Bonilla and José Silva Michelena, eds., *A Strategy for Research on Social Policy,* vol. 1. Cambridge: MIT Press, 1967.
    A psychologist's report of interviews he conducted with a Venezuelan revolutionary who had been released from prison.

3238. Somit, A. ''Biopolitics.'' *British Journal of Political Science* (April 1972): 209-238.

3239. ———. ''Toward a More Biologically Oriented Political Science.'' *Midwest Journal of Political Science* 12 (November 1968): 550-567.

3240. Stanciu, V. V. ''Macrocriminology: Terrorist Psychology.'' *Revue internationale de criminologie et police technique* 26 (April-June 1973): 189-198.
    Argues that tyranny and terrorism go hand in hand.

3241. Stevenson, H. M., and Wilson, W. ''Gunshot Wounds of the Trunk.'' *British Medical Journal* 1 (1975): 728ff.

3242. Storr, Anthony. ''Violence as Individual Human Response.'' Paper presented to the Conference on Terrorism in the Contemporary World, April 26-28, 1976, at Glassboro State College. Published as ''Sadism and Paranoia,'' in Marius Livingston, ed., *International Terrorism in the Contemporary World* (Westport, Conn.: Greenwood Press, 1978), pp. 231-239.

3243. Strassmen, H. D.; Thaler, Margaret B.; and Schein, E. H. ''A Prisoner of War Syndrome: Apathy as a Reaction to Severe Stress.'' *American Journal of Psychiatry* 112 (1956): 998-1003.

3244. Strentz, Thomas. ''The Sociopath.'' Unpublished manuscript. Quantico: FBI Academy, 1974.

3245. ———. "The Terrorist Organizational Profile: A Psychological Evaluation." In Yonah Alexander and John Gleason, eds., *Terrorism: Behavioral Perspectives*. New York: Pergamon, 1980.

3246. Tagiuri, R. "Differential Adjustment to Internment Camp Life." *Journal of Social Psychology* 48 (1958): 103-109.

3247. Tan, E. S., and Simons, R. C. "Psychiatric Sequelae to a Civil Disturbance." *British Journal of Psychiatry* 122 (January 1973): 57-63.

3248. Tanner, J. M., and Jones, M. "Psychological Symptoms and Physiologic Response to Exercise of Repatriated Prisoners of War with Neurosis." *Journal of Neurology, Neurosurgery and Psychiatry* 11 (1948): 61-71.

3249. Tas, J. "Psychical Disorders among Inmates of Concentration Camps and Repatriates." *Psychiatry Quarterly* 25 (1951): 679-690.

3250. "The Terrorist and His Victim." Hearing before the Subcommittee on Criminal Laws and Procedures of the Committee on the Judiciary, U.S. Senate. 94th Cong., 1st sess., July 21, 1977.
Testimony by H. H. A. Cooper, who argues that terrorists seek justification for their acts by turning to revolutionary rhetoric. The real causes for their actions may be sex and drug related.

3251. Thompson, Clara. "Identification with the Enemy and Loss of the Sense of the Self." *Psychoanalytic Quarterly* 8 (1940): 15-21.

3252. Toch, H. *Violent Men: An Inquiry into the Psychology of Violence.* Chicago: Aldine, 1969.

3253. Toppe, Alfred. *German Methods of Interrogating Prisoners of War in World War II.* Koenigstein, Historical Division, European Command, 1949.

3254. Torre, M. "How Does Physical and Mental Illness Influence Negotiations between Diplomats?" *International Journal of Social Psychiatry* (Summer 1964): 170-176.

3255. Torre, M., and Glaser, W. *The Effect of Illness on Diplomatic Intercourse.* New York: Research Institute for the Study of Man, 1963.

3256. Torrie, A. "Return of Odysseus: Problem of Marital Infidelity for Repatriates." *British Medical Journal* 2 (1945): 192ff.

3257. Tubbs, N. ''A Comparison of Deaths from Injury, 1947-56 Compared with 1962-71.'' *Injury* 7 (1976): 233ff.

3258. Tureen, L. L., and Palmer, J. O. ''Some Group Differences in Personal Values between American Soldiers and German Prisoners of War.'' *Journal of Social Psychology* 42 (1955): 305-313.

3259. Vaughan, Elizabeth J. ''Adjustment Problems in a Concentration Camp.'' *Sociology and Social Research* 32 (1947-1948): 513-518.

3260. ———. *Community under Stress: An Internment Camp Culture.* Princeton: Princeton University Press, 1949.

3261. Wallace, A. F. C. *Human Behavior in Extreme Situations.* Washington, D.C.: National Academy of Sciences, National Research Council, Publ. No. 390, 1956.

3262. Wallach, M., and Kogan, N. ''Aspects of Judgment and Decision Making: Inter-Relationships and Changes with Age.'' *Behavioral Science* 6 (January 1961): pp. 23-36.

3263. Waller, J. A. ''Emergency Care for Fatalities from Injury and Illness in the Nonhighway Setting.'' *Journal of Trauma* 13 (1973): 54ff.

3264. Walt, A. J., and Wilson, R. F. *Management of Trauma: Pitfalls and Practice.* Philadelphia: Lea and Febiger, 1975.

3265. Waterworth, T. A., and Carr, M. J. T. ''An Analysis of the Post-Mortem Findings in the 21 Victims of the Birmingham Pub Bombings.'' *Injury* 7 (1976): 89ff.

3266. ———. ''Report on Injuries Sustained by Patients Treated at the Birmingham General Hospital Following the Recent Bomb Explosions.'' *British Medical Journal* 2 (1975): 25ff.

3267. Watson, Peter, and Moynahan, Brian. ''The Mind of the Terrorist.'' *Sunday Times-Spectrum*, August 19, 1973, p. 8.

The authors note the great number of international terrorists who appear to have been attracted to terrorism because of their psychoses rather than for political reasons. Attention is given to hijackers, the Japanese Red Army, Italian anarchists, Argentina's Angel Bengochea, Brazilian death squads, the Baader-Meinhof group, and Wolfgang Huber's Socialist Patients' Collective.

3268. Welford, A. "Age and Skill: Motor, Intellectual, and Social." In A. Welford and J. Birren, eds., *Decision Making and Age*. Basel: Karger, 1969.

3269. Wenner, M. W. "Biological and Environmental Factors as Political Variables." Paper presented to the annual convention of the American Political Science Association, September 1971.

3270. Wertham, F. "New Dimensions of Human Violence." *American Journal of Psychotherapy* 23 (July 1969): 374-380.

3271. West, L. J. "Psychiatric Aspects of Training for Honorable Survival as a Prisoner of War." *American Journal of Psychiatry* 115 (1958): 329-336.

3272. Westermeyer, J. "Grenade-amok in Laos: A Psychosocial Perspective." *International Journal of Social Psychiatry* 19 (Autumn 1973): 251-260.

3273. ———. "On the Epidemicity of Amok Violence." *Archives of General Psychiatry* 28 (June 1973): 873-876.

3274. Wiegele, Thomas C. "Decision-Making in an International Crisis: Some Biological Factors." *International Studies Quarterly* 17 (September 1973): 295-335.

Argues that such factors as fatigue, age, drugs, circadian rhythms, and general health can affect decision making under stressful situations. Methods of researching his propositions are suggested.

3275. ———. "Toward a Psychophysiological Variable in Conflict Theory." *Experimental Study of Politics* 1 (July 1971): 51-81.

3276. Weigele, Thomas C., and Plowman, Sharon. "Stress Tolerance and International Crisis: The Significance of Biologically-Oriented Experimental Research to the Behavior of Political Decisionmakers." *Experimental Study of Politics* 3 (December 1974): 63-92.

3277. Wilkins, J. L.; Scharff, W. H.; and Schlottman, R. S. "Personality Type, Reports of Violence, and Aggressive Behavior." *Journal of Personality and Social Psychology* 30 (August 1973): 243-247.

3278. Wilson, I. V., and Tunbridge, R. E. "Pathological Findings in a Series of Blast Injuries." *Lancet* 244 (1943): 257ff.

3279. Winokur, G. "The Germ Warfare Statements: A Synthesis of a Method for the Extortion of False Confessions." *Journal of Nervous and Mental Disorders* 122 (1955): 65-72.

3280. Wolf, S., and Ripley, H. S. "Reactions among Allied Prisoners Subjected to Three Years of Imprisonment and Torture by the Japanese." *American Journal of Psychiatry* 104 (1947): 180-193.

3281. Wolfenstein, E. *The Revolutionary Personality.* Princeton, N.J.: Princeton University Press, 1967.

3282. Wolff, H. G. "Commitment and Resistance." In A. D. Biderman and H. Zummere, eds., *Special Reports of Study SR 177-D.* Washington, D.C.: Bureau of Social Science Research, 1959.

3283. Woods, S. M. "Violence: Psychotherapy of Pseudohomosexual Panic." *Archives of General Psychiatry* 27 (August 1972): 255-258.

3284. Wright, M. D., and Paszek, L. J., eds. *Science, Technology and Warfare.* Proceedings of the Third Military History Symposium. Washington, D.C.: U.S. Government Printing Office, 1970.
        Included are items on medical aspects of terrorism.

3285. Yinger, J. Milton. "Anomie, Alienation, and Political Behavior." In Jeanne N. Knutson, ed., *Handbook of Political Psychology.* San Francisco: Jossey-Bass, 1973.

3286. Zimmer, H., and Meltzer, M. L. *An Annotated Bibliography of Literature Relevant to the Interrogation Process.* Washington, D.C.: Georgetown University Medical Center, 1957.

3287. Zuckerman, S. "Experimental Study of Blast Injuries to the Lungs." *Lancet* 2 (1940): 219ff.

3288. ———. "The Problem of Blast Injury." *Proceedings of the Royal Society of Medicine* 34 (1943): 171ff.

    For additional reading, see entries 161, 377, 424, 572, 575, 943, 989, 990, 2055, 3410, 3414, 3519, 3524, and 3535.

GUERRILLA WARFARE

3289. Aaron, Harold Robert. "The Anatomy of Guerrilla Terror." *Infantry* 58 (March-April 1967): 14-18.

3290. Asprey, Robert B. "Terrorism as an Aspect of Guerrilla Warfare." In "Guerrilla Warfare." *Encyclopedia Britannica—Macropaedia* 8 (1974): 459.

3291. ———. *War in the Shadows: The Guerrilla in History.* Garden City, N.Y.: Doubleday, 1975. 2 vols.

3292. Barclay, C. N. "Countermeasures against the Urban Guerrilla." *Military Review* (January 1972): 83-90.

3293. Bell, J. Bowyer. *Besieged: Seven Cities under Attack.* Philadelphia: Chilton, 1966.

3294. ———. "Guerrilla Analysis: Present Directions." *Military Affairs* 37 (December 1973): 155-157.
Reviews the major works of 1971-1973, finding three schools of analysis: sympathy, conventional analysis, mixed traditional and quantitative analysis.

3295. ———. *The Myth of the Guerrilla: Revolutionary Theory and Mal-practice.* New York: Alfred A. Knopf, 1971. 285 pp.
Reviewed briefly in *Foreign Affairs* (January 1972). Bell finds that the myth of the courageous hero in charge of the situation is false and that he is generally a frightened boy. He notes various revolutionary theories of Mao, Giap, and Che and uses case studies to point of their failings in southern Africa, Palestine, and Bolivia.

3296. ———. *On Revolt: Strategies of National Liberation.* Cambridge: Harvard University Press, 1976.

3297. Black, Harold, and Labes, Marvin J. "Guerrilla Warfare: An An-alogy to Police-Criminal Interaction." *American Journal of Orthopsychiatry* 37 (July 1967): 666-670.

3298. Caine, P. D. "Urban Guerrilla Warfare." *Military Review* 50 (1970): 73-78.

3299. Calvert, Michael. "The Characteristics of Guerrilla Leaders and Their Rank and File." *Practitioner* (London) (December 1973).

3300. ———. *The Pattern of Guerrilla Warfare.* Allen Lane.

3301. Calvert, Peter. *A Study of Revolution.* Oxford: Clarendon Press, 1970.
     Suggests that the technical improvement of weapons that enable persons to kill each other at greater distances will tend to prevent the aggressive instinct from being dampened by face-to-face contact.

3303. Civil Insurgency: A Bibliography with Abstracts, NTIS/PS—75/002/6GI, 5K. Order from National Technical Information Service, Springfield, Virginia, U.S.Department of Commerce. Mentioned in *Government Reports Index*, March 21, 1975.

3304. Clutterbuck, Richard Lewis. *Guerrillas and Terrorists.* London: Faber and Faber, 1977. 125 pp.

3305. Condit, D. M. "Modern Revolutionary Warfare: An Analytical Overview." American Institutes for Research, Kensington, Maryland, May 1973. Contract DAAH91-72-C-0908, ARPA Order-2066.
     Focuses on governments supporting, preventing, or fighting revolutionaries, as well as how the United States can deal with the future of the problem. Five theories of revolutionary violence, particularly as they apply to the United States in the mid-1970s, are described.

3306. D. M. Condit, et al. *A Counterinsurgency Bibliography.* Washington, D.C.: Special Operations Research Office: American University, 1963.

3307. Condit, Doris M., and Cooper, Jr., Bert H. *Challenge and Response in Internal Conflict.* Washington, D.C.: American University Center for Research in Social Systems, 1967-1968.

3308. Cross, James Eliot. *Conflict in the Shadows: The Nature and Politics of Guerrilla Warfare.* London: Constable and Company, 1964. Garden City: Doubleday, 1963.

3309. Crozier, Brian. *A Theory of Conflict.* London: Hamish Hamilton, 1974. 239 pp. New York: Scribner's 1974. 245 pp.

Readers are given fragments and insights from a conservative political philosophy, with much musing on how this might relate to the contemporary scene. Crozier touches on many subjects but is unable to treat any of them with the depth that they require.

3310. Daly, William T. *The Revolutionary: A Review and Synthesis.* Beverly Hills: Sage, 1972.

3311. Dubbin, Sidney M. "Urban Insurrection: The Time Frame Factor for Military Intervention in a Counterinsurgent Environment." Carlisle Barracks, Penn.: Army War College, October 1973. AD-A002 530 15/7 5/4.

Polarization of political forces has led to the breeding of urban revolutionaries, who finds the complex city a vulnerable target. Dubbin finds that military incursion has been the most effective short-range method of combating urban guerrillas.

3312. Eckstein, Harry, ed. *Internal War.* New York: Macmillan, 1964. 339 pp.

A collection of readings by major U.S. academics studying the problem.

3313. ———. "On the Etiology of Internal Wars." *History and Theory* 4 (1965): 133-163.

3314. Ellis, John. *A Short History of Guerrilla Warfare.* New York: St. Martin's Press, 1976. 220 pp.

3316. Fairbain, Geoffrey. *Revolutionary Guerrilla Warfare: The Countryside Version.* Harmondsworth: Penguin, 1974. 395 pp.

Discusses the theory of revolutionary warfare as practiced by Chinese, Malayans, Viet Cong, Cubans, Palestinians, and T. E. Lawrence. Considers questions of peasant support, legitimacy, and international law.

3317. Faleroni, Alberto D. "What Is an Urban Guerrilla?" *Military Review* 67 (1969): 94-96.

3318. Feldman, Arnold S. "Violence and Volatility: The Likelihood of Revolution." In Harry Eckstein, ed., *Internal War: Problems and Approaches,* pp. 111-129. Glencoe: Free Press, 1964.

3319. Fraser, M. "At School During Guerrilla War." *Special Education* 61 (June 1972): 6-8.

3320. Gann, Lewis H. *Guerrillas in History.* Stanford, Calif.: Hoover Institution Press, 1971.

3321. Greene, ed., T. N. *The Guerrilla and How to Fight Him.* New York: Praeger, 1962.

3322. Greene, Thomas H. *Comparative Revolutionary Movements.* Englewood Cliffs: Prentice-Hall, 1974. 172 pp.
    Discusses the characteristics of such groups, including leaders, followers, ideology, organization, techniques, and external support, as well as theories about their causes, including preconditions and accelerators. An extensive bibliography is included.

3324. Guerrilla Warfare: A Bibliography with Abstracts. NTIS/PS—75/001/8GI/15G. Order from National Technical Information Service, Springfield, Virginia, U.S. Department of Commerce.

3325. Harrigan, A. "Combat in Cities." *Military Review* 46 (1966): 26-30.

3326. Hillard, J. Z. "Countersubversive Operations in Urban Areas." *Military Review* 6 (1966): 12-19; 47 (1967): 27-35.

3327. Hodges, Donald, and Abu Shanab, R. E. eds. *National Liberation Fronts, 1960-70.* New York: William Morrow, 1972.

3328. Horowitz, Irving Louis. ed. *The Anarchists.* New York: Dell, 1964.

3329. Hyde, D. *The Roots of Guerrilla Warfare: A Background Book.* Chester Springs: Dufour Editions, 1968.

3330. Internal Defense: Bibliography. Fort Leavenworth, Kan.: U.S. Army Command and General Staff College, May 31, 1977.
    Heavily concentrates on insurgencies, with particular emphasis on the Vietnam war.

3331. Jenkins, Brian Michael. "The Five Stages of Urban Guerrilla Warfare: Challenge for the 1970s." Santa Monica: RAND Corporation, P-4670, July 1971.
    Discusses violent propaganda, organizational growth, guerrilla offensives, mass mobilization, and urban uprising, as well as constraints and environments of guerrillas.

3332. ———. ''An Urban Strategy for Guerrillas and Governments.'' Santa Monica: RAND Corporation, P-4670/1.

Looks at a five-stage model of guerrilla operations and suggests government countermeasures that center on legitimacy and superior resources.

3333. Johnson, Chalmers. ''Civilian Loyalties and Guerrilla Conflicts.'' *World Politics* 14 (July 1962).

3334. ———. *Revolutionary Change*. Boston: Little, Brown, 1966. 191 pp.

3335. Johnson, Charles. *Autopsy on Peoples' War*. Berkeley: University of California Press, 1973.

Argues that each decade has its own revolutionary paradigm, which appears to have worked in one context and is slavishly followed by revolutionaries in other areas.

3336. Jones, W. M. ''Predicting Insurgent and Governmental Decisions: The Power Bloc Model.'' Santa Monica: RAND Corporation, RM-6358-PR, December 1970.

3337. Klonis, N. I. [pseudo] *Guerrilla Warfare: Analysis and Projections*. New York: Robert Speller, 1972. 400 pp.

Traces the history of the phenomenon in some detail, concentrating on tactical aspects.

3338. Knorr, Klaus. ''Unconventional Warfare: Strategy and Tactics in Internal Strife.'' In J. K. Zawodny, ed. ''Unconventional Warfare.'' *Annals of the American Academy of Political and Social Science* (1962).

3339. Kossoy, Edward. *Living with Guerrilla: Guerrilla as a Legal Problem and Political Fact*. Geneva: Librairie Droz, 1976. 405 pp.

Reviewed briefly by Christiane Shields Delessert, *American Journal of International Law* 71 (April 1977): 373-374.

3340. Kutner, Luis. *Due Process of Rebellion*. Chicago: Bardian House, 1974. 163 pp.

3341. Laqueur, Walter. *Guerrilla: A Historical and Critical Study*. Boston: Little, Brown, 1976. 462 pp.

3342. ———, ed. *The Guerrilla Reader: A Historical Anthology*. Bergenfield, N.J.: New American Library, 1976, and Philadelphia: Temple, 1977, 246 pp.

3343. ———. "The Origins of Guerrilla Doctrine." *Journal of Contemporary History* 10 (July 1975): 341-382.
Surveys concepts offered by European theorists of small wars between 1750 and 1900.

3344. Lortequy, Jean. *The Guerrillas.* New York: World, 1970.

3345. McCuen, John J. *The Art of Counter-Revolutionary War.* Harrisburg, Penn.: Stackpole; London: Faber and Faber, 1966.
Argues that terrorism is frequently used when the terrain is unsuitable and/or the political and military organization of the insurgent group is not sufficently developed for complete guerrilla warfare or it can be used as a supplement to that total warfare.

3346. Andrew R. Molnar, et al. *Undergrounds in Insurgent, Revolutionary, and Resistance Warfare.* Washington, D.C.: American University Special Operations Research Office, 1963.

3347. Nasution, Abdul Haris. *Fundamentals of Guerrilla Warfare.* New York: Praeger, 1965.

3349. Orlansky, Jesse. "The State of Research on Internal War." Rept. No. RP-p-565, Contract: DAHC15-67-C-0011, Project ARPA Assignment-20, Monitor: IDA/HQ-69-10919. Institute for Defense Analyses, Science and Technology Division, Arlington, Virginia, August 1970.
Reviews the literature of internal war, discovering that the crucial conceptual issues are still being developed. He believes that further research should look at longitudinal, attitudinal, postrevolutionary combat issues.

3350. Osanka, Franklin, ed. *Modern Guerrilla Warfare.* Glencoe, Ill.: Free Press, 1962.
An early and influential collection of readings by academics and military officers.

3351. Paret, Peter, and Shy, John W. *Guerrillas in the 1960's.* Rev. ed. New York: Praeger, 1962.

3352. Pearse, George A. "Similarities and Differences in the Guerrilla Strategies of Mao and Lawrence." Student essay. Carlisle Barracks, Penn.: Army War College, December 29, 1973.
Looks at variables of personal philosophy, time, geographical area, and political, military, and strategic concepts.

3353. Proceedings of the Second International Conference on the History of the Resistance Movements, Milan, Italy, March 26-29, 1961. New York: Macmillan, 1964.

3354. "Revolutionary War: Western Response." *Journal of International Affairs* (Columbia) 25 (1971): entire issue.

3355. Russell, D. E. H. *Rebellion, Revolution, and Armed Force: A Comparative Study of Fifteen Countries with Special Emphasis on Cuba and South Africa.* New York: Academic Press, 1974. 210 pp.

3356. Sarkesian, Sam C., ed. *Revolutionary Guerrilla Warfare.* Chicago: Precedent, 1973. 623 pp.
    Reviewed by Richard Eder, *New York Times*, December 14, 1975. A collection of readings on political, military, strategic, moral, and reactive aspects of revolutionary warfare.

3357. Schlaak, Thomas M. "The Essence of Future Guerrilla Warfare." *Marine Corps Gazette* (December 1976): 18-26.

3358. Scott, Andrew M. *Insurgency.* Chapel Hill: University of North Carolina, 1970. 139 pp.

3359. Silverman, Jerry M., and Jackson, Peter M. "Terror in Insurgency Warfare." *Military Review* 50 (October 1970): 61-67.
    The authors discuss the use of terrorism as part of an insurgent campaign. Terrorism's uses against the government, the population, and the group's own members are outlined. The authors conclude that it is useful in the early stages of an insurgency but becomes counterproductive if it becomes indiscriminate and if the group is unable to present itself as a viable alternative to the present authorities.

3360. Singh, Baljit, and Ko-Wang, Mei. *Theory and Practice of Modern Guerrilla Warfare.* New York: Asia Publishing House, 1971.

3361. Soderland, W. "An Analysis of the Guerrilla Insurgency and Coup d'Etat as Techniques of Indirect Aggression." *International Studies Quarterly* 14 (December 1970): 335-360.

3362. Spjut, R. J. "Review of Counterinsurgency Theorists." *Political Quarterly* (January 1978): 54-64.

3363. Stupack, Ronald J., and Booher, D. C. ''Guerrilla Warfare: A Strategic Analysis in the Superpower Context.'' *Journal of Southeast Asia and the Far East*, November 2, 1970, pp. 181-196.

3364. Sully, François. *Age of the Guerrilla: A Study of the New Warfare.* New York: Avon, 1968. 222 pp.

3365. Taber, Robert. *The War of the Flea: A Study of Guerrilla Warfare Theory and Practice.* New York: Citadel, 1970. 160 pp.

3366. Thayer, Charles W. *Guerrilla.* New York: Signet, 1965.

3367. Thompson, R. *Defeating Communist Insurgency.* London: Chatto and Windus, 1966.
  The author was directly involved in the Malayan insurgency.

3368. Tinker, Hugh. ''The Future of Guerrilla Warfare: Can Urban Guerilla Warfare Succeed?'' *Current* (May 1971): 52-57.

3369. Weller, Jac. ''Guerrilla Warfare.'' *National Guardsman* 24 (1970).

RELATED STUDIES

3370. Alker, Jr., Hayward R. ''Measuring Inequality.'' In his *Mathematics and Politics*, pp. 29-53. New York: Macmillan, 1965.

Alker discusses Lorenz curves, equal share coefficients, minimal majority, Schutz's coefficient of inequality, and Gini index and demonstrates their use in cases of inequal votes, taxes, and school studies.

3371. Alker, Hayward R., and Russett, Bruce M. ''On Measuring Inequality.'' *Behavioral Science* 9 (July 1964): 207-218.

The authors introduce the equal share coefficient, which measures the percentage size of the underprivileged population (the point at which the slope of the Lorenz curve equals one).

3372. Allen, Robin. ''Student Revolt.'' *Economist Brief* 16 (1969).

3373. Allen, Vernon L. ''Ghetto Riots.'' *Journal of Social Issues* 26 (Winter 1970): entire issue.

3374. Allison, Graham T. *Essence of Decision: Explaining the Cuban Missile Crisis*. Boston: Little, Brown, 1971. 338 pp.

Posits two alternative methods to the traditional way of viewing international behavior, pointing out the importance of bureaucratic bargaining and organizational processes in the creation of foreign policy responses.

3375. Alper, Benedict Solomon, and Boren, Jerry F. *Crime: International Agenda*. Lexington, Mass.: Lexington Books, 1972. 221 pp.

A history of actions and discussions by international organizations on definitons of and responses to crime.

3376. Antunes, George. ''Socioeconomic, Political, and Violence Variables as Predictors of Government Expenditures in Nations: 1955, 1960, 1965.'' Ph.D. dissertation, Northwestern University, 1971.

3377. Archer, Dane, and Gartner, Rosemary. ''Some Aspects of Reliability and Validity in Comparative Crime Data.'' Unpublished manuscript. University of California, Santa Cruz, 1975.

3378. ———. "Violent Acts and Violent Times: A Comparative Approach to Postwar Homicide Rates." *American Sociological Review* 41 (December 1976): 973-993.

The authors use data on crimes committed in 110 nations between 1900 and the early 1970s to test seven competing theories of the relationship of war to criminal behavior. Nations participating in wars show an increase in their homicide rates, especially if the nation was victorious and experienced a large number of combat deaths.

3379. Arendt, Hannah. "Reflections on Violence." *Journal of International Affairs* 23 (1969).

3380. ———. *On Violence.* London: Penguin, 1970. New York: Harcourt, Brace and World, 1970. 106 pp.

3381. Bailey, C.; Martin, J.D.; and Gray, L. N. "Crime and Deterrence." *Journal of Research in Crime and Delinquency* 11 (July 1974): 124-143.

3382. Bailey, William C. "Homicide and a Regional Culture of Violence: Some Further Evidence." In Marc Riedel and Terence P. Thornberry, eds., *Crime and Delinquency: Dimensions of Deviance*, pp. 59-73. New York: Praeger, 1974.

Attempts to relate, by means of multiple correlation analysis, the relationship between three types of homicide offenses and degree of "Southerness," controlling for other demographic factors.

3383. Baker, Robert K., and Ball, Sandra J. *Mass Media and Violence: A Staff Report to the National Commission on the Causes and Prevention of Violence.* Washington: U.S. Government Printing Office, November 1969. 614 pp.

3384. Baldwin, D. A. "Thinking about Threats." *Journal of Conflict Resolution* 9 (1971).

3385. Ball-Rockeach, S. J. "Values and Violence: A Test of the Sub-Culture of Violence Thesis." *American Sociological Review* 38 (December 1973): 736-749.

3386. Barnett, Randy. E., and Hagel III, John, eds. *Assessing the Criminal: Restitution, Retribution, and the Legal Process*, Cambridge, Mass.: Ballinger, 1977.

3387. Bay, Christian. "Violence as a Negation of Freedom." *American Scholar* 40 (Autumn 1971): 634-641.

3388. Becker, Gary S. "Crime and Punishment: An Economic Approach." *Journal of Political Economy* 76 (March-April 1968): 169-217.

Analyzes the cost of crime, cost of apprehension and conviction, number and frequency of crimes, punishments, fines, and collusion using mathematical techniques normally found in economics.

3389. Becker, Gary S., and Landes, William M., eds. *Essays in the Economics of Crime and Punishment.* New York: Columbia, National Bureau of Economic Research, 1976. 268 pp.

This series of readings employs economic science approaches to the study of the deterrent effects of criminal sanctions, court functions, bail systems, behavioral effects of legislations, and legal decision making.

3390. Bedau, Hugo Adam, ed. *The Death Penalty in America: An Anthology.* New York: Doubleday, 1967.

3391. Berk, R. A., and Aldrich, H. E. "Patterns of Vandalism during Civil Disorders as an Indicator of Selection of Targets." *American Sociological Review* 37 (October 1972): 523-547.

3392. Bersani, Carl A., ed. *Crime and Delinquency: A Reader.* London: Collier-Macmillan, Ltd., 1970. 575 pp.

3393. Bertelsen, Judy S., ed. *Non-State Nations in International Politics: Comparative System Analyses.* New York: Praeger, 1977. 272 pp.

Reviewed briefly by Jacques Fomerand, *Perspective: Monthly Reviews of New Books on Government/Politics/International Affairs* 6 (September 1977): 147. Bertelsen presents systems studies of Palestinians, the prestate Zionists, Welsh nationalists, Kurds, Croats, Basques, and Navajos to generalize about objectives, strategies, and international impacts.

3394. ———. "The Strategies of Non-State Nations in Shaping Trans-National Policies." Summary in William D. Coplin, ed., *The Analysis of Transnational Policy Issues: A Summary of the International Relations Panels of the 1974 American Political Science Convention,* pp. 16-17. St. Louis: University of Missouri, Consortium for International Studies Education, 1974.

Nonstate nations are national groups that do things normally done only by sovereign nation-states (such as raise an army, conduct foreign relations, act as party to a treaty), but are not generally recognized nation-states. A systems framework for studying them is outlined.

3395. Betz, Joseph. "Violence: Garver's Definition and a Deweyan Correction." *Ethics* 87 (July 1977): 339-351.

3396. Biderman, A. D. "Surveys of Population Samples for Estimating Crime Incidence." *Annals of the American Academy of Political and Social Science* 374 (1967): 16-33.

3397. Bienen, Henry. *Violence and Social Change: A Review of Current Literature.* Chicago: University of Chicago Press, 1968. 119 pp.

3398. Bittner, Egon. "Radicalism and the Organization of Radical Movements." *American Sociological Review* (December 1963).

A psychological approach to the study of the individual's perceptions of his relation to an extremist group.

3399. Blackey, Robert. *Modern Revolutions and Revolutionists: A Bibliography.* Santa Barbara: Clio, 1976.

3400. Blechman, Barry M. "The Impact of Israel's Reprisals on Behavior of the Bordering Arab Nations Directed at Israel." *Journal of Conflict Resolution* 16 (June 1972): 155-191.

Blechman uses two measures of events—frequency of events and number killed—to assess how Israeli reprisals affected the Arab nations and Palestinian guerrillas by deterrence, positive compellence, and negative compellence.

3401. Boulding, Kenneth E. *Conflict and Defense: A General Theory.* New York: Harper, 1962. 349 pp.

Shows how game theory, economic models, and other formal theoretical techniques can be used to piece together an all-encompassing view of conflict. Unfortunately Boulding's propositions are at such a high level of abstraction that few of his suggestions have been tested.

3402. Boydell, C. L., and Grindstaff, C. F. "Public Opinion toward Legal Sanctions for Crimes of Violence." *Journal of Criminal Law and Criminology* 65 (March 1974): 113-116.

3403. Brustein, Robert. *Revolution as Theatre: Notes on the New Radical Style.* New York: Liveright, 1971. 172 pp.

A collection of articles by the dean of the Yale School of Drama on the student uprisings of the late 1960s. He argues that stylistically much of what they do has theatric intent and these staged happenings have less content than their perpetrators believe them to.

3404. Buckman, Peter. *The Limits of Protest.* London: Panther, 1970. 286 pp.

3405. Bull, Hedley. ''Civil Violence and International Order.'' *Adelphi Papers* Part II (London) International Institute for Strategic Studies, 1971, pp. 27-36.

Views international terrorism as a series of nuisances to governments but not as a coordinated nonmilitary threat.

3406. Burki, S. J. ''Social and Economic Determinants of Political Violence: A Case Study of the Runjab.'' *Middle East Journal* (Washington, D.C.) 25 (August 1971): 465-480.

3407. Bwy, Douglas P. ''Political Instability in Latin America: The Cross-Cultural Test of a Casual Model.'' *Latin American Research Review* 3 (Spring 1968): 17-66. Reprinted in Ivo K. Feierabend, Rosalind L. Feierabend, and Ted Robert Gurr, eds., *Anger, Violence and Politics: Theories and Research* Englewood Cliffs, N.J.: Prentice-Hall, 1972, pp. 223-241.

3408. Calder, Nigel, ed. *Unless Peace Comes: A Scientific Forecast of New Weapons.* New York: Viking, 1968.

3409. Cameron, J. M. ''Changing Patterns in Violence.'' *Medical Science Law* 13 (October 1973): 261-264.

3410. Cameron, Paul. ''What Is the Least Amount of Money You Would Take to Push a Button to Kill a Person inside a Black Box. (No One Would Ever Know What You Did)?'' Paper presented to the annual convention of the National Federation of Catholic Physicians' Guilds, 1976, at Oak Brook, Illinois.

Cameron found a distressing disregard for life in his questionnaire responses and that those who had previously killed someone (usually in military service) were only about half as inclined as nonkillers to kill for a fee, as well as continue life-support systems for the chronically ill.

3411. Campbell, James S. *Law and Order Reconsidered: A Staff Report of the National Commission on the Causes and Prevention of Violence.* New York: Bantam, 1970. 659 pp.

3412. Camus, Albert. *The Rebel: An Essay on Man in Revolt.* New York: Alfred A. Knopf, 1956.

3413. Candela, C. *Decisionmaking during Crisis: A Literature Review.* Baltimore: Bendix Corporation Applied Science and Technology Division, August 1974.

3414. Cantrill, Hadley, et al. *The Invasion from Mars: A Study in the Psychology of Panic.* New York: Harper and Row, 1966.

3415. Caporaso, James. ''Methodological Issues in the Measurement of Inequality, Dependence, and Exploitation.'' In S. J. Rosen and J. R. Kurth, eds., *Testing Theories of Economic Imperialism,* pp. 87-114. Lexington, Mass.: D. C. Heath, 1974.

3416. Choucri, Nazli. ''Population Dynamics and International Violence: Propositions, Insights, Evidence.'' Paper presented at the annual convention of the American Political Science Association, September 1972, at Washington, D.C. Available as MIT C/73-8, August 1973, as well as FAR 16201-P.

3417. Clinard, Marshall B., and Abbott, Daniel J. *Crime in Developing Countries: A Comparative Perspective.* New York: Wiley-Interscience, 1973. 319 pp.
   Presents numerous tables of incidence of crime in selected countries, as well as some attempts at the statistical analysis of the causes of crime.

3418. Clinard, Marshall B., and Quinney, R. *Criminal Behavior Systems: A Typology.* New York: Holt, Rinehart and Winston, 1967.

3419. Clor, Harry M., ed. *Civil Disorder and Violence: Essays on Causes and Cures by the National Commission on the Causes and Prevention of Violence.* Chicago: Rand McNally, 1972.

3420. Cocozza, J. J., and Steadman, J. H. ''Some Refinements in the Measurement and Prediction of Dangerous Behavior.'' *American Journal of Psychiatry* 131 (September 1974): 1012-1014.
   The authors found that age and previous dangerous behavior were related to subsequent dangerous behavior. They created a legal dangerousness scale, based on four aspects of previous criminal activity: presence of a juvenile record, number of previous arrests, presence of convictions for violent crimes, and severity of offense.

3421. Cohan, A. S. *Theories of Revolution: An Introduction.* London: Nelson, 1975.

3422. Cooper, Mark N. ''A Reinterpretation of the Causes of Turmoil: The Effects of Culture and Modernity.'' *Comparative Political Studies* 7 (October 1974): 267-291.
   Cooper adds two new variables, culture and modernity, to Gurr's analysis of the causes of turmoil, defined as ''relatively spontaneous, unorganized

strife with substantial popular participation.'' Quantitatively studying 114 nations, representativeness, interest articulation configuration, and relative deprivation are seen as having important effects.

3423. Corning, Peter A., and Corning, C. H. ''Toward a General Theory of Violent Aggression.'' *Social Science Information* 11 (1972): 7-35.

3424. Coser, Lewis. *The Functions of Social Conflict.* New York: Free Press, 1956. 188 pp.
A sociological perspective on the role of conflict in social organizations, reviewing much of the then-current literature.

3425. Couzens, Michael. ''Reflections on the Study of Violence.'' *Law and Society Review* 5 (May 1971): 583-604.

3426. Cressey, D. R. ''A Confrontation of Violent Dynamics.'' *International Journal of Psychiatry* 10 (September 1972): 109-130.

3427. Crick, Bernard, and Robson, William A., eds. *Protest and Discontent* Penguin: Harmondsworth, Middlesex, England, 1970. 220 pp.
Twelve of these essays appeared in *Political Quarterly* (October-December 1969).

3428. ''Data Sources for Social Indicators of Victimisation Suffered by Individuals, with Special Reference to the Potential of Victim Surveys.'' Special Studies No. 3. OECD Social Indicator Development Programme Series 81 76 05 1. November 1976.

3429. Davies, James Chowning. ''Toward a Theory of Revolution.'' *American Sociological Review* 27 (February 1962).
An early presentation of the author's J-curve hypothesis on the effects of relative deprivation.

3430. ———, ed. *When Men Revolt and Why: A Reader in Political Violence and Revolution.* New York: Free Press, 1971. 357 pp.

3431. Denton, Frank H. ''Factors in International System Violence: 1750 to 1960.'' Santa Monica: RAND Corporation, P-4216, October 1969.
A progress report, explaining data-collection problems and initial findings on how these conflicts relate to the overall political system and to political group behavior.

3432. Deutsch, Karl. ''The Theoretical Basis of Data Programs.'' In Richard L. Merritt and Stein Rokkan, eds., *Comparing Nations: The Use of Quantita-*

tive Data in Cross-National Research (New Haven: Yale University Press, 1966), pp. 27-55.

Deutsch calls for three levels of theorizing and a renewed concentration upon the collection of reliable data for the testing of theories.

3433. "Developments in the Law: The National Security Interest and Civil Liberties." *Harvard Law Review* 85 (1972): 1130ff.

A review of the debate regarding the justification of partial abrogation of constitutional protections due to threats to national security.

3434. Domenach, Jean-Marie. "The Ubiquity of Violence." *International Social Science Journal* 30 (1978): 717-726.

3435. Drew, Paul. "Domestic Political Violence: Some Problems of Measurement." *Sociological Review* 1 (February 1974): 5-25.

Attacks social science methods of coding violent acts, arguing that the scientist's definition of what constitutes a political act may differ from how it is understood contextually. What should be studied is the corpus of rules for determining what is a violent, political act.

3436. Dror, Yehezkel. "War, Violence and Futures Studies." *Futures* 6 (Fall 1974): 2-3.

Argues that futurists must consider issues outside of ecology, such as violence, to increase the usefulness of the discipline.

3437. Dugan, Maire A. "The Relationship Between Pre-Independence Violence and Nonviolence and Post-Independence Political Repression." Paper presented at the annual convention of the International Studies Association, 1979.

3438. Dunn, John. *Modern Revolutions: An Introduction to the Analysis of a Political Phenomenon.* Cambridge: Cambridge University Press, 1972.

3439. Eckstein, Harry. "Internal War: The Problem of Anticipation." In *Social Science Research and National Security.* Washington, D.C.: Smithsonian Institution, 1963.

3440. "Effects of Rapid Population Growth on Political Change in the Less Developed Countries." Washington, D.C.: Department of State external research study C1033L2 FLD: 5D, 5K, 56C USGRDR7313 April 20, 1973.

Participants at a conference suggested that quantification would establish an empirical relation between rapid population growth and domestic conflicts.

3441. Ehrlich, Isaac. "Capital Punishment and Deterrence: Some Further Thoughts and Additional Evidence." *Journal of Political Economy* 85 (August 1977): 741-788.

3442. ———. "Participation in Illegitimate Activities: A Theoretical and Empirical Investigation." *Journal of Political Economy* 81 (May-June 1973): 521-565.

3443. Ehrlich, Isaac, and Gibbons, Joel C. "On the Measurement of the Deterrent Effect of Capital Punishment and the Theory of Deterrence." *Journal of Legal Studies* 6 (January 1977): 35-50.

3444. Eisinger, Peter K. "The Conditions of Protest Behavior in American Cities." *American Political Science Review* 67 (March 1973): 11-28.

3445. Ekman, P., and Friesen, W. V. "Detecting Deception from Body or Face." *Journal of Personality and Social Psychology* 29 (1974): 288-298.

3446. Elliott, Mabel A. *Social Disorganization.* 3d ed. New York: Harper, 1950.

3447. Endicott, Stephen L. "Germ Warfare and 'Plausible Denial': The Korean War, 1952-1953." *Modern China* 5 (January 1979): 79-104.
A study of the credibility of charges that the United States used biological warfare during the Korean conflict.

3448. Endleman, Shalom, ed. *Violence in the Streets.* Chicago: Quadrangle, 1968. 471 pp.

3449. Epting, Robert L. "Dealing with Unruly Persons in the Courtroom." *North Carolina Law Review* 48 (1970): 878ff.

3450. Erskine, Hazel. "Fear of Violence and Crime." *Public Opinion Quarterly* 38 (1974): 131ff.

3451. Feierabend, Ivo K., and Feierabend, Rosalind L. "Aggressive Behaviors within Polities, 1948-1962: A Cross-National Study." *Journal of Conflict Resolution* 10 (1966): 249-271.

3452. ———. "The Relationship of Systematic Frustration, Political Coercion, International Tension and Political Instability: A Cross-National Study." Paper presented at the annual meeting of the American Psychological Association, 1966, at New York City.

3453. ———. "Systemic Conditions of Political Aggression: An Application of Frustration-Aggression Theory." In Ivo K. Feierabend, Rosalind L. Feierabend, and Ted Robert Gurr, eds., *Anger, Violence and Politics: Theories and Research* (Englewood Cliffs, N.J.: Prentice-Hall, 1972), pp. 136-183.

3454. Feierabend, Ivo K.; Feierabend, Rosalind L.; and Nesvold, Betty. "The Comparative Study of Revolution and Violence." *Comparative Politics* 5 (April 1973): 393-424.

3455. Feld, Werner J. "Transnational Policy Analysis: A Framework for Assessing the Role of Nongovernmental Organizations in World Politics?" Paper presented at the annual meeting of the International Studies Association, February 1975, at Washington, D.C. Available as FAR 22411-P.

3456. Ferracuti, Franco, and Wolfgang, Marvin E. *The Subculture of Violence.* London: Social Science Paperbacks, Associated Book Publishers, Ltd., 1967. 387 pp.
    Subcultures advocating violence as a method of resolving personal problems can exist in societies with general norms prohibiting violence.

3457. Field, Stanley H. "The Right to Dissent: Protected in the Courtroom." *St. John's Law Review* 44 (1970): 591ff.

3458. Finch, G. A. "Piracy in the Mediterranean." *American Journal of International Law* 31 (1937): 659ff.

3459. Firestone, Joseph M. "Continuities in the Theory of Violence." *Journal of Conflict Resolution* 18 (March 1974): 117-142.
    A review of several theoretical works.

3460. Flacks, R. "The Liberated Generation: An Exploration of the Roots of Student Protest." *Journal of Social Issues* 23 (1967).

3461. Flaum, Joel M., and Thompson, James R. "The Case of the Disruptive Defendant: Illinois v. Allen." *Journal of Criminal Law, Criminology and Police Science* 61 (1970).

3462. Forman, E. M. "Civil War as a Source of International Violence." *Jounal of Politics* 34 (November 1972): 1111-1134.

3463. Forst, Brian E. "The Deterrent Effect of Capital Punishment: A Cross-State Analysis of the 1960s." *Minnesota Law Review* 61 (May 1977): 743-768.

3464. Forster, Arnold. "Violence on the Fanatical Left and Right." *Annals of the American Academy of Political and Social Science* 364 (March 1966): 141-148.

3465. Frank, Robert S. "The Prediction of Political Violence from Objective and Subjective Social Indicators." Edinburgh: International Psychoanalytical Congress, 1976.

3466. Friedenberg, Edgar Z. "The Privilege of Violence." *Ramparts* (September 1975): 41-44. Adapted from the *The Disposal of Liberty and Other Industrial Wastes* (New York: Doubleday).

3467. Friedrich, Carl J. "Opposition and Government by Violence." *Government and Opposition* 7 (1972): 3-19.

3468. Garfinkel, H. "Conditions of Successful Degradation Ceremonies." *American Journal of Sociology* 61 (March 1956): 420-424.
    Studies social rituals used to label criminals as socially unacceptable.

3469. George, Alexander L., and Smoke, Richard. *Deterrence in American Foreign Policy: Theory and Practice.* New York: Columbia University Press, 1974. 666 pp.
    A massive review of American policies of deterrence in several major episodes.

3470. Gerlach, Luther P. "Movements of Revolutionary Change: Some Structural Characteristics." *American Behavioral Scientist* 14 (July-August 1971): 812-836.

3471. Geschwender, James A. "Explorations in the Theory of Social Movements and Revolutions." *Social Forces* 47 (December 1968): 127-135.

3472. Gillespie, J. V., and Nesvold, Betty A., eds. *Macroquantitative Analysis: Conflict, Development, and Democratization.* Beverly Hills: Sage, 1971.

3473. Gilula, M. F., and Daniels, D. N. "Violence and Man's Struggle to Adapt." *Science* 164 (1969).

3474. Gleason, John M., and Barnum, Darold T. "Crime Does Pay: An Analysis of the Burglary Profession." *Interfaces* (May 1977): 55-60.

The authors attempt to estimate the imputed wage rate for time spent in prison by burglars. Much time is spent in examining sources of error in crime statistics. Estimates are then made for various jurisdictions, noting probabilities of arrest, charge, trial, conviction, and imprisonment.

3475. Gostkowski, Zygmunt. "The Evolution of Developmental Gaps between Rich and Poor Countries, 1955-65: A Methodological Pilot Study." *International Social Science Journal* 27 (1975): 38-52.

3476. Graham, Hugh Davis, and Gurr, Ted Robert. *The History of Violence in America: A Report to the National Commission on the Causes and Prevention of Violence.* New York: Bantam, 1969. 822 pp.

3477. ———. "Violence in Perspective: A Review Essay." *Journal of Human Relations* 20 (1972).

3479. Grofman, Bernard N., and Muller, Edward N. "The Strange Case of Relative Gratification and Potential for Political Violence: The V-Curve Hypothesis." *American Political Science Review* 67 (June 1973): 514-539.

3480. Gross, Feliks. *The Seizure of Political Power in a Century of Revolutions.* New York: Philosophical Library, 1958.

3481. Gurr, Ted Robert. "A Causal Model of Civil Strife: A Comparative Analysis Using New Indices." *American Political Science Review* (December 1968): 1104-1124.

A pioneering article using aggregate data in an attempt to explain the cause of different types of manifest political conflict within the nation state.

3482. ———. "New Error-Compensated Measures for Comparing Nations: Some Correlates of Civil Violence." Princeton: Princeton University, Center for International Studies, Research Monograph 25, 1966.

3483. ———. "Psychological Factors in Civil Violence." *World Politics* 20 (1968): 245-278.

3484. ———. "Sources of Rebellion in Western Society: Some Quantitative Evidence." *Annals* 391 (1970): 128-144.

3485. ———. *Why Men Rebel.* Princeton: Princeton University Press, 1970. 421 pp.

The seminal work on the effects of relative deprivation on polities.

3486. Gurr, Ted Robert, and Duvall, Raymond. ''Civil Conflict in the 1960s: A Reciprocal Theoretical System with Parameter Estimates.'' *Comparative Political Studies* (July 1973): 135-170.

The authors present an eleven-variable, bloc-recursive, simultaneous equation model of the causes of manifest political conflict. Its multiple correlation coefficients are quite high, and the model appears to provide an excellent start in empirically testing a formal theory of civil strife.

3487. Gurr, Ted Robert; Grabosky, Peter N.; Hula, Richard C.; Peirce, David; Persson, Leif; and Sperlings, Sven. *The Politics of Crime and Conflict: A Comparative Study of Four Cities.* Beverly Hills: Sage, 1977. 792 pp. Abridged version available as Ted Robert Gurr, *Rogues, Rebels and Reformers* (Beverly Hills: Sage, 1977), 192 pp.

The authors explore crime in London, Stockholm, Sydney, and Calcutta over the last two hundred years, surveying origins of contemporary policies and institutions for public order, class interests, and political circumstances behind changes in criminal justice systems, the relation between crime and civil disorder, and applications to a general theory of public order.

3488. Gurr, Ted Robert, and Ruttenberg, Charles R. ''The Conditions of Civil Violence: First Tests of a Causal Model.'' Princeton: Center for International Studies, Princeton University, Research Monograph 28, 1967.

3489. Gurr, Ted Robert, and Weil, Herman. ''Population Growth and Political Conflict: A Correlational Study of Eighty-four Nations.'' Report supported by the National Science Foundation, Guggenheim Foundation, and U.S. Department of State INR/XR, July 1973. Available as USC/FAR Prof. No. 1565/72 and FAR 19451-G.

3490. Haggman, Bertil. ''The Vulnerable Modern Industrial Society.'' *Jerusalem Journal of International Relations* 3 (Summer 1978): 1-18.

3492. Halleck, S. ''Hypotheses of Student Unrest.'' In J. Foster and D. Long, eds., *Protest: Student Activism in America.* New York: William Morrow, 1970.

3493. Harris, Paul. ''The Concept of Violence.'' *Political Science* 25 (December 1973): 103-114.

3494. Hatcher, Christopher. ''Practical Issues in the Treatment of Religious Cults.'' Paper delivered to the Conference on Moral Implications of Terrorism, March 14-16, 1979, at UCLA.

3495. Hermassi, Elbaki. "Toward a Comparative Study of Revolutions." *Comparative Studies in Society and History* 18 (April 1976): 211-235.

3496. Hibbs, Jr., Douglas A. *Mass Political Violence: A Cross-National Causal Analysis.* New York: Wiley, 1973. 253 pp.
    Reviewed by Stanley B. Greenberg, "Social Differentiation and Political Violence." *Journal of Conflict Resolution* 19 (March 1975): 161-184. A quantitative attempt to create a multiequation causal model.

3497. Hirsch, Herbert, and Perry, David C., eds. *Violence as Politics.* New York: Harper and Row, 1973.

3498. Hobsbawm, Eric. *Bandits.* New York: Delacorte, 1969. 128 pp.
    Hobsbawm sees a difference between common bandits, social bandits who seek to right individual wrongs within the established system, and revolutionaries who wish to change society itself.

3499. Hofstadter, Richard. "The Future of American Violence" *Harper's* (April 1970).

3500. Hood, E. Ellsworth. "Violence and the Myth of Quantification." *International Philosophical Quarterly* 9 (December 1969): 590-600.
    Hood attacks social science methods as not addressing the fundamental question of what is man's being, reducing theory to mere description. He sees this as being the reason why violence is chosen, as men have lost their ability to see others as human and see only quantification.

3501. Hopper, R. D. "The Revolutionary Process: A Frame of Reference for the Study of Revolutionary Movements." *Sociological Forces* 29 (1950): 270-279.

3502. Horn, J. L., and Knott, P. D. "Activist Youth of the 1960s: Summary and Prognosis." *Science* 171 (1971).

3503. Horowitz, Donald L. "Direct, Displaced, and Cumulative Ethnic Aggression." *Comparative Politics* 6 (October 1973): 1-16.

3504. Horowitz, Irving Louis. *The Struggle Is the Message.* Berkeley: Glendessary, 1970.

3505. Hudson, Michael C. "Conditions of Political Violence and Instability: A Preliminary Test of 3 Hypotheses." *Sage Professional Papers in Comparative Politics* 1 (1970). 56 pp.

3506. ———. "Political Protest and Power Transfers in Crisis Periods: Regional, Structural and Environmental Comparisons." *Comparative Political Studies* (October 1971): 259-294.
Assesses the behavior of political systems before, during, and after periods of political violence.

3507. Huntington, Samuel P. "Patterns of Violence in World Politics." In his *Changing Patterns of Military Politics*. Glencoe: Free Press, 1962.

3508. Iglitzin, Lynne B. *Violent Conflict in American Society*. San Francisco: Chandler, 1972.

3509. Ilfeld, Jr., Fred W., and Harris, R. F. "Alternatives to Violence: Strategies for Coping with Social Conflict." In D. N. Daniels et al., eds., *Violence and the Struggle for Existence*. Boston: Little, Brown, 1970.

3510. Isaacs, Harold R. *Idols of the Tribe*.
An exploration of separatism.

3511. Jacoby, J. E. "When 'The People' Take Over a Hospital." *Medical Times* 101 (September 1973): 71.

3512. Johnson, D. H. N. "Piracy in Modern International Law." *Transactions of the Grotius Society* 43 (1957): 63ff.

3513. Johnson, E. "Organized Crime: Challenge to the American Legal System." *Journal of Criminal Law, Criminology and Police Science* 54 (1963).

3514. Joll, James. *The Anarchists*. London: Eyre and Spottiswoode, 1964.

3515. Kaplan, Lawrence J., and Kessler, Dennis, eds. *An Economic Analysis of Crime*. Springfield, Ill.: Thomas, 1975. 410 pp.

3516. Karber, Phillip A. "Armed Attack as a Unit of Analysis." Paper presented before the International Studies Association convention, March 1973.

3517. Kerr, Louise. "Youth Gangs—A Comparative Historical Analysis of Their Evolution from Recreation to Terror." Paper presented to the Conference on Terrorism in the Contemporary World, April 26-28, 1976, at Glassboro State College.

3518. Kirchheimer, Otto. "Asylum" *American Political Science Review* 53 (1959): 985ff.

3519. Kisker, George. *The Disorganized Personality.* New York: McGraw-Hill, 1964.

3520. Kitsuse, J. I., and Cicourel, A. V. "A Note on the Uses of Official Statistics." *Social Problems* 11 (1963): 131-139.

3521. Kittrie, Nicholas. "In Search of Political Crime and Political Criminals." *New York University Law Review* 50 (April 1975): 202-209.

3522. Knudten, R. D. *Crime in a Complex Society: An Introduction to Criminology.* Homewood, Ill.: Dorsey, 1970.

3523. Korpi, Walter. "Conflict, Power, and Relative Deprivation." *American Political Science Review* 68 (December 1974): 1569-1578.

3524. Krauss, Robert M.; Geller, Valerie; and Olson, Christopher. "Modalities and Cues in the Detection of Deception." Paper presented at the annual meeting of the American Psychological Association, September 2, 1976, in Washington, D.C.

Psychological experiments were run to examine the ability of individuals to test verbal, visual, and other cues in deception, as well as to note what cues lying individuals believe they are using. Some noteworthy results obtained, of significance for hostage situation negotiators contemplating badfaith bargaining. Cues can be effectively manipulated to create a deception. Individuals are generally unaware of the cues they use and do not use those they believe to be effective.

3525. Kritzer, Herbert M. "Political Protest and Political Violence: A Nonrecursive Causal Model." *Social Forces* 55 (March 1977): 630-640.

3526. Kuper, Leo. *The Pity of It All: Polarisation of Racial and Ethnic Relations.* Minneapolis: University of Minnesota Press, 1977. 302 pp.

3528. Land, Kenneth C. "Theories, Models and Indicators of Social Change." *International Social Science Journal* 27 (1975): 7-37.

3529. Lapp, Ralph E. *The Weapons Culture.* New York: Norton, 1968.

3530. Leiden, Carl, and Schmitt, Karl M. *The Politics of Violence: Revolution in the Modern World.* Englewood Cliffs: Prentice-Hall, 1968. 244 pp.

3531. Leites, Nathan C., and Wolf, Jr., C. *Rebellion and Authority: An Analytic Essay on Insurgent Conflicts.* Chicago: Markham, 1970.

3532. Lenoir, James J. "Piracy Cases in the Supreme Court." *Journal of Criminal Law, Criminology and Police Science* 25 (1934): 532ff.

3533. Lerner, Daniel; de Sola Pool, Ithiel; and Schueller, George K. "The Nazi Elite." In Harold D. Lasswell and Daniel Lerner, eds., *World Revolutionary Elites: Studies in Coercive Ideological Movements.* Cambridge: MIT Press, 1965.

3534. Letkemann, Peter. *Crime as Work.* Englewood Cliffs, N.J.: Prentice-Hall, 1973. 182 pp.
Based upon interviews with forty-five Canadian property offenders, Letkemann views crime within the literature of the sociology of professions and discusses acquisition of skills and reputation in the trade, alternative courses of action, and other subjects.

3535. Lichtenstein, S.; Slovic, P.; Fischhoff, B.; Layman, M.; and Combs, B. "Perceived Frequency of Low Probability Lethal Events." *Decision Research Report* 76 (1976).

3536. Lipsky, William E. "Comparative Approaches to the Study of Revolution: A Historiographic Essay." *Review of Politics* 38 (October 1976): 494-509.

3537. Lockhart, Charles. "Bureaucratic Politics and the Obsolescence of War." Paper presented to the Panel on Terrorism of the annual meeting of the Southwest Region of the International Studies Association, March 30-April 2, 1977, at Dallas, Texas.

3538. ———. "The Efficacy of Threats: International Interaction Strategies" 02-023. *Sage Professional Papers in International Studies.* Beverly Hills: Sage.
In international conflict, threats can be counterproductive because they cannot be implemented indiscriminately and effectively. Lockhart illustrates this by referring to the 1911 Agadir crisis and the literature of misperception.

3539. Lupsha, Peter A. "On Theories of Urban Violence." *Urban Affairs Quarterly* 4 (March 1969): 273-296.

3540. Malcolm, Benjamin. "The Self-Proclaimed 'Political Prisoner.' " Paper presented at the 102d annual Congress of Corrections of the American Correctional Association, 1972. Reprinted in "Revolutionary Target: The

American Penal System,'' Report by the Committee on Internal Security, U.S. House of Representatives, 93d Cong., 1st sess., House Report 93-738. pp. 155-160.

3541. Mandel, Robert Michael. ''Political Gaming and Crisis Foreign Policymaking.''Ph.D. dissertation, Yale University, 1976.
Explores some hypotheses about misperception in international relations using political games from Yale, MIT, Rand, and various government agencies.

3542. Manheim, Jarol B., and Wallace, Melanie. *Political Violence in the U.S., 1975: A Bibliography.* New York: Garland, 1975.

3543. Mansback, Richard W.; Ferguson, Yale H.; and Lampert, Donald E. *The Web of World Politics: Nonstate Actors in the Global System.* Englewood Cliffs: Prentice-Hall, 1976. 326 pp.
Surveying multinational corporations, revolutionary movements, and nongovernmental organizational activity, the authors present a framework for studying nonstate actors.

3544. Marx, G. T. ''Thoughts on a Neglected Category of Social Movement Participant: The Agent Provocateur and the Informant.'' *American Journal of Sociology* 80 (September 1974).
Origins, motives, and roles of informants and how they become provocateurs.

3545. Mascotti, Louis H., and Bowen, Don R., eds. *Riots and Rebellion: Civil Violence in the Urban Community.* Beverly Hills: Sage, 1968.

3547. McGee, Jr., Henry W. ''Arrest in Civil Disturbances: Reflections on the Use of Deadly Force in Riots.'' *Rutgers Law Review* 22 (1968): 717ff.
A discussion of the limits on the official use of force in emergencies.

3548. McLennan, Barbara N. ''Cross-National Comparison of Political Opposition and Conflict.'' In Barbara N. McLennan, ed., *Political Opposition and Dissent*, chap. 12. New York: Dunellen, 1973.

3549. McNown, R. F., and Singell, L. D. ''A Factor Analysis of the Socio-Economic Structure of Riot and Crime Prone Cities.''*Annals of Regional Science* 8 (1974).

3550. McPhail, C. ''Civil Disorder Participation: A Critical Examination of Recent Research.'' *American Sociological Review* 36 (December 1971): 1058-1073.

3551. McPhee, William. *Formal Theories of Mass Behavior.* New York: Free Press, 1962.

3552. Megargee, Edwin I., and Hokanson, E., eds. *The Dynamics of Aggression: Individual, Group and International Analyses.* New York: Harper and Row, 1970. 271 pp.

3553. Meier, R. L. ''Some Thoughts on Conflict and Violence in the Urban Settlement.'' *American Behavioral Scientist* 10 (1966): 11-12.

3554. Menkes, Joshua. ''On the Politics of Violence: Part I.'' Arlington, Va. Institute for Defense Analyses, Science and Technology Division, November 1968. Contract: DAHC15-67-C-0011 Report No. RP-P439-Pt. 1.
    The abstract states: ''Political violence is treated as one of the manifestations of a lack of communication betwen the government and the populace. A highly simplified model is proposed to represent the interaction between value determined behavior and value-free government functions.''

3555. Migdal, Joel S. *Peasants, Politics and Revolution: Pressures toward Political and Social Change in the Third World.* Princeton: Princeton University Press, 1974. 300 pp.

3556. Milburn, Thomas W. ''The Nature of Threat.'' *Journal of Social Issues* 33 (1977): 126-139.

3557. Miller, L. ''Identity and Violence in Pursuit of the Causes of War and Organized Violence.'' *Israeli Annals of Psychiatry* 10 (March 1972): 71-77.

3558. Miller, Norman, and Aya, Roderick, eds. *National Liberation: Revolution in the Third World.* New York: Free Press, 1971.

3559. Miller, P. R. ''Revolutionists among the Chicago Demonstrators.'' *American Journal of Psychiatry* 127 (December 1970): 752-758.

3560. Mitchell, Edward J. ''Relating Rebellion to the Environment: An Econometric Approach.'' Santa Monica: RAND Corporation, P-3726, November 1967.
    Mitchell develops a procedure to test theories about the determinants of rebellion and applies it to Vietnam and the Philippine Huk uprising, and suggests it could be applied to Thailand.

3561. Montgomery, J. E. G. ''The Barbary States in the Law of Nations.'' *Transactions of the Grotius Society* 4 (1918): 87ff.

3562. Morgan, Patrick M. *Deterrence: A Conceptual Analysis.* Beverly Hills: Sage Library of Social Research, March 1977. 216 pp.

Distinguishing between "pure" or "immediate" deterrence and "general deterrence," Morgan looks at the former in terms of current world events, finding that it is unreliable as a foundation for national security.

3563. Morrison, Stanley. "A Collection of Piracy Laws of Various Countries." *American Journal of International Law Supplement* 26 (1932): 887ff.

3564. Mueller, Carol. "The Potential of Riot Violence as a Political Resource." Paper presented at the Annual Meeting of the American Sociological Association, August 1975, at San Francisco, California. Available as FAR 23001-N.

3565. Muller, E. N. "Test of a Partial Theory of Potential for Political Violence." *American Political Science Review* 66 (September 1972): 928-959.

3566. Nardin, Terry. "Conflicting Conceptions of Political Violence." In Cornelius P. Cotter, ed., *Political Science Annual: An International Review*, 4: 75-126. Indianapolis: Bobbs-Merrill, 1973.

3567. ———. "Violence and the State: A Critique of Empirical Political Theory." 2 01-020 *Sage Professional Papers in Comparative Politics* (1971).

3568. Nie, Norman H.; Hull, Hadlai; Jenkins, Jean G.; Steinbrenner, Karin; and Bent, Dale H. *SPSS: Statistical Package for the Social Sciences*, 2d ed. New York: McGraw-Hill, 1975. 675 pp.

The most readable introduction to statistics currently on the market. A knowledge of the package is essential in using ITERATE, which is written with SPSS setups.

3569. Neiburg, Harold L. *Political Violence: The Behavioral Process.* New York: St. Martin's Press, 1969. 184 pp.

Discusses the relevance of violence, critiques common theories, and notes process and polity, escalation and reintegration, men, groups, and the state, and the politics of confrontation.

3570. ———. "The Uses of Violence." *Journal of Conflict Resolution* (March 1963): 43-55.

3571. O'Neill, Bard E.; Alberts, D. J.; and Rossetti, Stephen J. *Political Violence and Insurgency: A Comparative Approach.* Boulder, Colo.: Phoenix, 1975.

3572. Parvin, Manoucher. "Economic Determinants of Political Unrest: An Econometric Approach." *Journal of Conflict Resolution* 17 (1973): 271-296.

3573. Passell, Peter, and Taylor, John B. "The Deterrent Effect of Capital Punishment: Another View." *American Economic Review* 67 (June 1977): 445-451.

3574. Patrick, James. *A Glasgow Gang Observed.* London: Byre Methuen, 1973. 256 pp.
Reviewed by Ronald Thomson, "Violent Youth Gangs Change in Glasgow." *Washington Post*, August 17, 1975. Patrick infiltrated one of the hoodlum gangs of Glasgow, attempting to get a look at this subculture. More than fifty groups receive mention.

3575. Patridge, Eric. "History of Pirates." Quarterly Review 262 (1934): 142 ff.

3576. Pearlman, A. L. "Chemical Weapons on the Home Front." *New England Journal of Medicine*, August 21, 1969, pp. 442-443.

3577. Powell, E. H. *The Design of Discord: Studies of Anomie.* New York: Oxford University Press, 1970.

3578. "Principles as to Disruption of the Judicial Process of the American College of Trial Lawyers." *Arkansas Law Review* 24 (1970).

3579. Radzinowicz, Leon. *Ideology and Crime.* New York: Columbia, 1975. 160 pp.

3580. Radzinowicz, Leon, and King, Joan. *The Growth of Crime: The International Experience.* New York: Basic Books, 1977.

3581. Ranly, B. W. "Defining Violence." *Thought* 47 (August 1972): 415-427.

3582. Raser, John. "Theories of Deterrence." *Peace Research Reviews* 3 (February 1969).
Among Raser's insights is that "deterrence is only meaningful in the context of nations' perceptions of one another."

3583. Report of the National Advisory Commission on Civil Disorders. New York: Bantam, 1968. 609 pp.

3584. "The Revolt of the Young Intelligentsia." In R. Aya and N. Miller, eds., *The New American Revolution*. New York: Free Press, 1971.

3585. Rights in Conflict: *The Walker Report to the National Commission on the Causes and Prevention of Violence—The Violent Confrontation of Demonstrators and Police in the Parks and Streets of Chicago during the Week of the Democratic National Convention*. New York: Bantam, 1968. 362 pp.

3586. Robinson, James A. "Crisis Decision-Making: An Inventory and Appraisal of Concepts, Theories, Hypotheses and Techniques of Analysis." *Political Science Annual* 2 (1969-1970): 111-148.

3587. Robinson, J. P. "Public Reaction to Political Protest: Chicago 1968." *Public Opinion Quarterly* 33 (Spring 1970): 1-9.

3588. Rose, T. "Violence as Political Control and Revolt." *International Review of History and Political Science* 5 (1968): 106-141.

3589. Rosenau, James N., ed. *International Aspects of Civil Strife*. Princeton: Princeton University Press, 1964.

3590. Rubenstein, Richard E. *Rebels in Eden: Mass Political Violence in the United States*. Boston: Little, Brown, 1970. 201 pp.

3591. Russett, Bruce M. "Inequality and Instability: The Relation of Land Tenure to Politics." *World Politics* 16 (April 1964): 442-454.

3592. Salerno, R., and Tompkins, J. S. *The Crime Confederation: Cosa Nostra and Allied Operations in Organized Crime*. Garden City. N.Y.: Doubleday, 1969.

3593. Salert, Barbara. *Revolutions and Revolutionaries: Four Theories*. New York: Elsevier, 1976. 170 pp.
     Salert critiques rational choice theory, psychological theory, structural functionalism, and Marxism.

3594. Schelling, Thomas C. "Economics and Criminal Enterprise." *Public Interest* (Spring 1967).

3595. Scheuch, Erwin K. "Cross-National Comparisons Using Aggregate Data: Some Substantive and Methodological Problems." In Richard L. Merritt and Stein Rokkan, eds., *Comparing Nations: The Use of Quantitative Data in Cross-National Research*, pp. 131-167. New Haven: Yale University Press, 1966.

3596. Schmidt, C. F. ''Multidimensional Scaling Analysis of the Printed Media's Explanations of the Riots of the Summer of 1967.'' *Journal of Personality and Social Psychology* 24 (October 1972): 59-67.

3597. Schneider, P. R., and Schneider, A. L. ''Social Mobilization, Political Institutions, Political Violence.'' *Comparative Political Studies* 4 (April 1971): 69-90.

Using ten highly developed nations, the following independent variables were used to predict political violence: institutionalization, social mobilization, economic development, ratio of social mobilization to institutionalization, and the ratio of social mobilization to economic development. 95 percent of the variance was accounted for. Authors concluded that political violence is more apt to occur in those nations where change is outrunning the development of adaptable, legitimate, and complex institutions.

3598. Schurman, F. ''On Revolutionary Conflict.'' *Journal of International Affairs* 23 (1969): 36-53.

3599. Schwartz, David C. ''On the Ecology of Political Violence: 'The Long Hot Summer' as a Hypothesis.'' *American Behavioral Scientist* 11 (July-August 1968): 24-28.

3600. Schwartz, M. M. ''The Use of Force and the Dilemma of Violence.'' *Psychoanalytic Review* 59 (1972-1973): 617-625.

3601. Scolnick, Jr., Joseph M. ''An Appraisal of Studies of the Linkage between Domestic and International Conflict.'' *Comparative Political Studies* 6 (1974): 485-510.

3602. Shaffer, Jerome A., ed. *Violence: Award-Winning Essays in the Council for Philosophical Studies Competition.* New York: David McKay, 1971.

3603. Short, Jr., James F., ed. *Modern Criminals.* New Brunswick, N.J.: Transaction Books, 1973. 302 pp.

Articles include works on public and criminal responses to disasters, assassinations in the Middle East, and war crimes.

3604. Sigmeth, G. F.; Dean, G. L.; and Patula, E. F. ''A Note on Lacrimator Weapons.'' *American Journal of Hospital Pharmacy* 26 (January 1969): 41-42.

3605. Skolnick, Jerome H. *The Politics of Protest: A Report Submitted by the Task Force on Violent Aspects of Protest and Confrontation of the National*

Commission on the Causes and Prevention of Violence. New York: Ballantine, 1969. 420 pp.

3606. Snyder, D., and Tilly, Charles. "Hardship and Collective Violence in France, 1830 to 1960." *American Sociological Review* 37 (October 1972): 520-532.

3607. Sperber, Manes. "Violence from Below." *Survey* 18 (Summer 1972): 189-204.

3608. Spiegel, J. P. "The Dynamics of Violent Confrontation." *International Journal of Psychiatry* 10 (September 1972): 93-108.

3609. ———. "Theories of Violence: An Integrated Approach." *International Journal of Group Tensions* 1 (January-March 1971): 77-90.

3610. Stark, M. J.; Raine, W. J.; Burbeck, S. L.; and Davison, K. K. "Some Empirical Patterns in a Riot Process." *American Sociological Review* 39 (December 1974): 865-876.

3611. Starr, Richard F., ed. *Yearbook of International Communist Affairs, 1974*. Stanford: Hoover Institution Press, 1974.

3612. Stone, Lawrence. "Theories of Revolution." *World Politics* 18 (1966): 159-176.

3613. Strauss, Harlan. "Revolutionary Types." *Journal of Conflict Resolution* 17 (1973).

3614. Sutherland, E. H. and Cressey, D. *Criminology*. 8th ed. Philadelphia: J. B. Lippincott, 1970.

3615. Tanter, Raymond. "International Crises Behavior: An Appraisal of the Literature." *Jerusalem Journal of International Relations* 3 (Winter-Spring 1978): 340ff.

3616. Tanter, Raymond and Midlarsky, Manus. "A Theory of Revolution." *Journal of Conflict Resolution* 3 (September 1967): 264-280.
    Four types of revolution—palace revolution, reform coup, revolutionary coup, and mass revolution—are ordered on the basis of increasing intensity. The Cuban revolution provides support for the hypothesis that revolution intensity, measured by level of domestic violence, is associated with a long-term increase in achievement, followed by a reversal in expectations im-

mediately prior to the revolution. Correlational analysis provides evidence that the intensity of Asian revolutions in general and Middle Eastern revolutions in particular is associated with the rate of increase in economic development (a measure of achievement) prior to the revolution. Educational attainment is found to be inversely related to revolutionary intensity. With the exception of Cuba, none of these findings applies to Latin America. Societies that underwent successful revolutions in the period under investigation (1955-1960) experienced significantly lower expectations, as measured by the Gini index, than did countries that had no successful revolutions. A derivative finding is that the causes of palace revolution may differ from those of the other forms of revolution.

3617. Taylor, Charles Lewis, and Hudson, Michael C. *World Handbook of Political and Social Indicators*, 2d ed. New Haven: Yale University Press, 1972. 443 pp.

This is the most widely respected academic compilation of characteristics of national entities. A computer data set is available from the Inter-University Consortium for Political and Social Research.

3618. Tedeschi, J. T., et al. "A Paradigm for the Study of Coercive Power." *Journal of Conflict Resolution* (1971).

3619. Terchek, Ronald. "Personal Violence and Political Violence: In Search of Linkages." Paper presented to the panel on Violence and Terror of the Conference on Complexity: A Challenge to the Adaptive Capacity of American Society, sponsored by the Society for General Systems Research, March 24-26, 1977, at Columbia, Maryland.

Using correlation analysis of survey responses, Terchek finds little relation between experience of violence and political attitudes and gives several reasons for this conclusion.

3620. Tilly, Charles. "The Analysis of a Counter-Revolution." *History and Theory* 3 (1963): 30-58.

3621. ———. "Revolutions and Collective Violence." In Nelson Polsby and Fred Greenstein, eds., *Handbook of Political Science*, vol. 3: *Macropolitical Theory*, pp. 483-555. Reading, Mass.: Addison-Wesley, 1975.

3622. Tobin, R. L. "More Violent Than Ever: Preoccupation with Bad News in the Mass Media." *Saturday Review*, November 9, 1968, pp. 79-80.

3623. Todoroff, Kostia. "The Macedonian Organization Yesterday and Today." *Foreign Affairs* 6 (1928): 473-482.

3624. Trice, Robert H. "The Political Activities of Non-Governmental Actors Project: Codebook and Manual." Ohio State University, Department of Political Science, January 1976. Available as FAR 24657-N.

3625. Tullock, Gordon. "The Paradox of Revolution." *Public Choice* 11 (Fall 1971): 89-99.

3626. Turner, R. H. "The Public Perception of Protest." *American Sociological Review* 34 (December 1969): 815-831.

3627. Tyler, G. *Organized Crime in America.* Ann Arbor: University of Michigan Press, 1962.

3628. U.S. National Commission on the Causes and Prevention of Violence. *Staff Reports.* Washington, D.C.: U.S. Government Printing Office, 1969.

Volumes 1 and 2: Hugh Davis Graham and Ted Rober Gurr, *Violence in America: Historical and Comparative Perspectives*; Volume 3: Jerome H. Skolnick, *The Politics of Protest*; Volume 4: *Rights in Concord: Response to Counter-Inaugural Protest Activities in Washington, D.C., January 18-20, 1969*; Volume 5: Louis H. Masotti and Jerome R. Corsi, *Shoot-Out in Cleveland: Black Militants and Police*; Volume 6: William H. Orrick, Jr., *Shut it Down! A College in Crisis: San Francisco State College*; Volume 7: George D. Newton, Jr. and Franklin E. Zimring, *Firearms and Violence in American Life*; Volume 8: James F. Kirkham, Sheldon G. Levy and William J. Crotty, *Assassination and Political Violence*; Volume 9: David L. Lange, R. K. Baker, and S. J. Ball, *Mass Media and Violence: A Report*; Volume 10: James S. Campbell, Joseph R. Sahid, and David P. Stang, *Law and Order Reconsidered*; Volumes 11-13: Donald J. Mulvihill, Melvin M. Tumin, and Lynn A. Curtis, *Crimes of Violence.*

3629. ———. *To Establish Justice, to Protect Domestic Tranquility: Final Report.* New York: Bantam, 1970.

The Eisenhower commission report, noting that violence is a historical phenomenon in America, suggests a number of solutions.

3630. Verkko, V. "General Theoretical Viewpoints in Criminal Statistics Regarding Real Crime." In *Transactions of the Westermarck Society*, pp. 47-75. Copenhagen: Munksgaard, 1953.

3631. ———. "Survey of Current Practice in Criminal Statistics." *Transactions of the Westermarck Society*, 3:5-33. Copenhagen: Munksgaard, 1956.

3632. Vold, G. B. *Theoretical Criminology.* New York: Oxford University Press, 1958.

3633. The Vulnerability of the Computerized Society. Stockholm: Ministry of Defense, Preliminary Report by a Swedish Government Committee, 1978.

A survey of how dependent Swedish society is upon computers and how military organizations or terrorist groups could attack computer facilities, with the aim of destroying hardware and information, or tapping that information.

3634. Wade, Francis C. ''On Violence.'' *Journal of Philosophy* 68 (June 1971): 369-377.

3635. Wade, Nicholas. ''Going Public with VX Formula—A Recipe for Trouble?'' *Science*, February 7, 1975, p. 414.

Recent studies have shown that it is possible to make VX, a deadly nerve agent, with recently declassified information.

3636. Walter, Eugene Victor. ''Power and Violence.'' *American Political Science Review* 24 (June 1964): 350-355.

3637. Ward, W. J. ''Dimethyl Sulfoxide: A New Threat in Public Figure Protection.'' *Assets Protection* 1 (1976): 11-15.

Considers the possibility of mixing poison with DMSO, which is absorbed through the skin. Such attacks on public figures are viewed as remote though not impossible.

3638. Weil, Herman M. ''Domestic and International Violence: A Forecasting Approach.'' *Futures* (December 1974): 477-485.

Consolidated Analysis Centers is attempting to use futures research to ιook at nonenvironmental issues of politics and the military. A regression-based forecasting model and simulations are used to generate long-range forecasts for Europe.

3639. Weiss, Edith Brown. ''Weather Control: An Instrument for War?'' *Survival* 17 (March-April 1975): 64-68.

Weiss observes that small-scale fog dispersal, rainfall stimulation, typhoon modification, diversion of the jet stream, and the melting of polar ice could all be used as weapons in the future. She discusses such techniques and their military applications, deterrence, and diplomatic initiatives on these questions.

3640. Werthan, F. *A Sign for Cain: An Exploration of Human Violence.* New York: Macmillan, 1966.

3641. West, D. J.; Wiles, P.; and Stanwood, C. *Research on Violence.* London: University of Cambridge Institute of Criminology, n.d.

3642. West, Louis. "Cults and Liberty: Guyana and Mind Control in Light of the First Amendment." Paper presented to the Conference on the Moral Implications of Terrorism, March 14-16, 1979, at UCLA.

3643. Whang, Paul K. "Anti-Piracy Measures." *China Weekly Review,* September 2, 1933, p. 24.

3644. Wheeler, S. "Criminal Statistics: A Reformulation of the Problem." *Journal of Criminal Law and Criminology* 58 (1967): 317-324.

3645. White, A. G., and Vance, M. " Organized Violence in Urban Areas: A Selected Bibliography." Washington, D.C.: Council of Planning Librarians, 1973. Includes 135 references.

3646. Whiteside, Thomas. *The Pendulum and the Toxic Cloud: The Course of Dioxin Contamination.* New Haven: Yale University Press, 1979.
Reviewed by Odom Fanning, *Washington Post Book World* April 15, 1979, p. H5. Whiteside visited Seveso, Italy, the scene on July 10, 1976, of an industrial accident that released a herbicide on the town.

3647. Wilcox, Leslie D.; Brooks, Ralph M.; Beal, George M.; and Klonglan, Gerald E. *Social Indicators and Societal Monitoring: An Annotated Bibliography.* San Francisco: Jossey-Bass, 1972. 464 pp.
A computer printout of items that primarily concentrate on measures of domestic activities.

3648. Wilkinson, Burke, ed. *Cry Sabotage.* Scarsdale, N.Y.: Bradbury, 1972. 265 pp.

3649. Wilkinson, Paul. "Social Scientific Theory and Civil Violence." In Yonah Alexander, David Carlton, and Paul Wilkinson, eds., *Terrorism: Theory and Practice,* pp. 45-72. Boulder: Westview, 1979.
Wilkinson debunks many popular theories (such as those of Freud, Dollard, Lorenz, Gurr, and Skinner) on the causes of violent behavior.

3650. Williams, Peter C. "Rights and the Alleged Right of Innocents to Be Killed." *Ethics* 87 (July 1977): 383ff.

3651. Williams, R. W.; Burns, G. P.; Anderson, M.; Reading, G. P.; Border, J. R.; Mindell, E. R.; and Schenk, Jr., W. G. "Mass Casualties in a Maximum Security Institution." *Annals of Surgery* 179 (May 1974): 592-597.

3652. Wolf, P. "Crime and Development: An International Comparison of Crime Rates." *Scandinavian Studies in Criminology* 3 (1971): 107-121.

3653. Wolff, Robert P. "On Violence." *Journal of Philosophy* 66 (October 1969): 601-616.

3654. Wolfgang, M. "International Crime Statistics: A Proposal." *Journal of Criminal Law, Criminology, and Police Science* 58 (1967): 65-69.

3655. Worchel, Philip; Hester, Philip G.; and Kopala, Philip S. "Collective Protest and Legitimacy of Authority: Theory and Research." *Journal of Conflict Resolution* 18 (March 1974): 37-54.

3656. Yablonsky, Lewis. *The Violent Gang.* Baltimore: Penguin, 1966. 256 pp.
    A study of violent urban youth culture.

3657. Yough, Syng Nam. "Political Violence: A Cross National Analysis." Ph.D. dissertation, Texas Tech University, in preparation.

3658. Zartman, I. William, ed. *The 50% Solution: How to Bargain Successfully with Hijackers, Strikers, Bosses, Oil Magnates, Arabs, Russians, and Other Worthy Opponents in This Modern World.* Garden City: Anchor, 1975.

3659. ———. "Negotiations as a Communications Process." Paper presented at the annual meeting of the American Political Science Association, September 3, 1976, at Chicago.
    Argues that most theories of negotiations miss empirical patterns of the process. He suggests that the prevailing models are coalition (numerical aggregation, judication), hierarchical selection, and negotiation (value combination). A concession-convergence approach (formula/detail) reflects reality more accurately.

3660. Zimring, Frank. "Is Gun Control Likely to Reduce Violent Killings?" *University of Chicago Law Review* 35 (Summer 1968): 721-737.
    Using aggregate data on crime, Zimring compares the murderous intent of knife and gun wielders.

EVENTS DATA RESEARCH

3661. Aldrich, John and Cnudde, Charles F. "Probing the Bounds of Conventional Wisdom: A Comparison of Regression, Probit, and Discriminant Analysis." *American Journal of Political Science* 19 (August 1975): 571-608.

A very useful article showing which technique is appropriate and most powerful, depending upon the level of measurement and research question involved.

3662. Andriole, Stephen J., and Daly, Judith Ayres. "Computerized Crisis Forecasting." *Air Force Magazine* (July 1979): pp. 88-92.

A discussion of how the Advanced Research Projects Agency plans to develop software for the World Event/Interaction Survey (WEIS) data set.

3663. Attina, Fulvio A. "Analysis of International Events: An Application for Descriptive Purposes of Edward Azar's Thirteen-Point Scale." *International Interactions* 2 (1976): 121-124.

3664. Azar, Edward E. "Analysis of International Events." *Peace Research Reviews* 4 (November 1970).

Azar summarizes the work of the WEIS project and shows how his research at Michigan State is complementary to WEIS by measuring events rather than classifying them. Differences among coders regarding sex, age, education, and specialization are noted, as well as problems of source coverage. Azar then shows applications of event data analysis, such as his three-phase model of voluntary political unification and his signal accounting model.

3665. ———. "Behavioral Forecasts and Policy-making: An Events Data Approach." In Charles W. Kegley, Jr., Gregory A. Raymond, Robert M. Rood, and Richard A. Skinner, eds., *International Events and the Comparative Analysis of Foreign Policy*, pp. 215-239. Columbia: South Carolina University Press, 1975.

After a review of suggestions that have been made in the evaluation of forecasting models, Azar discusses the creation of his signal accounting model, based upon the Conflict and Peace Data Bank (COPDAB) project's data.

3666. ———. "The Dimensionality of Violent Conflict: A Quantitative Analysis." Paper presented to the conference on the Middle East Conflict, Peace Research Society (International), June 1970, at Cambridge, Massachusetts.

3667. ———. "An Early Warning System of Internation Violence." Paper presented to the conference on Forecasting in International Relations, Peace Research Society (International), 1973, at Cambridge, Massachusetts.

3668. ———. "The Problem of Source Coverage in the Use of Events Data." *International Studies Quarterly* 16 (December 1969).

3669. ———. "Profiling and Predicting Patterns of Inter-Nation Interactions: A Signal Accounting Model." Paper presented to the 66th annual convention of the American Political Science Association, September 7-12, 1970, at Los Angeles, California.

3670. ———. "The Quantification of Events for the Analysis of Conflict Resolution." Paper presented to the 7th Research Conference, Peace Research Society (International), November 1969, at Ann Arbor, Michigan.

3671. ———. "Quantitative Events Research at the University of North Carolina." *International Studies Notes* 1 (Spring 1974): 28-30.

3672. Azar, Edward E., and Ben-Dak, Joseph D., eds. *Theory and Practice of Events Research.* New York: Gordon and Breach, 1975.

3673. Azar, Edward E.; Bennett, J.; and Sloan, T. "Steps Toward Forecasting Models of International Interaction." Paper presented to the North American Peace Science Conference, Peace Science Society (International) 1973 at Cambridge, Massachusetts.

3674. Azar, Edward E.; Cohen, Stanley H.; Jukam, Thomas H.; and McCormick, James M. "Methodological Developments in the Quantification of Events Data." Paper presented to the Michigan State University International Events Data Conference, April 15-16, 1970, at East Lansing, Michigan. Published as Michigan State University Cooperation/Conflict Research Group Report 70-2. Republished as "Making and Measuring the International Event as a Unit of Analysis," in "International Events Interaction Analysis: Some Research Considerations," 1, 02-001 *Sage Professional Papers in International Studies* (1972), pp. 59-77.

The authors describe the development of their conflict and peace data bank, detailing their thirteen-point scale, types of data sources, and demographic factors, which determine reliability between coders.

3675. ———. "The Problem of Source Coverage in the Use of International Events Data." *International Studies Quarterly* 16 (September 1972): 373-388.

A comparison of the *New York Times* and *Middle East Journal*'s coverage of that region, with substantive and methodological issues discussed.

3676. Azar, Edward E., and Koeller, G. "The Potential of Events Research in International Relations." Paper presented to the British Section of the Peace Science Society (International) Annual Convention, August 25-26, 1972, at London.

3677. Azar, Edward E., and Sloan, Thomas J. *Dimensions of Interaction: A Source Book for the Study of the Behavior of 31 Nations from 1948 through 1973.* International Studies Occasional Paper No. 8, 1975. 537 pp.

A description of Azar's conflict and peace data bank.

3678. Banks, Arthur S., and Textor, Robert B. *A Cross-Polity Survey.* Cambridge: MIT Press, 1963. 1386 pp.

An early attempt to quantify the attributes of nations.

3679. Beal, Richard. "Systems Analysis of International Crises: Event Analysis of Nine Pre-Crisis Threat Situations, 1948-1962." Ph.D. dissertation, University of Southern California. 1977.

3680. Blake, D. H. "The Identification of Foreign Policy Output." Paper presented to the meeting of the Midwest Political Science Association, 1969, at Ann Arbor, Michigan.

3681. Bloomfield, Lincoln P.; Beattie, Robert; and Moulton, G. Allen, with Mandel, Robert M.; and Spear, John J. "Revised CASCON II: Computer-Aided System for Handling Information on Local Conflicts, Users' Manual." Cambridge, Mass.: Arms Control Project, Center for International Studies, MIT, C/72-14, September 1972.

Explains how to use a fifty-two-case data set on conflicts, including a long listing of conflict-reducing policies that can be tested.

3682. Bobrow, Davis B. "Data Banks, Foreign Affairs, and Feasible Change." Paper presented to the Conference on Data Banks for International Studies, 1971, at Washington, D.C.

3683. ———. "International Indicators." Paper presented to the annual convention of the American Political Science Association, September 1969, at New York City.

3684. Brey, Gary G. ''Event Data Reliability: A Computer Coding Technique.'' Paper presented to the annual meeting of the International Studies Association, February 1975, at Washington, D.C. Available as FAR 22460-P.

3685. Brody, Richard A. ''International Events: Problems of Measurement and Analysis.'' Paper delivered to the Events Data Conference, April 15-16, 1970, at Michigan State University. A revised version appeared in ''International Events Interaction Analysis: Some Research Considerations'' 1, 02-001 *Sage Professional Papers in International Studies* (1972), pp. 45-58.

Discusses the uses of event data, the units of analysis, and the question of unidimensionality of acts. Brody notes the problem of distinguishing between the same act emanating from different sources, whether acts that come from the area of shared repertoire but that represent different levels of effort for two nations should be considered the same, and assumptions of independence of events. He notes that the relaxation of the latter assumption entails ''an absolute and total prohibition against tests of significance based on independent probability models for any score, mean, and so on. It directs our attention to difference scores, change scores, or other measures which are independent of the trend.'' He also suggests that this means we might question our unit of analysis, offering discrepancies from trends, ranges on dimensions, and the most prominent act in a period as candidates. He suggests that we should consider the context of the sequence of signals between nations in analyzing events.

3686. ———. ''Problems in the Measurement and Analysis of International Events.'' In Charles W. Kegley, Jr., Gregory A. Raymond, Robert M. Rood, and Richard A. Skinner, eds., *International Events and the Comparative Analysis of Foreign Policy*. Columbia: University of South Carolina Press, 1975.

A revision of his Sage Professional Paper.

3687. Burgess, Phillip M. ''Nation-Typing for Foreign Policy Analysis: A Partitioning Procedure for Constructing Typologies.'' In E. H. Fedder, ed., *Methodological Concerns in International Studies*, pp. 3-66. St. Louis: Center for International Studies, University of Missouri, 1970.

3688. Burgess, Phillip M., and Lawton, Raymond W. ''Evaluating Events Data: Problems of Conception, Reliability, and Validity.'' In Charles W. Kegley, Jr., Gregory A. Raymond, Robert M. Rood, and Richard A. Skinner, eds., *International Events and the Comparative Analysis of Foreign Policy*. Columbia: South Carolina, 1975.

A revision of their Sage paper, excluding several of the original's tables.

3689. ———. ''Indicators of International Behavior: An Assessment of Events Data Research.'' 1, 02-010 *Sage Professional Papers in International Studies* (1972).

Survey of the major events data studies, showing criteria for comparisons of the data sets, and evaluating the overall direction of this field. A very extensive bibliography is appended, including preliminary research results, prospectus drafts, and similar material.

3690. ———. ''The Study of International Events Behavior.'' In Edward Azar and Joseph D. Ben-Dak, eds., *International Events*. New York: Gordon and Breach, 1973.

3691. Burgess, Phillip M.; Lawton, Raymond W.; and Kridler, T. P. ''Indicators of International Behavior: An Overview and Re-examination of Micro-Macro Designs.'' Paper presented to the International Studies Association annual convention, March 14-18, 1972, at Dallas, Texas.

3692. Burgess, Phillip M., and Munton, D. J. ''An Inventory of Archived and Fugitive International Relations Data.'' Paper presented to the Conference on Data Banks in International Studies, May 1971, at Washington, D.C.

3693. Burrowes, Robert. ''I Dreamt I Was Collecting and Coding Event Data in my Matrix-Form Brain.'' Paper presented to the annual meeting of the International Studies Assocation. 1970, at Pittsburgh, Pennsylvania.

3694. ———. ''Multiple Time-Series Analysis of Nation-Level Data.'' *Comparative Political Studies* 2 (January 1970): 465-480.

Argues that political research is moving toward the consideration of questions that would make time-series studies appropriate and advantageous.

3695. ———. ''Problems of International Events Coverage.'' Paper presented to the Michigan State University International Events Data Analysis Conference, April 1971, at East Lansing, Michigan.

3696. Burrowes, Robert; Muzzio, D.; and Spector, B. ''Mirror, Mirror, on the Wall . . .: A Source Comparison Study of Inter-Nation Event Data.'' Paper presented to the International Studies Association Annual Convention, March 1971, at San Juan, Puerto Rico. Reprinted as Robert Burrowes, ''Mirror, Mirror, on the Wall . . . A Comparison of Event Data Sources,'' in James J. Rosenau, ed., *Comparing Foreign Policies* (New York: Wiley, 1974), pp. 383-406.

Compares the individual event yields of several sources of event data for their absolute yields, unique contribution to a data pool, effectiveness when used with other sources, types of selective reporting regarding types of events and targets of coverage, and ease of use of sources. The Middle East Conflict and Cooperation Analysis (MECCA) project used *Cahiers de l'orient contemporain*, the *New York Times* index, the *New York Times* daily edition, the *Middle East Journal*, the *Times of London* daily edition, the *Asian Recorder, Facts on File, Keesings' Contemporary Archives*, and *Deadline Data*, with their total yield of all events being in that order. He concludes that source selection will affect substantive conclusions, and that using even three sources will greatly increase dataset validity.

3697. Burrowes, Robert; Muzzio, D.; and Spector, B. "Sources of Middle East International Event Data." *Middle East Studies Association Bulletin* 5 (May 1971): 54-71.

3698. Calhoun, Herbert L. "Exploratory Applications to Scaled Event Data." Paper presented to the International Studies Association Annual Convention, March 15-17, 1972, at Dallas, Texas.

3699. ———. "The Measurement and Scaling of Event Data Using the Semantic Differential with Theoretical Applications." Ph.D. dissertation, University of Southern California, 1977.

3700. ———. "A Situational and Psychological Analysis of Events." Paper presented to the 19th annual convention of the International Studies Association, February 22-25, 1978, at Washington, D.C.

3701. Chessler, R. "INTERACT: A Computer Model for International Behavior." Paper presented to the Michigan State University International Events Data Analysis Conference, April 1971.

3702. Corson, Walter. "Conflict and Cooperation in East-West Crises: Measurement and Prediction." Paper presented to the Michigan State University International Events Data Conference, April 1970.

3703. ———. "Conflict and Cooperation in East-West Relations: Measurement and Explanation." Paper presented to the American Political Science Association annual convention, September 1970, at Los Angeles, California.

3704. ———. "Measuring Conflict and Cooperation Intensity in International Relations." Paper presented to the Michigan State University International Events Data Conference, March 1969.

3705. ———. ''Measuring Conflict and Cooperation Intensity in East-West Relations: A Manual and Codebook.'' Mimeographed. University of Michigan, 1970.

3706. Deutsch, Karl W., and Merritt, Richard L. ''Effects of Events on National and International Images.'' In Herbert Kelman, ed., *International Behavior: A Social-Psychological Analysis.* New York: Holt, Rinehart, and Winston, 1965.

3707. Doran, Charles F.; Pendley, Robert E.; and Antunes, George E. ''Reliability of Cross-National Measures of Civil Strife and Instability Events: A Comparison of Indigenous and Secondary Sources.'' Paper presented to the International Studies Association annual convention, March 1971, at San Juan, Puerto Rico.

3708. ———. ''A Test of Cross-National Event Reliability: Global Versus Regional Data Sources.'' *International Studies Quarterly* 17 (June 1973): 175-203.

Using sophisticated statistical techniques, a comparison was made of the Feierabends' data with those collected by the authors. Issues related to the proportional and nonproportional bias in data are discussed.

3709. Dow, John; Taylor, Charles L.; Russett, Bruce M.; and Sullivan, John D. ''Computer Routines for Arraying Aggregate Data.'' *International Studies Quarterly* 16 (September 1972): 389-398.

A description of the computer programs that accompany the second version of the *World Handbook*, which include capabilities to compare events cross-nationally.

3710. East, Maurice A.; and Salmore, Stephen A.; eds. *Theoretical Bases for Comparative Foreign Policy Studies.* Beverly Hills: Sage, 1976.

3711. Eley, J. W. ''Events Data and Foreign Policy Theory: An Analysis of American Foreign Policy Toward Internal Wars, 1945-1970.'' Paper presented to the meeting of the International Studies Association, 1973, New York City.

3712. Farley, L. T. ''Situational Dimensions in the Scaling of Event Data.'' Paper presented to the International Studies Association-West Annual Meeting, March 22-24, 1972, at Portland, Oregon.

3713. Feierabend, Ivo K., and Feierabend, Rosalind E. *A Cross-National Data Bank of Political Instability Events.* San Diego: San Diego State College, Public Affairs Research Institute, January 1965.

3714. Fitzsimmons, B.; Hoggard, Gary; McClelland, Charles; Martin, W.; and Young, R. "World Event-Interaction Survey Handbook and Codebook." World Event/Interaction Survey Technical Report 1, University of Southern California, January 1969.

3715. Fowler, William Warner. "Data Bases and Information Processing Systems: Developing a Semantics of International Relations Data." Paper presented to the annual meeting of the International Studies Association, February 22-25, 1978, at Washington, D.C.

Argues that rectangular data structures must be replaced by hierarchical systems.

3716. Funkhouser, G. R., and Parker, E. B. "Analyzing Coding Reliability: The Random-Systematic-Error Coefficient." *Public Opinion Quarterly* 32 (Spring 1968): 122-128.

3717. Galtung, Johan, and Ruge, Mari Holmboe. "The Structure of Foreign News." *Journal of Peace Research* 2 (1965): 64-91.

3718. Gurr, Ted Robert. "The Neo-Alexandrians: A Review Essay on Data Handbooks in Political Science." *American Political Science Review* 68 (March 1974): 252-254.

3719. Hayes, Richard E. "Identifying and Measuring Changes in the Frequency of Event Data." *International Studies Quarterly* 17 (December 1973): 471-493.

Looks at the problem of identification and measurement of changes in event data, suggesting that characteristics of event data sets reduce the utility of traditional measures and that the Poisson-based comparison avoids this problem.

3720. Hazelwood, Leo A., and West, Gerald T. "Bivariate Associations, Factor Structures, and Substantive Impact: The Source Coverage Problem Revisited." *International Studies Quarterly* 18 (September 1974): 317-337.

The authors argue that there is little impact of source differences upon pattern delineation and general hypothesis testing.

3721. Hermann, Charles F. "Bureaucratic Politics and Foreign Policy: A Theoretical Framework Using Events Data." Paper presented to the annual meeting of the International Studies Association, 1973, at New York City.

3722. ———. "Comparing the Foreign Policy Events of Nations." In Charles W. Kegley, Jr., Gregory A. Raymond, Robert M. Rood, and Richard A.

Skinner, eds., *International Events and the Comparative Analysis of Foreign Policy*, pp. 145-158. Columbia: South Carolina University Press, 1975.

Hermann used typologies by Rosenau to create eight basic nation types. He then used CREON data to note differences in the types of actions such nations engage in.

3723. ———. "Conceptualizing Foreign Policy Behavior Using Events Data." In James N. Rosenau, ed., *In Search of Global Patterns*, pp. 354-360. New York: Free Press, 1976.

A how-we-did-it piece on the CREON project.

3724. ———. "Policy Classification: A Key to the Comparative Study of Foreign Policy." In James N. Rosenau, Vincent Davis, and Maurice A. East, eds., *The Analysis of International Politics*, pp. 58-79. New York: Free Press, 1972.

3725. ———. "What Is a Foreign Policy Event?" In W. F. Hanrieder, ed., *Comparative Foreign Policy*, pp. 395-421. New York: David McKay, 1971.

Thirty-six rules on coding foreign policy events.

3726. Hermann, Charles F., and Salmore, Stephen. "Coding Events: A First Step in the Comparative Study of Foreign Policy." Paper presented to the International Studies Association annual convention, April 1970, at Pittsburgh, Pennsylvania.

3727. ———. "The Recipients of Foreign Policy Events." Paper presented to the annual convention of the Peace Research Society, 1971, at Ann Arbor, Michigan.

3728. Hermann, Charles F.; Salmore, Stephen A.; and East, Maurice. "Comparing Foreign Policy Behavior with Events Data." Paper presented to the Michigan State University International Events Data Analysis Conference, April 1971.

3729. Hoggard, Gary D. "An Analysis of the 'Real' Data: Reflections on the Uses and Validity of International Interaction Data." Paper presented to the International Studies Association annual convention, March 17, 1972, at Dallas, Texas.

3730. ———. "Differential Source Coverage in Foreign Policy Analysis." In James N. Rosenau, ed., *Comparing Foreign Policies: Theories, Findings, and Methods*, pp. 353-381. New York: Wiley, 1974.

Compares four major data sources for one major international relations episode and finds that one's conclusions change depending upon the source used for data. Deadline Data was found to be particularly deficient in its addition to the coverage sources.

3731. Holsti, K. J. "The Use of Objective Criteria for the Measurement of International Tension Levels." *Background* 7 (August 1963): 77-95.

3732. Howell, Llewellyn D. "A Comparative Study of the WEIS and COPDAB Data Sets." Paper presented to the 1979 annual convention of the International Studies Association.

3733. Jukam, Thomas. "Computer-Based Scaling of International Events." Paper presented to the Michigan State University International Events Data Analysis Conference, April 1971.

3734. Kegley, Jr., Charles W. "The Generation and Use of Events Data." In Charles W. Kegley Jr., Gregory A. Raymond, Robert M. Rood, and Richard A. Skinner, eds., *International Events and the Comparative Analysis of Foreign Policy*, pp. 91-105. Columbia: South Carolina University Press, 1975.
Reviews the literature of events data, noting that the field has been more concerned with problems of cleaning data than with substantive conclusions. Kegley points out the limits of the uses of events data and that such research must be bolstered by other considerations. Events data cannot by itself give a general theory of foreign policy.

3735. ———. "Selective Attention: A General Characteristic of the Interactive Behavior of Nations." Paper presented to the 1974 meeting of the Southern Political Science Association, at New Orleans.

3736. Kegley, Jr., Charles W.; Raymond, Gregory A.; Rood, Robert M.; and Skinner, Richard A., eds., *International Events and the Comparative Analysis of Foreign Policy*. Columbia: South Carolina University Press, 1975.

3737. Kegley, Jr., Charles W.; Salmore, Stephen A.; and Rosen, D. "Convergence in the Measurement of Interstate Behavior." In Patrick J. McGowan, ed., *Sage Yearbook of Foreign Policy Studies*, 2: 309-342. Beverly Hills: Sage, 1974.

3738. Lanphier, V. "Foreign Relations Indicator Project." Paper presented to the International Studies Association annual convention, March 1972, at Dallas, Texas.

3739. Leng, Russell. "The Future of Events Data Marriage: A Question of Compatability." *International Interactions* 2 (1975).

3740. ———. "Problems in Events Data Availability and Analysis." Paper presented to the New England Political Science Association annual convention, April 1972, at Kingston, Rhode Island. April 1972.

3741. Leng, Russell, and Singer, J. David. "Toward a Multi-Theoretical Typology of International Behavior." Paper presented to the Michigan State University International Events Data Conference, April 1970.

3742. Markham, J. W. "Foreign News in the U.S. and South American Presses." *Public Opinion Quarterly* 25 (Summer 1961): 249-262.

3743. McClelland, Charles A. "Access to Berlin: The Quantity and Variety of Events, 1948-1963." In J. David Singer, ed., *Quantitative International Politics: Insights and Evidence*, pp. 159-186. New York: Free Press, 1968.

3744. ———. "Action Structures and Communication in Two International Crises: Quemoy and Berlin." *Background* 7 (February 1964): 201-215.

3745. ———. "The Acute International Crisis." *World Politics* 14 (October (1961): 182-204.

3746. ———. "D-Files for Monitoring and Forecasting Threats and Problems Abroad." Paper presented to the annual convention of the International Studies Association, 1978, at Washington, D.C.
    McClelland notes several disadvantages of the WEIS (and other) events data files that miss the important details of certain situations. D-Files would be aimed at spotting trends that may be clues in predicting future disasters.

3747. ———. "An Inside Appraisal of the WEIS." In James N. Rosenau, ed., *In Search of Global Patterns*, pp. 105-111. New York: Free Press, 1976.
    An impressionistic essay reviewing the course of the WEIS project, from McClelland's initial readings of the original general systems theorists to the data collection and analysis with a number of his graduate students.

3748. ———. "Some Effects on Theory from the International Event Analysis Movement." In "International Events Interaction Analysis: Some Research Considerations" 1, 02-001 *Sage Professional Papers in International Studies* (1972), pp. 15-43. Originally appeared as a paper delivered to the Events Data Conference, April 15-16, 1970, at Michigan State University.

Finds events studies to be a rediscovery of international relations as a historical discipline. Discusses how this new focus may aid in studying international conflict, the international system, and foreign policy.

3749. ———. "Some Local Properties in International Event Flows." Paper presented to the 19th annual convention of the International Studies Association, February 22-25, 1978, at Washington, D.C.

3750. McClelland, Charles A., and Hoggard, Gary D. "Conflict Patterns in the Interactions Among Nations." In James N. Rosenau, ed., *International Politics and Foreign Policy*, pp. 711-724. New York: Free Press, 1969.

3751. McClelland, Charles A.; McGowan, Patrick J.; and Martin, Wayne R. "Threat, Conflict and Commitment: Threat Recognition and Analysis Project." University of Southern California, Department of International Relations, ONR contract NR 170/773, September 1976.

The authors show how to monitor a nation's "threat burden" through the use of dangers files. Southern Africa is used as an example.

3752. McClelland, Charles A.; Tomlinson, Rodney G.; Sherwin, R. G.; Hill, G. A.; Calhoun, Herbert L.; Fenn, P. H.; and Martin, J. D. *The Management and Analysis of International Event Data: A Computerized System for Monitoring and Projecting Event Flows*. Los Angeles: University of Southern California Press, 1971. 383 pp.

A report on WEIS methods of data collection, storage, analysis, and simulation.

3753. McGowan, Patrick J. "A Bayesian Approach to the Problem of Events Data Validity." In James N. Rosenau, ed., *Comparing Foreign Policies: Theories, Findings and Methods*, pp. 407-433. New York: Wiley, 1974.

Reviews the previous source coverage literature, noting that sources vary on their total event yields and do not overlap in their coverage. Disagreeing with the rest of the field, McGowan argues that merely increasing the total number of events counted does not increase content validity. Rather one should note how the data alters our posterior probabilities (Bayesian degrees of certainty) about specified substantive hypotheses. Data sets that strengthen our prior beliefs have content validity.

3754. ———. "The Unit-of-Analysis in the Comparative Study of Foreign Policy." Paper presented to the Michigan State University International Events Data Conference, April 1970.

3755. Merritt, Richard L., and Rokkan, Stein, eds. *Comparing Nations*. New Haven: Yale University Press, 1966. 584 pp.

An early collection of papers on the quantitative comparison of nations.

3756. Moore, James A., and Tanter, Raymond. "CACIS I: Computer-Aided Conflict Information System I: A Report of the International Security Analysis Project, Consolidated Analysis Centers, Inc.," Paper delivered to the 1973 annual convention of the American Political Science Association, September 4-8, 1973, at New Orleans, Louisiana.

Explains how historical events, the organizational process models of Cyert and March, and subjective expected utility are incorporated into CACIS. A brief discussion is given of event validity of its models, using 1961 Berlin crisis data.

3757. Moses, L. E.; Brody, Richard A.; Holsti, Ole R.; Kadane, J. B., and Milstein, Jeffrey S. "Scaling Data on Inter-Nation Action." *Science*, May 26, 1967, pp. 1045-1059.

3758. Mowland, Hamid. "A Paradigm for Source Analysis in Events Data Research." *International Interactions* 2 (1975).

3759. Munton, D. "Waiting for Kepler: Event Data and Relational Model Explanations of Canadian Foreign Policy Behavior." In Patrick J. McGowan, ed., *Sage International Yearbook of Foreign Policy Studies*, vol. 3. Beverly Hills: Sage, 1974.

3760. O'Leary, Michael K. "Needs and Prospects in the Analysis of International Events." Remarks to a round-table of the Events Data Conference, April 1971, at Michigan State University.

3761. ———. "The Role of Issues." In James N. Rosenau, ed., *In Search of Global Patterns*, pp. 318-325. New York: Free Press, 1976.

3762. Pearson, F. "Events Data and Conflict: Dynamics of 'Middle Eastern' Conflict, 1963-1964." Paper presented to the International Events Data Conference, April 1971, at Michigan State University.

3763. Pearson, F. "Events Data and Conflict: Dynamics of 'Middle Eastern' Conflict, 1963-1964." Paper presented to the International Events Data Conference, April 1971, at the Michigan State University.

3764. ———. "International Events, Foreign Policy-Making, Elite Attitudes and Mass Opinion: A Correlational Analysis." Paper presented to the International Studies Association annual convention, March 1971, at San Juan, Puerto Rico.

3765. ———. `` Research on Research: Events Data Studies: 1961-1972.'' Paper presented to the International Studies Association annual convention, 1973.

3766. Phillips, Warren. ''The Theoretical Approaches in the Events Data Movement.'' *International Interactions* 2 (1975).

3767. ———. ''Theoretical Underpinnings of the Events Data Movement.'' Paper presented to the annual convention of the International Studies Association, 1973, at New York City.

3768. Richman, Alvin. ''Issues in the Conceptualization and Measurement of Events Data.'' *International Interactions* 2 (1975).

3769. ———. *A Scale of Events Along the Conflict-Cooperation Continuum.* Philadelphia: University of Pennsylvania Research Monograph Series, 1967.

3770. Riker, William H. ''Events and Situations.'' *Journal of Philosophy*, January 31, 1957, pp. 57-70.
    Riker is concerned with the problem of ambiguity of events, which leads to difficulties in the attribution of causation. He discusses several events that are possibly ambiguous and argues that social scientists should study much smaller events, a solution that would avoid ambiguity and allow the power of statistical techniques to aid in explanation.

3771. Rosenau, James N. ''Internal War as an International Event.'' In James N. Rosenau, ed., *International Aspects of Civil Strife*. Princeton: Princeton University Press, 1964.

3772. Rothe, Fred. ''Tranquility and Turbulence in the International System.'' Paper presented to the panel on International Event Analysis, 19th annual convention of the International Studies Association, February 22-25, 1978, at Washington, D.C.

3773. Rothman, J. ''The *New York Times* Information Bank.'' New York: New York Times Library and Information Services, n.d.

3774. Rummel, Rudolph. ''Dimensions of Conflict Behavior within Nations, 1946-1959.'' *Journal of Conflict Resolution* 10 (March 1966): 65-73.
    A seminal article, using factor analysis.

3775. ———. ''A Foreign Conflict Behavior Code Sheet.'' *World Politics* 18 (January 1966): 282-296.

3776. Russett, Bruce M.; Singer, J. David; and Small, Melvin. ''National Political Units in the Twentieth Century: A Standardized List.'' *American Political Science Review* 62 (September 1968): 932-951.

The authors offer a three-digit code, which is now widely used in the field, especially among contributors to the ICPSR International Relations Archive at the University of Michigan.

3777. Salmore, Stephen A., and Munton, Donald. ''An Empirically Based Typology of Foreign Policy Behaviors.'' In James N. Rosenau, ed., *Comparing Foreign Policies: Theories, Findings, and Methods*, pp. 329-352. New York: Wiley, 1974.

3778. Scolnick, J. M. ''Observations about Selected Aspects of the Use of Conflict Event Data in Empirical Cross National Studies of Conflict.'' Paper presented to the International Studies Association annual convention, March 14-18, 1972, at Dallas, Texas.

3779. Scott, W. A. ''Reliability of Content Analysis: The Case of Nominal Scale Coding.'' *Public Opinion Quarterly* 19 (Winter 1955): 321-325.

3780. Sigler, J. H. ''Reliability Problems in the Measurement of International Events in the Elite Press.'' Paper presented to the International Events Data Conference, April 1970, at Michigan State University.

3781. ———. ''Reliability Problems in the Measurement of International Events in the Elite Press.'' In John H. Sigler, John O. Field, and Murray L. Adelman, ''Applications of Events Data Analysis: Cases, Issues, and Programs in International Interaction'' 1, 02-002 *Sage Professional Papers in International Studies*, pp. 9-28. 1972.

Sigler attempted to replicate the procedures used in creating the WEIS data, using new data sources. Interproject coder reliability differed regarding the choice of items to be coded, as well as the coding of certain variables.

3782. Singer, J. David, and Small, Melvin. *The Wages of War, 1816-1965: A Statistical Handbook.* New York: Wiley, 1972. 419 pp.

The first compendium of data from the Correlates of War project.

3783. Sloan, Thomas J. ''A Summary Report on the Development of the Cooperation-Conflict Interaction Scale for Inter-Nation Events Data.'' *Review of Peace Sciences* 1 (1973).

3784. Smith, R. F. `` On the Structure of Foreign News: A Comparison of the New York Times and the Indian White Papers.'' *Journal of Peace Research* 6 (1969): 23-36.

3785. Stark, K. ''The Handling of Foreign News in Finland's Press.'' *Journalism Quarterly* 45 (Autumn 1968): 516-520.

3786. Tanter, Raymond. ''Dimensions of Conflict Behavior within and between Nations, 1958-1960.'' *Journal of Conflict Resolution* 10 (March 1966): 41-64.
   A replication of Rudolph Rummel's factor analysis.

3787. Tomlinson, Rodney. ''Analyzing the Change Characteristics and Patterns in the International Event Flow over the Years 1966-1975.'' Ph.D. dissertation, University of Southern California, 1977.

3788. ——. ''Monitoring International Behavior with an Eye-Ball Events Flow Model.'' Paper presented to the 19th annual convention of the International Studies Association, February 22-25, 1978, at Washington, D.C.

3789. Young, R. A. ''A Classification of Nations According to Foreign Policy Output.'' In Edward E. Azar and Joseph D. Ben-Dak, eds., *Theory and Practice of Events Research*, pp. 175-196. New York: Gordon and Breach, 1975.

3790. ——. ''An Events-Based Nation Typology.'' Arlington, Va.: Consolidated Analysis Centers, 1970.

3791. Young, R. A., and Martin, W. R. ''A View of Six International Event/Interaction Category and Scaling Methods.'' Mimeographed. University of Southern California, 1968.

FICTION

3792. Albert, Marvin H. *The Gargoyle Conspiracy*. Garden City, N.Y.: Doubleday, 1975. 278 pp.

An Arab terrorist bomb kills five. A U.S. State Department agent searches for the mastermind of this incident who intends to assassinate the U.S. secretary of state and the king of Jordan.

3793. Aricha, Amos, and Landau, Eli. *Phoenix*. New York: New American Library, 1979. 298 pp.

An assassin is paid to kill Moshe Dayan to destroy chances of an Arab-Israeli peace settlement.

3794. Atwater, James D. *Time Bomb*. New York: Viking, 1977.

Reviewed briefly by Michael Dirda, *Washington Post Book World*, January 8, 1978, p. E3. The IRA's top explosives expert tries to manufacture a bomb that England's best bomb expert cannot dismantle.

3795. Burns, Alan. *The Angry Brigade*. London: Quartet, 1973.

Six members of a commune turn to terrorism. Based upon the author-lawyer's tapes of terrorists.

3796. Camus, Albert. "The Just Assassins." In *Caligula and Three Other Plays*. Translated by Gilbert. New York: Vintage 1958.

3797. Carretero, José Maria. *The Terrorist: A Novel*. Madrid: Cabellero Andaz, 1933.

3798. Charles, Robert. *The Hour of the Wolf*. New York: Pinnacle, 1974. 188 pp.

Palestinians, the IRA, and the Japanese Red Army engage in favors for each other.

3799. ———. *The Prey of the Falcon*. New York: Pinnacle, 1976. 186 pp.
An intelligence officer conducts a vendetta against IRA bombers.

3800. ———. *The Scream of the Dove*. New York: Pinnacle, 1975. 182 pp.
Palestinians and the Japanese Red Army take over a supertanker.

3801. Conrad, Joseph. *The Secret Agent.* 1907.

Fictionalized account of the anarchist movement in England. The terrorist, an old professor, says, "I have always dreamed of a band of men absolute in their resolve to discard all scruples in the choice of means, strong enough to give themselves frankly the name of destroyers, and free from the taint of that resigned pessimism which rots the world. No pity for anything on earth, including themselves, and death enlisted for good and all in the service of humanity—that's what I would have liked to see . . . Madness and despair. Give me that lever and I'll move the world."

3802. Coppel, Alfred. *Between the Thunder and the Sun.* New York: Harcourt Brace, Jovanovich, 1971.

A half-crazed hijacker wishes to go to Cuba, but his route will take the plane into the path of a hurricane.

3803. Corley, Edwin. *Air Force One.* New York: Doubleday, 1978.

A novel pitting congressional concern for overspending by the executive, and a psychotic veteran with a grudge against the president's plane. The latter fires at AF 1 while flying a P-38.

3804. Cormier, Robert. *After the First Death.* New York: Pantheon, 1979.

A sixteen-year-old terrorist holds hostage a busload of American children.

3805. Crosby, John. *An Affair of Strangers.* New York: Stein and Day, 1975. London: Jonathan Cape, 1975.

Among the characters in this novel are Arab terrorists, Israeli intelligence agents, Middle Eastern oil barons, and international politicians. An Arab terrorist and an Israeli counterterrorist fall in love.

3806. Cussler, Clive. *Vixen 03.* New York: 1978. 285 pp.

Reviewed by Joseph McLellan, "Underwater Adventures-Deep in the Rockies," *Washington Post*, October 24, 1978, p. C-7. Quick Death—a CBW agent—is involved in a blackmail scheme between black revolutionaries and a white government in South Africa.

3807. Dan, Uri, and Mann, Peter. *Carlos Must Die.* New York: Norton, 1978. 240 pp.

The Israeli authors view Carlos as an agent of the Soviet Union, which directs him to attack Saudi oil wells. Israeli agents make several unsuccessful attempts to kidnap or kill Carlos.

3808. Debray, Regis. *L'Indésirable.* Paris: Le Seuil, 1975.

About an intellectual who becomes an arms smuggler and dies for a movement.

3809. Delaney, Lawrence. *The Triton Ultimatum.* New York: Crowell, 1977.

Terrorists seize a nuclear missile site, aiming the twenty-four warheads at world capitals.

3810. DeLillo, Don. *Players.* New York: Knopf, 1977.

Terrorists are used as a comment upon rules and the role of individuals. Reviewed by Diane Johnson, ''Beyond Radical Chic,'' *New York Times Book Review*, September 4, 1977, pp. 1, 16.

3811. De Mille, Nelson. *By the Rivers of Babylon.* New York: Harcourt Brace Jovanovich, 1978.

An Israeli peace delegation's plane is downed by terrorists. The delegation battles the guerrillas in the deserts. Reviewed by Robert J. Serling, ''Captive in Babylon: A New Thriller with an Old Twist,'' *Washington Post*, August, 1978, B1-B2.

3812. DiMona, Joseph. *The Benedict Arnold Connection.* New York: Dell, 1977, 287 pp.

The Deep Men, a group of rightist superpatriots, steal three nuclear bombs from a maximum security Air Force silo in Minot, North Dakota. A two hundred-year-old map signed by Benedict Arnold with the legend ''For revenge of Nancy'' is found at the scene of the crime. A subplot concerns a Justice Department lawyer's love for a descendant of Benedict Arnold.

3813. Dostoyevsky, Fyodor. *The Possessed (The Devils).* Translated and with an introduction by David Magarshack. Harmondsworth: Penguin, 1962.

The classic story of a terrorist, based upon the life of Nechayev.

3814. Duane, Allan. *The Hadrian Ransom.* New York: Putnam, 1979. 275 pp.

Reviewed by Michael Demarest, ''Malice in Wonderland,'' *Time*, April 16, 1979, pp. 114-117. Pope Hadrian IX is kidnapped by three Americans and an Italian, whose caper is complicated by Red Brigades interference.

3815. Forbes, Colin. *The Stone Leopard.* Greenwich: Fawcett, 1975, 286 pp.

A novel of the Soviets and a Carlos-like figure who plans the assassination of the French president.

3816. ———. [pseudo.] *The Year of the Golden Ape.* New York: E. P. Dutton, 1974.

Arab and French terrorists place a nuclear device aboard a hijacked oil tanker, which sails into San Francisco Bay.

3817. Forsyth, Frederick. *The Day of the Jackal.* New York: Bantam, 1971.

The OAS hires a British assassin to kill De Gaulle. In a model of the modern genre, Forsyth establishes the structure for other novels of terrorism, beginning with a few examples of the group's other exploits, their germ of a plan, the elaborate preparations for the incident, the first leaks that begin the police search for them, and the final confrontation between the ace detective and the terrorist mastermind. The novel also furnished the nickname for the real-life Carlos, a Venezuelan PFLP terrorist leader.

3818. Frankel, Sandor, and Mews, Webster. *The Aleph Solution.* New York: Stein and Day, 1978, 241 pp.

Palestinian terrorists take over the U.N. General Assembly to force U.N.-sanctioned destruction of Israel. The Israeli Aleph rescue squad saves the day. Reviewed by James Grady, ''Terrorists in the U.N. and the Israelis to the Rescue,'' *Washington Post*, January 8, 1979.

3819. Freeling, Nicolas. *Gadget.* New York: Coward, McCann, Geoghegan, 1977.

Terrorists hold a nuclear physicist for ransom, demanding a homemade nuclear bomb.

3820. Gilbert, Michael. *The Empty House.* New York: Harper and Row, 1979, 245 pp.

Reviewed by Michael Demarest, ''Malice in Wonderland,'' *Time*, April 16, 1979, p. 114. A secretive genius discovers a formula that alters chromosomes. The British army, the Israelis, and Arab guerrillas begin hunting for the inventor.

3821. Granger, Bill. *The November Man.* Greenwich: Fawcett, 1979.

Noted briefly in the *Washington Post Book World*, September 23, 1979, p. 13. An Irish Republican Army faction plans to kill the queen's rich, elderly cousin in a bomb-rigged boat, a scenario quite similar to the killing of Lord Mountbatten.

3822. Green, Gerald. *The Hostage Heart.* Chicago: Playboy, 1976.

Terrorists hold hostage an operating room team during open-heart surgery on a famous millionaire.

3823. Greene, Graham. *The Honorary Consul.* London: Bodley Head, 1973, 334 pp.

A bungled kidnapping by Latin American guerrillas. Greene believes that the morality of such actions depends upon the circumstances.

3824. Grogan, Emmett. "Final Score." *Oui* (November 1976): 59ff.

Three individuals plan a thirteen-step operation to steal plutonium from a New York nuclear power plant. This excerpt from Grogan's novel details the theft of the plant's security plans.

3825. Haley, Arthur. *Overload.* New York: Doubleday, 1979.

A consumer-financed terrorist sabotages electric power plants.

3826. Harris, Leonard. *The Masada Plan.* New York: Crown, 1976, 314 pp.

In 1979, the Israelis have lost a war to the Arabs. The plot revolves around a possible terrorist nuclear device and the machinations of Arab terrorists against Western interests.

3827. Harris, Thomas. *Black Sunday.* New York: Putnam, 1975, 318 pp.

Black September and a crazed American veteran hijack the Goodyear blimp and attempt to kill 84,000 people, including the U.S. president, at the Superbowl.

3828. Hartley, Norman. *The Viking Process,* New York: Simon and Schuster, 1975.

A corporation uses terrorism to destroy its rivals.

3829. Hilton, James. *Lost Horizon.* New York: Morrow, 1933.

A hijacking to the mythical Asian paradise, Shangri-la.

3830. Household, Geoffrey. *Hostage: London, The Diary of Julian Despard.* Boston: Atlantic-Little, Brown, 1977.

A terrorist defector tries to stop his comrades from destroying London.

3831. Jacks, Oliver. *Assassination Day.* New York: Stein and Day, 1976.

Soviet leader Brezhnev is the target.

3832. Kalb, Marvin, and Koppel, Ted. *In the National Interest.* New York: Simon and Schuster, 1977.

Palestinian terrorists kidnap the wife of a Kissinger-like figure.

3833. Katz, William. *North Star Crusade.* New York: Harcourt Brace Jovanovich, 1977.

Reviewed by Ray Walters, *New York Times Book Review*, February 5, 1978, p. 41. A U.S. Navy officer leads a group that hijacks a nuclear submarine to start a war between the United States and the Soviet Union. New York and Boston, viewed as centers of pacifist corruption, are threatened.

3834. Kiefer, Warren. *The Kidnappers.* New York: Harper and Row, 1977, 312 pp.

Leftist terrorism versus right-wing death squads in Argentina.

3835. Koestler, Arthur. *Thieves in the Night.* London: Macmillan, 1946. 357 pp.

A novel of the Irgun Zvai Leumi and the Stern group.

3836. Lancaster, Graham. *The Nuclear Letters.* New York; Atheneum, 1979, 233 pp.

Reviewed by Michael Demarest, "Malice in Wonderland," *Time,* April 16, 1979, pp. 112-114. Plutonium-239 is stolen in 1972 from a storage center in Washington State. A series of threatening letters sent to Western heads of state turn out to be part of a hoax by the Soviets to take over West Berlin.

3837. Lewis, F. *One of Our H-Bombs Is Missing.* New York: McGraw-Hill, 1967.

3838. Lippincott, David. *Salt Mine* New York: Viking, 1979, 333 pp.

Reviewed by Michael Demarest, "Malice in Wonderland," *Time,* April 16, 1979, p. 117. Soviet dissidents take over the Kremlin's Oruzheinaya Palata, taking hostage fifty tourists and Lenin's corpse.

3839. Ludlum, Robert. *The Matarese Circle.* New York: Marek, 1979, 601 pp.

Reviewed by John Marks, *Washington Post Book World,* March 18, 1979, p. E3. A conspiracy hatched in 1911 aims at assassinating world leaders to further the group's hopes of world domination. A CIA and KGB agent team up against the plotters.

3840. MacInnes, Helen. *Prelude to Terror.* New York: Harcourt Brace, Jovanovich, 1978. 368 pp.

Paintings from the Iron Curtain are sold in the West. The proceeds are used to provide terrorists with laundered money. Reviewed by Joseph McLellan, "Good Story, Well Told," *Washington Post,* September 21, 1978, p. B-17.

3841. Malraux, André. *La condition humaine.* Paris: Gallimard, 1946.

Malraux creates an archetypal terrorist, Ch'en, who is a Westernized Chinese with his own ideology of violence.

3842. Mather, Berkley. *With Extreme Prejudice.* New York: Scribners, 1976.

A novel linking international terrorists with a criminal organization.

3843. MacLean, Alistair. *The Golden Gate*. Greenwich: Fawcett, 1976. New York: Doubleday, 1976.

The president's motorcade, escorting two Arab heads of state, is hijacked.

3844. ———. *The Satan Bug*. Greenwich: Fawcett, 1962. 224 pp.

A deadly toxin is stolen from a germ warfare laboratory.

3845. McCarthy, Mary. *Cannibals and Missionaries*. New York: Harcourt Brace Jovanovich, 1979. 369 pp.

Reviewed by Ann Tyler, "Mary McCarthy: Terrorism, Trinkets and the Function of Art," *Washington Post Book World*, October 14, 1979, pp. 4-5. A plane flying to prerevolutionary Iran is hijacked to an isolated Dutch farm, where negotiations begin. The chief of the terrorists holds Western liberals to attack the West's "pious notion of itself," and art collectors for their paintings.

3846. Mills, James. *The Seventh Power*. New York: Dutton, 1976. 236 pp.

A group of students manufacture a nuclear device and threaten to destroy Manhattan. Reviewed by S. K. Oberbeck, "Cooking up 'A Nuclear Julia Child,' " *Washington Post*, December 4, 1976, p E2.

3847. Newcomb, Kerry, and Schaefer, Frank. *Pandora Man*. New York: Morrow, 1979.

Terrorists kidnap the president-elect, planning to substitute a double.

3848. Oran, Dan, and Hoklin, Lonn. *Z Warning*. New York: Ballantine, 1979. 336 pp.

Reviewed by Michael Demarest, "Malice in Wonderland," *Time*, April 16, 1979, p. 112. Patients from a mental hospital team up with the mistress of a U.S. senator to steal eighty kilograms of plutonium dioxide.

3849. Osmond, Andrew. *Saladin!* New York: Doubleday, 1976.

About PLO-Israeli counterterrorist attacks after the Munich Olympics.

3850. Phillips, David Atlee. *The Carlos Contract: A Novel of International Terrorism*. New York: Macmillan, 1978. 252 pp.

Phillips, a former CIA case officer, shows how the agency would track down Carlos, the famed terrorist.

3851. Proud, Franklin M., and Eberhardt, Alfred F. *Tiger in the Mountains*. New York: St. Martin's Press, 1976, 336 pp.

Four men hijack an Air France jetliner to Hanoi to obtain the release of American prisoners of war.

3852. Reid, James. *The Offering.* New York: G. P. Putnam's Sons, 1977, 223 pp.

Reviewed briefly by Michael Mewshaw, *New York Times Book Review*, February 5, 1978, p. 33. A Catholic priest becomes involved in an underworld attempt to pass $1 million to the IRA.

3853. Reynolds, Mack. "Pacificist." In Martin Harry Greenberg and Patricia S. Warrick, eds., *Political Science Fiction: An Introductory Reader*, pp. 399-413. Englewood Cliffs, N.J.: Prentice-Hall, 1974.

A short story in which an antiwar group uses terrorist methods to intimidate politicians and researchers whose actions support war.

3854. Rowe, James N. *The Judas Squad.* Boston: Little, Brown, 1977.

Terrorists take over the Bartonsville Fast Breeder Reactor and threaten to destroy Pittsburgh if they are not given $50 million in cash.

3855. Sanders, Leonard. *The Hamlet Warning.* New York: Scribners, 1976.

An international terrorist group plans to explode a nuclear bomb in Santo Domingo to pressure the United States.

3856. Scortia, Thomas N., and Robinson, Frank M. *The Prometheus Crisis.* Garden City, N.Y.: Doubleday, 1975.

3857. Seymour, Gerald. *The Glory Boys.* New York: Random House, 1976.

A Palestinian assassination squad is sent to London to kill an Israeli scientist.

3858. ———. *Harry's Game.* New York: Random House, 1975, 281 pp.

Reviewed by Richard Howard Brown, "A Killer-for-a-Killer Thriller," *Washington Post*, November 25, 1975, p. B-2. The British intelligence and defense bureaux send an agent to kill the assassin of a British cabinet minister. Much attention is given to the feeling of what it is like to be part of the Ulster conflict.

3859. ———. *Kingfisher.* New York: Summit, 1977, 349 pp.

Reviewed by Godfrey Hodgson, "Morality on a High Plane," *Washington Post Book World*, January 22, 1978, p. F-6. Four young Jews shoot a Kiev policeman. One kills himself after capture to avoid torture, while the remaining two boys and one girl hijack a Soviet plane to the West. Western European governments are faced with a moral dilemma.

3861. Stahl, Norman. *The Assault on Mavis A.* New York: Random House, 1978, 258 pp.

Reviewed by Allan A. Ryan, Jr., "Disaster Story with Something for Everyone and a Natural Movie." *Washington Post*, October 20, 1978, p. E-8.
The IRA conducts a mass prison escape, seizes an oil tanker, and rams it against an offshore drilling rig.

3862. Swerdlow, Joel. *Code Z*. New York: Putnams, 1978, 275 pp.
Reviewed by Roderich MacLeish, "The Taste of Terror." *Washington Post Book World*, January 14, 1979, p. E-3. Unknown individuals plot to bomb three commercial airliners leaving Dulles for London, Paris, and Dakar in hopes of wrecking a Geneva Middle East peace conference. Under a special statute, a CIA agent is allowed to take over the federal bureaucracy during the crisis.

3863. Theroux, Paul. *The Family Arsenal*. Boston: Houghton Mifflin, 1976.
A novel about IRA terrorism in London's slums.

3864. Todd, Ian. *Ghosts of the Assassins*. New York: E. A. Seeman, 1976.
A contemporary terrorist group attempts to kill 3 million New Yorkers.

3865. Trew, Anthony. *Ultimatum*. London: Collins, 1975.
Arab terrorists smuggle a nuclear warhead into the center of London and demand the return of all the Palestinian territory Israel has captured, threatening detonation within seventy-two hours.

3866. Tuchman, Barbara. *The Proud Tower*. New York: Bantam, 1972.

3867. Wager, Walter. *Viper Three*. New York: Macmillan, 1971, 257 pp.
Five convicts take over a Minuteman site.

3868. Wahloo, Per, and Sjowall, Jam. *The Terrorists*. New York: Random House, 1976.
The last of the Beck series of police novels that study life in the Swedish welfare state. Beck must protect a right-wing U.S. senator from assassins in Sweden. Reviewed by Jean M. White, "Beck's Last Case," *Washington Post Book World*, November 21, 1976, p. E-6.

3869. West, Morris. *Proteus*. New York: Morrow, 1979. 324 pp.
Reviewed by Joseph McLellan, "Reluctant Terrorist in a Violent World," *Washington Post*, January 25, 1979, p. B-7. A corporation president is also head of a secret benign organization, Proteus. He and his group adopt terrorist tactics to survive against governments and ultimately threaten to unleash a bacteriological weapon unless all governments release political prisoners.

Also see entries 1382 and 1385.

BIBLIOGRAPHIES

3870. "Annotated Bibliography on Transnational Terrorism." 7th Security Assistance Symposium of the Foreign Area Officer Course, U.S. Army Institute for Military Assistance, Fort Bragg, North Carolina, n.d. [approx. 1974-1975], 27 pp.

Categories include "Books"; "Publications of the Government, Learned Societies and Other Organizations"; "Periodicals." Unfortunately it gives too much emphasis to journalistic accounts of separate incidents.

3871. Bander, Edward J., and Ryan, Margaret T. "Bibliography." In *Report of the Task Force on Disorders and Terrorism* pp. 596-634. Washington, D.C.: National Advisory Committee on Criminal Justice Standards and Goals, December 1976.

Many of the items are annotated. The bibliography includes much material on domestic terrorism and legal citations that is not included in other comparable compilations. Its scope is limited to articles that appeared before early 1976 and does not include many research reports of private research firms or papers presented to professional society meetings. It also does not include many citations found elsewhere in the report.

3872. Becker, Louise G. "Terrorism 1978: Selected Books and Documents." Washington, D.C.: Library of Congress, Congressional Research Service, April 11, 1978.

3873. Boston, Guy D.; Marcus, Marvin; and Wheaton, Robert J. "Terrorism: A Selected Bibliography." Washington, D.C.: National Criminal Justice Reference Service, National Institute of Law Enforcement and Criminal Justice, Law Enforcement Assistance Administration, U.S. Department of Justice, March 1976., 45 pp.

A short, annotated listing of 103 recently published items, covering many aspects of terrorism. Much of the material is geared to security officers faced with incidents. This listing is updated with 539 references in Guy Boston, O'Brien, and Palumbo, "Terrorism" (Rockville: National Criminal Justice Reference Service, Police Services 5/78, 1978, 323 pp., with a Supplement by Guy Boston.

3874. Cosyns-Verhaegen, Roger. *Present-Day Terrorism: Bibliographical Selection.* Wavre, Belgium: Centre D'information et de documentation de La L.I.L., 1973, 21 pp.

A listing of 131 works on terrorism, most of them in French. Headings include assassinations, skyjacks, repression of terrorism, terrorism in geographic areas, and·individual terrorist groups. Many of the articles come from magazines and newspapers.

3875. Coxe, Betsy. "Terrorism." Colorado Springs: U.S. Air Force Academy, 1977, 50 pp.

3876. Jenkins, Brian M.; Johnson, Janera; and Long, Lyn. "International Terrorism: An Annotated Bibliography." Santa Monica: RAND Corporation: R-1598-DOS/ARPA, 1975.

Concentrates on articles in news magazines with little attention to possible contributions of social science theories on violence.

3877. Kelly, Micheal J., and Mitchell, Thomas H. *Violence, Internal War and Revolution: A Select Bibliography.* Ottawa, Canada: Norman Paterson School of International Affairs, Carleton University Bibliography Series 3, June 1977, 57 pp.

Six hundred citations, unannotated, noting the multiple approaches to the problem. A separate section on terrorism is included. An appendix updates the bibliography.

3878. Kress, Lee Bruce. "Selected Bibliography." In Marius Livingston, et al., eds., *International Terrorism in the Contemporary World*, 469-502. Westport, Conn.: Greenwood Press, 1978.

3879. Lagergren, Thomas R., and Pitt, Kathleen A., eds. *International Criminology and Criminal Justice: A Selected Bibliography.* Washington, D.C.: National Institute of Law Enforcement and Criminal Justice, 1977, 36 pp.

3880. Mickolus, Edward F. *Annotated Bibliography on Transnational and International Terrorism.* Washington, D.C.: Central Intelligence Agency, Office of Political Research, December 1976, PR 76 10073U, 229 pp.

Designed to provide a comprehensive survey of nonjournalistic literature dealing with one or another aspect of transnational or international terrorism. It is not intended to be a complete listing of writings on terrorism, for it does not include domestic incidents having no international connection, nor does it deal with terrorist groups based in the United States or incidents within the United States.

3881. Norton, Augustus R., and Greenberg, Martin H. *International Terrorism: An Annotated Bibliography and Research Guide.* Boulder: Westview, 1979. 200 pp.

Lists approximately a thousand items and annotates one-third of them.

3882. Piasetzki, J. Peter. *Urban Guerrilla Warfare and Terrorism: A Selected Bibliography.* Monticello, Ill.: Council of Planning Librarians Exchange Bibliography 1098, August 1976, 16 pp.

A list of standard U.S. sources, with a few Canadian citations not found elsewhere.

3883. Readers Advisory Service. *International Terrorism and Revolutionary Warfare.* RAS #216. New York: Science Associates International, n.d. 3 pp.

An introductory bibliography.

3884. Sabetta, Anne, R. ''Annotated Bibliography.'' Prepared for Special Issue Devoted to International Terrorism. *Stanford Journal of International Studies* 12 (Spring 1977): 157-164.

3885. "A Select Bibliography on International Terrorism." United Nations: List No. 5/Rev. 1, October 25, 1972.

3886. "Selected Papers on Terrorism." Washington, D.C.: U.S. Department of State, Office of External Research, Foreign Affairs Research Documentation Center, July 1977, 13 pp.

According to the paper's abstract, ''This is a selected list of papers on terrorism that have been added to the collection of the Foreign Affairs Research Documentation Center between November 1971 and July 1977.''

3887. "Terrorism." Washington, D.C.: Library of the Department of State, October 1978, 5 pp.

Lists 101 recent articles, books, and reports on terrorism.

3888. U.N. Secretariat. *International Terrorism: A Select Bibliography.* September 26, 1973, 10 pp.

3889. U.S. Department of Justice. ''Terrorist Activities: Bibliography.'' Quantico, Va.: FBI Academy, 1975. 79 pp.

A listing of periodical treatments, law enforcement articles, newspaper items, and books on terrorism, skyjackings, and bombings. Three films on handling bomb incidents are summarized.

3890. U.S. Department of State. "Unclassified Bibliography on Terrorism." Washington, D.C.: U.S. Department of State, S/CCT, March 1976, 5 pp.

A short bibliography of public statements by the president and State Department spokesmen, as well as a few items produced by contractors working for State's Bureau of Intelligence and Research.

Also see entries 580, 581, 614, 737, 771, 772, 781, 943, 961, 1077, 1359, 1374, 1417, 1655, 1734, 3286, 3303, 3306, 3324, 3330, 3399, 3645, and 3647.

AUTHOR INDEX

Entries after each individual contributor's name refer to citation numbers rather than the pages on which they appear. The names of editors of collected works appear only once per book rather than being listed for each chapter written by others. *FNU* means "first name unknown."

TITLE INDEX

Entries after each citation refer to citation numbers rather than the pages on which they appear.

Comment: Hijacking. The Limitations of the International Treaty Approach, 2713

Comment: Juridical Control of Terrorism, 2338

Comment on Criminal Jurisdiction over Aircraft Hijacking, 2641

Comments from a member of the Office of the Ministry of Justice, Egypt, 1920

Comments on a Paper Presented by Dr. Brian Jenkins, 1451

Comments on a Paper Presented by Dr. Thomas P. Thornton, 186

Commitment and Resistance, 3282

The Common Features of the Armenian and Jewish Cases of Genocide: A Comparative Victimological Perspective, 2034

Communications Aspects of International Terrorism, 2945

Communist Attempts to Elicit False Confessions from Air Force Prisoners of War, 3018

Communist Techniques of Coercive Interrogation, 3019

Communist Terrorism in Malaya, 1763

Communities in Disaster: A Social Analysis of Collective Stress Situations, 2911

Community Development: Some More Lessons from the Recent Past in Northern Ireland, 1497

Community under Stress: An Internment Camp Culture, 3260

Comparative Approaches to the Study of Revolution: A Historiographic Essay, 3536

Comparative Revolutionary Movement, 3322

The Comparative Study of Revolution and Violence, 3454

A Comparative Study of the WEIS and COPDAB Data Sets, 3732

A Comparative Survey of the Anti-Terrorist Legislation in the FRG, France, England, and Sweden, and an Overview of the Legal Situation in the U.S., 2508

Comparing Foreign Policy Behavior with Events Data, 3728

Comparing Nations, 3755

Comparing the Foreign Policy Events of Nations, 3722

A Comparison of Deaths from Injury, 1947-56, Compared with 1962-71, 3257

The Compatibility of the Detention of Terrorists Order (Northern Ireland) with the European Convention for the Protection of Human Rights, 2524

A Compendium of European Theater Terrorist Groups, 1430

The Complaint of Yugoslavia against Hungary with Reference to the Assassination of King Alexander, 2827

The Complete Bolivian Diaries of Ché Guevara and Other Captured Documents, 1094

A Comprehensive System of Trauma Services: The Austrian Experience, 3030

The Computer: A Target, 336

Computer-Based Scaling of International Events, 3733

Computer Routines for Arraying Aggregate Data, 3709

Computerized Crisis Forecasting, 3662

A Concept for Antiterrorist Operatons, 2580

The Concept of Public Purpose Terror in International Law, 2339, 2340, 2341

The Concept of Revolutionary Terrorism, 187

The Concept of Terror, 260

The Concept of Terrorism, 231

The Concept of Terrorism and Its Relationship to Other Forms of Violence Such as Guerrilla War and Mass Insurrection, 445

The Concept of Violence, 3493

Concepts of Political Prisonerhood, 2282

Conceptualizing Foreign Policy Behavior Using Events Data, 3723

Conceptualizing Political Terrorism: A Typology and Application, 382

Concerted Actions against States Found In Default of Their International Obligations in Respect of Unlawful Interference with International Civil Aviation, 2541

Conclusions, 372

Conclusions d'une enquête sur le suicide dans les camps de concentration, 3035

La condition humaine, 3841

About the Compiler

EDWARD F. MICKOLUS is an Intelligence Analyst in the Office of Political Analysis, U.S. Central Intelligence Agency. His articles have appeared in the *International Studies Quarterly*, *Journal of Irreproducible Results*, *Orbis*, and many other journals and books. He is the author of *Transnational Terrorism: A Chronology of Events, 1948-1979* (Greenwood Press, 1980).